Coleridge's Submerged Politics

J. M. W. Turner, *Slave Ship (Slavers Throwing Overboard the Dead and Dying—Typhon Coming On)*, Henry Lillie Pierce Fund, Courtesy, Museum of Fine Arts, Boston.

Coleridge's Submerged Politics

The Ancient Mariner **and**
Robinson Crusoe

Patrick J. Keane

University of Missouri Press
COLUMBIA AND LONDON

Library of Congress Cataloging-in-Publication Data

Keane, Patrick J.
  Coleridge's submerged politics : The ancient mariner and Robinson
Crusoe / Patrick J. Keane.
      p.   cm.
  Includes bibliographical references and index.
  ISBN 0–8262–0942–4
  1. Coleridge, Samuel Taylor, 1772–1834. Rime of the ancient mariner.
2. Coleridge, Samuel Taylor, 1772–1834—Political and social views.
3. Politics and literature—Great Britain—History—19th century. 4. Defoe,
Daniel, 1661?–1731. Robinson Crusoe. 5. DeFoe, Daniel, 1661?–1731—
Influence. I. Title.
PR4479.K43 1994
821'.7—dc20   94–2291
                                                                                   CIP

∞™ This paper meets the requirements of the
American National Standard for Permanence of Paper
for Printed Library Materials, Z39.48, 1984.

Designer: Elizabeth Fett
Typesetter: Connell-Zeko Type & Graphics
Printer and Binder: Thomson-Shore, Inc.
Typeface: New Baskerville

For permissions to reproduce copyrighted material, see the last printed page
of the book.

This book is brought to publication with generous assistance from the
Francis Fallon, S.J., Professorship Fund of Le Moyne College and the
Le Moyne College Faculty Senate Committee on Research and Development.

To
David V. Erdman

———————

Contents

Acknowledgments

Aside from Carl Woodring and Thomas McFarland, the originally anonymous readers selected, most fortunately for me, by the University of Missouri Press, no one had suffered through the whole of this long book until M. H. Abrams read the revised manuscript in the fall of 1993. Several of my colleagues at Le Moyne (Barron Boyd, Douglas Egerton, Alan Fischler, Roger Lund, Clarence Taylor) have read portions. I am specifically grateful to Doug Egerton for insights that helped me improve Chapter 2 and to Professor Abrams for his generous, encouraging, and clarifying response to the introductions to both parts of this study. Others have listened to me, making suggestions as I tried out my ideas on them (Elizabeth Costello, David Lloyd, Jonathan Schonsheck, Bruce Shefrin). I also learned from a panel and audience discussion following the presentation of a version of the introductory chapter as a lecture under the sponsorship of *Salmagundi* at Skidmore College in April 1992.

The final stages of preparing the manuscript were made more than tolerable by the assistance of Faculty Secretary Sharyn Knight and by my own student assistant Jennifer Stanley, both of whom brought to the task competence, patience, and saving humor. In addition, the manuscript benefited from the editorial skill of Tim Fox. Once again, I am happy to thank the Le Moyne College Faculty Senate Committee on Research and Development for a series of grants, and the college itself for honoring me with an endowed chair, carrying with it a generous budget for travel and research as well as a course reduction that gave me the time to hammer this unwieldy work into a semblance of unity.

These are immediate acknowledgments; my deepest debts are, of course, to the work and, in some cases, the friendship and encouragement over years, of several men and women. The work of most of them appears in the Works Cited; but I would like particularly to acknowledge—along with M. H. Abrams, Thomas McFarland, and Carl Woodring—Harold Bloom, Robert Boyers, Marilyn Butler, Denis Donoghue, Kenneth R. Johnston, Alan Liu, Jerome J. McGann, Morton D. Paley, Nicholas Roe, M. L. Rosenthal, Edward Said, Michael Shugrue, the late E. P. Thompson, and Helen Vendler. Unfortunately, I read Professor McFarland's *William Wordsworth: Intensity and Achievement* (Oxford: Clarendon Press, 1992) too late to register affinities with his opening chapter, "The Clamour of Absence: Reading and Misreading in Wordsworthian Criticism."

Finally, I would like to add my gratitude to that of many others. Odd and imperfect though the final result may be, the inspiration for this project has been the extraordinary erudition and personal friendship of the great Romantic scholar to whom the book is dedicated.

Primary Works Cited

Coleridge

The works of Coleridge appearing parenthetically in the text and in footnotes are signified by the abbreviations in the following table. With the exception of the *Letters, Notebooks,* and *Poetical Works,* all are to be found in *The Collected Works of Samuel Taylor Coleridge,* general editor Kathleen Coburn, associate editor Bart Winer (16 Numbers. Bollingen Series 75. London: Routledge and Kegan Paul; Princeton: Princeton University Press, 1969–), hereafter abbreviated *CC.*

AR   *Aids to Reflection.* Edited by John Beer. No. 9 of *CC* (1993).

BL   *Biographia Literaria.* Edited by James Engell and W. Jackson Bate. 2 vols. No. 7 of *CC* (1983).

CL   *The Collected Letters of Samuel Taylor Coleridge.* Edited by E. L. Griggs. 6 vols. Oxford: Clarendon Press, 1956–1971.

CM   *Marginalia.* Edited by George Whalley (1984). 2 vols. (of a projected 5). Vol. 3, edited by H. J. Jackson and Whalley (1992). No. 12 of *CC.*

CN   *The Notebooks of Samuel Taylor Coleridge.* Edited by Kathleen Coburn. 4 vols. (of a projected 5). Bollingen Series 50. Princeton: Princeton University Press, 1957–.

CPW   *The Complete Poetical Works of Samuel Taylor Coleridge.* Edited by Ernest Hartley Coleridge. 2 vols. Oxford: Clarendon Press, 1912. (The standard edition until the *Poetical Works,* ed. J. C. C. Mays, is published in three vols. as No. 16 of *CC.*)

C&S   *On the Constitution of the Church and State.* Edited by John Colmer. No. 10 of *CC* (1976).

EOT   *Essays on His Times.* Edited by David V. Erdman. 3 vols. No. 3 of *CC* (1978).

F   *The Friend.* Edited by Barbara Rooke. 2 vols. No. 4 of *CC* (1969).

L 1795   *Lectures 1795: On Politics and Religion.* Edited by Louis Patton and Peter Mann. No. 1 of *CC* (1971).

LL   *Lectures 1808–1819: On Literature.* Edited by R. A. Foakes. 2 vols. No. 5 of *CC* (1987).

LS   *Lay Sermons.* Edited by R. J. White. No. 6 of *CC* (1972).

TT   *Table Talk.* Edited by Carl Woodring. 2 vols. No. 14 of *CC* (1990).

W   *The Watchman.* Edited by Louis Patton. No. 2 of *CC* (1970).

Several other Coleridge texts are cited. The first four are unpublished manuscripts in the British Museum (Additional MS 34225). Dating from 1825–1827, these fragments speculating on race are entitled "Solitary [as distinguished from] Gregarious," "Degeneration and Race," "On the Definition of Species," and "The Historic Race." A related fifth manuscript—an 1828 outline intended for Coleridge's projected but never completed grand treatise, the "Opus Maximum"—is in the Huntington Library in California (HM 17299, 132r–142r). Presumably, they will all eventually appear in either the *Collected Coleridge* or the *Notebooks.* In the meantime, they have been partially transcribed and cogently discussed by J. H. Haeger, "Coleridge's Speculations on Race," *Studies in Romanticism* 13 (1974): 333–57.

Coleridge's March 1819 "Lecture on Milton and the *Paradise Lost*" is quoted from *Coleridge on the Seventeenth Century,* ed. Roberta F. Brinkley (Durham: University of North Carolina Press, 1955). Coleridge's 1808 review of Clarkson's *History of . . . the Abolition of the African Slave-Trade . . .* and his two 1818 pamphlets supporting Sir Robert Peel's Bill to shorten the working hours of children in factories are quoted from *Inquiring Spirit: A New Presentation of Coleridge from his Published and Unpublished Writings,* ed. Kathleen Coburn (New York: Pantheon, 1951). Also cited: *Coleridge's Miscellaneous Criticism,* ed. T. M. Raysor (Cambridge: Harvard University Press, 1936); *Coleridge's Shakespeare Criticism,* ed. T. M. Raysor (London: Dent, 1960); "On Method," from *Samuel Taylor Coleridge's "Treatise on Method,"* ed. Alice D. Snyder (London: Constable, 1934).

Defoe

There is no definitive edition of the voluminous and varied writings of the prolific Defoe, whose production, much of it anonymous or pseudonymous, *may* amount to some 570 books, poems, journals, and pamphlets. That at least is the astonishing number of established and attributed items assigned in John Robert Moore's influential *Checklist of the Writings of Daniel Defoe* (Hamden, Conn.: Archon, 1971 [1960]), an establishment of the Defoe canon that, though still dominant, has been challenged by Rodney Baine (1974) and, most recently and fully, by P. N. Furbank and W. R. Owens in *The Canonization of Daniel Defoe* (New Haven and London: Yale University Press, 1988).

My page references to the best-known novel, originally entitled *The Life and Strange Surprizing Adventures of Robinson Crusoe, of York, Mariner,* are to *The Life and Adventures of Robinson Crusoe,* ed. Angus Ross (Baltimore: Penguin Books, 1965). Though it modernizes the capitalization, this is an otherwise accurate and accessible text. *The Farther Adventures of Robinson Crusoe,* also first published in 1719, is cited from the 14 volume Shakespeare Head edition (Oxford: Basil Blackwell, 1927), vol. 3.

My citations from Defoe are limited by the theme of the present volume. I deal briefly with his pious meditation on *Robinson Crusoe* in the third part of the novel, the miscellaneous *Serious Reflections during the Life and Strange Surprizing Adventures of Robinson Crusoe: with his Vision of the Angelick World* [1720], vol. 3 of *The Works of Daniel Defoe*, 16 vols., ed. G. H. Maynadier (Boston and New York, 1903–1904), and with three other Defoe novels: *The Life, Adventures, and Pyracies of the Famous Captain Singleton* [1720], ed. Shiv. K. Kumar (London: Oxford University Press, 1972); *The History and Remarkable Life of the Truly Honourable Col. Jacque, commonly Call'd Col. Jack* [1722], ed. Samuel Holt Monk (London: Oxford University Press, 1965); and *The Fortunes and Misfortunes of the Famous Moll Flanders* [1722], ed. G. A. Starr (London: Oxford University Press, 1971). I also refer to two long and important Defoe poems in heroic couplets, *Reformation of Manners: A Satyr* (London, 1702) and *Jure Divino. A Satyr. In Twelve Books* (London, 1706). Defoe's description of his terror of prison is cited from *The Letters of Daniel Defoe*, ed. George Harris Healey (Oxford: Oxford University Press, 1955); his observation about London's many prisons occurs in *A Tour Through the Whole Island of Great Britain* [1724–1727], ed. P.N. Furbank, W. R. Owens, and A. J. Coulson (New Haven and London: Yale University Press, 1991).

Defoe's nonfiction defending the slave trade includes *An Essay upon the Trade to Africa in order to set the Merits of that Cause in a True Light and Bring the Disputes between the African Company and the Separate Traders into a Narrower Compass* (London, 1711) and *A Brief Account of the Present State of the African Trade* (London, 1713). The need for slaves in colonial expansion is also a recurrent theme of Defoe in his *Review* (inaugurated in 1704), especially between 1706–1712, and in the *Manufacturer*, which he edited from October 1719–February 1720. The texts cited are *Defoe's Review*, intro. Arthur Wellesley Secord, Facsimile Text Society, 22 vols. (New York: Columbia University Press, 1938); and *Manufacturer*, intro. Robert N. Gosselink (Delmar, N.Y.: Scholars' Facsimiles and Reprints, 1978).

Against these may be set Defoe's 1702 verse satire, *A Reformation of Manners*, printed in *A True Collection of the Writings of the Author of the True Born Englishman*, 2d ed. (London, 1705), and "Of Captain Mission," in *A General History of the Robberies and Murders of the Most Notorious Pyrates* [2 vols., 1724–1728], ed. Manuel Schonhorn (Columbia: University of South Carolina Press, 1972). Though J. R. Moore's pivotal attribution of the *General History* has been challenged by Furbank and Owens, many scholars follow Moore in considering it part of the Defoe canon. In any case, in the same year (1728) that the final installment of that half-truth, half-fiction *General History* appeared, Defoe also published *Atlas Maritimus and Commercials*, in which slaves, far from being liberated by an egalitarian pirate, are regarded as African "produce." The juxtaposition, if in fact "Of Captain Mission" is from the pen of Defoe, offers a particularly striking example of the famous "ambivalence" with which he is said to have regarded those questions of slavery and the slave trade that are the principal concern of the first part of the present study.

Coleridge's Submerged Politics

Preface

Like a long-legged fly upon the stream
His mind moves upon silence.

Yeats

1

The book that follows consists of two independent but intimately related studies that, together, explore Samuel Taylor Coleridge's role in and response to several crucial issues of the revolutionary and post-revolutionary age: the tragic question of slavery and the Atlantic slave trade, which preceded and outlasted the dawning of "glad day" in France, and the rise and suppression of English radicalism during the decade of the French Revolution itself. J. M. W. Turner's *Slavers Throwing Overboard the Dead and Dying—Typhon Coming On* (1840) provides the visual image that links the two parts. Turner's thin-masted slave ship, luridly lit by a blood-red sunset at sea, was verbally re-created three years later in a celebrated passage in John Ruskin's *Modern Painters*. In turn, painting and description evoke for me that terrifying moment in *The Ancient Mariner* when, with "the western wave . . . all aflame," a bloody, setting sun peers through the skeletal masts of the spectre-bark, "as if through a dungeon-grate."

Several critics have seen in Coleridge's spectre-bark an abolitionist's allusion to the Life-in-Death horrors of a slave ship. I register that somber connection, in the process relating *The Ancient Mariner* to the slave-trading of Robinson Crusoe, and, in Part Two, go on to associate the blood-red sunset, a familiar Romantic-apocalyptic representation of the sanguinary "failure" of the French Revolution, with *counter*-revolution in England. More specifically, I link the dungeon-grate simile with Pittite repression, which intensified dramatically during the invasion panic of March 1798, the month Coleridge was completing his ballad and William Pitt was (successfully) urging renewal of the suspension of habeas corpus.

These interpretations need not be mutually exclusive, given not only their speculativeness but also the multiple meanings of Coleridge's images and the role he assigned to imagination itself as an "intermediate faculty" (*BL* I 124). Imagination, for Coleridge, was "a middle state of mind," a "hovering between images." As soon as the mind "is fixed on one image, it becomes [mere] understanding; but while it is unfixed and wavering between them, attaching itself permanently to none, it is imagination."[1]

However unfixable they may be, the images I've been discussing have something in common: historical resonance. But while the historical context of Turner's painting is overt, and documentable, *The Ancient Mariner,* despite the startling intrusion of that dungeon-grate, remains for virtually all its myriad readers utterly ahistorical, indeed—in Coleridge's own endlessly repeated description—a "supernatural" work of "pure imagination." Simply put, my argument (which participates in the current "demystification" of "the Romantic" *without* demeaning or dismissing aesthetic value) is that Coleridge's extraordinarily graphic and haunting image—while its continuing communicability derives, like Turner's, from artistic genius and depends upon our own intensity of response—also draws much of its power, overt and covert, from its historical context in the Age of Revolution.

This project, a historical as much as a literary study, had its origin in my surprise at what Coleridge *didn't* say in annotating Daniel Defoe's *Robinson Crusoe.* Thus, Part One begins by examining this marginalia, extended notes in which Defoe's hero, his slave-trading activities neither criticized nor even mentioned, is celebrated as humanity's "Universal Representative."

My initial curiosity about an abolitionist's failure to criticize Crusoe as slaver gradually became, in part, a "hook" enabling me to say what I thought needed to be said about Coleridge's own complex and shifting attitudes on race and slavery—as well as to take issue with most Defoe critics, who find their man considerably more "ambivalent" about these matters than I do. As for the "omission" in the marginalia, there are, of course, any number of possible explanations. It might be an instance of the inherent randomness of annotations; or of a possible exercise of "historical imagination" on the part of a sophisticated reader unwilling to fault Crusoe for a moral obtuseness more apparent to Coleridge's than to Defoe's age; or of what many poststructuralists—historicist, Marxist, or psychoanalytic—would call an ideologically determined repression or evasion. Related to the latter, and the most obvious possible explanation, the omission might be a reflection of the shift—religious, political, cultural, anthropological—in Coleridge's own position between his 1792 ode attacking the slave trade and his annotation of *Robinson Crusoe* thirty-eight years later.

The true reason why he did not talk of slavery in these marginal notes may be, *causa sui,* simply that he did not talk of it. But none of these possible explanations *fully* accounts for this silence in the marginalia, a lacuna that remains *some*thing of a curiosity in the annotations of a man who, whatever his oscillating movement from radical liberationist to anthropological racist, remained a lifelong abolitionist. My own search for answers led me to explore the attitude not only of Coleridge but also of Defoe toward slavery and the slave trade, both in their sociopolitical and economic thinking and in the context of

---

1. From the seventh in his 1811–1812 lectures on Shakespeare and Milton; in *Coleridge's Shakespeare Criticism,* ed. T. M. Raysor 2:103.

their two best-known literary works. Thus this first part of the volume offers, along with an account of Coleridge and Defoe on slavery and the slave trade, an examination of *aspects* of *Robinson Crusoe* and of *The Ancient Mariner.* I also provide a sketch of some recent treatments of the Crusoe-Friday story, treatments relevant, by way of contrast, to what Defoe and his merchant-adventurer never see and to what Coleridge, at least in his *Crusoe* marginalia, never says.

My discussion of *The Ancient Mariner* in Part One is limited to noting connections between the poem and *Robinson Crusoe* and to expanding the argument—first advanced in the 1960s by Malcolm Ware and William Empson, and further developed in the early seventies by Empson and J. B. Ebbatson—that Coleridge's poem of guilt, repentance, and continued punishment is covertly related to Western maritime expansion and the slave trade. In the second part, and the most original portion of the project, I propose an even more covert, or at least hitherto undetected, political dimension in *The Ancient Mariner.* Placed in historical and biographical context, several of its crucial images historicized and its significant silences scrutinized, this apparently apolitical work of "pure imagination" emerges as both an inscription and a reflection of its general milieu—the decade of the French Revolution—and of Coleridge's own dangerous political voyaging during the months when, supposedly "retired" from politics, he was simultaneously working on his ballad and, whether anonymously or under a pseudonym, writing anti-Pittite essays and verses for Daniel Stuart's Opposition newspaper, the *Morning Post.*

As these synopses indicate, *Coleridge's Submerged Politics* reflects the current ascendancy of "cultural studies," studies which, largely in reaction to the rebirth of New Criticism in the dehumanized and mandarin form of deconstruction, have restored the sociopolitical "referentiality" theoretically played down or dismissed by these two "isms" at their most formalist.[2] But, just as I try to steer between the excesses of Right and Left in our contemporary culture wars, I also try to strike a balance between "text" and "context." Even in the act of moving beyond the linguistic artifact to the history out of which it emerged, I remain wary of the sort of criticism which, in redressing those evasions that reduced history to "background" or the merely "extrinsic," itself becomes so politicized that it risks reducing works of art to culturally determined tokens of their material moment or to interesting but doomed attempts to escape the history and ideology in which they are inextricably embedded. The so-called "return" to history is a welcome development, so long as it does not become the occasion to put dead authors in the dock or, alternatively, to apparel them in the celestial light of anachronistic political correctness. In either case the result is to sacrifice poems and novels of the past to a present ideological program—an academic "activism" that remains largely aspiration and textual gesture with little or no consequence in the world of actual politics.

2. The status and future agenda of cultural studies can be traced in *Cultural Studies,* the massive survey (nearly fifty essays by diverse hands) edited in 1992 by Lawrence Gross, Cary Nelson, and Paula Treichler.

To return these generalities to the two works examined in the present proj-ect: though much attention is paid here to Defoe's text, and to subsequent treatments of the Crusoe-Friday story, readers of this first part will encounter less about aesthetic detail than about race, racism, slavery, and Western colo-nialism; and Part Two, while it includes close attention to crucial elements of *The Ancient Mariner*, goes into considerable detail about Coleridge's engage-ment with and disengagement from historical and political developments in the 1790s. Nevertheless, in the case of *The Ancient Mariner*, rather than an attempt to "demystify" a poem magnificently resistant to any and all attempts at reductive interpretation, my purpose has been to acknowledge, expand, and *multiply* that extraordinary richness of meaning.

I feel more uneasy about my treatment of *Robinson Crusoe*, which, on *this* occasion, I *do* subject to a rather narrow critique, one that may appear to accept the "new conventional wisdom based on emancipatory values and a dismissal of 'artistic' issues as inherently retrograde." I am quoting Frederick Crews, who, in the introduction to his latest book, welcomes the academic shift to neo-historicism but rightly warns against the critical procedures of the more zealous poststructuralist leftists, who tend to brush aside the overt themes of literary works, "cutting straight through to the racism, sexism, and class rule they regard as the liberal order's secret essence." Despite finding Crusoe and his creator men tainted by their association with slavery, I oppose (to anticipate "optical" imagery employed in the introductory chapter that follows) scrutiniz-ing literature through any single lens, and want no part of that critical "closed shop," as Crews calls it, "in which scholarly questions tend to be answered apri-oristically and in which only a small band of opinion is considered tolerable."[3]

For those on the cultural Left, at least the activist Left, Frederick Crews is a bourgeois conservative posing as a pluralist. But Crews is hardly alone. One thinks of M. H. Abrams, Harold Bloom, Frank Kermode, Robert Alter, Denis Donoghue, Helen Vendler, Edward Said, and Eugene Goodheart, among many less visible others: *very* different critics but passionate humanists all, united in testifying eloquently to the undeniable fact of aesthetic *experience* and in resist-ing those operating within the circumscribed limits of that small band of politi-cally tolerable opinion who are suspicious of, even hostile to, works of art. Marxist and other oppositional "theorizers of the discourse" are less interested in appreciating, illuminating, and evaluating than in "demystifying" aesthetic "objects." As America's leading Marxist critic noted in 1989, "virtually every-one" now "acknowledges the deep constitutive relationship between poetry and politics, between language and power." But there remains a distinction, and anyone who, however opposed to coercive domination, remains more passionately and professionally committed to art than to literary theory, to

3. *The Critics Bear It Away: American Fiction and the Academy*, xvii, xx, xxv. Crews advances a related critique of literary criticism by recent Marxist theorists in "Dialectical Immaterialism," in his *Skeptical Engagements*. For a response to Crews (and Sacvan Berco-vitch), see Donald A. Pease, "New Americanists: Revisionist Interventions into the Canon."

poems than to politics, is bound to resist movements that threaten to marginalize literature itself, subordinating works of the creative imagination to the Marxian imperative to change the world.[4]

2

Those familiar with Coleridge are no strangers to the device of the apologetic preface, a genre he made his own. At the risk of out-Coleridgeing Coleridge in defensiveness, I must acknowledge at the outset that this is an odd project. Ostensibly, I have, in what may seem an absurd and self-indulgent exercise, written at inordinate length about two phantoms: about what Coleridge *didn't* say in his annotations on Defoe's novel, and about "politics" in what would appear to be an utterly *apolitical* poem. To borrow that image Yeats borrowed from Coleridge, my mind has moved like a water-insect "upon silence"—only to break that silence by plunging beneath the surface of the stream.

But in fact, lying beneath both that surface and the genetic curiosity about absences, the real foci of my attention include (along with slavery and the general question of Western maritime expansion) the political turmoil attending the birth pangs of English Romanticism during the 1790s; the social and "internalized" aspects of the Romantic Imagination; the sociocultural context and subsequent critical history of both the Crusoe-Friday story and *The Ancient Mariner;* and, above all, the mind of Coleridge—early and late, receptive and creative, activist and quietist. Even if my initial angle of approach to them may seem idiosyncratic, these are not insignificant subjects.

I cannot deny that the project is self-indulgent in a second way. Emulating

4. Fredric Jameson, Foreword to Roberto Fernández Retamar, *Caliban and Other Essays,* vii. Among other signs of the politicized times and of the marginalization of literature, consider (along with the remarks of Barbara Herrnstein Smith I cite in my Introduction) these observations. The first is from Paul A. Bové's "A Politics of American Criticism." In attending to American literature in the context of "our imperial and oppressive cultural, social order," we must, according to Bové, "theorize the discourse with no advance regard for its 'accomplishments.'" Not that "such theorization should have no interpretive sympathy for its objects"—and Bové points us in a footnote to the remark of a *boundary 2* colleague (Daniel T. O'Hara) acknowledging that "the productive power of critical reading must be balanced by an appreciation for the achievement being read." This concession to aesthetic experience does not, however, get out of ideological hand: "Minus that sympathy," Bové explains, "even the critical understanding necessary to struggle cannot be achieved" (*In the Wake of Theory,* 61, 169*n*).

The second example, more immediately relevant to the concerns of Part Two, is taken from the editors' description of *Beyond Romanticism: Approaches to Texts and Contexts, 1780–1832,* a new collection of poststructuralist, feminist, and New Historicist essays demystifying "the Romantic" and its "dominantly aesthetic construction": "*Beyond Romanticism* represents a substantial challenge to traditional views of the Romantic period and provides a sustained critique of 'Romantic ideology.' The debates with which it engages have been under-represented in the study of Romanticism, where the claims of history have never had quite the same status as they have had in other periods, and where *confidence in poetic literary value remains high*" (Stephen Copley and John Whale, eds., i; italics added).

what Ezra Pound in the 59th of his *Cantos* called "periplum" (the experiential, rather than mapped-out, revelation of a coastline as "seen by men sailing"), I've "voyaged" where my pursuit of these Mariners seemed to take me. Gambling that my ideal readers, informed and interested though not necessarily special- ist, might become engaged by the things that engaged me in the process of researching and writing, I've explored certain historical, biographical, and theoretical details beyond what was necessary to push a thesis. I may have been seduced into too many byways or loaded my boat with too much pemmican.[5] It may be my "grievous fault," as it was Coleridge's as digressive monologist, that "my illustrations swallow up my thesis—[feeling] too intensely the omnipres- ence of all in each . . . [I] go on from circle to circle till I break against the shore of my Hearer's patience, or have my Concentricals dashed to nothing by a Snore" (*CN* II 2372).

Having mentioned both a snore and the even more ominous "theoretical," I hasten to assure the reader that I have *tried* not to contribute to the mass of dense, sometimes impenetrable prose that deforms so many works of current literary theory. Some technical terminology is necessary if we are to get on with the job, but, for the most part, I have steered clear of what Coleridge condemns as the "gypsie jargon" of a professional caste designed to repel all but an initiated coterie, holding instead to what he praises as "the middle style."

In the course of that steering, I move rapidly at times, pause and digress at others. Thus my mental process, though it *does* adhere to my main themes, consciously replicates that movement of Coleridge's "small water-insect on the surface of rivulets" propelling itself by "alternate pulses of active and passive motion": a motion predictably proposed in *Biographia Literaria* as "no unapt emblem of the mind's self-experience in the act of thinking." Coleridge offers, as a model for thinkers and readers alike, a similar emblem seven chapters later: the "motion of the serpent," that is, a willingness to be carried forward, not "by a restless desire to arrive at the final solution; but by the pleasurable activity of mind excited by the attractions of the journey itself" (*BL* I 124, II 14; cf. an earlier metaphor, in *The Friend,* in which philosophic method is described as the progress of a "serpent"). Though in this passage Coleridge frowns on being "carried forward . . . merely or chiefly by the mechanical impulse of curiosity," what eventually *became* this admittedly curious study *began* with curi-

---

5. My "sailing" is related not only to Poundian periplum, but also to the overladen canoe trip described by Claude Manceron in "The Historian and His Pemmican" in *The Wind from America, 1778–1781,* part of his *Age of the French Revolution.* Manceron blames his book's "shortcomings" on the "card-index" (the historian's version of transportable food or Indian pemmican) belonging to "any man crazy enough to set out on a solitary paddle through a quarter of a century in the hope of re-creating it." He soon found his pemmican "spilling over the gunwales of my canoe"; some of the pieces "swelled to such enormity that they nearly scuttled my little craft." He became "a victim of the density" and complexity of interrelated events, until "I was headed for shipwreck from over- weight" (xix, xx). So was I, a fate I hope has been avoided by emulating Manceron's solution, which was to divide a unified project into two parts.

osity, an evolution less mechanical than organic. My inquisitiveness concerned the impact of Coleridge's personal and political attitudes on both his *Crusoe* marginalia and his most celebrated poem, an inquisitiveness that eventually assumed the form of two distinct but equally political questions.

In the case of the marginalia, I was puzzled that a man on record as being morally, intellectually, and emotionally appalled by slavery and the traffic in human flesh should not only say nothing about Robinson Crusoe's slave-trading activities, but should actually propose him as the "Universal Representative" of humanity, an Everyman whose actions, thoughts, and emotions we can all imagine ourselves doing, thinking, feeling. Since I have never been persuaded by the argument, advanced by many Defoe critics, that Defoe, himself "ambivalent" about slavery, was "ironic" in his fictional handling of the subject, I had no great difficulty understanding why Crusoe, as mercantilist and imperialist as his creator, never expresses qualms let alone guilt about his participation in the slave trade. But why, I wondered, was *Coleridge* silent—not only about the very activity that led directly to Crusoe's shipwreck and consequent quarter-century of solitary existence, but also about the later relationship with the native who is both Crusoe's companion and willing slave: "I made him know his name should be Friday; . . . I likewise taught him to say Master, and then let him know, that was to be my name" (*Robinson Crusoe,* 209).

In the case of *The Ancient Mariner,* I wondered why it was that a poem, written and revised during a period of extraordinary political drama in England, should be, if we are to believe virtually all its readers, without even an oblique allusion to British or French politics. This, despite the fact that its author, the most politically astute of the great Romantics and the poet of the 1790s with the most politics in his poetry, was, though in "retirement," closely monitoring and commenting on international and domestic developments during the remarkably eventful and dangerous months he was working on *The Ancient Mariner:* November 1797–late March 1798, with the poem still in his possession and subject to tinkering until May, when it was given to Joseph Cottle, the publisher of *Lyrical Ballads.*

But an offshoot of that question soon emerged. The first part of my study takes off from a lacuna, the *absence* of something *expected;* the second explores a *presence:* the initially *un*expected intrusion into an "apolitical" poem of images either overtly or covertly "political." The crucial images—of dungeon-grate, slave, underwater convulsion, and spiritual or quietist benediction—are recurrent emblems in Coleridge's political lexicon, both in prose and in his millennial-apocalyptic poems referring to international and domestic political events from 1789 to 1798. But what were they doing in *The Ancient Mariner,* a supernatural, escapist poem repeatedly pronounced to be without the slightest reference to the body politic? Examined intrinsically and extrinsically, such images as the dungeon-grate and the subaquatic convulsion emerge as agitated whirlpools in the "stream" of association or, to adapt Freudian metaphors, as signposts on the royal road to the Coleridgean political unconscious, the repressed returning in unexpected figurative language contesting, or at least complicating, the moral argument of the poem and its later prose gloss.

3

That case, for which I have supplied an independent preface and introductory chapter, will be detailed in Part Two, which focuses on the crucial year, mid-1797 to mid-1798. Reversing chronology, the present examination—once past these remarks and a discussion of perspectivism, multiculturalism, and "political correctness"—begins by addressing the annotations on *Robinson Crusoe*, carefully inscribed by Coleridge in the margins of James Gillman's copy of the novel (the 1812 edition) in 1830. In trying to understand Coleridge's silence on Crusoe's slave trading and the master-slave relationship with Friday, I found myself embarked on a voyage in the wake of Coleridge's and Defoe's Mariners. Thus this first section is about—and round-about—two of the "best-loved," most widely read, and frequently reprinted works in all of English literature: at once critically acclaimed masterpieces and, in illustrated versions, perennial favorites among young readers.

Coleridge read *Robinson Crusoe* before he was six and "devoured" it many times before annotating it when he was near sixty, Defoe's age when he wrote the novel. Not surprisingly, Coleridge's most celebrated literary voyage, *The Rime of the Ancient Mariner,* was influenced in a variety of ways by Defoe's riveting work, which burst upon an instantly receptive world in 1719 as *The Life and Strange Surprizing Adventures of Robinson Crusoe, of York, Mariner.* Whatever their generic differences—one the prototypical realist novel, the other a Romantic "supernatural" ballad—both works rise out of their authors' fascination with the sixteenth- and seventeenth-century exploration voyages, the accounts that laid the ideological foundation of Western maritime expansion and the establishment of the great colonial empires. *Robinson Crusoe* is—"certainly not accidentally," as Edward Said notes—"about a European who creates a fiefdom for himself on a distant, non-European island."[6] *The Rime of the Ancient Mariner* is—and not only for readers persuaded by the arguments of Ware, Empson, and Ebbatson—enabled by and reflects the same Western momentum toward overseas expansion. I am also concerned in part with the more-than-titular similarities that link these two haunting "Mariner"-texts: their intertwined motifs of sea, sin, and existential solitude; of transgression, punishment, repatriation; and of at least partial redemption.

On occasion, there are imagistic "links" between the two works. Imagination is the crucial province of the creator, a faculty which, by definition, creates "images." Readers ("actualizers of the text," as we are called by practitioners of reception aesthetics and reader-response criticism) participate in the imaginative act as well, re-creating the poet's creations over time. My own fascination with Defoe's and Coleridge's Mariners has involved brooding—at least semi-creatively, as what Wolfgang Iser would call an "implied reader" completing the "gaps" within the "virtuality" of the unfinished text—over certain inadequately interpreted images. I have, for example, pondered the relationship between what Crusoe calls "this Death of a Life," the lot of "a prisoner locked up with

6. *Culture and Imperialism,* xii.

the eternal bars and bolts of the ocean" (*Robinson Crusoe*, 203, 125), and what Coleridge's Mariner sees: a spectre-bark whose masts resemble the bars of a "dungeon-grate" and whose nightmare passengers are a black-boned skeleton named "Death" and a leprous hag named "Life-in-Death." These graphic images, I suggest, have profound significance for Defoe and Coleridge, men haunted, not without reason, by the claustral fear of imprisonment, actual and emblematic.

But my primary interest lies in connections less overt. The "strange surprizing" silence of Coleridge on Crusoe's involvement in activities that morally revolted the man annotating the novel led me to reexamine Coleridge's positions on slavery and the slave trade. His poems of the 1790s, many of which include attacks on slavery and the trade, his eloquent Bristol lecture and *Watchman* jeremiad, "On the Slave Trade" (1795–1796), his laudatory 1808 review of his friend Thomas Clarkson's monumental *History of the Abolition of the African Slave-Trade*, his almost obsessive condemnations (published and unpublished) of the perversion of persons into things: all these had to be weighed against an increasingly conservative fear of rights without responsibilities and the gradual erosion of Coleridge's racial egalitarianism by what he took to be anthropological evidence to the contrary. That evidence derived largely from the pioneering work of the physical anthropologist J. F. Blumenbach. Though his famous craniological collection was shown to Coleridge in Germany as early as 1799, the poet's Blumenbachian position is most clearly presented in some speculations on race dating to 1825–1827. What emerges from study of these unpublished documents, now in the British Museum, and from passages in Coleridge's later prose and recorded conversations, is a complex picture of the man—still an abolitionist if no longer a racial egalitarian—who sat down in 1830 to reread one of his favorite books.

Study of the tangled racial theories beneath the surface of Coleridge's *essentially* justified reputation as a lifelong abolitionist, in turn, impelled me to probe beneath the verbal surface of the text of *The Ancient Mariner*, plunging into its "submerged," essentially unspoken political context and subtext. Having examined the poem in the light shed by Defoe's novel and the issue of slavery and the slave trade (Part One), I turned to its possible transformation, displacement, and resituation of the domestic political response to events in France: the subject of Part Two.

Together, these explorations sent me on a voyage combining déjà-vu with discovery. Working my way through the great Bollingen edition of the *Collected Works of Samuel Taylor Coleridge*, I found myself rereading material David Erdman had shown me more than twenty years ago and ten years before it was finally published. Cranking through the microfilm of Richard Kaplan's dissertation, "Defoe's Views on Slavery and Racial Prejudice," I found not only that it had been submitted in the same year and to the same institution that had accepted my own, but that it had been supervised by the same New York University professor, Michael Shugrue, for whom I wrote the first version of what eventually became the second chapter of the present volume.

There have been other coincidences and other critical debts, some predictable, some bizarre. Though this book does not rank even as a pinnace in the wake of that venerable four-master of Coleridgean *Quellenforschung,* John Livingston Lowes's *The Road to Xanadu,* I *have* been sailing in some strange waters.[7] Not all have been uncharted. But while others anticipated me in relating Coleridge's poem to maritime expansion, even to the slave trade, a plausible "political" reading of *The Ancient Mariner* as a whole has not yet been offered—either by the literary historians from whom I have learned most (David Erdman, Carl Woodring, E. P. Thompson, M. H. Abrams, Nicholas Roe) nor even by the so-called New Historicists, cultural and literary critics notably attuned to what Jerome McGann calls a poem's "repressed or invisibilized" content.[8]

Of course, fools rush in where angels fear to tread. Though I think I make my case, the argument of Part Two remains speculative despite the concrete detail, the minute particulars, I accumulate in its support. The same is true of Part One—however critically fashionable the pondering of "significant silences" or "not saids" has become in New Historicist, Marxist, and deconstructionist circles. Though I believe it reveals a good deal about Coleridge's political psychology, my puzzling over his marginal lacunae and the tracing of slavery-

7. A few random examples of the "journeying" involved in Part One: In addition to reading Defoe's economic defenses of the slave trade, along with horrifying descriptions of the slave ships that hauled their black cargoes across the Atlantic, I found myself (not alone) contemplating the connections linking James Thomson's description of slaves and their captors devoured by sharks with *The Ancient Mariner* and with J. M. W. Turner's painting, *Slavers.* Before I had done, I had perused such disparate curiosities as Coleridge's remarks on the last will and testament of George Washington; a list of Napoleon's projects while exiled on the island of Elba, including plans for the introduction of a silkworm industry; descriptions of "Golgotha," Blumenbach's craniological collection (the largest in the world at the time), along with those fragmentary manuscripts in which Coleridge speculates on Blumenbach's racial theories; poetic tributes to Defoe and Robinson Crusoe by Walter Savage Landor; and an excited account of his boyhood discovery of *Robinson Crusoe* by the Victorian linguist and adventurer George Borrow, as well as more sober assessments of Crusoe as symbol by Karl Marx, James Joyce, and Adolf Hitler.

The reassessment of Friday is by now almost a twentieth-century mini-industry. I was aware of Friday-centered treatments of Defoe's material by the French novelists Jean Giraudoux and Michel Tournier; Martin Green's timely book, *The Robinson Crusoe Story,* made me realize the astonishing proliferation of variations on the Crusoe theme. Shortly thereafter, I stumbled across a number of texts unmentioned by Green. The day after I read "Man Friday" by the Australian poet A. D. Hope, I ended up in the rare book room of the New York Public Library at Forty-second Street, enthralled by Charles Martin's poetic sequence, *Passages from Friday,* as well as by a charming little booklet, *Crusoe's Only Isle,* by L. A. M. Lichtveld, a former Dutch diplomat resident in Tobago, who was determined not only to establish that Caribbean island as the one Defoe had in mind, but to piece together the whole biography of "Crusoe's 'Man Friday'": a double task admirably accomplished, according to the chairman of the booklet's sponsoring organization, the Tobago Branch of the Trinidad & Tobago Society for the Prevention of Cruelty to Animals.

8. "Introduction: A Point of Reference," in *Historical Studies and Literary Criticism,* 4.

associated and other connections between *Robinson Crusoe* and *The Ancient Mariner* are not calculated to issue in certitudes.

Indeed, my esoteric "in-and-between-the-lines" approach both to Coleridge's marginalia and to his poem may seem at once a variant of New Historicism and a near reductio ad absurdum of the deconstructionist shifting of focus from center to periphery, from presence to absence. In the course of pursuing these absences, Pope's couplet (*An Essay on Criticism* II.326–27) has occasionally floated into mind: "Such laboured nothings, in so strange a style, / Amaze the'unlearned, and make the learnèd smile." I would not be inflicting my pursuit on the reader if I did not believe that, in violation of the old axiom *ex nihilo nihil fit*, in this case something of substance *does* emerge from "nothing." What emerges with some certainty from the examination undertaken in Part One is that Defoe's hero, hardly a "Universal Representative" of humanity, is far from representative of humane Coleridge himself, who—even as a radical turned conservative—thought, felt, and acted in ways markedly different from his proposed Everyman, that chilly epitome of the Age of Mercantilism, Robinson Crusoe.

INTRODUCTION

Parts of the Truth; or, Negotiating Common Ground in the Culture Wars

The whole truth is the best antidote to the Falsehoods
which are dangerous chiefly because they are half-truths . . .

(F II 124)

1

For the most part, theoretical considerations come into play only in the second part of *Coleridge's Submerged Politics,* which proposes a "political" theme of which Coleridge, like his Mariner, may himself have been largely "unaware." In the course of advancing that argument about what is currently referred to as the "political unconscious," I necessarily engage the New Historicists specializing in the Romantic period, especially those whose historicism is mediated by Marxist, psychoanalytic, and deconstructive approaches, and who have of late been emphasizing what such poets as Wordsworth and Coleridge *don't* say in their poems: the political content they allegedly repress as part of a "quietist" move, the Romantics' well-known "inward turn" away from the public and political to the private and imaginative realms.

Despite my emphasis on what *isn't* said in Coleridge's *Robinson Crusoe* marginalia, these critical interactions—involving both agreement with and departure from such contemporary Romantic scholars and historicists as Jerome McGann, Marilyn Butler, Marjorie Levinson, and Kenneth R. Johnston—figure most prominently in my discussion of a political layer of meaning in *The Ancient Mariner.* Fearing that these important but occasionally convoluted issues might add too much pemmican to my canoe or (still worse) congeal into a ponderous theoretical prolegomenon, a dragon at the mouth of the cave repelling precisely those readers I hoped to attract, I decided to concentrate on the poem's "submerged politics" *after* dealing with the chronologically later but more straightforward Coleridge-Defoe material.

At the same time, it would be disingenuous to say *nothing* about critical and political orientation when the primary subject matter of my first three chapters is slavery and the slave trade, race and racism. I've already indicated my general alignment with a "pluralist" like Frederick Crews, which, from the perspective of the adamantly oppositional Left, would situate me on the Right. Yet chapters 1–3 contain a rather harsh "post-colonialist" critique of Crusoe, Defoe, and, to a lesser extent, of Coleridge. To avoid misrepresentation, therefore, I should clarify my critical and political stance. The clarification that follows attends particularly to "perspectivism" and to two unfortunately intertwined contemporary phenomena, each of them distorted by friend and foe alike: I mean "political correctness" and "multiculturalism."

Though I hope the substance of these studies will outlive the moment, readers I am inviting to sail along with me in largely political pursuit of these ancient Mariners have a right to know where I am "coming from" in the context of the current culture wars. Whatever my project's genetic roots and its fate among future readers, the perspective presented here on *Robinson Crusoe* and *The Rime of the Ancient Mariner* cannot be utterly divorced from its immediate context. For the year in which most of this book was written, 1992, was the year of the Los Angeles riots following the original acquittal of the four white policemen tried in the beating of Rodney King; the televising of cultural politics (featuring the performances of Pat Buchanan and Pat Robertson at the Republican convention); the emergence from radio to TV and best-sellerdom of that purveyor of half-truths, Rush Limbaugh; and the resurrection of Malcolm X. And overarching all: the Columbus Quincentenary, which further politicized the debate raging in higher education and in society at large over the impact of cultural diversity on the traditional curriculum and canon—all of it involving such "postmodern" theories and movements as multiculturalism, deconstruction, feminism, academic Marxism, and New Historicism.

Some may think it unnecessary to tour contemporary battlefields scarred by the (equally excessive) debunking and defense of things "Eurocentric" (including the "traditional" canon) and by a new politics of separatism that threatens to reduce American diversity to mere divisiveness. Such readers, especially those less interested in the current culture wars than in Coleridge, may be tempted to skip ahead to Chapter 1. I hope they won't. The aspects of the contemporary scene now to be discussed provide the context for much of what follows, especially in Part One, while the attempt to mediate between perspectivism and the search for truth is at the heart of this as of every honest enterprise.

Given the occasional, if much exaggerated, danger these days of being labeled either politically correct or neanderthal, I'll make a few painfully obvious points at the outset. Like anyone likely to be reading this book, I am opposed to and appalled by racism in all its manifestations—let alone its most cruel and morally debased form, slavery. As an Irishman and an American, I am at least vicariously and empathetically aware of the historical experience of being oppressed and of the capacity of my ilk to oppress others, whether women or people of color, victimized individually and socially by prejudice and collectively through colonialist and literal enslavement of subject races. The present exploration amply demonstrates my commitment to a multiculturalism that, taking into account suppressed ethnic perspectives as well as the *human* experience we have in common, is sensitive to the racist sins of the past—and present. At the same time, I have not enlisted among those who sometimes seem eager to trash (in the name of broadening) the entire Western tradition via some current "ism"—whether the angrier forms of bourgeois-hating Marxism, or radical feminism, or that dogmatic intolerance and exclusionary tribalism that too often *masquerades* as multiculturalism.

Such extremism threatens but cannot undo the positive aspects of any of these perspective-altering ways of envisioning the world. The collapse of the brutal and dehumanizing Soviet version of communism does not invalidate crucial elements of the Marxian diagnosis of capitalism any more than genuine multiculturalism is discredited by what Henry Louis Gates, Jr.—W. E. B. Du Bois Professor of the Humanities and Director of Harvard's Institute for Afro-American Research— calls the "ethnic fundamentalism" of certain Afrocentrists who would resurrect and reverse the racist pseudoscience of the past to prove *black* superiority.

Above all, perhaps, the richest insights of feminism, transcending the necessary but transitional stages of premature assimilationism followed by monolithic sisterhood, have permanently changed the way we *all* see ourselves and our world, including the literature we thought we knew best. "Feminist" texts themselves, especially the writings that have enabled so many gendered *and gender-transcending* contemporary alterations and revisionings, cannot be ghettoized or relegated to "Women's Studies."[1] But neither does "taking feminist arguments seriously" require us, as James A. Winders claims, to "say farewell to the canon that has been the heart, soul, and viscera of the field of intellectual history," a field dominated by supposedly "objective, neutral guardians of humanist values" who are in fact "apologists for sexism, white racial superiority, class privilege, and American imperial hegemony."[2] Though this diatribe re-

---

1. A personal example. I'm now working on a book on W. B. Yeats's female personae in the Crazy Jane poems and the *Woman Young and Old* sequence, a study in part influenced by my reading of the work of such feminists as Julia Kristeva, Hélène Cixous, Luce Irigaray, Elaine Showalter, Susan Robin Suleiman, Wendy Lesser, and my Le Moyne colleague Susan Bordo. I'm far from certain that Yeats's female speakers embody *écriture féminine* or that Yeats (any more than Joyce in the "Penelope" episode of *Ulysses* or, more recently, Norman Rush in his 1991 novel *Mating*) has completely refuted the gender separatists by successfully meeting the Tiresian challenge male writers sometimes set themselves to create a fully realized female character. I *am* sure, however, that my book is less obtuse as a result of exposure to these feminist writings; and that, like Yeats himself in liberating what he called "the woman in me," I have, in the empathetic process of reading and writing, opened myself up to some degree to the "other half," my Jungian anima.

2. *Gender, Theory, and the Canon*, 12, 4. As a "first step" to a radical revision of the canon, Winders takes up the "wager" of the "right culture prophets" by rereading, "through the perspectives of feminist and other postmodern theories," five canonical texts—by Descartes, Marx, Flaubert, Freud, and Nietzsche—in order to expose their omissions and unstated gender assumptions and prejudices (17, 145).

peats the cant litanies typical of the school of indictment, such attention to covert structures of domination beneath the surface of liberal humanism is salutary—until it calls for the canonical books to be consigned to the flames, or, under the aegis of our postmodern "hermeneutics of suspicion," to be read largely as an exercise in demystification and sin exposure, or as "objects" to be engaged as part of the antihegemonic struggle.

That Western culture—Eurocentric and imperialist, racist, classist, and sexist—deserves much of the critique leveled against it no honest person would dispute, though such a person would—or should—add that the same culture that oppressed and enslaved also produced enlightened core ideas of tolerance and liberation. To focus for a moment on the primary subject of the three chapters that follow: It scarcely diminishes the horrors of the Atlantic slave trade to acknowledge that black slavery had for many centuries prior to European intervention been controlled by Egyptian pharaohs, Black African kings, and Arab (not, pace Louis Farrakhan, Jewish) traders, and that it was *only* (however belatedly) the nineteenth-century nations of Europe and North America, states shaped by the Enlightenment, that abolished slavery—facts glossed over by politically correct historians justifiably exercised by oppression, providing it is *Western* oppression. The disturbing interdependence of these opposites, indeed the thesis that "freedom was generated from the experience of slavery," is at the heart of Harvard sociologist Orlando Patterson's award-winning *Freedom,* the first of two projected volumes on that "supreme value of Western culture." There are other aspects of liberation; and a similarly paradoxical case can be made—Richard Tarnas makes it compellingly—that the Western project is not to be "rejected as an imperialist-chauvinist plot" since, "all along," the underlying goal of the West's dialectical development has been what many see as the imminent reunion of "the long-dominant but now alienated masculine and the long-suppressed but now ascending feminine."[3]

Pending that happy denouement, less teleological equanimity is to be expected from those still oppressed by patriarchy, or tired of being relegated to the peripheral and tribal by Europeans and Anglo-Americans claiming theirs as not only the superior but the "common" or "universal" culture. Yet many of the most passionate loathers of the West are not outsiders, but inner émigrés, leftists whose revolutionary impulses are usually confined to the library. To want to retributively level Western civilization itself—metaphorically or literally, as some radicals within the walls occasionally pretend—seems an apocalyptism quarried out of knowledge, righteous indignation, and a loving empathy for the West's historical victims, on the one hand, and frustration, *ressentiment,* and guilt-ridden self-hatred, on the other.

The history under assault, European and post-Columbian American, is both glorious and a series of slaughter-benches, an imposing edifice erected on ground often saturated with the blood of victims. Yet the death of the West is

---

3. See Tarnas's post-Jungian epilogue to *The Passion of the Western Mind: Understanding the Ideas that Have Shaped Our World View,* 443, 444.

hardly a consummation devoutly to be wished, especially when, as much of the current critique demonstrates, Western culture is itself uniquely characterized by a saving pluralist and critical tradition less "insular" than open to "foreign" influence, and less monolithic than internally subversive. Western conventions have been challenged from the Sophists and Socrates on; critique is an inherent part of the Western tradition, and the roots of democratic pluralism, indeed of multiculturalism itself, are distinctively Eurocentric. Those skeptical of everything but the guilt of Western liberalism and humanism inherit their skepticism, along with the freedom to exercise their inquiring spirit, from the very tradition they rather indiscriminately condemn.[4] Allan Bloom's contention that "only in the Western nations, i.e., those influenced by Greek philosophy, is there some willingness to doubt the identification of the good with one's own way" is vulnerable to riposte: "This is almost a Cretan liar's paradox," writes Michael Berubé, "from which it follows that the West is superior to other cultures because the West knows how to doubt its superiority to other cultures." Nevertheless, most scholars and teachers, including most of those who give conservatives unquiet dreams, welcome a multiculturalism out, not to bury the West, but (in Berubé's phrase) to "*enrich* our sense of Western culture."[5]

Less committed to that particular enrichment than to rectifying the injustices of the West, some radical educators, "cultural materialists" and other proponents of "oppositional" criticism, want the classroom and the curriculum to become instruments of revolutionary social transformation, conceived of as an essential part of a necessary revolt against the imperialist, racist, hegemonic, late-capitalist state and all its political, social, and cultural "apparatuses of domination." Transformative pedagogies of "the oppressed" or "of difference" or "of enablement" unsurprisingly depict the "official" Western canon—intended, claims Frank Lentricchia, "to exclude all but a single, continuing voice of the hegemonic classes"—as a fixed, static instrument of oppression and sinister

4. In the United States, the despised category of the "culturally comfortable" surely extends to those "oppositional" critics united in their contempt for Eurocentric liberal humanism. The situation is changing in Europe itself. In an article on the momentous transformation of Eastern Europe in 1989, Gerald Marzorati remarked in July 1990 that, following those extraordinary events, "the language of liberalism [which] has its roots in the European Enlightenment has been reclaimed by European intellectuals" who had until quite recently embraced "the variety of anti-liberal, anti-humanist modes of thought grouped under the rubric 'post-structuralism'" (*International Herald Tribune*, July 11, 1990). As Robert Hughes observes in *Culture of Complaint: The Fraying of America*, while the American academic Left was, in the late 1980s, "emptily theorizing" that "repression is inscribed in all language, . . . the longing for freedom and humanistic culture was demolishing the very pillars of European tyranny" (72).

5. In "Public Image Limited: Political Correctness and the Media's Big Lie," 129–30, 149, Berubé parries Bloom's (typically sweeping but nevertheless accurate) point made in *The Closing of the American Mind: How Higher Education Has Failed Democracy and Impoverished the Souls of Today's Students.*

socialization, reducing students, according to William V. Spanos, to "good" citizens, that is, "willing subjects and agents of hegemonic authority."[6]

An initial reaction would be to dismiss this as an overestimation of the impact of the canon—which, to begin with, is hardly "single"-voiced—on actual students, many of whom cannot construe complex sentences, follow arguments, or detect shifts in tone and diction, let alone so immerse themselves in Great Books as to become browbeaten into submissive citizenship. Yet advocates of "critical teaching," for whom "pedagogy *is* politics," and (of course) readers of Michel Foucault, are aware of the covert ways in which education, the institutionalized form of his indissoluble "power/knowledge" complex, reproduces "authorized" knowledge by imposing "political conformity" upon students through a "double repression"—excluding the oppressed and imposing "bars" even on those included and "normalized" within the discipline. For Foucault, "surveillance" and "the modern spirit of punishment" operate not only in prisons and factories, but among schoolchildren as well. Still, his distinction-blurring obsession with forms of perpetual control and his genealogical skepticism in general should not lead educators to abandon either the canon or canon-reform. The potential for genuine liberation, once teachers take their students beyond the passive literacy that provides society with docile and obedient citizens, is likeliest to be found in an evolving canon and curriculum that recover the voices and perspectives excluded or marginalized by the "dominant discourse" but which also preserve the cultural inheritance embodied in the great works of that terrible thing, Western civilization. And, so long as it does not become simply an excuse to replace literature with theory and politics, we should consider bringing our students into the discussion, possibly revitalizing education by exposing them to the tensions and ideological conflicts at the heart of today's debates over canon, curriculum, and the very purpose of teaching in a democracy.[7]

6. Readers of this paragraph's opening sentence will recognize the once-vivid language (now almost drained of force by numbing repetition) of Antonio Gramsci, Raymond Williams, Fredric Jameson, and Louis Althusser. The references to the "pedagogy of the oppressed," of "difference," and of "enablement" are to Paulo Freire, Henry Giroux, and Mas'ud Zavarzadeh, respectively. See Lentricchia's *Criticism and Social Change* for his definition of the canon as an effort at exclusion through the repression of difference and a "dematerialization" that hides "class conflict by eliding the text's involvement in social struggle" (128, 131). Spanos's phrase, from *Repetitions: The Postmodern Occasion in Literature and Culture,* is cited by Giroux in "Liberal Arts Education and the Struggle for Public Life: Dreaming about Democracy," 126. For a "genealogical"-radical interpretation of liberal humanist pedagogy "culminating" in the recently revised, "stabilizing" Harvard "core," see Spanos, *The End of Education: Toward Posthumanism.*

7. For a dozen oppositional essays urging teachers to train their students to recognize and resist the apparatuses of domination and socialization, see Maria-Regina Kecht, ed., *Pedagogy Is Politics: Literary Theory and Critical Teaching.* In addition to Foucault's *Discipline and Punish: The Birth of the Prison,* see his 1971 essay "Revolutionary Action: 'Until Now,'" in *Language, Counter-Memory, Practice: Selected Essays and Interviews,* 218–33, especially 219.

Gerald Graff's imperative, repeatedly advanced since 1987, is that we "teach the conflicts"; that educators, agreeing to disagree about the issues that divide us in the

The imposition of power comes in many forms, often cloaked as Western humanism. But those who go beyond vigorous confrontation of the Western tradition to indulge in routine canon-bashing occasionally forget that the canon is anything but monolithic, and that the ideas in many Western masterworks were at odds with the received wisdom of their own day. Of course, as neo-Marxists and other critics of imperialism and "deceptive" liberal pluralism insist, capitalist societies shaped by Western culture tend to produce and reabsorb their own countercultural antagonists, at once permitting and defusing radical ideas—a neutralization also visible in the fixing of "specializations" in the contemporary university. Edward Said is hardly alone in noting a consumer culture's "phenomenally incorporative capacity, which makes it possible for anyone in fact to say anything at all, but [by means of which] everything is processed either toward the dominant mainstream or out to the margins."[8] But is that process, specifically when it comes to the canon, conspiratorially directed from on high? And is co-optation inevitable? While few can doubt the power exercised by a dominant, disciplining ideology and its market forces, it seems reductive (and defeatist) for so many on the Left to dismiss *all* the political radicalism, skepticism, heterodoxy, and dissent in the existing European, English, and American canons as instances of Antonio Gramsci's "passive revolution," or of what Herbert Marcuse (in a related oxymoron first employed in 1968) used to call "repressive tolerance."

Both were referring to dissent orchestrated, controlled, and finally "dissipated" by those in power, or (more subtly) by what Gramsci—that least reductive, least orthodox, and therefore most attractive of Marxists—called "hegemony," the true power of which lies in making bourgeois domination seem natural, even preordained. Though Gramsci saw that the power of bourgeois hegemony resided in its control of the very ways of thinking, speaking, living, hoping, and fearing, so that the subject many *accept* a system that serves the interests of the powerful few, he also saw a way out: a way for the proletariat, recognizing and resisting *this* hegemony, to defeat and replace it with its own hegemony, a supposedly just social order enabling men and women to become free and fully human.

His is the position taken by many recent oppositional critics who find those who acknowledge the perpetual capacity of the "system" to foster and "contain" subversive forces unduly pessimistic and quietist. Though these contem-

---

current culture wars, make the clash pedagogically productive by including our students in the canonical and ideological debate. There are always such dangers as pedagogical self-indulgence or taming a debate by institutionalizing it, but the risks may be worth it. See Graff's *Beyond the Culture Wars: How Teaching the Conflicts Can Revitalize American Education*. In this paragraph I also echo Northrop Frye's remark that society "supports compulsory education because it needs docile and obedient citizens." Such "passive acquirements" as learning to read traffic signs and make out our income tax exhaust society's interest in literacy. "Teachers take over from there: their task is to transform a passive literacy into an active postliteracy, with the responsibility and freedom that is part of any world we want to live in" ("Literary and Linguistic Scholarship in a Postliterate World," in *Myth and Metaphor: Selected Essays, 1974–1988*, 18).

8. *Culture and Imperialism*, 323–24.

porary oppositionalists often lack Gramsci's commitment and his antideterministic defense of human freedom, they share his conviction that knowledge can change the given—even in a capitalist culture that transforms radical ideas into consumer products destined for a short shelf life ending in planned obsolescence. Such critics, including but not limited to more action-oriented *marxisant* historicists, are either optimistically insistent or desperately hopeful about the power of oppositional forces—both in their own political criticism and in the literature of the past—to effectively challenge the existing order through "authentic breaks," efforts that are (in Raymond Williams's Gramscian phrase) independent and "free" in the sense that they are "irreducible to the terms of the original or adaptive hegemony."[9] Such efforts—to return to the question of the canon—can find sustenance in the very citadels of high culture. Indeed, many implications in canonical works, not all intended by the original authors, retain their subversive potential—a potential "actualized" when the texts are engaged by attentive readers. Such readers include those open to the "counter, original, spare, strange" things that constitute the "pied beauty" of the *actual*— rather than the allegedly "hegemonic" or "monolithic"—canon, as well as those adept at reading classics against the grain, at detecting ideologically significant silences, and at "read[ing] between the lines to recover the opinions of those who wrote in censoring societies."[10]

While some "appropriating" readers distort or reinvent works of art to serve their own political agendas, remaking texts when the body politic proves recalcitrant, at least certain time-tested and indispensable works—gradually joined by marginalized and new works—are still being *engaged*. But what if that long-sustained dialogue breaks down, and continuity and commonality disappear, splintered by the laudable "diversity" championed by populist and multicultural elitists who, conversant with the major ideas and texts themselves, paternalistically inform their students that the Western conversation is irrelevant to *them?* The tragic and predictable result would be precisely, and ironically, what all educators work against: student marginalization and ignorance. Those who justifiably attack neoconservative simplifications, distortions, and omissions regarding the Western legacy seldom tell us why our students come to, and often leave, college knowing so little. And as the neopragmatist philosopher Richard Rorty (hardly a conservative despite the endorsement of individual freedom implicit in his engagement in "the conversation of the West") points out in defending the sensible but much abused cultural-literacy reforms advanced by E. D. Hirsch, Jr., "you cannot liberate a tabula rasa."[11]

9. For a discussion of Gramsci's concept of hegemony and of authentic opposition, see Raymond Williams, *Marxism and Literature,* 108–27.

10. Annabel Patterson, Introduction to *Reading between the Lines,* 7. See also her *Censorship and Interpretation.* The other text quoted is, of course, Gerard Manley Hopkins's poem "Pied Beauty."

11. "Two Cheers for the Cultural Left," 237. Rorty's model of philosophy, alternative to a foundational search for Truth, is that of a continuing "conversation," especially "the conversation of the West" (*Philosophy and the Mirror of Nature,* 394).

The truth of that axiom is powerfully confirmed by two of the classic texts I engage in the present project: C. L. R. James's *The Black Jacobins* and E. P. Thompson's *The Making of the English Working Class* (which appeared in 1963, the same year as the revised edition of James's 1938 study of Toussaint Louverture). James, a black West Indian Marxist historian who is both anti-imperialist and rooted in the Western European heritage, shows how Toussaint's own struggle for liberation from French colonialist slavery was informed by study of French writings (the Declaration of the Rights of Man, the ideas of Diderot, the Abbé Raynal, Robespierre, Danton, and, especially, Rousseau and Mirabeau), while Thompson reminds us of the importance of English literature, Shakespeare above all, to the culture that nourished nineteenth-century British radicalism. Precisely this point about the cultural and political work of these two anti-imperialist historians has recently been made by Edward Said, perhaps the most prominent of our politically engaged literary critics, and by Robert Hughes, that Australian cosmopolite whose *The Fatal Shore* (1987) bears the traces of his reading of James and Thompson.

Reaffirming the advances made by the demystification of Eurocentrism and patriarchy while attacking the poststructuralist reduction of works of literature to mere "texts" totally determined by their historic situation and further limited by similarly determined readers, Said mounts an impressive defense of literary excellence as a criterion of evaluation and of the liberatory—humanist and antiseparatist—potential of canonical works. "One of the greatest pleasures for those who read and study literature," he writes,

> is the discovery of longstanding norms in which all cultures known to me concur: such things as style and performance, the existence of good as well as lesser writers, and the exercise of preference. What has been most unacceptable during the many harangues on both sides of the so-called Western canon debate is that so many of the combatants have ears of tin and are unable to distinguish between good writing and politically correct attitudes, as if a fifth-rate pamphlet and a great novel have more or less the same significance. Who benefits from leveling attacks on the canon? Certainly not the disadvantaged person or class whose history, if you bother to read it at all, is full of evidence that popular resistance to injustice has always derived immense benefits from literature and culture in general, and very few from invidious distinctions made between ruling-class and subservient cultures.

"After all," he continues, "the crucial lesson" of such works as those by James and Thompson

> is that great antiauthoritarian uprisings made their earliest advances, not by denying the humanitarian and universalist claims of the general dominant culture, but by attacking the adherents of that culture for failing to uphold their own declared standards, for failing to extend them to all, as opposed to a small fraction of humanity. . . . It does not finally matter *who* wrote what, but rather *how* a work is written and *how* it is read.[12]

---

12. "The Politics of Knowledge," reprinted in Paul Berman, ed., *Debating PC: The Controversy over Political Correctness on College Campuses*, 188. Said's remarks here are

More than most, Said has been eulogized and castigated. A "professor of terror" to those who oppose his support of the Palestinian cause, he has been a hero to most on the anti-imperialist and activist Left. But even here there are signs of a recent shift. Some were disturbed by his distinction, at the 1992 Modern Language Association convention in New York City, between political engagement outside the classroom, which of course he advocates, and politicized pedagogy, which he spoke against; and, as he reports in "The Politics of Knowledge," he was recently attacked for devoting most of a paper to dead European white males while failing ("How could you do such a thing?" asked one hostile member of the audience) to utter the names of any politically approved and modish "Others." This is almost to reverse the famous travail of Lafayette, forced in 1792 to escape from France as a reactionary only to be thrown into an Austrian dungeon as a dangerous radical. Said's is a unique case, but the audience responses just mentioned are exemplary not only of the role of perspective but of what Said calls "caricatural reductiveness" in the current culture wars—including "clamorous dismissals and swooping assertions" regarding the canon.[13]

Still, as *Culture and Imperialism* reconfirms, Said remains a politically committed man. Others are not; and the "consequence," as Byron said, of "being of no party" is to "offend all parties" (*Don Juan* IX.xxvi). From the perspective of the hard Right, those who, however wary of politicized pedagogy, seek a conciliatory middle ground will seem altogether too friendly with the enemy; while, from the perspective of the radical Left, ameliorative pluralists and "aesthetes" resemble those Young Hegelians so devastatingly exposed by Marx in *The German Ideology:* culturally comfortable bourgeois conservatives deluded by their own dialectical and liberatory rhetoric. Though committed to the fruitful tension between past and present, tradition and innovation (it is, notes Blake, "the thankful receiver" who "bears a plentiful harvest"), I am not about to endorse Coleridge's utopian vision of a civilizing and conserving "clerisy." Yet the essentially Coleridgean, "humanistic," and even conservative nature of my stance can be conveyed in imagery suggested by this project's focus on two celebrated literary mariners. Rather than a political, cultural, or pedagogical capsizer, I am what Donald Reiman has called Coleridge: a "true trimmer," a balancer of the boat inclined by nature as well as seamanship to shift to the less populated, and less noisy, side of the vessel.

---

fleshed out in his capstone work, *Culture and Imperialism* (see 245–48 for more on C. L. R. James). While he continues to insist on the distinction between good and bad literature and defends aesthetic value, he calls there (in imagery reflecting his own passion for music) for a "global, contrapuntal analysis" in which texts and "worldly institutions" are seen as "working together," not (as previously) on the model of a "symphony," but rather as an "atonal ensemble" (318). Connecting the West's "estimable and admirable" works of art with "the imperial processes" in which they participated is not a simple act of condemnation; indeed, what we learn in this way "actually and truly *enhances* our reading and understanding of them" (xiv).

13. "The Politics of Knowledge," 172–75, 183.

This may also make me a "trimmer" in the worst—Dantesque—sense. But the trimming I have in mind is not just an acknowledgment of the partial validity of both sides of an argument; and it is less a matter of equivocation than of mediation. Such a mediating "Yes but"—resembling the "Yea *but* Nay" doubling attributed to Coleridge by Alan Liu as well as the dialectical function of what Blake called in *The Marriage of Heaven and Hell* the "reprobate"—is a closure-denying opposition that, privileging *neither* of the terms in fashionable binary polarities, provides instead a progress-engendering pluralist "contrary" to the usual facile political alternatives presented by Right and Left.[14] Though, as Blake said, "Contraries are Positives," not negations, and "Without Contraries is no progression,"[15] a contrarian dialectic *can* produce an admittedly tedious sequence of "on-the-other-hands." At the risk of being at once obvious and offensive, here are some examples drawn from the present volume.

Exercising—though, I believe, not utterly bound by—my own perspective, I have not rigorously resisted the temptation, in chapters 2 and 3, to pass indignant or "moralistic" judgment on both Defoe and Robinson Crusoe. Nor have I (in chapter 1) ignored Coleridge's later sorry lapses from his early racial egalitarianism. To be *completely* judgmental would be to succumb to ahistorical smugness, a self-righteous measuring of Defoe and Coleridge by contemporary standards, moral or ideological. On the other hand, to pass *no* judgment would be to accede to an au courant cultural relativism and historical determinism according to which no one can be expected to glimpse *any*thing beyond one's limited horizon, one's own socioeconomic and cultural milieu.

What seems needful is a balance, an act of mediation combining "historical imagination" with an equally empathetic capacity to be disturbed by cruelty and injustice. A major test case, immediately relevant to the issues raised in the three chapters that follow, is offered by the master Mariner himself, Christopher Columbus, under intense scrutiny (books, documentaries, two feature films, at least one "politically correct" novel) during the quincentennial of 1492. If, as has been recently remarked, "Columbus was mugged on the way to his own party," the muggee was not a completely innocent victim.[16] Though the quincentennial year produced less complex mediation than acrimonious polarization, the reassessment finally took into account—along with Columbus's misconceived but brilliant seamanship, spirit of enterprise, and apparent affection for many of the indigenous peoples he encountered—his fifteenth-century worldview: ethnocentric, Christian, and imperialist. Meeting the inhabitants of Tortuga, though "they did not understand me nor I them," Columbus somehow "gathered" from what the young "king" and some of his "counsellors" said that

14. See Liu, *Wordsworth: The Sense of History*, 422.

15. "Contraries are Positives. A Negation is not a Contrary," is engraved in reverse on the title page of *Milton: Book the Second;* the more famous axiom is from Plate 3 of *The Marriage of Heaven and Hell* (*The Poetry and Prose of William Blake*, ed. David V. Erdman, 128, 34).

16. Kenneth Maxwell, "¡Adiós Columbus!" 38.

"the whole island was at my command," one of those "marvellous possessions" of which Stephen Greenblatt has recently written.[17]

Like Robinson Crusoe, who turned his island into a miniature England, completed by his eventual transformation of a native into a slave-servant, the quincentennial Columbus emerges as less the discoverer of a New World than a man of his time who brought an Old World vision across the sea with him. That vision, shaped by a quest for souls and gold, ended up quickly depleting the supply of both, focusing greed instead on (what would become Crusoe's crop) sugarcane, thus institutionalizing indigenous and, soon, imported plantation slavery. Any thoughts Columbus had of a profitable trade in slaves from the New World back to Europe were undone by the extermination of much of the Antillean population from disease and the shattering of their physical environment, an unintended holocaust that led, in turn, to the importation of enslaved Africans to fill the labor vacuum in the islands. We are, all of us, still living with the consequences; but, here again, what are needed are studies (like those of James Lockhart, Robert Royal, David J. Weber, and Richard White) that rightly empathize with the Amerindian and African victims of the European invasion without succumbing to the more egregiously naive, anachronistic, politically correct forms of moralizing.[18]

Though, in my sometimes indignant, sometimes flippant critique of Defoe

17. *Marvellous Possessions: The Wonder of the New World*, 13. Quoting this passage from the diary of the first voyage, Greenblatt writes: "I am fascinated by the move, here and elsewhere, from knowing nothing . . . to imagining an absolute possession, . . . a legitimate appropriation."

18. Slavery existed in the Americas before the arrival of Columbus—a point glossed over by such anti-Columbians as Kirkpatrick Sale, in whose readable but politically correct *The Conquest of Paradise: Christopher Columbus and the Columbian Legacy,* Columbus, representative of the evil Old World, shatters the idyllic harmony of the New—as if indigenous slavery, warfare, bloody sacrifice, and cannibalism were myths invented by Europeans. In fact, the Arawaks, when Columbus "discovered" them, were being eaten with some frequency by the Caribs, their neighbors from the Lesser Antilles. Nevertheless, Columbus not only prepared the way for the importation of African slaves, but also enslaved some of the natives he encountered. The passages that follow are quoted (from Cecil Jane's 1930 translation of Columbus's log and other documents pertinent to the first voyage) by George P. Horse Capture in "An American Indian Perspective": "And as soon as I arrived in the Indies, in the first island, which I found, I took by force some of them." Writing to his sponsors, "their highnesses," Columbus promises gold and other riches, including unconverted "slaves, as many as they shall order to be shipped and who will be from the idolators" (189, 191). Largely because of disease, that potential "many" soon dwindled to very few.

The Columbus Quincentenary inspired an avalanche of studies legitimately seeking to redress the Eurocentrism of the past. But some revisionists have erred on the other side, presenting a romanticized, pristine world of saintly Noble Savages contaminated and killed by invariably evil white men. For example, in describing "the Americas through Indian eyes, since 1492," Ronald Wright, in *Stolen Continents,* narrates a poignant and crucial tale. In doing so, however, he sometimes substitutes for one myth, the Eurocentric, another, which is far more appealing but almost as one-sided, simplistic, and incomplete.

and his hero, I am not only analytic but also accusatory, I have for the most part tried to balance moralizing with mediation. Reflecting common decency and our own cultural milieu, this volume participates in the modern recuperation of the mute and marginalized—in this case, of Friday (a fictional descendant of Caribs, who were first and accurately described as cannibals by an initially skeptical Columbus). But in negotiating that act of balancing and recuperation, I do not, as a "true trimmer" or Blakean "reprobate," ally myself with those extremists on the politically correct cultural Left who, in rightly seeking empowerment of the victimized, proclaim a new, segregated hierarchy—a "privileging" both contemporaneous and historically retrospective. The new separatism is not, like the old, brutally inflicted by whites; and since it neither dominates nor persecutes, its practitioners and semantic apologists deny that it is "racist." It does matter which haters and name-callers have power, and a commitment to redress historical injustice and to resist discrimination requires us to be discriminate in our indignations. Nevertheless, black self-segregation can be as dogmatic and supremacist as white racism, too often simply reversing the "privileged" and "demonized" groups—in the most notorious recent case, exalting black over white, superior "sun people" or people of color over demonic European "ice people."

The latter contrast, largely indebted to the Afrocentrist Egyptologist Cheikh Anta Diop, is that of Leonard Jeffries, the controversial but hardly isolated chairman of African American Studies at the City University of New York, who claims that melanin, the dark skin pigment, gives blacks intellectual and physical superiority over whites. "Our thesis," he told his students in 1990, "is that the sun people, the African family of warm communal hope, meets an antithesis, the vision of ice people, Europeans, colonizers, oppressors, the cold, rigid element in world history."[19]

There are echoes here, not only of Diop, but of the old Third World concept of *négritude*, defined by one of its leading developers, Senegalese poet and statesman Léopold Senghor, as the "sum total of the values of the African world," one of which is "communal warmth." But Jeffries has none of Senghor's integrationist emphasis. He is in fact one of the "new pharaohs" and xenophobic loose cannons warned against by Gates and Cornel West,[20] cultural pluralists

19. First reported in the New York *Newsday* in 1990, Jeffries' now famous "thesis" was repeated in *Time* (August 26, 1991), 19–20. The controversies surrounding Jeffries came to a head when he chose a conference sponsored by New York State to lash out at movie moguls and other "rich Jews," and to repeat charges made in that Nation of Islam pseudohistory, *The Secret Relationship between Blacks and Jews,* that Jewish merchants often dominated the Atlantic slave trade (baseless charges refuted in 1992 by Harold Brackman). In the wake of demands for action on the part of many, including Governor Mario Cuomo, Jeffries was dismissed from his chairmanship in the spring of 1992. He claimed violation of his civil rights, sued in federal court, and, rightly winning a case botched from the outset by the university, was reinstated in his chair and awarded $300,000 in damages.

20. See Gates, "Beware of the New Pharaohs" and his 1992 collection, *Loose Canons:*

who seek what Gates and an increasing number of recent commentators—including Benjamin Barber, Morris Dickstein, Robert Hughes, and even Edward Said—have been advocating as "a middle way" between the Manichaean extremes presented by polarized "reactionaries" and "radicals." Gates's "middle way" is between the equally untenable and "vulgar" nationalist polemics of a Jeffries on the one hand and an Allan Bloom or William Bennett on the other, between "the mindless celebration of difference for its own sake" and "the nostalgic return to some monochrome homogeneity." As for the invocation of Otherness associated with Jeffries, Gates writes: "Bogus theories of 'sun' and 'ice' people, and the invidious scapegoating of other ethnic groups, only resurrects the worst of 19th century racist pseudoscience—which too many of the pharaohs of 'Afrocentrism' have accepted without realizing."[21]

Notes on the Culture Wars. Writing in 1991, in *Democratic Left,* Cornel West, Professor of Religion and Director of the Afro-American Studies Program at Princeton, makes this balanced point: "Within the multicultural debate, leading Afrocentric and Africanist thinkers Leonard Jeffries and Molefi Asante articulate a critical perspective that says they are tired of the degradation of things African. On this particular point, they're absolutely right. However, they don't have a subtle enough sense of history, so they can't recognize ambiguous legacies of traditions and civilizations. They refuse to recognize the thoroughly hybrid culture of almost every culture we have ever discovered. In the case of Jeffries, this lack of subtlety slides down an ugly xenophobic slope—a mirror image of the Eurocentric racism he condemns" ("Diverse New World," 327–28). In "The Crisis of Black Leadership," a 1988 *Z Magazine* essay reworked for *Race Matters,* West remarks that "much, though not all, of Afrocentric thought" entails black expression of racist white hierarchies, with "rhetoric a substitute for analysis" (43).

21. *Loose Canons,* xvi, xix; "Beware of the New Pharaohs," 47. Bennett and Bloom, though "vulgar," are treated with relative civility by Gates. The "dynamic duo of the new cultural right," they are the "'feel good' targets . . . we all love to hate" (*Loose Canons,* 17–18). But his hatred is as nothing compared to the deep hostility and apoplectic rage with which many on the cultural Left responded to Bennett's *To Reclaim a Legacy* (National Endowment for the Humanities, 1984) and Bloom's *Closing of the American Mind.* Even Hirsch's apparently benign *Cultural Literacy: What Every American Needs to Know* has been widely condemned. Leaving aside Bloom's openly elitist jeremiad and Bennett's pamphlet, Hirsch's short book resembles Diane Ravitch's 1990 *American Scholar* essay, "Multiculturalism: E Pluribus Plures," and *The Disuniting of America: Reflections on a Multicultural Society,* by Arthur Schlesinger, Jr., in that all three speak of a common American culture formed by the commingling of diverse cultures in a single nation—a "privileging" of similarity felt by many to be indistinguishable from that assimilative erasure of "difference" intolerable to multiculturalists.

Cogent discussions of these issues may be found in three studies published in 1992, and in three lectures given that year by Robert Hughes, since expanded and published as *Culture of Complaint.* Writing with his usual passion, verve, and satiric wit, Hughes calls, like Schlesinger, for a reknitting of an American cultural fabric frayed by the ludicrous excesses of both Left and Right, extremes that meet and that he diagnoses as symptoms of a single puritanical malaise. Of the other three books alluded to, the first and most relevant is Benjamin R. Barber's *An Aristocracy of Everyone: The Politics of Education and the Future of America.* In his crucial fourth chapter, Barber stresses "the fine balance required to preserve a union rooted in difference," a middle way between an "under-

I dwell on an extremist like Jeffries not only because he presents a mirror image of the white racism I focus on in the first part of the volume that follows, but because of a provisional convergence. That what Hamlet's Horatio would call a "piece" or "part" of me is sympathetic to aspects of Jeffries' admittedly invidious "thesis" will be clear from my treatment of the contrast between frigid, domineering Crusoe and warm, appealing Friday—an antithesis present even in Defoe's novel and certainly emphasized in such later "anti-Robinsons" as the works I discuss by Jean Giraudoux, Michel Tournier, A. D. Hope, J. M. Coetzee, and Charles Martin. These are all white authors, and their theses, though more benign than the reverse racism of Jeffries and his followers, are perhaps no less partial. The modern exaltation of Friday at the expense of Crusoe, a revisioning in which I "part"-icipate, is certainly understandable; it is an attempt to give voice to those silenced by the racism and colonialism that is a tragically large *part*, but not the whole, of the truth about the West. But it also reflects a contemporary cyclopean perspective with troubling implications for both historical balance and the resolution of social and racial conflict.

For Jeffries, all whites, even "very nice white folks," are guilty of history-distorting "racial pathology. They are as diabolical as that."[22] An allied, if apparently benign, form of pathology—that of a politically correct elite consisting mostly of very nice white folks—involves an exaltation of nonwhite races similar to that of Jeffries, though closer still to the celebrations of "native" values to be found in Giraudoux's or Tournier's rhapsodizing over Friday, or in the romanticizing of Native Americans in the books mentioned above by Kirkpatrick Sale and Ronald Wright, and in Kevin Costner's appealing if facile film, *Dances with Wolves,* winner of a shelf of Oscars in 1990.

The warmhearted who keep their heads are not rushing to the defense of history's oppressors when they express misgivings about that aestheticizing, sentimentalizing, glamorizing—and consequent trivializing and dehumanizing—of "minorities" and the "marginal" typical of the more doctrinaire elements of the PC Left (as well as of some self-appointed captains of what has become a victimization industry, in which equal treatment somehow compounds the original oppression). "Victimhood" and marginality, Edward Said insists, "are not to be gloried in; they are to be brought to an end, so that more, and not fewer,

---

differentiated America," which "pretends to a unity that actually excludes many," and an "overdifferentiated America," which "falls to pieces, sacrificing what it means to be an American to a passion for inclusiveness," what Barber calls "hyperpluralism" (126). In the preface, introduction, and (especially) the imaginary dialogue with which he concludes *Double Agent: The Critic and Society,* Morris Dickstein applies and exemplifies the intellectual "balance" epitomized by the earlier cultural criticism discussed in the body of his book. In *Politics by Other Means: Higher Education and Group Thinking,* a closely reasoned pox-on-both-your-houses study focusing on higher education and the sterile anti-intellectualism of group thinking, David Bromwich rejects any "middle way" but does advocate a return to a tradition of rigorous and independent thought he finds betrayed by both Left and Right in the heat of the culture wars.

22. Reported in *Time,* August 26, 1991, 19.

people can enjoy the benefits of what has for centuries been denied the victims of class, race, and gender."[23] "Marginality and oppression are never glamorous for those who are indeed marginal and oppressed," Daniel Harris reminds us in a "true-trimmer" essay of 1991 criticizing "the excited attempts" of the educated and radically chic to "deify the downtrodden." The politically correct, he argues, minimize and camouflage real social and racial conflict through cosmetic and sanitizing verbal and behavioral etiquette. (In a related point about such PC-speak as *physically challenged* and *differently abled,* Robert Hughes writes: "We want to create a sort of linguistic Lourdes, where evil and misfortune are dispelled by a dip in the waters of euphemism.") Though Harris's unflattering psychological explanation of what motivates the politically correct may be reductive, it contains truth enough to illuminate this kinder, gentler mirror image of what Jeffries calls history-distorting racial pathology. By "privileging" the underprivileged and exalting any and all victimized "minorities," PC elitists, professing multicultural diversity and pluralism but practicing groupthink, actually exploit ethnicity as a guilt-alleviating "antidote to their own sense of culpability."[24]

One needn't be neoconservative to prefer not to participate in various "politically correct" reversals of the old binary oppositions, or in the related reversal involving new variations on that discredited racist pseudoscience accurately characterized by biologist Stephen Jay Gould as the Eurocentric and white-racist "mismeasure of man." In the present volume I criticize later Coleridge for his susceptibility to a quack anthropology based in part on craniological measurement and for his racist denial that "the thick lips" could accurately refer to Othello (a Moor, later Coleridge insists, "not a Negro"). I therefore have no desire to cheer on those contemporary Afrocentrists who reject the demonstrably multiracial nature of ancient Egypt (and even measure the presumed nostril-width of noses said to have been deliberately chiseled off ancient Egyptian statues by racist defacers, including Napoleon, who allegedly shot off the nose of the Sphinx to prevent its being recognized as Negroid) in a misguided effort to "prove" the Black-African, rather than multiracial or, worse, Aryan-Greek, origins of Western culture and civilization.

This curious identification with the oppressor is avoided by those who, like

23. "The Politics of Knowledge," 189.

24. Harris, "What Is the Politically Correct?" 50–52. Hughes, *Culture of Complaint,* 18. However ironic the term may have become for those on the Left unaffected by the need to toe any Leninist party line, "political correctness" still exists, even when it is ridiculed as a conservative myth. Indeed, one of its more amusing if typically anecdotalist gadflies, Roger Kimball, the author of *Tenured Radicals,* noted, after attending the 1990 MLA convention, the spawning of "a new sub-variety of political correctness that consists in subscribing to all the politically correct pieties while loudly denying that such a thing exists." "The Periphery v. The Center: The MLA in Chicago," which first appeared in 1991 in the neoconservative journal *The New Criterion,* may be found in Berman, ed., *Debating PC,* 61–84 (70). See also Patricia Aufderheide, ed., *Beyond PC: Toward a Politics of Understanding,* and the 27 essays on the "politics" of PC in *Partisan Review* 4 (1993).

Cheikh Anta Diop and Molefi Asante, advance the even more curious—and racialist—argument that any civilization worthy of the name is African in origin. This caricature is a sad falling off from that earlier African "politics of identity," *négritude*. As developed by Senghor, and even by the more militant Caribbean poet Aimé Césaire, this is best understood as a redemptive *first* stage leading to *reintegration:* a vision projected by Césaire at the climactic turning point of his surrealist epic of colonial oppression and ultimate liberty, *Cahier d'un retour au pays natal* (1939). Having already established his commitment to a *négritude* that "stood up for the first time and swore by its humanity" in Haiti and in "a little cell in the Jura mountains," the prison in which Napoleon confined "A single man defying the white cries of white death / (TOUSSAINT LOUVERTURE)," Césaire affirms that his love for his own people "is not out of hatred for other races," that one can transcend self-limiting vision, indeed, that "No race possesses the monopoly of beauty, of intelligence, of force, and there is a place for all at the rendez-vous of victory."[25] This is the true legacy of Toussaint's own multiracial vision.

The deep-rooted myths that feed white racism—a racism doubtless reflected in and fed by the nineteenth-century European downplaying of the traditional, Herodotus-based view of Egypt's contributions to Classical Greece—are pernicious.[26] But to recognize and condemn "bias" in either the old or the new rac-

25. *Cahier d'un retour au pays natal,* 66, 68, 124, 138–40.

26. On the fall of the "Ancient Model," which stressed the contribution of Egypt, and the rise of the "Aryan Model" among nineteenth-century students of the origins of Classical Greece, see the first volume of Martin Bernal's *Black Athena: The Afroasiatic Roots of Classical Civilization.* In both volumes, Bernal emphasizes the relatively neglected "Afroasiatic" roots of Classical Civilization. But his final ("Revised Ancient") position—though he is too quick to cry conspiracy, accepts uncritically the testimony of Herodotus, and has unintentionally spawned a generation of Afrocentrists lacking his linguistic range and scholarship—is syncretic, *not* exclusionary. In volume 2, he even acknowledges, "with some surprise and distress," the validity of aspects of the Aryan Model.

As for the pigmentation of the ancient Egyptians: Bernal noted at a 1989 conference on *Black Athena* that *his* title was *African Athena,* and that "Black" was substituted by his publisher as more appealing, commercially and ideologically, to Afrocentrists. In acknowledging uncertainty or accepting the hybrid nature of Egyptian culture, Bernal parts company with such Afrocentrists as Asa Hilliard, whose "African-American Baseline Essays" have provided dubious support for a number of curriculum "reforms," Cheikh Anta Diop (*The African Origin of Civilization, Civilization or Barbarism: An Authentic Anthropology*), G. M. James (*Stolen Legacy*), and Indus Khamit Kush (*What They Never Told You in History Class*). Yet Afrocentrist Molefi Kete Asante continues to assert that Egypt as a Black African culture is "no longer a controversy among reputable scholars . . . nor should it be to those familiar with the evidence." To prolong *this* monochrome myth, and to call Jeffries a responsible curriculum planner, is to undermine Asante's own crucially important point that the "primary" and "fundamental" objective of Afrocentrism is not "to raise self-esteem" but "to provide accurate information." See his 1991 *American Scholar* response to Diane Ravitch, "Multiculturalism: An Exchange," in Berman, ed., *Debating PC,* 310–11, 307.

ism makes little sense absent a norm of "disinterestedness." Since (despite Foucault's historically conditioned, power-based "regime of truth") I cling to the unfashionable notion that one can at least *seek* the truth, a pursuit not *necessarily* coterminous with the quest for power, I oppose both the conspiratorial confusion of error with deliberate falsification and the fabrication of counter-myths that prolong racial divisiveness and, ironically, distract from genuine accomplishments.

2

Of course, nowadays to so much as mention the "pursuit of truth" in some quarters is to be pitied or dismissed as chimerical, or condemned as a "hubristic objectivist," a "hegemonic reactionary," or—worst of all—a "liberal humanist." To let the word drop without the obligatory smirk or bemused smile is to risk ridicule by ideologues for whom "truth" is not merely a disputed rather than a given term, but just another lobby, a mask for bourgeois oppression. After Marx's *The German Ideology,* and, more recently, Leo Strauss's epilogue to *Essays in the Scientific Study of Politics* (1962), Thomas Kuhn's *The Structure of Scientific Revolutions* (1962, 1970), and Jürgen Habermas's *Knowledge and Interests* (1971), not to mention Nietzsche's genealogical tracking of the will to power and the whole of Foucault's project, only the most naive could imagine that power and interests were not implicated in allegedly "objective," "neutral," "value-free" truth-seeking. But that is not to say (and most of these thinkers do not make the claim) that reason is *always mere* rationalization and knowledge *simply* a function of "dominant paradigms" or local, vested interests.

The cultural Left counts among the proudest accomplishments of its ideological critique the exposure of reason—especially allegedly objective, disinterested humanist scholarship—as a tool deployed to perpetuate classist, sexist, and racist oppression rather than a principal guide to humane progress. Given radical poststructuralism's antifoundationalist subversion of truth and of objectivist canons of logic and evidence, compounded by the Marxist assumption of inevitable conflict between self-interested, incompatible, locked-in perspectives, this unmasking and demystification of reason is itself not only perspectival but blatantly ideological. Further, as many "progressives" on the action-oriented Left have recently been charging, such corrosive skepticism is cynical, nihilistic, and—worse yet—politically quietist. Much-maligned liberal humanists, holding a wide variety of positions regarding political insurgency, *are* committed to the accommodation and rational testing of diverse perspectives. *Their* "progressivism" takes the form of resistance to the profoundly *anti*progressive, nihilist extinction of at least the *ideal* of a rational search for truth. "When reason is polluted by interest and power," as Benjamin Barber rightly insists, "the remedy is not to jettison but to cleanse it. The remedy for hypocrisy is not less but more reason. Rationalization is evidence of reason abused, not proof that there is no reason. The object of questioning is to test and strengthen rather than to annihilate the idea of the rational."[27]

27. *An Aristocracy of Everyone,* 124. Earlier (89–91), Barber wittily reminds such "children of Leo Strauss" as William Bennett and Allan Bloom of the "ironies" involved in

Barber's twin theme is the politics of education and the future of America. In his intelligently pragmatic and "provisional" view, education is a training in "the middle way between the dogmatic belief in absolutes and the cynical negation of all belief." Students who are well-taught

> learn to suspect every claim to truth and then to redeem truth provisionally by its capacity to withstand pointed questioning. They learn that somewhere between Absolute Certainty and Permanent Doubt there is a point of balance that permits knowledge to be provisionally accepted and applied . . . and allows conduct to be provisionally evaluated in a fashion that makes ethics, community, and democracy possible. There is much illusion in this fragile middle ground. Civilization, Yeats reminds us [in "Meru"], is tied together by a hoop of illusion. It would be dangerous to pretend that the illusion is real, but it is fatal to dispense with it altogether. Justice and democracy are illusions that permit us to live in comity. Truth and knowledge are the illusions that permit us to live commodiously. Art and literature are the illusions that make commodious living worthwhile.

And, after sounding rather like the Nietzsche who balanced his fierce skepticism with a theory of "necessary fictions" and an effort to surmount the very nihilistic abyss he opened at our feet, Barber concludes his subchapter (entitled "Hyperskepticism: Prudent Doubt or Fatal Nihilism?") by calling for a moderate middle way alien to those who trace their own ancestry back to Nietzsche at his most skeptical and relativistic. "Deconstruction," says Barber, "may rid us of all our illusions and thus seem a clever way to think, but it is no way to live at all." In particular, educators cannot teach

> when offered only the choice between dogma and nothingness; between orthodoxy and meaninglessness; between someone's covert value hegemony and the relativism of all values. The first business of educational reformers in schools and universities— multiculturalists, feminists, progressives—ought to be to sever their alliance with esoteric postmodernism; with literary metatheory (theory about theory); with fun-loving, self-annihilating hyperskepticism. As pedagogy these intellectual practices court catastrophe. They proffer to desperate travelers trying to find their way between Scylla and Charybdis a clever little volume on Zeno's paradoxes. They give to people whose very lives depend on the right choice a lesson in the impossibility of judgment. They tell emerging citizens looking to legitimize their preferences for democracy that there is no intellectually respectable way to ground political legitimacy.[28]

My agreement with Barber easily overrides one necessary caveat, in defense of the most rigorous of American deconstructionists. In a passage that *might*

---

their assailing of the Leftist critique of the alleged objectivity of centrist political scientists, a critique brilliantly "foreshadowed" by their mentor. In his 1962 essay, conservative Strauss had exposed the "unavowed commitment" to "liberal democracy" which was "built into the new political science" (Epilogue to *Essays in the Scientific Study of Politics,* 326). Thus, today's conservatives—now champions of liberal democracy and "objectivity," and ideological adversaries of the diabolical concept of knowledge compromised by unavowed interest—would, if they had "longer memories," give "the devil his due by acknowledging their own kinship with him."

28. *An Aristocracy of Everyone,* 124, 125.

temper Barber's perspectivally justified assault on deconstruction, Paul de Man, balancing chaos with coherence, textual indeterminacy with the need for intellectually grounded argument in literary interpretation, notes: "What makes a reading more or less true is simply the predictability, the necessity of its occurrence, regardless of the reader or of the author's wishes. . . . It depends, in other words, on the rigor of the reading as argument. . . . This does not mean that there can be a true reading, but no reading is conceivable in which the question of its truth or falsehood is not involved."[29]

Like most of the truth bemockers, I do not believe that one can attain pure objectivity, absolute truth, or any transcendental signified: quixotic ideals that evade the real issue. But as a "true trimmer," or what Barber would call a provisionalist trying to navigate between a dogmatic Scylla and nihilistic Charybdis, neither do I believe that the impossibility of attaining the ideal releases the individual, especially the scholar, from what the distinguished classical historian Peter Green calls "the harsh obligation of striving for it to the best of his or her ability. To do otherwise is as though (to draw a theological parallel) the concept of inherent human sinfulness and fallibility were taken as a self-evident reason neither to pursue virtue, nor to avoid error; or, worse, as indicating that the terms 'virtue' and 'error' had no significant meaning."[30]

Green, writing in 1990, was alluding to the poststructuralist ethos that threatened to dominate, and that still pervades, some American universities: a climate of thought in which scholarship is seldom or never a "disinterested" project; in which "facts" (that is, "interpretations") can be cooked or altered or "spun" to serve a political purpose; in which ethnicity, gender, and other collectively "subjective" factors are "privileged" over scholarly "objectivity." Most on the cultural Left assume that contemporary theories, displacing outmoded ideals, have demonstrated that "claims of disinterest, objectivity, and universality are not to be trusted and themselves tend to reflect local historical conditions." The new claim, as John Searle and others have noted in criticizing it, is not merely that these ideals are difficult or impossible to attain, but rather "that the very enterprise of trying to attain such things is misconceived from the beginning, because there is no objective reality for our objectivist methodology to attain, . . . no independently existing set of objects and features of the world to which such statements correspond."[31]

Since much of this rejection of the correspondence theory of truth, and most of modern perspectivism itself, derives from Nietzsche, it is worth remind-

29. Quoted by Dickstein in the dialogue that concludes *Double Agent*, 183.
30. *Alexander to Actium: The Historical Evolution of the Hellenistic Age*, xvi.
31. The first citation is from *Speaking for the Humanities*, a 1989 pamphlet produced by the American Council of Learned Societies and authored by six humanists justifiably responding to criticism from the Right but sounding rather too smugly confident that supposedly unattainable truth has in fact been attained—by the new theories and movements favored by the Left. The second quotation is from John Searle's synopsis of the Left's position, in his 1991 review-essay, "The Storm over the University," reprinted in Berman, ed., *Debating PC*, 109.

ing ourselves that this endlessly dialectical thinker was a cognitivist as well as a noncognitivist, and that he passionately sought, whatever the personal and cultural consequences, the very "truths" he more than anyone else put in radical question. To be sure, at his most noncognitivist, Nietzsche was a radical perspectivist, utterly skeptical of metaphysical realism. To quote several of the most familiar of the fragments posthumously collected in *The Will to Power:* there are no "facts, only interpretations" (§481); were "optics" or perspectives on the world to be "deducted," nothing would "remain over" (§567); "'Truth' is not something there, that might be found or discovered—but something that must be created" (§552).

This Nietzschean perspectivism has punctured much essentialist afflatus and provided a tonic corrective to disembodied Cartesian rationalism, to Kantian "pure reason" or knowledge of any "thing-in-itself," to Matthew Arnold's depiction of the function of criticism as "seeing the object as in itself it really is," and to Leopold von Ranke's futile attempt to describe history "as it really was." Yet in one of the pivotal passages in which he advised his fellow philosophers to "guard against" such absolutist "snares," Nietzsche insisted on *two* points. His usual "optical" emphasis—"There is *only* a perspective seeing, *only* a perspective 'knowing'"—was amplified by the following significant addendum, still optical but expansive: " . . . and the *more* affects we allow to speak about one thing, the *more* eyes, different eyes, we can use to observe one thing, the more complete will our 'concept' of this thing, our 'objectivity,' be."[32]

Here Nietzsche, a relativist who nevertheless ranks values, clearly values the attempt to *approximate* a never-fully-attainable "objectivity" by gathering together as many viewpoints and angles of potential access as possible. Whether considered as vantage points on what is actually "there," determinate and determinable, or as no more than heuristic methodologies, the more perspectives we generate and bring to bear, the more we *multiply* rather than prematurely delimit and regularize differences, the more likely we are not only to increase our access to new or forgotten ways of seeing, but actually to see *more,* and *better.* Writing precisely a century ago, American educator Anna Julia Cooper declared that "woman's strongest vindication for speaking" was not to set women—white, black, brown, or red—against each other, or woman against man. No, the strongest vindication was and is "that the world needs to hear her voice." Having registered this crucial truth, she shifted from oral and auditory to bodily and optical imagery: "The world has had to limp along with the wobbling gait and the one-sided hesitancy of a man with one eye. Suddenly the bandage is removed from the other eye and the whole body is filled with light. It sees a circle where before it saw a segment. The darkened eye restored, every member rejoices with it."[33]

---

32. *On the Genealogy of Morals,* Third Essay, §12.

33. *A Voice from the South,* xiv. Ocular and body language resembling Nietzsche's and Cooper's turns up, appropriately enough, in a recent collaborative study of Nietzsche by a philosopher (Bernd Magnus) and two literary critics (Stanley Stewart and Jean-Pierre

This call for binocular vision, originally voiced in the service of Cooper's work for suppressed women and black Americans, remains a liberating call to *try* to see a circle rather than a segment, to be open to other perspectives, to see better, more holistically. Since, like most works about Romanticism in the past twenty years, this project's second part builds on, even when it veers from, M. H. Abrams's landmark study, *Natural Supernaturalism: Tradition and Revolution in Romantic Literature*, it seems appropriate to recall a portion of *his* "optical" response to the critics of that volume, remarks relevant to the present point about seeing more and differently.

Abrams readily acknowledged that his was not the only plausible history of Romanticism, that he could easily "imagine" other (more skeptical or ironic) versions, indeed could "almost imagine" writing one—a book he would "ungrudgingly accept" as "valid." His somewhat anxious argument that this would not mean acceptance of "relativity," at least not "in any dismaying sense of that word," would in *part*, I think, resonate with Nietzsche and Anna Julia Cooper. Acceptance of an alternative history would not, says Abrams, "obviate the claim" that both books would "tell a story which is true." What would "seem 'contradictory'" wouldn't be since the "disparate judgments" about the "representative quality and greatness" of Wordsworth's poetry would follow

> from different controlling categories which effect a different selection and ordering of the historical facts and implicate a different set of criteria by which to assess what is representative and great. The insights and assessments of each book, in other words, are relative to the vantage point chosen by its author, and each tries to make us see selected goings-on in the Romantic era in a certain way; but these diverse goings-on are there to be seen in that way. Each, that is, tells only a *part* of the truth, but it is a part of the *truth*.[34]

Mileur). The authors' diversity of specialization "became an instrument for multiplying perspectives in a way perhaps uniquely appropriate to a thinker like Nietzsche." Their book attempts to "suture the body of Nietzsche's institutionally dismembered literary/philosophical thought," in order to attain "a genuine recuperation, a convalescence, a restoration" of that dismembered body, in "a kind of healing" (*Nietzsche's Case: Philosophy as/and Literature*, 2, 4).

34. "Rationality and Imagination in Cultural History: A Reply to Wayne Booth," 459–60; italics in original. In the immediately preceding essay, Booth had defended *Natural Supernaturalism* against several critiques, the most thorough of which was that of J. Hillis Miller in *Diacritics*. To Abrams's paradigm of original unity, fall, and redemptive recovery, a literary displacement of a spiritual pattern reflected in the initial enthusiasm, disillusionment, and reconstituted recovery marking the Romantics' response to the revolutionary upheaval of their era, Miller proposed an alternative model of original dispersal, decentering, and displacement: a deconstructive scattering that would expose Abrams's unitary and coherent "Romanticism" as no less multiple and ambiguous than the period's "dialogical" and "undecidable" texts. While Abrams resisted, and still resists, a deconstruction that leaves poems and periods alike incoherent, he accepted the valid point about alternative histories. Wayne Booth had ended his praise of *Natural Supernaturalism* by challenging any critics who claimed they could write a history of Romanticism alternative to Abrams's which was as plausible and as faithful to the mass of

Nietzsche would applaud Abrams's thrice-repeated "different" and his "opti-cal" metaphors ("vantage point," "make us see . . . in a certain way") to describe access to diverse facets of the subject under scrutiny. He would, at his most characteristic, certainly place the words *facts* and *truth* in quotation marks and dispute the ontological claim that "these diverse goings-on are *there* to *be* seen." But he would agree with the spirit of Abrams's concluding sentence, and with Abrams's insistence elsewhere that the pluralistic "bringing to bear on a subject of diverse points of view, with diverse results" is "not only valid, but necessary to our understanding of literary and cultural history: in such pursuits the conver-gence of diverse points of view is the only way to achieve a vision in depth."[35] The purpose of the "more" and "different" eyes called for in the *Genealogy* is not, after all, an infinite dissemination of isolated and contradictory perspectives, but a genuine advance in understanding, a fuller and deeper "seeing."

Whatever logical difficulties are caused by the Nietzschean claim that noth-ing objective is there to *be* seen, his metaphor of "seeing" emphasizes the perspectival nature of any knowledge, ours or that of others. Yet perspectivism, which does preclude absolute truth, "does not preclude objectivity." The for-mulation is that of Eugene Goodheart, who goes on to qualify it. Denying, not the "presence and force" but the "omnipresence and omnipotence" of ideol-ogy, Goodheart has recently described the "essential task of intellectual work" as the need "to resist and minimize ideological motives in the interests of objectivity, or at least in the interests of marking out the limit of one's own perspective and allowing the claims of other perspectives."[36]

In identifying liberal humanism with "a perspectivism" not only tolerant of other perspectives but entailing "a belief in the possibility of objectivity," Good-heart goes beyond Nietzsche; yet the philosopher would have little problem with the following distinction: "The mark of an ideological mind is not that it is perspectival (all minds are perspectival), but that it is *enclosed* within a particular perspective for unacknowledged (to oneself as well as to others) reasons of self-interest. In contrast, the unideological mind is open to the claims of other perspectives." And Nietzsche might recognize, though Goodheart doesn't, an echo of his own *Genealogy* aphorism in the insistence that "what is not ideologi-cal" is the "heuristic view of multiple perspectives, in which no perspective is *a priori* privileged."[37]

The philologist in Nietzsche would even find congenial Goodheart's stress on "seeing" as suggesting "the need for a check against the unseen structures of interpretation that reinvent the text to advance one ideological program or another." In fact, opposing subjective reinvention at the cost of a genuine

---

data: "Go try" (439). Abrams, in effect, took up the challenge, at least in the thought experiment described above. Something like the "ironic" or "skeptical" study Abrams envisaged appeared four years later: Anne K. Mellor's *English Romantic Irony.*

35. "The Deconstructive Angel," 237.

36. Afterword to *The Skeptic Disposition: Deconstruction, Ideology, and Other Matters,* 190.

37. Ibid., 185; and, for the citation in the sentence that follows, 190.

"desire to understand," Nietzsche occasionally claims that, unlike "things," *texts* (perhaps because they are humanly designed artifacts) *can* be "read off"— transparently, objectively—"without interposing an interpretation" (*The Will to Power* §479). In *The Antichrist* (§52), he actually calls this philological ability to patiently and delicately "read facts without falsifying them by interpretation" the rare "art of reading well."

For the most part, however, he is committed to his "no-facts, only-interpreta- tions" axiom, and to a perspectival seeing. Nevertheless, even for radical Nietz- sche, the lines of sight, while they do not converge on a univocal objective "truth" or independent "thing-in-itself," cumulatively come together to pro- duce an ampler, better-balanced, more "complete" account in which Abrams's "parts" verge toward a whole, a "circle" rather than a "segment"—an ideal and therefore unattainable "truth" or "objectivity" toward which we strive, pre- cisely *through* more and different perspectives. "'Tis all in pieces, all cohaerence gone," cried John Donne, anticipating the centrifugal imagery both of Nietz- sche's madman at God's funeral (*The Gay Science* §125) and of the Yeatsian speaker in "The Second Coming." But the Nietzsche of *Genealogy* 3:12 invokes no "mere anarchy" in which "things fall apart," but a centripetal, multiple perspectivism in which diverse vantage points converge on "one thing" in a near-holistic and, yes, more *accurate,* apprehension of something far more—if never fully—interfused and "complete."

One can, of course, opt for radical perspectivism, for isolated viewpoints rigidly dependent on contexts in which each of us, as individuals or as groups, is said to be inescapably and incompatibly embedded, with no "common" ground, only "difference." It is, writes our most lucid and engaging antifounda- tionalist, "*difference all the way down.*"[38] So be it. But to emphasize *that* over- differentiated extreme rather than this practical and fruitful Nietzschean multi- perspectivism—what the great physicist Niels Bohr called "complementarity," or what Fish himself *seems* to mean by "interpretive communities"—is to license and even validate *any* "subjective" ideological position, no matter how atomis- tic, internally inconsistent, and unsupported by plausible evidence. And then mere anarchy *is* loosed upon the world. Even demonstrable error becomes *someone's* unassailable "truth" when "truth" is not only influenced or inflected but totally *determined* by, say, one's culture or ethnicity. Dead white males who long conflated "the way things are" with their own myopic but hegemonic perspective have spawned, as merely *apparent* opposites, more conscious though equally biased successors. "We deal," says Jeffries with lofty finality, "with the African truth." End of conversation.[39]

38. Stanley Fish, "The Common Touch; or, One Size Fits All," 247. That our students would catch the (popular) allusion in his characteristically witty title, but probably not the (canonical) allusion to the famous Turtle-and-Elephant origin-myth in the line cited, would not disturb an anti-elitist champion of popular culture for whom "democracy is simply a name for the canon-making process" (261).

39. Jeffries, who adds, "We can't worry about the consequences," is quoted from

Gender-separatists and uniculturalists operating under a bogus banner of diversity pose a related danger in the aesthetic realm. Art communicates. A principal function of literature, music, drama, dance, and the visual arts is their transhistorical or transcultural capacity to illuminate *shared human* experience *as well as* to open us up to the diverse experiences of other selves. To emphasize "those things we have in common," an ideal admittedly tainted by liberal lip service, is to deny, not "difference," but inevitable and permanent ideological enclosure within our own perspective and entrenched interests. In terms of writers and readers, creators and audiences: from the fact that "every work and every judgment . . . *emerge* from certain interests, it does not follow," as David Bromwich rightly insists, "that a given work or judgment must *serve* the same interests."[40] Because we start from a particular ethnic and cultural context we need not, to reverse John Donne's rondure, "end where [we] begunne." This is particularly true in the case of the arts. Through imaginative exploration and an effort and "desire to understand," the creative artist can cross supposedly irremediable gaps: barriers of gender, race, class, and culture. And those who enter into the works can gain access to artists and forms emerging from very different cultural situations than their own.[41]

Biological determinists and ethnic separatists are unenthralled by such humanistic aspirations of the liberal tradition, or by what Nadine Gordimer (winner of the 1991 Nobel Prize for literature, a white woman who has communicated to us with rare power the lives of men and women, blacks and whites, living in South Africa) calls "imaginative extensions as a gift of insight that writers are trying to pass on to other people."[42] To many self-segregationists on

---

Newsweek, September 23, 1991, 45. Others have been, and are, worried about the consequences of scholarship by ethnicity. In a 1963 essay ("The Dilemma of the American Negro Scholar") and in a 1971 lecture, both reprinted in his 1989 collection *Race and History: Selected Essays, 1938–1988,* John Hope Franklin exposed the white racism that had forced black scholars to retreat from other fields into "the study of Negroes," and warned that "ethnicity," a transition to general assimilation for whites, had, by 1969, become a trap, "a terminal point for blacks." C. Vann Woodward quoted both passages in his *New Republic* review (April 30, 1990) of Franklin's book and returned to them a year or so later in the *New York Review of Books* (September 26, 1991). In this exchange, he expressed the wish (76) that his "old friend" and fellow-historian of the segregationist South "would find a pulpit from which to preach that gospel to some of the current black advocates of ethnicity and Afrocentricity, with their doctrine of self-segregation, and culture and scholarship determined by race." (Intriguingly, Woodward transposes the nouns in Franklin's title. Was it merely a proofreader's or a Freudian slip that turned *Race and History* into *History and Race?*)

40. *Politics by Other Means,* 211.

41. So-called "irremediable gaps" have recently been reduced to unanswerable axioms: the T-shirt slogan of the late 1980s, "It's a black thing. You wouldn't understand," or the phrase taken by many to epitomize the Anita Hill/Clarence Thomas confrontation: "Men just don't get it."

42. Asked in October 1991 about objections to whites portraying blacks, or women men, Gordimer responded that "such complaints" arise out of "astonishment, a puzzled

the cultural Left such imaginative extensions are simply another form of imperialist exploitation—in this case, "stealing the discourse of the Other." The barrier-crossing function (and glory) of art, empathetic and communicative, is denied by those adamant not only that races, cultures, and the genders are fundamentally distinct, but that one cannot hope to understand the Other; that, for example, the female or the black "experience" is at once internally monolithic and beyond the ken of even the most curious and motivated outsiders who would try to appreciate, let alone dare to criticize or presume to imaginatively trespass upon, the artistic expressions of that experience.

There can be no legitimate objection to placing works of art in their particular cultural contexts, or to redressing past insensitivity to diverse perspectives, or—needless to say—to presenting an ampler *and more accurate* account of Western culture itself by seeing through "more" and "different" eyes, especially those eyes that have been only recently unbandaged. Quite the contrary. But the more strident dogmatists of "difference" and apostles of *alteritas* go well beyond correcting a history distorted by Eurocentric bias, even beyond benign (if pedagogically ineffectual) esteem-enhancing ethnic or gender celebration, to a crass politicization of the arts that dismisses artistic merit as a compelling criterion of evaluation,[43] and to the even more ominous abandonment of any vestigial hope of cross-cultural understanding, let alone of an integrated human community. Valuing difference is one thing; prescribing dichotomy and dismissing, in the name of democracy, even minimal commonality quite another.

One does not have to be a conservative to realize that some of the critics of multiculturalism, whatever their own agendas, have raised what Catherine R. Stimpson conceded in a front-page piece in the *New York Times Book Review* in 1991 is "a profound moral and political question: What are the commonalities

---

feeling, about what writers do." Citing, as an example of the artistic invention of other selves, Joyce's Molly Bloom soliloquy in *Ulysses,* she added that for those who "appreciate literature at all," this "extraordinary, inexplicable faculty that writers have if they're any good" should be taken as "a gift of insight" artists are trying to pass on to the rest of us. ("The Power of a Well-Told Tale," 92).

43. This ideological marginalizing of literature is resisted not only by those damned as part of the canonizing "establishment," but by an anti-imperialist like Edward Said, who has retained his love (and ear) for literature. The rejection of intrinsic aesthetic criteria is reflected in the work of many others, perhaps most notably (or notoriously) Barbara Herrnstein Smith, Braxton Craven Professor of Comparative Literature and English at Duke. Presumably echoing Nietzsche's bemused exclamation in aphorism §567 in *The Will to Power:* "As if a world would still remain over after one deducted the perspective!" Smith wondered in a 1987 article on "Value" (incorporated the following year in her *Contingencies of Value: Alternative Perspectives for Critical Theory*) "whether anything *is* left over when all . . . other forms of value and interest"—such forms as market value, utility, historical and personal interest, and of course, political and ideological interest—"are subtracted" from a work of art (448). Precious little attention is given, as Eugene Goodheart remarks, "to the search for new grounds for what seems to me undeniable, aesthetic experience, whether or not we have a persuasive theory to explain it" (*The Skeptic Disposition,* 193).

that a multicultural society must have if it is to be a society?" Those who have effectively given up on an integrated America range from know-nothing racists, white and black, to, say, Derrick Bell, whose multigenre *Faces at the Bottom of the Well* is a challenging, disturbing work urging blacks, in the face of majority white attitudes, to acknowledge "the permanence of racism" in this country, "not as a sign of submission, but as an act of ultimate defiance."[44]

For Bell, in effect, we in this country are back to a pre-Mecca Malcolm. He may be right. But the chaos of much of the post–Cold War world provides grim evidence of the dangers glibly overlooked by those less thoughtful "separatists" who would destroy what hope remains for American mutuality by raising recognized differences into what Robert Hughes calls "cultural ramparts." Confronted, for example, by the racial, cultural, genocidal dismembering of the former Yugoslavia, we see again what that supposedly "dead metaphor, 'balkanization,' . . . once meant and now means again":

> A Hobbesian world: the war of all on all, locked in blood-feud and theocratic hatred, the *reductio ad insanitem* of America's mild and milky multiculturalism. . . . Against this ghastly background, so remote from American experience since the Civil War, we now have our own conservatives promising a "culture war," while ignorant radicals orate about "separatism." They cannot know what demons they are frivolously invoking. If they did, they would fall silent in shame.[45]

What more is there to say? Only that we must not let the lunacies of the extremist Left and Right either tempt us into censorship or dissuade us from submitting their claims to rational scrutiny and intellectual debate. As Jefferson said of those who might "wish to dissolve this Union or change its republican form, let them stand undisturbed as monuments of the safety in which error of opinion may be tolerated where reason is left free to combat it." Barring "fighting words," the same principle holds when the opinions expressed are repugnant—racist and sexist, let alone simply "insensitive." Freedom of speech is currently under intense assault, not least by humanitarians and egalitarians sensitive to the feelings of minorities. The motivation is laudatory, as is the compassion and appeal to civility. *Some* limits there must be; but to take the position that speech and ideas should be policed by university codes or state laws on the ground that "hurtful words" are no less "violent" than clubs or knives is to blur the crucial distinction between matricidal Nero and Hamlet, who, confronting his mother, "will *speak* daggers to her, but *use* none."[46]

44. Stimpson, "Multiculturalism: A Big Word at the Presses." In the year his book was published, 1992, Derrick Bell was a visiting professor at NYU law school following his much-publicized refusal to continue teaching at Harvard until its law school hired a black woman in a tenure-line position.

45. *Culture of Complaint,* 13. The last two sentences seem to me, as they do to Alfred Kazin ("The Way We Live Now," 3), the "most striking" in Hughes's book: a book whose second section (83–151) focuses on cultural separatism as the antithesis (not, as some conservatives would have it, the inevitable result) of real multiculturalism. Rejecting dialogue and exchange, separatism is "multiculturalism gone sour" (84).

46. *Hamlet* III.ii.382. In *Kindly Inquisitors: The New Attacks on Free Thought,* Jonathan

The defense of free speech need not deteriorate into name-calling at a higher level. At their creative and democratic *best,* egalitarian advocates of multiculturalism, feminism, and perspectivism in general are not the relativistic mind-closers, illiberal educators, tenured radicals, and imposters in the temple of current hyperbole. At their best, they reflect the realities of a changing world, exciting, enriching, and challenging us all just as they academically destabilize—by re-scrutinizing, criticizing, revising, and expanding, rather than simply repudiating—the traditional canon. But at their destructive and divisive *worst,* soured by an understandable resentment at past or present exclusion and marginalization, and allied with new forms of particularism, territoriality, and a "politically correct" stifling of honest dialogue in the name of "sensitivity," proponents of the new theories and movements can lead, the champions of the oppressed becoming near-oppressors in their turn, to more of the same old hatred: variants of that individuality-denying group-separatism that always threatens to exchange one set of mind-forged manacles for another. To replace one demonized group, or stereotyping canon, with another is hardly progress.

Combat, when it is the Jeffersonian combat of free reason, is a learning experience, and there are recent hopeful signs in the culture wars—some recognition of complacency-disrupting facts by conservatives, some back-pedaling by poststructuralists embarrassed by their canon-bashing disciples. In addition, many ideologues on the Left are now painfully aware of just how out of touch they are with the mainstream "masses." It would, however, be premature to conclude that peace is about to break out. (Nor *should* it, if the price is a politically correct suppression of ideas and words, which, posing no credible threat to a community's core values, are simply deemed offensive.)

The mediating task, requiring both humane expansiveness and critical rigor, is to persist in the current effort to get beyond the caricatures presented by simplifying "conservatives" and "radicals" mouthing routinized elitist and egalitarian pieties, beyond the polarizing cross fire of armed camps each confident as to whose side the angels are on, and who the enemies are. Leaving aside the utterly unaccommodating positions of the *most extreme* radicals and reactionaries, surely those who keep an open mind can continue to learn from one another. Though less exuberantly caustic than Robert Hughes, a born puncturer of the balloons of both the Left and the Right, I am a flawed practitioner of the moderation I preach. But, along with a willingness to listen to the other side, a toning down of our own jargon-riddled and inhospitable rhetoric would seem the right place to begin to find a middle ground. If the "culture guardians" on the hard Right can stop panicking and confusing reality with nostalgic myth, perhaps the hard-liners on the Left can adjust *their* overwrought rhetoric

---

Rauch passionately and rigorously defends—against the attacks of both fundamentalist absolutists and well-intentioned humanitarians—free inquiry, free speech, and the free development of knowledge, only attainable by unfettering, and then choosing between, conflicting views. Jefferson's observation, quoted from his first inaugural address, recalls Milton's insistence, in *Areopagitica,* that truth and falsehood should "grapple" without prohibition, since "who ever knew truth put to the worse, in a free and open encounter?"

so that perspectives meant to challenge and liberate do not themselves deterio-
rate into a self-righteous intolerance pouring ideological salt into the very
cultural wounds—racism and sexism—they hope to heal. *Parts* of the truth
ought, ideally, to become parts of the *truth*, segments forming a circle.

I feel somewhat less uncomfortable pontificating in this way since my first
published article, "On Truth and Lie in Nietzsche," reveals far less attraction to
Cartesian objectivity than to Nietzschean perspectivism, especially that perspec-
tivism emphasizing not merely "*more* eyes," but "different eyes." Coleridge
makes the same "optical" point in criticizing that "Order of Intellects, who like
the Pleuronectae [flat-fish] in Ichthyology that have both eyes on the same
side, never see but half of a subject at one time" (*AR* 403; cf. *CM* III 132). They
mistake what Abrams calls "only a *part* of the truth" for the whole, Cooper's
"segment" for a "circle"—a danger rarely risked by Coleridge, whose notorious
yet admirable binocular tendency to see both sides of virtually every issue I
describe, and to some extent emulate, in the first chapter. I'll conclude these
introductory remarks by briefly recording the more general impact of current
critical trends and reading strategies on *Coleridge's Submerged Politics,* a project
conceived from the outset as both multiperspectival and as a work of mediation
between opposed views.

As a reader shaped in part by Nietzsche, I recognize not only the inevitability
of "interpretation" but even the force of radical linguistic skepticism, and do *in
part* believe it. Whether accepting or resisting, I have, like every thoughtful
reader, been affected by the contemporary impact of Nietzschean "optics." As
the very omnipresence of Nietzsche indicates, few of the theories, critical and
political, are as novel as their more ahistorical practitioners pretend; one wearies,
for example, of the false claim, implicit or explicit, that what preceded them was
a monolithic and dogmatic commitment to cyclopean, "correct" interpretation
of either "facts" or "texts." And given the poststructuralist repudiation of objec-
tivist certitude, one can only wonder, along with Denis Donoghue, at the tenden-
tious assertiveness, "the remarkably insistent terms," in which supposedly skepti-
cal and speculative discourse is conducted these days. "Reading essays in critical
theory," Donoghue remarked in the first of his two Bucknell lectures in 1992,

> I often find myself wondering about the authors: where have they found such con-
> viction, in the declared absence of any ground of ultimacy? They tell me that
> nothing can be established, but they show no misgiving in producing a tone of
> certitude in the admonition. Having rid themselves and us of certainty, they seem
> unwilling to act upon the diminished thing or to learn a tentative style from a de-
> spair. It begins to appear that theory denotes not an affiliation of theorists in
> search of tenable theories to establish whatever it is that exerts a claim upon
> them; but, on the contrary, a concatenation of largely independent ideologies as
> blatant as the certitudes they begin by undermining.[47]

47. "The Status of Theory," in *The Pure Good of Theory: The Bucknell Lectures in Literary
Theory,* 37.

It is true, as Donoghue says on the preceding page, that many of the theorists "share nothing but a prejudice that they have certain enemies in common," and that their "favored terms of reference and agency are far more likely to threaten than to invite." Nevertheless, the best of the new theorists (and "post-theorists") have, like Nietzsche himself, introduced an exhilarating, dust-stirring breeze. The most rigorous have sharpened any number of analytical tools and made us all rethink certain facile and complacent assumptions—about power, culture, race, and gender; about concepts and values less permanently fixed than variable, historically situated, and culturally contingent; about language, silence, and the problematic relation of rhetoric to reality; about the impossibility of pure Cartesian "objectivity," especially given the tendency to universalize personal or cultural biases. Professionally, I now cast a colder eye on the belief, or pretense, of some academicians that only feminist and minority-studies courses have "political" content; and even on canon formation—though without abandoning esteem of the intrinsic aesthetic value that seems to have been the sole criterion of the original *kanon*-establishers in the Alexandrian library, and which I once thought not only the principal but the *exclusive* determinant of admission into the open-doored pantheon of works that have "pleased many and pleased long."

Despite the ideological conformity, even lockstep *uni*formity, that too often characterizes the advance of these liberating forces, I have found many of the "New Readers" (Abrams's term) personally liberating, sanctioning (for example) what I used to think my perverse tendency, despite my loyalty to intrinsic criticism, to wander away from the immediate texts of works I was studying. I found support in "cultural studies" generally, especially in the New Historicists, led by Jerome McGann, specializing in the Romantic period. At its best, McGann's balance (exposure of the poets' ideological "illusion" joined with praise for their heroic struggle rather than crude accusations of reactionary evasion) is matched by his attention to both text and context. But the New Historicists in general frequently turn away from the verbal details of the poetic text in order to make their points. It is a procedure recently sustained at length, and in depth, by Alan Liu, whose explorations of Wordsworth's "poetics of denial, of reference lost,"[48] converge at many points with the reading strategies of deconstructionists and New Historicists specializing in Romanticism, and whose 1989 book, surely among the most important contemporary studies of Wordsworth, bulges with detailed excursions (historical, cultural, theoretical) contextualizing—and occasionally overwhelming—the poems he discusses.

His methodology—a synthesis of contemporary formalist, deconstructionist, and historicist approaches—has made me more comfortable about my own excursions. Nevertheless, as a "true trimmer," or boat balancer, I remain vestigially troubled about the degree to which I have sacrificed balance in what follows. Like Alfred Kazin, steering a half-century ago between dogmatic Marxism and New Critical formalism, I have "never been able to understand why the

48. *Wordsworth*, 35.

study of literature in relation to society should be divorced from a full devotion to what literature is in itself, or why those who seek to analyze literary texts should cut off the act of writing from its irreducible sources in the life" of actual men and women.[49] While I am—like the older practitioners of cultural criticism, or, now, like the New Historicists—incapable of treating works of art as if they were hermetically sealed off from their context in the actual world, I also continue to value intrinsic criticism and to pledge primary allegiance to the work of art. Therefore, despite the considerable validity in current arguments about the intrinsic-extrinsic dichotomy breaking down, I regret the extent to which (to borrow Stephen Greenblatt's terms) historical "resonance" has seduced me away from the linguistic "wonder" of the works I am ostensibly examining in the present project.

Though my speculative voyaging has brought to port perspectives worth salvaging on these authors and their masterworks, my spirit's bark has been driven far from the immediate pleasures of the text—especially in Part Two, where for long stretches the visible, public text of *The Ancient Mariner* is an almost *in*visible shoreline. Indeed, throughout, I've been driven, literally, to the marginal: to Coleridge's marginalia on *Robinson Crusoe;* to contemporary writers and their re-imaginings and recuperations of the marginalized Friday; to what Defoe might have called "the allusive allegorick history" of the events of 1797–1798 as encrypted in *The Rime of the Ancient Mariner;* and to Coleridge's prose gloss, added to the poem's margins in the *Sibylline Leaves* edition—published in 1817, a century after that other notable Mariner, Robinson Crusoe, sailed into shipwreck and into the world's imagination.

In speculating about the relationship between Coleridge and Defoe's Crusoe, or between Coleridgean politics and *The Ancient Mariner,* what initially engaged my curiosity were the "gaps"—the "not saids"—in Coleridge's poem as well as in his *Crusoe* marginalia. Since I believe that art is as much the antidote to, as the continuation of, politics, I do not intend to reductively politicize *Robinson Crusoe,* still less *The Ancient Mariner,* especially since it is precisely "politics" that that poem overtly omits. Even granted the significance and seductiveness of repressed and unconscious materials, what is actually said by an artist, or even an annotator, has a rather obvious prima facie claim over what is not.

Nevertheless, I have chosen on this occasion to focus on silences I continue to find significant—beholding, like Wallace Stevens's listener in the snow, "Nothing that is not there and the nothing that is." I hope that what follows—a listening to what is just below the threshold of hearing and a saying of those "not saids" by one reader—will engage the imaginations of other readers. At the same time, I believe that some new light, not all of it peripheral, has been cast on what is present, not merely absent, in both these canonical texts, each of them—as Coleridge said of *Robinson Crusoe* in 1820—"not only enjoyed but acknowledged as a rich jewel in the treasury of our permanent English Literature" (*CM* III 484).

49. Preface to *On Native Grounds: An Interpretation of Modern Literature,* xi.

PART ONE

———————

Crusoe, Slaves, and Coleridge

Reflections on Lacunae in the *Robinson Crusoe* Marginalia

1

Coleridge, Race, and Slavery

1

Robinson Crusoe was one of the books—along with the *Arabian Nights* and a Crusoe-like curiosity by an "Edward Dorrington" entitled *The English Hermit,* and ascribed to "Mr. Philip Quarll"—that Coleridge claimed to have read before he was six. As with generations of readers before and after him, the book made a profound impression on his youthful imagination, and he thought enough of it to reread and carefully annotate it when he was near sixty: Defoe's age when he *wrote* the book (*CL* I 347, VI 979). Approximately a century later, his marked copy was rediscovered—"on a second-hand book-stall"—by one F. D. Klingender, who reported his finding in the *Times Literary Supplement* of February 1, 1936.

Coleridge's *Crusoe* annotations are included—indeed, almost all his annotations, some eight thousand notes recovered from almost seven hundred volumes, will eventually be included—in the multivolumed *Marginalia* compiled by the greatest student of the poet's reading, the late George Whalley. As Professor Whalley stresses in the introduction to his masterly edition, as well as in his moving essay "On Editing Coleridge's Marginalia," the annotations repeatedly demonstrate both Coleridge's extraordinary perceptiveness as a reader and his imaginative participation in the act—his close adherence to the details of a text and his independent pursuit of ideas, particularly ideas of either a philosophic or moral nature.[1]

Knowing what kind of man Coleridge was, and knowing, with the help of George Whalley, what kind of *reader* he was, certain expectations are set up. Of *Robinson Crusoe*, Virginia Woolf wrote, we have "before we open the book" a sense of what "we expect it to give us. We read; and we are rudely contradicted on every page."[2] Similarly, before reading a word of the *Crusoe* marginalia, we

---

1. Professor Whalley died while working on the proofs of the second of his five projected volumes. Those two volumes, however, comprise over two thousand pages, and a third, published in 1992, adds another eleven hundred pages. Some of Coleridge's marginalia, including that on *Robinson Crusoe,* had earlier been published in the first volume of *Literary Remains of Samuel Taylor Coleridge,* ed. H. N. Coleridge, 4 vols. (London, 1836–1839) and, a century later, in *Coleridge's Miscellaneous Criticism,* ed. T. M. Raysor; see 292–300 for the *Crusoe* notes.

2. *Second Common Reader,* 54.

imagine we know what in *Robinson Crusoe* would have fascinated Coleridge and what would have repelled him; at the least we feel we know what aspects of the novel would have attracted his attention and critical comments. To a considerable extent, however, our expectations are, again, rudely contradicted.

For example, the student of economics, youthful cosponsor (with Robert Southey) of a Pantisocratic colony in America, and lifelong advocate of organic community as opposed to selfish economic individualism, is silent not only on the question of Crusoe's basic egocentricity and single-minded acquisitiveness, but also on the more provocative general questions of the economic and, later, political development of Crusoe's island. There is one significant exception: the question of "right of possession" of the island fascinated Coleridge almost as much as it did Crusoe. Alongside Crusoe's claim to sovereignty—his pleasurable thought that "this was all my own, that I was king and lord of all this country . . . and had a right of possession" (*Robinson Crusoe*, 114)—Coleridge jotted, "By the bye, what *is* the law of England re[specting] this? Suppose I had discovered, or been wrecked [on an] uninhabited island, would it be mine or t[he] K[ing's?]."[3] Such curiosity had been fruitful in the past. A notebook entry years earlier in which Coleridge had reminded himself to "examine into the Laws upon Wrecks as at present existing" refers back to a fourth-century Latin Epistle of Paulinus, Bishop of Nola, a document suggested as early as 1853 as a source for the idea of having the ship in *The Ancient Mariner* guided by a troop of angelic spirits.[4] But there is little speculation of this sort in Coleridge's notes on Defoe's novel.

There are gaps on the emotive side as well. The deeply affectionate man who insisted on the link between "filial" love and "universal Benevolence" (*L 1795* 46), who chose *The Friend* as the title for his periodical essays, and who wrote in anguish, "To be beloved is all I need, / And whom I love, I love indeed" (*CPW* I 391), only once comments on the frigid Crusoe's personal feelings, singling out an uncharacteristic passage, a eulogy on his departed (but nameless) wife, to praise for its warmth! This is all the more curious since the passage Coleridge refers to occurs not in *Robinson Crusoe* itself, but in its sequel, the *Farther*

---

3. *CM* I 161. Like Raysor, Whalley follows the *Literary Remains* (I, 192) in supplying words from the missing corner of the leaf. The answer to Coleridge's question is that, providing the discovery was properly and publicly recorded, the found land became a possession, not of the discoverer, but of the country the discoverer represented. The economic and political questions relating to Crusoe's island are explored in detail in the work of Maximillian E. Novak. See *Economics and the Fiction of Daniel Defoe* and "Crusoe the King and the Political Evolution of His Island," which appears little altered in Novak's *Defoe and the Nature of Man*, 50–64. A recent penetrating study of the novel's expansive political economics is Richard Braverman's "Crusoe's Legacy."

4. Paulinus tells the story of a storm-tossed ship abandoned by everyone except an old man; the Lord takes pity on him and sends a band of angels to steer the ship safely to harbor. That Coleridge borrowed from this letter—a suggestion first made in an anonymous article, "The Original Ancient Mariner," in *Gentleman's Magazine* (October 1853)—is now generally accepted. See John Livingston Lowes, *The Road to Xanadu: A Study in the Ways of the Imagination*, 258–62.

Adventures—rushed into print later in the same year, after *Robinson Crusoe* had gone through four printings in as many months. Coleridge's response to what he called "De Foe's comprehensive Character of the Wife, as She Should be" is understandable since, as is suggested by his altering of "my" to "his" in transcribing the passage, he had long since concluded that his own wife could not fulfil the roles specified by Crusoe: "the strong Supporter, the Comforter, . . . the Soul's living Home!" (*CM* I 166).

But Coleridge has no comment on the fact that, toward the end of the first volume, the undersexed Crusoe had squeezed marriage ("not either to my disadvantage or dissatisfaction"), procreation (two sons and a daughter), and the death of his wife into a single unfeeling sentence that ends with our hero setting off on another voyage (298). Likewise, when he returns home after a thirty-five-year absence to find his parents and his brothers "extinct," his only grievance is that there had been "no provision made for me" (274). In short, the deepest emotions of Robinson Crusoe, an unloving and sexually apathetic mercantilist, are stirred by money, and his friends tend to be those with whom he has some economic arrangement—the widow in England, the Portuguese Captain, his partner in Brazil (280). As Charles Nodier wrote in 1870, favorably comparing J. D. Wyss's immensely popular *Swiss Family Robinson* (1818) to the original: "What is lacking [in Defoe] are those tender anxieties, those mutual solicitudes, those alarms, those joys we share with others."[5]

And then, of course, there is Friday. The emotional contrast between man and master is most graphically revealed when Friday is reunited with his father, rescued along with the Spaniard. The reunion is so dramatic that Crusoe, who had heartlessly left his own parents without a farewell (31), feels himself admonished. Finding his old father, Friday "kiss'd him . . . hugg'd him, cry'd, laughed, . . . jumped about, danced, sung," and so on. Even Crusoe is "moved . . . to see what extasy and filial affection had worked in this poor savage, at the sight of his father, and of his being delivered from death" (237–38). A similarly ecstatic scene occurs when, Crusoe and Friday having returned to the island after an absence of eight years, father and son are once again reunited (*Farther Adventures* 3:55).

Crusoe's relationship to Friday will later be discussed in detail, but worth mentioning at this point is Charles Dickens's observation on Crusoe's response to the death of Friday in the *Farther Adventures* (3:73, 75). Ordered by Crusoe to the deck of the ship to palaver with natives in canoes off the coast of "the Brasils," Friday is killed in a hail of arrows. Dickens, who thought *Robinson Crusoe* "the only instance of an universally popular book that could make no one laugh and could make no one cry," claimed: "There is not in literature a more surprising instance of an utter want of tenderness and sentiment, than the death of Friday. It is as heartless as *Gil Blas,* in a very different and far more serious way."[6] Dickens overstates the case, but while Crusoe does refer to his

---

5. Introduction to *The Swiss Family Robinson.*
6. Quoted in John Forster, *The Life of Charles Dickens* 3:135*n.*

"inexpressible grief" at the death of Friday, and feels fully "justify'd before God and man" for the bloody revenge he takes, he seems at least as much disturbed by the loss of his "old servant" as by the gratuitous extinction of the "companion of all my sorrows and solitudes." Revealingly, he instantly thinks about capturing another cannibal as a substitute slave. As with all the other instances of Crusoe's essential lack of tenderness, Coleridge seems not to notice.

Nor does the Romantic poet seem much disturbed by what Ian Watt has called Crusoe's "blindness to aesthetic experience," his preference for "exploitation" rather than "adoration" of nature. In this novel, as Virginia Woolf said, "Nature must furl her splendid purples." For Crusoe, "Nature does not exist" except as a utilitarian entity, and even then it is "snubbed back with ruthless commonsense." As Frank H. Ellis notes, "Tropical islands in the Caribbean and the Pyrenees in winter unfold their beauties in vain before his unseeing eyes." If it is not quite true that, as Diana Neill put it, he "never once remarked on the beauty of nature," it is certainly true that Crusoe never gets carried away. Yet this "prosaic realism" did not (as she claims) "discredit [Defoe] with a romantic age"—at least not with Coleridge, who seized on the description of the "delightful cavity or grotto" Crusoe discovers (the floor of which was "dry and level, and had a small loose gravel upon it" [184]), in order to remark with enthusiasm: "How accurate an observer of Nature De Foe was!"[7] The comment Coleridge adds—"The reader will at once recognize Prof. Buckland's caves and diluvial gravel"—is a typical revelation of his grasp of contemporary science and his characteristic penchant for synthesis.[8] But, again, Coleridge's notes on

7. Watt, *The Rise of the Novel: Studies in Defoe, Richardson, and Fielding,* 70. Woolf, *The Second Common Reader,* 54, 55. Ellis, Introduction to *Twentieth-Century Interpretations of "Robinson Crusoe,"* 5. Neill, *A Short History of the English Novel,* 51. *CM* I 164. Crusoe does respond to nature occasionally. His aesthetic apogee comes early. He finds the morning after the storm "the most delightful that ever I saw" (32); and on the island finds a "delicious vale" (113). His interest in the cave he describes as "a most delightful cavity or grotto" is less aesthetic than economic: the walls seem to glitter with "diamonds" or "gold" (184). Nowhere does Coleridge comment upon Crusoe's feeble response to the beauty of his "exceedingly pleasant, fruitful" island (167)—an aesthetic insensitivity reflecting that of Defoe, whose own *Tour* of Great Britain reveals him as oblivious to the beauty even of the Lake District.

8. Coleridge refers to William Buckland, in whose *Reliquiae Diluvianae* (1823) gravel on cave floors provides evidence supporting the biblical story of the Deluge. Such allegedly "un-Romantic" attention to detail is typical of Coleridge's own approach to nature. His poems bristle with observations (backed up by scientific footnotes) on such phenomena as flowers that emit flashes, the mysteries of the Simoom, and the creaking quill-feathers of the Savannah Crane, to mention a few of the more esoteric items (*CPW* I 99–100, 119, 181). For lucid discussions of the poet's "*Naturphilosophie*," see Raimonda Modiano, *Coleridge and the Concept of Nature,* and Ian Wylie, *Young Coleridge and the Philosophers of Nature.* As Wylie demonstrates, Coleridge's attack on mechanism should not be taken, as it usually is, as establishing a necessary conflict between poetry and natural philosophy. Coleridge's perceptive marginalia in scientific books and his *Notebooks* for 1816–1828 have been closely studied by Trevor H. Levere, *Poetry Realized in Nature: Samuel Taylor Coleridge and Early Nineteenth-Century Science.* Levere emphasizes the poet's remarkable, even "unique," grasp

Robinson Crusoe omit more than they include on the subject of nature, whether apprehended aesthetically, religiously, or scientifically.

Among all these curious omissions, one lacuna or "not said" will seem particularly inexplicable to those most familiar with Coleridge's warmhearted nature and early political activism. Perhaps the best way to approach it is to focus on one important aspect of the novel upon which Coleridge *does* comment at some length. Attention to that point, Crusoe's "universality," leads to the central critical and moral statement Coleridge makes about Crusoe, and that, in turn, should invite the resistance of many readers. What is most remarkable is that few such readers will be able to claim, mutatis mutandis, greater moral sensitivity to the issue Coleridge apparently overlooks than Coleridge himself.

Crusoe's spectrum of activities, as numerous critics have pointed out, constitutes one of the novel's major sources of interest for readers living in an age of economic specialization, when the division of labor has rendered most of us ignorant of the basic skills.[9] The championship of human integrity against the forces of division is, of course, a fundamental Romantic theme. But Crusoe's description of his activities as potter, tailor, carpenter, farmer, etc., must have been especially fascinating to a Romantic who, anticipating the early Marx on "alienation," deplored the spiritual and intellectual effects of specialization; who had planned as a young man to set up a self-sufficient colony in the transoceanic wilderness; and who, at the time he wrote his greatest poems, lived as a philosophical (though far from depoliticized) farmer at Stowey, subsisting primarily on his own potatoes, pigs, and poultry (*CL* I 277, 305). Indeed, in the course of a lecture on the slave trade (published first in the volume containing his Bristol lectures of 1795 and a year later as the most dramatic piece in his short-lived periodical, *The Watchman*), Coleridge pauses to dwell on the lot of the "happy and innocent" Africans of the interior, and his remarks permit us to see just *how* much this aspect of *Robinson Crusoe* must have appealed to him:

> The peaceful inhabitants of a fertile soil, they cultivate their fields in common, and reap the crop as the common property of all. Each family . . . spins, weaves, sews, hunts, fishes, and makes baskets, fishing-tackle, and the implements of agriculture: and this variety of employment gives an acuteness of intellect to the Negro which the Mechanic whom the division of labor condemns to one simple operation is precluded from attaining. (*W* 134)

Coleridge's focus is characteristically on community rather than individualism, but such a vision reveals one source of his abiding interest in Crusoe—a man whom Fate had released from the daily tedium of the one simple opera-

---

of contemporary science and his capacity for synthesis. It might be added that Coleridge was too quick to accept a few forms of pseudoscience, including phrenology and racial classifications based on dubious anthropology.

9. For a brief summary and expansion of T. H. Green's thesis that the division of labor has created particular needs in the modern audience, see Watt, *The Rise of the Novel*, 71–74.

tion, at a high price to be sure. But notice Coleridge's emphasis in discussing Defoe's treatment of Crusoe's activities: "Even so very easy a problem as that of finding a substitute for ink is with exquisite judgment made to baffle Crusoe's inventive faculties. Even in what he does, he arrives at no excellence . . . Basket-work . . . Carpentering, Tailoring, Pottery, are all just what will answer his purposes—and those are confined to needs that all men have, and comforts that all men desire" (*CM* I 165).

Is *that* how we remember Crusoe? Does he not, rather, seem a paragon of efficiency, exceptional in his capacity to manage on his own? Rousseau, who thought the book "a complete treatise on natural education," was not alone among his contemporaries in being impressed by Crusoe's practical ingenuity; and Coleridge's friend Wordsworth, correcting what he thought a general un-derestimation of Crusoe's "uncommon merits," ascribed the "chief interest" of the story to "the extraordinary energy and resource of the hero under his difficult circumstances," qualities "far beyond what it was natural to expect, or what would have been exhibited by the average man."[10]

Yet Coleridge is essentially right, and if he goes too far in disparaging Crusoe's technical accomplishments, he is at least getting his information straight from the horse's mouth. Crusoe, with moderately self-deprecating humor, often ridi-cules his own technical efforts: he is an "awkward" maker of "misshapen ugly" pots, a "bad carpenter" and "worse taylor," etc.[11] However, for a man who had "never handled a tool" in his life, and who started with "want of tools, want of help, and want of skill," he does more than moderately well—despite his fail-ure, as Coleridge *would* note, to devise a substitute for ink.[12] Even though "time and necessity" combine to make Crusoe, as he declares, "a compleat natural

10. In *Émile* (1762), Rousseau pronounces *Robinson Crusoe* (at least the island section, the only portion of the novel he considers) the "first book" his imaginary pupil "shall read"; indeed, "for a long time," it will constitute "his whole library" (2:57). Words-worth's remarks are recorded in "Reminiscences of the Rev. R. P. Graves, M.A.," in *The Prose Works of William Wordsworth*, ed. Alexander B. Grosart (3:468).

11. Not that this self-disparagement gets out of hand. Crusoe tells us about the "many awkward ways" in which he raised paste for earthen vessels, and of the "odd misshapen ugly things" that resulted, but adds that with smaller items he enjoyed "better success" (131–32), and in time did manufacture jars that were "round and shapa-ble" (153). Reflecting back on his problems with tables and chairs while in the process of getting his new goatskin in shape, he remarks, "if I was a bad carpenter, I was a worse taylor" (145). But soon after, we learn that he "improved much" in his wickerware; improved, indeed, "in all the mechanick exercises," even becoming "a very good car-penter, especially considering how few tools I had" (153). John J. Richetti observes: "As generations of fascinated readers can testify, [Crusoe's] experiments are enthralling; they seem to reenact the trial, error, and accident by which we imagine technological progress has taken place in primitive times" (*Daniel Defoe*, 59).

12. *Robinson Crusoe*, 85, 127, 82. Despite the reference to "want of tools," however, Crusoe is aware that he would have perished without the supplies salvaged from the ship (141). These supplies, as Novak has said, have been a "stumbling block to economists who have wanted to use Crusoe as the hero of their parables." See "*Robinson Crusoe* and Economic Utopia," 477.

mechanic," Coleridge's essential point remains valid in this context, for Crusoe adds immediately, "as I believe it would do any one else" (89).

Coleridge's "essential point"—and it is this that we are after—is, then, Crusoe's universality: Crusoe as Everyman. In the course of an 1818 lecture, Coleridge digressed from a digression on the *Arabian Nights* to say a word about Defoe's hero: "Crusoe himself is merely a representative of humanity in general; neither his intellectual nor his moral qualities set him above the middle degree of mankind; his only prominent characteristic is the spirit of enterprise and wandering, which is, nevertheless, a very common disposition" (*Miscellaneous Criticism,* ed. Raysor, 194). The point is reaffirmed, and extended, in one of Coleridge's overarching comments on *Robinson Crusoe.* The author, he tells us, could have made Crusoe a natural scientist of sorts, with a consequent enrichment of one aspect of the book; but Defoe chose better, for then his hero would have ceased "to be the Universal Representative—the person, for whom every reader could substitute *himself*—But now nothing is done, thought, or suffered, or desired, but what every man can imagine himself doing, thinking, feeling, or wishing for" (*CM* I 165).

Crusoe as Everyman is, in Coleridge's scenario, responded to by the reader as Everyman. Many contemporary readers will resist this universalism, what James Sutherland could still refer to in 1971 as the novel's "appeal to the permanent feelings and essential interests of the human race." I am, in any case, less concerned here with Coleridge's essentialism and the blasé exclusion of women readers than with several even breezier, and rather un-Coleridgean, assumptions. Up to a point, we can agree that Coleridge's remark about readers sharing vicariously in Crusoe's thoughts and activities constitutes a penetrating and valid judgment, one accurate enough to be paraphrased ever since. "The reader identifies himself with the character," Angus Ross writes in his introduction to the Penguin edition; "Crusoe is Everyman. 'So,' we say, 'if I had been Crusoe, I should have behaved.'" The "form" chosen by Defoe, his most recent biographer writes, "maneuvered to assure that the reader would say, 'In his place, I, too, would . . .'"[13] But is it true, as Coleridge claims, that reading *Robinson Crusoe,* we are "all the while . . . touching or touched by, common Flesh and Blood" (*CM* I 167)? Do we agree that Crusoe does, thinks, feels, and desires nothing "but what every man can imagine himself doing, thinking, feeling, or wishing for"? Most significantly, are Crusoe's "moral qualities" really to be found at the "middle degree of mankind"?

One hopes not. There is, of course, much that is admirable about Crusoe; the "lessons" of the novel, as singled out by Defoe himself in his preface to the third part of *Robinson Crusoe,* the *Serious Reflections,* are the very qualities we associate with its hero: "invincible patience," "indefatigable application," and "undaunted resolution" (*Works* 3:xiii). Yet there is also a good deal that is distasteful about Defoe's Robinson Crusoe, flaws whose detection does not

---

13. Sutherland, *Daniel Defoe: A Critical Study,* 131. Backscheider, *Daniel Defoe: His Life,* 415.

require a twentieth-century sensibility. Defoe was pilloried during his life, and it would be ungenerous to repeat the punishment posthumously. While I have found it impossible not to pass *some* judgment, my real subject is not the mercantilist ethics of Defoe, or of Crusoe, as judged and found wanting by contemporary standards and sensitivities. I am interested, instead, in the reaction of a nineteenth-century reader. As a matter of fact, for those readers who think of him as essentially the poet whose genius flourished in the few years immediately preceding and following the turn into the nineteenth century, the warm-hearted young man who ardently embraced the libertarian if not the irreligious values of the French Revolution, Samuel Taylor Coleridge will seem—in terms of his own sensibility, personality, political principles, and "moral qualities"— so singularly well equipped to criticize Crusoe's human shortcomings that they may well wonder why he did not.

I've already mentioned Crusoe's cold, antiaesthetic, exploitative attitude toward the natural world and his fellow beings—as well as Coleridge's apparent reluctance to find fault. Now comes what I have described as the most glaring lacuna in the marginalia: Coleridge's failure to say a word about Crusoe's involvement in slavery and the slave trade.

Surprising in the marginal notes of a man on record as morally and intellectually appalled by European crimes against Africa and, indeed, by slavery in any form, that omission generated the question behind the present thoughts, thoughts that led me not only to reread *Robinson Crusoe* but also to reexamine Coleridge, especially later Coleridge. I remain vestigially perplexed by the omission, which, though it now seems considerably less surprising, is even more troubling. In any case, I hope the intellectual journey the question occasioned can be justified on its own terms; that, as Coleridge says in that characteristic passage from *Biographia Literaria* cited in my Preface and quoted fully in my Conclusion, "the reader [will] be carried forward . . . not by a restless desire to arrive at the final solution, but by the pleasurable activity of mind excited by the attractions of the journey itself" (*BL* II 14).

I have had my share of pleasurable activity in the reading for and writing of the present study. But if, like Coleridge's Mariner, I have returned at the end of this first part to much the same harbor from which I departed, the experience of the voyage has also made me, if not the sufferer of a sea change, something akin to the Wedding Guest: a sadder and a wiser man. For the issues involved proved, as I should have expected given the complexity of Coleridgean thought and the increasing conservatism of his politics, less straightforward than I had originally imagined—or hoped.

The tracing of that complexity begins with an attempt to reaffirm, with some necessary qualification, Coleridge's lifelong opposition to slavery without neglecting his shift in attitude toward egalitarianism and race. Pursuit of these issues, which necessitates rummaging through material Coleridge never published, provides a richer, if more complicated, image of the man who sat down, pen in hand, to read *Robinson Crusoe* in 1830. Having followed the troubled stream of Coleridgean thought on these issues, we can return to Defoe's novel, emphasizing the cultural, political, imperialist, and racial aspects of a central work of Western literature too often recalled, especially by those of us who read it as children and never again, as *simply* a great "adventure story."

2

I have already cited Coleridge's 1795 lecture "On the Slave Trade," published in *Conciones ad Populum* and *The Watchman*. That ardent and eloquent jeremiad predated by three years Coleridge's public recantation of his initially enthusiastic support of the French Revolution (in "France: An Ode," originally entitled "Recantation"), and came a third of a century before the annotations on *Robinson Crusoe*. In the course of those years, Coleridge's political and economic thinking—though his claim to a certain internal consistency is to a considerable extent justified—underwent an oscillating evolution from radicalism to conservatism.

Consistency or apostasy? Since that question is at the heart of discussions of two of the great minds encountering the French Revolution, it is worth having the judgment of one upon the other on this very point. In the course of noting the occasional "inconsistency" of Edmund Burke, Coleridge delivered what has recently and justly been described as "a towering tribute to Burke's consistency, of principle." "I do not mean," wrote Coleridge (divorcing himself from the endlessly repeated but superficial Foxite and radical charge that Burke had violated his own principles by condemning the French Revolution after having supported the American),

> that this great Man supported different Principles at different aeras [eras] of his political Life. On the contrary, no Man was more like himself. From his first published Speech on the American Colonies to his last posthumous Tracts, we see the same Man, the same Doctrines, the same uniform Wisdom of *practical* Councils, the same Reasoning and the same Prejudices against all abstract grounds, against all deduction of Practice from Theory. The inconsistency to which I allude, is of a different kind: it is the want of congruity in the Principles appealed to in different parts of the same Work, it is an apparent versatility of the Principle with the Occasion.[14]

Burke's most sustained defense of his own "consistency," the "virtue" he most valued in himself, occurs in *An Appeal from the Old to the New Whigs* (1791), where he mounts an impressive defense not only of his consistency but also of what he calls a "true natural aristocracy," a "wise and learned" bulwark against the leveling tendencies unleashed by the French Revolution. The *Appeal*, pre-

---

14. *F* I 123–24. The passage is cited by A. C. Goodson, "Burke's Orpheus and Coleridge's Contrary Understanding," 56, and by Conor Cruise O'Brien, *The Great Melody: A Thematic Biography and Commented Anthology of Edmund Burke,* who also makes the "towering tribute" remark (lxx). It should be added that Coleridge disagreed with Burke's consistent "opposition of Theory to Practice." Such an opposition is "absurd," since an "erroneous System is best confuted," not by ridiculing theory, but by detecting "Errors in the particular Theory. For the meanest of men has his Theory: and to think at all is to theorize" (*F* II 124).

dictably W. B. Yeats's favorite among Burke's writings, also "appealed," despite his intellectual struggle to resist Burke, to a Coleridge who—from the "radicalism" of "Religious Musings" to the much later call for a natural aristocracy in the form of a guiding "clerisy"—always feared the anarchic potential of the "outrageous mass" as much as he despised (at least throughout the 1790s) the Pitt Ministry.[15]

While Burke, combining conservative prejudice with almost clairvoyant insight, opposed the French Revolution from the outset, Coleridge, open for almost a decade to the potential of revolutionary liberation, eventually came to see that Revolution from an essentially Burkean perspective. He watched, with mingled hopes and fears, as events unfolded pretty much as Burke had predicted in *Reflections on the Revolution in France* (1790). With the rise of Bonaparte (the "master" and "popular general" with "the true spirit of command" foreseen in the *Reflections*), Coleridge moved away from egalitarian ideals betrayed by the French themselves. Now he was committed, not to Gallic *liberté* (revealed as "Licence"), but to Burkean "liberty," an orderly freedom inhering, as Burke said in the *Appeal*, in "good and steady government."

Even private property, condemned by young Coleridge as "beyond doubt the Origin of all Evil" (*CL* I 214; cf. *CPW* I 116–17), was now perceived as indispensable to a stable government and society—though without Burke's inordinate reverence for privilege and antiquity. Though a precise date is difficult to fix, before the decade of the 1790s was over, the former advocate of Pantisocracy had abandoned as premature that egalitarian social ideal. In "On the French Constitution," a November 1799 *Morning Post* article written soon after his return from Germany, Coleridge noted the gradual decline over the past four centuries of the "prejudices of superstition, birth, and hereditary right." The "empire of property" was "gradually establishing itself in their stead." Anticipating Marxist dialectic, he wondered "whether or no this too will not in a distant age submit to some more powerful principle." But that was "a subject fruitful in *dreams* to poetic philosophers; . . . to all present purposes it is a useless and impertinent speculation. For the present race of men Governments must be founded on property; that *Government is good in which property is secure and circulates;* that *Government the best, in which, in the exactest ratio, makes each man's power proportionate to his property.*" Perhaps in America, he continues, "where the great mass of the people possess property," universal suffrage is attainable, but "when the physical strength of a nation is in the poor, the Government must be in the hands of the rich" (*EOT* I 32).

15. *CPW* I 118. Inexplicably omitted from the French Revolutionary volume of *The Writings and Speeches of Edmund Burke, An Appeal from the Old to the New Whigs in consequence of some late discussions in Parliament* is here quoted from the twelve-volume Nimmo edition of Burke's *Works* (London, 1899), 4:92–103. Two recent informed studies trace the dialectic between Coleridge's radicalism and quest for elite leadership: John T. Miller, Jr., *Ideology and Enlightenment: The Social and Political Thought of Samuel Taylor Coleridge* (1987) and Nigel Leask, *The Politics of Imagination in Coleridge's Critical Thought* (1988).

"Once a Jacobin always a Jacobin," Pitt had declared in Parliament. Coleridge revealed—both here and in his October 21, 1802, *Morning Post* piece actually entitled "Once a Jacobin Always a Jacobin" (*EOT* I 367–73)—that he had learned from the process of revolution in experimental France that stable government had to be founded on something more dependable than shifting popular opinion or an abstract doctrine of the Rights of Man. He had also concluded, by 1799 at the latest, that when the bulk of the population was poor, redistribution of political power would inevitably lead to redistribution of wealth, which, in an economy of scarcity, would result in a leveling reduction of everyone to a subsistence level. A subsistence economy, in turn, would make unlikely or impossible that socioeconomic growth and intellectual development Coleridge thought indispensable to a genuine state. Given that premise, and given his attraction to humanistic culture (which he associated even before the turn of the century with landed property) rather than to "the commercial spirit," Coleridge saw the task ahead as one of *moderating* the inevitable shift of power from the landed aristocracy to the rising class, urbanized and mercantile: Defoe's people, in short.

One can deplore Coleridge's abandonment of a "premature" egalitarian ideal as itself premature, or applaud him for his insight in consigning it, in terms of practical politics, to the realm of the visionary. One can, but really shouldn't, dismiss him as an enthusiast turned reactionary by the evolving historical drama of the French Revolution and his own equivocation and opportunism, a man whose shifting positions between 1795 and (say) 1802 were simply the self-serving tergiversations of a political apostate. Max F. Schulz, sounding rather like Coleridge on Burke, has recently remarked "how easy it is for armchair academics to scold Coleridge for his apparent apostasy from principled positions, when in fact he was responding, like the practical politician and the practicing journalist, with versatile energy to world events." Thomas De Quincey attributed Coleridge's "Toryism" after 1798 to a justifiable commitment to resist Napoleon; Coleridge's perceptions of England, an island sea power, at war with Napoleonic France, a seemingly invincible land power, involved (in Schulz's words) "political realities at variance with the political stances of a youthful Bristol rebel of the 1790s." In the second part of this study, I will be arguing, as does Erdman, that Coleridge's rapid swings from "Yea" to "Nay" in his "arc of oscillation," particularly his abrupt shift in March 1798 away from Opposition, reflect his response less to developments in France than to menacing actions taken by an increasingly repressive Pitt Ministry. But caution and even fear need not *utterly* abolish principle, and it is the search for principles and the attempt to delineate their complex interaction with material history, the dialectic of the ideal and the real, that is at the heart of Coleridge's ambivalent engagements with and withdrawals from the political arena.[16]

16. Schulz, "The Many Coleridges," 24. De Quincey, *Recollections of the Lakes and the Lake Poets,* ed. David Wright, 104–10. Coleridge himself offers "Yea" and "Nay" as "an attempt to delineate an arc of oscillation" in his mental state (*EOT* I lxxv). The remark is

On the related but separable questions of slavery and racial equality, his position also shifted. Though there was minimal inconsistency in his continued opposition to slavery, it lessened in intensity, and he certainly rejected his earlier insistence on the equality of the races. The rejection is hardly remarkable for a man of the period. While racial egalitarianism is, in contemporary discussion, usually taken to be an immutable and eternal law, an assumption made by precisely those who deny every other absolute or transhistorical "truth," it is in fact a concept that emerged from a set of global conditions which have changed radically and which remain subject to further change. A perceptive and sympathetic reader of an earlier version of this volume suggested that, while I was "by no means slavish to 'political correctness,'" I seemed to have "internalized many of its arguments," most noticeably in assuming or accepting this monolithic "new morality." One result, in his opinion, was that I found "puzzling inconsistency to reside in Coleridge's attitudes, rather than seeing those attitudes as necessarily connected to the socioeconomic reality of Coleridge's milieu." To avoid making my work "time-bound," the reader suggested that I simply report "the variations of Coleridge's attitude toward race as neutral data, with no implied moral praise or censure." I've tried; and I had noted from the outset that such attitudes toward race were a commonplace position among even advanced thinkers of his period. Yet few reached it from the direction of Coleridge's original "radicalism," a fact that may make him, even

---

quoted by Erdman in his masterly introduction to *EOT* (I lix–clxxix). On Coleridge's thinking and rethinking as revealed in his political prose, see also John Colmer, *Coleridge: Critic of Society*, and Donald H. Reiman, both his "Coleridge and the Art of Equivocation" and his review-essay on *EOT*, available as "The Bollingen Coleridge," in his *Romantic Texts and Contexts* (see especially 75–79). A favorable survey is offered by John Morrow in "Coleridge and the English Revolution" and in his introduction (1–23) to *On Politics and Society*, vol. 1 of the new Princeton edition of *Coleridge's Writings*. Negative judgment has been passed by E. P. Thompson in *The Making of the English Working Class* and "Disenchantment or Default? A Lay Sermon" and (most intemperately) in his dismissal (in reviewing *EOT*) of the man those articles reveal.

Sophisticated accounts of Coleridge's political dialectic may be found in Carl Woodring's *Politics in the Poetry of Coleridge*, Kelvin Everest's *Coleridge's Secret Ministry: The Context of the Conversation Poems, 1795–1798* (97–145), Robert Sayre's "The Young Coleridge: Romantic Utopianism and the French Revolution," and in four essays—Jerome Christensen's "Once an Apostate Always an Apostate," Michael Fischer's "Morality and History in Coleridge's Political Theory," Raimonda Modiano's "Metaphysical Debate in Coleridge's Political Theory," and R. F. Storch's "The Politics of the Imagination"—in the special section "Coleridge: The Politics of the Imagination," in *Studies in Romanticism* 21 (1982), 447–74 (ed. Carl Woodring). A penetrating and more hostile account, based on Erdman and reflecting Christensen's conclusion that Coleridgean "equivocation . . . turns apostasy into a kind of power" (464), is offered by Liu in *Wordsworth*, 416–26. "It was not that Coleridge changed his mind from Yea to Nay," writes Liu (following Erdman's use of Coleridge's arc-points), but that he "consistently said Yea *but* Nay" (422). If "this was his genius," it was also the equivocation of a "philosophically slippery propagandist" who, "in dialectical terms," epitomizes the "problem of Romantic apostasy" (422, 416, 427).

mutatis mutandis, open to judgment, especially if the judgment is neither shrill nor accusatory.

During the 1790s, Coleridge was a zealous and committed egalitarian appalled by slavery and the slave trade— simultaneously abolished by England and the United States in 1807, though illegal trading and slavery itself persisted in British colonies until 1833, and beyond.[17] More than a decade after the abolition of the trade, an event that had the effect of dampening the ardor of many antislavery liberals, Coleridge was still referring enthusiastically to its outlawing as a "glorious" example of appropriate state intervention in commerce, and castigating those British merchants who continued, clandestinely and illegally, to profit from the trade. In the years that followed, though he continued to deplore slavery as an utter subversion of all morality, his attitude was increasingly less radical than paternalistic. In the years immediately prior to his annotation of *Robinson Crusoe*, Coleridge's thinking was demonstrably influenced, not only by political conservatism, but by the racial classification of the German physiologist and pioneer anthropologist Johann Friedrich Blumenbach. Coleridge's Blumenbachian speculations on race are troubling, but they cannot be ignored, especially since they seem related to his later suspicions that the class structure of society may be hierarchical almost by divine plan.[18]

The founder of physical anthropology and "one of those few scientists often cited in retrospect as cultural relativists and defenders of equality,"[19] Blumenbach, for whom the decisive factor was the influence of climate, argued against

17. For a full, recent survey, see James Walvin, *England, Slaves, and Freedom, 1776– 1838*.

18. Barbara Paul-Emile argues that his evolving conservative sense of "society as hierarchical by divine plan" caused Coleridge, an abolitionist from 1792–1798, to later resist any drastic change that might lead to social upheaval ("Samuel Taylor Coleridge as Abolitionist").

Whatever the root causes of the evolution in Coleridge's thinking on these matters, that thinking seems less focused on the issue of slavery than of race, and more than both on the question of religious edification and the inseparability of rights and duties. Paul-Emile's argument seems essentially correct; but even if so, she is wrong to limit Coleridge's abolitionist phase to six years in the nineties, though not at all precipitate in initiating his later "hierarchical" phase with the year 1808. In that year, he wrote a laudatory review of Clarkson's *The History of . . . the Abolition of the African Slave-Trade*, which nevertheless affirms white superiority and a civilizing responsibility. But he still ardently celebrated both Clarkson's book and abolition itself, which, ten years later, he was still praising as "glorious." For an earlier examination of Coleridge as an abolitionist despite a subsequent change in his racial attitudes, see Eva Beatrice Dykes, *The Negro in English Romantic Thought*, 75–80.

19. The phrase is Stephen Jay Gould's, in *The Mismeasure of Man*, 36. Actually, Gould observes a few pages earlier, "throughout the egalitarian tradition of the European Enlightenment and the American Revolution, I cannot identify any popular position remotely like the 'cultural relativism' that prevails (at least by lip-service) in liberal circles today. The nearest approach is a common argument that black inferiority is purely cultural and that it can be completely eradicated by education to a Caucasian standard" (32).

racial rankings on aesthetic grounds or presumed mental ability. No bigot (indeed, he assembled an important collection of books written by blacks), Blumenbach nevertheless viewed the "Caucasian" race, a term he originated in 1795, as the norm. From that standard or "center" his four other principal races (the Malayan, American, Mongolian, and Ethiopian) "deviated," with the Mongolian and the Ethiopian (that is, African blacks) the "two extremes."[20] This was the "enumeration of the races now generally adopted," a classification "we owe" to "Prof. Blumenbach." The accurate observation was made by Coleridge, in one of the British Museum manuscripts of 1825–1827 in which he speculates about race. In his Table Talk for February 24, 1827, Coleridge "figured" Blumenbach's hierarchical "scale of dignity" as a pyramid, with the "Caucasian or European" race at the apex, the "Malay" and "American" at the median points, and the "Negro" and "Mongolian" at the base (*TT* II 55, I 64–65).

During his trip to Germany in 1798–1799, Coleridge had met Blumenbach, attended his "delightful" lectures, and received from this "most interesting" man "*flattering* attention," including, eventually, a huge farewell party, at which Coleridge "dazzled all the professors and their wives with his brilliant talk and execrable pronunciation" of German.[21] Göttingen was then at its zenith as an intellectual center, a university notable for its superb library, its exhaustive scholarly professionalism, and the interest of its distinguished lecturers in biblical higher criticism, natural history, and questions of ethnicity and race. Coleridge matriculated in order to gain access to the library—"without doubt . . . the very first in the world," he wrote his wife (*CL* I 475)—and in order to attend Blumenbach's lectures on physiology and natural history. Singled out by the professor as a pupil both convivial and brilliant, Coleridge *may* have been shown Blumenbach's collection of black literature; he certainly saw his rather more famous collection.

In an 1811 notebook entry, he refers to Blumenbach having "collected 70 or 80 Skulls, each of a different race or nation, before he settled on the central one—& by the time he had a 110 (he has now, I believe, a 120) he had altered his arrangement a score of times at least." (This mixture of interest and skepticism is reflected in remarks Coleridge made years later: "Craniology very imperfect at present," he observed in 1827—"though some things could not be by accident" [*TT* I 75].) Blumenbach's array of "race-skulls"—to which, another traveler tells us, "his family have well given the name of Golgotha"—was the largest craniological collection in the world at the time, one proudly exhibited to curious visitors.[22]

20. *A Manual of the Elements of Natural History*, 37.
21. *CL* I 472, 494. For the account of Blumenbach's leave-taking party for Coleridge, see Clement Carlyon, *Early Years and Late Reflections* 1:161–62, and Richard Holmes, *Coleridge: Early Visions*, 236. The significance of Göttingen to Coleridge is discussed in the opening chapter of Levere's *Poetry Realized in Nature*.
22. *CN* III 4047. The other visitor cited inspected the collection in 1816; see *Life, Letters, and Journals of George Ticknor* 1:94. The context of Coleridge's own note, mockery of Scottish empiricists obsessed by the collection of "evidence," suggests that he

Coleridge's remark about Blumenbach's trying to settle on a "central" race is itself the crucial issue, since, unsurprisingly, the central historical race turned out to be white and European. Though few racial theorists of the day were either as sophisticated or as influential as Blumenbach, such racial ranking was almost universal among Enlightenment and nineteenth-century intellectuals in Europe and America. Hume, Kant, and Hegel; Franklin, Jefferson, and Lincoln, for example, had no doubt about its propriety, nor, incidentally, did Marx and Engels.[23] There are, however, distinctions to be made. Biologist Stephen Jay Gould speaks of "hard-liners" and "soft-liners."

Hard-liners held, not only that blacks were inferior, but also that "their biological status justified enslavement and colonization." The great "chain of being" itself provided a potential rationale, at once theological and pragmatic; Gould quotes Alexander Pope as if he were referring, not (as he is) to human faculties, but to "superior" and "inferior" races: "Without this just gradation, could they be / Subjected, these to those, or all to thee?"[24] The soft-liners, agreeing that blacks were inferior, held that "a people's right to freedom did not depend upon their level of intelligence." Thus, Jefferson—who advanced, though "as a suspicion only," his feeling that blacks were mentally and physically inferior to whites—also insisted in "Query XIV" of his *Notes on the State of*

---

is simultaneously attacking resistance to general "ideas" and the danger of drawing precipitous conclusions. In *De Generis Humani Varietate Nativa*, a book Coleridge annotated in 1828, Blumenbach records eighty-two skulls in his collection as of 1795. After his death in 1840, the collection (constantly added to) provided the nucleus of a Pan-German racist theory: a corruption of Blumenbach's work that reached its nadir when the Nazis came to power. For Coleridge's continuing interest in Blumenbach, see, e.g., *F* I 59, 154–56; *CN* I 1657, 1738, IV 4548, 4668, 4697, 4839, 4984; *CL* VI 723; *CM* III 948.

23. To restrict the racist litany to the first two names: In a footnote added in 1753 to his essay "Of National Characters" (1748), David Hume referred to "negroes" among others as "naturally inferior" to whites; Negro slaves are without "any symptom of ingenuity" (*Essays and Treatises on Several Subjects* 1:521–22). A decade later, expanding on Hume in a section devoted to "National Characteristics" in his *Observations on the Feelings of the Beautiful and the Sublime* (1764), Immanuel Kant declared the racial difference as great in terms of "mental capacities" as in terms of color. Just as Hume had dismissed a cultured black man in Jamaica (the poet Francis Williams) as resembling "a parrot who speaks a few words plainly," so Kant tells a story of a "Negro carpenter" who replied to a point with obvious intelligence and wit, only to dismiss it as unintentional; "The fellow was quite black from head to foot, a clear proof that what he said was stupid" (113). In both cases, the alleged stupidity is posited as inherent and—even in the face of empirical evidence to the contrary—as self-evident.

24. *An Essay on Man*, "First Epistle," 229–30. Gould's unfairness in quoting Pope out of context is compounded by the fact that, both in "Windsor Forest" and in the *Essay on Man* itself, Pope condemns the disruption of natural harmony epitomized by making "slaves of Subjects" from conquered lands. In the latter part of "Windsor Forest," added in 1713, Pope has a ringing apostrophe: "Oh stretch thy Reign, fair *Peace!* from shore to shore, / Till Conquest cease, and Slavery be no more" (ll. 407–8).

Virginia, "Whatever be the degree of their talents, it is no measure of their rights."[25]

The position of the later, "conservative" Coleridge was in accord with that of the "liberal" Jefferson. In 1828, two years before annotating Defoe's novel, Coleridge reread and annotated a 1798 German translation of the third edition (1795) of Blumenbach's *De Generis Humanae Varietate Nativa* (first published in 1775). "Without rejecting his Pentad," that is, Blumenbach's fivefold division of the races, Coleridge attributed to it essentially "the merit of being . . . convenient," pointing out in a notebook entry that his purely physiological classification offered no distinction "in respect of intellectual faculties, and moral predispositions." His own "modification" was based, as his Table Talk confirms (*TT* I 38, 64), on what he thought were Kant's "three great races of mankind"— Kant in fact distinguished four, confidently pronouncing "Americans" (that is, Indians) and "blacks . . . lower in their mental capacities than all other races." Coleridge's triadic scheme, an arrangement he thought at once "founded on history" and the Bible, was less dependent than Blumenbach's on "climate": a deterministic environmentalism he saw as a threat to the human soul. In this scheme, "the Negro," associated with the biblical Ham, was equated with the "unhistoric and Degenerous."[26]

The last word echoes Blumenbach, who, with the third edition of *De Generis,* became (along with Sir Joseph Banks), one of the principal promoters of the "degeneration" thesis. It was a thesis anticipated earlier in the century by the French naturalist G.-L. Buffon and, in a sense, by Robinson Crusoe, who, viewing another "collection" of skulls and other bones—the refuse of a human flesh-feast—is struck by the cannibals' "inhuman hellish brutality" and by "the horror of the degeneracy of human nature," a nature "entirely abandoned of Heaven," and acting "by some hellish degeneracy" (172, 176; this condemnation will later be moderated by Crusoe, as he becomes something of a cultural relativist).

The other designation, "unhistoric," is clarified by Coleridge's claim, in his

25. *Thomas Jefferson: Writings,* 256–75. Many years later (in a letter of February 25, 1809), Jefferson said that his "doubts"—based on "personal" and "limited" observations— were "expressed . . . with great hesitation," and that subsequent and frequent observation "of respectable intelligence in that race of men" encouraged him in anticipating not only "a complete refutation" of his own early doubts, but also "the day of [blacks'] relief."

The 1993 conference papers edited by Peter Onuf for *Jeffersonian Legacies* are dominated by issues of slavery and racism. But the real stain on Jefferson's greatness may have less to do with his own slaveholding than with his cooperation with Napoleon in the latter's crushing of Toussaint's revolt in 1802.

26. On the environmentalist threat to soul, see *CL* VI 723; *CN* IV 4548, 4668, 4697, 4839, 4984. Coleridge's attempts to develop a triadic modification of Blumenbach may be traced in *CN* IV 4548 and in the British Museum documents speculating on race. For the annotations on Blumenbach, see *CM* I 537–41, especially 539–40. In the first edition (1775), Blumenbach had distinguished four races; a fifth was added in the second (1781) edition. For Kant's four races, see *TT* I 38–39*n.*

1825–1827 fragment "The Historic Race," that "the Human Species consists of an Historic Race—and other Races." Later in the fragment, this becomes "*One* historic Race," a "central" race capable of "ameliorating," even "subliming," the "*several* others, . . . even where it leaves them in their peculiar orbit." Insisting that "even the central Race is a degeneracy" from the original human ideal, Coleridge argues that it "obtains its paramountcy by comparative *Generosity*— which confers the right negatively by the less degree of our degeneracy and positively by the direction in which we are moving." Elsewhere it is made clear that "that which in the central Race saves man from *Degeneracy*" is the Judeo-Christian ethic. Though these ideas on race remained unpublished during Coleridge's lifetime, they may be said to contain, as J. H. Haeger rather strenuously but justifiably puts it, "the premise of a master race leading to the doctrine of the white man's burden and the idea of ethical-moral progress," thus enunciating "the cultural assumptions of British imperialism later in the century."[27]

There's *some*thing to this, and one doesn't have to wait until later in the century to find partial evidence. In Malta in 1804, acting as "a sort of diplomatic Understrapper" (*CL* II 1146) to the British High Commissioner and de facto Governor, Sir Alexander Ball, Coleridge collaborated with the admiral on a series of papers that expounded an imperialist philosophy. Unpersuaded by the "exclusive" nature of the strategic argument that Malta was "the key to Egypt" and Egypt in turn "the key to India," Coleridge thought Egypt *itself,* with its "natural wealth, and commercial capabilities," a target for potentially profitable Napoleonic colonization. In versions of a document variously titled "Defense of Egypt" and "Observations on Egypt," which David Erdman describes as Ball's position papers intended for the Ministry but which may reflect, as Donald Sultana insists, Coleridge's own position, it is proposed that to prevent the French from seizing and colonizing Egypt, "we must take it ourselves." As Erdman remarks, "Coleridge detested slavery, but the calculations of the 'Observations on Egypt' are those of a master-race economist." At the same time, Erdman disputes Sultana's conclusion that "as a political journalist" Coleridge "was now committed to the cause of imperialism." Even if Sultana's characterization of these documents is accurate, to conclude that Coleridge (rewriting the white paper of a civil servant he happened to admire) was now journalistically "committed to imperialism" is to neglect what Erdman perceptively depicts as the "coil of resistance lurking in any Coleridgean commitment."[28]

In any case, Coleridge's temporary endorsement of imperialism did not include a justification of slavery. The paper on Egypt (*EOT* III 200–205), for example, drew in part on the recently published two-volume *Inquiry into the*

27. "Coleridge's Speculations on Race," 335, 348, 355. In this article, Haeger studies the five unpublished manuscripts mentioned in the Coleridge bibliography at the outset of the present volume.

28. *EOT* I cxxvi; Sultana, *Samuel Taylor Coleridge in Malta and Italy,* 128–29, 174, 177–78, 258, 308. In a mixture of admirably close reading and rather mean-spirited bickering with Erdman, Sultana returned to the subject in "Coleridge's Political Papers in Malta" (see especially, 215, 225–26, 229).

Colonial Policy of the European Powers (1803) by the twenty-five-year-old Henry P. Brougham, of whose activities in the movement to abolish the slave trade Coleridge was aware (*CL* VI 952). Coleridge's notes on Brougham's study (not in the margins since the volumes belonged to Ball) assert that an attentive reading of history reveals the incompatibility of colonial subordination and "Slavery" with any "genuine" colony, which would have to consist of free men.[29] As an anti-Bonapartist who in 1804 preferred British to French imperialism, Coleridge may have gotten a bit carried away with the "Observations on Egypt." As his Brougham annotations indicate, however, he had not forgotten his own May 1801 *Morning Post* parody of naval jingoism and maritime expansion, a sarcastic exposure of the political and economic domination coated with pious cant in Britain's policy of colonial slavery in the West Indies:

> "Rule, BRITANNIA! rule the waves!"
> Blacken your sugar isles with slaves,
> Speak mercy, preach devotion;
> On foaming billows rear your throne . . .
> (*EOT* I 262)

Still, admirers of Coleridge will find the race-speculation fragments, especially that entitled "The Historic Race," deeply disturbing—even, as Haeger says of the latter, "damning," at least when it comes to "its author's place in the history of ideas on race."[30] And there is other damning evidence.

In "Degeneration and Race," another of the 1825–1827 manuscripts, Coleridge, anticipating the 1828 annotations on Blumenbach, describes "the Negro" as descended, "historically or mythically," from Ham, the "post-diluvian Ham" standing "in the place of the pre-lapsarian Cain."[31] Even earlier, Noah's lineage had been discussed by Coleridge in several literary lectures of 1818. In the draft notes for one, a lecture on European literature, Coleridge refers to "the almost universal opinion of the learned that Africa was peopled by the posterity of Ham" (*LL* II 51). Noah's son Ham is the father of—indeed, because of editorial confusion, becomes almost interchangeable with—Canaan. Coleridge alludes to the passage (Gen. 9:20–27) in which Ham looks upon the nakedness of the drunken Noah, reporting it to his more discreet brothers, Japhet and Shem, who cover their father without looking on his shame. In consequence, Ham is, in Noah's curse, condemned to be subservient to his brothers and their posterity. Coleridge quotes the curse in the King James version: "God shall enlarge Japhet, and he shall dwell in the house [or "tents"] of Shem; and Canaan shall be his Servant" (Gen. 9:27). The whole passage,

29. The notes on Brougham's *Inquiry* are preserved in the British Museum (BM MS Egerton 2800 ff. 106–8); I am synopsizing Erdman's synopsis (*EOT* I cxxvii) of 2800 f. 108.

30. "Coleridge's Speculations on Race," 342.

31. British Museum, Additional MS 34225, 135r–136r. Coleridge refers to the "Idea" of the descendants of Noah (Shem, Ham or Canaan, and Japhet) and to "the Hebrew tradition, whether it be interpreted historically or mythical[ly]."

which doubtless entered Genesis as a justification of the Hebrews' enslavement of the Canaanites, has provided subsequent scriptural "justification" for the enslavement of the children of Ham.[32] However sketchy his thoughts in these notes, however consistent his published opposition to slavery, Coleridge's citation of Noah's curse, juxtaposed with his peopling of "Africa . . . by the posterity of Ham," is profoundly troubling.

Another disturbing passage occurs in fragmentary notes for a January 1819 discussion of *Othello,* one in the series of Shakespeare lectures given by Coleridge at the Crown and Anchor Tavern in London. Typically paying particular attention to the opening of the play, he at one point focuses, though he never quotes the actual phrase, on Roderigo's reference to Othello as "the thick lips" (I.i.66). This, writes Coleridge, is "the one if not the only justification of the Blackamoor Othello, namely as a Negro—who is not a *Moor* at all." Only his "rivalry" with Othello, says Coleridge, can explain Roderigo's "wilful confusion of Moor & Negro" (*LL* II 314).

By a "Moor," we, like Coleridge, would mean a North African Moslem of mixed Berber and Arab descent; it may well be, as Isaac Asimov contends, that "to Shakespeare a Moor was not clearly distinguished from a black," indeed that the "use of the term 'thick lips' is the first indication that Shakespeare is talking about a true black, rather than merely a Moor of North Africa, who, despite a swarthy complexion, would not be black."[33] That is not the distinction insisted upon by Coleridge, who apparently has no quibble with the *coloration* in Iago's description of Othello as "an old black ram . . . tupping [Brabantio's] white ewe" (I.i.88–89). *His* distinction is between "Moor" and "Negro," a distinction, he insists, of which Shakespeare was aware: "Can we suppose him to be so utterly ignorant as to make a barbarous *Negro* plead Royal Birth [I.ii.21–24]—Were Negros then known but as Slaves—on the contrary were not the Moors the warriors &c—" (*LL* II 314).

Thus, we "should complain of an enormity"—the theatrical tradition of

---

32. On this, as on most aspects of slavery, help can be found in Walvin's *England, Slaves, and Freedom,* and in two other solid studies: Winthrop D. Jordan, *White Over Black: American Attitudes toward the Negro, 1550–1812,* and David Brion Davis, *The Problem of Slavery in the Age of Revolution, 1770–1823.* On the long and bizarre history of the "curse of Ham" as it applies to slavery and blackness, see Davis, 539–41, and Jordan, 18–19, 35–37, 41–42, 54–56, 62n, 84, 243. Jordan quotes (in translation) four lines of Jacob Steendham, a Dutch poet who lived in Guinea before coming to New Amsterdam; the lines of fatherly lamentation are addressed to his legitimate mulatto sons in Africa: "Since two bloods course within your veins, / Both Ham's and Japhet's intermingling; / One race forever doomed to serve, / The other bearing freedom's likeness" (84). However painful the personal consequences, the biblical curse could apparently not be surmounted.

With the help of the biblical scholar Gerhard Von Rad's 1961 commentary on Genesis, Davis (who had earlier discussed the controversy over Ham and the curse of Canaan in *The Problem of Slavery in Western Culture*) explains the textual confusions that led to the identification of "the Negroes, the supposed children of Ham, as a people cursed with blackness because of their ancestor's disobedience or sexual transgression" (539).

33. *Asimov's Guide to Shakespeare* 1:609, 613.

Othello as Moor *and* Negro when he "cannot be both"—"built on one single word ["thick lips"]—in direct contradiction to Iago's '*Barbary* horse.'" Coleridge accurately takes Iago's adjective in the remark to Brabantio, "you'll have your daughter cover'd with a *Barbary* horse" (I.i.111), as a reference, not to Othello as a "*barbarous* Negro," but as a native of North Africa, a region that came to be known as "Barbary." He concludes that "Iago's speech to Brabantio implies merely that [Othello] was a *Moor*—i.e. black," but not "Negro."

That the distinction was not a casual one is confirmed before and after this 1819 lecture. In a lecture of November 9, 1813, Coleridge, on this occasion quoting Roderigo's phrase "the thick lips," found it unimaginable that Shakespeare could have intended us to think of Othello as Negroid, and "monstrous to conceive" of reciprocal romantic feelings between "a beautiful Venetian girl" and "a veritable negro." Othello *must* be a Moor, not a Negro, otherwise Desdemona's love would convict her of a "want of balance" (*LL* I 555). A decade later, in his Table Talk for January 6, 1823, Coleridge, discussing the character he thought perhaps Shakespeare's greatest, declared that "Othello was not a negro, but a high and chivalrous Moorish chief," whose "character" Shakespeare had learned from "the Spanish poetry . . . prevalent in England in his time" (*TT* I 25–26).

The one Coleridgean comment on *Othello* that everyone remembers, his alliterative characterization of Iago's soliloquies as "the motive-hunting of motiveless malignity," though often disputed, still has much to recommend it. Aside from his historical observation that Negroes were "*then* [that is, in Shakespeare's day] known but as Slaves," and his acknowledgment that Othello is "black," there is little to recommend these subliterary ruminations on Othello's race. In the present context, however, it is worth noting that Robinson Crusoe makes the same distinction. He considers Xury, the Moorish boy with whose help he escapes from enslavement in North Africa, neither a barbarian nor a Negro (45, 48)—though such nice distinctions do not dissuade him from selling the young man at the first opportunity. In this racial context, too, it is worth remembering that Friday does not have Negroid features. Since he is a Carib, a Native American rather than an African black, the seemingly "idealized" description of Friday has racial justification—though Defoe avoids the "Noble Savage" excesses of his precursor, Aphra Behn, whose enslaved African prince, the "ebony" but classicized Oroonoko, has a nose "rising and Roman instead of African and flat," and a mouth "far from the great turned lips, which are so natural to the rest of the Negroes."[34]

One comes to expect such Westernized portraits and simultaneous denigration of "the Negro" in the late seventeenth and early eighteenth centuries. Even Swift, through Gulliver, describes that "abominable Animal," the Yahoo, as possessing a "human Figure," yet with a face "flat and broad, the Nose depressed, the Lips large, and the Mouth wide," features "common to all savage Nations," though the cause of the facial "distortion" among those "nations," as

34. *Oroonoko; or, The History of the Royal Slave*, 9.

opposed to the clearly polygenetic Yahoos, is not "natural" but the result of nurture.[35] It *is,* however, disturbing to find Coleridge—the egalitarian of the 1790s but now a participant in the general rise of Eurocentric racism in the first half of the nineteenth century—insisting on such distinctions in discussing the noble Othello in 1813, 1819, and 1823. The ramifications of the French Revolution's betrayal of its own egalitarian and fraternal ideals—culminating racially, in 1802, in Napoleon's reinstitution of slavery in the West Indies, his destruction of Toussaint, and his expulsion of blacks from France—assumed a variety of forms in the thinking of its former devotees, concern about the thickness of lips being one of the sadder curiosities.[36]

What has to be borne in mind in the present context, however, is that Coleridge's later ethnic attitudes, painful though they may be to contemplate in the 1990s, do not irredeemably tarnish his credentials as an abolitionist. The annotations on Blumenbach, along with his various speculations on race, especially between 1813 and 1827, reveal that by the time Coleridge annotated *Robinson Crusoe* in 1830 he was more engaged by a philosophic and pseudoscientific schema than he was by the biological research on race emerging from the work of such men as Erasmus Darwin and Lamarck. They also reveal later Coleridge as what Gould would call a "soft-liner" and John C. Greene a "monogenist"—that is, one who holds that *all* the races, having descended from our common parents, had degenerated from Edenic perfection. Though late Coleridge, like so many in his milieu, held that "the Negro," mythically or historically descended from Ham-Canaan, had declined the most, he rejected, as Blumenbach did, the "polygenist" position that the human races constituted separate biological species. Therefore—

35. "A Voyage to the Houyhnhnms," in *Gulliver's Travels,* ed. Robert A. Greenberg, 199. Swift's, or Gulliver's, racism is mitigated since the "disfigurement" in the case of the humans derives from nurture rather than nature. In these nations, "Lineaments of the Countenance are distorted by the Natives suffering their infants to lie grovelling on the Earth, or by carrying them on their Backs, nuzzling with their Face against the Mother's shoulders."

36. Wordsworth characteristically dramatizes the Napoleonic ordinance of 1802. His sonnet "The Banished Negroes," first published in the *Morning Post* (February 11, 1803), describes a "fellow-passenger who came / From Calais with us" on the occasion of Wordsworth's return from seeing Annette Vallon and their daughter during the Peace of Amiens: "She was a Negro Woman driv'n from France, / Rejected like all others of that race, / Not one of whom may now find footing there; / This the poor Out-cast did to us declare, / Nor murmur'd at the unfeeling Ordinance." Immediately preceded by "To Toussaint L'Ouverture," this sonnet was published as number 9 among the twenty-six "Sonnets Dedicated to Liberty" in volume 1 of the 1807 *Poems.* Now entitled "September 1st, 1802," it was accompanied by the following headnote in the 1827 edition of Wordsworth's *Poetical Works:* "Among the capricious acts of Tyranny that disgraced these times, was the chasing of all Negroes from France by decree of the Government: we had a Fellow-passenger who was one of the expelled" (*Wordsworth's Poems of 1807,* ed. Alun R. Jones, 60, 164–65*n*). Though most critics pronounce the Wordsworth of these years a simple "conservative," these sonnets prove him otherwise; and unlike De Quincey and even Charles Lamb, the poet who wrote them does not seem to have been "infected" (as John Barrell has recently said of De Quincey) by racism.

despite the diminished intensity of his opposition to slavery and despite that one ominous adversion to Canaan as "Servant"—on scientific and moral grounds alike, Coleridge was adamant that, whatever the "inferiority" of certain races, it did not entitle "superior" races to mistreat let alone enslave them.[37]

That was the position not only of Coleridge, but of most "degenerationists," including Blumenbach himself, whom Coleridge particularly valued precisely because he was a naturalist opposed to "materialism" and to "the identification of Man with the Brute, in *kind*" (F I 154–56*n*). Furthermore, arguing that degeneration was essentially environmental and therefore reversible, Blumenbach insisted that, with opportunity, Negroes would equal Europeans in accomplishment; slavery was therefore a pernicious evil. He ranked blacks below European whites, "but so slightly inferior to the Caucasians, and so immensely superior to the intelligent animals, [that] the poor negro might justly class those of us who *philosophically* view him as merely a better monkey, or who desire to traffic in his blood, not only below himself, but below apes in intellect, and tigers in feeling and propensity."[38]

One could, in short, believe in white superiority and still struggle for the liberation of blacks in bondage and despise their brutal enslavers. If Coleridge became a racist, J. H. Haeger acknowledges, he "was not, in action or in policy, a virulent racist. In his youth, and lasting into his later life, he was solidly behind the Abolitionist movement."[39] Slavery was finally abolished by the British Parliament in 1833, and given certain remarks Coleridge was to make on that occasion, both in conversation and in the margins of a book he was reading on Africa, that adverb, *solidly,* may be too strong. But it is at least arguable that from the position Haeger attributes to him, despite some characteristic trepidation of the "Yes but" or "Yea *but* Nay" sort when abolition finally came, Coleridge never truly wavered.

Furthermore, however troubling his later racial theories based on Blumenbach, Coleridge had been familiar with the German anthropologist's work from at least as early as 1799. Neither then nor subsequently did his absorption and modification of Blumenbach's systematic racial "enumeration" make Coleridge anything less than passionately humanitarian, as Blumenbach himself was, in his response to the issue of black slavery. That response—not limited to the graphic horrors of the slave trade itself, but focused on that perversion of persons into things which epitomized slavery for Coleridge—remained essentially what it had been from his late teens: a moral revulsion that can be traced in his poetry and prose alike.

3

"From his college months on," as Carl Woodring observes, Coleridge "counted among the evidences of commercial excess in England the enormity of the slave

37. On "monogenists" and "polygenists," see the chapter "The Origin of Human Races" in John C. Greene's *The Death of Adam,* 221–45.
38. *The Institutions of Physiology,* 401–2.
39. "Coleridge's Speculations on Race," 356.

trade." His 1792 Cambridge Prize poem on the slave trade—focusing on the misery of slaves in the West Indies and calling on "Nemesis" to inflict "burning punishment" on those who trafficked in human flesh—was attacked by the great classicist Richard Porson in *Blackwood's* for its bad Greek, but "the poet stuck by its sentiments." As Woodring adds, between 1794 and 1799 Coleridge "wrote lines about 'Afric's wrong' into at least one poem every year."[40]

The poem quoted is the 1796 "Ode to [more accurately, "on"] the Departing Year," in which the "Spirit of the Earth" calls upon the "God of Nature" to "rise" and smite a "bloody" and "thankless" island corrupted by many things, "But chief by Afric's wrongs, / Strange, horrible, and foul!" (*CPW* I 164–65). Coleridge's greatest political poem, "France: An Ode," which first appeared in print as "The Recantation: An Ode" in the *Morning Post* in April 1798, originally included, Coleridge claimed, a ferocious attack on the hyena-like Pitt Ministry's complicity in the slave trade, a stanza allegedly deleted by the editor, Daniel Stuart, to the aesthetic if not the moral benefit of the ode. The stanza may have been intended rather than completed, but if he did delete it, Stuart, who had just been summoned before the Privy Council to answer questions about his radical sources, would have been exercising self-censoring caution during a period of strategic retreat from his paper's anti-Ministerial policy. The ode, however, was probably improved as a poem if not as a jeremiad. "Fortunately," as Woodring says, the lost stanza, which would have disrupted the unity of the poem, "led by figurative contrast in the succeeding stanza to one of Coleridge's finest denunciations of the French, as 'Slaves by their own compulsion.'" Three years later he would repeat the image in a description of France as "a natural Slave" bound in "her self-forg'd Chains," a phrase resembling the "mind-forg'd manacles" of Blake's "London" as well as a contemporaneous remark by the twelve-year-old William Hazlitt: "The man who is a well-wisher to slavery, is always a slave himself."[41]

40. *Politics in the Poetry of Coleridge*, 59. Anthea Morrison translates and discusses "Samuel Taylor Coleridge's Greek Prize Poem on the Slave Trade" in J. R. Watson, ed., *An Infinite Complexity: Essays in Romanticism.*

41. See Coleridge's "Ode to Tranquillity" (1801), in which, climactic among the now disgusting political things that allegedly "Disturb not me" are whatever "fancy figures" or false name "Half-thinking, sensual France, a natural Slave, / On those ne'er-broken Chains, her self-forg'd Chains, will grave" (*CPW* I 360n). The final stanza of the Recantation ode opens: "The Sensual and the Dark rebel in vain, / Slaves by their own compulsion! In mad game / They burst their manacles and wear the name / Of Freedom, graven on a heavier chain!" (*CPW* I 247). "To the stanza otherwise annihilated," Woodring remarks, "these lines owe part of their excellence and even their existence. From the linked subject of France and Liberty why not omit Africans compelled into slavery? Jacobins who follow Reason slavishly are 'Dark' enough, and self-compelled. The force of the implications in 'own compulsion' and 'Dark' reached the poem through the rejected stanza on the slave trade" (*Politics in the Poetry of Coleridge*, 59, 183–84). If he actually wrote the stanza (which has never come to light), Coleridge, whether for political or aesthetic reasons, never restored it to the poem. Its tone can be judged from stanza VI of the poem as it first appeared in the *Post;* apologizing to "Afric," it refers to

From these poems of the nineties, and the eloquent public address and essay "On the Slave Trade," through the *Lay Sermons* of 1816–1817, and well beyond, Coleridge, attacking slavery as both a specific wrong to its African victims and in the sense of any "perversion of a Person into a Thing," made it clear that he was morally, emotionally, and intellectually appalled by what he described as the "most pernicious" evil "that ever degraded human nature," an "eating ulcer," a "slow poison . . . one long continuous crime, involving every possible definition of evil: for it combined the wildest physical suffering with the most atrocious moral depravity."

This passage, which might have come from the *Narrative* of Frederick Douglass or from a *Liberator* article of William Lloyd Garrison, is in fact from the opening of Coleridge's lengthy July 1808 *Edinburgh Review* essay on his friend Thomas Clarkson's monumental *History of the . . . Abolition of the African Slave-Trade,* "the only publication," he told the author, "I ever wished to see my name in" (*CL* III 78). Coleridge had read the work in manuscript and wrote (May 23, 1808) to the editor of the *Edinburgh Review,* Francis Jeffrey, offering himself as a reviewer. The offer was accepted, though Coleridge later complained of editorial changes in his review, in particular an attack on William Pitt Coleridge claimed was not in his original manuscript and which amounted to "moral forgery."[42]

However it may have been "mutilated" by Jeffrey, Coleridge confirmed the accuracy of the essential thrust of the article. As this review makes clear, Coleridge's revulsion from "the horrors of the trade" and his detestation of slavery as an institution did not diminish his conviction that the European "race" was "superior" to that of the Africans, who were not "savages" but "(to speak classically) barbarians." He anticipates in Africa a "progress from barbarism to civilization," not by means of political or religious compulsion but through European example at its best, characterized not, as in the brutal past, by colonial greed and cruelty but by "justice and benevolence" (*Inquiring Spirit,* 373–74).

Writing ten years later, in the year Frederick Douglass and Karl Marx were born, Coleridge mentions (in pamphlets supporting Sir Robert Peel's bill to shorten the working hours of children in factories) the old laissez-faire argu-

---

the Ministers as loathed "Hyaenas, that in murky den / Whine o'er their prey and mangle while they whine" (*CPW* I 247*n*).

The observation of the precocious Hazlitt occurs in a letter written to his parents from Liverpool, where he had just dined with one of the wealthy Liverpudlians who had prospered in the slave trade. Quoted in Herschel Baker, *William Hazlitt,* 19.

42. *CL* III 112–13, 124–25, 148–49. For details on Coleridge's complaints about the "shameful mutilation" of his review (*Inquiring Spirit,* ed. Kathleen Coburn, 368–74), see Paul-Emile, "Samuel Taylor Coleridge as Abolitionist," 66–68. Whether or not Jeffrey altered judgments on Pitt (who had been opposed to the slave trade as early as 1792, the year of young Coleridge's prize ode), we can infer from Coleridge's silence on passages involving the atrocity of slavery and the slave trade, and on the colonizing of Africa, that these sections were left unembellished and unmutilated by the editor.

ments that had been used to justify noninterference with the slave trade. He appeals, in the peroration of the first pamphlet, to "the glorious precedent" of its abolition; in the second, he makes a passing reference to the slaves working and perishing in "a Surinam swamp." Like the "poor African hanging by hooks" (who, as Kathleen Coburn has noted, "haunts Coleridge's prose to the end"), that allusion indicates the lasting impression made on him by Captain John G. Stedman's *Narrative of a Five Years' expedition, against the Revolted Slaves of Surinam,* a two-volume work illustrated by William Blake and clearly reflected, as David Erdman has shown, in his *Visions of the Daughters of Albion.*[43] Coleridge had no knowledge of Blake's prophetic works, but his favorite among the few Blake poems he did know was, perhaps not coincidentally, "The Little Black Boy."

Coleridge was less explicit about abolition as the years passed. As his conception of society, always an organic one, increasingly emphasized the interdependence of fixed gradations of higher, middle, and lower classes, he became suspicious of abolitionists who appealed directly to blacks and who preached liberation without concern for education, rights without a balancing sense of responsibilities. Yet his detestation of slavery remains implicit, and often explicit, in his almost obsessive distinction between Persons and Things. Twice in *The Friend* he insists, and not for the last time, that

> all morality is grounded in the Reason. Every Man is born with the faculty of Reason: and whatever is without it, be the Shape what it may, is not a MAN or a PERSON, but a THING. Hence the sacred Principle, recognized by all Laws human and divine, the Principle indeed which is the *ground-work* of all Law and Justice, that a Person can never become a Thing, nor be treated as such without wrong. But the distinction between Person and Thing consists herein, that the latter may rightfully be used, altogether and merely, as a *Means;* but the former must always be included in the End, and form a part of the final Cause.[44]

That "be the Shape what it may" sounds as if Coleridge is remembering Swift's rational horses and irrational Yahoos in the fourth and final voyage of *Gulliver's Travels.* The whole passage, of course, recalls Kant, whose work Coleridge had studied closely for years (see, for example, *CM* III 236–366). In Kantian ethics, the moral law is inherent in reason itself, and the crucial distinction, implicit in the Categorical Imperative, is that one is to treat humanity, oneself or others, "in every case as an end and never as a means."

A fragment of 1811 intended for the *Courier* opens with the same Kantian

---

43. Coleridge's two pamphlets were *Remarks on the Objections to Sir Robert Peel's Bill* and *The Grounds of Sir Robert Peel's Bill Vindicated,* dated April 18 and April 24, 1818, respectively. They may also be found in *Inquiring Spirit,* 351–65 (358–59, 364). A letter that appeared about this time in the *Courier,* signed "Atticus," compared the "wretchedness" of the factory conditions to "that of a slave plantation under the torrid zone." On Stedman, see Erdman, *Blake: Prophet against Empire,* 230–31.

44. *F* II 125 (No. 9, October 12, 1809). The title of the essay in its original version— "On the Grounds of Government as Laid Exclusively in the Pure Reason" (*F* I 189–90)— reveals its philosophic source in Kant.

distinction, attended by a footnote in which Coleridge repeats the wording and the examples from *The Friend,* but adds: "A Slave is a *Person* perverted into a *Thing;* Slavery, therefore, is not so properly a deviation from Justice as an absolute subversion of all Morality" (*EOT* III 235). A half-dozen years later, referring us back to *The Friend,* Coleridge again repeats the Person-Thing distinction, stressing that only Things "may be *used*" (his italics). On this occasion, his sentence had begun with "Trade," from its "most innocent form to the abomination of the African commerce nominally abolished after a hard-fought battle of twenty years" (*LS* 219).

The "battle" Coleridge refers to had been fought at first principally by Granville Sharp and Thomas Clarkson, the friend to whom Coleridge referred as "a moral steam-engine" (*CL* III 179). Joined by William Wilberforce and the Evangelicals (Clarkson and Wilberforce founded the Society for the Suppression of the Slave Trade in 1787), the abolitionists had long struggled against Mammon and indifference, not to mention British cabinets more inclined, as Coleridge charged on a number of occasions, to condone than condemn the slave trade. In 1788–1789 Wilberforce's abolition bill failed; four years later, it passed the Commons before being thrown out by the Lords. By then, with the French essentially out of the business, British ships were transporting almost forty-five thousand Africans annually, more than half of the total trade. Up to the very eve of abolition in 1807, British volume and profit were high. During the brief coalition Ministry of "All the Talents" to which George III was compelled to submit in that year, the abolition legislation had finally been passed into law.

That achievement was less attributable to Wilberforce—"half-inclined," as Hazlitt accurately remarked, "to surrender" the issue into "Mr. Pitt's dilatory hands"—than to Clarkson, the "true Apostle of human Redemption on that occasion," the man that "effected it by Herculean labours of body and equally gigantic labours of mind."[45] As Wordsworth accurately put it in the first line of his congratulatory sonnet: "Clarkson! it was an obstinate hill to climb." But, as Coleridge's sarcastic "nominally" indicates, abolition was less than complete; despite Wordsworth's optimism in the sonnet, what he called "The bloodstained Writing" of slavery was *not* "for ever torn."

In June 1815, Wilberforce introduced a slave registry bill, claiming that the Abolition Act was "being continually evaded, and thereby rendered nugatory" by Spanish and Portuguese smugglers paid by British merchants to carry slaves into the colonies of those nations that had adopted abolition of the trade. The

45. Hazlitt's comparison occurs at the end of his brief but penetrating character of Wilberforce in *The Spirit of the Age,* a sketch echoing his earlier image of Wilberforce torn "between popularity and court favour, between his loyalty and his religion." (*The Complete Works of William Hazlitt,* ed. P. P. Howe, 17:15). On Wilberforce in general, see the biographies by Robin Furneux (1974) and John Pollock (1977), and Boyd Hilton's *The Age of Atonement: The Influence of Evangelicalism on Social and Economic Thought, 1795–1865.* On Wilberforce's manipulation by Pitt, see also C. L. R. James, *The Black Jacobins: Toussaint L'Ouverture and the San Domingo Revolution,* 53–54.

bill was defeated.[46] Wilberforce and a number of pamphleteers continued to protest the involvement of British subjects. The slave trade, the *Gentleman's Magazine* charged in February 1816, was "actually carried on to nearly an equal extent as ever by British Capital!! notwithstanding the Act of Legislature, and the vigilance of the Government." Wilberforce later claimed in the same periodical that in the years 1814–1816 Spain, with the help of British capital, carried more than twenty-five thousand slaves a year from Africa. It was during this period, June 24, 1816, to be precise, that Coleridge, who had not been keeping up with the editorial policy of Stuart's *Courier,* pronounced himself "really so shocked at the damnable immorality of the principles supported in that paper, which is now little more than a systematic advocate of the Slave-trade and all its West-India Abominations, besides every other mode of Despotism & Ministerial Folly, that I have resolved never to let an article of mine contribute to the sale of that paper" (*CL* VI 1041, Appendix B).

Over the next fourteen years, Coleridge had little to say about these "abominations," but they were not forgotten. During the period he was annotating *Robinson Crusoe,* Coleridge again employed his Person-Thing distinction—both in conversation (*TT* I 260), and in *On the Constitution of the Church and State* (1830), his last published prose work, and a mature synthesis of a lifetime of political and theological contemplation. In the opening chapter, in the course of discussing the "idea," rather than any unprovable historical "fact," of an original social contract, Coleridge observes that such an idea "is so certain and so indispensable, that it constitutes the whole ground of the difference between subject and serf, between a commonwealth and a slave-plantation. And this, again, is evolved out of the yet higher idea of *person* in contra-distinction from *thing*" (*C&S* 15).

Any violation of that distinction, Coleridge continues, aside from the case of criminals who forfeit their rights, constitutes a "grievous wrong." After yet another repetition of the *Friend* argument illustrated by the same examples, Coleridge adds that any government that permits a reduction of Persons to Things "is not worthy to be called a STATE." His two examples are instructive. The first was "unprogressive" Dahomey, a black kingdom societally based, as Coleridge knew, on slavery (he was also aware that human sacrifice was practiced there). The second, Russia, was an example of a genuine state "only by anticipation," a government advancing toward "a better and more *man-worthy* order of things": an obvious allusion to schemes already afoot to eventually liberate the serfs (*C&S* 15–16).

Though Coleridge elsewhere refers to American plantation slavery, and to the "almost universal corruption of manners" and "morals" in the states "in which slavery obtains" (*Inquiring Spirit,* 369), the United States and the "peculiar institution" of the South are not mentioned in this passage from *On the Constitution of the Church and State.* It is worth noting, however, that Coleridge,

---

46. Quoted by R. J. White in *LS* 220*n.* These notes are also the source of the passages cited from the *Gentleman's Magazine.*

who saw the United States as a democracy flawed by slavery, in 1800 praised George Washington for freeing and providing for his slaves in his will and, in an 1808 letter, cited the American Quaker opponent of slavery, John Woolman, as an example of a man who not only "believes in 'the voice within' but lives by it" (*CL* III 156).[47] Even more interesting, sometime *after 1829*, Coleridge, in the course of abusing Thomas Jefferson (who, in his first draft of the Declaration of Independence, had attacked George III for violating Negroes' "sacred rights of life and liberty," but was himself a slaveholder), also criticized the American Revolution itself as "preventive, & conservative not emancipative—or only emancipative *a priori!*"[48]

Some three years after he made this observation (and Coleridge was not the only British conservative in these years to cite slave welfare in dismissing American claims to moral superiority), there was an emancipative revolution closer to home. Yet when slavery finally *was* abolished in the British Empire, Coleridge's reaction was ambivalent. Nothing could be more characteristic. Our own reaction, however, must inevitably combine surprise and sadness with a recognition of Coleridge's endlessly dialectical thinking. One can find in this double-minded and self-divisive man evidence of instability, opportunistic equivocation, or plain apostasy—or, as Sara Coleridge did, proof of her father's "virtual consistency," a consistency of "spirit . . . amid all the variations and corrections of the letter." Such a recognition is "valid" (writes David Erdman,

47. In this *Morning Post* piece of March 1800 (*EOT* I 230), Coleridge, contrasting Washington to the now despotic "dwarf," Bonaparte, praised the American hero for the passage in his will expressing his "humane, earnest, and solemn wish concerning the emancipation of the slaves on his estate." The will explains, "with infinite delicacy and manly sensibility," Coleridge continues, "the true cause of his not having emancipated them in his life time; and should operate as a caution against those petty libellers, who interpret the whole of a character by a part, instead of interpreting a part by the whole." Washington's will reveals, says Coleridge, both his "deep and weighty feeling of the general principle of universal liberty" and his "veneration of those fixed laws in society, without which that universal law must forever remain impossible," as well as Washington's "affectionate attention to the particular feelings of the slaves themselves, with the ample provision for the aged and infirm." With the publication of the will, all the Washington slaves, including Martha's dowry Negroes, were freed. See also Coleridge's January 1800 *Morning Post* portrait of Washington (reprinted in the *Courier* in 1811), and David V. Erdman, "Coleridge on George Washington: Newly Discovered Essays of 1800."

48. *CM* III 133. The attack on Jefferson—recorded in Coleridge's marginalia in an 1829 edition of the former president's papers—reveals the annotator's double-minded sensitivity to both Anglophobia and moral pretention. In an 1814 letter deploring "the torrents of blood this man [Napoleon] is shedding in Europe," Jefferson hoped that—though it might place "our peace a little further distant"—the continental European nations, "and even England, may retain their independence." Coleridge asterisked and underlined *even England,* declaring it "monstrous" to find Jefferson one of those "Offspring of England" (the nation that was the "source" of the Anglo-Americans' "Laws, Religion, Language, Arts") who "expresses & owns a bitterness of unnatural hatred to their Mother Country." And this from revolutionaries whose own house was glass, whose revolution was "conservative not emancipative."

employing an "optical" image), providing we also recognize that Coleridge's dialectical thinking requires that "even while he speaks boldly on one side of a question he keeps a longing (or a roving) eye on the other sides of it." Erdman quotes with approval Sara's illustration: that her father, while vigorously *opposing* a movement for reform, "carefully recorded his protest in favor of reform, conducted judiciously" (*EOT* I lxiv).

The key, even when it came to abolition, was precisely that: reform, conducted *judiciously*. Donald Reiman, who finds "a greater stability and consistency in [Coleridge's] day-to-day political stance than has hitherto been recognized," calls him "a true trimmer," that is, "one who helps to keep a boat stable by moving or leaning toward the lighter side; a true trimmer—and Coleridge was often one—takes the less popular side of an argument merely to prevent ill-considered, precipitous action on the other side. Coleridge opposed Pitt, Fox, and Napoleon each at the height of his power and praised their good qualities when each was out of office."[49]

Coleridge had long denounced the slave trade and slavery itself. Now that the abolition movement had finally triumphed, he felt compelled to point out that the culmination of the long ordeal might still be "ill-considered" and "precipitous," especially since it seemed unaccompanied by principle, human wisdom, and, above all, religious faith. He now saw emancipation, in particular the Ministry's plan regarding manumission in the West Indies, less as the moral issue it had always been for him—even though, in 1801, he himself briefly considered emigrating to one of those "sugar isles" blackened with slaves—than as a crass conflict of contemporary political interests. Convinced of the general human inclination to "indolence" and less-than-vigorous "self-government," Coleridge feared, as had Milton and Edmund Burke before him, the removal of external government. Milton had argued that outer freedom was dependent on inner virtue, that whoever truly loves liberty "must first be wise and good." Annotating Sir George Beaumont's copy of the quarto edition of the ode on France, whose "misunderstood" final stanza meant that "true political Freedom can only arise out of moral Freedom," Coleridge said that that crucial point was nothing "but a dilation of those *golden* lines of Milton—'Licence they

49. "The Bollingen Coleridge," 78. Reiman, reviewing *EOT,* is referring to the earlier period of Coleridge's journalism, and has no comment on Coleridge's attitudes toward slavery and abolition. Coleridge's shifting responses to Fox, Pitt, and Bonaparte are at the heart of his political oscillations, of his integrity for some, his apostasy for others. I will be dealing, in Part Two, with Coleridge's reactions to Fox and Pitt in the 1790s. Bonaparte figures in Chapter 3, below. Briefly: though Coleridge recognized what he called in an 1800 *Morning Post* piece the Bonapartist "commanding genius," his attitude—which first became critical when the genius led an army into Switzerland, and soured when the "Saviour" (*CL* I 539) revealed himself in the Brumaire coup as a "Usurper" and destroyer of republican principles—turned completely negative after Bonaparte's aggressiveness became clear during the Peace of Amiens, thus seeming to vindicate the conviction and many of the hitherto repellent policies of the now out-of-office Pitt. (Of course, the British themselves violated the treaty by refusing to abandon Malta.)

mean, when they cry—Liberty! / For who loves that must first be wise and good.'"[50] Even if essentially sincere, Coleridge is also being somewhat disingenuous; not all the "objections" to this final stanza are, as Coleridge claimed in this note, "*unfounded*." Not only has the "slave-trade" stanza been omitted; Liberty itself is displaced from the political arena to the realm of nature.

"Control from without must ever be *inversely* as the Self-government of control from within"; consequently it was the virtuous who least required external control. Thus Coleridge in a June 1833 letter to Thomas Pringle, secretary of the Anti-Slavery Society (*CL* VI 940–41). "We must be men in order to be citizens," he had said three years earlier (*C&S* 43). By then he had long since been convinced not only that, as the ode on France insisted, no external government could free individuals who were "Slaves by their own compulsion" (*CPW* I 247), but that the alternative paradox of freedom within constraint was more than a trope. "Man is made [created] a Beast," he continued in the letter to Pringle; a slave "may be free with a freedom, compared with which his oppressor is a pitiable slave." "At Genoa," Coleridge once noted, "the word, Liberty, is engraved on the chains of the galley-slaves, & the doors of prisons" (*CN* I 206). This Pauline-Augustinian-Miltonic-Burkean lesson on the paradoxical but "true notion of human Freedom" as Christian liberty-within-restraint, even "Imperative Power in obedience" (*CN* II 3231), had certainly been learned by Wordsworth, who—having "felt the weight of too much liberty," and tired of an "unchartered freedom"—had in 1804 commended himself to "Duty," that Miltonic "Stern Daughter of the Voice of God" (cf. *Paradise Lost* IX.652–53) whose "Bondman" he longed to be.[51] Whether one endorses the emphasis on voluntary discipline and self-government as a genuine ethical and aesthetic insight or condemns it as individual repression and social oppression wrapped in a humanistic cloak,[52] this was the lesson preached to Pringle in person by Coleridge, who described himself in the letter as "an ardent & almost life-long Denouncer of Slavery."

50. John Milton, Sonnet XII ("I did but prompt the age . . ."), ll. 11–12, in *Poetical Works*, ed. Douglas Bush, 173. Coleridge's annotation (18) in Beaumont's copy, is quoted by Woodring, *Politics in the Poetry of Coleridge*, 185, and by Morton D. Paley, "Apocalypse and Millennium in the Poetry of Coleridge," 32.

51. "Prefatory Sonnet" ("Nuns fret not at their convent's narrow room"); "Ode to Duty." Sonnet and ode, both directly influenced by Milton, appeared in volume 1 of *Wordsworth's Poems of 1807*. In the same year, Coleridge was much concerned with "the sense of Duty" (*CN* III 3026), "the exact performance of Duty," especially that of "dear William! whose Path of Duty lies thro' vine-trelised Elm-groves, thro' Love and Joy & Grandeur" (*CL* II 553).

52. For many on the postmodern Left, their suspicions often fueled by Foucault, acceptance of one's own desire-restricting submission—the "fetishization of self-control, self-regulation, and self-discipline" characteristic of humanist "rhetoric"—"assures oppression by attempting to stabilize society in an image of harmony, restraint, and law" (Bové, *In the Wake of Theory*, 133). Of course, there is always the Orwellian reversal in which "Freedom *is* Slavery," but postmodernists seldom mention that Nietzsche is as insistent as Burke on the concept of liberty within restraint.

But, out-Wordsworthing Wordsworth on "Duty" as liberty under restraint, Coleridge now feared that emancipation might injure "humanity and freedom" as he conceived them. In Table Talk recorded at this time, he asked a visitor (almost certainly Pringle):

> Have you been able to discover any principle in this Emancipation Bill for the Slaves, except a principle of fear of the Abolition faction, struggling with a fear of causing some monstrous calamity to the Empire at large! Well! I will not prophesy, and God grant that this tremendous and unprecedented act of positive enactment may not do the harm to the concept of humanity and freedom which I cannot but fear! But yet what *can* I hope, when all human wisdom and counsel is set at naught, and Religious Faith—the only miraculous Agent amongst men—is not invoked or regarded! And that *unblessed* phase—the Dissenting Interest—enters into the question!! (*TT* I 389–90)

Despite this conflict of fears, including his own, and despite the inordinate number of dissenters from the Church of England who did in fact make up the Anti-Slavery Society, Coleridge could still refer to abolition as "this tremendous and unprecedented act of positive enactment." Attempting to synopsize this "twofold" final attitude, Barbara Paul-Emile describes Coleridge as desiring amelioration, yet wary of "any sudden freedoms" that "might upset the hierarchical pattern on which society is based."[53] I would supplement her characterization with Sara Coleridge's point about Coleridge favoring "reform, conducted judiciously," Reiman's boat-balancing "trimming," and with several additional considerations.

In 1831 (in Table Talk dated December 17), Coleridge attributed poor people's assertion of rights without responsibilities to an establishment enslaved to a false utilitarian philosophy that reduced men and women to objects: "When the Government and the Aristocracy of this country had subordinated Persons to things, and treated the one like the other: the Poor with some reason, and almost in self-defence, learnt to set Rights over Duties" (*TT* I 260). But whatever its causes, such learning was a dangerous thing. Similarly, racial egalitarianism was, for later Coleridge, an abstract concept unless, in practice, freed slaves were religiously instructed as to their proper duties. In Table Talk recorded for June 8, 1833, about a week before the rhetorical question posed to Pringle, Coleridge chastised his abolitionist visitor:

> You are always talking about the *rights* of the Negroes [in the West Indies];—as a rhetorical mode of stimulating the people of England *here*, I don't object, but I utterly condemn your frantic practice of declaiming about their Rights to the Blacks [themselves]. They ought to be forcibly reminded of the state in which their brethren in Africa still are, and taught to be thankful for the providence which has placed them within means of grace. I know no right except such as flows from righteousness, and as every Christian believes his righteousness to be imputed, so his right must be an imputed right. It must flow out of a Duty, and it is under that name that the process of Humanization ought to begin and to be conducted throughout. (*TT* I 386)

53. "Samuel Taylor Coleridge as Abolitionist," 74.

Such an observation, portions of which resemble Crusoe's conception of himself as providential savior of Friday, would seem to epitomize what Barbara Paul-Emile calls Coleridge's "passage from youthful abolitionism to settled conservatism," even to justify what some contemporary observers thought of as Coleridge's turncoat shift from opponent to defender of slavery.[54] It might be "calumnious untruth" that he had become a defender of slavery but, in the face of these remarks, it is hard to believe that Coleridge's objections to slavery were undiminished by his religiously oriented views on race and "rights." And Coleridge here goes beyond denouncing the abolitionist preaching of rights for the slaves in Jamaica. What are we to make of the insistence not only that those slaves ought to be "reminded" that their condition is preferable, physically and religiously, to that of their "brethren in Africa," but that they ought to be "*forcibly* reminded" of this providential situation?

And what of that "process of Humanization"? A week later, Coleridge was to refer to his own "concept of humanity and freedom," a concept that abolition may "harm." Here he speaks, even more ominously, of "Duty," under the aegis of which "the *process of Humanization* ought to *begin*." Coleridge is not suggesting that blacks are, literally, less than human to begin with, which would amount to a total betrayal of his otherwise consistent monogenist position. His use of the term is clarified by a rhetorical question raised in the first of his Bristol addresses. Referring to the "intolerable grievances of our poor brethren," the working poor of England who, brutalized by unjust economic and educational systems, had hardened their wounded hearts, he asked: "Can we wonder that men should want humanity, who want all the circumstances of life that humanize?" (*L 1795* 39). But a less sympathetic instance of brutalization occurs in an annotation on Lessing dating from about 1816; there the early Jews are referred to as "a Horde of emancipated quasi-Negroes—degraded & brutalized by a 500 years Slavery in Egypt" (*CM* III 658). Not only, apparently, does slavery pervert persons into things; during bondage and, for a time, even after being freed, it makes *any* race "quasi-Negroes."

Such remarks, especially those made to Pringle, by *later* Coleridge have caused me to look again at an incident involving *younger* Coleridge. I alluded above to his brief consideration of emigrating to the West Indies in 1801, when he was twenty-nine. That episode needs to be put in context, a context that includes William Wordsworth.

The two poets first met in Bristol in August or September of 1795. Considering that Coleridge had delivered on June 16 his Bristol address "On the Slave

54. Ibid., 74. "The Tory sophist was a man of little soul," declared Thomas Perronet Thompson in the *Westminster Review,* condemning Coleridge as a "Tory pensioner" and "puffed up partisan" reduced to "trampling on the labouring classes" and defending slavery and other forms of "harmful darkness" (537). Thompson was reviewing prepublication extracts from the 1835 edition of *Table Talk,* a quick review to which its editor, H. N. Coleridge, had time to reply in a footnote to his preface, accusing "the Westminster Reviewer," his "single object being to abuse and degrade," of uttering "calumnious untruth."

Trade," rightly taken by the Bristol *Observer* as "proof of the detestation in which he holds that infamous traffic," it is ironic that he and Wordsworth should have met not only in the city that was the center of the slave trade in England, but in the town house of John Pretor Pinney, a merchant whose wealth derived from his plantation on the West Indian "sugar island" of St. Nevis. Pinney was the father of a friend of Wordsworth's friend Basil Montagu, John Frederick Pinney, through whose generosity Wordsworth and his sister were shortly to live rent-free at Racedown Lodge, the Pinney country house in Dorset.[55]

Six years later, a financially and emotionally desperate Coleridge was hoping to emigrate with the Wordsworths and Southeys, possibly to the Pinneys' Nevis estate. He had, he wrote Robert Southey on July 25, 1801, "reason to believe" not only that the mansion was "at my disposal," but that the "expences of living there" could be halved since Pinney might "appoint us sine-cure Negro- drivers at a hundred a year each" (*CL* II 747–48). This is certainly strange talk from the man who only seven years earlier had passionately differed with his fellow-Pantisocrat, insisting that the Southey family's black servants, Shadrach Weeks and his wife, Sally, should not only join them in the New World but come on terms of total equality. "SHAD GOES WITH US," he had announced in emphatic capitals. "HE IS MY BROTHER" (*CL* I 103). Two months after the July 1801 letter to Southey, Coleridge, in a letter to William Godwin, reported "making the last effort by an application to Mr. John Pinney respecting his house in St Nevis, & the means of living there" (*CL* II 762). Admirers of Coleridge can only feel relief that the plans came to nothing; but that a genuine and passionate opponent of slavery, however desperate his straits at the time, should make such plans in the first place is a fact that cannot be ignored.[56]

And yet, neither those abortive plans in 1801 nor even the remarks to Pringle in 1833 make Coleridge simply a hypocrite or an apostate from his earlier republican ideals. There remains a certain continuity. Even early, "radical" Coleridge had insisted on the critical distinction he repeated to Pringle in 1833. There he condemned the abolitionists' "frantic practice of declaiming about their Rights" directly "to the Blacks." In his 1795 Bristol addresses, he was, he said, "pleading *for* the Oppressed, not *to* them" (*L 1795* 43), repeatedly emphasizing (as Colmer, Erdman, and Woodring have noted) the dangers of direct, emotive appeals to the poor, the ignorant, and the oppressed, let alone the enslaved.[57] Nor does his insistence to Pringle that "rights" flow out of a "Duty" represent a conservative shift from the thinking of his radical period.

55. Mary Moorman, *William Wordsworth: A Biography* 1:266–67.

56. On these and related matters, see Winifred F. Courtney's chatty account, stemming from her visits to the island in the 1980s: "Nevis, West Indies, and the English Romantic Writers."

57. Colmer, *Coleridge: Critic of Society*, 12, 135, 157–58; Erdman, *EOT* I clxx; Woodring, *Politics in the Poetry of Coleridge*, 79–80, 168, 210–11; and *TT* I 386*n*. For typical warnings by Coleridge, see, in addition to the whole of the passage at *L 1795* 43, *W* 11–14, 98–100; *EOT* II 376; *F* II 137 (I 210); and *BL* I 185. In print, the title even of the Bristol "Addresses to the People" was in elitist Latin, *Conciones ad Populum*.

He had also insisted, in this first of his Bristol addresses, that the truest reformer—one of the "small but glorious band" of "thinking and disinterested Patriots," combining "the zeal of the Methodist with the views of the Philosopher—should be *personally* among the poor, and teach them their *Duties* in order that he may render them susceptible of their *Rights*" (*L 1795* 40, 43).

The same point recurs in *On the Constitution of the Church and State*, though by 1830 this reciprocity between rights and duties had modulated into the instillation of a "civility" in the rude lower (and even middle) classes requiring almost docile obedience (inculcated by a National Church) to a state guided by a learned and civilizing "clerisy." Nevertheless, the function of that clerisy was to insure a balanced diversity in the state, especially in terms of rights and duties.

Not that the national church was to be too closely identified with the political state; indeed, it was to be the worldly kingdom's "appointed Opposite"—its "sustaining, correcting, befriending Opposite" (*C&S* 114), but its opposite nonetheless. Any closer relationship would undermine religion's role as a counterbalance to materialism and unbridled commercialism. In the *Lay Sermons* of 1816 and 1817, Coleridge had advocated a fusion of Platonic philosophy and Christian religion as a moral "counterpoise" to the landed classes' too eager embrace of "the spirit of commerce." Faced, in 1830, with the coalescence of landed and commercially derived wealth, Coleridge extended his conception of a state morally shaped by Platonized Christianity. By inculcating philosophic and moral values in the landed gentry, an educating clerisy would produce an intellectual rather than merely traditional aristocracy, a "polished" rather than a "varnished" culture. In this idealized scheme, a "guardian"-like clerisy, an elite "at the fountain heads of the humanities," was to help preserve the treasures of civilization, to bind present to past, and, by perfecting and adding to the cultural heritage, to connect the present with the future; but "especially to diffuse through the whole community, and to every native entitled to its laws and rights, that quantity and quality of knowledge which was indispensable both for the understanding of those rights, and for the performance of the duties correspondent" (*C&S* 43–44).

Though the national church of this 1830 treatise occasionally resembles an instrument to insure obedience to an organic state, the emphasis on religion as necessary and edifying is of course nothing new. Again, it would be quite wrong to infer that the points just emphasized were secondary elaborations, priorities of the later, conservative Coleridge having nothing to do with his earlier thought. He had, for example, *always* stressed, along with the reciprocity of rights and duties, the indispensable role of "Religious Faith" in social amelioration. In a 1794 letter to his brother George specifically addressing the issues of slavery and abolition, Coleridge observed:

I have been asked what is the best conceivable mode of meliorating Society—My Answer has been uniformly this—"Slavery is an Abomination to every feeling of the Head and the Heart—Did Jesus preach the *Abolition* of it? No! He taught those principles, of which the necessary *effect* was—to abolish all Slavery. He prepared the *mind* for the reception before he poured the Blessing—.["] You ask me, what the friend of universal Equality *should* do—I answer—["]Talk not of Politics—*Preach the Gospel!*" (*CL* I 126)

It is true that, on those occasions when Coleridge, young and Unitarian, preached amateur sermons from the pulpit, he rarely separated his (then) dissenting religion from his radical politics. In this letter, too, he wants to reassure his conservative clergyman brother that he was not the violent democrat some thought him. Nevertheless, what he says here is not insincere: Coleridge adhered all his life to the principle that the individual "mind" had to be prepared for any social "blessing," that moral edification and illumination were the necessary prerequisites to judicious political action.

It would also be inaccurate to *over*stress Coleridge's consistency. He had, he said on July 21, 1832, "no faith in Act of Parliament Reform. All the great, the permanently great, things that have been achieved in the world, have been so achieved by Individuals, working from the instinct of Genius or Goodness" (*TT* I 311). He had made the same point about individual illumination as more efficacious than parliamentary legislation many years earlier, in the "Prospectus" to *The Watchman* (*W* 4–5); but when, in Table Talk recorded for the same day, he *completely* dismisses parliamentary effectiveness regarding the slave trade, he is repudiating his own position as adumbrated in 1795–1796, and as clearly announced in 1808 and 1818, when he was praising the government's "glorious" intervention in abolishing the trade. In 1832 he claims retrospective clairvoyance, transporting his thoroughgoing skepticism back thirty-six years to *The Watchman:*

> The struggle about the Slave Trade and the Middle Passage excited my most fervent emotions. Yet I then stated in the Watchman—and I lost some friends by it—that no good will be done by applying to Parliament—that it was unjust—and that in twenty years after a Parliamentary Abolition—the horrors of the Trade would be increased twenty-fold. Now all acknowledge that to be true. *More* Africans are now transported to America for Slavery—the Middle Passage is more horrible—and the Slavery itself worse. (*TT* I 310)

As we have seen, Coleridge had, in 1817, referred sarcastically to the "nominal" abolition of the slave trade; but there is no prediction in *The Watchman* of future circumvention of the abolition legislation Coleridge then considered secondary to individual effort and which he was later to explicitly advocate. Still later, abolition seemed to become for Coleridge—as it did for Robert E. Lee—the work of Providence itself. In this 1832 conversation, he refers to the Middle Passage as having become, if anything, "more horrible" since the 1807 abolition of the slave trade. In 1833, the year of the abolition of slavery itself, Coleridge makes an extraordinary observation in the margins of an African voyage narrative he was reading. Annotating W. F. W. Owen's report of some Africans who, "it appeared, had voluntarily sold themselves to slavery in order to avoid the miseries of starvation" (one of several "accounts," as Coleridge put it, "of the state of the Negroes in their own country"), the former author of "On the Slave Trade" found it "pardonable to think, that if the power and wisdom of Law, enforced by powerful and wise Governments, had regulated the Middle Pas-

sage, and secured the right treatment, gradual Christianizing, and final eman-
cipation of the Slave after his arrival in the Colonies, the transportation would
have been a blessed Providence for the poor Africans!"[58]

Some readers may find H. J. Jackson's editorial note at this point rather too
defensive. "This is of course," she writes, "not a reversal of Coleridge's aboli-
tionist position (as stated in [for example, the "Lecture on the Slave Trade"])
but an acknowledgement of the preferability of controlled emigration to starva-
tion at home" (*CM* III 1082*n*). That acknowledgment might have added force
given the apocalyptic condition of much of sub-Saharan Africa (famine, drought,
war, AIDS, etc.) in 1992, the year this annotation was first published. In condi-
tions almost as horrendous a decade and a half earlier, the boxer Muhammad
Ali, after visiting Africa, joked that he was glad "my great grandaddy caught
that ship." However politically incorrect the offhand remark, Ali was enjoying
the benefits of a nation that, whatever its injustices, had freed its black slaves a
century earlier. Coleridge was writing in the very year of Parliamentary Aboli-
tion and thirty years *before* Lincoln's Emancipation Proclamation.

Thus, while conceding the point about "preferability," one has to wonder
about Coleridge's less-than-realistic hypotheses ("that if," ". . . had," "would
have been . . .") about controlling "emigration." Indeed, it would be hard to
find a more curious and inclusive mixture of Coleridge's social conservatism,
providential Christianity, and pervasive sympathy for the "poor Africans." The
marginal note amounts to a career-synopsizing hope, or pipe dream: slaves
humanely transported, Christianized, and—mirabile dictu—emancipated af-
ter arrival in the very plantations they had been enslaved to work! Coleridge
was not the only Christian to find transported blacks better off than in Africa or
to make a potentially providential case for the Atlantic crossing—both were
common sentiments among southern whites, even among those decent mem-
bers of the Virginia planter class who, like Coleridge, found slavery "a moral &
political evil in any Country."[59] But only a lifelong abolitionist whose heart had

58. This marginal note on a passage on page 218 in volume 2 of Owen's *Narrative of
Voyages to Explore the Shores of Africa, Arabia, and Madagascar* (2 vols. [London, 1833]),
appears in the third volume of the *Marginalia* (*CM* III 1082).

59. The phrase is from a celebrated letter (December 27, 1856) from Robert E. Lee
to his wife, Mary Custis Lee. But the future commander of the forces of the Confederacy
added, "The blacks are immeasurably better off here than in Africa, morally, socially &
physically"; the "painful discipline they are undergoing" is "necessary for their instruc-
tion as a race"; and the length of their "subjugation" is "known & ordered by a wise
Merciful Providence." Eventual freedom of the slaves, though a development advan-
tageous to whites as well as blacks, was in the hands, not of interfering northerners, but
of a God moving with all deliberate speed: "Their emancipation will sooner result from
the mild & melting influence of Christianity, than the storms & tempests of fiery
Controversy. . . . While we see the Course of the final abolition of human slavery is
onward, & we give it all the aid of our prayers & all justifiable means in our power, we
must leave the progress as well as the result in his hands who sees the end; who Chooses
to work by slow influences; & with whom two thousand years are but as a Single day."

As an American icon, Lee has traditionally been depicted as unsympathetic to gotten the better of his head could have expressed the fond wish that the horrific Middle Passage, transformed into a journey to freedom, could itself be a voyage marked by justice and wisdom. The whole marginal note, like his 1808 call for European kindness in Africa, exemplifies what I've referred to as Coleridge's sometimes rather desperate faith in a morally benevolent world order.

As this long excursus has been meant to demonstrate, despite his occasional adjustments of his own past and, here, of the history of the Atlantic slave trade itself; despite the changes, too, in Coleridge's social and racial attitudes over the thirty-five years between "On the Slave Trade" and *On the Constitution of the Church and State,* there remained what Sara Coleridge called "virtual consistency" in her father's position on the issue of slavery. His zeal had certainly diminished, evidence for the turncoat charge is there, especially in the 1833 comments to Pringle. Yet it is at least arguable that the young egalitarian, the Blumenbachian race-ranker, and the conservative theologian were, however different, essentially the same man when it came to lamenting "Afric's wrong" and categorizing human slavery as a moral abomination. Unfortunately, as Coleridge became increasingly conservative, the Gospel—always a crucial guide— became a less liberating than edifying text—until, finally, the Jesus who preached "principles" the effect of which would lead to emancipation seems to become institutionalized in a national church more interested in stability than liberation. As in the case of the Socrates re-created by Plato (the philosopher on whose mature thought Coleridge partially modeled his constitution of church and state), Coleridge evolved from a man publicly addressing the many to a sage whose lay sermons were meant for the few, an educated elite or guardian-like "clerisy."[60]

---

slavery, a tragic figure who condemned the very institution he was called upon to defend militarily. But, legend and his favoring of "gradual emancipation" notwithstanding, Lee was no real "opponent" of slavery, an institution he personally disliked but firmly *believed* in as necessary to the South at the time—however divine Providence might deal with it in the long run. The letter to his wife, quoted here from the original text in Douglas Southall Freeman's landmark four-volume biography, *R. E. Lee* (1:371–73), has been recently subjected to detailed and critical analysis by Alan T. Nolan in chapter 2 of his *Lee Considered: General Robert E. Lee and Civil War History,* especially pages 11–12, 25, and 29.

60. Coleridge's shift almost recapitulates several of the differences between the Socrates of the middle (or mature) as opposed to the early Platonic dialogues, differences listed in chapter 2 of the brilliant study—*Socrates, Ironist and Moral Philosopher*—with which the late Gregory Vlastos recently capped his distinguished career. While the Socrates of such early dialogues as the *Apology, Crito,* and *Protagoras* ("Socrates-E.") is a philosophic populist engaging those he meets in the street and defending an admittedly flawed (because *too* direct) Athenian democracy, "Socrates-M," the more "Platonic" Socrates of the middle period (from *The Republic* and *Phaedo* to the *Symposium* and *Theaetetus*), is a philosophic elitist whose lessons are restricted to the few and who advocates the rule of just such a philosophic elite—the "guardians" of *The Republic.* Both depictions of "Socrates," E and M, are Platonic re-creations; but if E is, as Vlastos persuasively argues, much closer to the "historical" Socrates, Plato's views developed and

4

On the Constitution of the Church and State was published in 1830, the same year Coleridge annotated not only *Robinson Crusoe,* but Bunyan's *Pilgrim's Progress* as well. He was more than ever absorbed by religion and moral issues—as is clear from the *Crusoe* annotations themselves. Thus, following his remarks about Crusoe's no-more-than-average technological accomplishments, Coleridge weaves his theme of universality into a final religious comment: "Crusoe rises only where all men may be made to feel that they might, and that they ought to rise—in religion, in resignation, in dependence on & thankful acknowledge-ment of the divine Mercy and goodness" (*CM* I 165). These remarks are relevant to the concept of Providence that dominates much of *Robinson Crusoe* (e.g., 107, 141, 181, 192, 194), just as it dominates Douglass's *Narrative of . . . an American Slave;* and, as usual, Coleridge has anticipated a good deal of modern discus-sion, in this case, of Crusoe as spiritual wayfarer.

While the spiritual import of the novel is undeniable, its realism "emblem-atic" of the "familiar Christian pattern of disobedience-punishment-repentance-deliverance" and its hero's isolation an epitome of the Puritan version of the human plight, I find myself less impressed than Coleridge and others have been by this particular pilgrim's progress. Not that I am as vigorously skeptical of Crusoe's religious dimension as such readers as Karl Marx, James Joyce, and Ian Watt. In discussing Crusoe as capitalist, Marx predictably took "no ac-count" of his "prayers and the like," dismissing them as superstructural trivia—"so much recreation." In his 1912 Italian lecture on Defoe, Joyce argued that the Puritan author, "perceiving rather tardily that . . . he had taken little account of the spiritual side of his hero," added, in the *Serious Reflections,* religious thoughts less integral than ornamental: they "decorate the figure of the rude sailor neither more nor less than the votive talismans which hang about the neck and from the outstretched hands of a miracle-working Ma-donna." Watt finds Defoe "sincere" enough, but "Crusoe's religion" uncon-vincing, a reflection of Defoe's own conflicted feelings. Though "otherworldly concerns do not provide the essential themes of Defoe's novels," they do, as in *Robinson Crusoe,* "punctuate the narrative with comminatory codas that demon-strate a lifetime of somewhat skeptical practice."[61]

While I share some of this skepticism, such scholars as J. Paul Hunter, G. A. Starr, Rodney Baine, and Leopold Damrosch have reminded us that the "Chris-tian pattern" they discuss is set up, as Hunter says, "in the first few pages of the book," and that the author's moral and ideological aims, though often re-

---

changed over the years in ways very similar to those of Coleridge. Coleridge's radicalism was never divorced from what has been called "his continuing search for an elite which would serve as a reliable guide to the nation's political society" (Miller, *Ideology and Enlightenment,* 31, 236). Still, he *was* committed for much of the 1790s to the "people" to whom he delivered his Bristol addresses.

61. Marx, *Capital: A Critique of Political Economy* 1:88. Joyce, "Daniel Defoe," 11–12. Watt, *The Rise of the Novel,* 81.

garded as Defoe's afterthoughts or rationalizations by modern scholars, are in fact an integral part of the structure of *Robinson Crusoe*. But I still retain vestigial doubts about the spirituality of both Crusoe and his creator. Perhaps the novel is, as Hunter argues, ultimately about man's spiritual development, with the events of Crusoe's life following what Starr calls "a conventional and regular pattern of spiritual evolution."[62] But the spiritual motif in the book is sporadic rather than pervasive, with Crusoe's emphasis on repentance and the workings of Providence notably diminishing as the novel goes on. Further, and more to the immediate point, Crusoe's extended bouts of spiritual introspection and retrospection, his meditations on the events of his guilty life, never extend to his participation in the practice of human slavery. That may be understandable in the case of Crusoe, or of Defoe, but Coleridge's apparent emphasis on the moral and religious dimension of *Robinson Crusoe* only makes his silence on the question of slavery, and Crusoe's involvement in that "atrocious moral depravity," the more striking.

As I remarked at the outset, there are many possible explanations. Annotations are by their nature wayward and random, and readers tend to focus on passages of particular interest to them in particular circumstances. Nor would Coleridge be unusual in failing to focus on slave trading in thinking about *Robinson Crusoe*. A man now sixty, Coleridge may have simply been settling down with a favorite book for a pleasant read. On the more serious level suggested by this chapter's tracing of context (the continuities and changes in Coleridge's political, humanitarian, anthropological, philosophic, and religious views), some readers may well conclude that Coleridge failed to express criticism let alone revulsion at Crusoe's attitude toward slavery and the slave trade precisely because, by 1830, he no longer found those attitudes repellent.

Though I have teetered on that brink, it is not my own conclusion. As I go on to argue in Chapter 3, the most—though still not fully—satisfactory solution to this "silence" lies in Coleridge's approach to *Robinson Crusoe*, which he read as a work, like *The Ancient Mariner*, "of pure imagination," a fiction at once moral

---

62. Hunter, *The Reluctant Pilgrim: Defoe's Emblematic Method and Quest for Form in "Robinson Crusoe,"* 19. Starr, *Defoe and Spiritual Autobiography*, 72. See also the books listed in the bibliography by Baine and Damrosch. Useful articles include Novak, "Robinson Crusoe's 'Original Sin,'" and William Halewood, "Religion and Invention in *Robinson Crusoe*." In the articles by Edwin B. Benjamin and Robert W. Ayers, Crusoe is seen as a spiritual wayfarer not unlike Bunyan's Christian. On the superficiality of Crusoe's Christianity, see, in addition to Marx, Joyce, and Watt, the articles by Hans W. Hausermann and Rudolph G. Stamm. Other recent examinations of "Providence" in the novel include the article by Lisa M. Zeitz and the German study by Wolfgang Mackiewicz.

In his marginalia, Coleridge praises Defoe/Crusoe for an able "vindication of Miracles" (*CM* I 161; in reference to the sprouting of the corn); and for presenting a "mighty motive for habitual prayer" (162; referring to Crusoe's admission that he used to pray to God only when "under great affliction," not realizing that prayer is "properly an act of the mind, not of the body"). On the other hand, both Defoe and his hero come under Coleridgean criticism (*CM* I 162, 164) for Crusoe's clear belief in a personal devil (*Robinson Crusoe*, 163, 183) and apparent belief in predestination (213).

yet not reducible to "*a* moral." This readerly response leads to the final partial explanation. For whatever else he was doing, this sophisticated reader, in remaining silent regarding Crusoe's slave trading and relationship with Friday, was implicitly exercising what we now call "historical imagination"—as in his rhetorical question about the period in which *Othello* was written: "Were Negro[e]s then known but as Slaves"? (*LL* II 314).

The question of "historical imagination" has recently come up in a context immediately relevant to this consideration of the response of a reader to the fictional depiction of slavery: a 1990 *New Republic* essay by Irving Howe and the response it drew from a correspondent. Discussing *Mansfield Park*, Howe confesses to an "uneasiness" about a "historical fact" which, while "not central to the action" of the novel, Jane Austen chose not to evade. With the plot requiring his absence, she sends Sir Thomas Bertram, the somewhat imperceptive but kindly baronet who is the "respected patriarch" of a solid family in the landed gentry, off to inspect his estate. The estate could have been anywhere, but Austen deliberately locates it in Antigua in the West Indies, which, in the historical circumstances, can only mean that Sir Thomas—like John Pretor Pinney of St. Nevis—owns slaves. Thus, while Howe does "not suggest that Austen approved of slavery," he is troubled:

> Sir Thomas profits from the exploitation of black labor and is nevertheless seen as a morally upright . . . figure. . . . The kind of problems presented in *Mansfield Park* can be found in many novels of the past . . . . If we are very sophisticated, we tell ourselves that . . . we ought to have enough "historical imagination" to enter unfamiliar settings and recognize the integrity of other moralities. . . . It's a splendid thing, this historical imagination, and everyone needs a supply of it, but the mere fact that we need to invoke it testifies to difficulties. We can no longer read some of these novels with a direct, spontaneous response. There must now be a complex act of "mediation" that entails all sorts of mental reserves.

Howe probably speaks for most of us in being made uneasy—especially since Jane Austen was writing as recently as the early nineteenth century. But there were morally upright slaveowners even that late, and we may wonder with E. A. Fry—who, in responding to Howe, mentions Washington, Jefferson, and Lee— if, "without regard to historical circumstances, a clubbable novelist is obliged to portray fictional slaveowners as scoundrels [and] never create fictional equivalents of those Virginians. Sins to which we are insensitive will be keenly felt by our descendants. Everyone's hope is to be measured by the whole of his work and not solely by the part that has fallen into disrepute."[63]

These considerations are even more apropos in the case of Defoe, an author writing a century before Jane Austen and in a mercantilist milieu largely insensitive to the sin of human slavery. Praising one of "those Virginians" (George Washington, who *owned* the slaves he emancipated in his will), Coleridge had also anticipated Fry's final point by cautioning us not "to interpret the whole of a character by a part" (*EOT* I 230). In passing over without marginal judgment

---

63. Howe, "History and the Novel," 33–34. Fry, "Correspondence," 4–5.

Crusoe's slave-trading activities, and Defoe's apparent approval, Coleridge *may* simply be refusing to indulge in ahistoricism or eschewing the currently fashionable notion that works of art ought to be submitted to a litmus test of "political correctness" based on contemporary standards, ethical or ideological.

To return to *Mansfield Park:* between condemnation of a "tainted" novel, on the one hand, and, on the other, insensitivity to "extrinsic" issues, there is a more sophisticated response—historical *and* aesthetic—that acknowledges the connection, however understated, between the injustice and harsh discipline of the distant slave plantation and the wealth, ease, and beauty of the slaveholder's estate in England. Exercising aesthetic "silence," Jane Austen—though familiar with slavery and the slave trade from her reading of Clarkson, her father's trusteeship of an Antigua estate, and graphic accounts by her sailor brother Frank of the "harshness and despotism" of West Indian slavery—provides no glimpse of Sir Thomas on his plantation, indeed only mentions Antigua a half-dozen times in the novel. Yet through those few references, and the "dead silence" that follows Fanny's question to Sir Thomas "about the slave trade," the world of Caribbean sugar and slavery enters into and, for Austen's modern readers, troubles the poised tranquillity of Mansfield Park: an estate and a commodious way of life paid for by the exploitation of slaves a hemisphere away.

As we have been reminded by Warren Roberts and, most recently, by Edward Said, this most amiable of novelists wrote in an age of revolution, *imperium,* and wealth derived from human slavery.[64] At the time of his annotations on *Robinson Crusoe* (recorded sixteen years after the publication of *Mansfield Park*), slavery still existed in lands under British control (and would for three more years), while Coleridge's attitude, however conservative on most social issues, remained for the most part one of moral revulsion when it came to slavery. His mixed response to abolition in 1833 suggests that the intensity of that moral revulsion had diminished and, certainly, that it had become complicated by his "Yes-but" fear that manumission without religious edification might prove injudicious. But none of this amounts to a reversal of Coleridge's abolitionist position. As a religious conservative and "true trimmer" rather than a simple backslider on the issue, he *should* still have been disturbed by Crusoe's slaving activities. And then there is Crusoe's assertion of mastership over his willing slave, "Friday." Quite aside from his shifting attitude toward the African Negro, and granting that he had become an anthropological racist, Coleridge should have had *something* to say about Crusoe's turning of Friday into his bondman; he, after all, was a Native American, not an African, and thus higher on the Blumenbachian "scale of dignity." But, again, though he thought that "a *willing* Slave is the worst of Slaves" (*CL* I 122), Coleridge has nothing to say in the margins.

64. Roberts, *Jane Austen and the French Revolution.* Said, "Jane Austen and Empire," one of the finest chapters in *Culture and Imperialism,* 80–97. See also Park Honan, *Jane Austen: Her Life,* 3, 21, 234, 341, and, for Frank Austen's 1811 denunciation of slavery, Edith C. Hubback, *Jane Austen's Sailor Brothers,* 192.

If we cannot reconstruct what was going through Coleridge's mind when he reread *Robinson Crusoe* in 1830, we can at least imagine the scene. He is sitting down, just three years before the long antislavery campaign was to come to fruition in the abolition legislation of 1833, to reread a favorite book. It is, to be sure, a great book, remarkable for its extraordinary endurance among critics and general readers alike—though I must confess that my own double response to *Robinson Crusoe* coincides precisely with that of John Richetti, who remarks that his critical study *Defoe's Narratives* is "an attempt to reconcile my entire pleasure in reading Defoe's novels with my divided and contradictory reactions after the enjoyable fact."[65] Granted that we are to measure a writer like Defoe by the whole of his work and not solely by the part that has fallen into historical disrepute—and that we are not to interpret the whole of such a character as Crusoe by a part—the question remains: what would Coleridge think of his childhood hero were he to examine Defoe's protagonist in the context of slavery? Could he still see him as the "Universal Representative" for whom "every reader could substitute himself"? A protagonist whose actions, thoughts, feelings, "every man" (including Coleridge) could "imagine himself doing, thinking, feeling"? Even making allowances for a relaxed moral censor (and Coleridge's was remarkably hair-triggered), for Coleridge's shift in political and racial attitudes, and for the exercise of historical imagination, let us consider the obstacles to empathetic identification Coleridge would have had to surmount.

65. Preface to *Defoe's Narratives: Situations and Structures*, i.

2

Crusoe, Defoe, and Friday

1

Crusoe's attitude toward slavery (except for his own, of course) is, to say the least, tolerant. His first voyage was made in the hope of procuring African slaves; when he returns, lured by his own prior experience and by other travelers' tales of gold, he and the rest of the crew are taken prisoner by Turkish pirates. Shipped to the Moorish port of Sallee in North Africa, they are sold as slaves. Crusoe escapes with the help of a fellow slave, Xury, having secured the young Moor's oath of fidelity as the alternative to his being thrown into the sea (*Robinson Crusoe*, 45). Xury, however, proves more than faithful; he becomes, in effect, *Crusoe's* slave. At one point, he offers to go on shore alone to fetch water, and when Crusoe asks why, "the boy answered with so much affection that [it] made me love him ever after. Says he, 'If wild mans come, they eat me, you go wey.' 'Well, Xury,' said I, 'we will both go, and if the wild mans come we will eat them, they shall eat neither of us.'" (47)

This camaraderie does not get out of hand. When the Portuguese captain who rescues them offers Crusoe sixty pieces of eight for Xury,[1] the bargain (though "I was very loath to sell the poor boy's liberty, who had assisted me so faithfully in procuring my own") proves too good to be resisted. The captain is an understanding man, though, and offers a compromise: "He would give the boy an obligation to set him free in ten years, if he turned Christian; upon this, and Xury saying he was willing to go to him, I let the captain have him" (54). Coleridge, who by 1830 would presumably be even more appalled by the selling of a Moor than a Negro, has nothing to say in the margins; perhaps he was mollified by the young man's "willingness" to turn Christian.

It is hard not to wonder what would have happened if Xury had *not* been willing. The "medium" Crusoe speaks of describes not only the deal but its nature: something between outright slavery and indenture, and a verbal contract made between the captain and Crusoe, acting as a "medium" or go-

---

1. Watt's remark—"twice Judas's figure" (*The Rise of the Novel*, 69)—seems more than witty. "Several circumstances," says Ayers, "suggest the possibility that Xury may be in some sense and to some degree a Christ figure. . . . [T]he name may be derived from a transliteration of the Greek monogram ☧ " ("*Robinson Crusoe*: 'Allusive Allegorick History,'" 404). If so, Crusoe, unlike Judas, never exhibits any remorse over his betrayal.

between. Of course, the Portuguese were notorious slavers, and there is no guarantee whatever that the captain will honor the bargain. Crusoe conveniently chooses to believe Xury will be enslaved for a mere ten years, in the collapsed timescale of this novel a drop in the bucket. Only twice does Crusoe reminisce about Xury—and in both cases he is thinking of him not as a person but as a slave who could have provided a useful pair of hands (55, 136). Many years later, rescued from the island and in Lisbon to find out about his Brazilian property, Crusoe tracks down the old Portuguese captain. "I enquired, you may be sure, after my plantation and my partner" (275). Nothing could be surer; but not once in the course of several days' "farther conference" (277) does he inquire about the boy who had "made me love him ever after." Whether the oversight is to be attributed to Defoe's short memory in regard to offstage characters, or to his hero's lack of interest, seems less important than the fact that it is typical of Crusoe.

Having invested his sixty pieces of eight in that Brazilian plantation, Crusoe finds that "I had done wrong in parting with my boy Xury" (55). But the "wrong" is economic, not moral. His only motive, as just indicated, is that he is short of manpower—a problem quickly rectified, for as soon as he can afford it, and in order to achieve the "advancement of my plantation, . . . the first thing I did, I bought me a negro slave, and an European servant also" (57–58). But a steady increase of wealth over four years only whets Crusoe's appetite. Accordingly, he now plants quite another crop than sugarcane: an idea. He tells his fellow planters and merchants about his experiences trading trinkets with the Negroes off the "Guinea" coast—that is, the western or "Slave Coast" of Africa. "They listened always very attentively to my discourses on these heads," he blandly observes, "but especially to that part which related to the buying negroes, . . . a trade at that time not only not far entred into, but as far as it was, had been carried on by the assientoes, or permission of the kings of Spain and Portugal,[2] and engrossed in the publick, so that few negroes were brought, and those excessive dear" (59).

After speaking "particularly earnestly" on the subject, Crusoe is "approached" with a proposal to go on a voyage to secretly procure slaves: "In a word, the question was, whether I would go their super-cargo in the ship to manage the trading part upon the coast of Guinea. And they offered me that I should have my equal share of the negroes without providing any part of the stock" (59).

2. Granted by the king of Spain, the *Asiento* was an extremely lucrative term contract for a monopoly to trade slaves in Spain's American colonies. In granting the British free trade with Spanish America for thirty years, the Anglo-Spanish Treaty of Utrecht (1713) also gave the famous South Sea Company (whose "bubble" was to burst in 1720) a monopoly of the Spanish slave trade. Defoe was skeptical that the provision would be honored by Spain, but for six years—until the renewal of war with Spain in 1719, the year *Robinson Crusoe* was written—the South Sea Company did in fact, under the contract of its single genuine trading transaction, operate under the *Asiento* to carry slaves to the Spanish colonies. England's increased participation in the slave trade after acquiring the *Asiento* is discussed by Richard B. Sheridan in *Sugar and Slavery: An Economic History of the British West Indies, 1623–1775*, 249–53 and passim.

As the details suggest, the author of this passage knew a good deal about his subject. We may leave Crusoe to contemplate this proposal for a moment and turn to Defoe, who is often described as having a more enlightened attitude regarding these matters.

In the same year he wrote the novel, Defoe, concerned about the sudden disruption of the South Sea Company's trade with Spanish America because of the new war with Spain, was urging the company, whose "charter begins at the River Oroonoque," to exploit the very area in which Crusoe's island was fictionally located. As the site of Sir Walter Raleigh's dreamed-of El Dorado, the basin of the Orinoco had long haunted Defoe's colonizing imagination. Now, with the resumption of war with Spain, his attention was refocused on the region. In the item I am citing (from the *Weekly Journal* of February 7, 1719), written while he was also working on *Robinson Crusoe,* Defoe spoke of a South Sea Company plan, similar to one he had proposed to William III three decades earlier, "for erecting a British Colony . . . upon the Terra Firma, or the Northernmost side of the Mouth of the great River Oroonoko, . . . the same Country and River discovered by Sir Walter Raleigh, in former Days, and that which he miscarried, which may now easily be prevented."

Crusoe's later governorship of his island and the plans, in the *Farther Adventures,* for an island colony must have been, as Maximillian Novak has said, "the product of one of Defoe's oldest daydreams."[3] But the daydream, even in the fiction, quickly became a pipe dream, and within two years of the *Weekly Journal* piece, Defoe's colonial prospectus was being couched in terms of sarcasm and nostalgia. Having sold his own South Sea stock the year before, Defoe was, by August 1720, contrasting the contemporary stock companies to more glorious precedents:

> Our Projects are all Bubbles, and calculated for *Exchange-Alley* Discoveries, not for enlarging our Commerce, settling Colonies, and spreading the Dominions of our Sovereign. . . .
>
>   Why has no bold Undertaker follow'd the glorious Sir *Walter Raleigh* up the River of *Amazon,* the *Rio Parano,* and the Great *Oroonoque,* where thousands of Nations remain undiscover'd, and where the Wealth . . . exceeds all that has ever been conquer'd or discover'd in the *American* World? (*Manufacturer,* August 10, 1720)

Still, the rhetorical question and the lure of wealth remained to beckon "bold undertakers."

Any such undertaking, Defoe was well aware, would involve the use of slaves. It was a subject on which Defoe was well versed and which cannot be evaded by readers of his most celebrated work. Slavery and the slave trade, described by Michael Seidel as a "seemingly tangential issue" in *Robinson Crusoe,* nevertheless "hovers like something of a curse over the narrative." And the "curse" was

3. "Imaginative Islands and Real Beasts: The Imaginative Genesis of *Robinson Crusoe,*" 27.

almost inevitable given Defoe's long-standing connections, direct and indirect, with the slave trade. His first patron and a man who had a significant influence on Defoe's life, Sir Dalby Thomas, had been agent-general of the African Company on the Guinea Coast; Defoe himself invested in the African Company, and the Guinea or "Slave Coast" was where Crusoe "carried on his first commercial venture and toward which he was returning when he met with his great disaster." As John Robert Moore adds, "if [Defoe] wrote a novel in 1719, it would have something to say of the slave trade."[4]

Defoe is not Crusoe, but on this issue there seems little to choose between the positions of creator and creature. Either that, or I simply fail to see what others have described as Defoe's "irony" regarding slavery and the slave trade. Even his alleged "doublemindedness" or "ambivalence" is somewhat suspect. Defoe is indeed "ambivalent" to the extent that he reflects, may even be said to epitomize, a conflict common to many thinkers of his era: that between ethical and commercial considerations. But as has been demonstrated by Hans Anderson, Maximillian Novak, and Richard Kaplan, when it came to slavery and the slave trade, Defoe consistently subordinated the moral to the mercantile. Though many sophisticated readers, far more knowledgeable about Defoe than I, insist on his doublemindedness on these issues, surely some of those who emphasize his ambivalence mistake Defoe's criticism of the cruelty inflicted by traders and owners (and even that criticism is usually utilitarian rather than altruistic) for condemnation of the institution of slavery itself. They then compound the misperception by translating that "ambivalence" into authorial "irony" when slavery and the slave trade feature in the fictional works.[5]

Footnoting his remark that Defoe "held curiously contradictory opinions as to the justifiability of the slave trade," Samuel Holt Monk refers to Anderson's well-known 1941 article on "The Paradox of Trade and Morality in Defoe." Anderson cites fictional characters as well as passages in pamphlets and in Defoe's *Review* expressing, from a religious perspective, condemnation of the slave trade. But, in Monk's succinct synopsis of Anderson's thesis,

> from the economic point of view [the slave trade] is held to be at least expedient, and therefore justifiable, since it increased the national wealth and was both profitable and necessary for the well-being of the colonies. Defoe was aware of the contradiction, but appears not to have been much troubled by it. If a choice between religion and trade confronted him, he habitually chose what was advantageous to trade.[6]

4. Seidel, *"Robinson Crusoe": Island Myths and the Novel,* 106. Moore, *Daniel Defoe: Citizen of the Modern World,* 224.

5. The observations of Anderson, Novak, and Kaplan are discussed in the text. Laura Brown is currently working on this question as part of a feminist "liberationist project." Presumably she will apply to her study of Defoe, slavery, and the slave trade the same interest in Marxian and poststructural theory she brought to bear in 1987 on Aphra Behn's *Oroonoko* in "The Romance of Empire: *Oroonoko* and the Trade in Slaves."

6. Introduction to the Oxford Edition of Defoe's *Colonel Jack,* x. Defoe's position is hardly unique in Western history. For example, though doubts about the justice of

In his dissertation, Richard Kaplan documents Defoe's defense of the slave trade in such nonfiction works as the *Essay upon the Trade to Africa* (1711), *A Brief Account of the Present State of the African Trade* (1713), *The Compleat English Tradesman* (1725), *A Plan of the English Commerce* (1728), and the *Review*, especially during the years 1706–1712. Even when, as in *The Compleat English Tradesman*, social equality is a prominent feature, ethical and humanitarian concerns are clearly subordinated to practical, capitalist considerations. But Kaplan's is a double thesis, an argument that puts him in the camp of those who insist on Defoe's "ambivalence." While Defoe condemned some of its injustices and cruelty, slavery was so critical to England's financial structure that, writes Kaplan, "economic and practical factors outweigh humanitarian objectives"— in the nonfiction. Defoe's *fiction*, on the other hand, "demonstrated and implemented" the reforms and alternatives his nonfiction "only suggested." Though I have learned from Kaplan's well-researched thesis, I think he is too generous regarding the fiction; he is surely too ingenious in arguing, for example, that *Captain Singleton,* a depiction of the most brutal aspects of slaving, is an "unintentionally caustic attack," a "scathing" if not quite conscious "satire," on Augustan middle-class values.[7]

There *are*, to be sure, "provisional" improvements suggested in *Colonel Jack,* some twenty pages of which are devoted to proposed reforms of the slave and indentured servant systems in America, and there is, of course, Captain Mission, of whom more in a moment. It is also true that the creative imagination often enhances empathy; the Muse is a nobler lady than that prose "slut who keeps the till." Thus apologists for Defoe frequently cite his 1702 poem in heroic couplets, *A Reformation of Manners. A Satyr,* in which the poet chastises those who "barter Baubles for the *Souls of Men.*" But more than this is required to justify Frank Ellis's claim, in his excellent introduction to a collection of critical essays on the novel, that Crusoe and Defoe "differ . . . in their attitudes toward slaves and slavery," and that "Defoe's attitude seems to have been completely ambivalent." It is true that in *A Reformation of Manners,* Defoe castigates the "more than *Spanish* Cruelty" of slavers, who do not kill their victims, but the "ling'ring Life of Slavery preserve," and so "Torment the Body, and

---

slavery were occasionally voiced in ancient Greece, the institution seemed (to free Greeks) indispensable to their leisured civilization. Aristotle, in the first book of the *Politics,* actually defended slavery as both "necessary" and "natural." The perennial question he tried to settle was the extent to which "a worthwhile life for some people involves the imposition of suffering on others." I am quoting Bernard Williams, who in 1993 analyzed the tortured Aristotelian argument to demonstrate "the truth that if there is something worse than accepting slavery, it consists in defending it." Aside from Aristotle, nobody in ancient Greece mounted such a defense, but neither was slavery condemned. Williams's conclusion can be readily applied to Defoe's position on slavery: "considerations of justice and injustice were immobilized by the demands of what was seen as social and economic necessity." See chapter 5, "Necessary Identities," of Williams's penetrating study *Shame and Necessity.*

7. "Defoe's Views on Slavery and Racial Prejudice," 130–31, iii, 15.

debauch the Mind." But outside that sincerely reformist poem, Defoe never attacks slavery as an institution, and even there his target remains essentially the cruelty of the slavers rather than their chosen profession. Indeed, while he is certainly critical of the slavers' inhuman treatment of their victims, Defoe, in the lines immediately preceding the base bartering of baubles for the souls of "harmless Natives," is almost as disturbed by the slavers' recklessness: frying in the "insufferable Heats" of "*Africk's* Torrid Zone," they "run vast *Risques* to see the Gold, *and die.*"[8]

In any case, a single poem, even one of Defoe's most important, cannot outweigh the series of essays, especially those published between 1709 and 1713, in which Defoe defended the slave trade as the "potentially most Useful and Profitable Trade . . . of any Part of the General Commerce of the Nation." He appealed for continued public support of the trade as a lucrative exchange of thousands of Negroes for "many thousands of Ounces of Gold" in a 1711 pamphlet whose full title tells all: *An Essay upon the Trade to Africa in order to set the Merits of that Cause in a True Light and Bring the Disputes between the African Company and the Separate Traders into a Narrower Compass.*

In short, Defoe, like most of his contemporaries, thought the slave trade a perfectly respectable business and, as noted above, bought stock himself in the Royal African Company, which, along with the South Sea Company, was engaged in this traffic. As Novak has said, Defoe "admired the profits made" from the slave trade "and would have been the last person to advise its abolition." Defoe, he continues in a footnote, "has sometimes been mistakenly praised as an opponent of slavery. Actually he regarded slaves as 'produce' of Africa." Since he was convinced of the indispensability of slave labor to British colonialism, Defoe's humanitarian impulses on the issue of slavery are, writes Seidel, "akin to being against the treatment of the cocks in cock fighting but not against the activity itself. Defoe's attitude is regulatory not abolitionist." Whatever his inner feelings, and despite occasional public disapproval of the cruelties inflicted by slavers, when it came down to the issue of financial investment, Defoe was committed, not at all ambivalent, in casting his vote for baubles rather than the souls of men.[9]

Certainly there is neither irony nor ambivalence in many of the pieces Defoe published in his *Review* between 1706 and 1712. It might be unpleasant to buy and sell human beings, but the money was good. "Our colonies in America . . . could no more be maintained, the *Islands* especially, without the supply of *Negro* slaves carried thither from *Africa,* than London could subsist without the River of *Thames*" (*Review* 5:559). So the trade *must* be carried on, even if "*Sword in Hand*" (6:552). The following notorious passage on English slaveholders in

---

8. Ellis, Introduction to *Twentieth-Century Interpretations of "Robinson Crusoe,"* 5–6. Defoe, *A Reformation of Manners,* in *A True Collection of the Writings of the Author of the True Born English-man,* 77–78.

9. Novak, *Economics and the Fiction of Daniel Defoe,* 104, 167, quoting Defoe's *Atlas Maritimus and Commercials* (1728). Seidel, *"Robinson Crusoe,"* 106.

Barbados, from the May 22, 1712, number of the *Review,* adds to sword-in-hand acquisition whip-in-hand subjugation:

> The Negroes are indeed Slaves, and our good People use them like Slaves, or rather like Dogs, *but that by the way:* he that keeps them in Subjection, whips, and corrects them, in order to make them grind, and labour, *does Right,* for out of their Labour he gains his Wealth: But he that in his Passion and Cruelty, maims, lames and kills them, is a *Fool,* for they are his Estate, his Stock, his Wealth, and his Prosperity. (7:730)

Excessive cruelty, in short, is unprofitable; maiming, laming, and murdering are bad for business. As with Crusoe, humanitarian concerns, if they arise at all, are clearly subordinate to those of utility. The slaveholder who "does Right" in this passage, like the Crusoe who "did wrong" in selling Xury, is functioning in an economic rather than ethical realm. In a 1963 essay reprinted a quarter-century later in his *England, Their England,* Denis Donoghue refers to this passage, and passes the decent moral judgment we all feel. What bothers Donoghue in general, as Frederick Pollack has noted, is how distressingly at one with his age's mercantile worldview Defoe really was, an accordance reflected in such ungenial and selfish characters as Moll and Crusoe. Donoghue is right, perhaps even quantitatively right, in saying that Defoe novels featuring such characters— however comfortable they and *he* may be working within their own "set of terms"— ignore "two-thirds of human existence," since the terms "cancel all aspects of human consciousness to which the analogies of trade are irrelevant." We can, in short, agree completely with Donoghue, who cites most of the cold-blooded passage from the May 22 *Review* as an indication of Defoe's "moral obtuseness," even as we recognize, as Pollack does, that Donoghue is "forced to fill the gap between his sensibility" and that of Defoe and his characters by "moralizing."[10]

We can therefore acknowledge the point made by Thomas Keith Meier in responding to Donoghue's original article: that the attitude toward slavery and the slave trade to be found in the *Review* and elsewhere was "hardly unique to Defoe." The most morally repellent example of the reduction of the human to the mercantile was, of course, enslavement. But Meier complains that the position of such critics of Defoe's morality as Donoghue and Hans Anderson "is firmly rooted in nineteenth- and twentieth-century attitudes toward Negro slavery," and that they "do not broaden their charge to include such contemporaries of Defoe as the Members of Parliament who voted to preserve the Africa trade or the Ministers who successfully negotiated for the Asiento." Meier's final point is that "while it is socially reprehensible to advocate slavery in the twentieth century, it was socially acceptable to do so in the eighteenth."[11]

---

10. Donoghue, "The Values of *Moll Flanders,*" 291–93. In his review "To the Unknown Reader," Pollack writes: since Moll and Crusoe are perfectly at home in their mercantile worldview, "Donoghue is forced to fill the gap between his sensibility and theirs by moralizing" (498). Despite the tone of this sentence, Pollack agrees that Donoghue does not miss "anything important about Defoe and *Moll Flanders*" (499); Pollack doesn't mention Crusoe and slavery.

11. *Defoe and the Defense of Commercials,* 82–83.

This is a bit glib since there was *some* opposition, beginning with the Quakers as early as 1671. Furthermore, not everyone in the eighteenth century found slavery acceptable. The French *philosophes,* along with Adam Smith and other leaders of the Scottish Enlightenment, condemned it and the trade that sustained it; in England its opponents included the Methodist John Wesley and such major literary figures as Addison, Pope, Samuel Johnson (who drank a toast to slave insurrection), and James Thomson—who condemns the slavers in a passage of *The Seasons* discussed below in connection with *The Ancient Mariner* and J. M. W. Turner's painting *Slavers.* Still, despite its extent and inhumanity, the slave system aroused only sporadic protest in England prior to the *later* eighteenth century, when, in the wake of Britain's shattering defeat in America, moral disapproval became widespread.

For that defeat seemed to many the verdict of God upon a guilty nation. In 1783, the Quakers presented the first antislavery petition to Parliament. The Society for Effecting the Abolition of the Slave Trade was founded in London in 1787 (a year before the founding of the first continental abolition society, the *Amis des Noirs*). In 1788–1789, William Wilberforce, initiating the antislavery debate in the Commons, specifically raised the specter of guilt, warning that, whatever the short-term economic benefits, no nation that countenanced the sin of slavery could long flourish. Even for Wilberforce and other Evangelicals, the solution was to convert the heathens rather than sell them. In the earlier part of the century, in Defoe's period, as C. A. Moore, Richard Kaplan, and Meier himself have shown, the attitude of literary figures and their audiences was in general insensitive to the issues of slavery and the slave trade. "For most of the 1700s," as Linda Colley observed in 1992, "Britons had seen no inconsistency whatever between trumpeting their freedom at home and buying men, women, and children from trading-posts in Africa to sell into slavery abroad."[12]

The first of my own two points, one anticipated by Novak and Donoghue, is that, in the latter's words, "far from exerting a critical irony in *Crusoe,* Defoe's attitudes are strictly continuous with Crusoe's; there is no irony at all." Author and character alike are enthusiastic about the commercial value of slavery. As Novak says of the novels in general, "in Defoe's fiction the ability and the willingness to exploit slaves are signs of the superior entrepeneur class."[13] There are, it is true, varying degrees of kindness to be found in Defoe's characters involved with slaves. I am not thinking of the pseudobenevolent Quaker surgeon William Walters, whose motive in persuading Singleton to spare a cargo of mutinous slaves is his plan, later carried out, to sell the slaves for his own profit (*Captain Singleton* [1720]). Rather, I have in mind the hero of *Colonel Jack* (1722) and, above all, Captain Mission, hero of one of the longest and most intriguing sections of *A General History of the . . . Pyrates* (1724–1728). Still, with

12. Moore, "Whig Panegyric Verse." Colley, *Britons: Forging the Nation, 1707–1837,* 351–52.

13. Donoghue, "Values in *Moll Flanders,*" 293. Novak, *Economics and the Fiction of Daniel Defoe,* 114.

the exception of Mission, Defoe's heroes, like their creator, criticize only the cruelty involved, and then from a utilitarian rather than a humanistic perspective.

Crusoe—who sells Xury, owns at least one slave in Brazil, has thrice engaged in slave trading, and keeps Friday as slave-servant for life—certainly feels no moral uneasiness about slavery as an institution—as William, a Quaker, *should* have. In Defoe's fiction, such scruples are reserved to Captain Mission, an idealist who actually liberates black slaves. Freeing the seventeen blacks aboard the *Niewstadt,* the Dutch ship he and his pirates capture, Mission proclaims, to the "general applause" both of his own men and the freed slaves, his belief

> that the trading for those of our own Species, cou'd never be agreeable to the Eyes of divine Justice: That no Man had Power of the Liberty of another; and while those who profess'd a more enlightened Knowledge of that Deity, sold Men like Beasts, they proved that their Religion was no more than a Grimace [and that] they differed from the *Barbarians* in Name only, since their Practice was in nothing more humane: For his Part, and he hop'd, he spoke the sentiments of all his brave Companions, he had not exempted his Neck from the galling Yoak of Slavery, and asserted his own Liberty, to enslave others. That, however these Men were distinguish'd from the Europeans by their colour, customs or religious Rites, they were the Work of the same omnipotent Being. . . . He desired [the slaves] might be treated like Freemen (for he wou'd banish the Name of Slavery from among them).[14]

Discussing Mission's theory and the colony of "Libertalia" he establishes on Madagascar, Novak drily observes that Defoe "believed that egalitarianism and communism, though morally excellent, ignored the realities of human nature."[15] Certainly, neither Jack nor Crusoe share Mission's advanced theories about the immorality of slavery. Indeed, when Jack, himself indentured, advocates a policy of kindness on the plantation (*Colonel Jack,* 127–46), it is in order to win the gratitude and better service of his master's slaves—slaves who remain in bondage when he is eventually freed. Jack's aim is to find

> that happy Secret, to have good Order kept, the Business of the Plantation done, and that with Diligence, and Dispatch, and that the *Negroes* are kept in Awe, the natural Temper of them Subjected, and the Safety and Peace of [the master's] Family secur'd. [These aims are to be achieved] as well by gentle Means, as by Rough, by moderate Correction, as by Torture, and Barbarity; by a due Awe of just Discipline, as by the Horror of unsufferable Torments. (*Colonel Jack,* 134)

Everything we know about Defoe indicates his approval of this kind of paternalistic efficiency. Like Jack, he preferred moderate to harsh treatment of slaves; but, aside from *A Reformation of Manners,* Defoe never criticizes slavery as an institution and, of course, takes white superiority for granted. As for Crusoe, though he had himself experienced that "galling Yoak of Slavery," he,

---

14. "Of Captain Mission," in *A General History of the Robberies and Murders of the Most Notorious Pyrates,* 403–4. Mission frees seventeen slaves; precisely seventeen cannibals are killed when Crusoe and Friday free the Spaniard and Friday's father (237). As noted above, p. xiii, Defoe's authorship of the *General History* has been seriously challenged.

15. *Economics and the Fiction of Daniel Defoe,* 110.

unlike Captain Mission, has no compunction, once his own liberty is secured, about enslaving others. Defoe seems to approve of this as well.

Of course, it may be argued that he seems also to approve of Mission, in whose liberationist doctrine he may have forecast changing Augustan attitudes, may even, as Kaplan humanely argues, have prophesied "the abolition of slavery and the creation of a universal brotherhood of man."[16] But, as my Le Moyne colleague Douglas Egerton, a specialist in pre–Civil War U.S. history, points out, Mission's criticism of slavery on human grounds

> does not mean that there was a side of Defoe that was critical of bondage, only that he knew enough about pirates to understand that Mission would be. Eighteenth-century Anglo-American pirates tended to be egalitarian and democratic (they elected their captain, split the shares equally). They were also very tolerant of Africans. Indeed, many runaway slaves from Barbados signed on as pirates. Pirates really did turn the world upside down. In other words, it seems likely that Mission is an exception in Defoe's work because he was based on a realistic character, and not because he represented some small doubt lurking in Defoe's mind about the injustice of slavery.

While some small doubt did presumably lurk in the mind of the "ambivalent" Defoe, Egerton, whose observations tally with Marcus Rediker's brilliant social history, *Between the Devil and the Deep Blue Sea,* seems closer to the truth than Kaplan.[17] Even if we were to see in the story of Captain Mission some authorial prophecy of abolition and brotherhood, Defoe's final, and notably "realistic," comment on Mission's utopianism seems implicit in the fate of the experiment: the natives of Libertalia rise up and massacre the benefactors who had trusted rather than enslaved them (437–38).

My second point is that *Coleridge,* writing on the slave trade in the years straddling the end of the eighteenth century and the beginning of the nineteenth, would have found himself "represented" on this issue only by Mission among Defoe's characters: a man whose "Libertalia" resembled his own visionary Pantisocratic community, and whose "monogenist" theory Coleridge, early and late, would have embraced, albeit with diminishing liberationist ardor as the years passed. The crucial point is that Coleridge's attitudes toward slavery and the slave trade were, from radical beginning to conservative end, antipodal to those of Robinson Crusoe.

Whatever Defoe's final position on these same issues, "strictly continuous with Crusoe's" or not, Crusoe's own attitude is clear enough. His only cause for hesitation regarding the planters' proposition—for "This was a fair proposal, it must be confessed"—is his concern about leaving the plantation and the wealth he has already accrued. But documents are signed to secure these, and, claim-

16. "Defoe's Views on Slavery and Racial Prejudice," iii.

17. Egerton, letter to author, December 13, 1991. Rediker, *Between the Devil and the Deep Blue Sea: Merchant Seamen, Pirates, and the Anglo-American Maritime World, 1700–1750,* chapters 5 and 6, especially, for the egalitarianism of the pirates, 245–49, 261–62, and 286–87.

ing as usual to be "obey[ing] blindly the dictates of my fancy rather than my reason," but motivated in fact by what he himself admits was "a rash and immoderate desire of rising faster than the nature of the thing admitted" (58), he sets out ("with all my heart") on the fateful voyage that ends in shipwreck on the island.

The tempest that drives his ship on the rocks, leaving him (at the symbolic age of precisely thirty-five) the sole survivor stranded on an unknown island, might strike some of his Puritan persuasion as an act of divine retribution. The point was in fact raised by a contemporary of Defoe, Charles Gildon, in *Robinson Crusoe Examin'd and Criticis'd* (1719). In this witty riposte, both parody and critique, Gildon is alternately trivial and trenchant, never more so than when he observes that, although Crusoe later proves "scrupulous" about killing the cannibals, "yet he neither then nor afterwards found any check of Conscience in that infamous Trade of buying and selling of Men for Slaves; else one would have expected him to have attributed his *Shipwreck* to this very cause."[18] He doesn't; nor does Defoe, who of course had the fictional option of avoiding the issue altogether by enlisting Crusoe in another line of work.

A recent commentator observes that when Defoe, who "says nothing" in *Robinson Crusoe* about the "inhumanity" of the slave system, has his protagonist "cast ashore alone after a slave trade disaster," the "scene itself speaks silently."[19] This *may* be another instance of what the New Historicists would call a "significant silence." But that he should be shipwrecked so soon after setting forth as a slave trader is a matter of no moral significance whatever to Crusoe, and if it had any for Defoe, authorial judgment would seem to fall, not on his hero's occupation, but on his private and illegal pursuit of it. As many items in the *Review* indicate, Defoe had always opposed Parliament's decision in 1698 to allow private traders to vie with the Royal African Company, chartered a quarter-century earlier to handle the rapidly growing slave trade. I have already quoted his 1711 pamphlet appealing for support of the slave trade while simultaneously trying to settle disputes between the Royal African Company and the "Separate Traders." Two years later, in *A Brief Account of the Present State of the African Trade* (1713), Defoe indignantly attacked unlicensed traders whose "private Gain of Clandestine Trade is so sweet a Thing . . . that . . . they care not what Injury they do to the Trade in General" (52).

He had personal reason to complain, having lost a great deal of money on his own slave-trade investments (selling at less than £100 a share stock he had bought at £400 per share) because of the widespread intervention of such clandestine operators as Robinson Crusoe. Kaplan suggests that Defoe—"not openly condemning the slave trade," but aware of its "unpleasant aspects"— presented Crusoe's shipwreck "as a warning to other Englishmen about to embark on a similar expedition." Perhaps, though it seems to me more likely that the fate of his hero's expedition was Defoe's ironic way of punishing the

18. *Robinson Crusoe Examin'd and Criticis'd,* 94; italics in original.
19. Seidel, *"Robinson Crusoe,"* 106.

private traders responsible for one of his own financial "shipwrecks": a recurrent Defoe metaphor for financial disaster, and a trope that becomes literal in *Robinson Crusoe*. With this one exception, however, Defoe's attitude toward slavery and the slave trade can hardly be said to differ from that of Crusoe. As James Sutherland has said, Crusoe is another, and the greatest, of Defoe's "authentic individuals, with something of the strong smell of Defoe still clinging to them." Though Sutherland, writing in 1971, also called Crusoe an "ordinary decent man," the authorial aroma that clings to him is offensive—at least (when it comes to Defoe/Crusoe's shared attitude toward slavery and the slave trade) in our twentieth-century nostrils and, one would have thought, in Coleridge's.[20]

Crusoe's only criticism regarding the slave-procuring project—at the time or in retrospect—is that it was imprudent; and, to repeat, there is not the slightest indication, during his years of hand-wringing spiritual contemplation on the island lamenting his "dreadful misspent life," his "wicked and hardened" past (107, 142), that his eagerness to traffic in human flesh was one of the things troubling his conscience. Quite the contrary. On the one occasion when he juxtaposes the thought of "just punishment" for his "sins" with his earlier slave-trading "expedition on the desart shores of Africa," it is merely to regret that he "never had so much as one thought" about "a God or a providence" to protect *him* from the "danger" of "voracious beasts" and "cruel savages" (103–4).

As that sincere but obtuse passage indicates, a thematic connection between slavery and sin, or rather the *possibility* of one, is present in the novel almost from the outset, at least from the moment when Crusoe is himself enslaved by the natives of Sallee in North Africa. As David Blewitt observes,

> the appearance of the motif of slavery in the Sallee episode stirs an important undercurrent in the novel. The motif of slavery is part of the larger theme of imprisonment, later to develop into one of the chief sources of imagery in the island section; it links Crusoe's enslavement in Sallee, his escape with the slave boy Xury (who foreshadows Friday), his need for slaves in Brazil, and the subsequent African slaving trip on which he is shipwrecked for the last time. Together these forms of slavery lend ironic emphasis to Crusoe's bondage in sin and his eventual imprisonment on the island.[21]

The problem is that the "ironic emphasis" is not a conscious irony on either Defoe's or Crusoe's part—despite the persistent imagery of imprisonment and bondage; the irony has to be lent by perceptive readers like Blewitt. Similarly, Michael Seidel, conceding that neither Defoe nor Crusoe "have excessive qualms about slavery," asserts that "the larger action in the narrative is set up in such a way that Crusoe appears to undergo some kind of penance for the moral vacuum of past actions." Since "slave trading and cannibal killing frame his island stay," one might argue, as Seidel does, that Crusoe's repatriation "comes only after he deals with his own murderous impulses in light of cannibal rights,

20. Kaplan, "Defoe's Views on Slavery and Racial Prejudice," 142. Sutherland, *Daniel Defoe: A Critical Study*, 228, 224, 244.

21. *Defoe's Art of Fiction: Robinson Crusoe, Moll Flanders, Col. Jack, and Roxanne*, 32.

which are, by implication, natural rights for the natives of South America just as there ought to be natural rights for the native African."[22] It is a perceptive point, but finally too hedged round with inferences, appearances, "almosts" and "oughts" to be fully persuasive. Seidel—"moralizing" *on behalf* of Defoe—cannot clinch his argument any more than Blewitt can develop the connection between the slavery "motif" and the larger themes of "imprisonment" and "Crusoe's bondage in sin" for the simple reason that Defoe never develops it.

Nor does Crusoe, for whom the slave-trading expedition was merely reckless, not at all sinful. Ian Watt, giving a modern twist to Crusoe's theological term, identifies Crusoe's "original sin" as in fact "the dynamic tendency of capitalism itself, whose aim is never merely to maintain the *status quo,* but to transform it incessantly."[23] But this is a modern, even Marxian, perspective. Coleridge himself—hardly an ally of Mammon, though he was as a young man considerably more repelled by the commercial spirit—finds no fault with what he calls Crusoe's "spirit of enterprise," which he describes as "a very common disposition," inexplicably overlooking the specific form that enterprise took. What Crusoe himself sees as his "original sin" (198) remains disobedience. He is referring to his rebellion against his gout-ridden father's loving but all-too-sedentary command to stay at home and to adhere to "the middle station" (29), the "station wherein God and nature" had placed him (198), and which apparently contributed to Coleridge's moral positioning of Crusoe at the "middle degree of mankind."

This "rash and immoderate desire to rise" above that middle station—Coleridge's "spirit of enterprise and wandering," Watt's "dynamic tendency of capitalism itself"—is echoed twenty-four years later when, lamenting the fact that he was not blessed with "confined desires," our merchant-adventurer makes his sole specific reference to the project that was the direct cause of his shipwreck and consequent solitary existence:

> What business had I to leave a settled fortune, a well-stocked plantation, improving and increasing, to turn supra-cargo to Guinea, to fetch negroes, when patience and time would have so encreased our stock at home, that we could have bought them at our door, from those whose business it was to fetch them? and though it had cost us something more, yet the difference of that price was by no means worth saving at so great a hazard. (199)

In general, Crusoe's habit of "balancing" his existential books, placing "Evil" over against "Good" in double columns, is perfectly understandable, even admirable. He is "cast upon a horrible desolate island, void of all hope of recovery." But he is "alive, and not drowned as all my ship's company was." Though he is "singled out" and "separated . . . from all the world to be miserable," he is "singled out too from all the ship's crew to be spared from death; and He that miraculously saved me from death, can deliver me from this condition." If he is a "solitaire," he is at least "not starved and perishing on a

22. *"Robinson Crusoe,"* 107.
23. *The Rise of the Novel,* 65.

barren place"; he has no clothes, but is in a hot climate; he is defenseless, but has not been cast up in a place with "wild beasts to hurt me, as I saw on the coast of Africa; and what if I had been shipwrecked there?" And then there is the crucial fact that "God wonderfully sent the ship in near enough to the shore, that I have gotten out so many necessary things as will either supply my wants, or enable me to supply my self even as long as I live." Balancing his books, he concludes that "there was scarce any condition in the world so miserable, but there was something negative or something positive to be thankful for in it, . . . that we may always find in it something to comfort ourselves from, and to set in the description of good and evil, on the credit side of the accompt" (83–84).

We can approve of this early mixture of prudent accounting and gratitude to Providence; but the passage about "fetch[ing] negroes" makes it unpleasantly clear that Crusoe's vaunted religious evolution over a quarter of a century, however much Coleridge and others have been impressed by it, had left credit and debit bookkeeping enshrined more firmly than ever in his soul—the soul, however religious, of a shopkeeper. Since Crusoe can be as self-righteous as any caricature of a Victorian, and since it is with the Victorian age that we associate the ideology of salvation through hard work, it is perhaps not irrelevant to recall that that age's laureate, Tennyson, declared: "We, likewise, have our evil things; / Too much we make our Ledgers, Gods." Marx himself, in *Capital,* the treatise researched in the British Museum of the Victorian era, describes how Crusoe, "having rescued a watch, ledger, and pen and ink from the wreck, commences, like a true-born Briton, to keep a set of books."[24]

Crusoe's retrospection about the fatal plan to "fetch negroes" ends with acknowledgment of only one error: his leaving a "settled fortune" to capture slaves instead of leaving the job to those whose "business" it was, for though it would have "cost" more, "yet the difference of that price was by no means worth saving at so great a hazard." Given *this* example of credit and debit bookkeeping, it is understandable but also misleading for Novak to stress Crusoe's "lack of economic prudence," and (in referring to Crusoe's rhetoric—"O drug . . . what art thou good for?" [75]—about the "uselessness" of the ship's gold on the island) to say that he "can afford to sneer at a commodity which he never pursued with any steadiness."[25]

At once creature of impulse and calculating *homo economicus,* Crusoe may be reckless in many ways, but it is all aimed at "rising faster." Even his famous sneer at the gold is short-lived. As Coleridge was the first to point out, Crusoe, "upon second thoughts," in fact "took it away"—and with only a semicolon to separate

---

24. *Capital* 1:88. Tennyson's lines, from the 1852 version of "Hands All Round," were dropped thirty years later when the poem was completely recast on the occasion of Queen Victoria's birthday. But compare the speaker in *Maud* (also 1852), condemning a time "When the poor are hovelled and hustled together, each sex, like swine, / When only the ledger lives, and when only not all men lie" (*The Poems of Tennyson,* ed. Christopher Ricks, 1002, 1310–11, 1042).

25. *Economics and the Fiction of Daniel Defoe,* 32, 51.

this from his next equally prudent activity. "Worthy of Shakespeare," Coleridge enthused of the realism and authorial irony of the whole passage, "and yet the simple semi-colon after it, the instant passing on without the least touch of reflex consciousness, is more exquisite & masterlike than the Touch itself" (*CM* I 160).

The acuteness of Coleridge's point is a bit dulled by the fact that the semi-colon in his edition (the 1812) had been a comma in the first edition of *Robinson Crusoe,* and that the rambling sentence has lots of other commas and stops. "This seems to be hiding the effect a little too much," as Ian Watt drily remarks responding to Coleridge.[26] There has been enough subsequent discussion of the passage to make it perhaps the principal critical crux of the novel. Whether or not Defoe was being intentionally ironic, Crusoe's unemphatic prudence eventually pays off. Twenty-eight years later, leaving the island at last, "I forgot not to take the money . . . which had lain by me so long useless," as well as the money he'd later salvaged from the wreck of the Spanish ship (273–74): both prologues to the moment when, like Job, he discovers that his "latter end . . . was better than his beginning." His Brazilian properties having flourished in his absence, he finds himself rather a rich man and almost expires, so powerful is his "sudden surprize of joy." "It is impossible," exclaims an un-sneering Crusoe, "to express here the flutterings of my very heart . . . when I found all my wealth about me."[27] With "patience and time," he ends up, after all, "on the credit side of the accompt."

2

Finally, there is Crusoe's relationship with "Friday." In most readers' memories, I suspect, this relationship is preserved in amber, aureoled by a soft, nostalgic glow. There is something to be said for Richard Kaplan's argument that critics like Anderson and Novak miss "the emotional, social, and human aspects" of Defoe's fiction in general and, in particular, of the relationship of Crusoe with Friday. In this sociological two-person drama, says Kaplan, Defoe endeavored to eliminate preconceptions, to "break through the barriers of racial prejudice and simultaneously dispel erroneous ideas about primitive man."[28] We can agree that Defoe's realism represents a quantum leap over, on the one hand, Aphra Behn's idealization of the noble savage, Oroonoko, and, on the other, the racist caricatures to be found in such proslavery propaganda as William Bosman's grotesquely mistitled *A New and Accurate Description of the Coast of Guinea* (1705). Nevertheless, Defoe's attempt, in the relationship between Crusoe and Friday, to "break through" racist barriers is severely limited by his, and Crusoe's, time and temperament.

26. *The Rise of the Novel,* 120.
27. *Robinson Crusoe,* 279–80. This is an expanded version of his first reference to his island enclave, once it has been barricaded and filled with goods salvaged from the ship, as "home": "I was gotten home to my little tent, where I lay with all my wealth about me very secure" (57).
28. "Defoe's Views on Slavery and Racial Prejudice," iii, 13–14, 22, 134–64.

Since Charles Dickens's remark about Crusoe's insensitive response to Friday's death has earlier been noted, it may be appropriate to begin with that, especially since Friday's end may be said to be implicit in his beginning.

Most critics seem unbothered by Crusoe's truncated obituary for his "faithful servant"; others explain it away. Perhaps the least persuasive moment in Geoffrey Sill's refreshingly independent reading of the novel occurs in this context. Alluding to Crusoe's dream, just before the rescue of Friday, about finding a "pilot" to help him escape from the island, Sill writes of Friday's death years later: "The loss of Crusoe's 'pilot,' Friday, while on his last visit to the island colony, leaves Crusoe with no guide but himself through the moral wilderness of the world, but the scope of the world that Crusoe now has before him exceeds even Friday's knowledge, and so his services, though once highly valued, are not missed." However intriguing, even attractive, the idea of Friday as the guide with whose help Crusoe becomes an independent moral agent, this comment finally seems more appropriate to the disappearance of the Fool in *King Lear*, or to what happens in the 1988 film *Crusoe*, discussed below, than to the rapid eclipsing of Friday from Crusoe's memory in Defoe's novel.[29]

In fact, the reaction of Crusoe to Friday's death is of a piece, a lack of sustained sentiment obvious from the outset of their relationship. Watching through his telescope the cannibals who have begun to visit his island (it is now eight years since his dominion-shattering discovery of the famous footprint in the sand), Crusoe sees one of their native prisoners break away, followed by three pursuers. In the very instant he determines to save the life of the "poor wretch," Crusoe, who has at this point spent twenty-three years in solitude, makes it quite clear what kind of a relationship he is seeking: "It came very warmly upon my thoughts, and indeed irresistibly, that now was my time to get me a servant"—"and," he adds with the diminished warmth of an afterthought, "perhaps a companion or assistant" (206).

Crusoe fires his musket, killing one cannibal and frightening off the others in the act of saving the man he had earmarked as potential servant. Once rescued, the new man pays ritual obeisance; he not only "kneeled down" and "kissed the ground"; but he "laid his head upon the ground, and taking me by the foot, set my foot upon his head . . . in token of swearing to be my slave forever"—a gesture repeated after he has rested, when he makes to Crusoe "all the signs . . . of subjection, servitude, and submission imaginable, to let me know how he would serve me as long as he lived." (207, 209) "By saving the life of Friday," Novak observes, "Crusoe gains absolute dominion over him. At all times Crusoe has the right to kill" him. Friday "is Crusoe's slave because Crusoe has spared his life." Though it may be true, as Kaplan insists, that Defoe would not have assumed Crusoe's "absolute sovereignty over another human being," Crusoe does make it clear to his new acquisition, who was "still a cannibal in his

---

29. *Defoe and the Idea of Fiction, 1713–1719*, 166. This is from the final chapter of the book, "Ideology and the Island," and Sill's subheading, "Crusoe as a Model for Mankind," puts him in the "Universal-Representative" camp.

nature," that if he attempted ever again to eat human flesh, "I would kill him."[30] And Friday, like Xury, is always "willing" to sacrifice himself. He proves a "faithful, loving, sincere servant" who eventually gives "many testimonials" that "he would have sacrificed his life for the saving mine upon any occasion whatsoever" (211).

In short, the subjection is just about as complete as Novak asserts. A subjection Crusoe clearly relishes, it, together with his initial firing of the musket, forms what Martin Green calls, in his new study of *Robinson Crusoe* and its vast literary progeny, "the supreme sign of white imperialism":

> In the first case, the white man speaks in thunder and lightning, with the voice of a god, and the black man falls down dead. In the second, the good native approaches the white man on his stomach and makes himself his willing slave. This category of motif is concentrated in the last part of the story, but it had premonitions in Crusoe's own experience of slavery, and his dealings with Xury, so it is far from being a single event.[31]

What *is* Crusoe's primary motive in rescuing Friday? Letting the rescued, yet also captured, cannibal know "I was very well pleased with him" (209), Crusoe, as a number of readers have pointed out, echoes the voice of God at the baptism of Jesus. This baptismal symbolism, though critical to the salvation theme of the novel, only partially justifies Paula Backscheider's conclusion that, when Crusoe names Friday, "he is not committing an imperialist act but 'christening' a man given not only his mortal life but hope for eternal life."[32] Crusoe had, to be sure, added to his thoughts about acquiring a "servant" or "perhaps a companion or assistant," the conviction that "I was called plainly by Providence to save this poor creature's life" (206). He soon turns him—an example of Crusoe's prudishness rather than any Defoe parody of the Augustan tradition of rigging out black servants in outlandish costumes—into a decently clothed "Protestant" (241) and, upon reflection, remarks that his own grief was lightened to have been made "an instrument under Providence to save the life, and, for ought I knew, the soul of a poor savage, and bring him to the true knowledge of religion." Reflecting on this, he feels a "secret joy run through every part of my soul, and I frequently rejoyced that ever I was brought to this place, which I had often thought the most dreadful of all afflictions that could possibly have befallen me" (222).

Nevertheless, anticipating developments in the later nineteenth century, the evangelist remains an imperialist. Though the allegedly repentant sinner has undergone a spiritual conversion on the island, he treats Friday pretty much as he had Xury many years earlier. This may be attributable in part to genre, to

30. *Robinson Crusoe*, 210. Novak, *Defoe and the Nature of Man*, 52. Kaplan, "Defoe's Views on Slavery and Racial Prejudice," 20.

31. *The Robinson Crusoe Story*, 23. Green traces the proliferating lineage of the Crusoe story through an astonishing number of English, American, German, French, Swiss, and Scottish versions. However, of the Friday-centered materials I later deal with, Green discusses only Coetzee's *Foe*.

32. *Daniel Defoe: His Life*, 420.

"the static presentation of character in travel narratives." But even Ian Bell, who makes this generic point, concedes that "the parallels between the treatment of Xury and Friday are disquieting, if Crusoe's religious conversion is thought to be effective."[33]

In fact, Crusoe's initial motive in rescuing Friday was less religious than political, and more utilitarian than either. In the dream preceding the rescue, Crusoe had told himself that any cannibal he might save could serve as a "pilot" to help him escape from the island over which he no longer feels himself to be absolute sovereign. There is, of course, no question as to *relative* sovereignty. When he awakens, dejected, to find his dream is only that, Crusoe resolves, since this is the "only way" escape seems possible, "to get a savage into my possession" (203). Later, as a "first" step in communication, having let the rescued man "know his name should be Friday, . . . I likewise taught him to say Master, and then let him know, that was to be my name."[34]

They are, then, to be master and slave, with Friday treated as Kantian or Coleridgean "means" rather than "end"; continuing to dream of escape, Crusoe thinks, "this poor savage might be a *means* to help me" (218). They work together, but the most menial tasks fall to the servant; indeed, as "Friday," the new man may be said to initiate Crusoe's sabbath, the biblical day of rest. No amount of subsequent affection, even "love," changes this fundamental relationship, Friday having sworn by abject gesture, as Crusoe twice tells us, "to be my slave for ever" (207). One leading Defoe critic, noting parallels between *Robinson Crusoe* and *The Tempest,* suggests that in their overcoming of adversities on the island, Crusoe and Friday resemble Shakespeare's Prospero and Ariel.[35] True enough, though in terms of cultural and racial resonances, the contemporary poet Charles Martin, whose *Passages from Friday* is discussed below, seems closer to the truth in associating Master Crusoe and Man Friday with Prospero and Caliban—the latter sharing with Friday a principal role in English literature as symbol of the subject races and, in a number of cultural reclamations by Caribbean writers, as an "inaugural figure." Crusoe's "new companion," however well treated, remains, unlike Ariel, a permanent slave or servant, a "creature" taught "every thing that was proper to make him useful, handy, and helpful" (213).

His status as a Thing rather than a Person, means rather than end, is confirmed in a way that would be most telling to Frederick Douglass, who ends his *Narrative* by triumphantly signing his name. Revealingly, Crusoe, who remains uninterested in his servant's language, never over the years inquires as to "Friday"'s real name. Even after they arrive in England, where they spend five years in which Friday is only once mentioned, he remains a bondman to his master, who, far from rewarding his faithful service by offering to free him, retains him as willing slave,

33. *Defoe's Fiction,* 105.

34. *Robinson Crusoe,* 209. Similarly, when Captain Singleton and his men capture an African prince, the first words they teach him are *Yes, sir* (*Captain Singleton,* 60).

35. John Robert Moore, "*The Tempest* and *Robinson Crusoe.*"

continuing to call him by the label he first pinned on him. Iago is talking about reputation, but his remark is not inappropriate: stolen money is nothing,

> 'Twas mine, 'tis his, and has been slave to thousands;
> But he that filches from me my good name
> Robs me of that which not enriches him,
> And makes me poor indeed.
>
> (*Othello*, III.iii.159–61)

Friday's finale has already been discussed. Crusoe does grieve at the loss of his "old servant," but his final comment after burying Friday at sea—"So ended the life of the most grateful, faithful, honest, and most affectionate servant that ever Man had" (*Farther Adventures* 3:76)—anticipates, though without Samuel Beckett's irony, Hamm's nonchalant "I'm obliged to you, Clov. For your services," as *Endgame*, another variation on the master-slave motif, comes to its close. Almost as painful is the fact that the most sustained episode in which Friday is the featured player involves more-than-Beckettian buffoonery. I mean the encounter with the bear, an episode that must be placed in context.

Having spent ten months, from July to the following April, in England, Crusoe ships to Lisbon to find out more about his Brazilian plantation. Crusoe's addendum—"my man Friday accompanying me very honestly in all these ramblings, and proving a most faithful servant upon all occasions" (275)— comes as a surprise, since Friday's presence during these months was passed over in silence. Though one can imagine all sorts of fictional possibilities in Friday's initiation into this alien world (possibilities explored by later, more empathetic writers), both Defoe and Crusoe seem to have forgotten his very existence. Indeed, when, in their major "rambling," man and master cross "the Pyrenean mountains," Crusoe notes how "poor Friday was really frighted" by the snow and "cold weather, which he had never seen or felt before in his life" (284), forgetting that Friday had just spent an entire winter in England!

Then comes the rather lengthy and novelistically unassimilated interlude with the bear (288–93). Promising to divert Crusoe and his party ("O master! You give me te leave! . . . Me make you good laugh"), Friday, in a display of courage, high spirits, dexterity, and clowning for the white folk, dances round, confuses, and finally shoots the bear, capping off his performance with a fib about having killed bears in his own country. The sole exception to Friday's scrupulous and repeatedly mentioned "honesty," this obvious lie can only have been included to round out his performance as comic entertainer.[36]

36. Friday's claim cannot be an example of yet another Defoe "slip." Earlier in the narrative, Crusoe does report seeing "lyons and tygers" on the Guinea coast (47), but while there are no tigers in Africa, the word, as Angus Ross notes in the Penguin edition, "was applied to the leopard, panther, and animals of similar kind" (315). Defoe would have been as aware as Friday is that there are no bears in the Caribbean.

Friday's shooting of the bear is, incidentally, prefigured by Xury's similar dispatch (muzzle to the animal's ear) of a lion wounded by Crusoe in Africa (49): another of the conscious or unconscious links between Crusoe's black servants.

And it is in a kindred role, that of "white" interpreter, that Friday dies. It may have been for the best. Just as Defoe/Crusoe had forgotten about Friday in England, so he becomes insignificant when he returns with Crusoe to the island after an eight-year absence. Having served his primary purposes, the faithful servant is in the process of becoming just another in a crowd of native faces when he is singled out for one last task by his master. Answering, as always, the call of duty, he dies—heroically, to be sure, but, more in keeping with Crusoe's requirements, "useful, handy, and helpful" to the end.

The Crusoe-Friday relationship shows, among other things, how "the quest for the white man's burden tends to end," as Ian Watt once remarked, "in the discovery of the perfect porter and personal servant." It would almost seem that Defoe—angry enough to write a diatribe entitled *The Indolence and Insufferable Behavior of Servants in England, Duly Inquired Into*—invented the perfect servant in Friday. The cultural and emotional cost to the servant—never duly inquired into by Defoe, or by Coleridge—has been imaginatively explored by, among others, two French novelists: Jean Giraudoux, writing in the 1920s, and Michel Tournier, writing in the 1960s. More recently, the centrality of Friday has been stressed by Charles Martin, in his book-length poetic sequence, *Passages from Friday* (1983); by Elizabeth Bishop, in a poem written in the immediate wake of her years in Brazil; and by several contemporary non-European writers, including the Australian poet A. D. Hope and the South African novelist J. M. Coetzee. In the sections that follow, I will discuss these works, as well as the 1988 film, *Crusoe*.

3

A number of modern Caribbean and Latin American poets, novelists, and literary critics have written their own versions of the Columbus story as well as of Shakespeare's *The Tempest* and Defoe's *Robinson Crusoe*, acts of cultural repossession recently documented by Peter Hulme in *Colonial Encounters*. As Edward Said has noted, such adventures, which "stand guard over the imagination of the New World," have been reinterpreted, not merely in a vindictive or assaultive way, but as imaginative, intellectual, and figurative ways of "reseeing and rethinking the terrain common to whites and non-whites."[37] For example, Aimé Césaire (in *Une Tempête*) and the Cuban critic Roberto Fernández Retamar (in *Caliban and Other Essays*) contend with Shakespeare, choosing Caliban over Prospero and Ariel. Related interventions have resulted in reinterpretations of the Crusoe-Friday story.

I had originally intended to cover, in addition to Giraudoux's *Suzanne et le Pacifique* (1921) and Tournier's prize-winning *Vendredi: ou Les limbes du Pacifique* (1967), a number of modern works that favorably contrast Friday to Crusoe. But the relationship between *Robinson Crusoe* and *Vendredi* has been frequently discussed; and these and other "anti-Robinsons" are briefly synopsized by Pat

---

37. Said, *Culture and Imperialism*, 212. Peter Hulme, *Colonial Encounters: Europe and the Native Caribbean, 1492–1797*.

Rogers and ably treated in Martin Green's 1990 study of the many retellings of the Robinson Crusoe story. As he shows, such fictions as those by Giraudoux and Tournier, as well as Jean Psichari's *Le solitaire du Pacifique* (1922), Muriel Spark's *Robinson* (1958), and William Golding's two well-known novels, *The Lord of the Flies* and *Pincher Martin,* all launch attacks on the "merely" rationalistic values and simpler optimisms of the European Enlightenment.[38]

The French novels in particular satirize British empiricism and imperialism by castigating or simply ridiculing Crusoe's prosaic utilitarianism and colonialist assumptions, while—in appealing, but predictable and somewhat facile contrast—celebrating "native" values. As in Leonard Jeffries' Afrocentrist contrast between cold, materialistic, destructive "ice people" and warm, humanistic, superior "sun people," an antithesis discussed in my survey of the contemporary "culture wars" in the Introduction, the "privileged" term in the old binary opposition is simply reversed, leaving true trimmers mumbling our usual "Yes but. . . ."

With Crusoe condemned or spoofed, Friday emerges as the real hero. Thus, when Giraudoux's shipwrecked heroine, living in luxuriously idle solitude on her island, finds and reads a copy of *Robinson Crusoe,* she hates the main character: a "Puritan weighed down with rationality, certain that he was Providence's only toy," a drudge forever "fastening cords, sawing stakes, and nailing planks," an Englishman "already encumbering his poor island, as his nation would encumber the world, with tin-plate and rubbish," a soulless creature "never dreaming of a woman, devoid of divination, and without instinct." In contrast to the dull utilitarian Crusoe, Friday immediately appeals to this languid fantasist: "Friday plunged into me, to my very heart, by a shorter road than that of a pearl diver. Every thing that Friday thought seemed natural: what he did, [genuinely] useful."[39]

The postmodern Tournier, fully aware of Gallic *jouissance* and of the pleasures of the text, is even more ecstatic. Like Giraudoux's Suzanne, Tournier's Crusoe wants to learn from the natural grace and wisdom of Friday. In the third and final phase of the novel, associated with *l'extase solaire,* Tournier's Crusoe prays, like Nietzsche's Zarathustra, that sun-worshiping apostle of gravity-mocking laughter, to the source of all energy: "Sun, deliver me from gravity. Wash my blood free from its thick humours . . . which spoil the surge of my youth and snuff out my joy in living. . . . Instruct me in irony. Teach me lightness, the laughing acceptance of this day's immediate gifts. . . . Sun, make me like Friday."[40]

This Crusoe, who had formerly dressed to dine and had inscribed all over the island prudential moral maxims from Benjamin Franklin, now lets his hair grow long and becomes sun-bronzed and muscular. He longs for a face like the fifteen-year-old Friday's, "opened up by laughter," and a body like his, carried

38. Green, *The Robinson Crusoe Story.* Rogers, *"Robinson Crusoe,"* 10–16.
39. *Suzanne et le Pacifique,* 226–28.
40. *Vendredi: ou Les limbes du Pacifique,* 217.

with "natural majesty."[41] Tournier's friend, the poststructuralist critic and Nietzsche scholar Gilles Deleuze, writes in the essay published with *Vendredi*, that while Defoe's Crusoe was a limited being, solemnly determined to reproduce England on his island, Tournier's Crusoe opens himself up to the genuinely new and playful. In Deleuze's argument, a kind of postmodern valorization of that "profound superficiality" advocated by Nietzsche in *The Gay Science*, Tournier's Crusoe "discovers superficiality and discards the illusions of depth and weight. Those moral qualities, so suggestive of nineteenth-century humanism as a whole, have been the *bête noirs* of dandy and avant-garde writers for a century. Friday was already superficial, and that is why he could be a twin to Robinson, a double and not an other."[42]

Except for Coetzee's *Foe*, which he covers in two short paragraphs (204–5), Green does not mention the Crusoe "retellings" to which I now turn. Though an extension of what is already an excursus, this discussion adheres to my main theme. Indeed, Bishop's poem (written in the early 1970s) and these other works, written in the 1980s, may be thought of as continuing—like the novels of Giraudoux and Tournier before them—to fill in the moral, racial, and cultural lacunae in Defoe, as well as in Coleridge's annotations on *Robinson Crusoe*.

Hope's 1985 "Man Friday" is set (like Elizabeth Bishop's "Crusoe in England") back in Crusoe's native country—as is most of Coetzee's novel *Foe*, published the following year. In Hope's poem, "The gentle savage, taught to speak and pray, / On England's Desert Island cast away," is presented "handling alien fork or spoon," as "England, less unreal day by day, / The Cannibal Island, ate his past away." His "brooding eye" and "swarthy skin" still "witnessed to the Natural Man within," but gradually the years "Transformed the savage to an Englishman":

> Brushed, barbered, hatted, trousered and baptized,
> He looked, if not completely civilized,
> What came increasingly to be the case:
> An upper servant, conscious of his place,
> Friendly but not familiar in address
> And prompt to please, without obsequiousness,
> Adept to dress, to shave, to carve, to pour
> And skilled to open or refuse the door.

41. *Vendredi*, 221, 228.
42. Deleuze's essay, "Michel Tournier and the World without Others," is synopsized in Green, *The Robinson Crusoe Story*, 193. In an ironic finale to his chapter, Green adds that Tournier's success with the novel (which won an Académie Française prize) enabled him to publish a children's version of the book, translated as *Friday and Robinson: Life on Speranza Island*. This preserves "the nowadays orthodox stress on the importance of Friday," but it also includes "a new appreciation of Robinson's virtues." Thus, Green concludes, "Defoe triumphed over Tournier, and the story triumphed over the teller . . . because when we are thinking of our children and the heritage we bequeath them, we still prefer Defoe. As parents we believe, it seems, in those 'virtues' that we mock in our role as readers" (194–95).

The poem ends when Friday, having accompanied his master on (of course) "business," is awakened in their coastal inn by a sea-storm. "For the first time in all his exiled years / The thunder of the ocean filled his ears." He goes down to the shore and sees in the sand "a single naked footprint." Staring at the ocean,

> suddenly he saw those shores again
> Where Orinoco pours into the main,
> . . . .
> And all his years of exile fell away.

The following noon, Crusoe, following the footprints in the sand, "found / The clothes and shoes and thought his servant drowned":

> Much grieved he sought him up and down the bay
> But never guessed, when later in the day
> They found the body drifting in the foam,
> That Friday had been rescued and gone home.

Though the poet attributes somewhat greater grief to Crusoe than Defoe did on the actual occasion of Friday's death, he is faithful to Defoe's depiction of his hero; Hope's Crusoe, unlike Bishop's, remains unimaginative; he "never guessed. . . ."

In Elizabeth Bishop's "Crusoe in England," a repatriated Crusoe is as alienated in England as is Hope's Friday. Rather than a returning colonist as in Defoe, her Crusoe (like Bishop herself, recently returned from Brazil to New England) is more exiled in civilization than he was as a marooned solitaire. His

> poor old island's still
> un-rediscovered, un-renamable.
> None of the books has ever got it right.

This leaves him lord of his island only in memory and imagination, a faculty he exercised on that island to the extent not merely of reading poetry, but of anachronistically reading Wordsworth, though in a text "full of blanks." He recites

> "They flash upon that inward eye,
> Which is the bliss . . ." The bliss of what?
> One of the first things that I did
> when I got back was look it up.

The missing word is, ironically enough, "solitude" (the word completing the two magnificent lines that, amazingly enough, were supplied to "I Wandered Lonely as a Cloud" by Wordsworth's wife, Mary). But the major "blank" in "Crusoe in England" is the precise relationship between Crusoe and Friday. Just as the "books" are all wrong about the location of his island, so "accounts" of Friday are "all wrong." He "had a pretty body," Crusoe reminisces of "dear Friday"—who, we are informed in the poem's final lines, "died of measles / seventeen years ago come March." Crusoe wishes Friday "had been a woman"; but Elizabeth Bishop—who lived with a woman during her Brazilian years and is, as Octavio Paz once remarked, a splendid poet of "the unsaid"—leaves the rest to our own imaginations.[43]

Except for the haunting epilogue, the story of Coetzee's metafictional novel is "told" to Daniel Foe by Susan Barton, a woman who, cast adrift by Portuguese mutineers off the Brazilian coast, washes up on the shore of an island where she is discovered by a black man. Silently, he takes her to "Robinson Cruso, in the days when he still ruled over his island." She becomes "his second subject, the first being his manservant Friday," who, in this version (a kind of fusion of Xury and Friday), is an African who landed on the island with Cruso when their ship went down.[44]

Coetzee's Friday is mute, his tongue having been cut out either by Moorish "slavers," as Cruso claims (23), or by Cruso himself, as Susan sometimes suspects (84). Friday's lot seems tragic; but, as Cruso observes: "If Providence were to watch over all of us, who would be left to pick the cotton and cut the sugarcane? For the business of the world to prosper, Providence must sometimes wake and sometimes sleep, as lower creatures do" (23). Friday, though not mistreated, is clearly for Cruso such a lower creature—as he is for Susan, until she witnesses his mysterious scattering of flower petals on a seaweed-strewn patch of water near where his and Cruso's ship went down. The ritual signifies to her "a spirit or soul" under his dull exterior (32).

A year after her arrival on the island, they are rescued. Cruso, as reluctant to leave his realm as Kurtz was his in Conrad's *Heart of Darkness,* does leave, only to sicken on the sea-journey back to England. Conveyed ever farther "from the kingdom he pined for," Cruso weakens and, three days from port, dies. What remains is his story (44–45). Under the name of Mrs. Cruso (they *had* made love once), Susan settles into lodgings; Friday is bedded in the cellar, where he does the laundry and grows plump on porridge. She approaches Foe with her account of the history of Cruso and the island in the hope that he will work it up artistically ("you will know how to get it right"), "weaving" it into a "story," she tells Friday, "which will make us famous throughout the land, and rich too" (58). Her hope, hindered by the absence of Foe, who is hounded by bailiffs, is that a commercially successful book can be written "so that Friday can speedily be returned to Africa and I liberated from this drab existence I lead" (63).

The rest of the novel centers on words and the emblematic tonguelessness of Friday. Trying to educate him, Susan has to confess that she often "uses words" only to "subject him to my will. At such times I understand why Cruso preferred not to disturb his muteness. I understand, that is to say, why a man will choose to be a slaveowner. Do you think less of me," she writes Foe, "for this confession?" (60–61). Moving into Foe's vacated house, Susan begins to write the story herself, not only inventing the very details that make *Robinson Crusoe* such a fascinating novel (67), but speculating about such things as Friday's years of submission to Cruso, when he might easily have made the older man *his* slave: "Is there something in the condition of slavehood that invades the heart and

43. "Crusoe in England," 9–19.
44. *Foe,* 11. Subsequent references are made parenthetically in the text.

makes a slave a slave for life . . . ?" (85). She continues to wonder whether it was the slavers or "your master" who cut out Friday's tongue, but she cannot bring herself to look into his mouth.

Along with that silent mouth, what most intrigues her—making Friday least known and most poignant—is still his mysterious strewing of petals at the site of the original shipwreck. "On the sorrows of Friday, I once thought to tell Mr Foe, but did not, a story entire of itself might be built; whereas from the indifference of Cruso there is little to be squeezed" (87). But to Foe, even the story of Cruso seems, at best, an episode in a larger novel, the island material in itself lacking the "light and shade" required to hold the attention of readers. Susan tries to persuade him that "if the story seems stupid, that is only because it so doggedly holds its silence. The shadow whose lack you feel is there: it is the loss of Friday's tongue": "Foe made no reply, and I went on. 'The story of Friday's tongue is a story unable to be told, or unable to be told by me. . . . The true story is buried within Friday, who is mute. The true story will not be heard till by art we have found a means of giving voice to Friday'" (117–18).

Friday has taken to dancing in a kind of trance while wearing Foe's gown and wig; his whirling exposes his nakedness so that Susan can see whether or not he had been spared "a more atrocious mutilation." Though "my eyes were open to what was present to them," the revelation remains ambiguous (119). Susan tries to penetrate Friday's Otherness by entering his world of music, even playing Foe's flutes with him—in vain. Yet, she feels certain that Friday's "desires are not dark," that he "desires to be liberated, as I do too." Susan wants him to be free, but she doubts he could understand what the word means. At Foe's urging, she tries to teach Friday to read. In the meantime, she and Foe make love, twice. The second time she straddles him in (she whispers) "the manner of the Muse when she visits her poets" (140).

The "hard ride" inspires him to recall her description of Friday paddling into the seaweed to strew his petals. Foe imagines the bed of seaweed as the home of the fabulous kraken, whom he pictures "lying on the floor of the sea, staring up through the tangled fronds of weeds at the sky, its many arms furled about it, waiting. It is into this terrible orbit that Friday steers his fragile craft." Foe, almost slumbering, now "surmise[s]" that the ship that carried Cruso and Friday was "a slave-ship, not a merchantman, as Cruso claimed." "Well, then," he continues (140),

> picture the hundreds of his fellow-slaves—or their skeletons—still chained in the wreck, the gay little fish . . . flitting through their eye-sockets and the hollow cases that had held their hearts. Picture Friday above, staring down upon them, casting buds and petals that float a brief while, then sink to settle among the bones of the dead. . . . Till we have spoken the unspoken we have not come to the heart of the story. . . . I said the heart of the story . . . but I should have said the eye, the eye of the story. Friday rows his log of wood across the dark pupil—or the dead socket—of an eye staring up at him from the floor of the sea. He rows across it and is safe. To us he leaves the task of descending into that eye. Otherwise, like him, we sail across the surface and come ashore none the wiser, and resume our old lives.

"Or like a mouth," Susan says, amending Foe's metaphor. "Friday sailed all unwitting across a great mouth . . . that stood open to devour him. It is for us to descend into the mouth, . . . for us to open Friday's mouth and hear what it holds: silence, perhaps, or a roar, like the roar of a seashell held to the ear" (141–42). Foe, though he "intended something else," agrees: "We must make Friday's silence speak, as well as the silence surrounding Friday." Susan responds: "'But who will do it? It is easy enough to lie in bed and say what must be done, but who will dive into the wreck? On the island I told Cruso it should be Friday, with a rope about his middle for safety. But if Friday cannot tell us what he sees, is Friday in my story any more than a figuring (or prefiguring) of another diver?' Foe made no reply" (142).

That other diver, as mysterious as the androgyne in Adrienne Rich's "Diving into the Wreck," descends in the novel's poetic epilogue. This "I" (the empathetic imagination itself?) discovers a number of bodies in the wreck, including that of Susan Barton; but "in the last corner, under the transoms, half buried in sand . . . I come to Friday, . . . a chain about his throat." "What is this ship?" the speaker asks, passing a fingernail across Friday's teeth, "trying to find a way in. His mouth opens. From inside him comes a slow stream, without breath, without interruption. It flows up through his body and out upon me; it passes through the cabin, through the wreck; washing the cliffs and shores of the island, it runs northward and southward to the ends of the earth. Soft and cold, dark and unending, it beats against my eyelids, against the skin of my face" (157).

This symbolic stream,[45] imagined by a contemporary novelist writing out of the experience of apartheid, is still not speech, though it represents an imaginative and empathetic leap in humanity and even eloquence over the pidgin English to which Friday is restricted in Defoe's novel. True, Defoe's Friday "began to talk pretty well," indeed, "fluently, though in broken English" (*Robinson Crusoe*, 215, 223); but as Ian Watt remarks, exaggerating for legitimate

---

45. Magda, in Coetzee's 1982 novel *In the Heart of the Country*, recording in her diary that she knows of no act "that will liberate me into the world," describes herself as "a torrent of sound streaming into the universe, thousands upon thousands of corpuscles weeping, groaning, gnashing their teeth." A kind of infernal, "outer-darkness" variation (via Matt. 8:12) on the "luminous torrents" of feminine *jouissance* in Hélène Cixous and other contemporary feminists, this "torrent of sound streaming into the universe" anticipates by contrast the imaginative expansion of the universe-filling "stream" from Friday's mouth.

That "stream," finally irrepressible despite Friday's tonguelessness, finds an analogue in the irrepressible Salman Rushdie's latest novel, *Haroun and the Sea of Stories*. There, a tyrant, Khattam-shud, "the Prince of Silence and the Foe of Speech," rules over "a place of shadows, of books that wear padlocks and tongues torn out." He hates stories, this "Arch-Enemy of all Stories, even of Language itself" tells Haroun (the only son of Rashid Khalifa, the professional storyteller, known as "Rashid the Ocean of Notions"). The tyrant hates stories because "the world is for Controlling," and "inside every single story, inside every Stream in the Ocean, there lies a world, a story-world that I cannot Rule at all."

effect, a "functional silence, broken only by an occasional 'No, Friday,' or an abject 'Yes, Master,' is the golden music of Crusoe's *île joyeuse.* "[46] With Friday's silence at least symbolically spoken by another diver's art, the novel of "*Daniel Defoe, Author,*" to quote the "placque . . . bolted to the wall of the house" (*Foe,* 155), is finally finished—in a way Defoe could not have imagined, though it would have been within Coleridge's linguistic and moral range. And yet, though his perspective on the politics of enslavement was almost as different from Defoe's as is Coetzee's, Coleridge too was silent, at least in the margins of his copy of *Robinson Crusoe.* Silent on the whole question of Crusoe's involvement in the attempt to bring African slaves to Brazil, he also has nothing to say about Crusoe's "humane" but permanent enslavement of a man who, as an American aborigine, would have ranked just below a European even in Coleridge's Blumenbachian "scale of dignity."

Very different is the most recent treatment of the "Crusoe-Friday" relationship: the 1988 film *Crusoe,* directed by Caleb Deschanel and starring Aidan Quinn in the title role.[47] Here, Crusoe's background as a slaver is thematically crucial, and the island on which he is marooned is not in the Caribbean but off the coast of Africa. Most significantly, the screenplay, written by Walon Green and Christoper Logue, departs from Defoe's novel to give us a hero whose "conversion" is less religious than humanistic: a raising of consciousness that is specifically racial.

The film opens in Tidewater, Virginia. The year is 1808 and Crusoe, an ambitious young slave trader, is successfully tracking down a runaway slave. Shortly thereafter, and in a rare instance of fidelity to Defoe's novel, he sets sail for Africa as super-cargo on a slave-trading expedition, having persuaded a local shipowner that "the pens in Guinea are crammed."

As in the novel, he is the sole human survivor (a dog, "Scamp," swims ashore on his own) of a shipwreck—though, in this case, off the coast of an island located, according to the captain's log, a day's sail from "the Slave Coast." This Crusoe seems to spend about twenty-eight weeks rather than twenty-eight years on the island. Within a few days he finds a human skull and Scamp noses out another skull and assorted bones. Much to Crusoe's grief, and despite his prayers, the dog soon dies; listless and almost inconsolable after he has buried the animal, Crusoe is squatting and staring at the sea when he suddenly spots cannibals arriving in canoes. They bring ashore three victims, their bodies and faces painted for a ritual sacrifice. The throats of two victims are slit, but when Crusoe fires his musket, the third man slips away in the confusion. With the cannibals frightened off, Crusoe brings the man back to his camp.

Though he does not give the rescued man a name, he tells him his own: "Crusoe" and, more to the point, "Master. Can you say, 'Master'?" He feeds and

---

46. *The Rise of the Novel,* 69.

47. Earlier film adaptations, including the unsurrealistic version by surrealist Luis Buñuel, are discussed by Anne Hutta Colvin in her 1989 dissertation, "The Celluloid Crusoe: A Study of Cinematic Robinsonades."

clothes the man, but insists, at pistol-point, on proper table manners. Crusoe manacles his man for the night, but discovers the next morning that he has managed—painfully, as the drops of blood testify—to work himself free from his fetters. Tracking him, he finds the man's severed head lying on the ground near the painted heads of the two earlier victims, suspended like masks from a tree. Crusoe is himself soon suspended from a tree, having stepped into a trap set by another native, whose dress and body-paint identify him as one of the cannibals, apparently left behind when the others panicked.

With the first native, Crusoe had not only designated himself as "Master," but had also wryly joked to the uncomprehending man that he was doubly "lucky" in his new master since "I have no one to sell you to." With this second man, Crusoe's would-be captor (an athletic warrior played by Ade Sapara), there is no question of subservience. After some tense moments, including a desperate fight in quicksand, from which Crusoe is unsentimentally rescued, the two men gradually learn to share the island as equals. They pick up a bare smattering of each other's language, in particular bits of two songs. They also work together, building a canoe. An essentially unspoken understanding develops, including mutual respect. Though as unsentimental as Crusoe's rescue from the quicksand, the bond formed seems genuine.

After some weeks or months, a ship arrives. Crusoe's joy is shattered when, moments after sighting the vessel, he sees his native companion wounded and captured by members of the crew. Cut to the ship's cabin, where we hear that the captive is to be brought back to "civilization" and exhibited as a "cannibal specimen." Crusoe comes aboard, explains his situation, and is promised passage home. During the night he slips up on deck, liberates the prisoner from the pen in which he has been confined, and helps him clamber down to the canoe they built together. Aboard the ship, Crusoe had put on fresh clothes but prominently worn round his neck the captive's necklace of bones; now, as he helps him over the side, he places the necklace around the black man's neck, then watches as he paddles off toward the island.

The film has come full circle, and not only in the immediate sense that the rescuer has been rescued. The original voyage, which ended in shipwreck, had begun with Crusoe's greedy announcement that "the pens in Guinea are crammed"; the film ends with Crusoe, resembling Defoe's hero less than Mark Twain's in *Huckleberry Finn*, freeing a black captive from one such pen. One dozing sailor notices, but does nothing to prevent the liberation—a hint, perhaps, that Crusoe's conversion may be catching. If the Green-Logue screenplay departs wildly from Defoe's novel, it could hardly do otherwise in the 1980s and still be morally palatable on the race question. Despite its unevenness, the film is well intentioned. It is also visually beautiful, and distinguished by haunting music (by Michael Kamen). In the final shot, sound and image coalesce. The ship, with Crusoe aboard, moves off in the distance: a Turner-like seascape at sunrise, with the island in the foreground, water lapping softly on the shore to the plangent sound of the harp.

In terms of both cultural relativism and simple humanity, this film's contemporary credentials are impeccable. As in Tournier's novel, we get a Crusoe who *could* meet the criteria implicit in Coleridge's depiction of him as the Universal Representative, a man whose actions would fully justify Richard Kaplan's at best partially accurate claim that Defoe's novel was an attempt to "break through the barriers of racial prejudice" and "dispel erroneous ideas about primitive man." Linguistically, however—and this is perhaps inherent in the medium— the film is sadly deficient. The single vividly memorable phrase is Crusoe's about the pens in Guinea being crammed, and the only exchange of language on the island consists of two snatches of each other's songs. There remains the need for communication through speech. If in Coetzee's novel, Otherness is valued, this film is at least moving in the direction of Tournier's novel, in which Friday may become, as Deleuze says, "a twin to Robinson, a double and not an other." But the black man in the film—despite the acceptance of his culture made explicit in Crusoe's symbolic wearing of the necklace of human bones— has still not been given a fully human voice.

4

In recently describing deconstruction as not merely a dismantling but a poten- tially "restitutive criticism," Geoffrey Hartman has been advocating what he calls a "Philomela Project," defined as "the restoration of voice to mute classes of people." That call was anticipated by Jean-François Lyotard and, more im- portantly, by a number of contemporary creative writers.[48] In her powerful late novel *Wide Sargasso Sea* (1966), Jean Rhys gave to the young Bertha Mason (Mr. Rochester's first wife) the words Charlotte Brontë had denied her madwoman in the attic in *Jane Eyre*. A similar restitution was enacted about the same time when another writer born in the West Indies, black poet Derek Walcott (the 1992 Nobel Laureate) gave us Defoe's Crusoe as seen through the eyes of a descendant of Friday's. Walcott's Crusoe bears, like Columbus, "the word to savages," altering

> us
> into good Fridays who recite His Praise,
> parroting our master's style and voice
> . . . .
> converted cannibals
> we learn with him to eat the flesh of Christ.[49]

48. Hartman, "Criticism and Restitution," 31. In a 1984 review of Fredric Jameson's *The Political Unconscious: Narrative as a Socially Symbolic Act,* Lyotard calls on contempo- rary historians, no longer able to present history as Hegelian "narrative" and "represen- tation," to give voice to the claims, and redress the grievances of, the "unrepresented," the "mute" subjects and forgotten objects excluded from "traditional" history ("The Unconscious, History, and Phrases: Notes on *The Political Unconscious*").

49. Walcott, "Crusoe's Journal." In his Nobel lecture, "The Antilles: Fragments of Epic Memory," Walcott dwelt at length on the work of Alexis Saint-Léger Léger (St.-John Perse), the first Antillean to win the Nobel Prize (1960), referring not only to *Eloges* and *Anabase,* but also to Perse's first major poem, the 1904 "Images à Crusoe."

Friday finally got to tell his own story at sustained length in Charles Martin's *Passages from Friday*, which, though it refuses to indulge itself in victimization-mongering and the usual facile heaping up of guilt feelings to be borne as the contemporary white man's burden, resembles the restoration of voice to the mute advocated by Lyotard and Hartman. "Friday" actually speaks—indeed, more to Martin's mimetic point, *writes*—in this remarkable fourteen-part sequence, a long poem in uninsistently rhymed quatrains. Since *Passages from Friday*, originally published in a rare edition limited to 260 copies, is still not widely known, I will synopsize it at some length, trying not to sacrifice its tone and texture.[50]

The poem is preceded by an epigraph: the first teaching of Defoe's Crusoe, that *his* name was to be "Friday," and *my* name was to be "Master." Martin's Friday will, he tells us, write as his Master did,

> tho withowt Hope of Recovery
> from this inchanted Island to my owne
> Nation where taken in Captivity
> som Yeers a go.

Invoking Providence, he proceeds, beginning with a retelling of his rescue by Crusoe, a mountain-like man "cover'd all in Hair." Falling in a fright, he had wondered prophetically, "*Have I escap'd the Snell but for the Snare?*" When the "*Mountain* proves *Volcano*, belching Fire," felling one of his pursuers as the other flees from the gunfire, "I place the *Masters* Foot upon my Head": a deft fusion of that thunder, lightning, and willing subjection that Martin Green finds "the supreme sign of white imperialism."

Friday will give "*a true Account of owr Life together / in all Particulars.*" It turns out to have been an endless round of labor—wood-gathering, milking, weeding corn, fetching and laying out of Crusoe's clothes, preparation of goat-stew (Friday gets the leftovers), and heeding the "showt / *Bring him his Jugg.*" If all has "not been as he pleases / as like as not poor *Friday* will be beaten." It is "*because poor* Friday *is a sinner* / that he must *spend his Days gain-fully toiling, / my Master* tells me" (I–II).

Life on the island takes a mythological turn when, in Section III, Crusoe, as anxious as Defoe's hero to build a canoe to escape from the island, tries to cut down a tree Friday had detected groaning. As those versed in folklore and mythology might expect, it turns out to be "no Tree at all, but a Woman's Spryght imprison'd / which, as we cut it, moan'd so piteously" that their axes, "enchanted by / the Sownd," rebound in their hands.[51] Crusoe's hand is cut by the blade of Friday, who took the

---

50. The title poem fills most of the volume (15–40), with a two-page epilogue. (Subsequent references, to section numbers, are made parenthetically in the text.) Though republished in Martin's collection *Steal the Bacon*, and recently discussed by Daniel Hoffman in *Words to Create a World*, this sequence has still not had wide circulation. Charles Martin has, however, gone on to achieve deserved acclaim for his translation and brilliant study of Catullus.

51. Like Arthur's Merlin, Shakespeare's Ariel is magically imprisoned in a tree.

> wounded Hand in mine & lick'd
> the Blood a Way, as any Man wou'd do
> owt of meer Affection.

But Crusoe wrenches his hand away, throws Friday to the ground, and "drives me from him with repeated Kicks & Blows." Religious and practical instructions become more frequent, with Friday "putting the *Cannibal* of earlier Yeers / behind me." But Crusoe retains "Fears / of my Savage Nature. *This* Callibans *a Canniball,* he'd say: *No teaching him.*"

Friday is, of course, more than tractable, performing "even the meaner things he taught me to do," cooking, cleaning-up, sewing, mending, etc. Nevertheless, Crusoe's "Melancholy seem'd ownly to increes / as tho' in his Innards a low Feaver burn'd." Nodding off over his manuscript, Friday dreams of how Crusoe once murdered all their domesticated animals:

> He had slyt ther Throats
> & as they twitch'd and skitter'd on the Grownd
> he hack'd & slash'd at thes poor harm-less
> Goats.

Ordered to build a great fire into which the animals, some still living, were cast, Friday fearfully obeys, "sutch whippings & picklings as I receiv'd / whenever I objected or gainsay'd him."

Following this holocaustal digression, Friday returns in Section VI to his account of the tree they were cutting down for their canoe. That task is made possible when Friday casts a spell "to quieten the Womans Spirit," but as the canoe is shaped, the curved figure of "*the Woman that was hid*" becomes evident even to Crusoe. To Friday, she seems

> a Woman of my race
> by Virtue of her Colour, dark as the Grayn
> of that *Mahogonee* in which we found her.

Readers will recall Daphne fleeing from Apollo as Friday imagines her having escaped from cannibal captors,

> and running off as I did,
> but finding no *Master,* no Deliverance

Though *The Tempest* is explicitly alluded to in Charles Martin's poem, he seems also to be thinking of such mythological scenes as those we encounter in Virgil, Ovid, Dante (*Inferno XIII*), Ariosto, and Spenser. When, in the first canto of *The Faerie Queene,* the Redcrosse Knight plucks a bough to make a garland for his newfound lady's head, blood trickles from the rift and a "piteous yelling voyce" cries for mercy and warns the knight to flee, "for feare / Least to you hap, that happened to me heare" (I.ii.31). In an 1892 article on folklore, W. B. Yeats refers to the dramatic way in which Spenser's Fradubio, "once a man . . . now a tree," makes his presence known. One need not, Yeats wrote, go to Dante or Spenser to find stories of "living trees that cry and bleed if you break off a bough" (*Uncollected Prose by W. B. Yeats* 1:284). The spirit imprisoned in the tree in Martin's poem warns Friday to flee, and, eventually, even offers herself as the means.

> from her persuing Enemies, she hid
> her-self by taking leave of her Womans
>
> Body & becoming at once a meer Tree;
> her Roots sunk down, her Branches lifted high
> she blossom'd into a Security
> that lasted untill we 2 hapn'd by.
>
> (VI)

Of her "sever'd Branches," Friday later made seven *"European Figur Fetisches"* to ward off savages and to attract ships. These figures, "with Musket in one Hand & naked Blade / in the other, scowling ferociously," stood, "fix'd in ther Places as tho' in a Trance, / staring with painted Eyes at the great Ocean" (VII). But that was later; at the time, Friday's work consisted of most of the manual labor for preparing the inland canoe for launching. (In Defoe's novel, Crusoe laboriously carves a huge canoe out of a log—only to discover he has no way of transporting it to water [146].) Friday, Crusoe tells him, would be

> *a Beast of Burden, which do not complayn*
> *no matter how heavy the Tasks theyr made to do*
> . . . .
> Whenever Shoulders were needed, *Fridays* bent;
> whenever Decisions, *Master* decided.

The task proves difficult. In a passage reminiscent of those earlier "anti-Robinsons" by Giraudoux and Tournier, Friday sets Crusoe's Western mixture of religiosity, utilitarianism, and "mastery" over against native grace, animism, and kinship with the natural world:

> for nothing he ever did was done with Ease
> of Natur; for, according to *Providence,*
> all Things had Value ownly from ther *Use,*
> & had no *Feelings* nor *Intelligence,*
>
> which we call *Spirit;* and which they did withowt;
> he call'd me *Savage,* that I cou'd not see
> how Things were Tools & how thes Tools allow'd
> us to master mor Things; for it appear'd to me
>
> that it was them that master'd us. . . .
>
> (VIII)

After two months of work maneuvering the craft on rollers to a stream Crusoe knew became a torrent in the rainy season, they sling it between two trees. While Crusoe sleeps in a tent, Friday, sleeping hammock-like in the suspended canoe, dreams that he is slumbering in his mother's womb (perhaps suggesting a reunion of Shakespeare's Caliban and *his* mother, the Sycorax who had incarcerated Ariel in a tree, but now herself a benevolent victim). He is awakened by a sudden rush of water that launches him on the swollen river, at once depriving Crusoe of "his ownly Servant & his Deliverance." What happened after this, Friday rightly tells us, "was Wonder-full." As in his dream,

Wood melted into Flesh
& a warm Hand press'd me to the Hull
a Hull no longer.

    For the Flood releas'd
the Woman that was hid in the *Canoo*
& with me clinging tightly to her Waist
she swum & frollick'd like a *Whale* or *Sea Cow;*

I was no longer affraid now of Death,
tho' we dove down Water-Falls immensly high
into the deep Pools that had form'd beneath,
then let the Current take us by & by

the 2 of us at one with the Water
& she cavorting in it merrily
& the arch'd Trees echoing with her Laughter;
As *Dolphins* carry Children, she carry'd me

my Arms & Legs secure a bowt her fastned:
When she roll'd over on her Belly, I twin'd her
Hair in my Hands
               great Coils of black Hair glisten'd
like *Water-Serpents* streaming owt behind her.

                       (IX)

Those glistening "Water-Serpents" suggest a recollection of Coleridge's suddenly beautiful and "glossy" water-snakes at the crucial moment in *The Ancient Mariner,* but that is another story, one taken up in the second part of the present study.

Following this marvelous journey, the next section of the poem opens with Crusoe questioning Friday at the river's mouth. The servant tells his master that the canoe had "chang'd into the Woman who had been / trapp'd in the Tree," and that, when he "gather'd that she meant to quit / the Island altogether," and he was forced to "choose betwicks my *Freedom* & my *Master,* / to whom I ow'd so mutch" ("here, *Master* nodded"), he had prodded the Woman's "Flanks with my Toes to-wards the Island." Looking at him with a sad smile, "*as at a poor bedraggl'd pup,*" the Tree-Woman deposited him within swimming distance of the island, then disappeared. In a short and poignant statement, Friday says, "I never saw that Woman any more." Having listened skeptically to this tale, Crusoe "totter'd off on down the beach," returning with pieces of wood he said were "from the broaken-up *Canoo.*" "Not possible," says Friday, but empirical Crusoe ignores his account, which "*did not make Sense,*" and accuses his servant of trying to "*mock both him &* Providence" (X).

The loss of the canoe and thus of "Deliverance" prove "*1 Disaster / too many*" for Crusoe, who soon grows absentminded and given to "wandering off / into the Woods with his Jugg of Raisin Wine." On one such drunken expedition, he stumbles down a steep slope, a fall that shatters his jug and leaves him the helpless victim of a paralytic stroke, "incapable of Movement or Speech." Crusoe does not recover, despite the nursing of faithful Friday, who, preparing a "Ceremony proper to insure / his Souls Release," repeats Christ's words at the Last Supper: "*Take ye & eat / of my owne Flesh in the Remembrance of me.*" Hearing these words, speechless Crusoe is "mutch agitated," yet, claims Friday, "very pleas'd, as ownly I cou'd see" (XI). The possibility that Friday, reverting to cannibalism, eats of Crusoe's flesh is left hanging during the next section, a detailed set of instructions for the skinning of a goat, whose skin—cleaned, dried, and softened—"will mutch resemble his / & may be us'd as Parchment for your Quill" (XII).

Now entirely alone, without orders to obey and at a loss for something to do, Friday begins to carve the wooden figure fetishes mentioned earlier. Godlike, he creates Europeans and a ship; he adds "Heathens," made up of remnants of a cannibal feast, arranging in tableau "my brave Crew menac'd by *Cannibals* / & my larger Figurs watching from above." But "after a while," Friday, suffering an obvious crisis of identity and a proto-Marxian alienation from the artifacts created by his own labor,

> grew troubl'd in Mind,
> & my Heart pounded & I was mutch affraid;
> for when I look'd, no wher cou'd I find
> no Place for Friday in what Friday made;
>
> then I was suddenly stricken & the Sun
> seem'd to fly In-side my poor bursting Skull
> & I stumbl'd dizzily a while & then
> fell down the way that dead Mens Bodys fall.
>   (XIII)

In feverish dreams, self-divided Friday, pursued by fiends in human shape, runs "betwicks the Forest & the Ocean, / but burthen'd with my Masters Cloaths & Goods." He comes to that "Poynt in the Woods" where Crusoe originally "lept out to my Assistance," but now there is no Master to deliver him from the howling fiends closing in on him. He can only try to run faster, though encumbered by Crusoe's clothes and alien gear, including a musket he dare not pause to load. Seized, he is

> *flung upon my Back*
> *environ'd by Cannibals that pin me down*
> *whil others of them commence to chop & hack;*
> *the Savage Face I look into is mine*
>
> *no longer.*

Friday awakens to find himself "in Bed, unhurt." Though "puzzl'd, per-plex'd, *as in the deepest Doubt,*" he is sufficiently recovered the following morn-ing to venture abroad, dressed (as in his dream) in Crusoe's goatskin and hat, and carrying "his Rifle & his Powder-Horn" and "his Umbrella." He feels driven by some mysterious Spirit to "*run a Way from Home,*" but why and where he cannot say:

for it was not I who set owt, nor was it him,
nor was it the both of us to-gether;
I know not who it was; but, as in my Dream
of the Night befor, when I was neither

Master nor *Friday,* but I partook of each,
so it was that Morning. Whatever my Intention
I find myself walking on that Beach
to-wards that Poynt which I have earlier mention'd

and when I pass it by un-harm'd, I collaps
upon the Sand   *I lay ther in great Fear*
for a great long Time   no Savage Shapes
assail mine Eye   no screeching payns mine Ear

(XIV)

Though, as the opening of the poem confirms, there is no hope of returning to his true "home," Friday, at poem's close, at last takes imaginative possession of the "inchanted Island" formerly ruled by Crusoe, of whom Friday may have "partook" in more senses than one. Appropriately, his passing of the critical Point "unharm'd" and his final assertion of liberation from savage sights and colonialist sounds ("no screeching payns mine Ear") recall dispossessed Caliban's imaginative possession of *his* enchanted island: his enjoyment of the sounds that "hum about mine ears" in the exquisitely unsavage passage beginning, "Be not afeard, the isle is full of noises, / Sounds, and sweet airs, that give delight and hurt not."[52]

Thus ends Friday's poem, but Martin adds an epilogue in heroic couplets entitled "Mr. Dorrington's Discovery, ca. 1727." The inside joke is that *The*

52. *The Tempest* III.ii.131–32. By having Caliban described by his sometime tutor, the gentle Miranda, as an "abhorred slave, / Which any print of goodness will not take" (I.ii.351–52) and by Prospero as "a born devil, on whose nature / Nurture can never stick" (IV.i.188–89), Shakespeare makes the ineducable "savage" a fit colonial subject or slave. At the same time, however, the brutish "gabble" of Caliban issues in what Stephen Greenblatt calls a "discordant voice," at odds with Prospero's mastery of an island Caliban's by right of inheritance: "This island's mine, by Sycorax my mother, / Which thou taks't from me, / . . . / Which first was mine own king" (I.ii.331–32, 342). Yes but. One sympathizes with Caliban, but both he and his anticolonialist critical supporters seem to forget that Sycorax originally took the island from Ariel, whom she imprisoned. Whether or not that freedom-loving and hardly possessive spirit can be called indigenous, his claim to the island would surely have priority. In any case, Caliban doesn't triumph in *The Tempest.* It would, as Greenblatt notes with writers like Césaire and Retamar in mind, "take different artists from different cultures—the postcolonial and African cultures of our own time—to rewrite Shakespeare's play and make good on Caliban's claim. But even within the powerful constraints of Shakespeare's Jacobean culture, the artist's imaginative mobility enables him to display cracks in the glacial front of princely power and to record a voice, the voice of the displaced and oppressed, that is heard scarcely anywhere else in his own time. If it is the task of cultural criticism to decipher the power of Prospero, it is equally the task to hear the accents of Caliban" ("Culture," 232).

English Hermit, that early Coleridgean favorite ascribed to Philip Quarll and dated 1727, was written by an unknown author using the pseudonym "Edward Dorrington," and pretending to have "lately discovered" Quarll on an uninhabited island.

In Martin's epilogue, an English crew, landing on "an unchartered / Island near the Mowth of the great River / *Oronooko*," finds "a very agreeable yong Savage, attir'd / in a Suit of Goat Skins." The native explains to them in their own language how a planter, who has since died, was his tailor. "Friday (for that was the name the Planter gave him)" identifies himself as a "Caribb *Prince*," who, having "escap'd" from cannibals, lived on the island for nearly fifteen years with this planter, who taught him English. "This evening," says Dorrington, the savage

> spoke of unseen Powers
> & rav'd delerious, for several Howres.
> Beside him lay a Goat Skin-Leather Cape
> roughly cut into a Mans own Shape.
> Earnestly he begg'd me to examine
> this Heathen Fetisch; but an inhumane
> Stench assail'd me when I try'd to do it,
> for a Multitude of Worms had tunnel'd through it,
> as Sappers do, to undermine a City
> & left it scribbl'd with their rude *Graffiti*.
> I ask'd, *Is this your own Divinity?*
> *All Things do say O to him*, was his reply. . . .

Thematic emphases to be developed later require a momentary pause at this point. For this "reply," here perhaps an openmouthed intimation of cannibalism, echoes *Defoe's* Friday, who, at the outset of his instruction "in the knowledge of the true God," tells Crusoe about his own native deity, *Benamuckee*. "*All things do say O to him*," says Friday, explaining (218) that the old god dwells atop a great mountain, whither the priests of his people "went to say *O* (so he called saying prayers). . . ."

The passage, in which Crusoe equates Benamuckee with "the devil" and tries "to clear up this fraud to my man Friday" (219), was recalled not only by Charles Martin but by Coleridge. He ends an untitled notebook poem of 1807 with the literally striking image of "a child beneath its master's blow," who "Shrills out at once its task and its affright." The uneven relationship—that of what Wordsworth called, in one of the lines of the Intimations ode criticized by Coleridge, "a master o'er a slave"—resembles that of Crusoe (at once missionary, instructor, and slave-master) and Friday, a potential convert who is also Crusoe's submissive bondman. In Coleridge's poem, though "all is blank on high" and "No constellations alphabet the sky," the Heavens *do* show "one large Black Letter." Despite his likely theme (the poem was later entitled by E. H. Coleridge "Coeli Enarrant" ["The heavens declare the glory of God"]), despite a passage in *The Friend* (I 512–13) in which an "unlettered African" or "rude yet musing Indian" confronting a Bible is instructed by a "friendly missionary," and despite the Pauline echo of a "whole world groaning for deliverance," Coleridge's final lines, governed by the simile of a frightened "child" crying out beneath its master's blows, suggest not so much illumination and deliverance as submission to a *divine*, Miltonic taskmaster. Just "as" the punished pupil "shrills out" his reading lesson and his fear, so "The groaning world now learns to read aright, / And with its Voice of Voices cries out O!"[53]

In this final metamorphosis, in "Mr. Dorrington's Discovery," the remains of the Crusoe worshiped by Defoe's Friday—a type of that "great Father" to whom, according to the ancient Mariner, each "bends"—is fetishized by Charles Martin's Friday. Martin's poem concludes with Friday giving the divine fetish to whom "*All things do say O*" to his rescuer, Dorrington,

> charging me to keep
> it for him safely. With that, he fell a Sleep
> and I remov'd my Self, taking his Parcell,
> which, as I say, reek'd like the very Devill
> and was, no Doubt, the source of his Feaver.
> I gave it to my Man to throw it over-
> board and now have some Hope he may recover.

At last separated from the worm-tunneled and devilishly reeking remnants of Crusoe, an all-too-human Benamuckee and the source of his fever in a more profound sense than Captain Dorrington and *his* "man" can imagine, "Friday" may well "recover." We know from the main poem, however, that he is "withowt Hope of Recovery" regarding "my owne / Nation," and that he will never again see that mythical Woman, the Tree Spirit whose wood had melted into flesh and who had held forth the promise of complete freedom.

---

53. *CN* II 3107; *CPW* I 486. A positive (or unsubverted) reading is offered by John Hodgson ("Coleridge's 'Coeli Enarrant' and a Source in *Robinson Crusoe*"), who also notes both the passage in *The Friend* and the echo of Friday's explanation of "O" to catechizing Crusoe. My alternative emphasis here is meant only to suggest darker possibilities relevant to connections made in Part Two, where I associate the conclusion of Milton's Adam ("I learn that to obey is best, / And love with fear the only God") with the sadistic boast of the Inquisitor in Coleridge's *Osorio* ("If a man fears me, he is forced to love me"), and with the simile in *The Ancient Mariner* in which the calmed ocean is said to be "Still as a Slave before his Lord"—a reverentially religious image subverted by a master-slave trope that may support my "political" reading of *that* poem.

3

Coleridge, Crusoe, and
The Ancient Mariner

1

In Charles Martin's poem, Friday—already elevated to a central position in a number of other twentieth-century retellings—finally speaks in a voice that seems as close to "his own" as literary convention will allow: pidgin English, but eloquent. Our central concern, however, remains Coleridge's silence in the margins of his copy of *Robinson Crusoe*. For the typical reader, Crusoe's slave-connected activities and master-slave relationship with Friday, both in *Robinson Crusoe* and in the *Farther Adventures,*[1] might be no more than a reflection of the mercantile times, the hero still emerging as the representative of mankind. But in this context, Coleridge was not a typical reader.

He would come in time to advance some racial theories based on a dubious anthropology in sorry conflict with his early egalitarianism. He would, as the years passed, have less to say explicitly on the abolition question, and even express the fears of an increasingly conservative "true trimmer" when that "tremendous" and "unprecedented . . . positive enactment," abolition, finally became law in 1833 (*TT* I 386). Though Coleridge never reneged on his commitment to the ideal of human freedom, the old man who expressed misgivings about manumission to Thomas Pringle was not the youth who had earlier embraced the French concepts of liberty, equality, fraternity. Nevertheless, in a long lifetime of writing on social and political subjects, Coleridge attacked nothing more passionately than slavery and the slave trade. The Bristol lecture and *Watchman* essay contains his most fiery outburst on the subject, but first a

---

1. After the old Crusoe returns to the island, in the second novel, he plans to turn a quick profit by selling the pacified cannibals as slaves. A priest persuades him to emancipate them; it is not humanitarianism, however, but an economic motive—population growth as a route to prosperity—that is the deciding factor. Though "grown old in affliction," the Crusoe of the *Serious Reflections* remains both a colonialist and a missionary. In the sixth section, Crusoe/Defoe proposes a crusade "to beat paganism out of the world." There would be "just and generous behaviour to the natives, or at least to such of them as should show themselves willing to submit" (*The Works of Daniel Defoe* 3:225, 240). For a recent discussion of colonialism in the *Serious Reflections*, see Fakrul Alam, "Religious and Linguistic Colonialism in Defoe's Fiction."

more personal illustration of his attitude during the 1790s may be of interest, especially since it provides a striking contrast to that of "Master" Crusoe.

One of the most revealing differences of opinion between the cofounders of Pantisocracy had to do with the status of the Southey family's black servants. Both Coleridge and Southey wanted Shadrach Weeks and his wife, Sally, to join them, but Coleridge insisted that the relationship be one of total equality: "SHAD GOES WITH US. HE IS MY BROTHER" (*CL* I 103). Southey, while he agreed on equality in the abstract, and had just completed a sequence of sonnets condemning the slave trade, failed to see why his aunt's servants should not continue as such—to perform, on the banks of the Susquehanna, "that part of labour for which their education has fitted them."[2]

Coleridge was deeply grieved. "*Southey* should not have written this sentence. My friend, my noble and high-souled friend. . . . Is every family to possess one of these unequal equals, these Helot Egalité-s?" (*CL* I 114). When Southey persisted in his inability to "*perceive* the error," Coleridge began to have prophetic doubts about the whole scheme of Pantisocracy. Out of his unhappiness came a noble statement on the "introduction of servitude into our society":

> Oxen and Horses possess not intellectual Appetites—nor the powers of acquiring them. We are therefore Justified in employing their Labour to our own Benefit. Mind hath a divine Right of Sovereignty over Body. But who shall dare to Transfer "from Man to Brute" to "from Man to Man"? To be employed in the Toil of the Field while we are pursuing philosophical Studies—can Earldoms or Emperor-ships boast so huge an Inequality? Is there a human being of so torpid a Nature, as that placed in our Society he would not feel it?—a *willing* Slave is the worst of Slaves—His Soul is a Slave.[3]

We can understand how the man who wrote this might be excited by Defoe's "Pantisocratic" intellectual, Captain Mission, discussed earlier, but it is strange, even given his later shift in attitude, that he would have nothing to say about the island emperorship and the willing slavery so lovingly detailed in *Robinson Crusoe*.

Quite aside from his relationship with Friday, Crusoe personally sells at least one human being, owns at least one other, had, before his captivity in Sallee, engaged in buying "Negroes . . . in great numbers," and is again on his way to becoming a full-scale slave trader when Providence deposits him instead on his island. Coleridge, in sharp contrast, spoke out against the slave trade with compassion and indignant wrath. In the course of "On the Slave Trade," he refers to "enormities, at which a Caligula might have turned pale," to a "tartarean conspiracy" of "kidnappers and assassins" (*W* 136–37). If his proposed solution—that people "leave off . . . Sugar and Rum" (138)—seems naive, we must remember, not only that the cause of the slave trade was the demand for

2. Coleridge quotes Southey to this effect in his letter of October 21, 1794 (*CL* I 114).
3. *CL* I 122. A quarter-century later Coleridge repeated that final phrase. To have no hope of a better life for one's children or grandchildren is to "have the Soul of a Slave" (*Inquiring Spirit*, 318; an 1819 note on a book by Heinrich Steffens). Cf. 35: what makes one a slave "is the being in a state out of which he cannot hope to rise."

its products, but also that, at the time he published this article (both in 1795, in *Conciones ad Populum,* and in 1796, in the *Watchman*), Coleridge believed the cure lay less in legislation than in a basic change of attitude on the part of individuals. Individual illumination as the necessary prerequisite to general social reform remained a central Coleridgean theme. That he later reversed himself in the case of the slave trade, arguing as late as 1818 that in this case legislation *was* necessary, indicates, if anything, the intensification of his opposition a quarter of a century after his ode and later Bristol address and article against the slave trade.

His proposal in "On the Slave Trade" that people boycott sugar and rum leads directly into one of the most violently purple passages in all of Coleridge's voluminous prose:

> Will God bless the food which is polluted with the Blood of his own innocent children? Surely if the inspired Philanthropist of Galilee were to revisit Earth, and be among the Feasters as at Cana, he would not now change water into wine, but convert the produce into the things producing, the occasion into the things occasioned. Then with our fleshly eye should we behold what even now Imagination ought to paint to us; instead of conserves, tears and blood, and for music, groanings and the loud peals of the lash!
>
> There is observable among the Many a false and bastard sensibility that prompts them to remove those evils alone, which by hideous spectacle or clamorous outcry are present to their senses, and disturb their selfish enjoyments. Other miseries, though equally certain and far more horrible, they not only do not endeavor to remedy—they support, they fatten on them. Provided the dunghill be not before their parlour window, they are well content to know that it exists, and that it is the hot-bed of their pestilent luxuries.—To this grievous failing we must attribute the frequency of wars, and the continuance of the Slave-trade. The merchant finds no argument against it in his ledger: the citizen at the crouded feast is not nauseated by the stench and filth of the slave-vessel—the fine lady's nerves are not shattered by the shrieks! She sips a beverage sweetened with human blood, even while she is weeping over the refined sorrows of Werter or of Clementina. (*W* 139)

I have quoted this passage at length because it confirms the depth and passion of Coleridge's loathing, and because the mention of the merchant and his "ledger" serves to point up the contrast between Coleridge and Crusoe—or between Coleridge and Defoe. Yet for the annotator, the author of *Robinson Crusoe* was "a true philanthropist" (*CM* I 163); guilt by association is extended, not to Defoe and Crusoe, but to the creators of Werther and Clementina. In alluding to the novel *Sir Charles Grandison,* our polemicist manages to drag the hyper-moral Samuel Richardson (whom Coleridge at once admired and despised) away from the delicacies of the escritoire into the very stench and blood of the slave ship. Fine, but if Coleridge wished to allude to an eighteenth-century novel in the context of an essay on the slave trade, he might well have spared poor Richardson and Goethe, and attacked instead Defoe and the hero of *Robinson Crusoe,* both of them directly involved in that traffic, Crusoe as slaver, Defoe as investor and apologist.

Of course, since Coleridge's immediate target is the refined, effeminate sensibility that falls short of genuine moral benevolence, *The Sorrows of Young Werther* and a novel of Richardson are more apropos. Revealingly, portions of this passage reappeared thirty years later, in *Aids to Reflection,* in an attack that relates "Sensibility" with "effeminate Selfishness"; the memorable image of the "dunghill" that is "not before their parlour window" is repeated, but *without* specific reference to slavery and the slave trade.[4] The omission seems another indication of Coleridge's attitudinal shift on the question. But even this does not explain the failure of a reader addicted to marginal commentary to jot so much as a word in the margins of a novel some of whose pages practically cry out for comment on the subject of slavery—especially when the reader was a man who spent years not only annotating books but inveighing against the slave trade as well, and whose transubstantiating imagination was once vivid enough to sweeten Milady's tea with the blood of black slaves.[5]

Whatever his shifting political and racial attitudes, Coleridge certainly never endorsed slavery. Yet he pronounces Robinson Crusoe humanity's *Universal* Representative, an odd designation for a man who met his fate as a direct result of his activities as a slave trader. There can be only one explanation—and it too proves inadequate—for so glaring an omission. Coleridge's silence on Crusoe as slaver (or, for that matter, as selfish economic hustler) becomes partially explicable when we read *Robinson Crusoe* as Coleridge read it. His approach to the book is anything but mysterious; and in its very simplicity it illuminates a relationship between this novel and Coleridge's greatest poem. I turn now to that relationship, and to the ineradicable differences that yet remain to separate Coleridge from Crusoe, this allegedly "Universal Representative" of mankind.

The essential and—it would *seem*—all-illuminating truth of the matter is that despite the fact that most of his marginal notes on *Robinson Crusoe* are of a religious nature, Coleridge saw the novel as a work of pure imagination, beyond mundane considerations of social morality. This despite the novel's "every-day matter-of-fact *Realness.*" The "Rob. Crusoe," Coleridge continued in his mar-

4. In *Aids to Reflection* (1825), Coleridge describes "sensibility" as an "ornament . . . of Virtue," which "may almost be said to *become* Virtue," but which remains "not even a sure pledge of a GOOD HEART." As a mere "quality of the nerves," it may or may not be founded on accurate moral perception. In addition to repeating the "dunghill" image, he also goes back to the mid-nineties to quote his 1795 poem, "Reflections on Having Left a Place of Retirement," which had attacked "sluggard Pity's vision-weaving Tribe," consisting of those "Who sigh for Wretchedness, yet shun the Wretched, / Nursing in some delicious solitude / Their slothful loves and dainty sympathies" (lines 55–59; *AR* 59).

5. Coleridge's fine lady who "sips a beverage sweetened with human blood" may have acquired her taste from one of Southey's six sonnets concerning the slave trade, poems written in Bristol in 1794. Number III addresses "Ye who at your ease / Sip the blood-sweetened beverage" while the poet feels his cheek glow with "indignation, when beneath the rod / A sable brother writhes in silent woe" (*The Poetical Works of Robert Southey* 1:66).

ginal note, "is like the Vision of a happy Night-mair, such as a Denizen of Elysium might be supposed to have from a little excess in his Nectar and Ambrosia Supper. Our imagination is kept in full play, excited to the highest; yet all the while we are touching or touched by, common Flesh and Blood" (*CM* I 167). The combination of food and reading recalls a strange remark made by Coleridge to James Gillman. "Conceive what I must have been at fourteen," said Coleridge, recalling his days as an orphan and exile at Christ's Hospital, often hungry and reading obsessively: "My whole being was, with eyes closed to every object of present sense, to crumple myself up in a sunny corner and read, read, read— fancy myself on Robinson Crusoe's island, finding a mountain of plum-cake . . . hunger and fancy!"[6] Only a few months before his death, in a letter of March 18, 1834, referring to "entertaining & fascinating . . . modern Travels & Voyages," Coleridge lists first his old favorite, *Robinson Crusoe* (*CL* VI 979).

His emphasis on *Robinson Crusoe* as an imaginative fantasy, an escapist romance, had earlier been made when, in the course of a rather random lecture touching on (among much else) the *Arabian Nights,* he paused to discuss, as another example of a book that "cause[s] no deep feeling of a moral kind," his other childhood favorite, *Robinson Crusoe.* "It always interests," he says, "never agitates." And, after noting again that Crusoe is "merely a representative of mankind," he concludes: "You will observe that all that is wonderful in this tale is the result of external circumstances—of things which fortune brings to Crusoe's hand."[7] Thus Crusoe is not only an Everyman, but an Everyman in a happy nightmare, a man more acted upon than acting, and thus, perhaps, incapable of being a moral agent. These comments are valuable, and not only because they suggest one possible explanation for Coleridge's failure to pass moral judgment on Crusoe. Because of what he says, and the context in which he says it, they also throw unexpected light on one of several connections between Defoe's novel and *The Ancient Mariner.*

Perhaps the single most famous comment on Coleridge's poem is his own reply to Mrs. Barbauld's obtuse complaint that it "had no moral." Though not the most accurate version, the response is best known in the form presented by Henry Nelson Coleridge in 1835:

> I told her that in my own judgment the poem had too much; and that the only, or chief fault . . . was the obtrusion of the moral sentiment so openly on the reader as a principle or cause of action in a work of such pure imagination. It ought to

6. Recorded in James Gillman, *The Life of Samuel Taylor Coleridge* 1:20.

7. *Miscellaneous Criticism,* 193–94. Coleridge once praised one of John Thelwall's political pamphlets on the ground that it "exert[s] the intellect without agitating the passions" (*CL* I 307). Only once, and then peripherally, does Coleridge become politically agitated in his *Crusoe* marginalia: he admires but cannot share Defoe's "philanthropy" toward the Spaniards, whose cruelty Coleridge insists cannot be acquitted, "in America, the Netherlands, the Inquisition, the late Guerilla warfare" (*CM* I 163). Defoe in fact levels a similar critique of "Spanish cruelty," both in *A Reformation of Manners* and in *Robinson Crusoe* (178); but, in general, he argued for amicable relations between England and Spain.

have no more moral that the Arabian Night's tale of the merchant's sitting down to eat dates by the side of a well, and, throwing the shells aside, and lo! a genie starts up, and says he *must* kill the aforesaid merchant *because* one of the date shells had, it seems, put out the eye of the genie's son.[8]

The specific reference to the *Arabian Nights* in Coleridge's response to Mrs. Barbauld, a reference enhanced by John B. Beer's connection of *The Ancient Mariner* with Richard Hole's *Remarks on the Arabian Nights' Entertainment* (1797),[9] taken together with Coleridge's previous linking of the *Arabian Nights* with Defoe's novel, make it possible for us (by a form of logical substitution) to say that Coleridge thought his poem "ought to have no more moral" than did *Robinson Crusoe*. Interestingly enough, the date of the famous remark to Mrs. Barbauld was 1830, the same year as the *Crusoe* marginalia.

A second link between poem and novel is forged when we join Coleridge's statements that Crusoe is a "representative of mankind in general" and that "everything wonderful in this tale is the result of things which fortune brings to Crusoe's hand," and compare these two points with Wordsworth's well known and ungenerous objections to the "Poem of my Friend." His two main complaints were "first, that the principal person has no distinct character . . . secondly, that he does not act, but is continually acted upon." One might object that the Mariner in fact does act at certain critical moments (as, incidentally, does Crusoe, who is, as a young man, less passive than he pretends) or reply, as Charles Lamb did in a letter to Wordsworth, that these were not defects, but qualities for which Coleridge had successfully striven.[10]

Bringing these scattered comments together suggests that Defoe's book and hero had a good deal to do with both the aim and the hero of *The Ancient Mariner.* That should come as no surprise given the works' shared and intertwined motifs of sea, sin, and solitude; guilt, remorse, deliverance, repatriation, and at least partial redemption. Furthermore, what David Blewitt refers to as the novel's "larger theme" of "imprisonment" and "bondage" in sin also fig-

---

8. As recorded by H. N. Coleridge, the comment (ascribed to May 31, 1830) consolidated a sentence dated May 30, 1830 ("The fault of the Ancient Mariner consists in making the moral sentiment too apparent and bringing it in too much as a principle or cause in a work of such pure imagination" [*TT* I 149]) with what would seem to be the actual response to Mrs. Barbauld, who "told me that the only faults she found with the Ancient Mariner were—that it was improbable, and had no moral. As for the probability— to be sure that might admit some question—but I told her that in my judgment the chief fault of the poem was that it had too much moral, and that too openly obtruded on the reader. It ought to have had no more moral than the story of the merchant sitting down to eat dates by the side of a well and throwing the shells aside, and the Genii starting up and saying he must kill the merchant, because a date shell had put out the eye of the Genii's son" (*TT* I 272–73).

9. Beer, *Coleridge the Visionary,* 154, 156.

10. Wordsworth's remarks, from his "Note" to the poem in the 1800 edition of *Lyrical Ballads,* may be found in the 1991 R. L. Brett and A. R. Jones edition of *Lyrical Ballads,* 276. Lamb's defense is in *The Letters of Charles and Mary Anne Lamb* 1:266; reprinted in *Lyrical Ballads: Wordsworth and Coleridge,* ed. Brett and Jones, 2d ed., 276–77.

ures in *The Ancient Mariner.* Coleridge's spectre-bark, whose ribbed rigging resembles a "dungeon-grate," together with the female passenger aboard that ghostly vessel (the "Night-mare LIFE-IN-DEATH"), resemble Crusoe's description of his island as a prison and his life there as "this Death of a Life" (203). In a moving recapitulation of his early years on the island, Crusoe describes how

> the anguish of my soul at my condition would break out upon me on a sudden, and my very heart would die within me, to think of the woods, the mountains, the desarts I was in; and how I was a prisoner, locked up with the eternal bars and bolts of the ocean, in an uninhabited wilderness, without redemption. In the midst of the greatest composures of my mind, this would break out upon me like a storm, and make me wring my hands and weep like a child. (125)

Such a passage makes us realize that what most profoundly, perhaps uniquely, unites these two works is not their narration of "strange surprizing adventures," but their depiction of existential loneliness. Indeed, referring to Coleridge's note about "the *desert island* feeling" in *Robinson Crusoe,* one Defoe critic remarks: "Coleridge was quite right in stressing what he called 'the *desert island* feeling'; nowhere in all literature before Defoe could one anticipate the cry of the Ancient Mariner, 'Alone, alone, all, all alone,/ Alone on a wide, wide sea.'" The Mariner's wide sea, like the "waste and empty sea" (*Oed' und leer das Meer*) imported from Wagner into *The Waste Land,* is precisely, as Florence Marsh once called it in an article comparing Coleridge's and Eliot's poems, an "ocean-desert."[11]

That Defoe's and Coleridge's terror of isolation, of solitary confinement, should express itself in concrete images of imprisonment is no accident. In Part Two, I will discuss the historical and autobiographical implications of Coleridge's image of the dungeon-grate. For Daniel Defoe no less than for Coleridge, the dungeon had both literal and symbolic significance. As an occasional secret service spy in the employ of Robert Harley and a more-than-occasional debtor, Defoe, from the time of his 1703 flight from incarceration as the author of that satire on the extreme Tory position, *The Shortest Way with the Dissenters,* was obsessed by thoughts of imprisonment. In the earliest of his letters to survive, a plea to Lord Nottingham, Defoe begged mercy for fleeing, pleading "a body unfit to bear the hardships of prison and a mind impatient of confinement." But in the summer of 1703 he had to submit to both imprisonment and three successive days in the pillory. Two decades later he reported that, "notwithstanding we are a nation of liberty," there were more prisons in London than in "any city in Europe, perhaps as many as in all the capital cities of Europe put together."[12]

In later years, he was terrified in particular by that most hopeless incarcera-

---

11. John Robert Moore, *Daniel Defoe: Citizen of the Modern World,* 227. For the "desert island feeling" remark, see *TT* II 295. T. S. Eliot, *The Waste Land,* line 42, borrowed from *Tristan and Isolde,* the third and final act. Marsh, "The Ocean-Desert: *The Ancient Mariner* and *The Waste Land.*"

12. *The Letters of Daniel Defoe* 1:1 (January 9, 1703); *Tour through the Whole Isle of Great Britain,* 157.

tion, imprisonment for debt. To judge from a letter in *Mercurius Politicus* of December 1718, this fear peaked just prior to the creation of *Robinson Crusoe*. Signing himself "Insolvent," Defoe lamented the plight of debtors, the *"only"* prisoners "condemned without Reprieve, without possibility of Pardon or room for Escape" (756–57). Defoe could be publicly, and ironically, defiant of those who threatened him with imprisonment or hanging—"Gaols, Fetters, and Gibbets are odd Melancholy things; for a Gentleman to *Dangle out of the World in a strang* has something so Ugly, so Awkward, and so Disagreeable in it, that you cannot think of it, without some Regret."[13] But what he calls in this letter in *Mercurius Politicus* (a monthly chronicle he edited from 1716–1720) the fear of "perpetual Imprisonment" seems relevant to Crusoe's anguished condition in the novel Defoe was about to start.

"It is as reasonable to represent one kind of imprisonment by another, as it is to represent anything that really exists by that which exists not," Defoe observed in his *Serious Reflections* on *Robinson Crusoe* (*Works* 3:3). Thus, on his island, Crusoe is both isolated and imprisoned, his terrible loneliness perhaps inevitably "represented" by that of "a prisoner, locked up with the eternal bars and bolts of the ocean." Defoe's other most notable creation, Moll Flanders, is actually born in London's Newgate Prison, and when she returns there, a convicted thief sentenced to hang, Newgate—the spectre of which was later to terrify Coleridge—becomes an "emblem" with particular private resonance for Defoe, who had spent much of the summer of 1703 confined there. Moll's nightmarish descriptions of "that horrid place"—"nothing could be filled with more horror . . . ; the hellish Noise, the Roaring, Swearing, and Clamour, the Stench and Nastiness, and all the dreadful croud of Afflicting Things I saw there joyn'd to make the Place seem an Emblem of Hell itself. . . . I thought of nothing night or day, but of Gibbets and Halters, evil Spirits and Devils" (273)— evoke Newgate as a horrific local version of that cosmic prisonhouse faced by both Robinson Crusoe and Coleridge's Mariner.

Still, when all is said, there remains a world of difference between Robinson Crusoe on the one hand and Coleridge and his partially redeemed Mariner on the other. If they share a terror of bolts and bars and dungeon-grates, they have very different attitudes toward nature and nature's creatures. In her admirable biography of Defoe, Paula Backscheider aligns Crusoe and Coleridge's Mariner as sharing "an affirmation of what nature offers": "Coleridge greatly admired *Robinson Crusoe*, and like his Ancient Mariner, Crusoe has learned to bless and find beauty in all God's creatures. At first terrified of the animals, the sea, and the earthquake, he learns to use nature to feed and clothe himself; his 'summer home' is in a beautiful natural setting, and he uses his knowledge to produce more food and even to capture the mutineers."[14]

13. Quoted by Bonamy Dobrée, *English Literature in the Early Eighteenth Century, 1700–1740*, 42. "It is," Dobrée adds, "the retort whimsical at its most effective, at least as a public gesture; and the order of the adjectives is masterly."

14. *Daniel Defoe: His Life*, 419.

While it is true that both characters learn to "bless" nature and affirm what it "offers," Crusoe, as Backscheider's passage makes abundantly clear, remains— necessarily but with no aesthetic or moral misgivings—a no-nonsense utilitarian. Indeed, the difference that separates Crusoe from both the Mariner and his creator can be demonstrated in something as seemingly trivial as the attitude toward Backscheider's first example of all God's creatures, "animals": a category made rather less trivial by its necessary inclusion of *human* animals. The poem, after all, even more than the novel (which Defoe later characterized as a "parable"), does have a moral—though an increasing number of readers have agreed with Coleridge that it is "too much," or, as an orthodox and inadequate synopsis of terrifying experiences, too little:

> He prayeth well, who loveth well
> Both man and bird and beast.

> He prayeth best, who loveth best
> All things both great and small;
> For the dear God who loveth us,
> He made and loveth all.
>   (lines 612–17 [1817 ed.])

Whether one accepts or rejects the moral, finds it banal or dramatically appropriate to a ballad, a sacramental affirmation of the "One Life" or a pseudoreligious sham, that "all" is essential. The crucial love is that for "man," though the poem itself pivots on "bird and beast." The spell of Life-in-Death that follows the Mariner's shooting of the albatross is only broken when he blesses the water-snakes "unaware," and the dead bird slides from his neck into the sea (lines 271–91).

On less exalted levels, Coleridge's own feeling for animals ranges from the fraternal to the endearing to the ridiculous. He concludes an October 1794 letter to Francis Wrangham, a young Cambridge don sympathetic to Pantisocracy, with this jocoserious peroration:

> If there be any whom I deem worthy of remembrance—I am their Brother. I call even my Cat Sister in the Fraternity of universal Nature. Owls I respect & Jack Asses I love: for Aldermen & Hogs, Bishops & Royston Crows, I have not particular partiality—; they are my Cousins however, at least by Courtesy. But Kings, Wolves, Tygers, Generals, Ministers, & Hyaenas, I renounce them all—or if they *must* be my kinsmen, it shall be in the 50th Remove—May the Almighty Pantisocratizer of Souls pantisocratize the Earth, and bless you and
> S. T. Coleridge! (*CL* I 121)

Had Lord Byron, himself an animal lover, seen the original version of the poem in which Coleridge hails a jackass "Brother!," he might have been inspired to come up with a still wittier sobriquet for Coleridge than "Laureat of the long-ear'd kind."[15] For the original manuscript of "To a Young Ass" (1794) sweeps to an even more hilarious finale than does the published text. In the

15. *English Bards and Scotch Reviewers*, line 264.

draft version, the poet imagines himself taking the jackass off to the Pantiso-
cratic valley of "Peace and mild Equality," where, among other personified
delights, "Mirth shall tickle Plenty's ribless side," where "Toil" will marry "Health
that charming lass" (the newlyweds have a truly rustic vanity table, employing
"sleek cows for a looking glass"), and "Where Rats shall mess with Terriers
hand-in-glove / And Mice with Pussy's Whiskers sport in Love."[16]

Elsewhere Coleridge has, fortunately, more felicitous variations on the ani-
malic imagery of millennial Isaiah, but in such passages we find the same
apparent commitment to "One Life," and the same essential love—even amid
the practicalities of daily life. Plagued by mice in his new cottage at Stowey, for
example, Coleridge cannot bring himself to disturb the harmony of the peace-
able kingdom by setting a trap. Swearing by "all the whiskers of all the pussies"
who have ever "mewed plaintively, or amorously," he cries out in a letter of
1797: " 'Tis telling a lie. 'Tis as if you said, 'Here is a bit of toasted cheese; come
little mice! I invite you!' when, oh, foul breach of the rites of hospitality! I mean
to assassinate my too credulous guests!" (*CL* I 322).

Beneath the lighthearted playfulness of such a statement—reminiscent of
the "universal good-will" of Sterne's Uncle Toby, who refuses to kill a fly[17]—
there is enough of what Matthew Arnold called "high seriousness" to satisfy the
most solemn critic. Such an "assassination" would be a "foul breach of the rites
of hospitality"; the Mariner in Coleridge's greatest poem "inhospitably killeth"
the albatross. I am quoting Coleridge's 1817 gloss to lines 81–82 of the poem,
but as early as his "Argument" prefacing the poem in the 1800 edition of *Lyrical
Ballads,* the central poem-synopsizing phrase is this: "how the Ancient Mariner
cruelly and in contempt of the laws of hospitality killed a Sea-bird and how he
was followed by many and strange Judgements" (*CPW* I 186*n*).

As a matter of fact, there is seriousness even in the letter, in the juxtaposition
of "assassinate" with the punning wordplay in the very next sentence: "I cannot
set a trap, but I should vastly like to make a Pitt-fall." In Part Two the implica-
tions of this sentence will be examined at length. For the moment, it is enough
to say that those familiar with Coleridge's anti-Pittite politics in the 1790s, as
well as his compulsive puns on the prime minister's name, know what serious-
ness underlies the joke. But there is seriousness along with comedy in the letter
to Wrangham as well, just as there is in the egalitarian-utopian vision of mice
sporting with pussy's whiskers in Pantisocratic Love. What comes through above
all is Coleridge's instinctive revulsion from murderous insensitivity to man,
bird, or beast.[18] Seven years after refusing to set a trap for the mice in his
cottage, Coleridge witnessed bored sailors shooting at an exhausted hawk from
the deck of the ship on which he was traveling to Malta. "Poor hawk!" he

16. These manuscript lines are dated October 1794. *CPW* I 75.

17. *Tristram Shandy* 2:12.

18. In his 1817 "Apologetic Preface" to "Fire, Famine, and Slaughter," which had
condemned the prime minister to Hell, Coleridge insists that, far from wishing Pitt any
real harm, he would have been ready, "had Mr Pitt's person been in hazard, to interpose
my own body, and defend his life at the risk of my own" (*CPW* II 1101).

exclaimed in his notebook. "O strange Lust of Murder in Man!—It is not cruelty / it is mere non-feeling from non-thinking" (*CN* II 2090). It was May 1804, and the same notebook reveals that Coleridge was reconsidering *The Ancient Mariner:* its details of shipboard life and the descriptions of the sea, not, apparently, the significance of its motif of a murdered seabird.

2

What a contrast all this provides to the decidedly unegalitarian island over which Robinson Crusoe reigns. True, he has his pets—parrot, dog, cats, tame goats. But they all, with the exception of the old dog, serve a utilitarian function: the goats provide meat, butter, cheese, and tallow; the parrot apparently supplies a feathery shoulder to cry on. The repetition of "Poll" and "Poor Robin Crusoe" make up the grand total of his oral accomplishment—the adjective *poor* a reflection of his master's ironic fate as a castaway rich in "useless" gold, but even more an echo of his egocentricity and intermittent expressions of self-pity. The cats serve in their traditional office of vermin control, and, when they multiply and become pests, are themselves treated like vermin and killed by Crusoe in great numbers (116). He restricts himself then to two cats, immediately drowning such kittens as are unfortunate enough to be born into his dictatorial household.

This last remark may seem the apotheosis of maudlin liberal sentiment. Yet Crusoe's own picture of his "little family" sitting down to dinner, however touched by humor ("It would have made a stoick smile . . ."), betrays his deepest feelings, and they are absolutist, even dictatorial: ". . . there was my majesty the prince and lord of the whole island; I had the lives of all my subjects at my absolute command; I could hang, draw, give liberty, and take it away, and no rebels among all my subjects" (157). You'd better believe it. Incidentally, we know from a previous passage (129) that Crusoe approves of the policy of hanging criminals and leaving their bodies on display to terrorize others. He continues in the "little family" passage: "Then to see how like a king I dined too, all alone, attended by my servants. Poll, as if he had been my favourite, was the only person permitted to talk to me. My dog, who was now grown very old and crazy . . . sat always at my right hand, and two cats, one on one side of the table, and one on the other, expecting now and then a bit from my hand, as a mark of special favour."[19]

19. In Luis Buñuel's brilliant film version of the novel (starring Dan O'Herlihy), Crusoe is gratuitously "humanized" by stressing his attachment to this dog. In fact, the most touching scene in the movie is that in which he tearfully buries his old "friend," an invention that transforms Defoe's hard-nosed protagonist into a Thomas Hardy lamenting the death of his "house-mate" in "Last Words for a Dumb Friend." In the 1988 film discussed earlier, the death of the dog, Scamp, is even more poignant. Crusoe nurses the sick animal, prays for it ("I beg you for my dog's life. He's such a good dog. I've come to need him. Without him . . ."), and, when the dog dies and is buried, seems on the verge of suicide. In the novel, Crusoe describes the dog, typically enough, as "a trusty *servant* to me many years" (82). That comes in the course of a passage that reveals the peripheral nature of Crusoe's pets, one of a series of typical Defoe "slips." After he has made twelve

There is, as James Sutherland insists, something of the "naive and playful delight" of children's make-believe in such a description.[20] And considering that his "subjects" are animals and Crusoe himself a goatskinned and monstrously mustachioed freak of nature who, as he admits, would have "rais'd a great deal of laughter" had any Englishman laid eyes on him, we may see in such a description self-deprecation and even an amused parody of absolute power. Crusoe surely is having at least *some* exuberant fun at his own expense. Nevertheless, the reality behind this fabulous tableau seems less childlike than adult, and less Aesopian than Orwellian, as is made clear once "my two new subjects" (241)—Friday's father and the Spaniard, rescued from cannibals three years later—have joined man and master to swell the local population to four. We are now dealing with human beings, but Crusoe, while he is willing to grant religious toleration, sees them in his mind's eye as precise equivalents of his obedient animals: a tame variant of his earlier equation of Africa's "voracious beasts" and "cruel savages" (103–4). Where the young Coleridge could at least play with the idea of raising an ass to the dignity of a human brother or, alternatively, insist that Southey's black servant Shadrach and his family go with them to America as equals on the ground that men and women are not "Oxen and Horses," Robinson Crusoe lowers human beings to the level of beasts and birds. Occupying a place analogous to the favorite Poll or to the nameless dog, Friday is treated, as Sutherland himself remarks, rather like a "pet":

> My island was now peopled, and I thought my self very rich in subjects; and it was a merry reflection which I frequently made, how like a king I looked. First of all, the whole country was my own meer property; so that I had an undoubted right of dominion. 2dly, my people were perfectly subjected: I was absolute lord and lawgiver; they all owed their lives to me, and were ready to lay down their lives, if there had been occasion of it, for me. (240)

That last point seems to be the sine qua non of a relationship with Crusoe. Xury (47) and Friday (212) earlier pass the test, much to the satisfaction of their

---

trips to the wreck, bringing ashore a horde of useful items, carefully enumerated, Crusoe is forced to mention details he had "omitted setting down before." Among other things, including pens, ink, and three Bibles, "I must not forget that we had in the ship a dog and two cats, of whose eminent history I may have occasion to say something in its place" (82). When he is finally rescued from the island, he takes the parrot aboard ship (273), forgetting that he had already said he had left him behind: "poor Poll may be alive there still, calling after *Poor Robin Crusoe* to this day."

20. Discussing Defoe's "talent for make-believe," his ability to revive "the memories of childhood" and "the games played by children," Sutherland cites this passage as exemplifying those "numerous occasions on which Crusoe contemplates his little kingdom with a sort of naive and playful delight." No doubt, but that there is more involved than "simple make-believe" is suggested by the very next example Sutherland offers: "Similarly, in the *Farther Adventures,* Crusoe tells us that his island dominion has been divided up in his absence into three colonies and that his old habitation under the hill was now 'the capital city'" (*Daniel Defoe: A Critical Study,* 130). Whatever playful delight that last statement demonstrates, the colonization of the island and the preeminence of Crusoe as governor are real enough.

"savior." Indeed, at the end of the *Farther Adventures,* long after Friday has been slain doing Crusoe's bidding, his master still counts the willingness of his subjects to "fight for me to the last Drop" as the ultimate proof of his "absolute Power" over them (3:200). The same point about the ultimate servile sacrifice is made in *Colonel Jack.* Advocating mercy and gentleness on slave plantations, Jack argues that, were kind treatment to be practiced, an appreciative "*Negro* or Servant . . . would not only Work for you, but even Die for you" (145–46). In the case of Robinson Crusoe, who actually saves Friday's life, it may be true that Crusoe is, as Novak says, once again merely following the "pattern of natural law which Grotius sets forth in *De Jure Belli et Pacis.*"[21] But Crusoe, unlike (say) the Swift of *Gulliver's Travels* or the Voltaire of *Candide,* reveals little awareness of at least some of the forms of tyranny that remain inhumane, even though sanctioned by the laws of warfare. Crusoe is neither cruel nor unjust, but what matters essentially is that he be "absolute lord"—and master—of subjects good to the last drop.

Just as many critics find, or profess to find, ambivalence and irony in Defoe's discussions of slavery, so many, probably most, readers find Crusoe's jocular descriptions of himself as absolute ruler of his little island humorous rather than off-putting, instances of harmless, even appealing, self-mockery. Perhaps critics like Maximillian Novak and Manuel Schonhorn make too much of "Crusoe the King," reading into the novel what Schonhorn calls Defoe's "natural hostility to parliamentary government," based in turn on his fear of the "fragmented will of innumerable self-seeking individuals." Yet Crusoe's own habitual language reveals his monarchical and possessive instincts. "One can," as Schonhorn says, "very early almost make out a crown on Crusoe's head, and he can be seen as a putative sovereign of an island commonwealth."[22]

Before he has been on "this unhappy island" a year, he surveys a green valley "with a secret kind of pleasure (tho' mixed with my other afflicting thoughts) to think that this was all my own, that I was king and lord of all this country indefeasibly, and had a right of possession" as complete "as any lord of a mannor in England" (113–14). In his fourth year on the island, he again pronounces himself "lord of the whole mannor; or if I pleased, I might call myself king or emperor over the whole country which I had possession of," with "none to dispute sovereignty or command with me" (139). William Cowper's famous lines, "I am monarch of all I survey, / My right there is none to dispute," are imagined spoken, not by Robinson Crusoe, but by the self-marooned sailor Alexander Selkirk, long familiar to readers as Defoe's most immediate proto-

21. *Defoe and the Nature of Man,* 52.
22. Novak, "Crusoe the King," and Schonhorn, "Defoe: The Literature of Politics and the Politics of Some Fictions," 22, 35, 32. Schonhorn argues that the novel presents the "necessity for . . . a unitary executive sovereignty." Crusoe militarily earns the right to monarchy over the island, including, to begin with, Friday, whose rescue demonstrates "the latent monarch actualiz[ing] the potential necessary for his role as communal leader." For a full discussion of Defoe's thoughts on the creation and maintenance of monarchy to achieve a beneficent political order, see Schonhorn's 1991 study, *Defoe's Politics: Parliament, Power, Kingship, and "Robinson Crusoe."*

type for Crusoe.[23] Interestingly, Cowper's lines are quoted by Henry David Thoreau in describing what the cover blurb to the Signet Classic edition of *Walden* refers to as *his* "Robinson Crusoe existence." But the differences between Thoreau and Crusoe go well beyond the fact that the American's isolation was chosen. Thoreau, who "never got my fingers burned by actual possession," cites Cowper's lines, italicizing "survey," in order to affirm imaginative, rather than material, "possession" of a "landscape."[24]

It is true that Crusoe's numerous references to himself as king, lord, master, emperor, majesty, prince, and, later, as "*generalissimo*" and "governour" (264), are usually accompanied by irony and humor. But the "merry reflection" is indeed "frequent," almost pathologically so, and the attendant irony is not quite that of Cowper's "Verses Supposed to be Written by Alexander Selkirk," nor that of Swift. At a level not very far beneath the surface of Crusoe's daydreaming, Defoe was, as Pat Rogers notes, "indulging . . . in a fantasy of himself as colonial proprietor. . . . There are, at the very least, buried sympathies for Crusoe's colonial experiment in the store of his creator's memories and desires."[25]

I am not trying to reduce Crusoe to an advocate of untempered tyranny, a position that would be repellent to his creator. Defoe, who strategically arranged that Crusoe's years of island exile (1659–1687) should coincide almost precisely with the Stuart Restoration (1660–1688), was hostile to abusive monarchical power. His defense of toleration was of a piece with his antagonism to tyranny, a case made in his twelve-book anti-Stuart poem *Jure Divino* (1706), at once a defense of monarchy and an assault on Jacobite absolutism. Defoe's ideal was a lawful rather than an absolutist monarchy. But despite that, and despite Crusoe's ultimate conclusion, many years after the island sojourn, that true sovereignty is mastery over oneself rather than others (*Farther Adventures* 3:200–201), there is little in the first volume to indicate that Defoe was exploiting his diplomatic experience to satirize either monarchical institutions or the piety-masked power-hunger of the colonizing imperialism so devastatingly reduced and exposed by Swift in the final voyage of *Gulliver's Travels*.[26] As an

23. Cowper, "Verses Supposed to be Written by Alexander Selkirk." The poem continues, with painful irony: "From the centre all round to the sea / I am lord of the fowl and the brute. / Oh, solitude! where are the charms / That sages have seen in thy face? / Better dwell in the midst of alarms / Than reign in this horrible place."

24. *Walden: or, Life in the Woods,* chapter 2, "Where I Lived, and What I Lived For."

25. *"Robinson Crusoe,"* 45.

26. By the end of Part IV, "A Voyage to the Country of the Houyhnhnms," even the obtuse Gulliver has "conceived a few scruples with relation to the distributive justice of princes upon those occasions." In his bland example, "a Crew of Pyrates" are driven ashore by a storm; they "rob and plunder . . . give the country a new name . . . [and] take formal Possession of it for the King." This is what happens to Crusoe's island, though at first he insists on his own absolute sovereignty. Through Gulliver, Swift presents the consequence: "Here commences a new Dominion acquired by Divine Right. Ships are sent with the first Opportunity; the Natives driven out or destroyed, their Princes tortured to discover their Gold; a free Licence given to all acts of Inhumanity and Lust; the Earth reeking with the Blood of its Inhabitants; and this execrable Crew of Butchers

Anglo-Irishman, Swift was somewhat skeptical of British imperialism. For Defoe, as demonstrated throughout his career and culminating in such late works as his 1724 fusion of imagination and propaganda, *A New Voyage Round the World,* or in *Atlas Maritimus and Commercials* (1728), British colonialism was commercial enterprise at its heroic best.

Nor is there compelling evidence that Crusoe's whimsical afflatus involves genuine self-mockery: that is, that he sees himself as truly ridiculous. No doubt, as Martin Green observes, the semimockery reflects the fact that *Robinson Crusoe* is both an imperialist and an anti-imperialist story, on the "side of self-help," the "Protestant conscience and the democracy of labor," rather than "official authority" and "empire." But as Green also notes, Crusoe's "jokes" about being the island's "king or governor, with subjects, . . . conceal, or ensure against hubris, a swelling excitement." Here, as in Kipling's "The Man Who Would Be King," the idea of kingship, even godhead, is "officially disinfected by the jocular ambivalence of tone Kipling and Defoe . . . maintain."[27]

Furthermore, as John Richetti notes, "Crusoe's little joke" about being "king and lord of all this country" "becomes deadly serious later in the book when he kills the cannibals and metes out justice to the English mutineers. . . . Crusoe is transformed from an introspective, cautiously defensive settler to an aggressive adventurer and domineering colonial overlord." Crusoe's "merry reflection" about his absolute sovereignty over Friday, Friday's father, and the Spaniard, as well as his undoubted power of life and death over others who intrude on his island, relate, as Richetti adds, "to Defoe's colonial propaganda, but they also point to [Crusoe's] more generalized resonances as a cultural archetype, a representative of European imperial expansion as it reached out for raw materials and slaves."[28]

Exactly, though one mustn't, of course, forget Crusoe's *particular national* resonance. Two short poems written by Walter Savage Landor within a decade of Coleridge's death confirm a tradition already in place and provide early examples of what would become an even more widespread Victorian tendency

---

employed in so pious an Expedition is a *modern Colony* sent to convert and civilize an idolotrous and barbarous People" (*Gulliver's Travels,* ed. Robert A. Greenberg, 258). While neither Defoe nor Crusoe would approve all such acts of inhumanity and lust, both would envisage them as part of an unfortunate but acceptable price to be paid to secure a profitable colony. What appalled Swift would seem only common sense to the ultra-commercial Defoe and his character Crusoe, who, even at the end of his long religious experience, has conceived far fewer "scruples" than Gulliver on these subjects.

Like Dr. Johnson, Coleridge valued *Robinson Crusoe* over *Gulliver's Travels,* a work clearly influenced by the most popular novel of Swift's rival propagandist for the Harley ministry. On at least two occasions, Coleridge declared his preference for the sympathy-inducing Defoe over the satirical Swift. In the *Crusoe* marginalia, he bases his argument on—again—Crusoe's "Universality": "he, who makes me forget my *specific* class, character, & circumstances raises me into the Universal *Man*—Now this is Defoe's Excellence, you become a Man while you read" (*CM* I 158–59).

27. *The Robinson Crusoe Story,* 22–23.
28. *Daniel Defoe,* 62–66.

to find in "persecuted, brave Defoe" and, particularly, in "staunch Crusoe" patriotic precursors of British maritime expansion and naval glory. In the first poem, from which I have just quoted, we are told that

> Achilles, in Homeric song,
> May, or he may not, live so long
> As Crusoe
> . . . .
> A Rodney and a Nelson may
> Without him not have won the day.

The second concludes:

> Never hath early valour been imprest
> On gallant Briton's highly-heaving breast
> So deeply as by Crusoe; therefore Fame
> O'er every sea shall waft your social name.[29]

A decade later, again speaking for many in hailing the "spirit of De Foe," the Victorian linguist, adventurer, and novelist George Borrow described *Robinson Crusoe* (which he, like Coleridge, first encountered at the age of six) as "having exerted over the minds of Englishmen an influence certainly greater than any other of modern times, . . . a book, moreover, to which, from the hardy deeds which it narrates, and the spirit of strange and romantic enterprise which it tends to awaken, England owes many of her astonishing discoveries both by sea and land, and no inconsiderable part of her naval glory." In *The Friend* for January 25, 1810, Coleridge, anticipating both Landor and Borrow, offers an example, one among many of those inspired by Defoe to go to sea in the service of the British Empire.[30] Coleridge's example was Sir Alexander Ball, the man for whom, on Malta, he had rewritten the notorious "Observations on Egypt." A commander of one of Nelson's ships at the Battle of the Nile and victorious conductor of the two-year siege of Malta, Ball "went into the Navy at an early age, . . . as he himself told me, in consequence of the deep impression and vivid images which were left on his mind by the perusal of *Robinson Crusoe*" (*F* II 288).

As a native of the island most intimately affected by the hardy deeds of British colonial expansionism, James Joyce, equally impressed by the symbolic role of Defoe's hero, cast a considerably colder eye in 1912:

> European criticism has striven for many generations, and with a not entirely friendly insistence, to explain the mystery of the unlimited world conquest accomplished by that mongrel breed which lives a hard life on a small island in the

29. Written around 1840, these verses to Defoe were first published in 1897. See *The Complete Works of Walter Savage Landor,* ed. Stephen Wheeler, 3:216.

30. Borrow, *Lavengro: The Scholar, the Gypsy, the Priest* 1:38–39. In his study of Defoe, the French writer Paul Dottin credits *Robinson Crusoe* with creating many vocations at sea. Martin Green writes that, while "there is of course no way to demonstrate how many such careers were inspired by Defoe, . . . the assertion is made in dozens of autobiographies and biographies. And the fact that such declarations seem plausible *is* a demonstrable fact, and an important one" (*The Robinson Crusoe Story,* 29).

northern sea. . . . The true symbol of the British conquest is Robinson Crusoe, who, cast away on a desert island, in his pocket a knife and a pipe, becomes an architect, a carpenter, a knife grinder, an astronomer, a baker, a shipwright, a potter, a saddler, a farmer, a tailor, an umbrella-maker, and a clergyman. He is the true prototype of the British colonist, as Friday (the trusty savage who arrives on an unlucky day) is the symbol of the subject races. The whole Anglo-Saxon spirit is in Crusoe: the manly independence; the unconscious cruelty; the persistence; the slow yet efficient intelligence; the sexual apathy; the practical, well-balanced religiousness; the calculating taciturnity. Whoever rereads this simple, moving book in the light of subsequent history cannot help but fall under its prophetic spell.[31]

In these penetrating observations, Joyce has caught precisely both the tone of Defoe's book and its significance as symbolic and historical prophecy: a prophecy inherent not only in Crusoe's indefatigable industry but also in his increasingly domineering lordship over his kingdom and its subjects, including the "trusty savage who arrives"—not on a providential—but "on an unlucky day." Judging from the similar if less extended observations by another Irishman, George Moore; the distaste for Defoe and Crusoe expressed by the most prominent contemporary Irish literary critic, Denis Donoghue; and related remarks by other "outsiders," being a colonial victim of the British "world conquest" of which Robinson Crusoe is the "true symbol" helps one to recognize other victims.[32]

Those who may still think that—in the context of so tiny and remote an island—Crusoe's grandiose language of lordship provides prima facie evidence that he is merely having fun at his own expense might change their minds were they to read a few of the letters—at once admirable and pathetic, funny and frightening—written by Napoleon Bonaparte while exiled on the island of Elba. In them, the fallen but unconquerable emperor (had he read *Robinson Crusoe*, which Maxim Gorky was later to call "the Bible of the Unconquerable"?) speaks of "the Fleet" (it consisted of one small cutter), the "naval Budget" (600 francs), and "my Guard" (made up of eighteen Marines, ten mariners more than the squadron commanded by "Generalissimo" Crusoe against the English mutineers).

As the distinguished historian who edited these letters remarks in the intro-

31. "Daniel Defoe," 25.
32. In *Avowals*, Moore, attacking the prosaic and unimaginative nature of English culture, observes, "Nobody was more *terre à terre* than Crusoe. England seems to have expressed herself in her first narrative uncommonly well" (8). Martin Green notes that Irish writers, "who stand at a little distance from England, have often been the ones to see the powerful way Crusoe represents his country—the way he, rather than John Bull, should be its symbol" (*The Robinson Crusoe Story*, 29). Writing in 1924, another outsider, the French critic Paul Dottin, declared that this one novel of Defoe, that shaper of the colonial imagination, "helps to maintain the cohesiveness of the great British Empire" and "contributes to the growth of the Anglo-Saxon hegemony in the world" (*Daniel Defoe et ses romans* [Paris, 1924]; quoted in Green, *The Robinson Crusoe Story*, 98).

duction to his appropriately titled volume *Napoleon Self-Revealed,* "few periods in Napoleon's career are more illuminating than the months during which he was organizing a tiny island and a skeleton navy on the scale of a world empire." As organized, "enlightened," constructively energetic, practically efficient, and ruthlessly determined as ever, Napoleon adapted to his enforced nine-month exile by turning a small island of a few thousand inhabitants into a miniature empire complete with armed forces, balanced books, defense-works, fisheries, cleared forests, new roads, even a silkworm industry. Except for the courtly and erotic intrigue that swirled around the marooned emperor, his domain bears some practical resemblance to that of Defoe's exiled but indefatigable islander.[33] While Crusoe's expressions of imperialistic grandeur are less solemn than Bonaparte's (though an air of unintended comedy hovered over Lilliputian Napoleonism as well), they are not utterly unrelated.

Nor are Crusoe and Napoleon unrelated when it comes to the question of slavery. Whereas Coleridge praised George Washington for emancipating his slaves in his will (*EOT* I 230), two years later, in the same *Morning Post,* he condemned Washington's opposite number, Bonaparte, for overturning the Revolutionary declaration of freedom (1795) that had liberated the men and women led by Toussaint Louverture. Coleridge's moral outrage at Bonaparte's reinstitution of slavery in the French colonies took the form of bitter irony. The decree reestablishing slavery came in May 1802; six months later, wondering aloud in a public letter to Charles James Fox, who had, Coleridge charged, become "the temporary courtier of Bonaparte," he sarcastically asked the reformer which of the First Consul's exploits had won him over: "Was it the reestablishment of the Slave Trade, and his truly Corsican faith to the Blacks in St. Domingo, which have recommended him by any bond of sympathy to the great FRIEND and ADVOCATE of the unhappy AFRICANS?"[34]

33. *Napoleon Self-Revealed: Three Hundred Selected Letters,* ed. and trans. J. M. Thompson, 354–55, xii. See also Robert Christophe, *Napoleon on Elba.* Crusoe, like Defoe, would have applauded Napoleon's many projects "to improve life on the island, and also to make it more pleasant," especially the commercial projects listed on page 83 of Christophe, a list that includes the introduction of the silkworm industry.

34. "Letter II. To Mr. Fox" (November 9, 1802, *EOT* I 393). With "political liberty" dead both at home and abroad in early 1802, Fox *did* at one point pronounce "Bonaparte . . . the fittest person on earth to be master." The great Whig was enthusiastically received on the occasion of his visit to France during the Peace of Amiens; but despite lavish praise to his face by the First Consul himself, Fox remained unresponsive. The longtime enthusiast of the French Revolution was, among other things, profoundly disturbed by the hardly republican atmosphere and pageantry surrounding Bonaparte, with whom he actually quarreled. See John Drinkwater, *Charles James Fox,* 346–47, and Stanley Ayling, *Life of Charles James Fox,* 213.

The Peace of Amiens and the cooperation of the Jefferson administration enabled Napoleon to launch a full-scale assault on Saint-Domingue and the movement led by Toussaint. Though he knew "we shall perish," Toussaint fought valiantly until he was captured and deported. The struggle continued, "no longer a war" (said the French commander, Napoleon's brother-in-law, Victor Leclerc) but "a fight of tigers." Accord-

Ten days earlier, in a *Morning Post* article comparing Napoleonic France with imperial Rome, Coleridge wrote, tongue in cheek, of what Bonaparte might do with Toussaint (who had been taken prisoner through treachery and shipped back to France in chains) or at least with the prisoner's soldiers. "It is well known, that Negroes are beyond measure fascinated with splendid vestments and ornaments of dress. It is worthy, therefore, of being hinted to the First Consul . . . whether the late soldiers of Toussaint might not be drafted to France, presented with rich regimentals," and established as a Consular Guard "more to be relied on than native Frenchmen." The Negroes would not be "addicted to certain detestable vices," but whether "in the present state of the morals of France, this would plead for or against the Negroes, is a difficult question, which we do not pretend to decide" (*EOT* I 332).

In fact, the imprisoned Toussaint *had* offered his services. Stressing his loyalty and integrity, he had appealed to Napoleon for mercy: "Let your sensibility be touched at my position, you are too great in feeling and too just not to pronounce on my destiny."[35] Anticipating Aimé Césaire, Coleridge's friend Wordsworth had pronounced on both his destiny and his legacy in "To Toussaint L'Ouverture," a sonnet of August 1802 whose sestet echoes the opening stanza and the resonant peroration of Coleridge's "France: An Ode." Though "fallen" himself, "never to rise again," Toussaint is to "Live, and take comfort":

> Thou hast left behind
> Powers that will work for thee; air, earth, and skies;
> There's not a breathing of the common wind
> That wilt forget thee; thou hast great allies;
> Thy friends are exultations, agonies,
> And love, and man's unconquerable mind.

But Napoleon—who in 1802 also ordered, as Wordsworth reminds us in his next "Sonnet to Liberty," the expulsion of all blacks from France—remained equally untouched by his Haitian captive's agonies and his direct appeal. Humiliated, maltreated, and slowly starved, Toussaint died (April 7, 1803) in a Napoleonic prison in the Jura mountains. Years later, himself imprisoned on St. Helena, the dethroned emperor confessed that he had made a mistake in not governing Saint-Domingue through Toussaint, a man he persisted in calling a "revolted

---

ing to the *Annual Register* for 1803 (237–41), forty thousand French troops may have been lost, mostly to disease. Atrocities inflicted on the black rebels included being suffocated in the holds of ships, being drowned, and being torn to pieces by savage dogs in gladiatorial spectacles. See Roger G. Kennedy, *Orders from France: The Americans and the French in a Revolutionary World, 1780–1820,* 157. Within six months of Coleridge's article, Toussaint was dead and France had given up trying to reenslave his followers, who renamed their half of the island "Haiti." Though the only truly independent state to come into being as a result of the French Revolution, Haiti was soon to be dictatorially ruled by one of Toussaint's former lieutenants, Jean Jacques Dessalines. Proclaiming himself Emperor Jacques I, he decreed a new massacre of whites.

35. Quoted in James, *The Black Jacobins,* 364.

slave" and leader of "gilded Africans." But even then his concern was exclusively power, not liberation—and especially not *black* liberation.

Though Defoe's and France's generalissimos share more than a few racial and imperial concepts, on one crucial point Crusoe would have represented for Coleridge, early and late, the very antithesis of Napoleon. Alongside Crusoe's repetition of his father's paean to the "middle station" as less "exposed" to "the calamities of life . . . shared among the upper and lower part of mankind," Coleridge noted: "Alas, the evil is, that such is the pressure of the Ranks on each other, and with exception of the increasing Class of Paupers so universal is the ambition of Appearances, that morally & practically we scarcely have a Middle Class at present!—S.T.C. 1830" (*CM* I 159). As George Whalley observes, directing us to passages in Coleridge's *The Friend* (I 231) and *EOT* (II 76, 348), "one of Coleridge's chief objections to Napoleon was that he had destroyed, as far as was within his power, the one source of civilization—the middle class."[36] (Of course, even on this point, Coleridge was of two minds. Less than two years later, distressed—though less apocalyptically and apoplectically than Wordsworth— by provisions of the Reform Bill of 1832, he lamented the throwing of "all political power into the hands of that class—the shopkeepers, which in all countries and in all ages has been, is now, and ever will be the least patriotic, of any." The "evil" was not the extension of the franchise per se, but its extension "to *such* classes and in *such a manner* that a disenfranshisement of all above and a discontenting of all below the favored class are the unavoidable result" [*TT* I 266, 267].)

It may have been a feature of "Defoe's Excellence" that, as Coleridge said in the *Crusoe* marginalia, he "makes me forget my *specific* class, character & circumstances" and "raises me into the Universal Man . . . while [I] read" (*CM* I 158–59). Nevertheless, as his initialed and dated note confirms, Robinson Crusoe was for Coleridge, as he has been for so many generations of readers, the very epitome of the practical, hardworking, resourceful middle-class Englishman. The bourgeois Briton as culture hero: if it is finally *this* that makes Crusoe—who was for James Joyce the "true symbol of the British conquest"— Coleridge's "Universal Representative" of mankind, the annotator had come a long way indeed from the classless radicalism to which, in its blissful dawn, he had been stirred by the promise of the French Revolution. He *had* come a long way, though readers of the early Coleridge may still be somewhat surprised to encounter in 1830 so complete an endorsement of a "spirit of enterprise" uncomfortably close to that "commercial spirit" he had warned against in the *Lay Sermons* of 1816–1817.

Such an identification of Crusoe with a temporarily approved middle class

36. *CM* I 159*n*. Coleridge's changing responses to Bonaparte can be tracked in his articles in the *Morning Post*. For his response not only to Napoleon Bonaparte but also to "heroes" in general, see David P. Calleo, "Coleridge on Napoleon," and Liu, *Wordsworth*, 26–27, 419–23. Coleridge's (perhaps justified) fear that he was being trailed through Italy by agents of Napoleon in 1804 is discussed in Part Two.

would resolve some, hardly all, of the questions I've been puzzling over. Even if
one accepts J. H. Haeger's suggestion that Coleridge's speculations on race in
the mid-1820s adumbrated "the cultural assumptions of British imperialism
later in the century," as well as Barbara Paul-Emile's argument that abolition
became less important for later Coleridge than the preservation of social stabil-
ity and stratification, there would still remain an abyss between Crusoe and his
marginal celebrator. For the man who annotated the novel was, however changed,
not quite a reactionary Urizen, the petrified form of the Orc who had written
"On the Slave Trade" and *The Ancient Mariner.* Indeed, those two texts clarify
the distinction between Coleridge and Crusoe.

3

For example, Crusoe's delight in finding himself "rich in subjects," both ani-
mals and people, over whom he has an "undoubted right of dominion," may
remind us not only of Coleridge's eventual bête noire, Napoleon, but—again,
and by way of contrast—of the Coleridgean "moral" pronounced by the An-
cient Mariner: "He prayeth well, who loveth well / Both man and bird and
beast." His gratuitous killing (resembling the "motiveless malignity" of Iago in
destroying Othello) of the harmless albatross, who is described as having "loved"
in particular the very man who later shot him, as well as the turning point
signaled by his intuitive blessing of the water-snakes he had previously cursed,
fully explain the Mariner's emphasis on the need to love "bird and beast."[37]
But where in Coleridge's poem do we have violence toward "man," and there-
fore a need for redeeming love?

What made the killing of the albatross, in the Mariner's own words, "a hellish
thing" (line 91) was not only that the "murder" violated the rites of hospitality
(the bird responded in friendly trust to the sailors' greeting of it as "a Christian
soul," played with them, shared their food, participated in their evening prayers,
and "loved" its eventual killer), but also that it violated the very harmony of the
universe, the profound relationship unifying humanity and, in turn, humanity
with the natural world. This is of course a central Romantic theme. The crucial
point in the context of the present argument is that there is some evidence in
the poem that this sacramental bond may include the human bond most bru-
tally violated by the negative bondage inflicted not only by those who capture,
transport, and own black men and women who ought to be their brothers and
sisters, but also by those who benefit from slavery and so become accomplices

37. The reversal is in fact fully symmetrical. The man who killed the bird and hated
the slimy sea-snakes comes to a new appreciation not only of the creatures of the deep
but of the sky. The "sweet sounds" that issue from the breathless mouths of his dead
crewmates reverberate in the heavens, and in the midst of this spiritual music the
Mariner hears another music, angelic but natural: "Sometimes a-dropping from the sky
/ I heard the sky-larks sing; / Sometimes all little birds that are, / How they seemed to
fill the sea and air / With their sweet jargoning!" (358–62). Antipodal to the slaying of
the albatross, this loving sensitivity to the beauty and beauty-making power of the birds
of the air complements the regenerative blessing of the water-snakes.

in *that* "hellish thing." The obvious symbolic association of the albatross with Christ may even link that sacrificed creature with Crusoe's Xury, "in some sense and to some degree a Christ figure": a young man sold by Crusoe for "sixty pieces of eight" rather than thirty pieces of silver, and whose very name, as we have seen, suggests a transliteration of the Greek monogram for Christ.

If we turn for a third and final time to Coleridge's lecture and article on the slave trade, we find two passages that, added to other evidence, suggest that he may have been thinking about the slave trade when he wrote *The Ancient Mariner,* indeed, may actually have incorporated some phrases from the article into the poem.

He argues in the essay, for example, that the consumer is as guilty as the slave trader because "the guilt of all, attaches to each one who is knowingly an accomplice" (*W* 138). This may be echoed—admittedly, it would be years later— in the gloss Coleridge added to the lines of the poem in which the members of the crew, reversing their earlier condemnation, "justify" the murderous act of the Mariner, "and thus make themselves accomplices in the crime" (gloss to lines 99–102). Though added to the poem in the 1817 *Sibylline Leaves* edition, we do not know when this gloss was actually written. Closer to the slave-trade article, in time and subject, is a contribution to the *Morning Post* of October 14, 1800, in which Coleridge again uses the operative word, *accomplice.* "Avarice," he writes, "can make a man an African slave-trader," who then resides, not among "the fathers, brothers, husbands, and wives, of the men, women, and children, whom he was in the habit of carrying into slavery" and who "detected his guilt," but "among his *accomplices. . . .*"[38]

Again, in the lecture and article "On the Slave Trade," advocating and exercising the "truth-painting imagination" that would put us in genuine contact with the horrors of a slave ship, Coleridge rhetorically asks his readers: "Would you choose to be sold? to have the hot iron hiss upon your breasts, after having been crammed into the hold of a Ship with so many fellow-victims, that the heat and stench, arising from your diseased bodies, should rot the very planks?"[39] In the poem, the Mariner looks upon the "rotting deck" of his own ship (line 242), and in an unpublished manuscript correction scribbled in a

38. *EOT* I 253. ". . . among his *accomplices,*" Coleridge continues, "or at least among those who are enjoying the luxuries he procures, without having their bodily sympathies disturbed by the miseries which he creates." And not only would the victims detect his "guilt"; if the slave-trader lived among them rather than among his "accomplices," he would be faced by people capable of making him feel not only *moral* guilt, but "possessed" of "all the *physical* power of the country to punish it." In an eerie way, the passage is reminiscent of Crusoe's thought that, while he has little in the way of defense, he is "cast on an island where I see no wild beasts to hurt me, as I saw on the coast of Africa; and what if I had been shipwrecked there?" (84)

39. 38. *W* 138. For graphic descriptions of the horrors of slave ships, see Daniel P. Mannix and Malcolm Cowley, *Black Cargoes: A History of the Atlantic Slave Trade, 1518–1865,* and James Pope-Hennessy, *Sins of the Fathers: A Study of the Atlantic Slave Traders, 1441–1807.*

copy of the first edition of the poem, Coleridge described the spectre-bark as a "*plankless* thing, / —A bare Anatomy! / A plankless spectre," while the charnel-crusted bones of the skeleton Death were originally, and perhaps racially as well as gothically, "*Jet-black*" (*CPW* I 193*n*, 194*n*).

Back in 1964, in what seemed at the time an idiosyncratic aside, William Empson, arguing that the poem's main theme was European maritime expansion and consequent guilt about the cruel exploitation of other civilizations, suggested that Coleridge's horror at the idea of a slave ship provided both images and motifs for *The Ancient Mariner,* written two years after "On the Slave Trade" was published in *The Watchman*. He expanded his argument in 1972, noting that the poem internalizes the largely unfelt guilt of colonialist "maltreatment of natives" as epitomized in the slave system and the trade that supplied it: "Horror of the Slave Trade does I think echo into the *Mariner* at one point, early on . . . before the lady [Life-in-Death] gets close enough, [the Mariner] recognizes the *ship:* 'Alas (thought I, and my heart beat loud). . . . Are those *her* sails? . . .' He is having a premonition of the Slavers."[40]

Empson's fascination with *The Ancient Mariner,* a forty-year obsession that ended only with his death, continued in a characteristically cantankerous response to Robert Penn Warren's celebrated essay on the poem. In this paper, posthumously published in 1993, Empson expands on several points he had made in 1964 and 1972. Not only has the Mariner had "a premonition of a Slaver, with its planks rotted off by the insanitary exudation of the dying slaves"—slaving was going to be "the final result of his heroic exploration, and well might his 'heart beat loud.'" The impact of the spectre-ship on the poem's most immediate readers would also be "fierce." Indignation was building in Bristol over the horrors of the slave trade, against which Coleridge had inveighed in his fierce attack—twice printed in Bristol, in 1795 and again the following year in *The Watchman*. "Thus many of [the] first readers [of *The Ancient Mariner*] would feel certain he had glanced at the Slave Trade at this point in the poem, even if he had not wanted to. But I expect he did want to." Referring specifically to the dungeon-grate comparison, Empson adds: "Coleridge must have had some reason for making it a prison window, and the likely one at the time would be to define the Ghost-Ship as a Slaver."[41]

In Part Two, I propose an equally "likely" reason "at the time" for the appearance of the dungeon-grate image (an historical reference Coleridge may or may not have consciously "wanted" to get into the poem). Nevertheless, Empson's hint has been taken up by J. B. Ebbatson and Chris Rubenstein. Though Empson either didn't know it or chose not to mention the fact, his suggestion, even in 1964, was not original. He had been anticipated, in sub-

40. Part 3 of Empson's long introduction to Empson and David Pirie, eds., *Coleridge's Verse: A Selection,* 29.

41. "*The Ancient Mariner:* An Answer to Warren," 167, 168. Coming to light too late to be included in *Argufying,* a 1987 collection of Empson's essays on literature and culture edited by John Haffendon, the essay (also edited by Haffenden) appeared in the Winter 1993 issue of *The Kenyon Review.*

stance if not in tone, by Malcolm Ware. Bringing together a number of contemporary works dealing with the slave trade, Ware, writing in 1961, had gone so far as to suggest that the "spectre-bark" of the poem *is*—like Crusoe's fatal vessel—a slave ship, and that Coleridge, "by referring to a slave ship, wished to demonstrate the consequences of violating the natural bonds of man to man, to justify thereby the moral stated, and to give his allegory a universality and scope quite consistent with the traditional Romantic concept of the oneness of nature and with Coleridge's own mature theory of the transcending unity of all creation."[42]

Whatever individual readers may make of Ware's suggestion, there is surely *some* reason for the otherwise unexpected comparison of the spectre-bark's rigging to a "dungeon-grate" through which the sun peers. I go on in Part Two to propose a number of elaborate parallels that make it at least plausible that the image is an "intrusion" from the world of domestic politics in which the poem was written, an intrusion that *visibly* imports into *The Ancient Mariner* the dungeon-grates and clanking chains of Pittite repression. But that certainly does not rule out Ware's suggestion. *The Ancient Mariner* also includes the even more "intrusive" simile in which the windless ocean is said (by the mysterious "Second Voice") to be "Still as a slave before his lord" (line 414). Ware might also find support for his suggestion in a later Coleridgean fusion of dungeon and slave ship. In a May 1808 lecture on education given at the Royal Institution, Coleridge memorably compared harsh discipline inflicted on children to the worst terrors he could conjure up: "fear of Newgate" and "horror at the thought of a slave ship!"[43] In addition, the Nightmare-Hag "Life-in-Death," whose name may well echo Crusoe's description of his existence in his island prison as "this Death of a Life" (203), would certainly be an accurate personification of human slavery.

The images linking slavery and *The Ancient Mariner* may be visual as well as verbal. In the past few years, three cross-disciplinary critics have stressed analogies between the coloration and imagery of Coleridge's poem and J. M. W. Turner's seascapes, especially the celebrated *Slavers Throwing Overboard the Dead*

---

42. "Coleridge's 'Spectre-Bark': A Slave Ship?" 593.

43. *CN* III 3291*n*. The target of Coleridge's indignant attack was not the use of corporal punishment, but the moral degradation he thought attended the infliction of public humiliation upon children. His implicit connection of Joseph Lancaster's educational methods, including humiliating punishments, to the horror of a slave ship aroused considerable controversy. Ironically, one of the members of the Royal Institution interested in Lancaster's *System of British Education* (1810) was none other than Thomas Clarkson, Coleridge's great abolitionist friend. At the point in the lecture at which he exclaimed, "No boy who has been subject to punishments like these will stand in fear of Newgate, or feel any horror at the thought of a slave ship!" Coleridge (perhaps emulating Edmund Burke's famous "dagger-speech") threw down Lancaster's book "with a mixture of contempt and indignation," leading to charges by Lancaster's supporters of "stage-tricks and clap-trap." R. A. Foakes cites Southey's account in "'Thriving Prisoners': Coleridge, Wordsworth, and the Child at School," 194; and see below, Chapter 7, note 6.

and Dying—Typhon Coming On. Exhibited at the Royal Academy in 1840, the painting was widely ridiculed, by individuals and in the pages of *Punch.* But it made a profound impression on William Makepeace Thackeray and John Ruskin. "The most tremendous piece of colour that was ever seen," said Thackeray; "it sets the corner of the room in which it hangs into a flame." Though painted in 1840, *Slavers* re-created an incident (described in Clarkson, whose book Turner was reading) that occurred before England's abolition of its colonial slave trade. In 1783, Captain Collingwood, master of the *Zong,* a British slave ship bound for Jamaica, ordered 133 epidemic-smitten blacks to be thrown into the sea alive, some shackled. Running low on water and aware that insurance could be collected only on slaves "lost" at sea and not on those who perished of disease, he simply dumped his expendable cargo.[44] At the time, the atrocity was not condemned; Collingwood went unpunished and his decision, seen in an economic rather than moral context, was described (by Lord Mansfield) as equivalent to throwing horses overboard in an emergency. It would be hard to find a more vivid example of Coleridge's fusion of "the wildest physical suffering with the most atrocious moral depravity," or of what he called the profit-motivated "perversion of a Person into a Thing."

The artist fused the anguish of the innocent victims with the churning and weirdly lit waters to produce a nightmare epic in oil. "The noblest sea that Turner has ever painted," said Ruskin (whose father later purchased the painting for his son), "and, if so, the noblest certainly ever painted by man." The storm is subsiding, as he notes in his description of the canvas, and between the swells, "the fire of the sunset falls along the trough of the sea, dyeing it with an awful but glorious light," an "intense and lurid splendor which burns like gold and bathes like blood." In two astonishing sentences Ruskin re-creates Turner's painting in words, describing the

> whirling water, now lighted with green and lamp-like fire, now flashing back the gold of the declining sun, now fearfully dyed from above with the indistinguishable images of the burning clouds, which fall upon them in flakes of crimson and scarlet, and give to the reckless waves the added motion of their own fiery flying. Purple and blue, the lurid shadows of the hollow breakers are cast upon the mist of night, which gathers cold and low, advancing like the shadow of death upon the guilty ship as it labours amidst the lightning of the sea, its thin masts written upon the sky in lines of blood, girded with condemnation in that fearful hue which signs the sky with horror and mixes its flaming flood with sunlight, and—cast far along the desolate heave of the sepulchral waves—incarnadines the multitudinous sea.[45]

Ruskin's description conjures up for us, and may have for him, memories of *The Ancient Mariner* at its most "hellish," with the "death-fires" dancing at night as "The water, like a witches' oils, / Burnt green, and blue and white," or as the

44. See Albert Boime, *The Art of Exclusion: Representing Blacks in the Nineteenth Century,* 67–70.
45. *Modern Painters* 2:161–62.

setting sun, the "western wave . . . all a-flame," peers "With broad and burning face" through the "dungeon-grate" of the spectre-ship's thin masts. In a footnote to his adjective *guilty* to describe the ship, Ruskin observes: "She is a slaver, throwing her slaves overboard. The near sea is encumbered with corpses." Whether looking at Turner's painting or reading Ruskin's remarkably evocative sentences, it is difficult *not* to think of the Mariner's guilty ship, in whose "huge shadow," the "charméd water burnt alway / A still and awful red," symbolically dyed by the innocent blood of the slain albatross (lines 269–71).

That terrifying red may derive its power from Jungian racial memory—"The word 'red' has a soul of terror that has come to it through a history of the race," writes Maud Bodkin in a famous passage on the *Mariner*[46]—or simply from its association with blood and fire. It is only one of the many colors (white, yellow, orange, green, blue, purple, black) present in both poem and painting, but it incarnadines the painting just as it does the poem—once the Mariner has shot the albatross and the sun, source of all colors, turns "bloody."

At the level of the poem's genesis, that blood-red may be connected with the color of black slaves. At the poem's turning point, the sea in the shadow of the ship is an infernal red, reflecting the original "hellish" crime, the shooting of the creature whose innocent blood stains sun and sea, as well as the Mariner's guilty soul. The long passage quoted earlier from "On the Slave Trade" began and ended with the food and drink of the trade being "polluted" with the "Blood" of God's "innocent children," the enslaved Africans. At the end of his horrifying voyage, the Mariner prays that the good Hermit will "shrieve" his soul and "wash away / The Albatross's blood" (lines 512–13). We tend to picture the innocent victim of the poem as the Wandering Albatross, a huge, almost completely snow-white bird. (Its very size—it has the widest wingspread among living birds—makes it an unlikely candidate to be hung about anyone's neck.) Though Coleridge never specifies the bird's color, we know his primary source. In his account of the genesis of *The Ancient Mariner,* conceived in the course of the famous November 1797 walking tour during which the poem was first planned as a joint venture, Wordsworth tells us

> I had been reading in Shelvocke's Voyages, a day or two before, that, while doubling Cape Horn they frequently saw Albatrosses in that latitude, the largest sort of sea-fowl, some extending their wings twelve or thirteen feet. "Suppose," said I, "you represent him as having killed one of these birds on entering the South Sea, and that the tutelary Spirits of those regions take upon them to avenge the crime." The incident was thought fit for the purpose and adopted accordingly.[47]

The adoption might have been particularly swift if Wordsworth's suggestion stirred Coleridge's recollection of an episode in the strange "Surprizing Adventures" Edward Dorrington ascribed to Philip Quarll in the Crusoe-like book Coleridge also read before he was six. After shooting a beautifully colored

---

46. "A Study of *The Ancient Mariner* and of the Rebirth Archetype," in her *Archetypal Patterns in Poetry: Psychological Studies of Imagination,* 43–48.

47. *Poetical Works* 1:361.

seabird with a homemade bow, the Hermit immediately regrets having "destroyed" a varicolored creature "made for Nature's diversion." That Coleridge, after having the passage in Shelvocke brought to his attention by Wordsworth, read it himself is almost certain. If he did, he would have found that the original "crime" had been committed by a "melancholy" sailor named Hatley, who, imagining "from its color, that it must be some ill omen," and hoping (vainly, as it turns out) that a "fair wind" would follow the sustained "foul weather," shot a "disconsolate *black* Albitross" (my emphasis).[48]

Even if the bird in Shelvocke's account was black, the poem's richly symbolic albatross cannot of course be reduced to an allegory of slavery. Still, though De Quincey may have been excessive in describing the incident as "the germ" of *The Ancient Mariner*, it is, as Lowes says, this incident in Shelvocke that "set the action of 'The Ancient Mariner' going," indeed "crystallized the structural design of the poem."[49] And it *is*, after all, the albatross's innocent blood that incarnadines the nightmare world of the poem.

As earlier mentioned, the coloring shared by *The Ancient Mariner* and Turner's painting, *Slavers*, has evoked a number of recent comparisons. "The setting sun," James A. W. Heffernan writes, "sends its influence to every part of the picture, and though the bleeding of the slaves is more implicit than explicit, the colors are essentially those of fire and blood." Noting Coleridge's use of "the same kind of coloring" forty-two years earlier, Heffernan remarks that in *The Ancient Mariner*,

> the color of blood is diffused through the sea and the sky—as if the entire seascape had been bloodied by the mariner's deed. . . . Like Turner's *Slavers*, . . . the seascape of *The Ancient Mariner* is dominated by the color of fire and blood. Mirroring at once the guilt of the Mariner and his purgatorial suffering, the pervasive redness in this poem also unifies the many-colored elements of his world.[50]

In the same volume (*Images of Romanticism*), Ronald Paulson, after discussing *The Ancient Mariner* and Turner's "use of similar lighting effects," concludes: "If he thought about Coleridge's sun I am sure it meant to him God's wrath and

48. Philip Quarll, *The English Hermit . . . Surprizing Adventures of Mr. Philip Quarll*, 157. Captain George Shelvocke, *A Voyage round the World by the Way of the Great South Sea*, 72–73. Lowes (*The Road to Xanadu*, 485–86) argues convincingly that Coleridge, characteristically following up Wordsworth's suggestion, read the passage himself. He wasn't alone. Coming across the same pages in Shelvocke in 1810, De Quincey "at once" saw in it "the germ" of Coleridge's poem, and put the question to the author. From De Quincey's slightly cryptic account, it must be inferred that Coleridge denied that it was the poem's "germ" but can hardly have denied knowing the passage to which, as De Quincey confirmed, Wordsworth had directed him. It was well known, Wordsworth told De Quincey, "that Coleridge had derived, from the very passage I had cited, the original hint for the action of the poem." De Quincey's observations, which first appeared in *Tait's Edinburgh Magazine* (September 1834, page 511), may be found in that compendium of his *Tait's* pieces, *Recollections of the Lakes and the Lake Poets*, 38–39.

49. *The Road to Xanadu*, 206, 208.

50. "The English Romantic Perception of Color," 146–47.

the mariner's conscience, bloodying the sky in *Slavers*." In his seascapes, says James B. Twitchell, who devotes most of a chapter to "aspects of the sublime" connecting Turner's painting and Coleridge's poem, Turner "takes us visually to that same point where the redeeming action of *The Rime* occurs; he takes us to the line where sea and sky cleave. . . . In both painting and poem, it is the blood-red sun that shatters the horizon and breaks the separation between natural and supernatural, real and daemonic."[51]

Intriguing as these observations are, they stay at the level of analogy or striking parallel. While such comparative exercises tend to be inconclusive, going beyond the analogical relation to suggest more than coincidence is, without solid evidence, highly speculative. Perhaps Turner had Coleridge's poem in mind, perhaps not; either way, it is the coloration, even if it has a profound moral dimension, not the slavery theme that links poem and painting for all three critics. Yet there may be more here than similar coloring, something that would explain the connection Heffernan, Paulson, and Twitchell note between the lurid hue of *Slavers* and the Mariner's "guilt," his "conscience," and the question of "God's wrath."

As it happens, Turner did have at least one poetic precursor for *Slavers*. The lines appended to his painting as an explanatory footnote are his own, from his sententious epic, *The Fallacies of Hope*. But, like the rest of his gloomy opus, these lines of Turner—in which "Yon angry setting sun and fierce-edged clouds / Declare the Typhon's coming," as the slavers prepare to "throw overboard / The dead and dying," heedless of "their chains"—are in the style of his poetic master, James Thomson. Their obvious source, and the literary (as opposed to historical) source for *Slavers*, is the storm passage (lines 980–1025) of the *Summer* section of Thomson's *The Seasons*. Thomson's "circling typhon, whirled from point to point" (line 984), anticipates the whirl of Turner's painting, as well as the spelling of *Typhon* in both his subtitle and in his poetic footnote. Following a reference to Vasco da Gama

> labouring round the stormy Cape,—
> By bold ambition led, and bolder thirst
> Of gold,

and to "The rising world of trade" becoming "unbounded commerce" (lines 1003–6, 1012), Thomson presents a vignette of the slave trade. His moral outrage breaks through the Miltonic blank verse, syntax, and diction:

> Increasing still the terrors of these storms,
> His jaws horrific armed with threefold fate,
> Here dwells the direful shark. Lured by the scent
> Of steaming crowds, of rank disease, and death,
> Behold! he rushing cuts the briny flood,
> Swift as the gale can bear the ship along;
> And from the partners of that cruel trade

51. Paulson, "Turner's Graffiti: The Sun and Its Glosses," 178. Twitchell, *Romantic Horizons: Aspects of the Sublime in English Poetry and Painting, 1770–1850*, 101, 105.

Which spoils unhappy Guinea of her sons
Demands his share of prey—demands themselves.
The stormy fates descend: one death involves
Tyrants and slaves; when straight, their mangled limbs
Crushing at once, he dyes the purple seas
With gore, and riots in the vengeful meal.[52]

Thomson's passage—its storm and wrecked slave ship reminiscent of the roughly contemporaneous *Robinson Crusoe*—puts into poetry, and moralizes, an incident recorded in Jean Barbot's *Description of the Coasts of North and South Guinea,* and, as T. R. S. Boase has demonstrated, Turner put Thomson into paint in *Slavers.*[53]

Of course, *The Seasons* had also been read by Coleridge. His "truth-painting imagination" in "On the Slave Trade" presented us with slaves "crammed into the hold of a ship with so many fellow-victims, that the heat and stench, arising

52. James Thomson, *"The Seasons" and "The Castle of Indolence,"* ed. James Sambrook, 64–65 (lines 1013–25). In a section (632–897) that appears earlier in *Summer,* but which was added to the poem in 1744, Thomson described the exotic "wonders of the torrid zone," including the "rocks rich in gems" and the sun-engendered gold that led to these regions being exploited (which Thomson deplores) and "civilized" (which he applauds). In one passage, drawing on *Purchas, his Pilgrimage* (1617) and Book IV of *Paradise Lost,* sources later to be mined by Coleridge in "Kubla Khan," Thomson directs his Muse to the "Nubian mountains" and "Abyssinia" (751–52). Addressing that Muse, he says: "Thou art no ruffian, who beneath the mask / Of social commerce, com'st to rob their wealth; / No holy fury thou, blaspheming Heaven, / With consecrated steel to stab their peace" (753–56).

After describing the Nile and the Niger, "In which the full-formed maids of Afric lave / Their jetty limbs" (823–24), he turns westward, to South America, including the "isles" (one of which was Crusoe's) over which "the branching Oronoque / Rolls a brown deluge" (834–35). This world, Thomson continues, was a pagan paradise, "The seat of blameless Pan, yet undisturbed / By Christian crimes and Europe's cruel sons" (854–55). But, just as India had been despoiled of her gems and "Afric's golden rivers" drained by Europeans, so the New World's "fatal treasures" drew the Spanish and Portuguese. He speaks of "sad Potosi's mines / Where dwelt the gentlest children of the Sun" (871–72), alluding to the Bolivian silver mines where native workers were cruelly treated by the Spanish, and to the sun-worshiping Incas of Peru.

But Thomson remains hopelessly ambivalent. The tropical zone's "ill-fated race" (875) knows nothing of "Progressive truth," including the true religion; nothing of European thought, "laws, / And all-protective freedom" (878–82). With no apparent irony, he concludes, "The parent Sun himself/ Seems o'er this world of slaves to tyrannize." Love, tenderness, sensibility, "the ineffable delight / Of sweet humanity: these court the beam / Of milder climes—in selfish fierce desire / And the wild fury of voluptuous sense / There lost. The very brute creation there / This rage partakes, and burns with horrid fire" (884–97). Given this solar mandate for European enslavement of these ill-fated folk, it is well that Thomson reminds us, four verse paragraphs later, of "that cruel trade / Which spoils unhappy Guinea of her sons."

53. For Barbot, see Churchill's *Collection of Voyages,* V (1732), 225–26; cited by A. D. McKillop, *The Background of Thomson's Seasons,* 165. Boase, "Shipwrecks in English Romantic Poetry."

from [their] diseased bodies, rot the very deck." That description may recall "the scent / Of steaming crowds, of rank disease, and death"—the stench that lures the slavers' predatory partner in crime, the shark, in Thomson's lines. The suggestion is not all that far-fetched. Southey seems to have recalled Thomson's lines in the sonnets opening his 1794 sequence condemning the slave trade. The first has "Niger's tainted flood" rolling "to the ravenous shark his banquet slain," and calls for "fire and sword" to wreak vengeance on "yon treacherous vessel, and her godless crew," while the second cries out for the God of justice to

> bid the wind
> Whelm that cursed bark beneath the mountain-wave,
> And bless with liberty and death the Slave![54]

Coleridge, sharing rooms with Southey at the time, was reading Thomson at least as early as 1795, when we find him (*CL* I 154–55) quoting lines to which he has a "Yes but" (lines which, I suggest in Part Two, he may have re-presented in nightmare form in the dungeon-grate stanza of *The Ancient Mariner*).

That passage is from *The Castle of Indolence,* but Coleridge also knew *The Seasons* well enough to borrow from it for "The Destiny of Nations," a poem with aquatic and political links to *The Ancient Mariner.* Visiting Nether Stowey in May–June 1798, William Hazlitt joined Coleridge for a walking tour down the Bristol Channel. He records drawing to Coleridge's attention "the bare masts of a vessel on the very edge of the horizon and within the red-orbed disc of the setting sun, like his own spectre-ship in the *Ancient Mariner.*" Seven sentences later, he tells us that in the parlour of a small inn they discovered a "little worn-out copy of *The Seasons* lying in a window-seat." "That is true fame!" exclaimed the poet who had recently completed *The Ancient Mariner.*[55]

The remark confirms Coleridge's knowledge and high evaluation of *The Seasons.* Perhaps Thomson's sea dyed purple with the mingled gore of innocent slaves and tyrants whose "cruel trade . . . spoils unhappy Guinea of her sons" provided, as it later would for Turner, both blood-red coloration and thematic content for Coleridge's poem. Certainly, Thomson's eye of the storm—"a cloudy speck / Compressed," which he himself tells us is "called by the sailors the ox-eye, being in appearance no bigger" (Thomson's note to lines 987–88)—resembles the Mariner's sighting of the tiny "cloud" that turns out to be the spectre-bark, which both Ware and Empson suggest Coleridge envisioned as a slave ship:

54. *Poetical Works of Robert Southey* 1:65–66. Sonnet V in the sequence (67) justifies, indeed celebrates, a slave who has taken bloody vengeance; and, the next year, in an atypically taut invocation "To the Genius of Africa" (1:68–70), Southey calls for that avenging power to collectively arise: "By the rank, infected air / That taints those cabins of despair; / By the scourges blackened o'er, / And stiff and hard with human gore; / By every groan of deep distress, / By every curse of wretchedness; / The vices and the crimes that flow / From the hopelessness of woe; / By every drop of blood bespilt; / By Afric's wrongs and Europe's guilt,— / Awake! arise! avenge!"

55. "My First Acquaintance with Poets," in *The Complete Works of William Hazlitt* 17:120.

> I saw a something in the Sky
> *No bigger* than my fist;
> At first it seemed a *little speck* . . .
> (lines 139–41, 1798 version)

At that point, we are confronted with the sun peering through the ship's masts as if through a "dungeon-grate"—something strikingly different from Thomson's open "Windows of the Sky / Through which the Morning shews her dewy face" (*CL* I 154–55).

Whether or not Coleridge had Thomson's lines from *The Seasons* in mind, Turner did. Ruskin's unforgettable description of *Slavers* also ends with an allusion, neither to Thomson's *Seasons* nor Coleridge's *Ancient Mariner,* but to Shakespeare's *Macbeth*. His point in doing so, however, is one that would be endorsed by Thomson, Southey, Coleridge, and Turner alike:

> What hands are here? Ha! they pluck out mine eyes.
> Will all great Neptune's ocean wash this blood
> Clean from my hand? No, this my hand will rather
> *The multitudinous seas incarnadine,*
> Making the green one red.[56]

Painting in 1840, on the eve of London's hosting of the first International Anti-Slavery Convention, Turner was doubtless reflecting the newfound moral superiority of the British, whose 1833 abolition of slavery had recently (August 1838) resulted in actual emancipation of all West Indian slaves. Yet the final lines of the poem he attached to *Slavers*—"fallacious Hope! / Where is thy market now?"—refer, not to the

> commercial failure of the slavers' enterprise but, in an extended sense, to the moral bankruptcy of the trade that deals in human beings. Even more specifically, [*Slavers*] is a critique of a whole economy which will buy and sell anything, which has turned the profit motive into the ultimate bond between people—an ultimate bond which, as we see in the painting, is all too easily severed.[57]

In *Modern Painters,* written three years after *Slavers* had been exhibited, Ruskin placed his description in the "Truth of Water" section, properly elevating the painting's daring aesthetic conception above its historical reference. Nevertheless, his famous prose seascape is as much a *paysage moralisé* as Turner's original dramatization of historical cruelty, set as it is during the sinking of that blood-red sun. Furthermore, by alluding to Macbeth's guilty cry about his murderous hand incarnadining the sea, Ruskin (who eventually sold the painting, finding it too painful to repeatedly contemplate) verbalizes what he takes *Slavers* to convey: the conviction that until slavery and its legacy truly cease, no washing of hands will cleanse us of collective guilt, even complicity.

"We are all guilty," William Wilberforce had warned the Commons back in 1789, initiating both the antislavery debate and the evangelical age of atone-

---

56. *Macbeth* II.ii.60; italics added.
57. Wolfgang Kemp, *The Desire of My Eyes: A Life of John Ruskin,* 104.

ment. As Coleridge had said in his 1795 diatribe against the slave trade, "the guilt of all, attaches to each one who is knowingly an accomplice"—just as the Mariner's crew, by justifying his murderous act, the killing of an albatross that was "black" in Coleridge's source, "make themselves accomplices in the crime." With the multitudinous seas themselves incarnadined, more is blood-red than the tea sipped by Coleridge's refined lady oblivious to the fact that her beverage is sweetened by the produce of Britannia's "sugar isles" blackened "with slaves."

Those West Indian islands appear in an unpublished gloss to the lines in *The Ancient Mariner* describing the sudden sinking of the sun and the no-less-sudden departure of the terrifying spectre-bark:

> The Sun's rim dips; the stars rush out;
> At one stride comes the dark;
> With far-heard whisper o'er the sea
> Off shot the spectre-bark.
>
> (lines 199–202)

The terse and beautiful gloss that now accompanies this stanza—"No twilight within the courts of the sun"—was added only in 1828, the single new addition to the poem's gloss since 1817 and the final result of at least four earlier attempts. An intriguingly specific and far more ominous manuscript version (inscribed "Highgate, 29 July 1820") is preserved in a copy of *Sibylline Leaves* at Harvard University: "Within the tropics there is no twilight. At the moment, the second, that the Sun sinks, the Stars appear all at once *as if at the word of a command announced by the evening Gun, in our W. India Islands*" (italics added). If the poem's sinking, "bloody Sun" and this sudden darkness *are* covertly linked with black slavery, *The Ancient Mariner* curiously anticipates Ralph Ellison's jocoserious mingling of blackness, blood, and the sun in the parodic sermon "The Blackness of Blackness" in his 1952 novel *Invisible Man*:

> *"Brothers and sisters, my text this morning is the 'Blackness of Blackness'."*
> *And a congregation of voices answered: "That blackness is most black, brother, most black . . ."*
> *"In the beginning . . ."*
> *"At the very start," they cried.*
> *". . . there was blackness . . ."*
> *"Preach it . . ."*
> *"and the sun . . ."*
> *"The sun, Lawd . . ."*
> *". . . was bloody red . . ."*
> *"Red . . ."*
> *"Now black is . . ." the preacher shouted.*
> *"Bloody . . ."*
> *"I said black is . . ."*
> *"Preach it, brother . . ."*
> *". . . an' black ain't . . ."*
> *"Red, Lawd, red. He said it's red!"* [58]

58. *Invisible Man*, 9.

4

There are related "political" implications beneath the visual surface of *The Ancient Mariner.* Robert Lowell, in a class he gave at Harvard, described Coleridge's "opium poem" as a work full of "phantasmagoria" and "fetters clanking."[59] I think myself that both the dungeon-grate, which is present in the text, and the fetters Lowell heard clanking in the subtext, found their way into the poem, not only because of covert connections with slavery, but also as a result of the personal and political history of the months during which *The Ancient Mariner* was being written and revised—months during which Coleridge, supposedly retired from politics, became publicly active again only to find himself dangerously exposed during a period of sudden and intensified domestic repression that saw many of the Pitt government's opponents (and Coleridge, as a contributor to the *Morning Post,* was known to be one) transported or imprisoned without benefit of habeas corpus. The fetters of oppression were still clanking, but this time closer to home than "Afric's" raided shores.

Part Two of the present project, which advances this argument, comes perilously close to twisting an apparently apolitical poem into a political allegory. An extended but less extreme attempt to place *The Ancient Mariner* in a socioeconomic context, relating it to Coleridge's "political awareness," is J. B. Ebbatson's "Coleridge's Mariner and the Rights of Man," which attributes the harsh punishment inflicted on the Mariner and his shipmates to "European racial guilt, and the need to make restitution." Though I focus more on domestic political events and he, like Ware and Empson, on Coleridge's attitude to mercantile expansion, especially the slave trade, our political readings are not mutually exclusive. "Ideas and images existed symbiotically in Coleridge's teeming imagination," as Ebbatson notes; "there is an interaction between them, and a multiple range of meanings."[60]

I bring all this up because the "allegory" I later trace, and the "allegory" given "universality and scope" by what Malcolm Ware detects as Coleridge's reference in *The Ancient Mariner* to a slave ship, are considerably different from what Defoe later—in the *Serious Reflections*—called the "allusive allegorick history" of the life of Crusoe. Whatever the Puritan allegory of sin and redemption woven into, or superimposed upon, *The Life and Strange Surprizing Adventures of Robinson Crusoe, of York, Mariner,* Crusoe himself, despite the fact that he is shipwrecked while engaged as a slave trader, never, in his long years of religious introspection on the island, devotes so much as a passing thought to

59. As reported by Helen Vendler, "Lowell in the Classroom," 26.
60. "Coleridge's Mariner and the Rights of Man," 198–99. In the 1964 *Critical Quarterly* article, Empson declares that despite critical sighs of "relief that the fanciful reverie is so free of politics," *The Ancient Mariner* actually "appeals to a proud national tradition and evokes a major historical event, the maritime expansion of the Western Europeans." He might be describing *Robinson Crusoe.* One cannot speak for the brilliantly outrageous Empson; but, like Ware and Ebbatson, far from wanting to impoverish the poem, I merely want to draw attention to a few more of its myriad elements—some of them political.

the possibility that commerce in human flesh might have been part of the sin for which he was being punished. Why not, if his creator was at least "ambivalent" toward slaves and slavery? But Crusoe never attains even the modest moral high ground reached by Defoe in the *Reformation of Manners,* where sympathy is expressed for the "harmless Natives" whose souls are bartered for baubles: baubles which, on most occasions, Defoe justifies as fair profit.

It may be true, as Meier says, that advocacy of slavery was "socially acceptable" in the earlier eighteenth century; it may even be that Coleridge, in annotating *Robinson Crusoe,* was simply acknowledging that historical fact. But neither this, nor his oscillating evolution from libertarianism to social conservatism, can *fully* explain Coleridge's silence in the margins. Quite aside from his own sensitivity to the moral atrocity of slavery and the slave trade, Coleridge had read works, written in the mid- and later eighteenth century, that both resemble and depart from Defoe's presentation of the slavery "theme" in *Robinson Crusoe.* Coleridge seems not to have read Captain Stedman's account of the slave revolt in Surinam until 1799, but two other books, both by the Reverend John Newton, appear to have become part of the extraordinarily complex genesis of *The Ancient Mariner.*

The first, Newton's *Authentic Narrative* (1764), probably influenced, as Bernard Martin has argued, the crime-repentance-atonement theme of the poem.[61] In the second, *Thoughts Upon the African Slave Trade* (1788), Newton again purges guilt, guilt specifically incurred on a slave vessel, through the same kind of public confession engaged in both by Coleridge's Mariner and by Robert Southey's "Sailor Who Had Served in the Slave Trade."

Both Malcolm Ware, in his speculation that the spectre-bark might be a slave ship, and Chris Rubenstein, in a paper delivered at the 1990 Coleridge Summer Conference, connect Coleridge's with Southey's ballad. In "A New Identity for the Mariner," Rubenstein suggests that Coleridge's Mariner, like Southey's sailor, had formerly been a crewman aboard a slave ship. Certainly, the resemblances between the two poems are striking. Both, to begin with, are ballads, and both have framing narratives. Southey's poem opens with a "Christian minister" (combining the roles of Coleridge's Wedding Guest and shrieving Hermit) going "forth at eve amid the fields / Near Bristol's ancient towers."

The location is significant. Bristol was the center of the English slave trade. In 1798, the year Southey's poem and *The Ancient Mariner* were written, income derived from the West Indies was four times as great as that drawn from the rest of the world, and as noted by Eric Williams (historian and later prime minister of Trinidad and Tobago), much of that wealth accrued to Bristol as a slaving

61. *"The Ancient Mariner" and the "Authentic Narrative."* Martin's short book (only forty-four pages of text, followed by a reprint of *The Ancient Mariner* and excerpts from the *Authentic Narrative*) establishes Wordsworth's knowledge of Newton's work, unmistakably echoed in *The Prelude* and *The Excursion.* While there are no such persuasive verbal parallels in the case of *The Ancient Mariner,* Newton's repentance and public confession-atonement almost certainly—directly or via Wordsworth—provide some of the background for *The Ancient Mariner.*

port: "Sumptuous mansions, luxurious living, liveried menials, were the produce of the wealth made from the sufferings . . . of the slaves bought and sold by Bristol merchants. . . . [The sugar trade] was worth to Bristol twice as much as all her other overseas commerce."[62]

It is in this context that Southey's Christian minister hears, breathed from "a lonely out-house" in sight of the sumptuous city, a "voice of woe," and groans less of pain than of "wretchedness":

> Heart-rending groans they were, with words
>   Of bitterest despair,
> Yet with the holy name of Christ
>   Pronounced in broken prayer.
>
> The Christian minister went in,
>   A sailor there he sees,
> Whose hands were lifted up to Heaven,
>   And he was on his knees.

Asked what is wrong, the sailor cries out, "I have done a cursed thing!" ("I had done a hellish thing," the Mariner acknowledges in reporting the words with which his shipmates cursed him after he had slain the albatross.) The cursed thing that "haunts" Southey's sailor "night and day" involves his past service on a slave ship:

> I sailed on board a Guinea-man,
>   And to the slave-coast went:
> Would that the sea had swallowed me,
>   When I was innocent!

But he is no longer innocent. The cursed act he needs to confess—appropriately enough, to a minister outside the slaving port of Bristol—is his having flogged to death, at the captain's orders, a recalcitrant female slave. In a passage that, more overtly than *The Ancient Mariner,* anticipates Turner's *Slavers Throwing Overboard the Dead and Dying,* her body was thrown overboard. The sailor "saw the sea close over her," yet he still sees and hears her:

> she is still in sight;
> I see her twisting every where;
>   I hear her day and night.
>
> Go where I will, do what I can,
>   The Wicked One I see;
> Dear Christ, have mercy on my soul!
>   O God, deliver me![63]

Southey's straightforward ballad, so close in ways to Coleridge's, almost confirms a shared if covert slavery theme in *The Rime of the Ancient Mariner.* The poems certainly share, along with the ballad form, the theme of lost innocence, demonic pursuit, and their anguished protagonists' need to confess their guilt to

62. *Capitalism and Slavery,* 53.
63. *Poetical Works* 1:72–75.

a "Christian minister." Southey's ballad was published in the same year, 1798, that the poem of his former fellow-Pantisocrat appeared in *Lyrical Ballads*—only to be dismissed by Southey as an unintelligible "Dutch attempt at German sublimity."[64]

In addition, Coleridge's partner in *that* enterprise, *Lyrical Ballads*, wrote in the same year "The Discharged Soldier," haunting lines on a ghostly, blighted veteran, discharged and suffering from diseases contracted while serving in "the tropic isles": soldiering, that is, in those "sugar isles" blackened "with slaves." That was Coleridge's sardonic description of "our W. India Islands," the area he had specifically targeted in his anti–slave trade ode of 1792. Wordsworth, too, though he wrote no ode on the subject, registers in *The Prelude* the extent to which, in 1792–1793, the "whole Nation" was "crying with one voice" against "the traffickers in Negro blood" (X.212, 206 [1805]). The task of Wordsworth's pestilence-stricken veteran, like that of virtually all British soldiers assigned at that time to the West Indies (thousands of whom died of yellow fever), must have included the grim work of subduing the slave rebellions ignited in British islands by the formidable Jacobin, Victor Hugues. Most of "The Discharged Soldier," never printed as a separate poem, was incorporated in weaker form at the conclusion of Book IV of *The Prelude*. In powerful lines inexplicably omitted from *The Prelude*, this wasted figure is described as

> Forlorn and desolate, a man cut off
> From all his kind, and more than half detached
> From his own nature. He was alone. . . . [65]

If this solitary apparition, who now puts his "trust . . . in the God of Heaven," anticipates the Leech Gatherer of "Resolution and Independence," he also resembles Coleridge's guilty Mariner, "alone, alone, all, all alone," until partially redeemed by that blessing of the water-snakes that enables him to pray. Indeed, the ghastly figure in "The Discharged Soldier"—a poem begun in January–February 1798, after Wordsworth had withdrawn from his brief collaboration on *The Ancient Mariner,* and finished before Coleridge completed his

64. "Lyrical Ballads," 201.
65. "The Discharged Soldier," lines 58–60. For the original text, see Beth Darlington, "Two Early Texts: *A Night-Piece* and *The Discharged Soldier*," 433–37. "He was alone" is retained in the 1805 *Prelude* (later dropped); but both the 1805 and the 1850 *Prelude* omit the other lines quoted. (Here and in Part Two I cite, unless otherwise specified, the 1805 version of *The Prelude*.)
Between 1793 and 1798, when Wordsworth wrote this poem, some forty thousand British soldiers had been lost to yellow fever, with an equal number rendered unfit for further service (according to the estimates of British army historian Sir John William Fortescue). The West Indian strategy, aimed both at putting down slave rebellions on the British islands and at capturing French islands, was based on the expectation that this would destroy the power of France. The British discovered, too late, that they had practically destroyed their own army. The West Indian campaigns had also been a near fatal distraction. By 1798, Britain "could not mobilize sufficient strength in Europe to put the republican genie back in the bottle. The way was open for Napoleon" (Kennedy, *Orders from France*, 139).

ballad—is Wordsworth's direct response to his friend's Mariner. But while Paul Magnuson devotes a dozen pages of his recent study of the poetic "dialogue" between Coleridge and Wordsworth to a persuasive demonstration of the relationship of these two haunted figures,[66] he never speculates on why Wordsworth chose to quietly, yet historically, trace his veteran's emaciation of body and soul to the West Indian campaigns, a solitary figure "Remembering the importance of his theme, / But feeling it no longer" (lines 145–46). Perhaps the condition of *both* wasted men—the veteran "lank, . . . long & lean," and the aged Mariner (in a phrase Wordsworth contributed to Coleridge's poem) "long, and lank"—has *something* to do with the guilt incurred by connection, actual or symbolic, with slavery and the slave trade: a guilt shared by Southey's sailor, who, having killed in the course of his service in that trade, ends up bemoaning his crime and seeking forgiveness from a cleric in a cowshed outside Bristol. In sharp contrast—to say it one last time, and at the risk of being forced, like Denis Donoghue, to fill the gap between my sensibility and Crusoe's by "moralizing"— Robinson Crusoe's slave-associated activities play no part in the sense of guilt and need for redemption that figure in what one critic rightly calls "Crusoe's warmest and most characteristic emotion, his anxiety for his soul."[67]

While there is little in Crusoe's unimaginative character to stir the *reader's* soul, most would probably agree with Sutherland that "as far as morality can be said to exist" in a story whose "actions are oddly removed from the moral world, . . . Crusoe is a thoroughly moral man" who, later, "becoming religious, . . . takes to reading his Bible."[68] For Coleridge, apparently, this odd removal of the novel's action from the moral world did not prevent him from making numerous observations of a moral and religious nature in the margins, while, simultaneously, allowing him to designate Crusoe at once a Universal Representative of mankind and a moral figure somehow beyond morality. We are back, in short, to the point raised in the 1818 literary lecture in which Coleridge declared that "The charm of De Foe's works, especially of *Robinson Crusoe,* is founded on the same principle" as many tales in the *Arabian Nights:* they "cause no deep feeling of a moral kind" (*CM* I 159).

This resembles the point Coleridge made in the response to Mrs. Barbauld, in which he said that *The Ancient Mariner* "ought to have no more moral" than one of the more arbitrary tales in the *Arabian Nights.* The two comments are close but not identical, for, as Humphry House insists in his concise and penetrating study of Coleridge's major poems, "Coleridge never said or meant that the 'Mariner' neither had nor was meant to have a moral bearing or a 'moral sentiment.' He said that the fault was '*the obtrusion* of the moral sentiment *so openly* . . . in a work of pure imagination.'"[69]

The more accurate version of Coleridge's response (actually separate obser-

66. *Coleridge and Wordsworth: The Lyrical Dialogue,* 84–95.
67. William Halewood, "Religion and Invention in *Robinson Crusoe,*" 339.
68. *Daniel Defoe: A Critical Study,* 232.
69. *Coleridge: The Clark Lectures, 1951–1952,* 90–91.

vations cobbled together by H. N. Coleridge) is ambiguous: Coleridge said "the poem . . . had too much moral, and that too openly obtruded on the reader" (*TT* I 272–73). Perhaps he was more aware of his own moralizing tendency than recent critics have suggested. Nevertheless, most readers will tend to agree with House, who, noting the moral ingredients even in the *Arabian Nights*'s tale of "The Merchant and the Genie," emphasizes only Coleridge's "possible dissatisfaction with the summary of the 'moral' as a kind of didactic epigram towards the end" of *The Ancient Mariner.* Many modern readers have been put off not only by the didactic epigram, but also by the systematic moralizing imposed on the poem by the Mariner in dialogue with the Wedding Guest and, especially, by Coleridge as later theologian-glossist. To some, that Christian overlay has seemed as much an excrescence, or "afterthought," as the religious theme of *Robinson Crusoe* seemed to James Joyce and Ian Watt. Nevertheless, being the work of a profoundly moral man, Coleridge's poem—however wonderfully and terrifyingly remote from the everyday world, however fantastic a voyage—could hardly be without *some* moral bearing or "moral sentiment," even if it had to be forcibly imposed on recalcitrant—or, as Southey said, disconnected, "absurd or unintelligible"—materials.

We need not find a slave ship in the text to confirm the poem's moral sentiment—though I was struck by a related "application" of the moral by Martin Gardner. Writing in 1965, during the civil rights movement in the United States, Gardner focused the final portion of his discussion on the "moral" of the poem—the "final question, and one that has troubled critics for more than a century and a half." What we make of it, he writes, "depends on whether we accept the symbolic religious theme." Not all readers do; but Coleridge did, Gardner rightly concludes, and he quotes from a letter written two weeks before the death Coleridge knew was imminent, in which the dying man reaffirms as "the originating, continuing and sustaining wish and design of my heart," the desire "to exalt the glory" of God; "and, which is the same thing in other words, to promote the improvement of mankind." Repeating the "moral" quatrain,

> He prayeth best, who loveth best
> All things both great and small;
> For the dear God who loveth us,
> He made and loveth all,

Gardner concludes by placing us in a rather different church than the one in which Ellison's preacher held forth on "The Blackness of Blackness":

> At present, Christian churches in this country are suddenly discovering the moral's application to the racially "small" in our midst, our Negro minority. "He prayeth best who loveth best. . . ." How fare, one wonders, the prayers of our southern Catholics and Protestants who refuse to take communion if the person next to them has skin of a different color? Cross-bows come in all shapes and sizes.[70]

70. "Interpretations," an essay appended to *The Annotated Ancient Mariner, Illustrated by Gustave Doré*, 228, 231–32.

Though the point would hold even if slavery and the slave trade were completely unconscious undercurrents in the poem, it would be more than poetic justice if Gardner's "application" of the "moral" of *The Ancient Mariner* had, as well, an objective justification in Coleridge's original if covert intention. Coleridge, after all, was as familiar as Southey's sailor with "Bristol's ancient towers," the most prominent of which is the tower of St. Mary Redcliffe's, a church with a history even darker than that of Gardner's in the segregationist South. Often, while the members of the prosperous merchant congregation, many of them engaged in the English sugar and slave trade, listened piously to the sermon in the upper church, in the basement down below groaning slaves were writhing in chains. Beneath the piety of Coleridge's moral and later theological gloss, a more specific moral theme may be writhing in the subtext of *The Rime of the Ancient Mariner.*

But if morality *is* a factor—preferably unobtrusive—in works of even the purest imagination, then we are back roughly where we started: wondering again, especially when we recall those very serious religious comments scribbled in the margins of the novel, why the annotator has nothing to say about what, from Coleridge's perspective even in 1830, was Crusoe's unquestionably *im*moral position, and practice, regarding human slavery. The novel, in other words, *should* have caused in Coleridge at least *one* "deep feeling of a moral kind."

We return to Crusoe—not to begin all over, but to end. I have been arguing that there is as much high seriousness behind Robinson Crusoe's dictatorial self-portraits as there is behind Coleridge's refusal to trap mice or shoot hawks (and, presumably, albatrosses). One man is a slave-master, the other someone opposed to cruelty of any sort, and the final joke is that neither man is joking. Consequently, we must see Crusoe and Coleridge, even later Coleridge, less as kindred than as antithetical spirits. Re-reading Defoe's novel, one of his youthful favorites, Coleridge must have realized that his Everyman, his alleged "Universal Representative," thinks, feels, and acts in ways alien to some of Coleridge's own most fundamental instincts and principles—not only as a youthful radical but as a venerable conservative who remained, if not an egalitarian, a humanitarian. Even if Defoe was oblivious to his hero's commodification of human beings as well as animals, and above all indifferent to, or in approval of, his reduction of black people to "produce" of Africa, how could *Coleridge*—who, despite his later speculations on race and growing political conservatism, remained an opponent of the slave trade and of slavery—have failed to remark on positions that must have seemed to him reprehensible or, at the very least, less than personally and universally "representative"?

Clearly, if it were not for his willing if selective suspension of the "moral" category as he re-read *Robinson Crusoe* in 1830, Coleridge would have found serious obstacles even to Sutherland's depiction of Crusoe as an "ordinary decent man," let alone to his own repeated proclamation of him as a Universal Representative with whom we can all identify. John Richetti is not alone in finding Crusoe "shallow-hearted and self-seeking": along with such Defoe characters as Moll and Singleton, "not the sort of [person] one might trust or even care to know."[71] The gulf between Crusoe and the youthful Coleridge, for example, might well be measured by the distance between hailing a jackass "Brother!" and the relegation of "both man and bird and beast" to hierarchically structured classes of "servants," "subjects," and "slaves": a hierarchy formally established on Crusoe's island in the *Farther Adventures*. It is true that, finally, Crusoe's wanderlust supersedes even his love of rule; off on what he acknowledges to be "a Wild Goose Chase" around the world, he leaves behind the island to which he had returned after an eight-year absence and which he had ruled as an absolute monarch, without, however, having taken "Possession of the Place [and] fortified and strengthen'd it in the Name of *England*" (*Farther Adventures* 3:80). In effect, less an imperialist than the same old adventurous individual, he admits to having failed his country in the role of successful colonist. Crusoe's colony, as Pat Rogers remarks, "is a poor advertisement for the ideology which imbued so much of Defoe's writing throughout his life. His fictional left hand seems not to trust the aspirations of his polemical right hand."[72] At the same time, sounding like a recent convert, Crusoe acknowledges, in this same passage in the *Farther Adventures*, having acted in the past "in a kind of haughty majestick way, like an old Patriarchal Monarch."

Toward the very end of this second installment of the novel, encountering in Siberia an exiled Russian minister, Crusoe at first boasts of his formerly benevolent but despotic rule, a sovereignty on his island greater than that enjoyed by the Czar since he had

> the absolute Disposal of the Lives and Fortunes of all my Subjects: That notwithstanding my absolute Power, I had not one Person disaffected to my Government, or to my Person, in all my Dominions. . . . That all the Lands in my Kingdom were my own, and all my Subjects were not only my Tenants, but Tenants at Will: That they would all fight for me to the last Drop; and that never Tyrant, *for such I acknowledged myself to be,* was ever so universally beloved, and yet so horribly feared by his Subjects. (*Farther Adventures* 3:200–201)

The philosophic courtier persuades him that "the true Greatness of Life was to be Master of our selves" (3:200); but this illumination comes later, long after the island chapters of the original *Robinson Crusoe*, the book the world has remembered. When one recalls the earlier Crusoe's mingled fearfulness and assertiveness, particularly evident in his erection of ever-more-secure fortifications and the assertion of his "dominion" over others, there is perhaps less reason to identify him with Everyman or the mythic Culture Hero than with their archetypal opposite—the Tyrant: a designation Crusoe himself acknowledges in the passage just cited.

But perhaps it is a case of Both/And rather than Either/Or: Everyman *as* Tyrant. *Robinson Crusoe* "gathered together in one man the history of all man-

71. *Defoe's Narratives: Situations and Structures,* i.
72. *"Robinson Crusoe,"* 45–46.

kind." Thus spake Adolf Hitler.[73] Years before he spoke with the Russian minis-
ter, back on his island, Crusoe had disabused the captain he saves from muti-
neers of any idea that he is "God" or an "angel"; he is, he insists, "a man, an
Englishman, and disposed to assist you" (253). But he is to the true captain and
his crew as God's Providence was to him when *he* landed on the island twenty-
eight years earlier. At such a moment Crusoe's lordship, cultural and political,
verges over into the theological, and he seems almost to identify himself with
the divine Providence to which he habitually defers.

In addition, and finally, we cannot see Crusoe as a prototype for Coleridge
himself in regard to the essential point: survival. Crusoe's long endurance, on
the face of it incredible, is made believable only by the realistic detailing of his
middle-class English virtues: the resolution and shrewd, practical, sustained
industry that enable him not only to survive but to triumph over fate and
hostile surroundings. Coleridge, who liked to talk about manual labor but
wasn't much good at it, and who would have affectionately but impractically
spared cats, kittens, maybe even mice and rats to "sport in Love" with "Pussy's
Whiskers," would not have survived, let alone thrived, on Crusoe's island.

Conjuring up the sort of tableau Crusoe so often presents, we might imagine
Coleridge suddenly deposited on that island in the mouth of the Orinoco.[74] We
might even imagine him joined in time by a black man—say, Shad, the Southey
family servant whom the young Pantisocrat had embraced as his "BROTHER."
The conservative Coleridge of 1830 was not that man, but surely—and espe-
cially since they would be removed from any precarious social organization—
theirs would be something very different from the absolute-Master/abject-Slave
relationship of Crusoe and Friday. That was a relationship even the later, Blu-
menbachian Coleridge would have found inadequate, even inhuman—no mat-
ter that it apparently fulfilled the every need, utilitarian and emotional, of the
taciturn and wintry Crusoe.

But what of our castaway faced with the challenges Defoe's hero had met and
mastered daily for "eight and twenty years, two months, and 19 days" (274)?

73. In *Hitler: The Missing Years*, the Führer's gossipy friend Ernst ("Putzi") Hanf-
tängel lists Defoe's novel among the more treasured books in Hitler's library. For a
discussion of Hitler's enthusiastic reading of a few English novels, *Robinson Crusoe* and
Gulliver's Travels among them, see Werner Maser, *Adolf Hitler: Legende, Mythos, Wirk-
lichkeit*, 199.

74. My invented scene is modest compared to that of the contemporary Irish poet
Paul Muldoon, who recently published a 250-page poetic sequence, *Madoc: A Mystery*
(1990), in which he imagines Coleridge and Southey (and Shad), having pushed on with
their Pantisocratic scheme, arriving in America only to have utopia quickly disintegrate,
a victim of the complex realities of imperialistic history. In addition to Iroquois and
Jeffersonian history, Muldoon is interacting with ancient Welsh material first exploited
by Southey in his nine-thousand-line epic, *Madoc*, whose hero is a twelfth-century Welsh
prince who founds a colony in the New World. The second and final part of Southey's
interesting but interminable poem opens with a description of the village of Caermadoc,
a New World settlement which is clearly an idealized vision of what he and Coleridge had
hoped to accomplish, Pantisocracy realized.

Coleridge *might* gradually learn to cope, but one doubts it. He was to write frantically to Tom Poole when he thought his friend was withdrawing his helping hand during the retirement at Nether Stowey: "Am I not ignorant, as a child, of everything that concerns the Garden & the Ground . . . who will instruct me?" (*CL* I 272). And, in fact, his eagerness to cultivate his acre and a half at Stowey quickly waned; as his friend the young Charles Lamb asked, rhetorically, though with affectionate recognition, "& what does your worship know about farming?"[75] But an islanded Coleridge would, one suspects, have outstripped the "compleat natural mechanick" in at least one technological feat—the finding of a substitute for ink[76]—and, having used it to full aesthetic, critical, philosophic, and theological advantage, surrounded by a teeming menagerie treated as pets rather than commodities, he would have died Coleridge. In that sense, the lovable but hapless S. T. C. would have proved himself inferior to Defoe's efficient and environment-mastering British burgher. Nevertheless, applying the sort of quantitative calculus Defoe and Crusoe teach us, we might find more human warmth in one Samuel Taylor Coleridge dead than in a dozen Robinson Crusoes living.

75. *Letters of Charles and Mary Anne Lamb* 1:87.
76. Coleridge found Crusoe's failure to insure his continued ability to write disturbing. One night, having made "5 or 6 pens just as I was going to Bed," Coleridge dreamed of a Robinson Crusoe making "an empire of pens" (*CN* II 2489).

PART TWO

"A Flash of Joy;
And Horror Follows"

Submerged Politics in
The Rime of the Ancient Mariner

Preface to Part Two

To examine a work of art . . . [is] to discover what the work omits as much as—if not more than—what it includes. This is surely the first step in any critical venture.

The epigraph, from René Girard's 1977 *Violence and the Sacred* (207), is an extreme formulation of a position associated with the neo-Marxists and soon to be advanced by the New Historicists, especially those reacting to what they perceived as traditional criticism's acceptance at face value of the Romantic poets' presentation of their own "ideology." I suspect that I am not alone in being torn between—to name the mighty opposites in this modern Romantic dialectic between inclusion and omission, presence and absence, literary text and political context—M. H. Abrams and Jerome McGann.

In the first part of *Coleridge's Submerged Politics*, I puzzled over the *absence* of something *expected:* some comment on the involvement of Robinson Crusoe, Coleridge's "Universal Representative," in slavery and the slave trade, an institution and an activity of which Coleridge, even at his most religiously conservative, hardly approved. In the present speculations about Coleridge's major poem, my curiosity was provoked by a *presence:* the initially *un*expected intrusion into the supposedly apolitical *Ancient Mariner* of images either overtly or covertly "political." The most overt, the simile of the ocean "Still as a Slave before his lord," in a way links the two parts. But with that phrase I deal only briefly, toward the end. My primary attention is given to three phenomena that gradually seemed to me signposts to what the poem was ostensibly *omitting*.

The first, though it occurs last in the poem, is the underwater "rumbling" preceding the convulsion that sucks down the Mariner's ship in a whirlpool: a sonic and whirling imagery I associate with the "rumbling," whirling, and sub-aquatic "up-thundering" accompanying revolutionary upheaval in Coleridge's explicitly political writings in both prose and verse in the 1790s. The second event I focus on is the encounter with the naked hulk bearing Death and the Nightmare Hag, Life-in-Death, my specific concern—as my title suggests—being the "flash of joy" instantly followed by "horror" when the "sail" the Mariner has sighted turns out to be the spectre-bark's bare masts, through which the sun peers "As if thro' a dungeon grate."[1] The third climactic event, a

---

1. *CPW* II 1035. It matters which version—according to Jack Stillinger, at least eighteen are extant—of *The Ancient Mariner* one cites. In Part One, I quoted from the text as

reversal transforming horror to equally sudden joy, is the crucial blessing of the water-snakes at the climax of the passage, which, from the first publication of the poem, has been singled out for particular, indeed virtually universal, admiration.

Sixty years ago, Irving Babbitt broke ranks by criticizing this pivotal passage as the most "extreme example" of the poem's "sham moral" and trivialization of Christian charity: the Mariner is "relieved of the burden of his transgression, symbolized by the albatross hung about his neck, . . . by admiring the color of water snakes." At once extending and reversing the attack launched by Babbitt along the lines later pressed by Edward E. Bostetter and William Empson, the mercurial, iconoclastic, and Bloomian Camille Paglia has recently been predictably audacious enough, in one of the finest chapters in her alternately penetrating and outrageous book *Sexual Personae,* to criticize the blessing of the water-snakes as not only pseudomoralistic but regressive and prompted by fear.[2] Though, aside from Empson, these critics proceed in apolitical ways, these are precisely the points I take up. As far as I am aware, however, no one

---

first published under Coleridge's name in *Sibylline Leaves* (1817), and (essentially) repeated in the 1828, 1829, and 1834 editions of his poems—the last being the text on which E. H. Coleridge based his 1912 Oxford edition, the standard *Poetical Works* until it is replaced by the edition being prepared for the *Collected Coleridge* by J. C. C. Mays. Since the chapters that follow deal with personal and political events of 1797–1798, I cite the poem as first published in *Lyrical Ballads.* But I hasten to add that while I agree with R. H. Tawney that "it is less important" for a historical researcher "to discover new material than to see the meaning of old," I have no intention of reducing *The Ancient Mariner* to its allegedly "real" (that is, political) "meaning" circa 1797–1798. See Stillinger, "The Multiple Versions of Coleridge's Poems: How Many *Mariners* Did Coleridge Write?" 130, 134; and Tawney, "The Study of Economic History," 58.

In 1993, Martin Wallen produced an "Experimental Edition" of *The Ancient Mariner,* printing the three "primary" versions of the poem (1798, 1800, and 1817) horizontally across the page. In fact, Wallen takes into account all six published versions, in addition to manuscript variants and a final gloss, added in 1828. Urging us to read not "*into* but rather *across* or *between* texts," Wallen intends to "avoid allowing any version to achieve privilege over any other, to prevent the suggestion of a final, authoritative text." Since Coleridge's compulsive retelling of *The Ancient Mariner* spans the entire Romantic period, the purpose of his edition, says Wallen, is to call into question any and all allegorical readings of the poem that confirm "a singular moral context," as well as to compel readers to "evaluate anew the alignment of Coleridge's moral and philosophical development along with the meaning of Romanticism" (*Coleridge's Ancient Mariner: An Experimental Edition of Texts and Revisions, 1798–1828,* xvii, xviii, 113, 124).

Incidentally, the hag is not named "Life-in-Death" until 1817, and the sudden reversal, "A flash of joy; And horror follows," is, of course, from the gloss, also added in 1817. My justification for employing it as this section's title is that, as in several other instances (most marvelously the moon-gloss itself), this particular marginal synopsis directly expresses the Mariner's emotion and has a vivid immediacy strikingly different from the "learned" glosses increasingly felt to be not only inadequate to the Mariner's astonishing experiences but an orderly and orthodox falsifying of their irreducible complexity.

2. Babbitt, "The Problem of the Imagination: Coleridge," 120. Paglia, *Sexual Personae: Art and Decadence from Nefertiti to Emily Dickinson,* 326–27.

has preceded me in drawing attention to events in 1797–1798 that might re-
inforce these negative critical responses.

There *is* a family resemblance linking mine with two recent theses. In the
first, advanced in 1988, Daniel P. Watkins argues that the poem's "narrative is a
symbolic formulation of the contradictions and struggles within history," and
that the "Christian structures of authority governing the Mariner's world,"
apparently static and universal, are in fact "in vital conflict with antagonistic
and apparently demonic forces which refuse to remain in the obscurity into
which they have been cast," forces that decisively "undermine the idealized and
uncritical assumptions of love, God, family, and community that prevail in the
Mariner's world." Taking the New Historicist line first advanced by Jerome
McGann in the article I synopsize below, Watkins argues that the poem's narrative

> presents as blackly and blindly demonic the pressing (historical) forces of change
> that make themselves felt despite all refusals to acknowledge their power or even
> their presence. . . . [The poem's "horror elements" are to be seen as] a displace-
> ment of the pressures and fears arising from the rapidly shifting social ground
> during the Romantic period. . . . Because [Coleridge's] conservative vision was in
> large measure a *response* to a historical situation, it was compelled to address the
> various elements in that situation, to explain them and, if possible, to defuse them
> by integrating them into a larger and more palatable scheme. Coleridge could
> never, in the *Rime* or elsewhere, simply write history out of the picture . . . and
> this meant that history was always present not only to shape but also to challenge
> and even to undermine the vision of ideal Christian goodness that he wanted to
> offer.[3]

My argument, in close accord with this general position, is fleshed out in a very
different way. Watkins's focus is on the restructuring of social and personal
relations during the period from 1780 to 1832; mine is on the immediate
political context of the months during which Coleridge was working on *The
Ancient Mariner.*

The second thesis referred to was presented in 1989 by Robert M. Maniquis.
Relating the killing of the albatross to the French Terror of 1793–1794, he
describes the redemptive snake-blessing as a "thaumaturgic act of love" that
enables the Mariner to "get beyond . . . both violence and its sacrificial sub-
limations"—though, as he adds, "Coleridge himself thought that injunction an
inadequate issue out of the poem's symbolic complexity."[4]

The comments of Watkins and Maniquis, along with several recent questions
raised by Paul Magnuson,[5] and the earlier arguments connecting the poem to
Western maritime expansion and the slave trade, have to be taken into ac-
count. But my claim to originality holds, despite these remarks and despite the
fact that there have been two wider "historical" readings of the poem in recent

3. "History as Demon in Coleridge's *The Rime of the Ancient Mariner,*" 24, 25, 30, 33.
4. "Holy Savagery and Wild Justice: English Romanticism and the Terror," 391.
5. Magnuson's "dialogic" connection of *The Ancient Mariner* with Wordsworth's ex-
plicitly political "Adventures on Salisbury Plain" is referred to below, in Chapter 5.

years. In order to establish the points of continuity and departure represented by my own study, I discuss, in the Critical Introduction that follows, Jerome McGann's 1981 essay "The Meaning of *The Ancient Mariner*," which offers an "historical analysis" of both the poem and its ongoing critical reception, as well as Peter Kitson's "Coleridge, the French Revolution, and *The Ancient Mariner*" (1989), which locates the *Rime* in the context of Coleridge's changing response to that upheaval. But Kitson ends up depoliticizing the poem, while McGann, soon to become the pioneer New Historicist specializing in the Romantic period, may not have been ready in 1981 to detect a covert but specifically political level of meaning.

In the first part of this study, I tried to avoid postmodernist jargon. But in suggesting slavery and the slave trade as an unspoken motif—a covert, suppressed, or effaced level of meaning—in Coleridge's *Crusoe* marginalia and, more importantly, in *The Ancient Mariner* itself, I was not unaware of recent attention to "not saids" in the work of historicists focusing on the Romantic period. In the critical preamble that follows, I comment on recent work by New Historicists who have emphasized the effacement of politics by Wordsworth and Coleridge in such apolitical—"quietist" or "privatized"—poems as "Tintern Abbey," the Intimations ode, and "Kubla Khan." Though no historicist critic, so far as I know, has examined *The Ancient Mariner* from this perspective, my methodology resembles theirs. What distinction there is involves my borderline balancing on the question of conscious authorial intent and my rejection of any claim, implicit or explicit, either to have "decoded" the "text" or to have "caught" Coleridge in some sinister act of sociopolitical suppression.

Despite this disclaimer about having discovered the poem's "real," hidden meaning, I may appear to be seeking out and elaborating a cryptic meaning Coleridge squirreled away in his ballad. Foucault called this hermeneutic approach to reading "allegorical." But my approach is allegorical neither in the Foucauldian nor the Coleridgean sense. I am not claiming that *The Ancient Mariner* "says" one thing and "means" another, and that the *Rime*—which appears to be about an isolating act followed by a partially redemptive reintegration into the world from which the protagonist had become alienated—is "really" about Coleridge's political voyaging in 1797–1798. Anyone engaged in "reading between the lines" is aware of *writing* between the lines and therefore of the distinction between the exoteric and the esoteric, what is openly said and what is privately meant. But to declare that a covert meaning Coleridge "put into" the poem has at last been recovered by *me*, the first reader to have plucked out its mystery, would be presumptuous and foolhardy. It would also be antipoetic, since one could make such a "demystifying" or "repoliticizing" claim only by failing to engage the poem in the very specificity that makes it the compelling, thrilling, disturbing, imaginative, *literary* thing it is, reducing it instead to a proof-text for a predetermined hermeneutic, deconstructive, or neohistoricist view of textuality.

Nevertheless, I *do* claim to have traced in *The Ancient Mariner* a layer of political meaning, and to have demonstrated its covert presence. As I suggest below, Coleridge himself was probably only partly conscious of "politics" in his apparently apolitical poem. Indeed, it is a "theme" so unobtrusive as to have gone undetected—not only by "amateurs" leafing through the ballad of a winter's night, but also by historically oriented professional critics like E. M. W. Tillyard (who in 1948 pronounced *The Ancient Mariner* "a poem of six hundred lines without the glimmering of a reference to any body politic");[6] by the New Historicists; and even by Carl Woodring, *il Maestro di color che sanno* when it comes to politics in the poetry of Coleridge. On this question of any recoverable "reference" to the body politic, *The Ancient Mariner* and its readers are equally mute. Whatever the consequence, genuine discovery or critical shipwreck, I am "the first that ever burst / Into *that* silent sea."

At the same time, this study can be seen as the (perhaps aberrant) development of a seed planted many years ago by David Erdman, who, in *Blake: Prophet against Empire,* referred in passing to Coleridge "objectifying the dereliction and dismay of the times in an imaginatively controlled nightmare *The Ancient Mariner.*"[7] Professor Erdman, now over eighty but still displaying that energy Blake called eternal delight, has just compiled a massive chronological compendium— with the working title of "The Political Coleridge"—of Coleridge's political utterances from the outbreak of the French Revolution to the advent of Victoria. Would anything I say here have persuaded him to include passages from *The Ancient Mariner* in "The Political Coleridge"?[8] Erdman is not averse to speculation based on detective work, a knowledge of the period, and imagination. While there is no excuse for recklessness on the one hand, or Procrusteanism on the other, timidity can also be despicable. "Prudence," Blake tells us, "is a rich ugly old maid courted by incapacity." While my questionings issue in possibilities rather than certitudes, my courtship of Prudence may seem too sporadic for so meticulous an historian as David Erdman. Yet, in many ways, he has been the main if not the "onlie begetter" of these speculations.

Though I devote most space to establishing a political context for the poem's "dungeon-grate" image, my most novel speculation involves the "political" interpretation of the blessing of the water-snakes at the principal turning point of *The Ancient Mariner.* Stated baldly, the suggestion of politics in this supremely Romantic and much-beloved moment, even politics at a submerged or unconscious level, may seem unpersuasive, even aesthetically repellent. It is one thing to advance political interpretations of the dungeon-grate image and the sinking of the Mariner's ship, or to associate the spectre-bark with a slave ship or

6. *Five Poems, 1470–1870,* 80.

7. *Prophet against Empire,* 268. The point is repeated, with "objectifying" changed to "Having objectivized," in the third edition, 293. Though this remark proved stimulating, my thesis that contemporary politics are (consciously or unconsciously) reflected in the poem is elaborated with a specificity beyond anything intended by Erdman's generalization.

8. Unsurprisingly, the poem is not excerpted, or even mentioned, in a similar compendium published in 1991. The opening volume of the new Princeton series—*Coleridge's Writings,* John Beer, general editor—is entitled *On Politics and Society.* It is edited by John Morrow, who also supplies an informed introduction.

the shooting of the albatross with contemporary political terror, foreign or domestic. It is quite another to cast doubt on the implications of the blessing of the water-snakes, the "redemptive" moment upon which the artistic integrity and imaginative power of *The Ancient Mariner* primarily depend. A negative reading of this crucial event would seem to deny the internal plausibility and coherence of the poem as a powerful and effective work of literary art.

The blessing, like the poem's moral and subsequent gloss, may be "problematic." But it is not enough to note the conflict between professed faith in divine benevolence and the irrepressible consciousness of evil, between a providential intervention and a daemon/or demon-ridden world—a contingent, unpredictable world of evil, fear, and retribution. That clash is, after all, indigenous to the Christian paradigm inherited by Coleridge, particularly given his ballad's late medieval setting and its Roman Catholic religious context. Similarly, that God acts (through the agency of the "kind saint") while the protagonist remains "unaware" allies the blessing of the snakes, as I later note, with the whole post-Pauline concept of redemptive grace, conversion, and salvation. A New Historicist might (McGann *does*) argue that modern readers must begin with "disbelief" in Coleridge's own faith (as mediated in the poem and its later gloss) in this Christian-sacramental vision. A deconstructionist would argue that since language, as such and in general, always already subverts itself, the blessing dissolves into incompatible meanings. While I share some of the skepticism of both camps, my contrary claim (to quote M. H. Abrams's succinct synopsis of my position) "is that Coleridge's individual and particular political (and psychological) preoccupations or obsessions intrude (mainly unconsciously) into his overt narrative, and, in oblique or masked form, manifest themselves as meanings that supplement, but may be entirely compatible with, his overt meanings."[9]

The political level of meaning I find in *The Ancient Mariner* is nothing if not strange and surprising. Yet in only one instance, my reading of the blessing of the water-snakes, do I advance a hypothesis that seems incompatible with, or at least not complementary to, the poem's manifest level or literal meaning. Though my argument, as I repeatedly stress, is tentative rather than exclusionary, it does risk subverting the poem. I am not quite a New Historicist, let alone a deconstructionist, yet here my corroborative evidence derives less from the images, plot-pattern, and "world" of *The Ancient Mariner* than from the sociohistorical situation of the man who wrote the poem. Still, the suggestion of a covert political meaning lurking behind the snake-blessing is the inevitable climax of thoughts stemming from a single question stimulated by the progress of the poem itself: Is *The Ancient Mariner* a conscious or unconscious "inscription" of Coleridge's political oscillations in 1797–1798?

I deal with the "unconscious" and intentionality in the chapter that follows.

---

9. Abrams, letter to author, July 2, 1993. Here and in his formulation of "the genetic fallacy," Professor Abrams was responding to manuscript versions of the chapters introducing each of the two parts of this project.

Here I concede that my "political" reading of the snake-blessing does not meet even Stanley Cavell's expanded conception of artistic intention. Having noticed that a character in Federico Fellini's *La Strada* can be seen as a reference to the Philomel legend, Cavell imagines a conversation with Fellini in which the director says that though he was unaware of the legend, it does capture the sense he had of the character while he was shooting, and that he *now* accepts the Philomel story as a part of the film he made.[10] Would Coleridge retrospectively accept my suggestion of an "unaware" political dimension in the blessing of the water-snakes: a different reading that is not complementary but contradictory to both his manifest intention and the standard interpretation of generations of readers?

And yet, within that same religious paradigm Coleridge inherited, snakes symbolize, from Eden on, enmity with humankind rather than filial love. Further, on an immediate political level, as toxic water-snakes in a rotting sea, these creatures suddenly blessed by the Mariner are allied with the slimy things flourishing in the "pestful calms" of despotism in Coleridge's contemporaneous political imagery—a freedom-stifling brood presided over by that Satanic serpent William Pitt, a "cockatrice" resembling Coleridge's female snake in the garden, the lamia in *Christabel*. These connections are elaborated in Chapter 8; all I can do at this point is request that skeptical readers suspend their disbelief until then.

Of course, *The Ancient Mariner* is far too rich and protean for that psychologically complex benediction scene to be reduced to mere "politics," especially the negative politics of accommodation and capitulation. The temptation of a New Historicist, as of a psychological, criticism is to succumb to what M. H. Abrams calls "the genetic fallacy"; that is, "the presumption that the meanings of an accomplished literary product are determined by (or in extreme formulations reduced to) the conditions of its genesis." Any such reductive interpretation should stimulate resistance. I have resisted a political reading of this pivotal passage myself, and even now offer it as only one among many possibilities—though that possibility seems to me reinforced by a number of more overt but unexplained "intrusions" of political imagery into what Coleridge called this "work of pure imagination." In any case, I am less interested in proving that I am "right" on this or any other particular point than I am in inviting readers to wonder along with me if even English literature's most celebrated poem of "pure" imagination may not, failing to utterly transcend its historical situation, carry with it not only the general context of the French Revolutionary period, but a cryptic account of its author's contemporaneous political voyaging as well—including, to cite the "Argument" introducing the first edition of the poem, "in what manner he came back to his own Country."

Tracking Coleridge's political twists and turns during the period of the poem's gestation and composition led me, as every reader of *The Ancient Mari-*

---

10. See Stanley Cavell, *Must We Mean What We Say?* chapter 8, and Ronald Dworkin's discussion of "Interpretive Concepts" in his *Law's Empire*, especially 56–58.

ner has been led, to focus on this blessing. As the act that transforms the Mariner, the blessing of the water-snakes may be the primary poetic example of what Kitson calls "moral revolution," or of what Coleridge himself called the transformation of politics into "spiritual Revolution." In Shelley's *Prometheus Unbound,* which, in the appendix, I connect with the Mariner's sudden outpouring of love for these "living things," the transfigured world is reported by the Spirit of the Earth as having been "somewhat changed" (III.iv.71). The Shelleyan understatement is urbane; I'm only being partly ironic when I say that, for good or ill, readers of this book will find *The Ancient Mariner* "somewhat changed."

4

Critical Introduction

1

My approach in this study is contextual and historical if not quite historicist. Engaging the interaction between literary criticism and sociopolitical and "cultural studies," this exploration is continuous with Part One of the present project and with my earlier books. Two of those studies have *interactions* in subtitle or title (*A Wild Civility: Interactions in the Poetry and Thought of Robert Graves* [1980] and *Yeats's Interactions with Tradition* [1987]), and a third is even more obviously interdisciplinary and historically anchored: *Terrible Beauty: Yeats, Joyce, Ireland, and the Myth of the Devouring Female* (1988). These books, and my favorite among my own essays—"Revolutions French and Russian: Burke, Wordsworth, and the Genesis of Yeats's 'The Second Coming'"—fall into the broad category of intellectual history, combining historical scholarship and literary criticism.

Though my primary mentors have been those indispensable literary historians of the Romantic period (David Erdman, Carl Woodring, E. P. Thompson, and the less political, or more "quietist," M. H. Abrams), their work has been supplemented by that of contemporary historical or historicist critics. Briefly, my position is an eclectic mixture of tradition and innovation: a mediation that maintains my formative connection with the earlier Romantic literary historians without (a) neglecting the more ironic and subversive tendencies of our own "Spirit of the Age," in particular those opposed yet often related poststructuralist movements, deconstruction and New Historicism, and without (b) succumbing to the tendency of both movements to "pass," as Coleridge put it, "an act of *Uniformity* against Poets."[1]

1. In 1796, Coleridge repeatedly and rhetorically asked his new friend, the leading English Jacobin John Thelwall, "Why pass an act of Uniformity against Poets?" (*CL* I 215, 279). As for the "opposed yet related" observation: Given the deconstructionist demotion of social actuality and almost of history itself, one can understand the opposition of the New Historicists. But their reaction can also be extreme, especially the recent tendency to present a literary work as a manifest content masking, displacing, and suppressing a latent—and invariably political—subtext. However covert or occluded, this subtext can run but it cannot hide; its existence predetermined, it will always be found out by its seekers, critics whose readings, however informed and brilliantly argued, tend to be self-confirming. At this point, ironically enough, the more radical historical determinists merge with those against whom they reacted—in particular the

177

Part of the contemporary and increasingly widespread movement to reinstate historical context as a ground of literary interpretation, this study also participates in the "demystification" of what both historicist Jerome McGann and deconstructionist Paul de Man refer to as the "illusion" inherent in "the Romantic ideology." I have, however, reservations, sharing what Tillotama Rajan calls "the Romantic poet's sense of the *limits* of demystification as an attitude to life," and agreeing with her that what de Man claims is "inherent in language"—the "tendency of Romanticism to relapse into illusions it sees through"—is not simply "an intermission in the drama of irony," but "something specific to Romanticism: an upsurge of the idealistic impulse."[2] Yet, this idealistic upsurge—relevant to the "spring of love" that gushes in the Mariner's breast immediately prior to his impulsive blessing of the water-snakes—is not naive but problematic: a precarious faith maintained by artists acutely aware of the "darker elements" threatening to deconstruct their affirmative vision, poets experiencing in "fear and dread" what the Mariner at perhaps his most Coleridgean calls "a frightful fiend [that] / Doth close behind him tread."

My own reservations about the transformative ideology of redemptive Romanticism—doubts manifest in my placing of that apparent locus classicus of redemption, the snake-blessing, in its political context—are part of an empathetic skepticism that restores the Romantic period's matrix by fusing the horizon of that revolutionary past with the horizon shaped by current critical and sociocultural insights, an approach that *questions* the past from present perspectives without, however, imposing *answers* from the present.[3] And though

---

deconstructionists, who seek, and invariably find, linguistic gaps and slippages ("aporias") that subvert what a poem "seems" to say, including what its author intended.

It is an interesting poststructuralist phenomenon that so many of those who pronounce texts indeterminate in theory, in practice claim to be decoders, revealing what authors "conceal," correcting what has been "distorted." Who, as Richard Levin has recently asked, cocking a mischievous eye, is more guilty of what indeterminists dismiss as "hubristic objectivism": those critics who believe that literary works are written by actual authors whose meanings are there in the text, open to interpretation, or those for whom the "hermeneutic vacuum" left by the supposedly liberating Death of the Author must be filled by "a universal law . . . that dictates what one must look for, and must find, in every [text]?" ("The Poetics and Politics of Bardicide," 502). Though the author of *The Ancient Mariner* was a politically obsessed young man, the remarks to Thelwall cited above give us his answer to Levin's rhetorical question about applying any "universal" law to literature, including the more recent New Historicist insistence that, whether overtly or covertly, Romantic texts are inevitably "political." And yet the New Historicists—especially when their revelations are not merely accusatory—*are* illuminating.

2. *Dark Interpreter: The Discourse of Romanticism,* 21–22.

3. To hold that literary texts are referential, that they reflect and are influenced by the social and historical contexts in which they are complexly anchored, and that they require readers, similarly influenced, to actualize them in what Hans George Gadamer calls in *Truth and Method* a hermeneutic or dialogic "fusion of horizons" (320) does not mean that history is to be reduced to any contemporary perspective. As Christopher Hill, veteran of many ideological and historicist wars, puts it in his most recent book: "It is right and proper that historians should ask new questions of the past, and such

such an approach does not neglect "intrinsic" attention to the text, it does, for particular purposes on particular occasions, emphasize the poem's relation to "extrinsic" reality. While neither the old New Critics nor even the better balanced among the deconstructionists seem, in practice, as consistently "non-referential" as historicists usually claim,[4] such immanent or text-centered approaches tend to play down or even bracket out the sociohistorical context of literary works, treating poems as lyric icons whose "beauty" is a joy forever precisely because they are kept chastely separate from the knotty, temporal details of biographical and sociopolitical reality. To that extent, however they may illuminate the "autonomous" verbal constructs they scrutinize, such antihistorical theorists limit the range of criticism.

That range has been restored—indeed, expanded—by the New Historicists, especially those specializing in the Romantic period. Much of the most probing work is being done by critics who adopt specifically Marxian methodology and values—critics who are, as McGann notes, "Marxist and Marxist-influenced" and/or feminists, both schools practicing "necessarily . . . a hermeneutics of a repressed or invisibilized [sociohistorical] content."[5] As the language reveals, the Marxian explanation of cultural phenomena as determined by underlying structures of historical "necessity" is here fused with Freudian mechanisms of displacement and repression by means of which writers disguise, evade, or reject their awareness of historical reality; thus the "silences" of a poet—often less an autonomous communicator than a conscious or unconscious medium of historical, class, and gender conflict—become as "significant," perhaps even more pregnant with meaning, than his or her overt statements. Untroubled by the fact that their political subtexts are so often unspoken, the "new" Romantic historicists who have supplanted such "old" Left literary historians as David Erdman and E. P. Thompson not only make the marginal central but what is textually absent thematically omnipresent. Though the results are often fascinating and illuminating, the methodology and unabashedly ideological stance of some New Historicists can also have a narrowing effect. Recontextualized poems *can* be read into near-invisibility themselves, their words decoded to expose occluded politics, the poet's voice and the poem's language replaced by silence, the "suppressed" or "canceled" historical context.

---

questions may well be stimulated by happenings in our own society. I see no harm in this so long as our *answers* do not derive from the present" (*A Nation of Change and Novelty: Radical Politics, Religion, and Literature in Seventeenth-Century England*, 244).

4. J. Hillis Miller, who has been recently insisting that deconstruction does touch base with "material reality," is cited later in this introduction. In a nice "touch," Alan Liu quotes one of the major New Critics, Cleanth Brooks, as the epigraph to his *Wordsworth:* "One wants to grant literature its autonomy, but one certainly doesn't want to cut it loose from the rest of the world, which in a thousand different ways it is constantly reflecting. What is the relation of literature to other things, the other things that men make and the other things that men do and think?" (Robert Penn Warren, "A Conversation with Cleanth Brooks," 1–2)

5. Introduction to *Historical Studies and Literary Criticism*, 4.

Thus, while I value, and to some extent here emulate, the neohistoricist detection of what such Marxist readers as Louis Althusser, Pierre Macherey, Terry Eagleton, and Fredric Jameson refer to as a work's "absences," "gaps," "rifts," "not-saids," and "silences," my position is distinguishable from that of the deconstructionists, deterministic Marxists, and more radical New Historicists. My principal hesitation has to do less with injury to the poem (any genuine poem will survive critical "demystification" and "repoliticization," and perhaps even be enhanced) than with the depiction—especially since Macherey's *A Theory of Literary Production*—of the "silences" in texts as linguistically and politically "necessary," inevitable: ideologically predetermined repressions of what is mutely present in the text's own, as opposed to its author's, "unconscious," and which it is the task of Marxist criticism to detect and make audible. "Like a planet revolving around an absent sun," in Macherey's memorable image, "an ideology is made out of what it does not mention; it exists because there are things which must not be spoken of."[6] A ramification of Marx's illusion-puncturing satire in *The German Ideology*, this is a seminal insight. In resisting that determinist "must," however, I am in accord with one of the Newreaders' principal critical opponents, M. H. Abrams—even though the subversive irony they have brought to bear on Abrams's monumental study *Natural Supernaturalism* has certainly trickled into my own detection of "silent" political undercurrents in *The Ancient Mariner.*

Having wrestled with Hillis Miller and other deconstructive angels, Abrams has more recently been defending poems from the political or politicized onslaughts of the New Historicists. The most notable example is the poem concluding the 1798 volume that opens with *The Ancient Mariner:* "Tintern Abbey," the recent critical history of which offers a striking example of the rewards and risks of historicist exegesis.

The New Historicists are not the only readers concerned about the curious relation of "Tintern Abbey" to the political developments encompassed by the "five years" thrice referred to in the poem's opening lines. Wordsworth's most recent biographer, Stephen Gill, expresses surprise that the poet should present 1793 as the time when nature was "all in all" and 1798 as the moment when "he felt himself most at one with the cause of humanity," for, as Gill notes, "in 1793 Wordsworth had been a radical patriot, his heart given to the people and the French cause, whereas in 1798 he was hymning Nature's power 'to feed this mind of ours, / In a wise passiveness.'"[7]

The continuity within which that shift occurred is explored in the contextual reading of Nicholas Roe, who explores the poem's "antiphonal relation" to Coleridge's "Fears in Solitude." Arguing persuasively that "the whole fabric of 'Tintern Abbey'—language, mood, philosophic bias—is grounded in Wordsworth's radical years," Roe concludes that "Tintern Abbey" expresses "the

6. *A Theory of Literary Production,* 132.
7. *William Wordsworth: A Life,* 154.

redemptive wish that he had shared with Coleridge and other friends of liberty." But, as is confirmed by Wordsworth's tentative phrasing ("such, perhaps," "Nor less, I trust," "If this / Be but a vain belief," "I would believe," "Nor perchance," "And so I dare to hope"), the poem achieves its triumph in "the context of a lasting vulnerability":

> "And so I dare to hope"—that was the common legacy of revolution to Wordsworth, Coleridge, and their contemporaries. Wordsworth's consciousness of human weakness and fallibility,
>
> The still, sad music of humanity,
> Nor harsh nor grating, though of ample power
> To chasten and subdue
>
> —was the hardest lesson of revolution, but for Wordsworth it proved most fruitful. More than the aspiration he felt with his generation,
>
>   —a time when Europe was rejoiced,
> France standing on the top of golden hours,
> And human nature seeming born again
>
> —it was failure that made Wordsworth a poet.[8]

Based on the poem's internalization of the Romantics' crucial political dialectic of hope, despair, and reconstituted recovery, and refusing to sacrifice text to subtext, such a reading enriches our understanding—providing that we are not *too precipitous* in accepting at face value "internalization" as a substitute for social concern. This is where the New Historicists are most valuable. Enrichment is also offered by their readings of the poem; but, as Emerson reminds us, nothing is got for nothing. That historicist insights often come at a high price has been the theme of a well-traveled lecture by Abrams, now available in his 1989 collection of theoretical essays, *Doing Things with Texts*.

Abrams defends "Tintern Abbey" from historicist critics who fault it for its alleged "suppression" or "evasion" of the contemporary sociopolitical dimension—no reference, in a poem set on the eve of Bastille Day, to the French Revolution, or to such persistent abuses and inequalities as the industrial pollution of the Wye and the presence of homeless beggars who took shelter in the ruined abbey. Abrams cites McGann ("from Wordsworth's vantage, an ideology is born out of things which [literally] *cannot* be spoken of"), Kenneth Johnston ("it may well be . . . one of the most powerfully *de*politicized poems in the language—and, by that token, a uniquely political one"); and Marjorie Levinson ("'Tintern Abbey' achieves its fiercely private vision by directing a continuous energy toward the nonrepresentation of objects and points of view expressive of a public—we would say, ideological—dimension." Wordsworth's evasive language creates "a reality that is self-contained . . . without reference to the observed scene or to the observer").[9]

---

8. Roe, "The Politics of 'Tintern Abbey,'" in his *Wordsworth and Coleridge: The Radical Years*, 268–75.

9. All citations but the last are from Abrams's "On Political Readings of *Lyrical*

But what of the "Tintern Abbey"—that sustained lyric meditation tracing the interplay between nature and mind—Wordsworth actually wrote? Generations of readers have responded to the joy and loss and recovery Wordsworth communicated in this great poem. Such readers have, in its own words, "felt / A *presence*" rather than castigated an alleged *absence*—the political "evasion" prosecutorial New Historicists are predisposed to find. Calling for "a more open—in political terms, a liberal—way of reading poetry," Abrams rejects closed, "must-be" or preestablished, theoretical impositions that reduce a poem to a culturally specific, time-bound "text" beyond the author's control, thus denying what so many readers have experienced, and continue to experience: the capacity of "Tintern Abbey" to "evoke a deep response because it speaks, in its innovative, ordered, and compelling way, to enduring constants amid the ever-changing conditions of what it is to be human."[10]

One can only agree with Abrams that a poet has the right to choose his own subject matter and theme, especially when, as in the case of Wordsworth, political complexities pervade much of the rest of his canon. "Wordsworth did not conceal (or 'repress' or 'exclude') in his poetry, taken as a whole, his political investments and his political disillusion; that he should be obliged to mention them in every poem, or even in *Tintern Abbey* alone, is a manifestly absurd requirement." I am quoting, not Abrams, but Helen Vendler, who, in an independent but related attack on the New Historicists, a polemic that dramatically polarized a 1990 conference on "Revolutionary Romanticism," fiercely rejected what she characterized as Levinson's vulgar assault on "Tintern Abbey."[11] By no means all, but surely too many, New Historicist readings, whatever their peripheral illuminations, are, as Abrams and Vendler insist, closed monoreadings that risk losing the palpable poem in the attempt to recover the political realities it supposedly tries to evade.

In the first place, who is to say what has been—in the pejorative sense intended by accusatory historicists—"evaded" in a poem? What would "count as evidence" in distinguishing between what has been artistically, even generically, excluded and what has been (in Levinson's hostile terms) "canceled" or

---

Ballads," 369, 374. See McGann, *The Romantic Ideology*, 91 (he is referring at this point to the Intimations ode); Johnston, "The Politics of 'Tintern Abbey,'" 13; Levinson, *Wordsworth's Great Period Poems: Four Essays*, 37–38, 41. Alan Liu has discussed the poem along similar lines (*Wordsworth*, 215–17, 579–80). See also Robert A. Brinkley, "Vagrant and Hermit: Milton and the Politics of 'Tintern Abbey.'" The Intimations ode, earlier put in historical context by Levinson, has recently received book-length historicist scrutiny in Jeffrey Robinson's *Radical Literary Education: A Classroom Experiment with Wordsworth's "Ode,"* a revisionary reading that also focuses on "absences," accusing the ode of "universalizing" its themes and adopting, in its final version, an "apolitical rhetoric" (123).

10. "On Political Readings of *Lyrical Ballads*," 377, 391.

11. "'Tintern Abbey': Two Assaults," 175; for citations in the paragraph that follows, see 183–85, 177. (The other "assault" is that of John Barrell, who in 1989 criticized the poem on gender grounds in *Poetry, Language, and Politics*.) Oddly, Vendler was unaware of Abrams's prior defense of "Tintern Abbey," and Abrams, a participant in the 1990 conference, was unaware of what Vendler was going to speak about until she began.

"suppressed"? "Tintern Abbey" is an example of lyric, a form of which Helen Vendler is perhaps our best close reader and most ardent defender. The compact form of lyric, she notes, privileges utterance at once private and general, personal and universal; we do not normally expect to find in lyric the kind of "factually mimetic" thick description of, say, a Dickens novel. Attacking the "always possible" but "always otiose" accusations of cultural materialists irritated to discover among the missing precisely those historical facts, "collective" and "materialist," they think *ought* to be present in a poem, Vendler remarks: one might "as truly say that a drawing 'cancels' the oil painting it might have been, or that a solo partita 'suppresses' the symphonic mode it might have been written in."

Faced with a choice between the ghostly paradigm of an unspoken political subtext and the poem's own body swayed to music, there can be little *aesthetic* difficulty in choosing. At the same time, as McGann argues compellingly in both *The Romantic Ideology* and *Social Values and Poetic Acts,* a price is also paid when attention is devoted exclusively to the words on the page, while ignoring how they got there and how they have been received, thus privileging timelessness and autonomy at the expense of genesis, reception, and the minute particulars of history. And McGann's argument is not extraliterary. The distinctive excellence of the "literary form of knowledge," he writes, is that it

> cannot deliver its knowledge in schematic or ideological forms without violating its own premises. This is the case because literary forms do not permit the archive of knowledge to be reduced to the abstractness of proverbs or the illusions of ideology. Literary forms deploy such abstractions and illusions all the time, but they dispel these ghostly shapes by transforming them into recognizable human forms: by incarnating them in words that are detailed, specific, and circumstantial. A thematizing hermeneutics which does not emphasize the sociohistorical particularities of the literary ideas and knowledge which it deploys runs a grave risk, therefore, of reproducing ideology rather than literature.[12]

Even when they are not presented with the balance McGann displays at his nonprosecutorial best, New Historicist insights do make audible possibly unspoken subtexts in the works whose silent surfaces they break through, even in so manifestly "apolitical" a poem as "Tintern Abbey." One argument implicit in the present volume is that such methods can be usefully deployed to burst into the "silent sea" of *The Ancient Mariner,* that even more "powerfully *de*politicized"— and intimately related—poem in the volume *Lyrical Ballads.*[13]

12. *Social Values and Poetic Acts: The Historical Judgment of Literary Work,* 107.

13. Referring to "Tintern Abbey," the last poem in the 1798 volume, R. L. Brett and A. R. Jones remark in the introduction to their edition of *Lyrical Ballads:* "Curiously it echoes the first poem in the collection, Coleridge's major contribution, *The Ancient Mariner.*" The two poems—the one overtly, the other covertly, autobiographical—"have a certain identity in the central experience they convey." Both move through "a dark night of the soul" with "a new self-awareness gained through suffering." And "there is the belief, as Coleridge put it [*CL* II 864], 'that every Thing has a life of its own, & that we are all *one Life*'" (xxvi–xxvii).

Still, such traditional respecters of genre as Meyer Abrams and Helen Vendler are not the only critics worried that in the process of restoring erased historical reference, salvaging "material reality," some historicists risk losing the very poems they contextualize. Such critics assiduously, often brilliantly, reconstruct the public dimension the original privatizing authors "evaded." But in stressing what one of the fathers of the movement, Renaissance scholar Stephen Greenblatt, has, in "Resonance and Wonder," called the "resonance" dependent on an object's enmeshment in a tangled temporal network, some historicists evade the resonances of the work of art itself, its *internal* "context," the poem taken in its full linguistic complexity and "wonder."

Greenblatt himself, in this the concluding and most recent essay in his *Learning to Curse: Essays in Early Modern Culture,* worries that those who have taken his critical path have elevated historical resonance at the expense of linguistic wonder. Writing in the same year, two prominent "Yale school" critics, drawn primarily though not exclusively to language and figuration, have more predictably criticized those "so much in touch with reality that they do not have to be in touch with language" (Geoffrey Hartman), ideologues who take "a linguistic reality for a material one" (J. Hillis Miller).[14] But Miller's remark itself comes with a history—a context and "resonance" worth establishing since it synopsizes recent theoretical wars, including attempts at a truce.

For those taking the post–New Critical "rhetorical" or "linguistic" turn in criticism, priority is accorded, not to the world supposedly represented by literature (the bailiwick of historicism and mimetic aestheticism), but to the act of representation itself. To consider otherwise is to "denature" literature. Thus Paul de Man, dismissing phenomenal referentiality in favor of literature's autonomy and rhetoricity, claims, "What we call ideology is precisely the confusion of linguistic with natural reality." That was in 1981, in the title essay in *The Resistance to Theory.* Defending that very theory (one under increased if often trivializing ad hominem assault in the wake of revelations about de Man's wartime articles in the collaborationist Belgian newspaper *Le Soir*), Miller echoes the master: "One of the major functions of literary theory is as a critique of ideology, that is, a critique of the taking of a linguistic reality for a material one."[15]

But Miller accommodates the New Historicists by trying to close the gap (as Greenblatt tries from the other side) between rhetoric and historical reality. De Man had ended the paragraph just cited—a paragraph Miller more than once quotes as answering historicist objections—on a note of hauteur: "Those who reproach literary theory for being oblivious to social and historical (that is ideological) reality are merely stating their fear at having their own ideological mystifications exposed by the tool they are trying to discredit. They are, in

14. The first remark is from the conclusion of Hartman's *Minor Prophecies: The Literary Essay in the Culture Wars,* the second from "Just Reading: Kleist's 'Der Findling,'" chapter 3 of Miller's *Versions of Pygmalion.*

15. De Man, *The Resistance to Theory,* 10. Miller, *Versions of Pygmalion,* 83.

short, very poor readers of Marx's *German Ideology*." The "ideology" Miller has in mind, similar to that so brilliantly satirized in the seminal work de Man flings back in the face of historicists given to citing it, is conservative and institutional, resulting in "assimilative rationalizing" and, in the specific case of reading, in conventional "passive interpretations of the manifest content" of texts that ought to be read actively, critically, rhetorically—or, as Harold Bloom would say, "strongly." Insofar as theory is "performative, political," its function, says Miller, is "to be an act of reading that is a productive event in the real world of material history." Thus, literature is treated as active rather than a merely reflective "passive mirroring" of "dominant ideologies"; and deconstructive theory, actively *applied* to what texts conceal as well as to what they reveal, is *not* out of touch with sociohistorical reality.[16]

That rejection of "passive mirroring," a centrally Romantic rejection, occurs in "The Function of Literary Theory," Miller's contribution to a 1989 collection of commissioned essays on the future of literary theory in the humanities. Miller concludes this essay, too, by insisting on "critical reading as the primary means of combating that disastrous confusion of linguistic with material reality, one name for which is 'ideology.'" But he also insists that deconstruction has been misrepresented as an elitist formalism—"cut off (so they say) from history and politics"—by those participating in the current "shift of focus" (which he describes as "massive" and "almost universal") "away from the 'intrinsic,' rhetorical study of literature" toward its "extrinsic" relations, its "placement within psychological, historical, or sociological contexts." While sympathetic to the "passion for social justice" that motivates much of the current paradigmatic shift, Miller wonders what and how it "has to do with the study of literature," and complains that the shift is "often accompanied by a false account of what is actually said about the extrinsic relations of literature by de Man, Derrida, or their colleagues." As one of the most prominent of those colleagues, Miller records his own contention that "the study of literature has a great deal to do with history, society, the self, but that this relation is not a matter of thematic reflection within literature of these extra-linguistic forces and facts, but rather a matter of the way the study of literature offers perhaps the best opportunities to identify the nature of language as it may have effects on what de Man calls 'the materiality of history.'"

Miller insists on the importance of "reading," in the sense of "a rhetorical analysis of the most vigilant and patient sort," and since such reading is in turn "indispensable to any responsible concern for the relations of literature to what is outside it,"

> it would be catastrophic for the study of literature if the insights of deconstruction, along with those of the New Criticism and of such critics as William Empson and Kenneth Burke, were to be forgotten or were to be relegated to an over-passed stage in some imagined historical "development," so that they no longer need to be taken seriously in the actual, present-day work of literary study. . . .

16. De Man, *The Resistance to Theory*, 11. Miller, *Versions of Pygmalion*, 83–84.

[T]o paraphrase de Man, "the task of literary criticism in the coming years," will be mediation between the rhetorical study of literature, of which "deconstruction" is by far the most rigorous in recent times, and the now so irresistibly attractive study of the extrinsic relations of literature.[17]

The paraphrase is rough, since what de Man had prescribed as the "task" in the coming years was the appropriation of all literature by deconstruction, which was, like Wallace Stevens's jar, to take "dominion everywhere." While it is difficult to grieve over the collapse of such hubristic overreaching, a fall manifest in the defensive tone of Miller's reaffirmation,[18] one can only applaud his—and Greenblatt's—call for "mediation" between "intrinsic" and "extrinsic" emphases.

These mutual attempts to find common ground between historicism and deconstruction, building on the strengths of each, are of considerable interest. But a gap remains, along with difficulties in both doctrines. The problem with the theorists of indeterminacy (especially with some American literary deconstructionists and reader-response critics) remains an inability at times to get beyond the disseminative play of nonreferential language and a more-than-occasional unwillingness to distinguish between "many" and "any" (equating multiple interpretations with infinite and contradictory possibilities).[19] The danger many New Historicists risk—despite the sophisticated "negotiations" implicit in their "reciprocal concern with the historicity of texts and the textuality of history"[20]—is the reduction of works of art, not to simplistic passive "reflections" of sociohistorical reality, but to "quietist" evasions and displacements of politics—or at least the conscious nudging of a work "toward a less literary register."

17. "The Function of Literary Theory at the Present Time," 111, 103, 102, 106, 104.

18. The defensiveness is explicit in the note Geoffrey Hartman supplies to "The State of the Art of Criticism," his essay in the same collection. That piece was written in 1986, before the de Man scandal. Chastened by those personally painful disclosures and more open to the historicist critique, Hartman says he would write differently now. "While I stand behind my essay, I am less certain that literary theory has a future. . . . [W]e may . . . have to overcome the suspicion that theory is but an exercise in ideology, or the opium of intellectuals who wish to evade political commitments and hard judgments" (86n). The evolution of his own work in the direction suggested here is reflected in Hartman's balanced study, *Minor Prophecies*.

19. As my qualification is meant to indicate, the positions of most of his American disciples should not be conflated with those of Jacques Derrida himself, at least with Derrida in philosophic context and (admittedly a tortuous demand) in toto. Despite his notorious and endlessly cited passages on "freeplay," with its "infinite" and contradictory interpretive possibilities, the founder of deconstruction is not quite—at least not consistently—the apostle of license so passionately celebrated by some and acrimoniously condemned by others.

20. This memorable chiasmus, an oft-cited synopsis of the New Historicist project, was first employed by Louis Montrose in a 1986 essay on Renaissance studies; it is quoted here from his "The Poetics and Politics of Culture," in the valuable collection, H. Aram Veeser, ed., *The New Historicism*, 20.

I am quoting a critic, Marjorie Levinson, whose historicism is mediated by deconstruction, and who in this passage (later discussed in detail) "histori-cizes" the "prison-house" of Wordsworth's Intimations ode by claiming that it "must" evoke the Bastille, the French Revolution being the "repressed" or "elided" political content of the poem. Despite my reservations (later spe-cified) regarding her political contextualization of Wordsworth's prison-house (as well as his Tree and Field in the preceding stanza), what Levinson says about these images as a return of the politically repressed anticipates the very point I make about the "dungeon-grate" in *The Ancient Mariner.*

But while his prison image is considerably more graphic, Coleridge's poem of "pure imagination" has not been given the full historicist treatment. Indeed, it has proven remarkably resistant to readers, including those on the imperial Left, who would assert their power over texts from the past. In my own case, in suggesting one more element among its myriad possibilities, I am not claiming to have lifted the burden of mystery borne since 1798 by *The Ancient Mariner,* a poem that has, as W. J. Bate said in 1968, "eluded reductionism more trium-phantly than any other . . . poem [of comparable length and coherence] in English."[21] A "nightmare" poem, especially one by a poet whose own night-mares were just beginning to reflect his opium addiction, might seem unusu-ally fair game for the sort of post-Freudian critical reading that dredges up a latent subtext concealed by the textual surface or manifest content. Yet my own study—which concludes by citing Frances Ferguson's protean and perspectival *Ancient Mariner* article, "Coleridge and the Deluded Reader"—is tentative and exploratory, not at all the assertion of a claim to have found a covert, and *therefore* the principal, meaning.

Despite accommodations and even fusions, deconstruction is in decline, historicism still on the march. That at least is the latest lit-crit word as of the day and hour I happen to be writing. It is therefore necessary to say more at the outset about the extraordinary amount of interesting historical and historicist thinking that has been focused on the Romantic poets, Wordsworth and Cole-ridge in particular—especially since much of it bears, directly or peripherally, on the poem under scrutiny.

As noted in Part One of the present work, in the 1960s and 1970s, Malcolm Ware, William Empson, and J. B. Ebbatson discussed *The Ancient Mariner* in the context of maritime expansion and the slave trade. Recent historical light has been cast on the poem by the two essays earlier mentioned: Jerome McGann's 1981 historicist analysis and Peter Kitson's 1989 article placing the poem in its French Revolutionary context. In addition, in several recent essays (1988–1990) restoring to prominence Robert Southey's marginalized epic *Thalaba the De-stroyer,* Marilyn Butler has noted an interaction between *Thalaba* and "Kubla Khan," an interaction stressing a politics-effacing move on the part of the more canonical poet.

21. *Coleridge,* 55.

A similar emphasis may be found in Alan Liu's massive *Wordsworth: The Sense of History*, in which the poet's inward turn from politics and history to nature and the "Romantic self," that cognitive and imaginative revolution influentially celebrated by M. H. Abrams two decades earlier in *Natural Supernaturalism*, is depicted as in part a "testament of social denial." Further, the very "denials of history are also the deepest realizations of history," so "strong" that every such denial—however determined the seeming "absence" or "negation" of history—becomes itself something to be studied as a "positive" fact, a "presence" influencing the poetry at the level of form, especially in terms of generic transformation.[22] What Liu calls Wordsworth's "poetics of denial, of reference lost," his depoliticizing effacements of contemporary historical detail, are treated more judgmentally in the New Historicist essays on "Tintern Abbey"—essays, as we have seen, persuasively if predictably attacked by Abrams and Vendler. Let me turn now to the *Ancient Mariner* articles by McGann and Kitson, then to Marilyn Butler's specifically New Historicist treatment of "Kubla Khan."

2

McGann's title, "The Meaning of *The Ancient Mariner*," is a daring one given the critical debate over the central question raised by the poem. The deadlock is familiar enough by now. There are those critics (Robert Penn Warren and others) who hold that the poem and its gloss present a sacramental, intelligible cosmos in which crime is followed by punishment and partial redemption, and those more skeptical readers who, in increasing numbers and following Bostetter and Empson, emphasize the dice-throwing arbitrariness of a nightmare world governed by "unpredictable despotic forces," forces that render the "pious moral . . . inescapably ironic" and the no-less-pious gloss an unreliable and desperately moralizing afterthought.[23]

McGann's essay subsumes and moves beyond this major crux in *Ancient Mariner* criticism. In addition, it steers a subtle course between authorial intention and critical interpretation, the reciprocity between readers and an only semideterminate (because historically developing) "text." For me, it offers as well a cultural perspective and a terminology I have recruited in the service of my own form of historicism. For I, too, want to employ "historical analysis" to "recover" what "the past" may have "sent us" in *The Ancient Mariner*. Combining traditional historical research with both intrinsic and "antithetical criticism," my study proposes its own version of what McGann calls "a thoroughly revisionist view of the poem, in which the entire ideological structure of its

22. Liu, *Wordsworth*, 304, 31–35.
23. Since these positions are elaborated in the text, there is no need to develop them here. The phrases quoted are from "The Nightmare World of *The Ancient Mariner*," by Bostetter, reprinted in *The Romantic Ventriloquists*, the earliest and most influential opponent of Warren's celebrated and much assaulted essay, "A Poem of Pure Imagination: An Experiment in Reading." As we have seen, Empson's iconoclastic position is developed in his 1964 article, in section 3 of his introduction to *Coleridge's Verse: A Selection*, and in his posthumously published response to Warren.

symbolist procedures would finally be able to be seen in their special historical terms"—not to "violate the past of its treasures," but rather to salvage one more possibility among this poem's innumerable sea-changed riches.[24]

My extended account of the "submerged politics" in *The Ancient Mariner* deals in part with what McGann calls the "special historical life" the poem has led in the course of its processional, critical career; and I am also concerned with dialectical, and dialogic, processes within the poem.[25] But I am still more concerned with a phenomenon related to this dialectic between actual experience and moralizing afterthoughts: the possible presence in the poem, in displaced form, of a "special historical life" replicating the lived rhythm of Coleridge's own political pattern of retirement/engagement/re-retirement. And here I take the argument a lengthy step beyond McGann as well as beyond Kitson's useful establishment of a general political context.

Retirement/engagement/re-retirement: that systolic-diastolic movement, resembling the Coleridgean water insect's "alternate pulses of active and passive motion" (*BL* I 124), was particularly marked in the poet's own "historical life" during precisely the months he was working on *The Ancient Mariner.* And those historical and personal developments may be inscribed in the poem, I suggest, as a dialectical movement from despair through hope to intensified despair followed by partial redemption and recovery. Like McGann and others, I question Coleridge's own "limited" reading of the poem, an essentially Christian reading reflecting a "faith" (poetic, religious, intellectual) evident in the text even in 1798 and particularly manifest in the attempt at a "complete" interpretation with the addition of the gloss in 1817. Whereas the New Historicists argue that we construct and construe already written texts, including our own, in line with our particular cultural and historical concerns, I go further on this occasion. I question that Coleridgean "faith" at the very moment of its initial and most sublime expression by raising the possibility of an ulterior, if less than fully conscious, political motivation behind the symbolic snake-blessing itself.

Here I depart from Kitson, whose acceptance at face value of the blessing of the sea-snakes as a religiously redemptive moment *may* mark his reading as too straightforward to be truly "Coleridgean" in pursuing the motif he himself

24. "The Meaning of *The Ancient Mariner,*" 66–67, 53; and 54, 65–66, for passages cited in the next few paragraphs.

25. Historicist narratology would focus, not on what may have "actually" happened on the fictional voyage, which can never be made available to us, but on those past events as re-presented in a story: the later version of that voyage as narrated to the Wedding Guest (one among many in an endless sequence of auditors, "ten-thousand," Coleridge later estimated in casual conversation [CN I 45n]) by a dramatic speaker who is an anguished, lonely, perhaps deluded old man incapable of fully understanding or at least of fully conveying his own terrifying and mysterious experiences. The gap between immediate experience and representation, even when the teller is (as he tells us) gifted with "strange power of speech," is reflected in the relation between the vivid evocations of lived experience and the more reflective, moralistic passages: a tension exacerbated for some, resolved for others, by the later addition of a prose gloss that tries to explain the ultimately inexplicable.

refers to as "Coleridge's retreat from politics."[26] If, "from our present vantage, . . . we must," as McGann says, "inaugurate our disbelief in Coleridge's 'poetic faith,'" specifically in his Christian-sacramental vision as mediated in this poem and its gloss, I focus my skepticism and "recovery" on the text's effacement of Coleridge's contemporary shift from anti-Ministerial activism to religious and loyalist quietism, a political retreat here symbolically transformed into what he called in a notebook entry, "spiritual Revolution" (*CN* II 2547). Though Kitson specifically, and Abrams generally, make a related point, both treat it positively; I will be arguing that, symbolically, the blessing of the water-snakes may be less a moment of internalized redemption than of individual and collective capitulation.

Thus, like McGann, I inaugurate my "disbelief" by "historicizing," if not "every aspect of the work," at least some of the most salient moments and symbols, which, in transformed but recognizable form, seem to convey political meaning. "The Mariner undergoes radical shifts in his physical circumstances, traveling through tumultuous arctic seas to oppressive tropic calm back to his pleasantly temperate home port."[27] A similar sequence of radical shifts can be traced in Coleridge's political life during the months he sent his Mariner voyaging; and both his and his Mariner's voyages end in submissive "repatriation." If my historicization imports politics into an "apolitical" poem, they are *Coleridge's* politics, signaled by intrusive images carried over from his overtly political poems and by a structural pattern symbolically replicating the activist-quietist dialectic recoverable by examining the details of the poet's political thoughts and actions during 1797–1798, particularly during the months he was writing and revising his ballad.

I will conclude my interaction with McGann, as McGann does his article, with the spectre-bark, which may simultaneously be a terror-induced "hallucination" *and* have "a basis in physical reality." It may be conjured up from something as meteorologically nebulous as McGann's "whisps of sea fog," yet something more tangible in terms of political symbolism. Judging from the 1798 text's reference to "a something in the Sky / No bigger than my fist," Coleridge was recalling Elijah's "little cloud out of the sea, like a man's hand," the harbinger of the "great rain" that finally ends the drought afflicting Israel (I Kings 18:44). Of course, in a horrifying reversal of joyful expectation, the Mariner's "something in the Sky" brings not rain but the spectre-bark and the strikingly graphic and unexpected analogy of the dungeon-grate. Salvific rain falls only after the blessing of the water-snakes, suggesting that the dungeon-grate and the snake-blessing are related, and that they may function as objective correlatives: images deriving from Coleridge's fears, in the spring of 1798, that (to reverse McGann's terms) the "symbolic" might give way to "the real"—that without the political equivalent of the blessing of the water-snakes, the possibility of a dungeon-grate intruding between *Coleridge* and the sun was a real and present danger.

26. "Coleridge, the French Revolution, and *The Ancient Mariner:* Collective Guilt and Individual Salvation," 205.
27. Karl Kroeber, *Romantic Fantasy and Science Fiction,* 75.

In discussing *The Ancient Mariner* in terms of Coleridge's changing response to the French Revolution, Peter Kitson emphasizes the poet's substitution of moral for political revolution, a Miltonic adaptation in which Coleridge moves from faith in a collective and political millennium to attainment of an individual "paradise within." Kitson traces this gradual loss of faith in the efficacy of political action from Coleridge's 1795 Bristol addresses to the people, through his millennial and apocalyptic poems "Religious Musings" (1795) and the "Ode on the Departing Year" (1796), until it appears as the dominant motif in the great political-withdrawal poems of the spring of 1798, "Recantation" (retitled, in 1802, "France: An Ode") and "Fears in Solitude."

The pattern of inward turn as a sublimated response to the failure of the French Revolution is familiar enough; Kitson's thesis is that this is the pattern—"collective restoration and national guilt" becoming "collective guilt and individual redemption"—that we find in the crime and individual restoration, through grace, of the Mariner:

> Coleridge's observation of the career of the French Revolution convinced him that humanity was inherently depraved and that any attempt by politicians to improve conditions would simply lead to an exacerbation of those conditions. . . . Coleridge came to realize that the millennium could never be realized in a collective sense given that the majority of mankind were sinful. The millennium could only exist as a state of mind, the "paradise within" of Milton's great epic. It is this sense of guilt and possible restoration experienced on an individual scale which informs "The Ancient Mariner."
>
> There have been almost as many readings of "The Ancient Mariner" as there are critics. Few, however, have made any real attempt to place the poem within the context of Coleridge's loss of faith in political action, a context which is demanded by Coleridge's other writings.

After distinguishing between Christian and non-Christian readings of *The Ancient Mariner,* the former emphasizing the "redemptive aspects" of the poem, the latter, the "strong sense of guilt it communicates," Kitson turns to Empson and J. B. Ebbatson, the two critics who have "made an attempt to locate the poem in Coleridge's political development." Subsuming rather than adjudicating among conflicting positions, Kitson places the poem "in the context of Coleridge's retreat from politics and his new-found sense of inward and individual restoration," a framework within which "the elements of redemption and guilt are of paramount importance."

Citing the important letter Coleridge wrote to his brother George on or about March 10, 1798, Kitson connects the "benevolence" Coleridge finds "growing within" him—as he responds with "love" to the "fields & woods & mountains," to the "beauty of the inanimate impregnated, as with a living soul, by the presence of Life" (*CL* I 397)—with the earlier alienated Mariner's recognition of the "beauty" of the water-snakes, which had "previously disgusted him."

> The mariner's imagination now perceives the water-snakes as beautiful and his sympathy with them leads to love of God. The curse is lifted. It is an act of grace that enables the mariner to begin the long process of restoration. . . . Thus "The

Ancient Mariner" shows the progress from motiveless sin to individual redemption achieved through the agency of natural forces "impregnated" with the divine. The millenarianism of "Religious Musings" which envisaged the collective regeneration of mankind through political action has been reduced to the process of individual and internal redemption. Collective national guilt is conflated with inherent, individual depravity and given a representative form in the mariner himself.

What, finally, is the precise relationship between *The Ancient Mariner* and the French Revolution? In a legitimate variation on the critical argument advanced by many of the New Historicists, Kitson concludes that the Revolution is omnipresent by its very absence:

> The French Revolution is not present in the poem, but it throws its gigantic shadow across it. No longer does Coleridge have faith in the possibility of improvement by political action which the Revolution promised, but the contribution of that event to [his] new faith in the restorative qualities of the imaginative perception of nature is substantial. In a sense the Revolution has been both naturalized and internalized. The millennium takes place in the mind of man and paradise becomes not a place on earth but a state of mind, "the paradise within" of *Paradise Lost*. "The Ancient Mariner" shows us the moral revolution, the necessity for which Coleridge has consistently pleaded . . . since his *Conciones ad Populum*. Without the experience of the French Revolution, "The Ancient Mariner" would not be the poem it is.

With much of this, especially the final statement, I concur; the evidence is there, in Coleridge's poems, essays, and letters. And yet this moral and cognitive naturalization and (ultimately) internalization of political revolution—reflecting *Paradise Lost,* Abrams's *Natural Supernaturalism,* and much of Romanticism itself—raises again the old charge of apostasy and that question posed more than twenty years ago by E. P. Thompson: "Disenchantment or Default?" Given what men like Coleridge and Wordsworth saw as the French Revolution's self-betrayal and failure, they were faced, as Coleridge told his friend in 1799, with the need to resist turning disillusionment and retreat from active politics into an excuse for rejecting "all hopes of the amelioration of mankind, and . . . sinking into an almost epicurean selfishness, disguising the same under the soft titles of domestic attachment and contempt for visionary *philosophes*" (*CL* I 527). For all its appeal, the "paradise within" *can* be vulnerable to that charge, as Kitson's verb, "reduced," inadvertently suggests—as does his formulation on the preceding page: "The millennium of 'Religious Musings' has not completely disappeared. Instead it has been subordinated to a process of individual restoration, a personal millennium."[28]

Imaginative internalization is obviously a crucial feature of Romanticism, but it is "an internalization made," as Harold Bloom noted in 1968, "for more than therapeutic purposes, because made in the name of a humanizing hope that approaches apocalyptic intensity." Yet this quest for "paradise within a renovated man" is "shadowed by a spirit that tends to narrow consciousness to

---

28. Thompson, "Disenchantment or Default? A Lay Sermon." Kitson, "Coleridge, the French Revolution, and *The Ancient Mariner,*" 198, 200, 204–7.

an acute preoccupation with the self," the solipsistic Blakean Spectre or Self-hood. For Bloom, the third and final stage of the Romantic quest, Abrams's "apocalypse of imagination," is the poet's achievement of a "widened consciousness" turning him away "not from society to nature, but from nature to what was more integral than nature, within himself," a paradoxically enlarged consciousness restoring him to his "former selfless self."[29]

Bloom's account reminds us that the Romantic "paradise within" cannot be reduced to a selfish retreat from social concern. (This crucial point may also apply to the ambiguous epic of Milton himself; beneath the poem's interiorizing transcendence of its author's political disillusionment and frustrated ideals, some acute readers of *Paradise Lost* have detected a continuing commitment to a defeated but still honorable political "Cause.") Indeed, if "internalization" is part of the Romantics' dialectic, so is their conviction that a principal function of poetry remains transformation and redemption of the social order. The bridge between the worlds within and without is Love.[30] In the 1795 Bristol address printed as the introduction to his *Conciones ad Populum* (and reprinted fifteen years later in *The Friend*), Coleridge insisted on the social and ethical indispensability of interest in "the welfare of others."

> The searcher after Truth must love and be beloved; for general Benevolence is a necessary motive to constancy of pursuit; and this general Benevolence is begotten and rendered permanent by social and domestic affections. Let us beware of that proud Philosophy, which affects to inculcate Philanthropy while it denounces every home-born feeling, by which it is produced and nurtured. The paternal and filial duties discipline the Heart and prepare it for the love of all Mankind. The intensity of private attachments encourages, not prevents, universal Benevolence. (*L 1795* 46)

This truth, strengthened by the exposure of a merely selfishness-masking "domestic attachment," was reaffirmed in the 1799 letter to Wordsworth—as it had been a year earlier, during the invasion panic of April 1798, the month of most overt Coleridgean political "retreat." His "Fears in Solitude," written in that dangerous month, does not conclude with the poet merely turning quietistically inward, to domestic affections and the bosom of nature. On the contrary, the minute particulars of village, cottage, family, the very "limits" of his native island's "rocky shores," are the necessary prerequisite to an *un-*

29. "The Internalization of Quest Romance," 15, 16, 21, 26. Describing this "former selfless self," Bloom adds, "One thinks of Yeats's Blakean declaration: 'I'm looking for the face I had / Before the world was made'" (26). Though the archetype-seeking speaker here is the female persona of *A Woman Young and Old,* the impersonal personality of the lyric self and the pattern of other-than-solipsistic inward turn is part of a larger Yeatsian dialectic. Jahan Ramazani writes in *Yeats and the Poetry of Death: Elegy, Self-Elegy, and the Sublime:* "To turn within . . . does not necessarily mean to turn from the political to the merely personal; it may also permit the articulation in the lyric of the complex forces and voices of history. In Robert Bly's typically Romantic assertion . . . 'the political poem comes out of the deepest privacy'" (74–75).

30. See J. Robert Barth, S.J., *Coleridge and the Power of Love.*

bounded love. Though activism to achieve political change in England is rather too conveniently dismissed as irrelevant (the source of evil being "our own folly and rank wickedness"), these private attachments—resembling Burke's filial affection for the "little platoon" and "the glove of neighborhood"—open Coleridge's heart to universal brotherhood and sisterhood and enable him to make his theme public, ending with gratitude

> that by nature's quietness
> And solitary musings, all my heart
> Is softened, and made worthy to indulge
> Love, and the thoughts that yearn for human kind.
>
> (*CPW* I 262, 263)

Writing in 1989, the same year Kitson applied the "paradise within" to the redemption of the Mariner, Jerome McGann (detecting, surprisingly enough, no political ambiguity in *Paradise Lost*) pronounced the Miltonic precedent finally inadequate, "contradicted by the actual practice of Romantic artists":

> Milton earlier established the model that, in place of a failed social order, one might establish the order of an inward paradise. But neither Blake nor Shelley— nor even Wordsworth, for that matter—accepted Milton's consolatory move. Their departures from Milton's model all differ somewhat, of course, but Blake's departure is especially significant because his work enacts an artistic practice that is committed to the transformation of society: the installation of the city of God (which for Blake means a *human* city) in England's green and pleasant land. . . . None of [the principal Romantic] imaginations are "inward" imaginations; they are emphatically political, institutional, even economic—as Blake's prose works repeatedly emphasize.[31]

As the shift to "prose works" may concede, in his later poetry Blake is less the celebrator of Orc, the fiery boy of historical revolution who too often petrifies into Urizenic tyranny, than of Los, the figure of capable imagination. In any case, Coleridge is not Blake. But neither is a commitment to universal benevolence and the welfare of others reducible to any world-dismissing "paradise within." And even if everything Kitson says about the centripetal, consolatory move in Coleridge were accurate, it is a movement less linear and inevitable than oscillatory and serpentine. What Woodring calls the Coleridgean "parabola from naturalistic Jacobinism to a reconciliatory faith in divine imagination" is no more orderly and smoothly patterned than history itself: "Day after day, year after year, he looped, back-tracked, redoubled, and reneged."[32] Indeed, I will be arguing that the epicycle of Coleridgean retreat from active politics, always subject to change, was temporarily reversed during the very period the poetic gardener supposedly "retired" to Nether Stowey was working on *The Ancient Mariner*. Thus I go beyond Kitson to argue that the poem, while it does reenact Coleridge's retreat from opposition politics, does so in a way that makes the blessing of the water-snakes more problematic than Kitson and most

31. "The Third World of Criticism," 96.
32. *Politics in English Romantic Poetry,* 52.

readers seem willing to acknowledge. For that blessing culminates in a develop-
ment in the poem that may reenact, consciously or unconsciously, the rapidly
shifting political events in England during the turbulent months Coleridge was
simultaneously working on his ballad *and* oscillating between withdrawal from
public life and some dangerous political voyaging of his own.

Recently, Marilyn Butler, Regius Professor of English at Cambridge, has
gone beyond her fine historical study of 1981, *Romantics, Rebels, and Reaction-
aries*, to claim that Coleridge does in "Kubla Khan" precisely what Levinson,
among others, has Wordsworth doing in "Tintern Abbey" and the Intimations
ode: deliberately privatizing political material to produce a quietist poem that
is nevertheless political because of that very move. She was not the first to see
the poem in these terms. In a political interpretation back in 1974, Norman
Rudich had read "Kubla Khan" as "Coleridge's flight from the political real-
ities of his day" having "all the markings" of his "reactionary politics": "The
poem is an exhortation to abandon political struggle for the sake of the highest
cultivation of the aesthetic, moral, and religious qualities of the soul. It sepa-
rates poetry from history, sublimating its meaning into the theological realms
of absolute Truth and eternal categories of Good and Evil."[33]
Marilyn Butler specifies this quietist retreat in terms of a specific poetic
interaction, arguing that what Coleridge left out of "Kubla Khan" is the revolu-
tionary politics of *Thalaba the Destroyer* by his former fellow Pantisocrat and
present brother-in-law, Robert Southey.[34] Though *Thalaba* wasn't completed
and published until 1801, Southey's drafts and elaborate notes were read by
Coleridge in October 1799, a month when (some have suggested) he was work-
ing further on "Kubla Khan."[35] Many of Southey's images and prose notes were
drawn from Purchas's *Pilgrimage*, best known to students of English literature as
the "source," according to Coleridge's 1816 preface to the poem, of "Kubla
Khan."
Certainly, there are many striking resemblances between the paradisal gar-
dens that so fascinated Southey and Coleridge. The difference is that in Southey's
fable of revolution, the pious Thalaba sees through and destroys the false
paradise, a garden created by Aloadin, a corrupting sorcerer and trainer of
assassins. By depopulating and depoliticizing Kubla's garden, Coleridge, ac-
cording to Butler, deliberately rewrote a narrative "previously in the public
sphere so that it becomes a private fable, political no longer." In addition,
when, in 1816, almost two decades after its composition, he finally published
the poem, Coleridge prefaced it with a commentary that "further impedes a
politicized reading by providing alternative 'sources' for the poem that lead

33. "'Kubla Khan,' a Political Poem," 52–53.
34. "Plotting the Revolution: The Political Narratives of Romantic Poetry and Criti-
cism." In the paragraphs that follow I quote 152–55. Southey's poem is also her example
of an influential but now marginalized text in "Repossessing the Past: The Case for an
Open Literary History."
35. See Richard Holmes, *Coleridge: Early Visions*, 168.

away from" Southey and the earlier and still well-known revolutionary text by the now conservative poet laureate.

Insisting that she is not "imposing" on "Kubla Khan" a "political reading which belongs to the consciousness of our period rather than of Coleridge's," Butler points to "Shelley's politicized retellings of Southey's political narratives." She is right to do so since Shelley, in *Queen Mab* and elsewhere, seems to fuse the radical progressivism of young Southey and young Coleridge (particularly as expressed in "Religious Musings") with the alternately limp and jerky metrics of *Thalaba*.[36] Though Shelley despised later Southey, he admired the hero of his early epic; indeed, though Butler does not mention the possible analogue, Shelley's Prometheus, who revokes his curse upon Jupiter, resembles Thalaba, whose mission is to avenge the death of his father, but who ultimately pardons rather than kills his murderer, the sorcerer Okba. Though it earns him paradise, this merciful gesture's but a trifle here since all—Thalaba included—perish in the apocalyptic cave-in of the ocean vault of "the Domdaniel," the submarine headquarters of the evil sorcerers (*Thalaba* XII.xxxvi).

Of course, for Byron, Southey's "tremendous Thalaba," the "rival of Tom Thumb," was less the destroyer of "mad magicians" than the "Illustrious conqueror of common sense," and *Thalaba* itself, according to Byron, "one of those poems 'which,' in the words of [Richard] Porson, 'will be read when Homer and Virgil are forgotten, but [as Byron felt compelled to add, unnecessarily]—*not till then.*"[37] Butler, however, wisely omitting any reference either to Byronic ridicule or to the Destroyer's sparing of Okba, stresses the revolutionary potential of Southey's poem, and so concludes that "in 1816 as much as in 1798, for Coleridge to *empty* the paradisal garden of people and of politics must also be read as a political move."

Her own political move is to broaden the charge. For such "quietist" poets as the Coleridge and Wordsworth who depoliticized "Kubla Khan" and "Tintern Abbey" have since been joined by similarly minded critics: "An issue that bears as centrally on the career of Paul de Man as of Wordsworth and Coleridge is that of the close relations throughout the modern period between sophisti-

---

36. John Thelwall, the radical activist who figures prominently in this volume, has an acute observation on Southey's metrics in *Thalaba* and *Kehama*. In *Biographia Literaria,* Coleridge compares the effect of some of the "*new metres* . . . attempted of late" to "galloping over a paved road in a German stage-wagon without springs." Annotating the passage, Thelwall notes, "Southey gives us plenty of the German Waggon in his new old measures (his Sapphics & his Dactylics)—in Thaliba [sic] & Kehama his wheels are frequently light enough & his springs sufficiently elastic; but he carries us thro roads so soft & so unequal that we are frequently slough'd up to the axle, & thrown fairly out by the jerk." See Burton R. Pollin, "John Thelwall's Marginalia in a Copy of Coleridge's *Biographia Literaria,*" 86. Thelwall's own metrics were rated highly by competent judges: "Mr. Coleridge and I," writes Wordsworth, "were of opinion that the modulations of his blank verse were superior to those of most writers in that metre" (*Letters: The Later Years, 1821–1853*, 959).

37. Byron's note to lines 211–20 of *English Bards and Scotch Reviewers.*

cated literature and hostility to politics, or quietism."[38] Unlike de Man, T. S. Eliot, for all his anti-Semitism, did not write collaborationist articles during World War II, but he emerges as a principal villain: pivotal because of his doctrine of the "autonomous" poem and his role in the particular critical esteem accorded to poets who were "religious and political conservatives." Finding a common denominator despite wide critical differences, Butler claims:

> Since Eliot's day New Criticism and its successor, the Yale-Cornell variant of depo-
> liticized deconstruction, has repeated that [conservative, quietist] discovery for
> the Romantics. From the late 1940s "Romanticism" has steadily risen in academic
> esteem, but a cluster of quietist poems has risen fastest of all. . . . The quietist
> poet and the quietist critic have this above all in common, a rejection of politics
> so comprehensive and doctrinaire that they appear to have left themselves no vo-
> cabulary in which to write analytically about their own sociopolitical positions.

As my reservations regarding Kitson's essay indicate, I share some of this suspicion about Romantic critics who seem almost as anxious as later Words-worth and Coleridge were to distance themselves from their own political radicalism during the 1790s, and to imaginatively transform hopes once invested in the French Revolution. But as readers of Byron and Shelley know, (and later there would be significant reminders from such major commentators as Erdman, Thompson, and Woodring), it did not take the *New* Historicists to make *that* point. The recent wrinkle has to do with the overt prominence of the Newreaders' Marxian or Marxist-influenced political positions; with their insistence that an artwork, whatever its creator's intention, necessarily reflects the dominant ideology (and, in the case of deconstructive New Historicists, the irrepressible logic of figurative language); and, above all, with a writer's evasion—sometimes deliberate but more often largely or completely unconscious—of historical and political conflicts and forms of oppression, evasions marked by detectable disguises and "significant silences." The New Historicist implication is that, even in the case of committed Marxians like Erdman and Thompson, the critical orientation of the old "historical scholars" of the Romantic period was simply too untheoretical and straightforward for them, then, to hear the inaudible.

Still worse, quietist and reactionary critics, it is charged, actually conspire with poets like Wordsworth and Coleridge, whose political shift from radicalism to reaction, or at least from activism to quietism, is inscribed in their self-reflexive and densely textured poetry. Unlike some historicists, whose clotted prose reflects more interest in theory than in poetry, Marilyn Butler, whose recent work is focused on poetic interaction, is not opposed to richly textured art. But, she insists, in making an "icon" of a literary artifact like "Kubla Khan"

---

38. Supporting evidence for Butler's point is certainly there, most pertinently perhaps in de Man's essay "Wordsworth and Hölderlin," which stresses—with de Man's implicit approval—the chastened poets' conclusion that they were deluded to have entertained hopes of translating their revolutionary ideals into an activist program capable of being fulfilled in the secular world of sociopolitical reality.

or "Tintern Abbey," its admirers "repeat even its significant silences in their criticism." As for the dialectic between Southey's *Thalaba* and "Kubla Khan," Butler has a final word:

> Coleridge's omission of the garden's inhabitants is a quietist maneuver representing in the apparent smallness of its scale the largeness of its implications. Without his subjects the ruler loses his malignity. . . . It is not marginal but central to observe that Coleridge refrains from telling *Kubla Khan* as a story about superstition or false consciousness imposed on numbers of people from above, or from describing the paradisal garden as though it could serve as a metaphor for a wicked court.

It should be noted that whatever Coleridge omitted or refrained from, it did not prevent Carl Woodring from seeing—more than thirty years ago, even before Rudich's political interpretation—connections between Kubla's pleasure dome and caves of ice and the tobogganing over mounds of snow and other iced luxuries enjoyed by the Russian court, especially by Coleridge's epitome of wickedness, Catherine the Great, who erected an ice palace to which Coleridge once alluded. Woodring also noted the resemblance between Kubla's decreed pleasure dome and "the spell-built palace of the state-magician"— to quote Coleridge's description of the oratorical skills of William Pitt. It was a palace, Coleridge continued, destroyed in debate by Pitt's principal parliamentary enemy, that "good genius," Charles James Fox, at the first touch of whose "wand," Pitt's deceitful palace "sunk into a ruinous and sordid hovel, tumbling in upon the head of the wizard that had reared it."[39]

Though the imagistic similarities are undeniable, and the revolutionary potential as striking as in any evasion of *Thalaba*, most readers, presumably including the New Historicists, will find Coleridge's Kubla a more benevolent despot than the British prime minister who, in fighting Jacobinism, initiated a domestic terror in England. From my perspective, the similar images suggest an *unconscious intrusion* into the poem of political concerns never far beneath the surface in the case of a poet and political lecturer who lived in justified fear of the Pittite Terror. Here I differ, perspectively at least, from those more accusatory New Historicists writing on Wordsworth and Coleridge who stress their *deliberate exclusion* of the political dimension.

Marilyn Butler's is a characteristic New Historicist essay of the most recent vintage. Like the readings of "Tintern Abbey" mentioned earlier, like Rudich's

---

39. *Politics in the Poetry of Coleridge*, 50–52. The description of Pitt's spell-built palace and its destruction occurs in a piece by Coleridge in the *Morning Post* of February 6, 1800 (*EOT* I 171). Coleridge, of course, demonized Catherine the Great, rejoicing at her death (as a sovereign, not a woman) "as at the disenshrining of a Daemon!, . . . as at the extinction of the evil Principle impersonated!" In addition to her political crimes, especially "the massacre at Ismail" and "her iniquities in Poland," he was appalled by her "poisoning of her husband," and refused to recall for readers of this exclamation-studded footnote to his "Ode on the Departing Year," the "libidinous excesses of her private hours! I have no wish to qualify myself for the office of Historiographer to the King of Hell—!" (*CPW* I 162–63*n*)

and Woodring's remarks on "Kubla Khan" (not mentioned by Butler), her essay illuminates textual and subtextual dimensions that cannot be dismissed—so long as they do not move from the margin to the center in ways that suggest that the poem, now that its deliberate evasions have been exposed, has been decoded, repoliticized, and, its critical hour come round at last, accurately read. Despite many points of similarity with the work of the New Historicists, my suggestion that there may be "submerged politics" in *The Ancient Mariner* does not include the more-than-occasional historicist claim that the suppression is deliberate and deplorably reactionary or that the "politics" I dredge up from beneath the surface of this apparently apolitical poem thereby constitutes its deepest layer of meaning, the meaning with greatest priority.

3

Two crucial, and related, questions remain to be addressed as preamble to the study that follows. The first is the most obvious: was Coleridge himself *aware* of a political dimension in *The Ancient Mariner?* And, second, even if the author may have been, like his Mariner, largely "unaware," does that compel us to conclude, as most deconstructionists insist, that language, particularly figurative language, is out of the control of the shaping artist? I can best respond to these questions—and to the overarching question about "intrinsic" and "extrinsic" approaches to a work of art—by employing what are, especially for my reading, the two crucial passages in the poem itself: the snake-blessing and the appearance of the dungeon-grate image.

Was Coleridge aware of a "political" dimension in the poem? No one, including Kitson, makes that claim. Neither do I, though one can never be certain. The question of intentionality, of distinguishing between conscious and unconscious processes in the creation of a work of art, is always problematic, especially in the case of a poet whose fascination with "the twilight realms of consciousness" was balanced by an insistence on the artist's active "power" and "*voluntary* purpose" (*BL* II 147, 65). But even if the politics in the poem remain "submerged," an unconscious motif would hardly be alien to a poem neither of whose pivotal events—the killing of the albatross and the blessing of the water-snakes—exemplify what Descartes called *cogitationis*, "conscious experience," by which he meant "everything that takes place within ourselves so that we are aware of it."

Twice in *Biographia Literaria*, Coleridge spoke of a crepuscular zone. He first described hidden "influences . . . at work" in an author's mind, spirits "walking in the *twilight* of his consciousness"; later, discussing the Intimations ode (and echoing and altering Wordsworth's Hartleian reference, in the "Preface" to the 1800 edition of *Lyrical Ballads*, to the "fluxes and refluxes of the mind"), Coleridge referred to "the flux and reflux" of the "inmost nature" of those who "venture at times into the twilight realms of consciousness" (*BL* I 230, II 147). Anticipating Freud (and his unacknowledged precursor, Nietzsche), Coleridge, Wordsworth, and the early German Romantics realized that, Cartesian rationalism notwithstanding, there is much within the human psyche of which we are unaware: dynamic activity that can be inferred from its traces but which itself remains—as Freud's term for the unconscious (*das Unbewusste*) indicates—inaccessible to direct inspection, "unknown."[40]

The Mariner blesses the water-snakes "unaware," an adverb repeated two lines later, when the impulse is attributed to a pitying "kind saint." The crucial water image is both Christian and proto-Freudian: "A *spring* of love *gushed* from my heart / And I blessed them unaware." Confessional literature is replete with born-again sinners whose conversion experience is attended by welling tears and springs gushing in the breast. Though less organic than mechanical, the "hydraulic" imagery Freud employs in describing the "dynamic unconscious" is also of pressure and release, a buildup of tension followed by a "pulsation" or "flow," energy released from hidden sources of which the subject is "not directly aware." The significance of attributing this impulse to an external, indeed orthodox, source is discussed below. For the moment, it is clear that the apparently spontaneous uprush of "love" that impels the Mariner to bless the snakes recalls (echoes and revokes) the equally unconscious act of cruelty that isolated him from his shipmates, indeed alienated him from all creatures in the universe: the dark impulse that drove him to kill the albatross, a bird affirmed, by the "First Voice" at the conclusion of Part V, to have "lov'd the man / Who shot him with his bow."

The killing of this innocent and loving creature is an act of unconscious, gratuitous cruelty, of what Coleridge elsewhere and famously called "motiveless malignity." Edgar Allan Poe—whose black cat is, like D. H. Lawrence's snake, kin to Coleridge's albatross—speaks of "the spirit of PERVERSENESS," one of the "primitive impulses of the human heart," an "unfathomable longing . . . to do wrong for the wrong's sake only." The narrator of "The Black Cat" first mutilates and then hangs Pluto precisely "*because*" the animal "had loved me, . . . *because* I knew that [in killing it] I was committing a sin—a deadly sin that would so jeopardize my immortal soul as to place it—if such a thing were possible—even beyond the reach of the infinite mercy of the Most Merciful and

40. "Freud's ideas about the unconscious were in the air in the nineteenth century and had already assumed some sophisticated guises. Poets and philosophers had been speculating about the notion of mental activities beyond the reach of awareness; a century before Freud began to occupy himself with the unconscious, romantics like Coleridge could speak of 'the twilight realms of consciousness,' while Goethe, that romantic classicist, had found the idea of depths beyond depths in the psyche extremely attractive. In his *Prelude* [1805], Wordsworth had celebrated the deep recesses in his heart as the realm in which he dwelt with pleasure. 'I held unconscious intercourse with beauty,' he wrote. '*Caverns* there were within my mind which sun / Could never penetrate' [I, 562–63; III, 246–47]. Some influential nineteenth-century psychologists . . . made much of this idea. And among the philosophers whose influence Freud resisted but could hardly evade completely, Schopenhauer and Nietzsche repeatedly cautioned against overestimating the conscious at the expense of the unconscious forces in the mind" (Peter Gay, *Freud: A Life for Our Time*, 366–67). For Freud himself, see especially his 1915 metapsychological paper, "The Unconscious," in *The Freud Reader*, ed. Gay, 572–84.

Most Terrible God."[41] Though this tension between punishment and redemption, terror and divine mercy, is at the agitated heart of *The Ancient Mariner,* one critical difference is that Coleridge's protagonist, when he shoots the albatross, is not conscious of yielding to the innate promptings of an evil "Imp of the Perverse," as Poe called it in the title of a related essay.

While the later gloss bristles with moral evaluation ("The ancient Mariner *inhospitably* killeth the *pious* bird of *good* omen"), the poem itself is notoriously and significantly silent as to "why" the Mariner kills the bird. He is interrupted, as deconstructionist Barbara Johnson has remarked, at "precisely the point where the motivation for the act ought to have been given." Indeed, the mystery is "transmitted by the very punctuation." The Wedding Guest's question, prompted by the suddenly ghastly appearance of the Mariner, is instantly followed by that haunted man's announcement of the deed, without explanation: "'Why lookst thou so?'—With my cross-bow / I shot the ALBATROSS." The "break" between the stunned question and the Mariner's resumption of his tale is "represented by the dash that marks the place where what is not known is evoked as the blank that makes the story go on forever."[42]

This inscrutability, strikingly similar to the "not-to-tell" moment in *Christabel* when a dash also marks the place between incipient revelation and mystery-prolonging obstruction,[43] contrasts sharply with the motivation attributed to the deed that partially atones for the murder of the albatross. When, in the Mariner's resumed tale, unconscious Evil is countered by unconscious Good, it is Good quickly rationalized in Christian terms. The distinction is revealing. Though the Mariner offers no speculation whatever about the unfathomable impulse that drove him to kill, he instantly attributes the snake-blessing impulse to his "kind saint," a guardian angel who has surely taken "pity" on him as a suffering sinner. Though the spring of love that gushes from his heart seems as mysteriously unconscious and autonomous as the evil act it reverses, the Mariner, in immediately turning to his guardian angel and to prayer, dismisses autonomy in favor of self-assurances of benign supernatural intervention, a religious sanction extending (most overtly in the "moral" and subsequent prose gloss) to the whole of the poem's otherwise uncanny and inexplicable universe.

This seems a later example of what J. Paul Hunter, discussing "Defoe's emblematic method and quest for form" in *Robinson Crusoe,* describes as the artistic adaptation of the characteristic Puritan conviction that all things have universal, spiritual significance. Construing history and biography according

41. *Prose Tales (First Series) by Edgar Allan Poe,* 420–21.
42. Johnson, Editor's Preface to "The Pedagogical Imperative: Teaching as a Literary Genre," vi–vii.
43. "Behold her [Geraldine's] bosom and half her side— / A sight to dream of, not to tell!" (*Christabel,* ll. 253–54). Of course, unlike Christabel, henceforth governed by a spell of silence, the Mariner, gifted with "strange power of speech," is compelled by fits of woeful agony to repeatedly "tell" his "ghastly tale." Still, he remains silent as to any motivation behind his slaying of the albatross. For Shelley's terrified response to the (revealing) manuscript version of these lines of *Christabel,* see Conclusion, note 13.

to their own lights and firmly committed to the workings of Providence, Puritan writers "'discovered' the divine patterns implicit in things and events, regarding life not as disordered, chaotic, and shapeless, but as one entire cosmic emblem of divine purpose and plan."[44] Coleridge clung to a similarly emblematic or symbolic perception of life, the "faith" that "*all things* counterfeit infinity" (*CL* I 349); that, as he imparts to his infant son in "Frost at Midnight," in the natural world we

> see and hear
> The lovely shapes and sounds intelligible
> Of that eternal language, which thy God
> Utters, who from eternity doth teach
> Himself in all, and all things in himself.
> (*CPW* I 242)

As Coleridge's vivid response to the nightmarish and horrific confirms, however, it was a benign, intelligible world and worldview under constant threat. Those committed to a spiritual or providential explanation, while they do not evade life's mystery, may not fully engage it either. Thus, in *The Ancient Mariner*, the snake-blessing, saint-thanking Mariner—and his even more anxious creator, Coleridge—in effect try to lift "the burthen of the mystery" from what Wordsworth, echoing and reversing in "Tintern Abbey" the phrase just quoted from "Frost at Midnight," calls "this *un*intelligible world." Coleridge, in short, struggles, religiously and perhaps reductively, to explicate the twilight workings of the unknowable unconscious, to "canonize" his Mariner's intuitive act by transforming an aesthetic response ("no tongue / Their *beauty* might declare") into an ethical event in a spiritually coherent universe.

While that would be in keeping with Coleridge's own response to natural beauty—his "love and adoration of God in Nature" (*CPW* I 244n) and his own refusal, like Poe's narrator, to believe that "such a thing were possible" as to be beyond God's mercy—the problematic nature of this "unaware" raises some questions. Given the chaotic universe of the poem, which seems rather more terrible than merciful, does the saint-inspired blessing, as opposed to the initial aesthetic response, reflect less love than fear—fear of the consequences of *not* blessing the snakes and then seeking an orthodox imprimatur? If so, the blessing is the thematic prelude to the poem's end, where, in the Mariner's fond vision of communal prayer, "each to his great Father bends," submitting in what Bostetter has coupled as "fear and enforced obedience" to a divine "despot."[45]

That fear and enforced obedience may, in turn, have something to do with the sociopolitical circumstances in which Coleridge wrote the poem, circumstances which may have entered his ballad without Coleridge being fully conscious of them—"unaware." In blessing the snakes, the Mariner unconsciously seeks reintegration into what he and Coleridge would like to believe is a benign and coherent universe. Political Coleridge—equally "unaware" of his poetry of

44. *The Reluctant Pilgrim*, 208.
45. "The Nightmare World of *The Ancient Mariner*," 114, 115.

displacement and repressing his fear that the world may not be providential—may be seeking in the snake-blessing a "loyalist" and "quietist" accommodation with the local branch of the cosmic tyranny: the arbitrary and repressive Pitt government of 1798, which had, according to "Fears in Solitude" (written in April of that year, when habeas corpus was suspended), "deemed" him an "enemy" (*CPW* I 262).

The present study is an attempt to provide the evidence that might support such a reading. To complete the immediate point: the "unconscious," as usual, achieves its goal—in this case, relative security in a hostile situation. The "method" would certainly be indirect, "displaced." In fact, in one of several anticipatory reversals of Freud, displacement is *down*ward, from the Pitt Ministry to the previously "slimy" water-snakes. It may all seem highly unlikely, or at least unintended. But if Coleridge is operating largely unconsciously, the question of intention need not deter us unduly, especially in its most obvious form: Why would a poet, unless he was, like Blake in his "Prophecies," engaged for safety's sake in deliberately arcane allegory, write a notably apolitical poem to address political issues? Woodring long ago observed that "If 'Christabel,' 'Kubla Khan,' and *The Ancient Mariner* are poems of escape, politics form a large part of what they escaped from."[46] In what would be a classic case of psychic repression, Coleridge may have fixed on a supernatural voyage as a way of avoiding thinking about contemporary domestic politics. Nevertheless, in a return of the repressed, politics surface in some of the figurative language, images that lead us back to unspoken concerns that persist beneath and agitate the fabulous surface of the ballad. Its presence betrayed by these traces of unconscious activity, the repressed material is exposed for rhetorical analysis buttressed by historical research. In short, and in provisional accord with the almost universal poststructuralist emphasis on the psychic or ideological necessities that disguise or occlude a text's "real" meaning, we can legitimately discuss a level of meaning of which Coleridge, like his Mariner, was perhaps "unaware."

The reference to rhetorical analysis and historical research raises once again that divisive matter of "intrinsic" versus "extrinsic" critical approaches. Despite the genuine tension between the terms in this opposition, it is a dichotomy that blurs for reasons I can best explain by returning to a crucial figure in the poem: an image which, for me, is as pivotal as the Wordsworthian prison-house historicized by Levinson, and which also demonstrates the *limits* of the unconscious in artistic creation.

As I read *The Ancient Mariner*, at least on this occasion, the principal signpost on the road to the Coleridgean political unconscious is the "dungeon-grate" through which the setting sun peers. The bars are the masts of the spectre-ship, "that strange shape" that "drove suddenly / Betwixt us and the Sun." In a bemused irrational or neoprimitive variation on Cartesian objectivism, Wallace Stevens, temporarily suspending his own disbelief, tells us that truth can exist

46. *Politics in the Poetry of Coleridge*, 223.

unmediated, independent of any informed perspective or point of view. "You must," he says in the "It Must Be Abstract" section of *Notes Toward a Supreme Fiction,* "become an ignorant man again / And see the sun with an ignorant eye." In its pure "idea," this abstract sun is "clean," "Washed in the remotest cleanliness of a heaven / That has expelled us and our images."

It is all very well to cleanse the doors of perception, but this Stevensian Windexing, if it were more than a phase, would ultimately remove perception itself, going beyond what Yeats in a related mood called "those great ignorant leafy ways" of prelapsarian bliss to a transcendent expulsion of the human altogether. Ignorance may be bliss; but for "us and our images" to be "expelled" would mean the washing away of concrete human experience, of our bodies, history, culture, tradition: everything that in actuality gets between us and the sun as a Kantian *ding an sich.* A skeleton ship's masts likened to a "dungeon-grate" intrude "Betwixt us and the Sun" in as dark and unblissful an experiential image as human history offers, and one far from remote for an Englishman of Coleridge's political views in 1797–1798. Along with his friend and collaborator Wordsworth, Coleridge had been spied on by government agents in 1797, and, as a new contributor of political essays and verses to the anti-Ministerial and widely read *Morning Post,* he felt himself exposed to the dangers of political imprisonment in the early spring of 1798.

In "Tintern Abbey," the poem that closes *Lyrical Ballads,* the volume that opened in 1798 with *The Ancient Mariner,* Wordsworth spoke of "sober," maturing experiences that alter our youthful perspective. In the Intimations ode,

> The Clouds that gather round the setting sun
> Do take a sober colouring from an eye
> That hath kept watch o'er man's mortality.

This, the "eye" of an anything but neutral or "ignorant" man, reports no purely independent objective reality perceived by a transparent eyeball, but a heavenly scene whose natural hues are also elegiacally colored by the adult observer's experience, at once personal and universal, of the pathos of mutability. That "sober colouring," as we shall later see, had its earlier, specifically political, analogue in the anchored vessels of the British fleet that "Darken with shadowy hulks" the otherwise tranquil and beautiful sunset Wordsworth saw from the Isle of Wight on the eve of war with France.

In *The Ancient Mariner,* sociopolitical reality also intrudes itself into the natural scene, with the masts of an even more ominous vessel crossing the face of the "setting sun." But whose perspective is being reported, whose experiential fears reflected, in the description of the setting sun glaring "As if through a dungeon-grate"? That simile, though cognate with the horrific "shape" of the spectre-ship as a whole, intrudes itself into the narrative in that it—like the later simile of the ocean submissive "as a slave" and the still later description of the violent convulsion that sinks the Mariner's ship—has less to do with the "normal" rhetoric of the nautical narrator, or of the mediating balladeer, than of the author, Coleridge.

The dungeon-grate, however, is not *simply* an "extrinsic" intrusion from mate-rial reality, specifically, from the period in which the poem was written and reflecting Coleridge's particular political situation in 1797–1798. Though an "in-trusion" from the political realm, the dungeon-grate is hardly incompatible with the imprisoning and penitential "world" of *The Ancient Mariner*. It is, however, at odds with the poem's moral, which presents that world as the creation and concern of a God of love. In that sense, as a striking and unexpected simile, the dungeon-grate may be seen by some as an example of that figurative language which, as deconstruction has shown if it has shown anything, tends to interfere with, or to subvert, the discursive level of language—the straightforward working of logic and syntax. For such readers, the discrepancy between this (and similar images) and the providential "moral" message of the poem as a whole would exemplify what deconstruction calls the gap or "aporia" between figure and grammar, between rhetoric as trope and rhetoric as persuasion.

Do such similes as masts resembling a "dungeon-grate" and an ocean still as a submissive "slave" have a mind of their own, an unconscious logic or Pas-calian reason that reason knows not of? Long before Derrida, John Thelwall, annotating *Biographia Literaria* in 1817, observed, "The similies of Coleridge are frequently much more luminous & logical than his arguments."[47] This may anticipate the deconstructionist point that figurative language has a logic of its own, subversive of and with presumed priority over discursive logic and autho-rial intent. Precisely that argument, one resumed in 1993, first surfaced a dozen years ago in a revealing interaction between M. H. Abrams and his poststruc-turalist colleague at Cornell, Jonathan Culler. The original occasion was a symposium in honor of Abrams, the immediate subject the similes and meta-phors of Coleridge.

Culler had contended that Abrams, in discussing Coleridge's organic "plant" metaphors, had punned on "tropes" and "tropics" in such a way as to reveal himself a precursor of Derrida. Experiencing a Wordsworthian "shock of mild surprise" at being pronounced an incipient deconstructionist, Abrams found the assertion "plausible," but only "within limits." The deconstructive puns *might* have been his, he conceded, but if so it was "unwittingly," by "an intention below the level of consciousness." For Abrams, acknowledging in effect that he had entered the Coleridgean twilight zone, it was a "borderline case," finally undecidable; either he *or* clever Culler might have made the puns. Culler's own deconstructionist position was that neither of them, "but language itself" was the punster since "language can lead a life of its own, even run wild" because "unable to control its own tropology." The logic of figurative language, Culler concluded, "invariably reveals a certain excess: something that doesn't fit." Coleridge himself, in an axiom once cited by Abrams in *The Mirror and the Lamp*, declared that "No simile runs on all four legs." For Derridean readers figures always outrun meaning, and any excess or surplus—operating autono-mously, beyond authorial control—moves in strictly linguistic ways its decon-

47. Pollin, "John Thelwall's Marginalia," 90.

structive wonders to perform.[48] Reasserting the "limits" of his agreement, Abrams rejected, in the name of "humanism," Culler's displacement of the author as an "originating consciousness" by the "deconstructive play of a language that is compelled by an inner entelechy, its 'autonomous logic'."[49]

The recourse to "humanism" is, of course, inevitable here, for one recognizes in Culler's position the familiar common denominators underlying most of the principal postmodern forms of critical "discourse." Whatever their differences, neo-Marxists, deconstructionists, and psychoanalytic critics, emphasizing the "precedence" and "mastery of language" and the "servitude" of "the subject," leave little or no room for a writer's control over his or her ideas and language. This deterministic dismissal of the conscious autonomy of the individual explains avant-garde assaults on "liberalism" and "humanism," indictments handed down with a contempt rivaling that of their apparent opposites: religious fundamentalists and right-wing Republicans. Over the past two decades, there have been post-Nietzschean funerals featuring Foucauldian and Barthean gloatings over the Death of the Author, and the End of Humanism, a humanism which, it is charged, is guilty on two rather different counts. Critically, it tends to limit a work's meaning to what a biographically defined author deliberately intended; while, politically, it cloaks the covert operations of power and prohibits even the subject's *desire* for power along with excluding any possibility of its being seized. Thus "demystified," Western liberal humanism stands exposed as both a constraining force that limits the exfoliating power of language and as a pseudoneutral ideology that, far from liberatory, actually stabilizes an unjust society by denying power to the oppressed.

While demystification has its indispensable uses, it also has its limits, and it is far from clear how advanced and supposedly emancipatory critical movements that ridicule "gestures" of autonomy and condemn in toto a flawed and incomplete yet rich and multifaceted humanist tradition can themselves lead to liberation rather than to hyperskeptical nihilism. In any case, the "humanist" position championed, and embodied, by M. H. Abrams would be applauded by Coleridge, for whom poetry was precisely the imaginative synthesis of determinism and freedom, nature and art: the "interpenetration of passion and of will, of *spontaneous* impulse and *voluntary* purpose."[50]

48. Again, some distinction must be drawn between the founding philosopher and the literary critics who have taken up deconstruction. For Derrida himself, authorial intention is not to be dismissed or discounted. Indeed, it is "an indispensable guardrail" protecting a reading from the excesses of that all-licensed "freeplay" popularly synonymous with deconstruction. At the same time, of course, given the problematic, figural nature of language with its catachreses and aporias, authorial intention is not *fully* determinative. The "guardrail has always only *protected*, it has never *opened*, a reading" (*Of Grammatology*, 158). Though, in the wake of Derrida, readings have become all *too* open, few if any of us would be willing to declare that complex texts inevitably say *precisely* what their authors *meant* them to say.

49. Abrams, "A Reply," 167–69.

50. *BL* II 65. The debate continues. Culler responded to Abrams's "What Is a Hu-

Those Coleridgean "plant"-images *do* pose the crucial dilemma: growth at once "inherently purposeful" *and* "fated in the seed," evolving into its final form "without the supervention of consciousness."[51] But the particular Coleridgean "plant"-passage that has haunted Abrams for decades—a wonderfully elaborated meditation from Appendix C of *The Statesman's Manual*—presents a growing plant as "the natural symbol" of the evolving "higher life of reason" and explicitly rejects not only mental mechanism but organic growth if conceived as excluding human freedom, purpose, consciousness. Despite their respect for the powers of the unconscious, the Romantics found the remedy to self-division and alienation from nature not in primitivistic regression but in knowledge itself; for as Hegel puts it in a celebrated dialectical image, "The hand that inflicts the wound is also the hand that heals it."[52] We have, says Coleridge (writing in 1816, the same year Hegel completed his *Wissenschaft der Logik*), "fallen" from a state of harmonious and unfallen nature to which we must "still become" reconciled. "But what the plant *is,* by an act not its own and unconsciously—*that* must thou *make* thyself to *become*" (*LS* 71–73).

"Where Id is," Freud was later to prophesy, "there shall Ego be." Celebrating the "*Esemplastic* power" to "shape into one" (*BL* I 168, 295) "my shaping spirit of Imagination" (*CPW* I 366), as opposed to organic unconsciousness or the associative chaos of language itself, Coleridge anticipates not only the Freudian vision but also the misconception George Orwell described in diagnosing our linguistic maladies as of 1946. While all could agree that, perverted as it was by politics, "the English language was in a bad state," Orwell rejected, at the very outset of "Politics and the English Language," the assumption that "we cannot by conscious action do anything about" its decline; for underlying that assumption is "the half-conscious belief that language is *a natural growth and not an instrument which we shape for our own purposes*" (italics added). The latter is the *fully* conscious belief-cum-dogma asserted by postmodernists proclaiming the Death of the Author, including deconstructionists who describe tropes as running wild, who (like Hillis Miller) "make the univocal equivocal . . . according to the law that language is not [a submissive] instrument or tool in man's hands," who locate control and autonomy essentially in language, denying both to agents whom such "humanists" as Coleridge, Orwell, and Abrams depict as "shaping" language to and for "our own purposes."[53]

---

manistic Criticism?," a lecture delivered at Cornell University on March 31, 1993, inaugurating the Heinrich and Alice Schneider Memorial Lecture Series, with "Human Limits: A Response to M. H. Abrams." While he neither eliminates nor denigrates authors, Culler once again casts doubt on their control of what they do and emphasizes the unconstrained "play of language." Both Abrams *and* Culler have subsequently been attacked by William V. Spanos, "The Genealogy of Humanism."

51. M. H. Abrams, *The Mirror and the Lamp: Romantic Theory and the Critical Tradition,* 173.

52. *The Logic of Hegel,* trans. W. Wallace, 56.

53. Orwell, "Politics and the English Language," 162. Miller, "The Critic as Host," 224.

Though fully aware that no artist has total control over language, Coleridge strenuously opposed any doctrine that would disempower this shaping self by reducing a "poor worthless I" to "the mere quicksilver plating behind a looking-glass" (*BL* I 119). The main culprit was David Hartley's doctrine of the "association of ideas," to which Coleridge had been strongly attracted in 1795–1796, even naming his child, born in the latter year, Hartley. Coleridge soon moved on from this too-passive associationism to that emphasis on mental activity he found in Berkeley (hence, his *new* son's name) and the Cambridge Platonists who, like Kant, emphasized the mind's creativity in perception. Influenced as much by Coleridge as by Edward Young's phrase about the senses that "half-create the wondrous world they see" (*Night Thoughts* VI.424), Wordsworth had referred in "Tintern Abbey" to the world of eye and ear, "both what they half-create, / And what perceive." But the "Preface" to the 1800 *Lyrical Ballads* relapsed into that language of Hartleian associationist psychology which Coleridge thought inadequate as an explanation of Wordsworth's own creative genius and to which he so strenuously objected years later in *Biographia Literaria*.

Doubtless he responded at the time. In excited letters written in the winter and spring of 1801, Coleridge reported meditating "vigorously" on "the Relations of Thoughts to Things"; declared "false" any "system," Hartleian or Newtonian, built on mental "passiveness," mind as a "lazy Looker-on on an external World"; and first announced that he had "overthrown the doctrine of Association, as taught by Hartley, and with it . . . the irreligious . . . doctrine of Necessity." "This I have *done*," he added, neglecting to mention that Kant had "done" it before him (*CL* II 672, 709, 706). These announcements to his friend Tom Poole may have been shared with Wordsworth, who seems to register Coleridge's objections in the lengthy speculation, focusing on the question "What is a Poet?," added to his "Preface" in the 1802 edition of *Lyrical Ballads*. In any case, the letters to Poole adumbrate Coleridge's later full-scale refutation of Hartleian associationism in the *Biographia* (*BL* I 89–128). There he affirmed a "will" not subject to "blind mechanism," active and "distinct powers, whose function is to controul, determine, and modify the phantasmal chaos of association" (*BL* I 116). And in the famous Chapter XIII, he distinguished limited, determined "Fancy" (which "must receive all its materials ready made from the law of association") from "Imagination," an "essentially *vital*" faculty, creative rather than merely associative (*BL* I 304–5).

Even when in the earlier nineties he had been most fascinated by "the streamy nature of association," it was a stream "curbed and ruddered" by "the disposing imagination."[54] This Coleridgean faith in mind's creative activity—a Romantic version of Berkeley and Kant shared by W. B. Yeats, who adopted both the "shaping imagination" phrase and the anti-"quicksilver plating" image—culminates in a "Constructive or Dynamic Philosophy in opposition to the merely mechanic" (*CL* IV 579). It was, in short, always a question of *when* rather than *if* Coleridge would repudiate the random streaminess of an associationism that reduced the mind to mirror-like, slavish passivity.

54. Lowes, *The Road to Xanadu*, 68.

Coleridge's trope of enslavement may have some connection with his addiction. He characteristically referred to the "dirty business of Laudanum" as that "*free-agency-annihilating* poison" (*CL* III 490); "a slave he was to this potent drug not less abject than Caliban to Prospero," De Quincey observed in an anonymous contribution to *Tait's Edinburgh Magazine* in 1833–1834. But the philosophic enemy remained enslaving mechanism, necessitarian and associationist. "Vulgar" and unthinking minds given to making irrelevant verbal connections were attacked by Coleridge, in an unpublished fragment now in the British Museum, as "the passive Slaves of Association" (Egerton MS 2800 f. 186). It was in his synopsis of the offending doctrine of the mind as a Lockean tabula rasa that Coleridge, examining the "necessary consequences of the Hartleian theory," spoke of "the mere quicksilver plating behind a looking-glass; and in this alone consists the poor worthless I!"[55] Thus, despite my emphasis on the "unconscious" dimension of *The Ancient Mariner,* a level revealed in its figurative language, I too resist—on Yeatsian, Orwellian, and, preeminently, *Coleridgean* grounds—the extreme position (beyond Derrida himself) that would minimize, or negate altogether, what Abrams calls authorial "consciousness, intention, purpose, design."[56]

Whatever the unconscious component in creativity, Coleridge—certain that the self was neither "crude egoismus" nor passive mirror, and that a poet like Shakespeare "never wrote anything without design"—never unconditionally surrendered authorial purpose and freedom to the uncontrollable play of non-referential language. Words were at least *intended* to relate "Thoughts to Things." Coleridge would even, as he told Godwin in 1800, "endeavor to destroy the old antithesis of *Words & Things,* elevating, as it were [,] words into Things, & Living Things too" (*CL* I 625–26). But a gap remained. Coleridge was painfully aware of language's frequent "inadequacy," even "impotence," in this regard: "O what then are Words," he cries out in a notebook, "but articulated sighs of a Prisoner heard from his Dungeon!" (*CN* II 2998).

Here again, this time anticipating our postmodern "prison-house of language" as described by Fredric Jameson and others, Coleridge employs a dungeon image. Now, however "unaware" he may or may not have been regarding a "political" level of meaning in *The Ancient Mariner,* Coleridge knew a dungeon-grate from a handsaw and cannot have been completely unconscious and purposeless in the selection and retention of such imagery, whether in his ballad or

55. *BL* I 119. Yeats (who insisted that the passive *mirror* must turn active *lamp*) inserted in his copy of *Biographia Literaria* at this page in chapter 7 (the same chapter from which he borrowed his image of the contemplative-creative mind as "a long-legged fly upon the stream") a small piece of paper on which he wrote, "plating behind a looking glass." In his correspondence with his friend Sturge Moore, Yeats deplored the turning of the "mind . . . into the quicksilver at the back of the mirror," and he declared in his essay on George Berkeley: "Something compels me to reject whatever—to borrow a metaphor of Coleridge's—drives mind into the quicksilver." For the references, see my *Yeats's Interactions with Tradition,* 39, 53.

56. "A Reply," 173.

in this striking notebook entry. And, deconstruction notwithstanding, he surely intended *The Ancient Mariner*'s dungeon-grate to refer, at some level, to a material reality "outside of language," beyond the endlessly contradictory play of a "*texte*" without external reference and unbridled by authorial intent. To imagine otherwise is to imagine a Coleridge willing to submit to the modern version of Hartleian associationism: a Saussurean or Lacanian theory of "arbitrary" signification that Coleridge the poet would be as predisposed to resist as Coleridge the young republican was to resist the "arbitrary" government of William Pitt, with its suspension of habeas corpus and the specter of the dungeon.

Of course, the desire to resist—even to defy—is not necessarily to escape, a grim truth with both linguistic and political ramifications. Though, in a well-known essay, Lacan tentatively depicts poetry as an escape from the linguistic prison house, even to resist is, he claims, ultimately and inevitably, to confirm our servitude.[57] Though there would be far greater resistance on Coleridge's part to the consciousness-preceding and "subject"-enslaving "tyranny" of signs as depicted in postmodernism, his images of the dungeon-grate and of the prisoner sighing "from his dungeon" suggest fear of a hopeless, impotent condition not unrelated to that contemporary prison house of language and the servitude of "the subject" to which antihumanist postmodernism seems committed. If an aporia *is* revealed by the Mariner's "dungeon-grate," or by the simile of the "slave" stilled "before his lord," it is the subversive gap or slippage between the free and spiritually coherent cosmos Coleridge longs for and the penitential nightmare world he fears and that—in images re-creating an ominous sociopolitical contemporary reality—rises irrepressibly to the surface.

Of course it is hardly necessary to invoke deconstruction to notice the obvious tension in *The Ancient Mariner* between the horrific and the benign, and the constant subversive threat to the latter presented by the former. The point is that whether we apply rigorous rhetorical analysis or stress the referential relation between the simile and the sociopolitical world from which it derives (and which it consciously or unconsciously reflects), the surprising analogy of the dungeon-grate cannot be "expelled" either from the Mariner's experience of that blood-red sunset or from the historical circumstances of the author who put this graphic image in the mouth of his protagonist in the first place. The dungeon-grate cannot be neatly "fitted" into the imagery of a poem repeatedly pronounced apolitical. Yet it cannot be dismissed, either by intrinsic readers who emphasize the organic unity of poems, by tracers of subversive tropes, or by those aware of the political Coleridge. Indeed, the Mariner's creator is an author whose other nineties' texts in verse and prose have more than their share of figurative and nonfigurative dungeons. Like Daniel Defoe, a sometime spy and lifelong debtor (among many other things), the Coleridge of 1795–1798 lived in sporadic fear of imprisonment.

A similar intrusion-subversion occurs with the convulsion and whirlpool that sink the Mariner's ship: an image Robert Penn Warren tried, and failed, to

57. *Ecrits: A Selection*, 155–56.

subsume under one of his two thematic categories in the best-known essay on the poem. The problem is that the image is allied with Romantic "political" symbolism—as, of course, is the rising and setting sun itself, that diurnal emblem of the course of the French Revolution for two generations of Romantic writers. Once incorporated in the literary work, such images become more than tokens of their sociopolitical origins. Thus, in the final analysis, the intrinsic-extrinsic polarity breaks down, or at least blurs. The extralinguistic signifieds (political oppression, political revolution) become linguistic signifiers (dungeon, rising and setting sun, underwater convulsion) subject to rhetorical, not only historical, scrutiny. By refusing to delimit the linguistic complexity of *The Ancient Mariner,* or to reduce it to a mere reflection of contemporary politics, while, at the same time, examining it in its experiential genesis, in its layers of mediation, *and* as a highly articulated verbal construct, we see the poem with an eye that is not "ignorant" and neither antihistorically "aesthetic" nor— necessarily and *narrowly*—"ideological."

5

The Political and Philosophic Context

1

While Peter Kitson, Daniel Watkins and Robert Maniquis have set the poem in its broad revolutionary context, David Erdman alone has related *The Ancient Mariner* to its *immediate* political milieu, describing it as "an imaginatively controlled nightmare . . . objectifying the dereliction and dismay of the times." Though even this isolated assertion, according to Carl Woodring, "goes beyond what we can demonstrate to the skeptical," Erdman repeated the thrust of his original Wordsworth-echoing sentence twenty-three years later in the third edition of *Blake: Prophet against Empire*.[1]

New Historicists, especially those of a Marxian persuasion, tend to shift what Erdman calls "control" away from the poet's imagination to history itself, which becomes, in Stephen Greenblatt's phrase, the artwork's "enabling condition, shaping force, forger of meaning."[2] This goes beyond the "intentional fallacy" excoriated by the old New Critics to a rejection of their own primary emphasis on intrinsic approaches to literature. Yet even the New Critics dominant in the second quarter of the twentieth century, though theoretically anti-historical in their emphasis on intrinsic or text-centered approaches, in practice acknowledged the importance for criticism of the work of literary historians. American deconstructionists like Paul de Man and Hillis Miller go further, ostensibly dismissing, as "the fiction of the referential," any text's literal connection to an actual world outside that text—though, as we have seen, Miller has been trying to close the gap Derrida opened between rhetoric and material reality, anything "outside of language."

Even though his three most celebrated poems fall into the category of the "supernatural," that gap between rhetoric and material reality is hard to maintain in the case of Coleridge—especially the *youthful* Coleridge, who not only wrote "Kubla Khan," *The Ancient Mariner,* and "Christabel," but also, in these same years (1797–1798), moved in and out of political activism, oscillating between retirement and engagement.

The Coleridge of the 1790s was certainly a politically minded man. "Coleridge, of the English Romantic poets, gave most thought to politics," writes

1. Woodring, *Politics in the Poetry of Coleridge,* 33. Erdman, *Prophet against Empire,* 293.
2. *Representing the English Renaissance,* viii.

Woodring in the opening sentence of the definitive study, continuing: "He had, no doubt, the most thought to give." In sermons, addresses to the people, pamphlets, short-lived periodicals, newspaper articles, and poems alike, he addressed the great political issues of the turbulent nineties, an English decade shaken by the international and domestic reverberations of the French Revolution. Yet it was in 1797–1798, which Marilyn Butler rightly calls "the fiercest year of the English counter-revolutionary reaction," that Coleridge "produced almost all his corpus of great poems," poems that are "rapt, intent and exclusive"—or, as Levinson said of "Tintern Abbey," "fiercely private." Butler continues: "The shift from a public to a private focus is in response to political events and has an acknowledged political significance—loyalism—a fact which is well demonstrated in Coleridge's most explicit 'private' poem of this sequence, 'Fears in Solitude. Written in April 1798, during the alarm of an invasion.'" Coleridge's lifelong tendency to internalize public events was perhaps most pronounced in "this rich year," when "he caught the fear in the public mood and availed himself of a moment when his own insecurity could be made the correlative of England's."[3]

Like Nicholas Roe and Alan Liu, neither of whom mentions the poem, Marilyn Butler does not examine *The Ancient Mariner* in the political context she establishes here. That is hardly surprising; as even Kitson acknowledges, *The Ancient Mariner* "has none of the political allusions which stud the contemporaneous 'France: An Ode' or 'Fears in Solitude.'"[4] Nevertheless, playing a variation on Butler's acute observation, I argue that some of the "fears in solitude" expressed in *The Ancient Mariner*—especially that "horror" rapidly succeeding the "flash of joy"—incarnate the public, political turbulences of the period. I'll also be suggesting that the "loyalism" to which she refers, though in large part genuine, was also in part the result of Coleridge's legitimate "fears," not so much of expansionist France as a potential invader, as of the increasingly repressive Pitt Ministry itself during that "alarm of an invasion."

While I shall propose that an anticipatory "loyalism," or repatriation,[5] may

---

3. Woodring, *Politics in the Poetry of Coleridge*, 3. Butler, *Romantics, Rebels, and Reactionaries: English Literature and Its Background, 1760–1830*, 85, 86.

4. "Coleridge, the French Revolution, and *The Ancient Mariner*," 197.

5. My term *repatriation,* equivalent to Butler's *loyalism,* is indebted to, and reverses, *expatriation,* Coleridge's term for early English commitment to the French, the seemingly "human," cause. In April 1796, in an article in which he first began to turn against the French, Coleridge looked back to a time when "each heart proudly expatriated itself, and we heard with transport of the victories of Frenchmen, as the victories of Human Nature" (*W* 269–70). Twenty years later, referring in *Biographia Literaria* to the decade beginning with the French invasion of Switzerland (1798) and climaxing with Bonaparte's campaign to put down the Spanish insurrection (1808), Coleridge wrote: "The youthful enthusiasts who, flattered by the morning rainbow of the French revolution, had made a boast of *expatriating* their hopes and fears, now disciplined by the succeeding storms and sobered by increase of years, had been taught to prize and honor the spirit of nationality as the best safeguard of national independence, and this again as the absolute pre-requisite and necessary basis of popular rights" (*BL* I 190). Human rights remain the sine qua non, but now to be achieved by repatriated loyalists, British nationalists.

even play a part in the blessing of the water-snakes, I have no intention of allegorizing *The Ancient Mariner*, a poem resistant to any reading that would reduce its bewildering variety to schematic order. That proved an impossible task, not only for Robert Penn Warren in the single most brilliantly comprehensive (and, for that very reason, most constantly assaulted) attempt at a categorical interpretation, but even for Coleridge, whose own gloss was at once a secondary elaboration and the first prose attempt to tame and order the poem. C. M. Bowra rightly and unpretentiously stressed its multiplicity, a "combination of different themes" reflecting Coleridge's own "complex vision of existence":

> For him life had both its dark and bright sides, its haunting responsibilities and its ravishing moments of unsullied delight. He saw that the two were closely interwoven and that, if he were to speak with the full force of his genius, he must introduce both into his poem. . . . The shadow cast by the Mariner's crime adds by contrast to the brilliance of the unearthly world in which it is committed, and the degree of his guilt and his remorse serves to stress the power of the angelic beings which watch over humankind. The result is a poem shot with iridescent lights. It appeals to us now in this way, now in that, and there is no final or single approach to it.[6]

Though Bowra's terms seem almost quaint given the ever-increasing complexity of critical approaches to this profoundly complex poem and its labyrinthine history, it is precisely the proximity of darkness and brightness, of shadow and iridescent brilliance, of fear and hope, that I am most interested in—particularly at the two moments of most dramatic change. The first, that sudden shift from hopelessness to "a flash of joy" instantly converted to an even more profound despair, may be thought of as the first turning point of the poem, when the "something in the Sky" is revealed as the horrifying spectre-bark, the burning sun peering through its masts "as thro' a dungeon grate." The second is the miraculous transformation in which the hitherto slimy and malignant water-snakes, suddenly revealed in all their iridescent beauty, are blessed by the suffering and apathetic Mariner—with the alleged help of one of those "angelic beings which watch over humankind."

I stress a "submerged" political dimension in interpreting both critical passages, though—again—in doing so I am far from succumbing to the delusion that such a political reading "decodes" a poem to which there is no "final or single approach." Indeed, in the very process of temporarily "foregrounding" a possible political undercurrent in *The Ancient Mariner*, I am simultaneously aware of innumerable details and actions that cannot be neatly arranged under this or any other interpretive diagram. "The poem's very richness," as one of its most perceptive critics has written, "at once tempts and defeats definiteness of interpretation; as we commit ourselves to the development of one strand of meaning we find that in the very act of doing so we are excluding something else of importance."[7] The admonition has particular force when the interpreta-

6. "*The Ancient Mariner*," 72.
7. Humphry House, *Coleridge: The Clark Lectures, 1951–1952*, 93.

tion to which I have been tempted on this occasion not only leads the reader "away from the poem into non-poetic areas of thought,"[8] but also focuses on something the text itself seems to be "excluding."

House's warning about developing one strand of meaning at the cost of excluding others is applicable by extension to even the most ambitious theories of Romanticism in general, in which "comprehension is achieved by definitional exclusion." Jerome McGann's remark was there directed specifically at the theses of M. H. Abrams and Anne K. Mellor, which stress, respectively, displaced theology and Romantic irony. In his brief but influential study, McGann delineates the various "artistic means" of evasion developed by Romantic poems to "occlude and disguise their own involvement in a certain nexus of historical relations," especially "the famous process of internalization" through which the world is subordinated to the poet's triumphant soul or mind, with the "conflicts" in a poem resituated "out of a sociohistorical context and into an ideological one." Despite my own resistance to ideology, I gradually discovered that I was, to a considerable extent, representing *The Ancient Mariner* as a poem that participates in McGann's ideological displacement. "The poetry of Romanticism," as he announces at the outset of his study, "is everywhere marked by extreme forms of displacement and poetic conceptualization whereby the actual human issues with which the poetry is concerned are resituated in a variety of idealized localities."[9]

I remain, however, less sure than are some *marxisant* New Historicists about rhetoric as a device by which reactionary Romantics masked their "apostasy" from their own earlier fellowship among the friends of liberty, or about the poetry as a necessary yet somehow culpable evasion of political complexity. Nevertheless, my argument in part coincides with their sense of denied history as a poem's "absent cause." That phrase, Louis Althusser's, is echoed by McGann's disciple Marjorie Levinson, who, in developing a theory of "deconstructive materialism," calls for an understanding of "the literary work as that which speaks of one thing because it cannot articulate another—presenting formally a sort of allegory by absence, where the signified is indicated by an identifiably absented signifier."[10]

8. Max F. Schulz's characterization of the biographical and Jungian interpretations of the poem in *The Poetic Voices of Coleridge: A Study of His Desire for Spontaneity and Passion for Order,* 54.

9. *The Romantic Ideology,* 89, 24, 82, 1.

10. *Wordsworth's Great Period Poems: Four Essays,* 8–9. Kevin Barry has recently compared Rousseau's definition of the musician as one who is "affected more by absent things as if they were present" with Wordsworth's definition of the poet as one who has "the ability of conjuring up in himself passions, which are indeed far from being the same as those produced by real events." Unpacking Barry's sentence with the help of New Historicist insights, Christopher Norris reads it as suggestive of "the changes wrought upon romantic ideology by the powerful conservative backlash that followed in the wake of the French Revolution," with the "architects of later romantic tradition—Wordsworth and Coleridge among them— . . . offering a kind of rearguard defence, a mystified

One absented signifier in *The Ancient Mariner*'s allegory by absence, the "fetters" Robert Lowell detected "clanking" in the subtext, isn't *all* that absent since those fetters link up nicely with the dungeon-grate simile. Like Erdman's remark about the poem objectifying a time of dereliction and dismay, Helen Vendler's 1979 report of Robert Lowell's characterization of *The Ancient Mariner* as an opium poem full of "phantasmagoria" and "fetters clanking" has haunted me.[11] While the poem, especially with its prose gloss added, is too willed, organized, and artful, too "imaginatively controlled" a nightmare, to be reduced to phantasmagoria, Lowell was, I think, uncannily accurate in his choice of metaphor. For Coleridge's masterpiece, whatever its slave-trade associations, seems to me a nightmare reflecting, in transformed but recognizable form, the personal and political history of the months during which the poem was written: a time, poetically and personally, of creative interaction with Wordsworth, but, politically, by the spring of 1798, of "dismay" and—precisely—of fetters clanking.

2

A political reading of *The Ancient Mariner* encounters difficulties. Aside from a few, apparently quite incidental "intrusions" of "political" imagery, there is nothing overtly political in it. E. M. W. Tillyard, in 1948, was one of the few critics who bothered to bring the subject up at all. The author of *The Elizabethan World Picture*, Tillyard was then thought of as the literary historian most interested in establishing the interconnections between a period's general culture and its literature—including analogies between the cosmos and the microcosmic "body politic," especially the "correspondence between disorder in the heavens and civil discord in the state." Yet he specifically remarked on the "total lack of politics" in *The Ancient Mariner*, a "poem of six hundred lines without the glimmering of a reference to any body politic."[12] Glimmerings touching on maritime expansion and the slave trade have since been detected by a few swimmers against the stream. Since those articles (discussed in Part One) first bridged the gap between *The Ancient Mariner* and "politics," they are precursors of my own argument here (though I relate the poem to domestic political developments) and so require brief rehearsal.

In 1961 Malcolm Ware tentatively identified the poem's spectre-bark as "a slave ship." In 1964 and 1972, William Empson described slavery as a concealed motif in *The Ancient Mariner*, a poem of "adventure and discovery" that "celebrates and epitomizes the maritime expansion of the Western Europeans." But the triumphant advances of colonialism incur transgression and guilt, in turn epitomized in the horror of the slave trade, a horror which, earlier denounced

---

doctrine of aesthetic value that precisely negates or collapses those hopes once vested in French political events" (Barry, *Language, Music, and the Sign: A Study of Aesthetics, Poetics, and Poetic Practice from Collins to Coleridge*, 179. Norris, *What's Wrong with Postmodernism: Critical Theory and the Ends of Philosophy*, 217).

11. "Lowell in the Classroom."

12. *The Elizabethan World Picture*, 90; *Five Poems*, 80.

in Coleridge's Bristol lectures, enters the poem with the arrival of the spectre-bark, for Empson "a premonition of the Slavers."[13]

Sounding rather like Karl Marx, James Joyce, and Ian Watt, all of whom pronounced the religious dimension of *Robinson Crusoe* a spurious afterthought, Empson in 1964 insisted that the Christian pattern of atonement-by-suffering was an excrescence, a theme essentially added by later Coleridge at the expense of blurring the poem's original socioeconomic context. That explains why, eight years later in their collaborative edition of Coleridge's poetry, Empson and David Pirie printed an "eclectic text," essentially though not quite the 1798 version of *The Ancient Mariner,* a poem closer to its original context and free of the prose gloss they thought a moralistic and distorting imposition. The gloss, described by Pirie as "the ageing Coleridge's own interpretation of his poem," amounts to a "perverting," distancing, third-person omniscient account: marginalia "by implication objectively true," but which "lie," make pious "nonsense of the poem at its very core," and so become the "most serious attempt to distract the reader from the poem."[14]

It is hardly necessary to agree with Empson that *The Ancient Mariner* is "a splendid poem . . . much mangled by its author for reasons of conscience."[15] Nor is it necessary to accept his and Pirie's too surgical severance of early from later Coleridge. Nevertheless, working (as they do) with the 1798 *Lyrical Ballads* edition of the *Mariner,* I follow up on Empson's hints, both about the exclusion of overt politics and the intrusion of Christian conscience.

In "Coleridge's Mariner and the Rights of Man," J. B. Ebbatson, taking an Empsonian line but stating his case more responsibly than Empson, also argued against reading the poem as a Christian epic, emphasizing instead its clandestine attack on European maritime expansion, colonialism, and the slave trade. But aside from these early speculations (and, most recently, Rubenstein's, Kitson's, Maniquis's, Magnuson's, and my own), Tillyard's denial of politics has been almost unanimously endorsed—implicitly or, as by Humphry House among others, explicitly. McGann offers and invites sophisticated analysis of the poem's "historical layerings"; Kitson establishes as a theme the internalization of the millennium; and there is that intriguing remark of David Erdman. But these have been treated as peripheral readings or undemonstrable speculations; social and political approaches have largely been dismissed as irrelevant to an appreciation of the poem.[16]

This dismissal occurs despite the general recognition that the social and political concerns of the Romantics tend to insinuate themselves, sometimes

13. "*The Ancient Mariner*"; Introduction to *Coleridge's Verse,* ed. William Empson and David Pirie, 28–29.

14. Pirie, "Textual Commentary," 214–15. The 1798 edition is also the text chosen by Jerome McGann for his *New Oxford Book of Romantic Period Verse* (Oxford and New York: Oxford University Press, 1993).

15. Introduction to *Coleridge's Verse,* 27.

16. In addition to House (*Coleridge,* 85), see Royal A. Gettman, Introduction to *"The Rime of The Ancient Mariner": A Handbook,* vii.

very subtly, into their poetry. Everyone knows, as well, that for the entire dec-
ade, from 1791 to 1800, almost everything Coleridge wrote, poetry included,
concerned politics and moral and social theory. But, as so many have observed,
the exception would seem to be the annus mirabilis (1797–1798), when Cole-
ridge, "retired" from politics, wrote almost all of the "imaginative" poetry for
which most readers remember him. The prize exhibit of a "work of pure
imagination" is of course *The Ancient Mariner,* so described by Coleridge him-
self in the most celebrated of all comments on the poem (*TT* I 180–81). Perhaps
it *is* "pure." Woodring has said that if Coleridge's supernatural poems are
poems of escape, "politics" form a large part of what they are escaping from;
but the most thorough scholar of politics in the poetry of Coleridge acknowl-
edges his failure to find even vestiges of it in his poet's masterpiece.[17]

Had Coleridge simply tuned out radical politics during the annus mirabilis,
the famous idyllic and creative period that coincided with his "retirement" to
Nether Stowey? The later Coleridge would have us believe so, even going so far,
in *Biographia Literaria,* as to conflate his move to Stowey (which took place on
December 31, 1796) with the French invasion of Switzerland (mid-February
1798) in such a way as to imply that for the *whole* of his retirement he was more
"vehemently" anti-French than anti-Ministerial, a simple soul "retired to a
cottage at Stowey," and harmlessly providing for his maintenance by "writing
verses for a London Morning paper" (*BL* I 187). He neglects to mention that
the newspaper was the prominent, anti-Ministerial *Morning Post,* and that his
untranquil contributions between December 1797 and the French invasion of
Switzerland were in fact far more vehemently anti-Ministerial than they were
anti-Gallican, climaxing in the publication of his celebrated attack on Pitt,
"Fire, Famine, and Slaughter: A War Eclogue."

Thus the short answer to the question about total withdrawal from politics is
No. But the period of the Stowey retirement, providing as it does the context in
which *The Ancient Mariner* was shaped, is so crucial to my argument that its early
phase (December 1796–July 1797) must be sketched in before later develop-
ments and their relationship to the poem can be discussed.

When he started *The Ancient Mariner,* in November 1797, Coleridge had been
at Stowey for eleven months, having arrived on the final day of the preceding
year in a flurry of resolutions about renouncing political activity as un-Christian
and seditious (*CL* I 240). He had come to the rustic retreat of his friend
Thomas Poole directly from his Bristol career as anti-Ministerial lecturer and
editor of *The Watchman;* but all that was allegedly over.

If we are to believe most of Coleridge's letters leading up to and on the very
eve of retirement, his intention was to sever himself utterly from politics, to
become a philosophic farmer—studying, reflecting, writing, and cultivating his
own bean row. Milton's trump, which had echoed over a morally and politically
renovated earth in "Religious Musings," the millennial poem Coleridge consid-

17. *Politics in the Poetry of Coleridge,* 223, 164–65.

ered his masterpiece, had been (not for the last time) diminished to a "squeaking baby-trumpet of sedition," duly "snapped," and its fragments hung up in the "chamber of Penitences" (*CPW* I 122–23; *CL* I 240, cf. 397). The journalistic *Watchman*, having "watched in vain" (his anti-Ministerial periodical failed in the spring of 1796, after ten numbers), had ceased to cry the state of the "Political Atmosphere,"[18] and mentioned for the first time a plan to go to Germany—only to settle instead at Stowey, near Poole's "Elysium" and "Dear Arbour!" (*CL* I 204). It was to Poole, a prosperous tanner with democratic and humanitarian political sympathies of his own, that he had lamented in a desperate letter of December 13 that he was, in heartbroken words later given his Mariner, "all, all alone." "My poetic Vanity & my political Furore have been exhaled," the former apocalyptic trumpeter exhaled to Poole; "and I would rather be an expert, self-maintaining Gardener than a Milton, if I could not unite both" (*CL* I 275).

Like the player queen in *Hamlet,* Coleridge doth protest too much, or at least enough to make us suspect the thoroughness of his disengagement. He was, after all—far from *exhalation*—on the verge of his most *inspired* poetic performances, some of which would overtly, some covertly, "unite both" poetry and politics. Both his withdrawal from public life and his continuing interest in the wide world are mingled in an important letter written on December 17, 1796, to none other than Citizen John Thelwall, the celebrated radical lecturer with whom Coleridge had been corresponding since April. Significantly, though "the Patriot," as he was known to his admirers, was a poet as well as a political activist, it was not Milton's trump that Coleridge passed to him on the eve of retirement, but quite another instrument:

> I doubt not, that the time will come when all our Utilities will be directed in one simple path. That Time however is not come; and imperious circumstances point out to each one his particular Road. Much good may be done in all. I am not *fit* for *public* Life; yet the Light shall stream to a far distance from the taper in my cottage window. Meantime, do *you* uplift the *torch* dreadlessly, and shew to mankind the face of that Idol, which they have worshipped in Darkness. (*CL* I 277)

The Idol was Liberty, seen as in a glass darkly, but soon face to face. The Darkness was popular ignorance; the candlelight shining from Coleridge's cottage-window that "Light of Philosophy" he hoped would illuminate "the Multitude" (*L 1795* 6). But more than philosophic light would seem to emanate from that italicized "torch" Thelwall was to uplift "dreadlessly." In the code-language of the period, that adverb allies the Patriot with Milton's "dreadless" Abdiel, the angel loyal to God in the battle with Satan and his apostates (*Paradise Lost* VI.1).[19] And the torch was being passed on to England's leading Jacobin agita-

18. For Coleridge's farewell, and the characteristic metaphor about the political weather, see the final number of *The Watchman* (*W* 374–75).

19. The almost obsessive adjective *dreadless* is applied by Coleridge to almost everyone on the "Patriotic" side in these years. A *dreadless patriot* is one who is loyal, not to the Pitt Ministry, but to the principles of liberty, equality, fraternity. In Coleridge's 1796

tor, the national figure who had defied the Treasonable Practices Act and more sweeping Seditious Meetings Act, certain clauses of which Pitt aimed at Thelwall, that "voice of tens of thousands" (*L 1795* 297)—the very man soon to be depicted in *Anti-Jacobin* cartoons with a torch of arson in his hand![20] If this is political retirement, it is not without a commitment to the continuation of the good fight, nor without the intrusion of imagery that, decoded, is unmistakably political: a phenomenon some have detected in *Paradise Lost,* and which is to be repeated in that ostensibly apolitical ballad, *The Ancient Mariner.*

There were to be other intrusions during the Stowey retirement. The first two converged in July 1797: the settling in of the Wordsworths and the visit of the "dreadless" Thelwall—welcome intrusions, at least to Coleridge if not to his rural neighbors, already uneasy about Poole's having settled the radical Coleridge in the neighborhood.

Most welcome, of course, was the long-anticipated arrival of Wordsworth, who had been living with his sister at Racedown in Dorset. The poetry he wrote there continued to be explicitly political—especially his revised "Adventures on Salisbury Plain," designed, he said, to "exhibit the vices of the penal law," a poem which, as Paul Magnuson has shown, stands in "dialogic relation" to *The Ancient Mariner.* In pondering that relationship, Magnuson raises the very questions my own study addresses. Both poems, as he notes, feature a sailor or mariner "persecuted by unjust powerful forces," but when Coleridge adopts Wordsworth's plot, his supernatural and late medieval setting seem

> to exclude the explicit references to contemporary events. Yet traces of Wordsworth's poem remain: persecution, injustice, and tyranny. In part *Ancient Mariner* is a poem of victimization, yet it is almost never read in its political context. . . . Does [Coleridge's] change of setting represent an evasion of political themes? Does his use of supernatural symbolism indicate a change of political views? . . . Why does Coleridge seem to be more concerned with a psychological rather than a social explanation of guilt?[21]

sonnet "To Earl Stanhope," that "unterrify'd" patriot is depicted pouring his "Abdiel warnings on the train / That sit complotting with rebellious pride / 'Gainst *Her* who from the Almighty's bosom leapt / With whirlwind arm, fierce Minister of Love!" (*CPW* I 89–90). The Satanic plotters are Pitt and his ministers; the italicized "Her" is identified in a footnote as "Gallic Liberty."

20. Writing on December 10, 1795, Pitt attacked "lectures on political subjects, where sedition was the source of livelihood of certain persons." As Pitt's biographer, John Ehrman, adds, the prime minister "had Thelwall obviously in mind" (*The Younger Pitt* 2:456). Thelwall was later cartooned as an arsonist in the *Anti-Jacobin.* The high point of Tory intelligence, effervescent wit, and a malice alternately brutal and urbane, the short-lived *Anti-Jacobin or Weekly Examiner* (ed. William Gifford and George Canning) appeared each Monday from November 1797 to June 1798. Southey, Coleridge, and even Charles Lamb (guilty by association) were lampooned as Pantisocratic fools and Jacobin knaves in its pages. It was succeeded by the *Anti-Jacobin Review and Magazine* (ed. "John Gifford" [John Richards Green]), which ran from 1798–1821.

21. "Teaching the Coleridge-Wordsworth Dialogue," 81. See also Magnuson's earlier cited (Chapter 3, note 66) *Coleridge and Wordsworth.*

Providing our answers are understood as speculative and exploratory rather than accusatory, these are the political questions I was asking myself before I read Magnuson.

As for Wordsworth, he was, even as he completed "Adventures on Salisbury Plain," becoming less politically engaged—despite having directly participated in events in revolutionary France, even considering, until he was financially "compelled" to return to England in late 1792, making "common cause" with the Girondist party.[22] As Coleridge was to put it fifteen years later in "To William Wordsworth," that richly allusive and psychologically complex interaction with the poet who had by then outdistanced him, 1792 was a time when

> France in all her towns lay vibrating
> Like some becalméd bark beneath the burst
> Of Heaven's immediate thunder, when no cloud
> Is visible, or shadow on the main.
> For thou wert there, thine own brows garlanded,
> Amid the tremor of a realm aglow,
> Amid a mighty nation jubilant,
> When from the general heart of human kind
> Hope sprang forth like a full-born Deity![23]

Much, if not all (as Coleridge implies in the next line), of that "dear Hope" had been "afflicted and struck down" by the time the two poets first met, in John Pinney's house in Bristol in August or September 1795. Since then they had been corresponding and reading each other's work in a spirit of mutual admiration. Wordsworth was familiar with *The Watchman,* copies of which he had been offered in the spring of 1796, and he had read Coleridge's *Poems* (published in April 1796), gratifying the author with his particular admiration of Coleridge's own favorite, "Religious Musings" (*CL* I 215–16). On March 20, 1797, Wordsworth received a large package of pamphlets and books, including Coleridge's *Conciones ad Populum* and his "Ode on the Departing Year," the jeremiad containing *both* Coleridge's most violently apocalyptic prophecy concerning his country *and* his most abrupt recoil into religious quietude. The package had been sent, at Wordsworth's request, by James Losh, another radi-

22. *Prelude* X.190–95. Wordsworth's return to England did not sever the latter connection. As has been noted by David Erdman, Carl Woodring, Nicholas Roe, and Kenneth Johnston ("Philanthropy or Treason? Wordsworth as 'Active Partisan'"), he was for a time involved with the Girondist British Club in London, and supported radical parliamentary reform. On Wordsworth's activities in France, including his involvement with the Jacobin club, *Les Amis de la Constitution,* see Erdman's "The Dawn of Universal Patriotism: William Wordsworth among the British in Revolutionary France," and his tour de force tracing of the fascinating and elusive John Oswald, *Commerce des Lumières: John Oswald and the British in Paris,* 223–54.

23. *CPW* I 405. For a splendid discussion of the interaction, via Milton, between this poem and the passages addressed to Coleridge in the version of *The Prelude* Wordsworth read to his friend and to which Coleridge is here responding, see A. Reeve Parker, "Wordsworth's Whelming Tide: Coleridge and the Art of Analogy."

cal reformer whose rhythm of political activism and withdrawal parallels that of many nineties radicals, including Wordsworth and Coleridge.[24]

Later that month, Wordsworth briefly visited his friend at Stowey, followed by the reciprocal and momentous visit in June to Racedown, where Wordsworth had settled with his sister, rent free, in Pinney's country house. During a fortnight's stay, Coleridge listened to Wordsworth's "absolutely wonderful" drama, *The Borderers*, which was to preoccupy its author for the rest of 1797, and was pleased that Wordsworth "admire[d]" his own tragedy of "displaced" politics, *Osorio*, which Coleridge had begun in February and would not finish until October.[25] He felt himself " *a little man by his* side," he told his publisher, Joseph Cottle; "& yet do not think myself the less man, than I formerly thought myself" (*CL* I 325). Coleridge, in turn, was judged "a wonderful man" by both Dorothy and William. It was a verdict that would survive all future conflicts and be repeated movingly by Wordsworth soon after the death, thirty-seven years later, of "the most *wonderful* man that he had ever known, wonderful for the originality of his mind & the power he possessed of throwing out in profusion grand central truths from which might be evolved the most comprehensive systems."[26]

During those two weeks at Racedown plans were laid for the personal and literary relationship that was to transform not only their lives but the history of English Romanticism. Now, in July 1797, Coleridge had succeeded, with the help of the always dependable Tom Poole (who, Coleridge informed Cottle, also thought Wordsworth "the greatest man he ever knew"), in bringing the poet, his sister, and the five-year-old Basil Montagu over from Racedown to Nether Stowey—that place, " *sanctum et amabile nomen!* rich by so many associations and recollections," as he was to say thirty years later, referring with fervent nostalgia to the annus mirabilis (*CPW* I 285). "I have *settled them,*" he announced triumphantly to Robert Southey, adding that by coincidence and luck he and Poole had secured for the Wordsworths a veritable "gentleman's seat" less than four miles northwest of Stowey and at a rent of only £23 a year, " *taxes included!*" (*CL* I 334).

With Poole standing security for the rent, Wordsworth and Dorothy leased

24. Moorman, *William Wordsworth: A Biography,* 1:309. On Losh, and the parallels noted, see Roe, *Wordsworth and Coleridge,* 241–43.

25. Both dramas displace their authors' not-quite-extinguished radicalism from the revolutionary 1790s to earlier centuries and other locales, the thirteenth-century Scottish border and Inquisition Spain. This pattern of displacement may be repeated in its most extreme form in the late medieval setting of that "supernatural" poem of "pure imagination," *The Ancient Mariner.* Neither *The Borderers* nor *Osorio* made it to the boards in the 1790s. Many years later, with Lord Byron's help, *Osorio* was successfully staged at Drury Lane under the title *Remorse.* Despite the change of title and a number of theatrically motivated revisions, Alhadra (unlike the other characters) retained her original name and her original revolutionary energy.

26. For the Wordsworths' pronouncement in 1797, see Moorman, *William Wordsworth: A Biography* 1:168. For the second observation (Robert Perceval Graves's report to Felicia Hemans of Wordsworth's conversation in August 1834, three weeks after Coleridge's death), see Christopher Wordsworth, *Memoirs of William Wordsworth* 2:288–90.

the mansion house at Alfoxden on July 7. But despite Coleridge's enthusiasm, there was trouble from the outset. Some in the neighborhood, village folk suspicious of outsiders, got it into their heads that this strange man and the woman "passing" as his sister were not only foreign but, ominously, French. The political atmosphere of the period must be borne in mind if we are to understand the neighbors' suspicions, suspicions that would lead, in March 1798, to the formal refusal to renew the Wordsworths' lease, clinching the decision of Coleridge, William, and Dorothy to depart for Germany.

Fear of a French invasion, which was to peak in March and April 1798, was already in the air in July 1797. In the very month Coleridge had retired to Stowey, a massive French expedition (forty-six ships carrying fifteen thousand troops) had eluded the Channel Fleet. Half of the storm-tossed ships reached Bantry Bay, on the southwest coast of Ireland. But after sixteen frustrating days of gales rising to a hurricane so severe that a landing proved impossible, and with the flagship blown far out into the Atlantic, the scattered and demoralized fleet had been forced back to Brest, its port of embarkation. As the United Irishmen leader Wolfe Tone remarked in his heartbreaking shipboard diary, England had had its greatest escape since the days of the Spanish Armada, that earlier victim of an Albion-saving storm.[27] Two months later, the same commander, General Hoche, pacifier of the Vendée, had ordered a smaller invasion aimed at taking the major city of Bristol—with what results we shall see later. In that same month, February 1797, there was a serious run on the Bank of England, triggered in part by an emergency loan to the Dublin government for the purpose of strengthening Irish defenses (fortifying the coast with Martello towers, extending the Militia Acts) against another invasion attempt by the French, abetted by the United Irishmen.

By then Austria had been knocked out of the anti-French coalition, leaving Britain, already counterrevolution's principal paymaster, to stand alone. What made invasion an even more terrifying prospect was the threat of full-scale mutiny in the Royal Navy, the only force that could prevent the French conquest not only of Ireland but of England itself. The great historian of sea power, Alfred Thayer Mahan, has made famous "those far-distant, storm-beaten ships, upon which the Grand Army never looked," but which "stood between it and dominion of the world."[28] But between April and June 1797, the Channel fleet moored at the Spithead anchorage off Portsmouth and the North Sea fleet at the Nore were immobilized by rebellious sailors. Wolfe Tone had long been urging Irish seamen in the Royal Navy to rise up and seize their ships, and there may have been some questionable, even treasonable, motivation in the case of Richard Parker, the leader of the Nore mutiny. Nevertheless, the cause of the uprisings was wretched conditions—deferred pay, abuses of discipline, and

27. The diary appears in the second volume of W. T. W. Tone, *Life of Theobold Wolfe Tone*, 205–447; for the parallel with the Spanish Armada, see page 266. See also Commander E. H. Stuart Jones, *The Invasion that Failed: The French Expedition to Ireland, 1796.*
28. *The Influence of Sea Power on the French Revolution and Empire* 2:118.

miserable rations—rather than political ideology. However aggrieved, the mutineers remained overwhelmingly loyal.

The government handled the first situation, more a sit-down protest than a rebellion, with concession, and the second, an altogether more volatile affair, with coercion and subsequent execution or transportation of the leaders. Not unreasonably, the Pitt cabinet suspected the subversive hand of the London Corresponding Society and other anti-Ministerial political "clubs," and of French agents in league with the United Irishmen. The oath-taking ceremonies of the Nore mutineers and the self-designation of Parker's movement as a "Floating Republic" fueled suspicions of a connection with Jacobins, whether English, French, or Irish. Despite repeated denials, even by Parker himself on the eve of execution, suspicion did not subside until October, when crews involved in the Nore mutiny participated, under Admiral Duncan, in the defeat of the French-allied Dutch fleet at Camperdown, thus living up to their pledge that disputes would be put aside if and when the enemy threatened.[29]

But back in the spring and summer, the panic was legitimate. At this moment of maximum danger, all radicals were suspect, including radicals in Parliament. The leader of the opposition, Fox, was depicted in cartoons as manipulating the Nore mutineers, even sketched sending telegraph signals to an approaching French fleet with no defending fleet in sight. In the final months of his life, Edmund Burke, registering the immediate impact of the Great Mutinies, wrote a friend that he would "not be suprized at seeing a French army convoyed by a British Navy to an attack upon this Kingdom" (May 12), a nightmare that explains his otherwise startling oral instructions, three days before his death in early July, that his body be buried in a (still) secret grave to prevent invading "*French Revolutionists*" from desecrating the corpse of their earliest, perhaps most adamant, and certainly most eloquent enemy.[30]

This was the nervous political perspective from which the good folk of Somersetshire looked askance at Coleridge and, especially, the alien-seeming Wordsworths, with their North-country accents ("a *burr*, like the crust on wine," according to Hazlitt) and strange ramblings at all hours. The worst fears must have seemed confirmed when, on July 17, the very day after the Wordsworths

---

29. For a succinct, informed account, including speculation (though "it is impossible, even now, to be certain") about the possible role of the LCS or its provincial offshoots in precipitating the mutinies, see Albert Goodwin, *The Friends of Liberty: The English Democratic Movement and the War of Ideas*, 406–11. See also chapter 4 of Roger Wells, *Insurrection: The British Experience, 1795–1803*, and chapter 9, "War against Europe, 1792–1797," in William Doyle, *The Oxford History of the French Revolution*, especially page 216. The report of the investigating committee of the House of Commons concluded that, while the mutinies were essentially a "breach of subordination and discipline," they were made dangerous by the continuing agitation of those grouped as English Jacobins (*Report of the Committee of Secrecy of the House of Commons, Ordered to be Printed 15 March 1799*, 18–19).

30. *The Correspondence of Edmund Burke* 9:332–40. Carl B. Cone, *Burke and the Nature of Politics* 2:507.

moved in, the neighborhood was treated to an even less welcome intrusion. The notorious John Thelwall arrived, responding to a vague but sincere invitation by the expansive Coleridge. Having arrived unexpected, Thelwall stayed the night at Coleridge's cottage, and the next morning walked over to Alfoxden with Sara to breakfast and converse with the Wordsworths and Coleridge—who had, for neither the first nor the last time, spent the night with William and Dorothy rather than with his wife.

The scene is now set for the first of the two most famous political anecdotes dating to the double retirement of Wordsworth and Coleridge in this eventful year, 1797–1798. I mean the verbal exchange in the "beautiful recess," second in celebrity only to the "Spy Nozy" episode, to be discussed later. Both concern Thelwall and both help us to understand the man who wrote, and years later glossed, *The Ancient Mariner.*

3

This first anecdote, though seemingly simple, itself requires some glossing. It is recorded in Coleridge's Table Talk for July 1830: "Citizen John Thelwall had something good about him. We were once sitting in Somersetshire in a beautiful recess. I said to him—'Citizen John! This is a fine place to talk treason in!' 'Nay! Citizen Samuel!' replied he, 'it is a place to make a man forget that there is any necessity for treason.'"[31]

This well-known anecdote is instructive, but problematic. The "beautiful recess," a "wild romantic dell," according to Thelwall's letter to his wife,[32] was located—in Wordsworth's proliferation of prepositions—"on the turf on the brink of a stream in the most beautiful part of the most beautiful glen of Alfoxden." This was the sylvan glen with rushing brook and "sequestered waterfall" that the Wordsworths had come upon in "a wander by ourselves," as Dorothy recorded on July 4, 1797, and which is often mentioned elsewhere in her delightful *Alfoxden Journal.* It was in this exquisite recess that Wordsworth was, in April 1798, to compose "Lines Written in Early Spring" and Coleridge, in the same month, "The Nightingale."

But the future poetic associations of Holford Glen are less important at the moment than the precise language and tone of Coleridge's account of the exchange with Thelwall in July 1797. The mutual employment, within the anecdote, of the address *Citizen,* indicating (like *Patriot*) an enthusiast of the French Revolution, seems less jocular than—to borrow again James Joyce's portmanteau word—jocoserious. It may even be *mostly* serious; certainly the term is used less sarcastically than affectionately in Coleridge's introduction of the story a third of a century after the event.

More importantly, the vignette suggests that of the two, it was Coleridge, not Thelwall, the notorious Jacobin and atheist, who was readiest to talk "treason"

31. *TT* I 180–81; July 24, 1830. In the 1835 edition, H. N. Coleridge dates it July 27, 1830, but Woodring, as usual, accurately follows the manuscripts.

32. Thelwall's letter, quoted below as well, is cited from Mrs. Henry Sandford, *Thomas Poole and His Friends* 1:233.

in July 1797. Whatever the mixed tonality, "treason" is a somewhat shocking word. Yet one is inclined to trust Coleridge's accuracy and memory on this particular occasion rather than Wordsworth's in the sanitized version of the story he recited to Isabella Fenwick in 1842–1843.

Half-joking, half-serious, the Coleridge of 1797 was speaking to the man who—along with Thomas Hardy, the shoemaker-founder of the London Corresponding Society, and John Horne Tooke, the revitalizer of the Society for Constitutional Information—had actually been tried for high treason in the famous, or infamous, State Trials of 1794. Nine others (including William Blake's friend, the engraver William Sharp, and the playwright Thomas Holcroft), had been charged but released without trial, the government having abandoned their prosecutions following acquittal of the first two defendants. But Thelwall, who had been observed by an informer blowing a head of foam from a pot of porter after an April 1794 LCS meeting with the regicidal proclamation, "So should all tyrants be served!"[33] and whose intercepted letters and public lectures made him more vulnerable than either Hardy or Tooke, became the third and (as it proved) the last of the accused to sustain trial at the Old Bailey. During the course of that five-day ordeal, Thelwall had scribbled a note to his defense counsel: "I'll be hanged if I don't plead my own cause"; Thomas Erskine responded curtly, "You'll be hanged if you do."[34] After deliberating for two hours on December 5, 1794, the jury returned a verdict of Not Guilty. Edmund Burke, still disgusted more than a year later, referred to the prosecutions in his brilliant if less-than-balanced *Letters on a Regicide Peace* as "little better than schools for treason; of no use but to improve the dexterity of criminals in the mystery of evasion."

But the "acquitted felons" had not evaded suffering and loss. Thelwall's private papers and a valuable collection of prints and engravings, seized by the government, were never returned. In addition, by the time he came to trial, the Patriot had spent five months in the Tower guarded by soldiers with fixed bayonets and another month in Newgate Prison, in (he tells us) "the dead-hole, or charnel house, where the corpses of such prisoners as died of diseases were placed before the burial."[35] The author of *The Ancient Mariner* may have remembered that description, as well as Thelwall's recollection (in "Maria," a poem written in October 1797) of himself gazing "thro' my grated dungeon." In addition to the dungeon-grate passage in *The Ancient Mariner*, and the depiction of Death with cracked and blackened bones patched with "charnel crust," the suffering Mariner later says that the deck of his ship, with the dead and stony-eyed sailors standing upright, was "For a charnel-dungeon fitter" (lines 171, 440; 1798 edition). Whether or not he would make these dungeon connections in his ballad some months later, the word *treason*, if he did use it in July 1797, was, Coleridge would have known, more than an abstraction to John Thelwall.

33. Philip Anthony Brown, *The French Revolution in English History*, 115.
34. Earl Stanhope, *Life of Pitt* 2:273.
35. *The Tribune* 1:90–91.

There would, of course, have been an ironic edge in the use of the word in 1797. It seemed to such men difficult for an opponent of Pitt or of the war against revolutionary France, or even for an advocate of parliamentary reform, *not* to be deemed guilty of treason in England in the years 1793–1798. Pitt himself was originally an advocate of parliamentary reform; then came the eruption across the Channel. Reacting to the contagion of democratic and reformist ideas epitomized by Paine's astonishingly popular *The Rights of Man* (200,000 copies sold by 1793) and to the military dimension of the revolutionary storm unleashed when France declared war on England on February 1, 1793, Pitt was no longer interested in such matters as Manhood Suffrage and Annual Parliaments. One did not—he declared, echoing Burke—try to "mend the roof in a hurricane." Since "terror was the order of the day" in 1794, when habeas corpus was first suspended, William Godwin, the author of *Political Justice*, withdrew the original preface to his novel *Caleb Williams* lest even a "humble" novelist "might be shown to be constructively a traitor."[36] And repression respected no genres; as late as 1803, the poet William Blake, having shoved a drunken soldier out of his garden with allegedly seditious execrations, found himself on trial for high treason. Like Hardy, Tooke, and Thelwall, Blake was acquitted; but, like them, he *might* have been found guilty, the penalty for which was to be hanged, drawn and quartered. The upshot, in any case, according to Blake, was that "every man is now afraid of speaking to, or looking at, a Soldier."[37]

Fear was hardly a new phenomenon. Traditional English law—public trial, independent jury, competent counsel—had triumphed in the State Trials in 1794, proving Britain a very different state than lawless France, Burke's "totalitarian democracy." Yet the Pitt Ministry had also achieved some of its aims. While the acquittals momentarily encouraged such radical clubs as the London Corresponding Society, founded by Hardy, the trials themselves, though legally unsuccessful, did succeed in isolating radicalism and fragmenting the Whig party. Tooke resigned from the SCI in 1795, and Hardy and Thelwall, both burdened by family responsibilities and wary of a second prosecution, resigned from the LCS—though Thelwall continued with his lecturing and later rejoined the soci-

36. *Caleb Williams*, 3d ed. (1797), 1:vii. The suppressed preface (significantly dated May 12, 1794, the day on which Hardy, Tooke, Thelwall, and the other accused "traitors" were arrested) was restored in the second edition, 1796. If we are to judge from *The Borderers*, Wordsworth read Godwin's novel as well as his *Political Justice*. For a perceptive account of the novel's political significance, see Marilyn Butler, "Godwin, Burke, and *Caleb Williams*."

37. *The Letters of William Blake*, 74. And this was *after* Bonaparte's violation (never mind that the British had violated it as well) of the Treaty of Amiens, proving him as insatiable as Pitt had always claimed. By 1803, the nation was completely solidified behind the war against France; now even Coleridge was a Pittite. The Blake episode, more important in literary than political history, figures symbolically in Blake's later Prophetic Books; still later, in the work of James Joyce; and, finally, in Tom Stoppard's play, *Travesties*. For details, see my "Time's Ruins and the Mansions of Eternity."

ety. In the aftermath of the State Trials, the clubs became smaller and extremist, since the "fear of similar proceedings, with the disgrace and the expense that they involved, helped to drive men of standing out of the radical movement."[38]

And there was a more visceral fear: the danger of the dungeon without benefit of indictment or trial at all. Coleridge's 1795 Bristol speeches against the war with France and against the Treason and Sedition Bills were, as we shall see, understandably obsessive about the Pitt Ministry's power to renew suspension of habeas corpus, to arrest and jail without trial even the most innocent among those opposed to government policies, domestic or foreign. Responding to the raising of an army against the French and to the Pittite repression at home, the Sheffield filemaker Joseph Mather caught the mood in a couplet: "Facts are seditious things, / When they touch courts and kings."[39] In his own political lectures of 1795, published in this and the following year in the *Tribune,* the acquitted Thelwall referred to the treason trials of 1794 as Pitt's attempt to establish a "system of massacre for opinion" (1:254). This may be *somewhat* hyperbolic. In a 1989 essay on British politics in the decade of the French Revolution, Clive Emsley, playing down the "Pittite terror" outside of Ireland, suggested that to "attribute defeat of reformers during the 1790s to Pittite repression . . . is to overrate both the scale of the latter and the intensity of support for the former."[40] This is a useful corrective to the emphasis in recent years; nevertheless, Thelwall's judgment has been largely validated, not only by leftist New Historicists, but by most modern historians. One of the most eminent has described the verdicts as a "timely check" on Pitt's expanding "reign of terror"; the acquittals, wrote G. M. Trevelyan in 1936, "saved England" from both a repressive bloodbath and, "perhaps ultimately from a retributive revolution."[41]

Even after this timely check, the passage of the Two Acts in December 1795 left, in Coleridge's phrase (*CPW* I 163–64*n*), little more than a "*remnant*" of the constitution. Recalling the preceding three years, James Losh complained bitterly, "The men who wish to be considered as peculiarly the friends of government in this country think that every man who denies the absolute perfection of our Constitution, must be a plotter of anarchy and confusion, and every

38. R. R. Palmer, *The Age of the Democratic Revolution: A Political History of Europe and America, 1760–1800* 2:480. On Pittite repression and the contemporary radical movements, see Simon Maccoby, *English Radicalism, 1786–1832;* Carl B. Cone, *The English Jacobins;* part one of Thompson's *The Making of the English Working Class;* and Goodwin's superb *The Friends of Liberty,* chapters 8–12. Recent discussions include David Erdman, "Treason Trials in the Early Romantic Period"; chapter 8 of Gerald Newman, *The Rise of English Nationalism: A Cultural History, 1740–1830;* and Iain McCalman, *Radical Underworld: Prophets, Revolutionaries, and Pornographers in London, 1795–1840,* which reassesses the radical movement, focusing on Thomas Evans, Robert Wedderburn, and George Cannon, as representative figures. The most recent study is David Worrall's *Radical Culture: Discourse, Resistance, and Surveillance, 1790–1820.*

39. Mather's lines are quoted in W. H. G. Armitage, "Joseph Mather: Poet of the Filesmiths."

40. "The Impact of the French Revolution on British Politics."

41. *History of England* 3:91.

republican, a plunderer and assassin.—Their great leader [Pitt] has even as-
serted, that, in some cases, opinions may be prosecuted with advantage."[42]

Looking back to the treason trials of 1794, to the Two Acts of 1795, to
Thelwall's "massacre of opinion," and perhaps to Coleridge's *Conciones ad Popu-
lum,* which Losh had read and sent on to Wordsworth, this footnote also looks
forward fifteen months to Coleridge's "Fears in Solitude": in particular to the
fear that men who do not rally round or, rather, "worship" the Pitt Ministry can
be pronounced "enemies / Even of their country! Such have I been deemed!"
(*CPW* I 262). Coleridge, writing during the intensified invasion panic of the
spring of 1798, was responding directly to the renewed suspension of habeas
corpus. But such an enemy of his country "Citizen John" had long since been
deemed. Long enough, he'd decided shortly before sharing this "beautiful
recess" with Coleridge and Wordsworth.

He had good reason to withdraw. Though, unlike Wordsworth, Thelwall had
not been in revolutionary France, his had been a truly dangerous and coura-
geous career of political activism. Before and after the treason trials, his meet-
ings had been interrupted by government goons. During his 1796 lecture tour
in East Anglia, Thelwall reported that he had "narrowly escaped assasina-
tion"[43] at the hands of church-and-king mobs. At Yarmouth, the hall was in-
vaded by "armed banditti," the crew of a man-of-war given shore leave and
outfitted for the evening with bludgeons, cutlasses, and pikestaffs. Yet Thelwall,
who drew a pistol in self-defense on this occasion and who now took to wearing
a cudgel-proof hat, had stood firm in the teeth of government repression,
continuing to lecture on politics (at King's Lynn, Wisbech, Derby, Stockport,
and Norwich) under the disguise of Roman history or, anticipating *Animal
Farm,* beast fables. As E. P. Thompson rightly insists, "Thelwall's defiance of the
Two Acts was a national event, a talking-point in the taverns and coffee houses.
Even the King was informed of his lectures." At the moment he arrived in
Stowey he was "the most notorious, if defeated, Jacobin in England."[44]

42. James Losh, in a January 1797 footnote in his translation of Benjamin Constant's
*Observations on the Strength of the Present Government of France, and of the Necessity of Rallying
Round It.* The passage (page 29) is quoted by Roe (*Wordsworth and Coleridge,* 242–43),
who points out that the footnote confirms Losh's "unaltered commitment to reform," a
commitment that continued "until the end of his life" (242). Roe also quotes a note of
December 31, 1798, which Losh wrote in the back of his diary. Though still committed to
liberty and opposed to government corruptions, he was "resolved to withdraw for ever
from Politics," at least active "party" politics. He would restrict himself to "calm discus-
sion" and "temperate arguments" to "promote those great truths which I consider as
essential to human happiness." And he ends on a note strikingly similar to Coleridge in
his phases of quietistic withdrawal: "Every species of war I consider as unlawful to a
Christian man, and all bitterness of contention, even in words, shou'd be abstained from
by a sincere follower of the humble Christ" (241). It certainly sounds as if Losh had read
all of Coleridge's "Ode on the Departing Year," especially the concluding Epode, before
sending the poem on to Wordsworth.

43. Preface to *Poems, Chiefly Written in Retirement,* xxx.

44. See Mrs. Cecil Boyle Thelwall, *The Life of John Thelwall by his Widow* (1837), and

But when he came to visit Coleridge and Wordsworth, Thelwall was a man in retreat. The *Tribune,* which had been printed at his own expense, was suppressed in April 1796; and he had been ejected in December from his lecture rooms at Beaufort Buildings off the Strand in London. Thelwall had become a muzzled agitator constantly harassed by government agents—in particular, by his nemesis, the spy James Walsh, who was also shortly to play a jocoserious role in the lives of the two poets. Tom Poole's observant and acid-tongued cousin Charlotte—always antipathetic to Coleridge, though she conceded his "brilliance" and "eloquence"—was accurately reflecting neighborhood feeling in confiding to her journal on July 23, "We are shocked to hear that Mr. Thelwall has spent some time at Stowey this week with Mr. Coleridge, and consequently with Tom Poole. Alfoxden house is taken by another of the fraternity. . . . To what are we coming?"[45]

But whatever the neighborhood was coming to, Thelwall had already come to the end of his political rope. True, immediately before and after the idyllic Stowey sojourn, Thelwall, on a pedestrian tour to gather information about the wages of factory workers, stopped at Bristol, where he met radicals who greeted him, he wrote his wife, with "some enthusiasm, & some *solid* friendship." But the man conversing with Coleridge and Wordsworth in Holford Glen was less interested in finding political allies with whom to conspire than human companions with whom to settle "far from the strifeful scenes / Of public life," in "some sequester'd dell" in "philosophic amity":

> some few,
> Still warm and generous, by the changeling world
> Not yet debauch'd, nor to the yoke of fear
> Bending the abject neck: but who, erect
> In conscious principle, still dare to love
> The man proscrib'd for loving human kind.[46]

The saving few included, preeminently, the two men courageous enough to put principle before servile fear and love a "proscrib'd" man: the poets with whom Thelwall was sequestered in July 1797—"Allfoxden's musing tenant" and, especially, "My Samuel, . . . best belov'd of friends!" as he referred to Coleridge in these verses composed at Bridgwater, as he journeyed away from his two friends "during" (as the subtitle tells us) "a long Excursion in quest of a

Charles Cestre's *John Thelwall: A Pioneer of Democracy and Social Reform in England during the French Revolution.* The Thompson quotation is from his "Disenchantment or Default?" 158, 160. In a final note (page 181), Thompson referred to "a forthcoming study of English Jacobins and English poets." Eight years later, in the third edition of *Prophet against Empire,* Erdman remarked in a footnote: "The extent of government espionage and suspicion of Coleridge, Wordsworth, and Thelwall, as a *foco* of English Jacobinism, is documented in the forthcoming book of studies of Blake and Wordsworth by E. P. Thompson" (293*n*). As of 1993, the year of Professor Thompson's death, this much-anticipated work had not appeared.

45. Sandford, *Thomas Poole and His Friends* 1:235.
46. Thelwall, "Written at Bridgwater . . . ," in *Poems, Chiefly Written in Retirement,* 139.

peaceful Retreat." Though still erect, all three knew something about the yoke of fear. Nor does Coleridge report Thelwall as saying that any temporary amnesia induced by the beauties of nature can erase injustice and repression. These things continue, and resistance to them (which the Pitt government equated with "treason") remains "necessary." It is just that—as his response to Coleridge's half-serious, half-bantering provocation accurately suggests—Thelwall himself felt he had no recourse left but retreat. The "trump of Truth," he complained in his poem to Coleridge, had been blown, only to awaken "the Ruffian Crew of Power / To deeds of maddest anarchy and blood." Passing on the torch passed to him seven months earlier by the retiring Coleridge, Thelwall was psychologically even more deeply attracted to rural retirement than "Citizen Samuel." Soon he and his wife would physically withdraw to a farm in South Wales—though even there he would be badgered by *Anti-Jacobin* cartoons and occasional government agents, as well as by a vicious local curate from whom he was partially shielded by a well-to-do sympathizer.[47]

As for Coleridge's depiction of himself as "Citizen Samuel": is the conservative Coleridge of 1830—the year of the *Robinson Crusoe* annotations and of *On the Constitution of the Church and State*—simply dramatizing or, alternatively, parodying his old radical self? Such retrospective glossing was almost second nature to him, and is certainly possible in this case—more than possible were we to accept Wordsworth's version of what was said. In *his* account, given almost a half century after the event, Coleridge's opening gambit was far from being radical, but was apolitical and harmless: "Coleridge exclaimed, 'This is a place to reconcile one to all the jarrings and conflicts of the wide world.'—'Nay,'" said Thelwall, 'to make one forget them altogether.'"[48]

Whose memory are we to trust? Though even Thelwall's response is softened in Wordsworth's retelling, both versions stress his relative quiescence: a state of mind reflected as well in the Patriot's own ecstatic account, in the letter to his wife, of "the Academe of Stowey" and the "delightful Society of Coleridge & of Wordsworth." Rambling "along a wild romantic dell," he told his female Citizen, he, Coleridge, and Wordsworth "philosophised our minds into a state of tranquility which the leaders of nations might envy and the residents of Cities can never know."[49] This is very close to Wordsworth's version, with Coleridge's words adopted by Thelwall. But perhaps these *were* Thelwall's words on this occasion, an occasion when Coleridge, not he, was being provocative.

4

It would be in character. For, odd though it may seem and though his poetic idiom was rarely adequate to his aesthetic response to nature, Thelwall was in 1797 even *more* susceptible to the intrinsic beauty and moral benefit of wild romantic dells than was Coleridge. This curious fact emerges from two letters

47. Cestre, *John Thelwall*, 148.
48. Wordsworth, *Poetical Works* 1:363; Moorman, *William Wordsworth: A Biography* 1:328.
49. Sandford, *Thomas Poole and His Friends* 1:233.

written on March 10 three years apart—letters in which Coleridge illustrates his thoughts and feelings by quoting other poets, and which figure in the discussion to come. But first Thelwall.

As early as 1793, in the *Peripatetic*, we find the Patriot praising the soothing and heart-ameliorating qualities of nature:

> I often shudder to reflect on the cruel and selfish dispositions which nature seemed at one time to have planted in my bosom. Nor was it 'till frequent opportunities of contemplating, with enamoured eye, the varied beauties of creation, in my eccentric rambles, and indulging the poetical studies to which they conducted, had soothed and meliorated my heart, that the blossoms of sensibility began to unfold themselves, and I awakened to a sympathetic feeling for every sentient tennant of this many-peopled sphere. (1:101)

Alongside these sentiments may be placed a 1795 letter in which Coleridge responds to his friend George Dyer's admission of misanthropic feeling growing from exposure to "illiberality." "Affected . . . greatly" by this alteration in his amiable, activist (and notoriously absentminded) friend, Coleridge, at the time committed to Hartley's emphasis on environment, attributes the embitterment of Dyer, then living in London, to our "being shaped & coloured by surrounding Objects." Living in "Great Cities" exposes us to that "moral Evil" upon which almost all physical evil "depends," and the "long-continued contemplation" of moral evil "does not tend to meliorate the human heart." Thus he recommends "rural beauties," from which we receive pleasures that "are of little Consequence compared with the Moral Effect of these pleasures—beholding constantly the Best possible we at last become ourselves the best possible. In the country, all around us smile Good and Beauty—and the Images of this divine καλοκἀγαθόα [a fusion of the Beautiful and the Good] are miniatured on the mind of the beholder, as a Landscape on a Convex Mirror" (*CL* I 154).

Coleridge immediately quotes the apostrophe in "that most lovely Poem," *The Castle of Indolence,* in which James Thomson tells "Fortune" that, whatever else "you me deny,"

> You cannot rob me of free Nature's Grace!
> You cannot shut the Windows of the Sky,
> Through which the Morning shews her dewy face—
> You cannot bar my constant feet to rove
> Through Wood and Vale by living Stream at Eve.
>
> (II.ii)

But, Coleridge instantly adds, "Alas! alas! she *can* deny us all this—and can force us fettered and handcuffed by our Dependencies & Wants to *wish* and *wish* away the bitter Little of Life in the felon-crowded Dungeon of a great City!" (*CL* I 154–55).

That was on March 10, 1795, a time when fetters, handcuffs, and dungeons implied more than being pent in any "great City." The political lecturer had informed Dyer, just a few days earlier, that he had been "*obliged* to publish" the first of his Bristol addresses, "it having been confidently asserted that there was

Treason in it," and now informs his friend, who was impressed by that first lecture, that the second and third were "superior to it in point of Composition," but that he has been "obliged by the persecutions of Darkness to discontinue" the series (*CL* I 152, 155).

Precisely three years later, Coleridge wrote a more celebrated letter with sentiments again remarkably similar to those expressed by Thelwall in the *Peripatetic*. Indeed, the Patriot, who was soon to know something about dungeons from firsthand experience, may be said to have anticipated by five years the crucial letter Coleridge wrote to his brother George on or about March 10, 1798. Though Thelwall, of course, has nothing to say about any "divine" *kalokagathia* in nature, his "sympathetic feeling" for all sentient things, an influx induced by "enamoured" contemplation of "the varied beauties of nature," parallels the nature-induced "benevolence and quietness growing within" Coleridge as reported in the letter to George, a letter in which, as in his response three years earlier to Dyer, he goes on immediately to quote lines of poetry—in this case from Wordsworth, the draft conclusion to "The Ruined Cottage":

> I love fields & woods and mounta[ins] with almost a visionary fondness—and because I have found benevolence growing within me as that fondness [has] increased, therefore I should wish to be the means of implanting it in others—& to destroy the bad passions not by combating them, but by keeping them in inaction.

> > Not useless do I deem
> These shadowy Sympathies with things that hold
> An inarticulate Language: for the Man
> Once taught to love such objects, as excite
> No morbid passions, no disquietude,
> No vengeance & no hatred, needs must feels
> The Joy of that pure Principle of Love
> So deeply, that, unsatisfied with aught
> Less pure & exquisite, he cannot chuse
> But seek for objects of a kindred Love
> In fellow-natures, & a kindred Joy.
> Accordingly, he by degrees perceives
> His feelings of aversion softened down,
> A holy tenderness pervade his frame!
> His sanity of reason not impair'd,
> Say rather that his thoughts now flowing clear
> From a clear fountain flowing, he looks round—
> He seeks for Good & finds the Good he seeks.[50]

As has been accurately observed by Stephen Gill, who thinks "Wordsworth never wrote more important lines than these," this philosophic passage on the

50. *CL* I 397–98. For the lines of Wordsworth quoted, part of the original conclusion of "The Ruined Cottage," see *Poetical Works* 5:400–401. Stephen Gill, quoted in the next paragraph, considered the entire passage important enough to include as the single appendix to his superb new biography of Wordsworth: *William Wordsworth: A Life*, 495–97.

moral life of the universe demonstrates "the creativity of the relationship be-
tween Wordsworth and Coleridge in the Alfoxden year." Indeed, the lines
emerge as poetry that could not have been written without the influence of
Coleridge's conversation and of poems like "Religious Musings" and "This
Lime-tree Bower my Prison." The "creative interaction" at work when Cole-
ridge quotes the lines in his letter is, as Gill later remarks, "fascinating": "Cole-
ridge's reading and thought has enabled Wordsworth to formulate complex
ideas in poetry. Wordsworth's poetry is so powerful that Coleridge seizes on it
as a means of conveying to his non-philosophic brother what he himself be-
lieves."[51] All these influxes of sympathetic feeling—Thelwallian, Wordsworthian,
Coleridgean—seem cognate with the Mariner's blessing of the water-snakes, in
which "aversion" and "hatred" are also replaced by "kindred love."

But there are two further points. First, in the earlier letter to Dyer, awareness
that the "wide world" can be contracted to "the bitter Little of Life" in the form
of a "felon-crowded Dungeon" certainly intrudes upon and complicates Cole-
ridge's response to the moralizing effect of "rural beauties": a recurrent History-
in-collision-with-Nature motif in the poetry of both Coleridge and Wordsworth.
Second, and less obviously, nature is doubly vulnerable because its "moral"
dimension is *not* intrinsic. On this point Coleridge differed sharply with men
like Thelwall, Hazlitt—and Wordsworth, to whose bucolic ballads and shorter
poems on such "trivia" as lesser celandines his friend was hostile. "Surely always
to look at the superficies of Objects for the purpose of taking Delight in their
Beauty, & sympathy with their real or imagined Life," Coleridge confided to his
notebook in 1803, "is as deleterious to the Health & manhood of Intellect, as
always to be peering & unravelling Contrivances may be to the simplicity of the
affections, the grandeur & unity of the Imagination" (*CN* I 1616). This remark-
able criticism of Wordsworth, whose sturdy "manhood" is usually emphasized
by a somewhat intimidated Coleridge, almost mechanizes the organic, equating
natural "superficies" with mechanical "contrivances"; it also tells us much
about why *The Recluse*, really more a Coleridgean than a Wordsworthian proj-
ect, was destined never to be completed, at least not in the form originally
intended.[52]

A similar point about the limits of nature, at least from the perspective of a
man whose vision was always *animae naturaliter Christianae,* was made at the time
we are discussing, late 1797. In a letter written two months after Thelwall's visit
to Stowey, responding to the Patriot's rhapsodizing about the sublime beauties

51. *William Wordsworth: A Life,* 134–35, 143.
52. In a full-scale textual and biographical study (including close attention to Cole-
ridge's role), Kenneth R. Johnston argued in 1984 that, far from being a "great failure,"
the *Recluse* exists, "not as an unrealized idea, but as a coherent though incomplete body
of interrelated texts, comprising nearly twenty thousand lines of poetry susceptible of
constructive reading" (*Wordsworth and "The Recluse,"* xi). This view of the *Recluse* as
shaping Wordsworth's canon and motivating the whole of his subsequent writing agenda
was extended in Alan Bewell's *Wordsworth and the Enlightenment: Nature and Society in the
Experimental Poetry.*

of nature, Coleridge informed his friend and "atheist reprobate" that his own response to nature was, unlike that of the Godless Thelwall (and, one must add, the "at least . . . *Semi*-atheist" Wordsworth),[53] less immediate than symbolic, mystical, religious:

> I can *at times* feel strongly the beauties, you describe, in—themselves & for themselves—but more frequently *all things* appear little—all the knowledge, that can be acquired, child's play—the universe itself—what but an immense heap of *little things?*—I can contemplate nothing but parts, & parts are all *little*—!—My mind feels as if it ached to behold & know something *great*—something *one & indivisible*—and it is only in the faith of this that rocks or waterfalls, mountains or caverns give me the sense of sublimity or majesty!—But in this faith *all things* counterfeit infinity!

In characteristic fashion, Coleridge goes on immediately to quote poetry, on this occasion the climactic moment in his own "This Lime-tree Bower my Prison": "'Struck with the deepest calm of Joy' I stand 'Silent . . . gazing round / On the wide landscape'" until all seems "a living Thing" clothing the "almighty Spirit, when he makes / Spirits perceive his presence!" These lines— later revised in ways that may alter the religious sentiment—anticipate the celebrated sublime passage in "Tintern Abbey," though Wordsworth, refusing to specify a personal "almighty Spirit," commits himself only to feeling a mysterious "presence." As for Coleridge, since, as he admits in the letter to Thelwall, it is "seldom that I raise & spiritualize my intellect to this height," he more typically longs for a tranquilizing passivity. It is a "feeling" put in "the mouth of Alhadra my Moorish woman," Coleridge tells Thelwall, going on to quote her wishful prayer that "The Raven & the Seamew were appointed / To bring me food," or, lot even more "divine," that she might be able to drift away "in some small skiff / Along some Ocean's boundless solitude."[54]

The recipient of these juxtaposed passages was a man who had gazed through an actual dungeon-grate, hoping to see, as schoolboy Coleridge would in "Frost at Midnight," the face of a beloved relative. But Thelwall's unmetaphorical dungeon was no classroom, and certainly no pleasant lime-tree bower. The gap between Thelwall's and Coleridge's "prisons" is considerably lessened, however,

53. Wordsworth was so described in Coleridge's letter to Thelwall of May 13, 1796 (*CL* I 216). Five weeks later, in the postscript to a June 22, 1796, letter inviting Thelwall to come to Stowey, Coleridge added: "We have an hundred lovely scenes about Bristol, which would make you exclaim, O admirable *Nature!* & me, O Gracious *God!*" (*CL* I 222).

54. *CL* I 349–51, quoting an earlier version of "This Lime-tree Bower my Prison," 38–43, and *Osorio* V.i.47–52. As Jack Stillinger points out in an essay based in part on J. C. C. Mays's forthcoming edition of the poems for the *Collected Coleridge,* both "manuscript and printed versions" of "This Lime-tree Bower my Prison" reveal "important differences concerning the spiritual significance of nature." The lines quoted in the letter were deleted in some subsequent texts. Those about the "Almighty Spirit" making "Spirits perceive his presence" were only temporarily dropped, but the idea of nature as a "living Thing" disappeared permanently from the "standard" text (Stillinger, "The Multiple Versions of Coleridge's Poems," 133, 142).

when we restore the original political context of "Frost at Midnight," written in February 1798 and appearing in a quarto text that year, a pamphlet issued by the radical publisher Joseph Johnson and containing only two other poems, both politically charged: the Recantation ode and "Fears in Solitude."[55] In *this* context, the passage from *Osorio* cited by Coleridge is particularly relevant to the conversation in Holford Glen since Alhadra's moonlight soliloquy is an interlude, a brief interruption in her inexorable progress to the deep-dungeoned Velez castle whither she is conducting a group of Moors to wreak physical vengeance on the çruel tyrant who has murdered her husband.

It would seem that for Coleridge in 1797, the things of nature, however beautiful, either "counterfeit infinity" or provide at best a momentary respite—intruded upon by death and dungeons—amid the jarrings and conflicts of the wide world. Whatever we make, in *Osorio*, of the residence of the "Almighty One" in "every gale . . . and wave," or of the thematic suggestion that nature teaches benevolence (*CPW* II 577, 591), the ambivalent response to nature Coleridge reveals in this letter to Thelwall, reiterated in his later notebook critique of Wordsworth's obsession with natural "superficies," should "give pause to any critic who would make him at this time too ready a believer in the power of nature to induce automatic moral benefits in man."[56] Oppression and injustice persisted, politics remained intrusive, and there was still the duty of resistance, even renewed activism, whatever the longing for "boundless solitude." To return these speculations to the exchange in Holford Glen: I suggest again that Coleridge's version, with the teasing invitation to talk "treason," may be at once the more dramatic and the more accurate account.

True, the Coleridge of Wordsworth's version seems a familiar S.T.C. This is the allegedly serene retirer from the political din; detector—despite the acknowledged fact that "It is most hard, with an untroubled ear / Thy dark inwoven harmonies to hear!"—of the Creative Spirit's cosmic harmonies played on "the wild Harp of Time" (*CPW* I 160); apostle of "the one Life within us and abroad" (*CPW* I 101): the Coleridge, one might add, who, as harmonizing glossist in 1817, reconciles his own inner divisions by explaining, and occasionally explaining away, the jarrings and conflicts *un*reconciled in the 1798–1800 text of *The Rime of the Ancient Mariner.* Significantly, *both* the famous "one Life" line and the even more famous gloss were retrospectively added to their 1790s texts, acts of revising that also become re-versionings.

55. See Paul Magnuson, "The Politics of 'Frost at Midnight.'"

56. John Beer, *Coleridge's Poetic Intelligence,* 164. Beer is referring specifically to the October 1797 letter to Thelwall; he does not mention the *Notebook* entry. In this as in most things, Coleridge expresses more than one perspective. In a September 1802 letter to William Sotheby, he criticizes William Lisle Bowles for "a perpetual trick of *moralizing* every thing—which is very well, occasionally—but never to see or describe any interesting appearances in nature, without connecting it with dim analogies with the moral world, proves faintness of Impression. Nature has her proper interest; & he will know what it is, who believes & feels, that every Thing has a Life of it's [sic] own, & that we are all *one Life*" (*CL* II 864).

I am not, of course, suggesting that the Coleridge who discoursed with Thelwall and Wordsworth in the glen in July 1797 was unaware of nature's more-than-occasional capacity to reconcile the human spirit to the turbulences of the "wide world." Coleridge is not, after all, Alhadra; if he were, he would have had no need to *create* her to act out his more vengeful political fantasies. Her Elijah-echoing reverie and temporary respite in the moonlight took the form, in Coleridge's case, of the ambiguous, conflicted, but nevertheless more permanent form of his various retirements—with the activist alternately calmed and agitated, as Elijah was on Mount Horeb, by the still small voice of God and, in Coleridge's case, restored by the healing power of nature. Again, the moonlit blessing of the water-snakes is not irrelevant.

Politically oriented scholars like Erdman and Thompson had always been skeptical, but until the advent of the New Historicists, this dialectic between inner and outer worlds, with the interiorizing imagination triumphant, was thought by most to be at the redemptive heart of Romanticism, not only in terms of the transaction between the mind and the external world of nature, but in terms of the reconciliation between the self and the "jarrings and conflicts" of a revolutionary era. Byron (it is no accident that both Erdman and McGann began their careers as scholars of Byron and that Abrams omits him from *Natural Supernaturalism*) anticipated the postmodern demystification of this quietist paradigm, charging that Wordsworth and Coleridge, like their more despicable fellow-"Laker," Southey, were political turncoats rather than Romantic philosophers.

Yet the transcendental model remains compelling, both for the Romantics and for their critics—an idealist paradigm built on even by those who challenge and subvert it. The *general* model is familiar. In specifically *political* terms, the imagination, healed by a restorative nature, accommodates the jarrings and conflicts of the French Revolution and its English sequelae by transforming them, turning political defeat—the failure of the revolutionary hopes of Wordsworth and Coleridge—into imaginative triumph. Brilliantly synopsized by Abrams, this is the "Miltonic" pattern that Kitson proposes as the historical context of *The Ancient Mariner:* a (de-)politicizing that simply reconfirms the victory of the Romantic Muse over material reality, of poetry over contemporary radical politics. Aside from the few great poems of Coleridge's annus mirabilis, and the later "Dejection: An Ode" and "To William Wordsworth," the poetic triumph was essentially Wordsworth's, but the pattern of that triumph was worked out theoretically by his friend, to whom the great poem we know as *The Prelude* was directly, and appropriately, addressed.

But those plans came after July 1797. I suspect that Wordsworth, in his account of what Coleridge said to Thelwall in the glen forty-six years earlier, is remembering their shared plans for his magnum opus, *The Recluse*, as expressed on many occasions, including the important letter of May 1815, when proprietary Coleridge spoke of the long-projected work as dialectical, embodying "a Fall in some sense," as attested to by "experience," but going on "to point out however a manifest scheme of Redemption" from conflict and division, of a *mental* "revolution" leading to "Reconciliation from this Enmity with Nature" (*CL* IV 574–75). Coleridge was—surely not coincidentally given the elaborate unity Wordsworth was claiming for his own work in the preface to his first collected *Poems,* published a month before this letter—extensively revising his own poems in 1815 and working on a gloss for *The Ancient Mariner,* a work that also needed to be "completed" if this spiritual pattern of fall, redemption, and reconciliation was to be made fully persuasive.[57]

This may be the Coleridge Wordsworth retrospectively transplants back into the dell of 1797 to exclaim that "This is a place to reconcile one to all the jarrings and conflicts of the wide world." In doing so, he glosses over the more-than-vestigial radicalism of a man who may have been "retired" from the wide world for half a year, but who remained painfully aware that that world was full of irreconcilable conflicts, some of which he had no desire to reconcile himself *to,* in the sense of acquiescently accommodating himself to evil. (Such an acquiescence, if it occurred, came in the spring of 1798, not the late summer of 1797.) We tend to think of Coleridge as epitomized by his Mariner in the crucial reintegrating event of his major poem: a supreme exemplar of reconciliation from the enmity with nature, of what Thelwall called the heart-ameliorating awakening to "a sympathetic feeling for every sentient tennant of this many-peopled sphere," celebrator of the sacramental bond uniting all life, of that affirmation, in "The Eolian Harp," of the "one Life within us and abroad," which has become—with Coleridge's help and powerfully reinforced by Warren's pivotal essay—the standard gloss on the Mariner's blessing of the water-snakes.

But, of course, that standard gloss is retrospective. The lines celebrating the "one Life" were added by Coleridge many years after he wrote "The Eolian Harp," thus—as Jack Stillinger remarks—"giving us ever afterward a memorable passage to help explain the action and theme of *The Ancient Mariner:* the Mariner's abrupt and seemingly motiveless shooting of the albatross now becomes a violation of the 'one Life' principle." And the importation of this after-the-fact unity creates an interpretive domino effect. In the light of the same memorable passage, the poet's lime-bower can be seen as "no prison at all but instead as a part of the 'one Life' available wherever one looks," while "This Lime-tree Bower my Prison" is, in turn, "revised to make the religious significance of nature more compatible with that conveyed in *The Eolian Harp* and

57. The year of Coleridge's most significant poetic revising, 1815, coincides with Wordsworth's recent and "highly publicized" preface to *The Excursion* (1814), in which he explained the massive unity and interrelatedness of his work, and the preface to *Poems* (April 1815), elucidating "the principles by which the poems were classified and arranged into categories." As Jack Stillinger remarks, "it would be a nice piece of biographical and textual criticism to explain Coleridge's most significant revisions as a reaction to these publications by Wordsworth. Such an explanation would inevitably involve seeing Coleridge the critical theorist turning theory into practical self-criticism as he revises to achieve in his own work the same kind of unity of effect that Wordsworth was in the process of accomplishing in his" ("Multiple Versions of Coleridge's Poems," 144).

Frost at Midnight."[58] In short, Coleridge's addition of the passage about "the one Life within us and abroad" functions in much the way his famous gloss does, later added to *The Ancient Mariner,* and similarly expanding the religious and moral significance of the poem, as well as adding to its perceived unity.

The theme of the "one Life" is also a standard, and—again—an essentially but not completely accurate, gloss on much of the collaborative thought and creative interaction engaged in by Coleridge and Wordsworth in 1797–1798. In "Tintern Abbey," Wordsworth referred to

> that blessed mood
> In which the burthen of the mystery,
> In which the heavy and the weary weight
> Of all this unintelligible world,
> Is lightened—

a "serene" state in which we "see into the life of things / . . . / with an eye made quiet by the power / Of harmony, and the deep power of joy." He was perhaps remembering, along with his poem's most immediate precursor, "Frost at Midnight," those opening lines of Coleridge's "Ode on the Departing Year" quoted above, as well as the lines Coleridge quoted to Thelwall from "This Lime-tree Bower my Prison." Wordsworth is also likely to be recalling "The Eolian Harp," where "one intellectual breeze" sweeps an "animated nature" composed of "organic harps diversely fram'd." In *Biographia Literaria,* published in the same year he added both the "one Life" phrase to "The Eolian Harp" and the gloss to *The Ancient Mariner,* Coleridge describes the "synthetic" and "magical" Imagination, revealing itself "in the balance or reconciliation of opposite or discordant qualities," as a "power" that brings "harmony" into being (*BL* II 16–17).

That is much, but not the whole, of Coleridge—especially not the Coleridge of the 1790s, a man also capable of skepticism not only about that counterfeiter of infinity, nature, but about the "one Life" and "harmony" as well. Discussing definitions of "Life" in an earlier letter to Thelwall, one written on the very day he moved into the cottage at Stowey, Coleridge quotes lines 44–47 from "my favorite of *my* poems," "The Eolian Harp"—

> And what if all of animated Nature
> Be but organic harps diversely fram'd
> That tremble into thought as o'er them sweeps
> Plastic & vast &c—

and then goes on immediately to what the "Metaphysicians" say of Life: "Plato says, it is *Harmony*—he might as well have said, a fiddle stick's end—but I love Plato—his dear *gorgeous* Nonsense!" Coleridge then concludes, inconclusively, that while he does "not know what to think about it," he suspects that "Life is I myself I! which is a mighty clear account of it" (*CL* I 295). Later, perhaps recalling Hegelian dialectic in the *Logic,* Coleridge was to praise Plato as a preparatory

58. "Mulitple Versions of Coleridge's Poems," 144.

philosopher who "leads the mind to see that contradictory propositions are each true—which therefore *must* belong to a higher Logic—that of Ideas. They are contradictory only in Aristotelian Logic" (*TT* I 98; March 31 1830).

Here, again, we encounter Wordsworth's reconciler, the theoretician of the synthesizing and harmonizing Imagination. But the man discoursing in Holford Glen in 1797, still somewhat skeptical about "nature" and the "harmony" of Life, was also aware of the "jarrings and conflicts" in the political world, and thus capable of proposing that he and the most famous radical in England talk constructive "treason." Of course, *any* serious opposition to the Pitt Ministry amounted to "treason" at the time, and Coleridge probably knew that the man he was speaking to was on the verge of headlong retreat. In this triple circumstance— the secrecy of a beautiful recess, a de-fanged radical, and an ironically muted term—he could safely use a normally dangerous, even potentially fatal, word. Judging from comments Thelwall would make in 1798 and, in a very different mood, in 1817, it was not Coleridge's sole instance of "reckless" talk during the Patriot's ten-day stay in the Alfoxden-Stowey neighborhood.

To some extent, Coleridge may have been "talking big," but that does not diminish the quintessential point detectable in his version of the incident. For the exchange succinctly epitomizes the *actual* similarity and distinction between Coleridge and Thelwall in July 1797, a time when, as Nicholas Roe observes, "Thelwall's political career had been 'concluded' by violent opposition whereas Coleridge seems to have anticipated continuing activity and involvement."[59] Roe "underlines the difference" between the retirees by citing the "well-known anecdote," adding that it "would be fascinating to eavesdrop on the rest of their conversation." But two things at least are clear from "this brief recollection":

> While admitting that much-needed reforms were at this moment equated with "treason," Thelwall was glad to be distanced from London and politics. Coleridge, on the other hand, was in a teaseful mood for conspiracy. He could afford to be: Coleridge had never faced organized violence as Thelwall had recently done in East Anglia,[60] nor had he been prosecuted for high treason. . . . [R]epression left him unscathed except, perhaps, for his financial loss on the *Watchman*.
>
> This was one obvious reason why Coleridge's support for reform and opposition to the war should have survived intact, until the French invasion of Switzerland on 13–14 February 1798. . . . [Up to that moment], his opposition . . . is markedly consistent. One should therefore be wary of any generalized pattern of retreat from politics into retirement.

To Roe's perceptive registration of the inconvenient facts that complicate "the reductive paradigm in which radical commitment is succeeded by 'with-

59. *Wordsworth and Coleridge*, 237–38.

60. True, though Coleridge *had* faced some violence, including death threats, during his Bristol lectures, and had been, as he tells Dyer in the letter quoted earlier, "obliged by the persecutions of Darkness to discontinue them" (*CL* I 155). According to Thompson, "Coleridge, with his lectures and his *Watchman,* was a sort of little Bristol Thelwall" ("Disenchantment or Default?" 159). Again, true; though Coleridge had a somewhat wider reputation, and faced greater dangers, than this description suggests.

drawal' or 'apostasy,'"[61] I would only add that Coleridge's deepening retreat into withdrawal in March 1798, following a period of renewed activism in the winter and spring of 1797–1798, was a response to ominous domestic developments as well as to the French invasion of democratic Switzerland: that shocking event memorialized in Coleridge's formal withdrawal of allegiance to the Revolution, "Recantation," later "France: An Ode."

5

Describing the context of the conversation in the glen, Jonathan Wordsworth has recently written: "Though they would hardly have put it to themselves in such terms, the three men were in the process of switching their energies from politics to poetry."[62] But, of course, Roe is, like William Hazlitt and others, right to chart the complications agitating this Coleridgean "retirement" of 1797–1798. Thelwall himself, writing in January 1798, described Coleridge good-naturedly as a scatterer of "levelling sedition and constructive treason"; and, years later, annotating *Biographia Literaria* in anything but good humor, insisted on the extreme radicalism of the man he met at Stowey. Alongside Coleridge's characteristic remark, "how opposite even then my principles were to those of Jacobinism or even of democracy" (*BL* I 184), an annoyed Thelwall commented: "Mr. C was indeed far from Democracy, because he was far beyond it, I well remember—for he was a down right zealous leveller."[63] And Thelwall underlined most of the following sentence two paragraphs later:

> Conscientiously an opponent of the first revolutionary war, yet with my eyes thoroughly opened to the true character and impotence of the favorers of revolutionary principles in England, principles which I held in abhorrence (for it was part of my political creed, that whoever ceased to act as an *individual* by making himself a member of any *society* not sanctioned by his Government, forfeited the rights of a citizen)—a vehement anti-ministerialist, but after the invasion of Switzerland a more vehement anti-gallican, and still more intensely an anti-jacobin, I retired to a cottage at Stowey. (*BL* I 187)

Asterisking the phrase ending, ". . . forfeited the rights of a citizen," Thelwall wondered rhetorically if Coleridge had forgotten his own earlier tribute in the form of a sonnet:

> "Some [,] Thelwall [!] to the patriot's meed aspire
> Who at safe distance, without wound or scar
> Round pictur'd strong walls waging mimic war
> Closset their valour, you mid thickest fire
> Leap on the perilous wall—Therefore I choose
> Unfading flowers that chastest odours breathe
> To weave for thy young locks the civic wreath"—&c.

& ending

61. *Wordsworth and Coleridge*, ix.
62. *Ancestral Voices: Fifty Books from the Romantic Period*, 122.
63. Pollin, "John Thelwall's Marginalia," 81.

"Blest if to my maturer years belong
Thy stern simplicity, & nervous song—"[64]

Underlining *Stowey,* Thelwall wrote in the right-hand margin: "Where I visited him & found him a decided Leveller—abusing the democrats for their hypocritical moderatism, in pretending to be willing to give the people equality of privileges & rank, while, at the same time, they would refuse them all that the others could be valuable for—equality of property—or rather abolition of property."[65]

Thelwall's account confirms Coleridge's commitment, as late as July 1797, to Christian egalitarianism and a communistic theory of property derived in large part from the Levellers and Diggers of the seventeenth-century Puritan Revolution. Coleridge's radicalism, religious in origin, *was* more "extreme" when it came to property than that of the atheistic Thelwall. In these annotations of 1817, Thelwall was dismayed and angered by what he, like many old reformers, took to be the youthful Pantisocrat's later *political* apostasy. While Coleridge was capable not only of backsliding but of defecating on his old enthusiasms,[66] he was also a dialectical thinker so aware of the complexity of issues, and so serpentine in his alternating commitments and recoils, that it is often hard to know what his precise political position is at a given time. "It is very unpleasant to me to be often asked if Coleridge has changed his political sentiments," wrote a confused Sara Coleridge to Tom Poole in March 1799, "for I know not properly how to reply. Pray furnish me." She was not alone. Four years earlier, before any "apostasy," many in his Bristol audiences must have been similarly perplexed by an ardent young man given to what he later described as "flame-coloured Epithets" (*L 1795 25n*), yet eschewing—on personal, religious, and legal grounds—any incitement to physical violence.

Against Thelwall's picture of Coleridge as an unreconstructed Pantisocrat as late as 1797 it is easy enough to set such endorsements of private property as Coleridge's *Morning Post* piece "On the French Constitution" (*EOT* I 32–33). But that was 1799, not 1797. And even if Coleridge's shifting response to the ever-more-ominous French Revolution and to domestic repression had clearly moved in this direction as early as 1797, that would not necessarily mean that Thelwall was lying twenty years later. Even if heightened by understandable

---

64. Pollin, "John Thelwall's Marginalia," 82 (77 for facsimile page). Significant variants from the text as printed in *CPW* II 1090 include (aside from punctuation) *distance* for *rage* and *wound* for *or rent* (line 2), *waging* for *sketching* (line 3), the addition of *perilous* to *wall* and *I* for *shall Freedom* (line 5), and, most curiously, *nervous* for *vigorous* in the final line.

65. Pollin, "John Thelwall's Marginalia," 82.

66. In memorable rhetorical questions about Coleridge's notorious reference, on two occasions, to his "squeaking baby-trumpet of sedition," Thompson asks: "Why the 'squeaking baby-trumpet'? Why defecate upon an enthusiasm whose ink has not yet dried?" ("Disenchantment or Default?" 153).

irritation, these marginal notes of 1817 were private and, therefore, the presumably honest reactions of a notably candid man.

One might legitimately surmise, taking at face value that remark about "a fine place to talk treason in," that chameleon Coleridge was, in July 1797, playing up his unpurged radicalism a bit for the benefit of the celebrated "Citizen John." But it is hard to know how to take the remainder of Thelwall's note on Coleridge's rejection of "Jacobinism": the charge that Coleridge was not only an economic leveler, but that "indeed in one of the worst senses of the word he was a Jacobin, a man of blood—Does he forget the letters he wrote to me (& which I believe I yet have) acknowledging the justice of my castigation of him for the violence, and sanguinary tendency of some of his doctrines—[?]"[67]

It is difficult to square these sanguinary charges with Coleridge's insistence, in his *Conciones ad Populum* of 1795, that Christians must enlighten rather than incite the people; that "general Illumination should precede Revolution"; that the "annals of the French Revolution have recorded in Letters of Blood, that

67. Pollin, "John Thelwall's Marginalia," 81. Thelwall began, "What Jacobinism may mean I cannot tell: if the principles of the first leaders of the Jacobin club, what friend of liberty [,] of human reason & human happiness would disown them? If the doctrines (or declamations [)], & the practices of the last, what friend of Man would not recoil from them with horror?" In "Once a Jacobin Always a Jacobin" (*EOT* I 367–73), he had, Coleridge later boasted in *BL*, anticipated even Burke in "distinguishing the jacobin from the republican, the democrat, and the mere demagogue" (*BL* I 217). Thelwall, who made a clear demarcation between early and later Jacobinism, was unpersuaded. Later in his annotations on the *Biographia*, responding to Coleridge's critique (*BL* II 221) of Charles Robert Maturin's Gothic tragedy *Bertram* (which ran in May 1816 at Drury Lane) as a "modern jacobinical drama" (on the basis of its "confusion and subversion of the natural order of things in their causes and effects"), Thelwall seized with legitimate irritation on Coleridge's gratuitous use of the adjective *jacobinical*, here and some pages later, where the fourth act of *Bertram* suggested to Coleridge that "the shocking spirit of jacobinism" was "no longer confined to politics" (*BL* II 229). "Nothing," wrote Thelwall in the margin, "betrays the destitution of principle more completely than the sophistical use of really unmeaning, but yet popular cant nick names. Thus Jacobin (a term of no definable signification, but conjuring up in the minds of alarmist & zealous royalists every emotion that belongs to the hatred of all crimes & enormities) is used by the consistent Mr C. in such way as to be apparently applicable to all reformers & *incliners* to republicanism—in short to all who are dissatisfied with the established systems of *legitimate* despotism: & then everything that is immoral & detestable in [the] arts literature manners & habits (by whatsoever class introduced, or by whatever classes countenanced & patronized) is to be called Jacobinical also; & the logical conclusion is expected to follow that everything immoral & detestable is concentrated & personified in the said reformers &c.—He does not call those from whom *he has deserted* "spawn of Hell"—He only endeavours to lead the minds of his readers to think (or at least to feel) of them as such. The reflections (so far as they are critical merely,) on the Germanised or modern melodramatized & farsicalized Drama, are very just, but what this abominable perversion of taste & morality has to do with Jacobinism, or what connection it has with those upon whom he is so assistant [insistent?] in affixing or in confirming that odious appelation, it would puzzle the Theban to discover" (Pollin, "John Thelwall's Marginalia," 93–4).

the knowledge of the Few cannot counteract the Ignorance of the Many"; that "a system of fundamental Reform will scarcely be effected by Massacres mechanized into Revolution"; and that all should be done, not in the fury of "revenge," but in the "spirit of Love" (*L 1795* 43, 6, 49). These were the very points Thelwall himself made in his speech to the London Corresponding Society at Copenhagen Fields on October 26, 1795. He urged "reform" of a corrupt "system," not "revenge upon individuals," citing (as did Coleridge in the Bristol addresses) the calamities that had befallen France, as a consequence of being "less influenced by principles than by faction."[68]

The positions of Coleridge and Thelwall (despite his famous foam-blowing gesture) were actually rather close at the time, positions that also coincided with that of Wordsworth, as expressed in the June 1794 letter in which he told his schoolteacher friend William Mathews, with whom he was planning to collaborate on a monthly miscellany he proposed to call *The Philanthropist*,[69] that their "detestation" of the Terror in France should be balanced by their "approbation" of such of the French "regulations and decrees as are dictated by the Spirit of Philosophy." He was, Wordsworth told his friend, "not amongst the admirers of the British constitution," a constitution subverted by the Ministry and by the new ideas regarding government "which within these few years have rapidly taken place in the minds of speculative men. . . . To the latter I would give every additional energy in my power." Yet he is fearful that "the destruction of those institutions" he condemned—that is, "all monarchical and aristocratic governments, however modified, and all hereditary and privileged orders"—appeared to be "hastening on too rapidly." As a Godwinian convinced that all social "improvements are necessarily slow and progressive,"

> I recoil from the bare idea of a revolution; yet, if our conduct with reference both to foreign and domestic policy continues such as it has been for the last two years how is that dreadful event to be averted? . . . [The people must be convinced]

68. *Peaceful Discussion, and Not Tumultuary Violence the Means of Redressing National Grievances*, 7–10. Thelwall had always responded more to the "principles" than to the actors and actions of the French Revolution. In the *Tribune*, he spelled out those principles—humane and Enlightened, but dangerous, even treasonable, to a frightened British Government at war not only against French arms but French ideas: "That which I glory in, in the revolution in France, is this. That it has been upheld and propagated as a principle of that revolution, that ancient abuses are not by their antiquity converted into virtues; that it has been affirmed and established that man has rights which no statutes or usages can take away; that intellectual beings are entitled to the use of their intellects; that the object of society is the promotion of the general happiness of mankind; that thought ought to be free, and that the propagation of thought is the duty of every individual; that one order of society has no right, how many years soever they have been guilty of the pillage, to plunder and oppress the other parts of the community, whose persons are entitled to equal respect, and whose exertions have been much more beneficial to mankind" (1:155–56).

69. An eight-page penny weekly of this title did appear, and Wordsworth probably contributed to it. For informed speculation on the subject, see Roe's appendix to *Wordsworth and Coleridge* and Johnston, "Philanthropy or Treason?"

that they can only be preserved from a convulsion by oeconomy in the administration of the public purse and a gradual and constant reform of those abuses which, if left to themselves, may grow to such a height as to render, even a revolution desirable. . . . After this need I add that I am a determined enemy to every species of violence?[70]

So was Coleridge. The nature of the battle he intended is explicit in his pronouncement on the eve of his first political reengagement. Conscious of his moral and political duty to "unnumber'd brethren" who "toil'd and bled" while he dreamed away his hours "On rose-leaf beds," Coleridge was "constrain'd to quit" his first place of "retirement," the "quiet dell" and "dear" honeymoon cottage at Clevedon. In time, he prayed, his pastoral bliss would become universal and millennial ("Speed it, O Father! Let thy Kingdom come!"); but in the meantime, he was returning to the political world as an activist engaged in what Blake would later call "mental fight," committed to religious, and specifically *un*sanguinary, principles:

> I therefore go, and join head, heart, and hand,
> Active and firm, to fight the bloodless fight
> Of Science, freedom, and the Truth in Christ.[71]

True, in the heat of his Bristol lecturing, Coleridge was sometimes carried away by his own ardor and gift for provocative metaphor. His most recent biographer, Richard Holmes, perceptively remarks that Coleridge's Bristol addresses "left his hearers (and perhaps himself) deeply confused as to his exact ideological position: at one moment a fiery democrat, at the next an unworldy Unitarian idealist preaching universal benevolence." But, as Holmes says, Coleridge never advocated violence (not, at least, in the printed versions of the addresses, and probably not as orally delivered). Thus, many pages later, in a footnote discussing Thelwall's marginal accusations of a "sanguinary tendency," and referring to Thelwall's own reference to letters Coleridge had sent him, Holmes remarks that "we do have those letters, but they do not bear Thelwall out."[72]

He is right as far as published letters are concerned (sixteen are extant), but Thelwall *may* be referring to others, which have not survived. Thelwall, in short, may not be (as Holmes concludes) "exaggerating and unreliable" in these

70. *The Letters of William and Dorothy Wordsworth: The Early Years, 1787–1805*, ed. Ernest de Selincourt, 128, 123–24.

71. *CPW* I 197–98. The systolic-diastolic rhythm of political withdrawal and engagement, and Coleridge's ambivalence, are epitomized by the alteration in the title of this poem. Originally entitled "Reflections on Entering into Active Life" when it appeared in the *Monthly Magazine* (2 [October 1796], 712–13), the poem was later retitled "Reflections on Having Left a Place of Retirement." For a cogent discussion of Coleridge's "Conversation Poems" as politically oriented statements setting the personal and familial against the disruptions emanating from the French Revolution and its social ramifications, see Kelvin Everest, *Coleridge's Secret Ministry: The Context of the Conversation Poems, 1795–1798*.

72. *Coleridge: Early Visions*, 93, 158n.

annotations. They may instead reflect, along with honest anger, the same con-
fused reaction as to Coleridge's "exact ideological position" experienced by so
many others in these years, Coleridge not always excluded. I suspect that Thel-
wall's underlinings, exclamations, and marginal notes—whose "fullness and
organization . . . tell us that he felt the significance of this confrontation with
his former friend"[73]—register with reasonable accuracy the picture Coleridge
presented to him in at least some letters and, especially, in person in July 1797.
Thelwall's notes provide, I suggest, fairly reliable testimony to the political
indignation still smoldering in 1797 in the breast of the gardener retired at
Stowey.

One must be skeptical of anecdotes and annotations, especially many years
after the event. I for one would be *more* skeptical of Coleridge's recollection of
his teasing invitation to John Thelwall to "talk treason," and of Thelwall's later
characterization of Coleridge's political position in 1797, if they were the *only*
evidence of the radicalism of the supposedly "retired" Coleridge in 1797. They
are not.

To begin with, England's most prominent radical did not come to Stowey out
of the blue; he was invited there by Coleridge, who hoped he would settle
permanently. Thelwall *did* turn up "unexpected" in the sense that he arrived at
Coleridge's cottage on a Sunday, his host with the Wordsworths and an aban-
doned Sara at her washtub. But he *was* expected. As proof we have the testi-
mony of Charles Lamb. Seeking peace and the company of his friend Coleridge
after the family tragedy ten months earlier in which his mother had been fatally
stabbed by his sister in a fit of madness, Lamb had spent the week of July 8–14 at
Stowey. In his bread-and-butter note, he told Coleridge, "I was looking out for
John Thelwall all the way from Bridgewater, and had I met him, I think it would
have almost moved me to tears." Thus W. J. Bate, among others, is quite mis-
leading when he writes: "A fly in the ointment was the unexpected visit of the
revolutionary and atheist, John Thelwall."[74] In fact, Coleridge and the Words-
worths were delighted that Thelwall had come (as was Sara, quickly won over by
her guest's energy and the attention he paid her); nor, as indicated by the
dinner party mentioned in Chapter 7, was Thelwall always averse to holding
forth on politics during these days, or Coleridge to hearing him on the subject.

And there is other evidence of Coleridge's unextinguished radicalism in
retirement: there is, for example, the most sustained creative work of the annus
mirabilis. In addition to tending his garden, pigs, and poultry, the retired
Coleridge employed himself in 1797 "on my Tragedy" (*CL* I 320). *Osorio*, Words-
worth's admiration of which encouraged Coleridge to continue working on it,
is dominated by the violently revolutionary Alhadra, a heroine not at all re-
stricted to the "bloodless fight," and given (as we shall see) Coleridge's own
obsessive images of his political hopes and fears: the whirlwind and earthquake

73. Pollin, "John Thelwall's Marginalia," 76.
74. Lamb, *Letters of Charles and Mary Anne Lamb* 1:117–18. (I correct Lamb's inadver-
tent transposition: "moved almost me. . . .") Bate, *Coleridge*, 39.

of revolution and the fetters and dungeon of repression. The project had been instigated by Richard Brinsley Sheridan, who, through a mutual friend, suggested that Coleridge write "a tragedy on some popular subject." "Gratified and somewhat elevated by the proposal," Coleridge promised Sheridan he would set right to work. "The phrase 'popular subject' has a little puzzled me," he notes, but his letter ends on a tribute less to Sheridan's theatrical than to his political stature; Coleridge was pleased "to add the feeling of individual obligation to the deeper and more lofty gratitude, which I owe you in common with all Europe" (*CL* I 304). Sheridan was still, as in Coleridge's 1795 sonnet to him (*CPW* I 88), Michael to Pitt's Lucifer, the "Apostate by the brainless rout ador'd," but doomed, as was "that elder fiend," to writhe "beneath great Michael's sword."

Unlike so many of his abortive projects, this was one Coleridge got hopping on immediately. Sheridan's request was clearly a catalyst for the suppressed political activism of its retired author. The finished play was less a call to action than a reflection of Coleridge's unextinguished ardor, partisan and revolutionary; and, eventually, the drama was rejected. But it is important to remember that *Osorio* was written for Sheridan: Pitt's opponent in the wars of Parliament and the newspapers, the man who had called the prime minister a "British Roberspierre" [sic] who, "to maintain his authority, kept the people in incessant alarm about plots and conspiracies, which were necessary to him to bind the nation in stronger shackles."[75]

The shackling machinery of the Inquisition in *Osorio* (a displacement transplanting to Spain the Pittite inquisition that had made a prison of contemporary England), as well as the revolutionary whirlwind and earthquake, reappear in the apolitical *Ancient Mariner,* begun a month after *Osorio* was completed. Furthermore, it is precisely *these* images—the rumbling convulsion and whirlpool that sink the Mariner's ship and the comparison of the spectre-bark's masts to a dungeon-grate through which the bloody sun peers—that are either ignored by the critics or treated hastily and unconvincingly. The dungeon-grate, for example, is the only image in *The Ancient Mariner* about which John Livingston Lowes has nothing to say, while Robert Penn Warren unpersuasively includes among his images associated with "imagination" the submarine rumbling and explosion attending the sinking of the ship. These images have to be accounted for, rather than evaded or explained away. Not in order to make a case for the total coherence of a poem that, though imaginatively controlled to a considerable degree, retains the phantasmagoric quality of nightmare, but because the dungeon-grate and the submarine rumblings seem—despite the "distancing" provided by its framed narrative and medieval/supernatural setting—to have intruded themselves into the poem from a region of Coleridge's conscious and unconscious mind which the imagery itself reveals to be notably "political."

I will also be making a case for possible political significance in the act most

75. Sheridan's comment (*Parliamentary Register* [1795] XLIII, 325) is cited in an editorial note discussing the title of Coleridge's *The Plot Discovered* (*L 1795* 283*n*).

readers consider the crucial moment of the poem: the blessing of the water-snakes. Since, on the level of the political theme, those previously loathsome creatures have associations with the Pitt Ministry (once despised, but by March–April 1798 embraced as part of God's providential universe), that blessing, too, may be, at least in part, an act of *enforced* love. For surely Coleridge's retreat from indignation against these instruments of evil has something to do with the fact that, by March 1798, the month he was finishing *The Ancient Mariner* and the fiercest month of what Marilyn Butler calls "the fiercest year of the English counter-revolutionary reaction," that Ministry had the power either to draft Coleridge into the militia or to imprison him as a suspected seditionist or potential fifth columnist.

Francesco, the Inquisitor in *Osorio,* tells us that a man, fearing him who has "the key" to his life, is "forced to love" his questioner and imprisoner (*CPW* II 560). This religious and political tyranny—including the theme of being forced to love those who hold keys that fit into literal dungeon locks—reappears in *The Ancient Mariner,* a mythic journey that, on the surface, is utterly removed from the political world. I will be arguing that this religio-political fusion of terror, tyranny, and submission entered, and came in a sense to dominate, the universe of *The Ancient Mariner* in part at least as a result of the political developments of the months during which Coleridge was working on the poem—the winter and spring of 1797–1798, when the political elements stirred slightly only to yield to the specter of clanking fetters and the dungeon-grate.

6

Pestful Calms and Whirlwinds, Rumbles and Earthquakes

1

The situation in the poem leading up to the "dungeon-grate" passage is nothing if not desperate. The ship is becalmed at the equator: "Down dropt the breeze, the Sails dropt down"; there is "ne breath ne motion"; the ship is "stuck," "idle." The "very deeps . . . rot"; "slimy things . . . crawl with legs / Upon the slimy Sea"; "Death-fires danc'd at night"; the sailors stand "dumb," every tongue withered through utter "drouth"; his shipmates have just hung the dead albatross about the Mariner's neck. As the text, after 1800, thrice informs the less observant, it is "a weary time."[1] We'll return to the slimy crawlers and dancing death-fires; for the moment, let me suggest a personal and political parallel to the situation in the poem.

Though Coleridge had retired to Stowey in December 1796 with high hopes, Elysium began to cloy or bore as early as March–April 1797, when we find him—back in Stowey after a visit to Bristol, the recent scene of his dangerous but heady political activities—writing to his publisher Joseph Cottle of a "depression too dreadful to be described." He has to resort to lines that Milton, himself with the Restoration's dangers compassed round, had given to his imprisoned and idle Samson:

> So much I felt my genial spirits droop!
> My hopes all flat, nature within me seem'd
> In all her functions weary of herself.
> (*Samson Agonistes*, lines 594–96)

Even the conversation of Wordsworth, on a brief visit to Stowey prior to his actual move into the neighborhood, could only rouse him "somewhat," for he was not the man he had been: "A sort of calm hopelessness diffuses itself over my heart."[2]

This sense of static hopelessness (suggesting in part the economic and emo-

---

1. "A weary time" was added in the 1800 edition. The other lines (103–32) are quoted from the 1798 text, as printed in *CPW* II 1031–48. As mentioned, since I am concerned with 1797–1798, I quote—aside of course from the gloss, added in 1817—from the 1798 text.

2. *CL* I 318–20. In quoting *Samson Agonistes* Coleridge cites a work that, as many verbal echoes indicate, was as political for him as it was for Milton.

tional difficulties of what a later generation might call an increasingly albatross-like marriage) resembles the becalmment in *The Ancient Mariner* and, more intimately, the smothering of Coleridge's "genial spirits" in the Dejection verse-letter and ode. But it also anticipates a January 1800 letter to his benefactor Tom Wedgwood, whose family's generous annuity had saved him in January 1798 from accepting a Unitarian ministry. He acknowledges that "private & personal" matters ought to occupy him more, and that "the dedication of much hope & fear to subjects which are perhaps disproportionate to our faculties & powers, is a disease." But he has had this political "disease so long, . . . that I know not how to get rid of it; or even to wish to get rid of it. Life were so flat a thing without Enthusiasm." By enthusiasm he means, as the letter makes clear, "a sort of heroism in believing the progressiveness of all nature, during the present melancholy state of Humanity," a "present state of human affairs [that] presses me for days together, so as to deprive me of all my chearfulness."[3]

The "calm hopelessness" he describes in the spring of 1797 also echoes Coleridge's 1795 denunciation of the Treason and Sedition legislation: a passage that recalls Milton's commitment—ironically, and defiantly, on the very eve of the Restoration—to a "Free Commonwealth," and to "the language of that which is not called amiss 'The Good Old Cause,'" even though, he concludes, what he has spoken "should happen . . . to be the last words of our expiring liberty."[4] Deploring the atmospheric smothering of freedom by Pitt's "gagging bills," Coleridge wrote his own epitaph on expiring liberty: "All political controversy is at an end. Those sudden breezes and noisy gusts, which purified the atmosphere they disturbed, are hushed to deathlike silence. The cadaverous tranquillity of despotism will succeed the generous order and graceful indiscretions of freedom—the black moveless pestilential vapour of slavery will be inhaled at every pore" (*L 1795* 289).

This linking of personal and political becalmed hopelessness may seem forced; yet in these same Bristol addresses, Samson, Milton's heroic avenger, is associated by Coleridge with the blind but strong French people, who had pulled down "Those two massy Pillars of Oppression's Temple, the Monarchy and Aristocracy" (*L 1795* 34). Retired from political activity, Coleridge Agonistes refers us, in the spring of 1797, to quite another Samson; and we can imagine the poet who, in "Religious Musings," had celebrated the patriotic "coadjutors of God" implementing "Love's wondrous plan" (lines 364–65), asking, as Milton's Samson does a few lines before those quoted in the letter:

> To what can I be useful? wherein serve
> My nation, and the work from Heaven imposed?

3. *CL* I 558. Shortly afterward, in his "Prefatory Memoir" to *Poems, Chiefly Written in Retirement* (1801), Thelwall, presenting himself as the "disciple of the Muses, not the Lecturer and Leader of Popular Societies now no more," referred to the political activism that had intruded on his literary aspirations as "diseased enthusiasm" (i–ii).

4. From the conclusion of Milton's 1660 pamphlet, ironically entitled *The Readie and Easie Way to Establish a Free Commonwealth*, in *The Works of John Milton* 7:387–88.

> But to sit idle on the household hearth
> A burdenous drone. . . .
>   (lines 564–67)

I am, in short, emphasizing quite another aspect of Milton than that stressed by Coleridge himself twenty-two years after his retirement at Stowey. The author of *Paradise Lost* was, says Coleridge in a lecture of March 4, 1819, "as every truly great poet has ever been, a good man; but finding it impossible to realize his own aspirations, either in religion or politics, or society, he gave up his heart to the living spirit and light within him, and avenged himself on the world by enriching it with this record of his own transcendent ideal."[5]

Such inner light Protestantism, the "paradise within" of Milton's epic, certainly had appeal for Coleridge, and it appeals as well to those who stress the positive imaginative fruit of failed political dreams. Peter Kitson, remarking that Coleridge's lecture on Milton and *Paradise Lost* "tells us a great deal about his own state of mind" in 1797–1798, argues that

> Coleridge had Milton's career very much in mind when writing "The Ancient Mariner." Like himself, the poet of *Paradise Lost* had witnessed the complete wreck of his hopes for a regenerated nation. . . . Although ultimately Coleridge hoped that his own [Miltonic] vengeance would be achieved by proxy in the Wordsworthian epic "The Recluse," "The Ancient Mariner" is an early attempt to enrich the world with a transcendent ideal forged, like *Paradise Lost*, from the wreck of his political aspirations.[6]

As his letters confirm, Coleridge certainly *did* have Milton's career in mind in 1797–1798. But, just as it violates immediate context to read the "one Life" theme back into poems written more than two decades earlier, it is also dangerous to judge the Coleridge of 1797–1798 in the retrospective light of his famous observation, also made two decades later, on Milton and *Paradise Lost*— a theory of interiorizing transcendence that has, incidentally, shaped much subsequent Miltonic interpretation. To do so is to underestimate the complex ambivalence of both Milton *and* Coleridge. This is not the place to rehearse the critical controversy about the extent to which Milton—compassed round by Restoration censorship and the danger of imprisonment, but still singing "with mortal voice unchang'd / To hoarse or mute, though fall'n on evil days" (VII. 24–25)—may have encoded in *Paradise Lost* his defiance in defeat and (beneath overt political disillusionment, Christian resignation, and the pious, "quietist" disclaimers in the final book of his epic) his continuing commitment to "The Good Old Cause."[7] It is worth mentioning that, echoing these lines of *Paradise Lost* ("fallen in evil days on evil tongues, / Milton appealed to the

---

5. "Lecture on Milton and the *Paradise Lost*," March 4, 1819. Lecture X (*Literary Remains* [London, 1836]); quoted in *Coleridge on the Seventeenth Century,* ed. Roberta F. Brinkley, 579.

6. "Coleridge, The French Revolution, and *The Ancient Mariner*," 197–98.

7. For a full discussion, tracing the positions of Milton's early readers, of Coleridge, and of such later Marxian critics as Christopher Hill and Fredric Jameson, see Annabel Patterson's "The Good Old Cause," chapter 7 of *Reading between the Lines,* especially pages 244–52, 256–61, and 270–72.

Avenger, Time"), Byron accurately notes that—unlike later Wordsworth, Coleridge, and that most contemptible apostate and "turncoat," Southey—Milton adhered to his original libertarian principles and did not curry favor with Charles II:

> *He* deigned not to belie his soul in songs,
>   Nor turn his very talent to a crime;
> *He* did not loathe the Sire to laud the Son,
>   But closed the Tyrant-hater he begun.
>   (*Don Juan*, Dedication, X)

The immediate point, and the specific point at which I part from Kitson, is that I am not fully persuaded that *Coleridge's* tyrant-hating appetite for "vengeance" in the form of political activism on behalf of national regeneration was either appeased or totally sublimated during the Stowey retirement, a period when he oscillated between oppositional engagement and quietist withdrawal, between hope, disillusionment, and a vestigial clinging to *his* version of the good old cause. In the January 1800 letter to Tom Wedgwood, still heroically "believing" in the possibility of progress and regeneration even "during the present melancholy state of Humanity," he was writing on the subject, "and no work, on which I ever employed myself, makes me so happy while I am writing" (*CL* I 558). Then, as in 1797–1798, the wreck of Coleridge's political hopes was considerable, but not "complete," perhaps not even beyond recuperation. Not if we are to judge by that "spot of time," the exchange with Thelwall in the glen at Alfoxden; by the revolutionary politics in *Osorio;* and, above all, by Coleridge's reentry into the battle as a political journalist in December 1797—a reentry that became vehement when, in January 1798, Pitt and his government were vulnerable.

That was, to be sure, a brief vulnerability and, consequently, a brief Coleridgean reengagement, one ending—in response not only to the French invasion of Switzerland but to the intensified Pittite repression accompanying the panic over an invasion of the British Isles themselves—in that far more profound withdrawal from politics immortalized in the Recantation ode and "Fears in Solitude." These major poems were written in the spring of 1798. But in the preceding spring, when he quoted *Samson Agonistes* to convey to Cottle the hopeless drooping of his genial spirits, Coleridge was not yet ready to forge any "transcendent ideals" from the wreck of his political hopes. In short, Coleridge in early 1797 was, if not eyeless at Gaza, otiose and impotent at Stowey, his genial spirits—oppressed by the cadaverous silence imposed by Pitt on the "sudden breezes and noisy gusts" of political controversy—drooping every bit as much as the breezeless sails of his Mariner's idle ship.

But at this point, there is, in the poem, a sudden movement of hope. "Surely," as Yeats would later put it, "some revelation is at hand"—though a revelation which, as my allusion to "The Second Coming" is meant to indicate, is soon to be ironically and disastrously reversed:

> I saw a something in the Sky
> No bigger than my fist;
> At first it seem'd a little speck
> And then it seem'd a mist:
> It mov'd and mov'd, and took at last
> A certain shape, I wist.[8]

Earlier, I associated this "speck" with James Thomson's lines in the storm-passage preceding the wreck of the slave ship in *The Seasons*. But the sudden appearance, during a tongue-withering drought, of a sign in the element "No bigger than *my fist*" unmistakably recalls Elijah's "little cloud out of the sea, like a *man's hand*," signaling the end of the drought afflicting Israel: "and it came to pass . . . that the heaven was black with clouds and wind, and there was a great rain" (I Kings 18:44). Though Coleridge's favorites were Isaiah and Ezekiel, Elijah is the most political of the Hebrew prophets, his career, like Coleridge's in the 1790s, remarkable for its oscillating rhythm of commitment and recoil, engagement and fearful or quietistic withdrawal.

Coleridge's awareness of a bond with Elijah, suggested by his own wish put in the mouth of Alhadra, who prays that she, like Elijah, be fed in the wilderness by heaven-sent birds (*Osorio* V.i.49–56), is confirmed by that crucially important letter to his brother of mid-March 1798, in which, having yet again "snapped [his] squeaking baby-trumpet of Sedition," he identifies the French Revolution with the wind, fire, and earthquake experienced by Elijah on Mount Horeb. In the letter, written on or about the day he and the Wordsworths decided to leave England for Germany, Coleridge, harkening to the "still small Voice" heard by Elijah, embraces "subdued & patient" withdrawal. Even here, however, divided Coleridge might be recalling that in the Bible the Lord's command, "still small Voice" notwithstanding, speeds Elijah's return to Palestine to incite a domestic revolution (*CL* I 395, 397; cf. *L 1795* 286).

The allusion to Elijah in Coleridge's presentation of drought and "cloud" (even though the shape in the sky turns out to be neither cloud nor "sail" but the naked-masted spectre-bark) suggests at least the possibility of covert politi-

---

8. *CPW* II 1034 (lines 139–44). In 1979 I suggested a correspondence between these (and the immediately following) lines of *The Ancient Mariner* and the Yeatsian "shape" suddenly "moving" its slow thighs in the desert, only to be revealed as a nightmare no less horrific than Coleridge's ("Revolutions French and Russian: Burke, Wordsworth, and the Genesis of Yeats's 'The Second Coming'"). I drew on a familiar paradigm: the transformation (from auroral to bestial) in the apocalyptic imagery of the politically disenchanted Romantics. In 1990 Greg Kucich traced the motif in the work of a number of writers and painters. He ended his essay "Ironic Apocalypse in Romanticism and the French Revolution" by observing that, finally, "Yeats has presented in our own era what may be considered the appalling culmination of an artistic motif bequeathed by the French Revolution" (85), thus completing his thesis: "The motif of a Second Coming turned unexpectedly and disastrously awry recurs in a wide variety of nineteenth-century artistic contexts, which incorporate the Revolution's own ironic millennial rhetoric to express the dislocated world-view which that spectacular, 'quasi-religious' failure helped to produce" (68).

cal significance both in the stagnant, infested sea endured by the Mariner and his shipmates, and in the sudden note of hope that enters the poem at precisely this point. As it happens, there are lines (part of an earlier poem Coleridge was ransacking in December 1797 for a *political* contribution to the *Morning Post*) that reinforce the political implications of the very situation described in *The Ancient Mariner.* The fragment, which follows directly the lines Coleridge chose to print in the *Post,* tells of "Love," the revolutionary spirit of social justice, rising and fluttering his wings, just as,

> after long and pestful calms
> With slimy shapes and miscreated life
> Poisoning the vast Pacific, the fresh breeze
> Wakens the merchant sail uprising.[9]

This was part of a passage singled out by Coleridge as "very fine," but "hang me, if I know or ever did know the meaning of [certain lines] tho' my own composition" (*CPW* I 140, manuscript note). Coleridge might have been hanged, or at least imprisoned for sedition, had his meaning been any clearer. For in the denouement of the poem, Joan of Arc bursts forth from the "brighter cloud / Returned more bright" (Charles Lamb was the first puzzled as to "what the devil Joan has to do . . . with the French and American revolutions," for these, in reversed order, are what the bright and brighter cloud represent), and, like the python-slaying Apollo Belvedere, lays siege to the "locust-fiends that crawled / And glittered in Corruption's slimy track." This pestiferous and short-reigned corruption sends up its "foulest fogs to meet the morn," but "The Sun that rose on Freedom, rose in Blood!"[10] No wonder Coleridge didn't publish *these* lines in December 1797, lines Thelwall might well cite as evidence of Coleridge's "sanguinary tendency." In any case, we have here, in an earlier poem squirming with revolutionary politics, the same pestilential calm, slimy crawling things, breeze, cloud-like sail, and "bloody Sun" that later find their way into *The Ancient Mariner.*

But a plausible case for the appearance, in transformed shape, of contemporary events in *The Ancient Mariner* stands or falls on the demonstrable presence of a sequence of political developments corresponding both to that sudden hopeful sign in the sky and to the poem's no-less-sudden blasting of that hope. I am not referring, at the moment, to the overarching paradigm of the age, the shattering of the impossibly idealistic expectations the early Romantics invested in the French Revolution. That ironic dialectic would, however, have

---

9. "The Destiny of Nations," lines 283–88 (*CPW* I 140). Lines 127–277 of this poem were published as "The Visions of the Maid of Orleans: A Fragment," which appeared in the *Morning Post* of December 26, 1797.

10. "The Destiny of Nations," lines 430–50 (*CPW* I 146). Lamb's comment (*Letters of Charles and Mary Anne Lamb* 1:102) is useful since, as Carl Woodring notes, it "informs us how a reader of that day would know at once that the two fair clouds following a pestilential vapour . . . represent the American and French Revolutions" (*Politics in the Poetry of Coleridge,* 172).

provided a tragic model for a domestic development related to the Revolution across the channel, and, writ small, taking the same form. For not only did just such a rapid rise and fall of political expectations occur in England; it occurred precisely during the period Coleridge was working on *The Ancient Mariner,* and the temporary improvement in the political atmosphere entered the poem, in my political reading, as that "something in the Sky."

2

In December 1797, a few weeks after Coleridge had begun working on his ballad, a sudden upsurge in popular opposition to Pitt's plan to triple the assessed taxes financing the war against France led some—including Pitt's great adversaries Fox and Sheridan, who abandoned their "secession" to return to Parliament at this critical juncture—to calculate that the move might bring down the government. The icy self-discipline of Pitt actually seemed on the verge of cracking. Seriously ill, taken aback by the double impact on the country of an unpopular war and even more unpopular methods of financing it, hooted at and insulted by a mob he had to be protected from by troops, the prime minister temporarily neglected the official documents, turning for consolation to theology.[11] Apparently, even workaholic Pitt was not utterly immune to the engagement-and-withdrawal pattern so characteristic of the *radicals*—those members of the internal dissension and spreaders of the contagion of ideas whose suppression preoccupied his Ministry almost as much as the threat of invasion and the cost of the war.

As for Coleridge: in the immediately preceding weeks, besides starting *The Ancient Mariner,* he had, for financial reasons (a guinea a week) and with neither personal enthusiasm nor political hope, signed a contract to supply "verses or political Essays" to Daniel Stuart's *Morning Post* (*CL* I 360). The first contributions, as Coleridge later implied in *Biographia Literaria,* were innocuous enough; but in the issue of December 26, we encounter a formidable Joan of Arc. Temporarily transferred from the revolutionary cloud from which she dispersed the slimy crawlers and pestful calms that now found a home in *The Ancient Mariner,* she is scourging—at a time when there was talk of a French invasion—the *English* "Invader." Four days later, in Coleridge's poem "Parliamentary Oscillators," Pitt's allies awake from their "long loyal dozing" with a "start," suddenly realizing that his Triple Assessment Bill had brought them all

---

11. On December 19, on the way to St. Paul's for the celebration of three naval victories, Pitt was jeered and threatened by an angry mob. The scene was dangerous, despite the fact that it has been historically dwarfed by the episode in October 1795 when the king, his coach surrounded by part of an enormous crowd of some 200,000 persons, had to be extricated from his subjects (hissing and roaring, "No war, no Pitt, no King!") after an object (a small stone or a bullet) broke one of the coach windows. At supper a few weeks later, Pitt had calmly remarked, "My head would be off in six months were I to resign." His immediate response to the attack on the king was to begin pushing through Parliament the Two Bills and to set loose in the land those spies and agents provocateurs that so appalled, and threatened, men like Wordsworth and Coleridge.

to the edge of the "precipice." But "Laberius" (Coleridge's pseudonym both here and in the "War Eclogue") mocks these "*quacking* Statesmen": their opposition to the bill is enfeebled because they share the prime minister's "alarms" about the presence of domestic radicals, epitomized as an infernal "imp" on "revolutionary broom-stick scampering" (*CPW* I 211–13).

In spite of the compromised but nevertheless intense opposition to what Coleridge calls in the poem "the ravenous *Bill*," identified in a footnote to "Parliamentary Oscillators" as "Pitt's 'treble assessment at seven millions' which formed part of the budget for 1798" (*CPW* I 212 and *n*), the bill carried. In the early hours of the day it passed, Fox spoke in vain against it (from midnight to 3 A.M. of January 5). "Opposition," Pitt told Lord Mornington on January 26, "added to the odium and disgrace of their secession by returning from it on this occasion."[12] But the fire kindled anew in Coleridge was not so quickly extinguished. In newspaper pieces of January 1798 newly and persuasively attributed to him in *EOT* by David Erdman, Coleridge recaptured the patriotic indignation of his Bristol addresses to the people, particularly the reforming zeal of his lecture against the Two Bills, and of some of the more ardent numbers of *The Watchman*.

The apogee of his—and the *Morning Post*'s—opposition to the government is reached in Coleridge's ferocious "Fire, Famine, and Slaughter: A War Eclogue," which appeared on January 8, three days after passage of the Triple Assessment. Probably written in December 1797 when the Ministry was at the precipice, this spirited poem places an unspecified but unmistakable Pitt ("Letters four do form his name") among his bosom companions, Fire, Famine, and Slaughter; prophesies that the suffering men and women of Ireland and England shall rend him; and finally condemns the miscreant to the flames of Hell, which shall cling to him "everlastingly." Pending that happy denouement promised by Fire, her sisters Famine and Slaughter, those "thankless beldames" for whom Pitt had done "so much," have their own plans. Since "Wisdom comes with lack of food," Famine promises to

> gnaw the multitude,
> Till the cup of rage o'er brim:
> They shall seize him and his brood—.

"They shall," chimes in Slaughter, completing the quatrain, "tear him limb from limb!"[13]

Flanking the dismembered and damned prime minister were three essays—run on January 2, 17, and 20. The first and last have been proven by Erdman, on internal and external evidence, to be Coleridge's; the second is, as he says (*EOT* I 9n), "almost certainly Coleridge's."

The first, Coleridge's inaugural essay in the *Morning Post*, opened by "sin-

12. Quoted in Arthur Aspinall, ed., *The Later Correspondence of George III* 3:4n.
13. *CPW* I 237–40. Though the poem may have been written as early as the *Watchman* period, C. G. Martin argues persuasively for December 1797 ("The Dating of S. T. Coleridge's 'Fire, Famine and Slaughter'").

cerely" wishing that "the opposition to the Assessed Taxes may be as perse-verant and vigorous, as it is wise." Though it will "increase the burthens of the people," the proposed tripling of taxes (on horses, carriages, dogs, male ser-vants, and a variety of house and window duties) will actually "diminish the sum total of the revenue." "Execrable" as these increased taxes appear, "worse and heavier measures" would follow, "UNLESS THERE BE A PEACE," without which, "folly may precipitate our destruction."

Now comes the theme announced in the essay's title ("On Peace. 1: Incom-patible Circumstances"); for there could be no peace while the Pitt govern-ment, committed to victory or a peace that would humble the French, re-mained in power. The French Directory, whose attitude toward England had stiffened since the royalist-purging coup of 18 Fructidor (September 4, 1797), "*will not conclude a Treaty honourable to this Country with the present Ministers.*" The emphasis is Coleridge's, and his proof comes in the form of a rhetorical ques-tion: How can the French be expected to negotiate with such men?—Ministers "who retain their hatred of the present order of things in that Republic," and who are determined, by force of arms and the employment of "English gold" in "exciting and supporting a counter-revolutionary spirit" in La Vendée, to "over-throw . . . the present Government in France." The essay ends on a mixed note of irony and judicious appeal to cost-counting reason: "We will grant, for a moment, that Mr. Pitt and his coadjutors possess all the talent, wisdom, and virtue which have been ascribed to them by their doubtless very *disinterested* advocates; and then entreat every man seriously to ask himself whether or no the People of England may not purchase their continuance in power at too high a price" (*EOT* I 7–10).

The essay of January 20, entitled "Lord Moira's Letter: Reform and Fox," also heartily approves of "the removal of the present Ministers," possibly to be replaced by a new administration headed by Francis Rawdon-Hastings, the Earl of Moira. But Coleridge rejects the arrangement whereby Charles James Fox is to be excluded from the new government. Without the Parliamentary reform cham-pioned by Fox, the three laudable goals of the projected new administration—peace with France, a solution to the financial crisis brought on by an unprece-dented increase in the national debt, and "the establishment of a just and lenient government in Ireland"—could not succeed. The threefold program simply could not be effected "without that radical reform, to the *prevention* of which so great a man was to have been sacrificed."

The bulk of this essay is devoted to the injustices visited upon Ireland, including "the unutterable atrocities which have been perpetrated by part of the English soldiery in Ireland," atrocities inflicted upon the United Irishmen and which had been witnessed and severely criticized by Lord Moira himself. Coleridge might have mixed feelings about the Jacobinical rationalism of the United Irishmen, but "Patriotic indignation is necessary to patriotic energy; and he who would suppress it, because it may hurry us to evil, choaks up the fountain of an hundred virtues, only because he fears that one virtue may overflow its banks." Why is the present Ministry unwilling to end the "organized massacres" in Ireland, to abolish the religious Test Acts,[14] and give "the Irish People a full, fair, and free representation in Parliament"? The answer is "evident." It could hardly grant to the "Sister Kingdom" blessings it continues to deny "at home." Rather than address injustice in both islands, Pitt and his Ministers "still cling to that system of corruption in our elections and legislature, which is the true source of all these evils." Once again, what is required to achieve peace with France, national solvency, and justice for Ireland is precisely that "radical reform" upon which the "salvation" of the country depends, and with which Fox is synonymous (*EOT* I 13–17).

The article of January 17 (*EOT* III 11–12), even more focused on the Irish crisis, takes the form of an ironic contrast between "Ireland and La Vendee," the latter the conservative district of France where Pitt was employing "English gold" in support of counterrevolution. In this essay Coleridge also called, as he had in the "War Eclogue" and as he would on January 20, for peace for a suffering Ireland. This, one must remember, was *the* year of the United Irishmen. Their leader, Wolfe Tone, had persuaded the French to try one massive invasion in December 1796. Though Coleridge, writing in January 1798, could not have anticipated later developments, the enemies of England (including Tone, dressed in a French uniform, armed with French principles, and aboard a French warship) were to try again in the summer and autumn of 1798, supported by a United Irishman rebellion that could have given the French their best opportunity ever for a successful invasion of the British Isles.[15]

Even if we were to take Coleridge's later "Apologetic Preface" to "Fire, Famine, and Slaughter" at face value, these contributions to the *Morning Post* offer, at their mildest, counterevidence to the inclusively retrospective and self-serving picture presented in 1803 to Sir George and Lady Beaumont: "I at Stowey, sick of Politics, & sick of Democrats & Democracy" (*CL* II 1001). Even if Coleridge *was* "out of heart with the French" in December 1796 (*CL* I 268) and "wearied with politics, even to soreness" (*CL* I 338) in the very week of Thel-

---

14. Catholic Emancipation had looked possible until 1795, when Earl Fitzwilliam, a sympathetic Lord Lieutenant of Ireland, was recalled. Fitzwilliam was committed to Burke's dream of Catholic Emancipation, a policy Pitt embraced six years later. It was to be liberality on the religious question, not war and near-bankruptcy, that finally, if temporarily, drove Pitt from power. As Woodring puts it with typical wit and concision: "Pitt resigned in 1801 because he had promised Irish Catholics what George III would go insane rather than grant" (*Politics in the Poetry of Coleridge*, 27).

15. It would prove unsuccessful. Though the December 1796 expedition, pounded by unrelenting storms, had failed to make a landing, Wolfe Tone continued to insist that, given a French invasion in sufficient force, the Irish would rise up against British rule. In 1798, the Irish revolution was defeated by precisely the French failure to send sufficient force. It was also, of course, defeated by a network of spies that had infiltrated the ranks of the United Irishmen, by the failure of a concerted rising to materialize, and by a massive influx of British military force, an army that by late 1798 numbered 140,000 soldiers, far more than ever faced the French on the continent. On the interaction of the United Irishmen and the French, see Marianne Elliott's *Partners in Revolution: United Irishmen and France*.

wall's visit in July 1797, these contributions, "vehemently" anti-Ministerial and Foxite, reveal a still reasonably radical author—a Coleridge who, if neither the self-confessed advocate of "treason" in recessed dells nor the "zealous leveller" Thelwall retrospectively claimed to find at Stowey at that time, was clearly a man reengaged and with plenty of "patriotic indignation" and anti-Pittite "political Furore" unexhaled.

That furor, mixed with religious fire, was evident in a sermon preached to a Unitarian congregation at Shrewsbury in January, at the height of his renewed political activism. It was a performance recalling the many earlier sermons Coleridge himself had described as "*peppered with Politics*" (*CL* I 176). Unlike them, and unlike the political sermon he preached at Christ Church Chapel in Bridgwater on January 7, 1798, this particular homily has been preserved for posterity. Present on the occasion was William Hazlitt, a young man not only spellbound by Coleridge's considerable charm and legendary eloquence, but also attracted to his anti-Ministerial politics. Coleridge's "War Eclogue," for example, was one of young Hazlitt's "favorite pieces," a poem he reprinted twenty years later in his *Political Essays* (1819) by way of reminding the older man and political "apostate" of what his earlier position really *had* been. According to Hazlitt's memorable account in "My First Acquaintance with Poets," the January 1798 sermon "was upon peace and war; upon church and state—not their alliance, but their separation—on the spirit of the world and the spirit of Christianity, not as the same, but as opposed to one another. He talked of those who had 'inscribed the cross of Christ on banners dripping with human gore.'"

We can be sure of Hazlitt's accuracy. This is the young Coleridge who had excoriated the war against France and the military perversion of Christianity in such poems as "Religious Musings" and in the heightened prose of the Bristol lectures; and here he is again, but *this* time during his period of supposed retirement from politics. The fiery candidate for this ministry at Shrewsbury went on, Hazlitt tells us, to make a "poetical and pastoral excursion" that enabled him to draw a "striking contrast" that sounds as if it might have been versified for a Wordsworthian contribution to *Lyrical Ballads*. Coleridge enthralled the congregation with the tale of a simple shepherd boy driving his team afield, only to be kidnapped, brought into town, made drunk at an alehouse, "turned into a wretched drummer-boy," powdered and pomaded, and "tricked out in the loathsome finery of the profession of blood" (Hazlitt, *Works* 17:108).

These public performances in January—the prose pieces in the *Morning Post,* this anti-Ministerial sermon against the war, "Parliamentary Oscillators," and, above all, the remarkable "War Eclogue"—cumulatively demonstrate that his smoldering republicanism, reignited by the same heightened opposition to the war and the reassessment of taxes that had caused Fox and Sheridan to abandon their "secession," also caused Coleridge to interrupt his already hardly halcyon retirement at Stowey. At the very least, calm, especially "hopeless calm," had been stirred up by the sudden change in the political atmosphere.

Meanwhile, Coleridge was also working away at *The Rime of the Ancient Mari-*

ner. Is the change in the political weather somehow registered on the complex barometer of the ballad? Though we mustn't expect, as Woodring notes in his study of politics in Coleridge's symbolic poetry, "perfect correspondence of fabular and historical details,"[16] my implied analogy is clear enough. Just as the moveless, cadaverous tranquillity—the pestful calm and deathlike silence that, for Coleridge, was England under Pitt's "gagging Acts"—corresponds to the rot and slime of the silent sea in which the Mariner and his tongueless ship-mates are becalmed, so this sudden widespread opposition to Pitt, his taxes, his despotism, and "his" war corresponds to the Mariner's hopeful sign in the sky, the "little speck" gradually assuming a "certain shape"—in Coleridge's case, a possible prelude to that "torrent of Democracy" (*EOT* I 21) which, like the French Revolution itself, he contemplated with mingled hope and dread. The January essays in the *Morning Post* indicate that his hopes for radical reform once again temporarily outweighed both his quietist despondency and his fears of revolution.

The hopes centered on the sine qua non both for peace and reform: the fall of Pitt; and Coleridge now saw, however brief the glimpse, a chance for a replication in fact of his fabulous hurling of Pitt into the Pit in the "War Eclogue," that fall over the "precipice" he envisaged in "Parliamentary Oscillators." In a spring 1797 letter earlier quoted (in the context of the difference between Coleridge's and Robinson Crusoe's attitude toward animals), Coleridge expressed his reluctance to bait and set a trap for mice: it is as if one said "'I invite you!' when, oh foul breach of the rites of hospitality! I mean to assassinate my too credulous guests! No, I cannot set a trap, but I should vastly like to make a Pitt-fall" (*CL* I 322). Mice are to be spared by this self-proclaimed brother of cats and owls, the fraternal lover of "Jack Asses," one of whom he notoriously imagined carting off to the Pantisocratic valley of peace and equality (*CL* I 121; *CPW* I 74–76). But the embrace of the "one Life" does not extend to that prime exemplar of "Wolves, Tygers, Generals, Ministers, and Hyaenas": the loathed prime minister, whom our retired gardener would "vastly like" not only to *see,* but to "*make,*" fall. The whimsy anticipates the 1800 "Argument" introducing *The Ancient Mariner,* in particular the new and operative phrase, "how the Ancient Mariner cruelly and in contempt of the laws of hospitality killed a Sea-bird. . . ." (*CPW* I 186*n*). At the same time, the compulsive pun on Pitt's name echoes Coleridge's hopeful prophecy, in the first of his Bristol addresses to the people, that the prime minister has "digged a pit into which he himself may perhaps be doomed to fall" (*L 1795* 10). By the winter of 1797–1798, he may even have believed that Pitt's policies had finally brought the nation, as he had predicted in a pamphlet published on the very eve of the Two Bills' enactment, "to a crisis which may convulse mortally" (*L 1795* 328).

Because of the passage of the Triple Assessment Bill, and of far more momentous developments to be examined shortly, that "convulsion"—a term repeatedly employed, by young Wordsworth as well as Coleridge, to describe

16. *Politics in the Poetry of Coleridge,* 135.

political revolution—did not take place. It may, however, have entered the poem in the transmuted form of the underwater convulsion and whirlpool that sink the Mariner's ship. Before focusing on the dungeon-grate suggested by the rigging of the spectre-bark, we might momentarily jump ahead in the poem to consider the submerged political implications of the mysterious destruction of the Mariner's own terrifying vessel.

3

The ship goes down in the seventh and final part of *The Ancient Mariner*. The skiff containing the Hermit, the pilot, and the pilot's son approaches the Mariner's ship, its planks "warped," its appearance "fiendish":

> The Boat came closer to the Ship,
>   But I ne spake ne stirr'd!
> The Boat came close beneath the Ship,
>   And strait a sound was heard!
>
> Under the water it rumbled on,
>   Still louder and more dread:
> It reach'd the Ship, it split the bay;
>   The Ship went down like lead.
>
> Stunn'd by that loud and dreadful sound,
>   Which sky and ocean smote:
> Like one that had been seven days drown'd
>   My body lay afloat:
> But, swift as dreams, myself I found
>   Within the Pilot's boat.
>
> Upon the whirl, where sank the Ship,
>   The boat spun round and round:
> And all was still, save that the hill
>   Was telling of the sound.[17]

The lines evoke several "political" parallels, among them a passage from Coleridge's greatest political poem, the recantatory ode on France. Discussion might begin, however, with another ode. "Death-fires," submarine explosions, and sinking things appear together publicly for the first time, not in *The Ancient Mariner*, but in Coleridge's most apocalyptic political poem, the "Ode on the Departing Year." In the penultimate stanza, Coleridge prophesies the destruction of his own country, a nation "Abandon'd of Heaven" since, amid its own wealth and insular security, it has "join'd the wild yelling of Famine and Blood" by leading the alliance combined against France. In keeping with his cherished epigraph (a Greek motto from Aeschylus's *Agamemnon*), Coleridge, a reluctant, powerless Cassandra for most of the ode, now emerges as a bard who, however ambivalent, reaches a crescendo of violent prophecy. In the letter (page 18) prefacing the 1796 quarto edition of the ode, his friend Tom Poole is said to

---

17. *The Ancient Mariner*, 1798 edition (lines 575–92). Except for punctuation and the archaic *ne* for *nor*, the passage is identical to the later texts (lines 542–59).

"*know* that although I prophesy curses, I pray fervently for blessings," and Coleridge wrote to the poem's publisher, "may God make me a foreboder of evils never to come" (*CL* I 313). Yet England's fate, destruction, is projected with energy, even zest, in a female image of political apocalypse so violent as to overwhelm any millennial sequel:

> The nations curse thee! They with eager wondering
> Shall hear Destruction, like a vulture, scream!
> Strange-eyed Destruction! who with many a dream
> Of central fires through nether seas up-thundering
>   Soothes her fierce solitude. . . .[18]

This was not the first appearance in Coleridge's poetry of this chiliastic wreaker of submarine vengeance. In manuscript lines originally intended for the apocalyptic peroration of "Religious Musings," "black Ruin" had been depicted

> Nursing th'impatient earthquake, and with dreams
> Of shatter'd cities & the promis'd day
> Of central fires thro' nether seas upthundering
> Sooth[ing] her fierce solitude—[19]

Transported to the "Ode," and no longer explicitly associated—as it was in "Religious Musings" (*CPW* I 121*n*)—with the whirlwind-armed French Revolution, "Destruction" similarly dreams of "central fires through nether seas up-thundering," and envisions Albion's "predestin'd ruins" as the necessary prerequisite to "the promis'd day." In his one specific connection of the imagery of the earlier poems with the imagery of *The Ancient Mariner*, Peter Kitson speculates that "'Strange-eyed Destruction' could be seen as a forerunner of the avenging agencies of the Polar Spirit and the Nightmare Life-in-Death from 'The Ancient Mariner.'"[20] I think he's right, and that the volcanic force "through nether seas up-thundering" may even have something to do with the sudden and violent sinking of the Mariner's ship.

The "Death-fires" dancing on the Mariner's rotting sea (lines 123–26) first trip the light fantastic in this "Ode" as well, as "Mighty armies of the dead" that "Dance, like death-fires" round the tomb of an equally rotten "Tyrant-Murderer," the recently deceased Catherine the Great (lines 141–48, 59–61). Mighty armies and seaquakes are in turn fused in *Osorio*, where, in order to "rouse a fiery whirlwind" in the conscience of his evil brother, Albert conjures up an imagi-

18. *CPW* I 167–68. In a 1992 article distinguishing between "Apocalypse and Millennium," Morton Paley notes that in *Sibylline Leaves*, where this ode is followed by "France: An Ode," Coleridge in effect creates a sequence, "signalling . . . abandonment not only of his former political convictions but also of his apocalyptic interpretation of history and of the millennial hope that had at one time accompanied it" ("Apocalypse and Millennium in the Poetry of Coleridge," 29).

19. British Museum MS. Add. 35343, ff. 65–66. The passage has been cited by Woodring, *Politics in the Poetry of Coleridge*, 179, and Ian Wylie, *Young Coleridge and the Philosophers of Nature*, 64.

20. "Coleridge, the French Revolution, and *The Ancient Mariner*," 201.

nary "whirling pillar" composed of a "mighty army" of dead spirits that creates, in a "becalmed" sea, an oceanic upheaval "whose sudden gulphs / Suck in, perchance, some Lapland wizard's skiff" (*CPW* II 549, 551). Albert's mental whirlwind, it is important to note, is a deliberate prefigurement of Alhadra's: the armed rebellion that physically destroys the tyrant-murderer Osorio, and in turn foreshadows universal revolution.

In fact, Alhadra is given revolutionary imagery ("Great evils ask great passions to redress them, / And whirlwinds fitliest scatter pestilence") earlier borrowed from Hosea by Coleridge for the Bristol lectures (*L 1795* 289) and *The Watchman* (*W* 241–42). Significantly, in *Osorio*, the images of political apocalypse now put in Alhadra's mouth (*CPW* II 528) are freed of cautious qualification. His empathetic identification with Alhadra, the one truly original character in the play, suggests that Coleridge was psychologically if not physically ready for action in late 1797. It is hard to detect much political disengagement in an author who has his "lower-class" Moorish heroine bring down the curtain—the curtain of a play he sent to Pitt's parliamentary enemy, Sheridan, and which he hoped would find a contemporary "popular" audience—by threatening that if she had

> an hundred men,
> Despairing, but not palsied by despair,
> This arm should shake the kingdoms of this world,

and set "earth groaning" beneath the "deep foundations of iniquity," the strongholds, temples, and towers of the aristocratic oppressors of mankind (*CPW* II 596–97). The author of these lines was the "Citizen Samuel" with whom Thelwall conversed in the "beautiful recess" and whom he resurrected twenty years later in the margins of his copy of *Biographia Literaria*.

This apocalyptic imagery of underground and underwater convulsion, like that of the whirling vortex, is obsessive, political, and—especially when the revolutionary cataclysm threatens to drag down the innocent—personal. In the poem from which Coleridge lifted his Joan of Arc fragment for the *Morning Post*, a "blameless fisher" is "absorb'd" in the explosion of a volcano whose

> fragments many and huge
> Astounded ocean with the dreadful dance
> Of whirlpools numberless.
> (*CPW* I 136, variant lines 144–46)

Coleridge's concern extended beyond Lapland wizards and blameless fishers. In December 1801, in the untranquil "Ode to Tranquillity" published in the *Morning Post*, Coleridge pictured himself as having abandoned his radical "bark, and blest the steadfast shore, / Ere yet the tempest rose and scared me with its roar" (*CPW* I 360)—lines anticipating his description of France itself

> vibrating
> Like some becalméd bark beneath the burst
> Of Heaven's immediate thunder.
> (*CPW* I 405)

Still later, in *The Friend* (I 223; II 146–47), he was to say that during the era of the French Revolution, he "did not remain unkindled in the general conflagration." He was "a sharer in the general vortex," though, he adds—insistent as ever on his "insulation" from the pro-French "patriotic" associations (*CL* II 1001)—"my little World described the path of its Revolution in an orbit of its own."

   This persistent image-cluster, to which might be added the fragment-hurling volcanic fountain that at once helps to create and threatens to destroy the pleasure garden of that benevolent despot Kubla Khan (*CPW* I 297), is to be traced to its biblical sources: Coleridge's constant identification of the French Revolution, and other possible eruptions, not only with the fireworks of the Book of Revelation, but with the pestilence-cleansing whirlwind of Hosea and the wind, fire, and earthquake of Elijah. The revolutionary earthquake in "Religious Musings" may have been derived from the Bible via Thomas Burnet or, with more political immediacy, from Joseph Priestley, the "patriot" depicted in that poem as a calm "sage" who, though "retired, / . . . mused expectant on these promised years" (*CPW* I 123). A year before, in early 1794, Priestley, the late eighteenth century's principal philosopher of human perfectibility, had compared events in contemporary Europe with "Ancient Prophecies" he'd garnered from the Bible. The violence of revolution, he noted, contextualizing if not justifying the recent Terror in France, is "frequently represented by *earthquakes*." Principal among those "Ancient Prophecies" is that ubiquitous biblical compendium of violent prophecy, the Book of Revelation, a prominent source, as H. W. Piper has observed, for the rotting-sea imagery of *The Ancient Mariner*—though Coleridge's "rot" and "slimy sea" echo as well the "slimy and other putrescent matter" identified by Priestley as the source of marine luminescence. Together, Revelation and Priestley surely contributed, not only to the specifically revolutionary earthquakes in Coleridge's millennial-apocalyptic poems, but to the underwater convulsion in *The Ancient Mariner*.[21]

   As both Lowes and Ian Wylie have shown, a source for Priestley as well as Coleridge was Thomas Burnet, whose occult speculations about the presence of "more invisible than visible things in the universe" provided the Latin epigraph Coleridge later placed at the head of *The Ancient Mariner*. While he never clarified the precise interrelation of political and natural events, Burnet did, as Wylie notes, "interpret the biblical Apocalypse as a prophecy of revolution in the natural order."[22] Indeed, the earthquake-and-apocalypse connection I've been tracing is powerfully reinforced by the similarity between the "sound"

   21. Piper, "*The Ancient Mariner*: Biblical Allegory, Poetic Symbolism, and Religious Crisis," 234–35. Priestley, Fast-day sermon of February 28, 1794, in *The Present State of Europe compared with Ancient Prophecies* (1794), 6. Priestley's observation on the "luminousness of the sea" arising from the "slimy and other putrescent matter with which it abounds" (576) occurs in "Of Light from Putrescent Substances . . . ," a chapter in his *Vision, Light, and Colours;* cited by John Ower, "The 'Death-Fires,' the 'Fire-Flags,' and the Corposant in *The Rime of the Ancient Mariner*," 203.

   22. *Young Coleridge and the Philosophers of Nature*, 63.

that "rumbled" on "Under the water" in *The Ancient Mariner* and passages from the second volume of Burnet's apocalyptic *Telluris Theoria Sacra* (1689), which, as his notebooks show (*CN* I 61, 174, 191*n*), Coleridge had read in 1796. Along with a "bloudy colour of the Sun," the Last Days were to be attended by

> Earthquakes and extraordinary commotions of the Seas. . . . Next to Earth-
> quakes, we may consider the *roarings of a troubled Sea,* . . . [an] ominous noise
> [which, because it is invisible, strikes] terrour into the inhabitants of the Earth.
> . . . These disturbances of the Sea proceed from below . . . partly by Earth-quakes
> in the very Sea it self; with exhalations and fiery Eruptions from the bottom of it
> . . . which makes it roar, as it were, for pain.[23]

Transported a century ahead to the 1790s, the specifically political character of these apocalyptic images becomes, of course, part of the Romantics' habitual application of biblical imagery to contemporary political events. The phenomenon is not restricted to the (usually, earlier) poems in which the political analogue is most explicit. Though I would lay greater emphasis on the complexity and flux of the transition from radicalism through quietism to reaction, M. H. Abrams has influentially observed that the great Romantic poems were written

> not in the mood of revolutionary exaltation but in the later mood of revolution-
> ary disillusionment or despair. Many of the great poems, however, do not break
> with the formative past, but continue to exhibit, in a transformed but recogniz-
> able fashion, the scope, the poetic voice, the design, the ideas, and the imagery
> developed in the earlier period. . . . Certain terms, images, and quasi-mythical
> agents tend to recur and to assume a specialized reference to revolutionary events
> and expectations: the earthquake and the volcano, the purging fire, the emerging
> sun, the dawn of glad day . . . [24]

Abrams's examples are drawn from Blake, Wordsworth, and Shelley; but the whirlwind, earthquake, and volcano are, if anything, even more obsessive with

23. *Telluris Theoria Sacra,* vol. 2, translated in 1690 as *Theory of the Earth* 2:92–95. The passages are quoted by Wylie (*Young Coleridge and the Philosopers of Nature,* 159, 160), who, perhaps because of his focus on the "young Coleridge," does not mention that later Coleridge adapted his epigraph for *The Ancient Mariner* from Burnet's *Archaeologiae Philosophicae sive Doctrina De Rerum Originibus* (1692).

24. "English Romanticism: The Spirit of the Age" (1963), now available in Abrams's *The Correspondent Breeze: Essays on English Romanticism,* 44–75 (62). For more recent accounts of nature metaphors "representing" the Revolution, see the opening chapter of Ronald Paulson's *Representations of Revolution* and chapters 3, 4, and 6 of Wylie's *Young Coleridge and the Philosophers of Nature.* Political implications are at the heart of Elizabeth Sewell's catalog of Coleridge's vortex images in "Coleridge on Revolution."

For an explication of a later Romantic's use of volcanic imagery, see G. M. Matthews, "A Volcano's Voice in Shelley." Shelley's question about the destructive and creative power manifest in the "frozen floods and unfathomable deeps" of the Mont Blanc glacier—"Is this the scene / Where the old Earthquake-daemon taught her young / Ruin?" ("Mont Blanc," 64, 71–73)—suggests to me a recollection of "Creation's Hag, black Ruin," who "sits / Nursing the impatient earthquake" in Coleridge's "Religious Musings" before she reappears as the dragon "Destruction" brooding over the "volcanic stream" through "nether seas up-thundering" in the "Ode on the Departing Year."

Coleridge. His "up-thundering" draconic Destruction "lies / By livid fount, or red volcanic stream" (*CPW* I 168), and, in the passage in "Religious Musings" in which Ruin first nursed "the impatient earthquake," the French Revolution was described as an empire-uprooting and corruption-purifying "whirlwind" (*CPW* I 121). "The French Revolution was a political eruption," Coleridge tells us in an 1803 *Morning Post* essay, its "lava" consisting of both "revolutionary principles" and "the patriotic enthusiasm of its armies, fighting for liberty and independence, which marked its progress with desolation and terror" (*EOT* I 422). Coleridge reminds his readers that "when the volcanic matter is exhausted, the effects of an eruption are surveyed with wonder and admiration, but cease to be objects of terror and dismay." The volcanic metaphor itself, however, was not so soon exhausted. Six years later, and even more judgmentally, the earthshaking event that had erupted across the English Channel is depicted as "the main outlet and chief crater of the revolutionary torrents" (*F* I 225).

The seismic convulsion in *The Ancient Mariner* seems to me one of Abrams's "transformed but recognizable" images. Certainly, it, like the dungeon-grate scrutinized in the next chapter, is less of a piece with the rest of the imagery in *this* poem than it is with the earlier, explicitly political poems—despite attempts to "fit" the strange sinking of the Mariner's ship into the symbolic pattern of the poem in which it occurs.

In the most notable attempt, Robert Penn Warren unsuccessfully tried to assimilate the undersea rumbling and sinking of the ship to his two-theme schema. As every Coleridgean knows, Warren's "primary theme," taking "the fable . . . at its face value as a story of crime and punishment and reconciliation," is what he calls "the theme of sacramental vision, or the theme of the 'One Life'"; the "secondary theme," concerned with "the context of values in which the fable is presented," is the "theme of the imagination." In his attempt to account for later parts of the poem admittedly not readily intelligible, Warren argues that the work's coherence requires a fusion of these two themes. Faced with "the terrific sound which sinks the Mariner's ship and flings the stunned Mariner into the Pilot's boat," Warren becomes both uneasy and inaccurate (in all versions of the poem, the Mariner's "body lay afloat" before "myself I found / Within the Pilot's boat"):

> In the logic of the symbolic structure this would be, I presume, a repetition of the wind or storm motif: the creative storm has a part in re-establishing the Mariner's relation to other men. Even if the destruction of the ship is regarded, as some readers regard it, as a final act of the Polar Spirit, to show, as it were, what he could do if he had a mind to, the symbolic import is not altered, for the Spirit belongs to the cluster of imagination, which has the terrifying and cataclysmic as well as benign aspect.

He then shifts ground, still enlisting the strange event in the "cluster of imagination," but arguing that the ship is sunk by the agency, not of the Polar Spirit, but of "the angelic troop." At the level of "the primary theme," the angels "wipe out the crime (i.e., the 'criminal' ship and the dead bodies); at the level of the secondary theme, they do so by means of the 'storm' which belongs to the symbolic cluster of the imagination."[25]

As Humphry House remarks, Warren "skates over" this whole episode "rather hastily," and, in the final attempt to accommodate both his themes, abandons the "coherent symbolism" of his system altogether, falling back on

> simple interpretation of the narrative in the light of decisions already made; for the clusters of symbols established earlier have borne some intelligible relation (either traditionally or in Coleridge's habitual associations) to what they symbolize: the creative wind is traditionally intelligible, and the moon and half-lights have special associations for Coleridge. But the method of the ship's destruction does not conform to the "logic" of such symbolism as this; and Warren's use of "I presume" points to his uneasiness about it. A submarine rumbling followed by a violent explosion is in a different key; it has a different sort of effect on the reader from that of the other items which Warren groups together as associated with the Imagination.[26]

The "effect" is different because the "key" seems less purely imaginative than political, a point House, who rules out politics in the poem, fails to make—though his reference to "Coleridge's habitual associations" might have led him to rethink that conclusion. The submerged currents connecting earthquakes, underwater volcanoes, revolutionary "fires through nether seas upthundering," whirlpools that suck in skiffs, and the sky- and ocean-smiting disturbance that sinks the "warp'd" and "fiendish" ship of the Mariner in a "whirl" upon which the Pilot's boat "spun round and round"[27] may be revealed in the lines in which the Mariner's ship sinks into the sea, as the albatross had, "like lead." To repeat the stanza describing the mysterious but thunderous and all-encompassing sonic sinking of the ship:

> Under the water it rumbled on,
>   Still louder and more dread:
> It reach'd the Ship, it split the bay;
>   The Ship went down like lead.

Earlier, the albatross the crew had hung about the Mariner's neck had, following his prayer, fallen off and sunk "Like lead into the sea" (lines 280–83). The only remaining physical evidence, the ship is also part of the evil past, its very planks drought-warped and tainted by the original crime, the Mariner's killing of the albatross. That innocent creature, which may have something to do with the victims of slavery, is also "the Bird / That made the *Breeze* to blow" (lines 91–92, italics added). If, as seems likely, the albatross is symbolic not only of Christian love and the creative imagination but also of the spirit of Liberty, we may detect in its murderer both a guilty Coleridge (who, in "retirement," may have seen himself as defaulting in his commitment to that political ideal)

25. "A Poem of Pure Imagination: An Experiment in Reading," 100.
26. *Coleridge*, 109–110.
27. Lines 562, 571, 589–90. Cf. line 66: "And round and round it [the Albatross] flew."

and its public assassin, the Pitt Ministry, which had hushed to "*deathlike* silence
. . . those sudden *breezes*" of freedom (*L 1795* 289). Whether interpreted soci-
etally or personally, the Mariner is criminal—and so is his ship, which "has a
fiendish look." Its destruction—whether the work of the Polar Spirit, the an-
gelic troop, or the Lord knows what—is a Gothic rather than a political finale;
and yet the *details* of its sinking have resonances of an unmistakably political
nature: enough to suggest at least some analogy with the allegorical Ship of
State Pitt was so frequently depicted as steering in cartoons of the period.

Though I am not claiming any conscious identification of the Mariner's
guilty ship with that piloted by Pitt, it would not be an impossibility. There is, I
think, a contemporary instance of such allegorizing on Coleridge's part. In
"The Raven," a cryptic political parable published in the *Morning Post* on
March 10, 1798 (perhaps the very day of the quietistic letter to his brother
George as well as the day Coleridge and the Wordsworths decided to go to
Germany), an avenging raven flies "round and round" a sinking ship made of
branches "sever[ed]" and "strip[ped]" from an oak in which the bird had
nested his family, now destroyed. The oak suggests the Liberty Tree an "arbi-
trary government" had "stripped of its boughs" (*L 1795* 61–62); the ship, in
turn, suggests the British Ship of State under that arbitrary government. Per-
haps, through the raven, no longer a bird sent from heaven to feed those who
have retreated into the political wilderness, Coleridge was vicariously enjoying
an event he had been hoping for since at least 1794: the downfall of the Pitt
Ministry. Such a reading would add a political to the personal dimension of the
raven's (and the poet's) glee—"They had taken his all, and REVENGE IT WAS
SWEET!"—when the ship strikes a rock and sinks, "injustice capsized."[28] The
fact that Coleridge later went out of his way to divorce himself from this un-
Christian relishing of vengeance reinforces suspicion that the British Ship of
State figures in the fable. That, in turn, would make the later retraction part of
the characteristic Coleridgean recoil from his anti-Ministerial position of 1794–
1798—or so, at least, I shall later suggest.

The sinking of a vessel in *any* way analogous to the British Ship of State
under Pitt would be, for Coleridge, both a consummation devoutly to be wished
and a national convulsion to be dreaded; he hoped, employing his characteris-
tic metaphors at the end of his first Bristol address, that "wisdom" might either
"heave" the "rocks" of the status quo from "their base," or, better yet, "might
produce the desired effect without the convulsion" (*L 1795* 48). In displaced
form, that anticipated yet dreaded violence enters *The Ancient Mariner.* That the
Mariner's ship goes down amid a submarine *rumbling* growing louder and more
dreadful is particularly significant, for this is the single occurrence in all of
Coleridge's poetry of a word (in any of its forms) that in his political prose is
part of the prolegomena to revolution. "Revolutions are sudden to the unthink-

---

28. *CPW* I 169–71. The last two words are Woodring's (*Politics in the Poetry of Coleridge*,
134), though his remarks on the poem tally with mine only in their insistence on the
"political immediacy" of "The Raven."

ing only," declared Coleridge in the Bristol address from which I have just quoted: "Strange Rumblings and confused Noises still precede these earthquakes and hurricanes of the moral World. The process of Revolution in France has been dreadful, and should incite us to examine with an anxious eye the motives and manners of those, whose conduct and opinions seem calculated to forward a similar event in our own country" (*L 1795* 36–37).

The next lines of the poem describe the Mariner as "stunn'd by that loud and *dreadful* sound, / Which *sky and ocean smote.*" Like *rumbled,* the final verb and its objects have (in this instance, virtually unmistakable) revolutionary reverberations. The second stanza of the Recantation ode, written (despite his dating of the poem "February") in late March 1798 when Coleridge was putting the finishing touches on *The Ancient Mariner,* opens:

> When France in wrath her giant limbs upreared,
> > And with that oath, which *smote air, earth, and sea,*
> > Stamped her strong feet and said she would be free,
> Bear witness for me, how I hoped and feared.
>
> > > > (*CPW* I 245)

Giantess France's declaration of freedom, though made manifest in the Tennis Court Oath, remains doubly conditional (she "*said* she *would* be free"), a qualification powerfully reinforced, as Morton Paley notes, by the crucial fact that "'*smote*' directs aggression towards 'earth, sea, and air,' which have already been declared the proper abodes of Liberty."[29] Even before the recantation proper (in stanza IV of the ode, introducing the "storms" of the Terror), Coleridge suggests that he had less hope than fear. The violence of revolutionary France, though itself a prodigious force of nature, is paradoxically directed *against* nature. The smiting "oath" is destined to degenerate into Jacobin "Blasphemy," and "The *name* / Of Freedom" (ironically graven on France's self-forged chains) will be revealed as a betrayal of the spirit of genuine "Liberty."

In *The Ancient Mariner,* the "loud and dreadful sound / Which sky and ocean smote" assumes a displaced form worthy of Coleridge's ambivalence about the principal event of his age. The Mariner's ship, the site of the poem's murderous crime, is eventually overwhelmed and destroyed by the natural forces that had been violated in the killing of the albatross. The historical referent may be the Revolution itself, or Coleridge's own radical "bark" (*CPW* I 360), this time lost in the whelming tide. But *some* readers of the Recantation ode, the "Ode on the Departing Year," "The Raven," and the Coleridgean fable of the Mad Ox, may join me in associating the Mariner's ship with the *counter*revolutionary Ship of State steered by a prime minister who set his nation against that force of nature, the French Revolution, in the process goading his foe to intensified

---

29. "Apocalypse and Millennium," 30 (quoting the final stanza, where the elements are reordered). Paley does not extend his point about *smote* to the verbally similar passage in *The Ancient Mariner.* On the ode's "central term, 'Liberty,'" see also Angela Esterhammer, "Speech Acts and Living Words: On Performative Language in Coleridge's Poems of 1798," 80–81.

violence and stifling freedom at home. Here, in a form disguised perhaps even from himself, Coleridge's revolutionary wrath, in a subaquatic return of the repressed, wreaks vengeance on the guilty.[30]

But the situation in the poem cannot be reduced to simple political allegory. For one thing, Coleridge's protagonist *is* the albatross-killer, the guilty party. Further, like that divided "patriot" Coleridge himself, he is aboard the doomed ship: a man who barely survives being drawn into the vortex, and who suffers the lifelong sentence of reenacting his "crime" and "penance." Though, again, no perfect correspondence is to be expected between the life and the work, the poem's fable and the history of the period, I would suggest that, on the political and biographical level, there are one or more plausible referents for this crime and repentance.

There is, to begin with, the sole "political" reading of the killing of the albatross, that proposed in 1989 by Robert Maniquis. The violence that initiates the central action of *The Ancient Mariner*—what he calls the "cosmically tiny, but ontologically giant act of killing the albatross"—seems to Maniquis, especially given the conferral of interpretive meaning that occurs when his crewmates become "accomplices," related to the French Terror. "The different orders of

30. There may be an illuminating contrast to the violent sinking of the Mariner's ship in *The Wine-Dark Sea* (1993), the sixteenth and most recent novel in Patrick O'Brian's justly celebrated epic series about two British seamen in the Napoleonic wars.

One of them, Stephen Maturin, ship's surgeon and presently intelligence agent for His Majesty's government, had been a medical student in Paris in 1789, "running about the streets . . . in the headiest state of happy excitement that could be imagined, or rather exaltation, in the dawn of the Revolution, when every disinterested, generous idea of freedom seemed on the point of realization, the dawn of an infinitely finer age." But "the confident system of his youth—universal reform, universal changes, universal happiness and freedom—had ended in something very like universal tyranny and oppression."

By the time he records his shifting response to the Age of Revolution, circa 1812, Dr. Maturin has long since sobered up from his youthful intoxication. If his disenchantment with the French Revolution parallels that of a generation of initially optimistic Britons (the generation of Wordsworth and Coleridge), Maturin's mature rejection of politics of the "Utopian pantisocratic kind" seems explicitly Coleridgean (Stephen is also a former opium-eater, addicted to laudanum).

But—precisely because their disillusionment *had* been preceded by "enthusiasm" and never entailed renunciation of "universal benevolence"—neither Wordsworth nor Coleridge would have endorsed the characteristically blunt dismissal expressed by veteran Royal Navy captain Jack Aubrey, the professional man of war in O'Brian's Aubrey/Maturin series: "Enthusiasm, democracy, universal benevolence—a pretty state of affairs," a utopianism beneath which lurked "wild, bloody, regicide revolutionary ideas," which a Burkean Jack associates with "Tom Paine and Charles Fox."

Though their frigate is—like the ship of Coleridge's guilty Mariner—rocked by a spectacular underwater volcanic eruption at the outset of *The Wine-Dark Sea*, the *Surprise*, manned by seamen guiltlessly conducting war for prize-money and against tyrannical Napoleon, does *not* sink. In terms of our "submerged" or submarine symbolism, one might say that Jack and Stephen are—*un*like the divided Coleridge of 1797–1798—beyond seduction, though not potential destruction, by the ambiguous energies originally unleashed by that force of nature, the French Revolution (*The Wine-Dark Sea*, 56, 63, 81, 170).

violence—massive violence of the French Revolution and the killing of a seabird—do not make this poem any less a poem of the revolutionary 1790s, when the interpretation of violence was a dominant political and psychological topic." While, for Maniquis as for me, *The Ancient Mariner* is no simple allegory of political violence, the poem may, as he says, "poetically concentrate the pervasive question of intellectual complicity in European reactions to the Terror."[31]

There are, I would suggest, at least three forms of political complicity or guilt that may find their transfigured way into the poem. The first has to do with what E. P. Thompson calls Coleridge's (and Wordsworth's) "default": their failure to persevere, whatever the terror and bloodshed in France, in their original commitment to egalitarian *liberté*. Wordsworth's famous complaint (in the preface to the 1800 edition of *Lyrical Ballads*) that Coleridge's Mariner "does not act, but is continually acted upon," may have something to do with that "liberal guilt"—"the guilt of feeling one should do, or should have done, something, but being unable to"—which, Kenneth Johnston has recently observed, was "very much Wordsworth's and Coleridge's as they contemplated their slender poetical and political hopes in the dreary climate of early 1798." He is thinking especially of February, when "news of Napoleon's invasion of Switzerland began to reach England"—the same February in which Wordsworth, in "The Ruined Cottage," and Coleridge, in *The Ancient Mariner,* were struggling to reconcile their narrators' "guilt feelings" in a final poetic if not political tranquillity.[32]

A related but distinguishable form of guilt would be particularly relevant to Coleridge—who, unlike the relatively nonactivist Wordsworth, had delivered political lectures until the passage of the Two Bills, had edited a political journal in 1796, and had just reentered the fray by writing anti-Pittite articles for the *Morning Post*. I refer to the possible guilt stemming from his fearful retreat from his commitment to liberty in the face of domestic repression, which became particularly ferocious following the invasion of Switzerland and the sensational discovery, on the final day of February 1798, of the proof of domestic treason Pitt had long been seeking (discussed in the next chapter).

Finally, and this would be quite another form of "liberal guilt," one no less relevant to Wordsworth (who in 1792 actually endorsed the idea of a French invasion of England), there is Coleridge's sense of collusionary guilt about having betrayed, in the earlier stages of his Gallic enthusiasm, the *genuine* "Liberty" celebrated both at the conclusion of the ascent of Mount Snowden in *The Prelude* and in the peroration of the Recantation ode.[33] His original com-

---

31. "Holy Savagery and Wild Justice," 390, 391.

32. "Wordsworth's Revolutions, 1793–1798," 196.

33. "Oh, who is he that hath his whole life long / Preserved, enlarged, this freedom in himself?— / For this alone is genuine liberty" (*Prelude* XIII.120–22 [1805]; XIV.130–32 [1850]). With the telescoped compression characteristic of his historical readings, Alan Liu (*Wordsworth,* 446) in effect locates this "genuine liberty" to the political right of Coleridge's "Liberty" at the end of the Recantation ode, identifying "the aesthetics of closure constructed at Snowden" as "one with Wordsworth's politics of patriotism. It was the volunteerism of his Mind." (Wordsworth did in fact join the Volunteers in 1803.)

mitment to France, despite Coleridge's later acts of distancing and "baby-trumpet" trivializing, was deeper than he usually admits. Even in the Recantation ode (written in the aftermath of both the French invasion of Switzerland and Pitt's arrest of British traitors at the end of February), in which he acknowledges his early allegiance to the French cause, his revolutionary commitment is reduced to private "dreams" and to things he "hop'd," "fear'd," and "sung." As Paley has recently remarked in "Apocalypse and Millenium," a "sensitive reader" of this ode "might well be expected to wonder why a poet who had [done no more than this] should feel so guilty." And even that guilt is purged in an act of total depoliticalization. In this poem, the poem with which I began these speculations, Coleridge records his powerful response to the mighty French oath that "smote air, earth, and sea" before precisely those smitten and violated elements, gathered together in the reconciliatory and "quietist" conclusion of the ode, were recruited in the service of a natural, spiritual, and individual Liberty far removed from any and all governments.

It is in late 1797 and, especially, early 1798—when international and domestic events were reaching their related crisis points and *The Ancient Mariner* was being written—that all these verbal associations coalesce. To gather them up: Like his Mariner, Coleridge had been stunned by a sky- and ocean-smiting explosion (in his case, reverberating across the English Channel); he too had

---

That move to the right is detectable in a specifically political context in Book X of the 1805 *Prelude*. When, echoing *Macbeth* (II.ii.32–28) in the crucial passage about the September Massacres, Wordsworth says, "I seemed to hear a voice that cried / To the whole city, 'Sleep no more!'" (*Prelude* X.82–84), he may be accepting Macbethian guilt by verbal association. Jonathan Wordsworth notes that, whatever Wordsworth's actual feelings when he was in France in 1792, by 1804, when this passage was written, "the language and its echoes are telling us loudly of the poet's sense of betrayal, and of his collusion in the violence that has taken place. In giving his heart to the people (country people chiefly, one suspects), he has become a party to murders committed by the Paris sanscullottes." In 1804, "Wordsworth associates his early commitment to the Revolution with murder, guilt and collusion." How important is the echo of *Macbeth* and how likely is it that it reflects "the poet's original feelings?" "We have no evidence outside *The Prelude,* but I think myself they probably do" ("Wordsworth's 'Dim and Perilous Way,'" 210, 215, 216). But who knows?

Also relevant here is Marjean D. Purinton's recent discussion of *The Borderers*. As she persuasively argues, the dramatic debate between Oswald and Marmaduke "echoes the justifications of factual revolutionaries who term 'murder' a necessary political expedient to a greater freedom"—a position initially taken in the pamphlets responding to Burke by (among others) Paine and Mary Wollstonecraft, as well as by Wordsworth in his *Llandoff* letter of 1793. But her essay does not endorse the idea that apocalypse is the necessary prerequisite to the millennium. Finally, Wollstonecraft, Paine, and Wordsworth agree that "mental and moral revolutions are the only ways to break the vicious cycle of tyranny that Oswald's and Marmaduke's reasoning perpetuates." This would be a truly "radical . . . revolution in human imagination," which, while it implies no "conservative endorsement of the status quo," "radically questions the mental structures that prompt the revolution-restoration cycle" ("Wordsworth's *The Borderers* and the Ideology of Revolution," 105, 106).

experienced a rumbling "Still louder and more dread" ("the process of Revolution in France has been dreadful"); and he *had* borne witness in a mixture of hope and fear, having "examined with an anxious eye the motives" of the most articulate and courageous of those working to forward "a similar event in our own country": our old friend, the "dreadless" John Thelwall.

4

Coleridge's relations with Thelwall following the Patriot's famous visit to Stowey and Alfoxden in July 1797 tell us a great deal about the period immediately preceding the composition of *The Ancient Mariner,* and about Coleridge's hopes and fears at the time. In the late summer and autumn of 1797, his eye was "anxious" in both an anticipatory and a cautious sense, for Coleridge, even at his most ardent, feared the "outrageous mass" ("Religious Musings," line 246) as much as he hated the Pitt government. Though he could tease his famous guest in July 1797 with suggestions that their quiet recess offered "a fine place to talk treason in," Coleridge had more prudential disagreements with the Patriot "on almost every point of religion, of morals, of politics, and of philosophy." But not only did he and Thelwall "like each other uncommonly well"; Coleridge had also concluded that this "very warm hearted honest man" was "the only *acting* Democrat that *is* honest," and in July and August of 1797 was hoping to discipline him in "patience" and "calculating spirit" just in case he did "forward," or emerge to leadership from, a "similar event in our own country" (*CL* I 339–42).

This tutelage of Thelwall would have been a practical application of Coleridge's guiding axiom from the Bristol lectures on, that "general Illumination should precede Revolution" (*L 1795* 43). Considering his emphasis in "Religious Musings" on the need for "eloquent men" with "patient eye serene" to monitor and shape the suffering masses in the event of revolutionary chaos (*CPW* I 118), his insistence on the need for reformers who were "thinking and disinterested Patriots" rather than popular demagogues whose direct incitement of suffering people might drive them to the bloody excesses witnessed in France (*L 1795* 37–40), and his borrowing of Mark Akenside's imperative, "To calm and guide / The swelling democratic tide," as an epigraph for the first of his 1795 *Moral and Political Lectures,*[34] this harping on Thelwall's need for "patience" and propriety (*CL* I 285, 341–42) might be expected. But was it warranted?

34. Lines 171–72 of Akenside's *Ode to the Right Honourable Francis Earl of Huntingdon* (1747). Akenside's immediately following references to a "servile Band" and a peace-wounding "Monster" are, I would agree with Harriet Devine Jump, adapted by Coleridge to those hostile to freedom in the 1790s, especially the monster, Pitt. For a thoughtful discussion of the "ingenuity" of this adaptation, see her "High Sentiments of Liberty: Coleridge's Unacknowledged Debt to Akenside," 211–12. Her hunch about "servile band" seems confirmed by Coleridge's use of "slavish band" in line 27 of the Recantation ode, a phrase that mightily annoyed such conservatives as the indignant critic who reviewed the poem in a Tory periodical in 1799: "We should like to know *where this slavish band existed.* There are none of that description in this country" (*British Critic* 13 [1799], 663; quoted in Donald H. Reiman, ed., *Romantics Reviewed* Part A, *The Lake Poets* 1:127).

It is true that Thelwall was not always judicious; he seems to have relished his notoriety, and was capable of self-dramatization and of gestures like the regicidal "beheading" of the foam on his pot of ale. However, as more than the exchange in Holford Glen reveals, Coleridge was as guilty as Thelwall on some of these counts. Furthermore, like Coleridge, Thelwall advocated reform, not violent revolution or genuine "treason." "There must be something in the constitution of this country," he wrote in *The Times* (December 6, 1794), "which a Briton will ever love and venerate." Like other contemporary radicals, Thelwall berated and petitioned Parliament, though always retaining (as most clubbists did) "a gut belief in the fundamental worth of the institution even as they called for its thoroughgoing reform."[35] Thelwall's title for a 1795 pamphlet is instructive: *Peaceful Discussion, and not Tumultuary Violence the Means of Redressing National Grievances.*

In this context, it is instructive to recall both Coleridge's and Thelwall's later characterizations of the similarities and differences between them; and it is not only instructive but amusing to read a *contemporary* comparison by Thelwall. In a letter written in March 1798, an exceedingly dangerous month for radicals in England, the Patriot wonders whether Coleridge has accepted or declined the offer of the Unitarian ministry at Shrewsbury. He didn't know that Coleridge had, the very morning after Hazlitt heard his sermon at Shrewsbury, turned down the post to accept the Wedgwood annuity, an enormously generous offer of £150 a year for life with no strings attached. But writing from his own enforced retreat in Wales, and sounding as if he had been sitting beside Hazlitt in the Unitarian chapel that morning, Thelwall hopes his friend "did not" accept the position: "I know he cannot preach very often without travelling from the pulpit to the Tower. Mount him but upon his darling hobby-horse, 'the republic of God's own making,' and away he goes like hey-go-mad, spattering and splashing through thick and thin and scattering more levelling sedition and constructive treason than poor Gilly [Gilbert Wakefield] or myself ever dreamed of."[36]

Nevertheless, seven months earlier, it was Coleridge who thought Thelwall, like the other English Jacobins, in need of lessons in prudence as part of his political reeducation. On August 20, 1797, he wrote a long and revealing letter to John Chubb, a friend who was also a former mayor and presently a leading merchant in Bridgwater. "I write to you on the subject of Thelwall," he began his plea to secure the Patriot a house in the area. His argument was a prudential one: if revolution should come, Thelwall, a man of undoubted talent, "activity & courage," would emerge as a leader, even if he was, like Coleridge himself, currently in the epicycle of retirement. Thus Coleridge was exerting himself mightily to obtain for Thelwall a cottage "*anywhere* 5 or 6 miles round

35. Colley, *Britons,* 336–37.

36. Quoted in Lawrence Hanson, *The Life of S. T. Coleridge: The Early Years,* 253. For a sympathetic portrait of Gilbert Wakefield, see Thompson, "Disenchantment or Default?" 164–67.

Stowey," arguing that, whatever the "odium & inconvenience," a duty to "Truth & Liberty" compelled him to try to settle his friend in the Quantocks, where he would find "the society of men equal to himself in talents, & probably superior in acquired knowledge," men who, like himself, Wordsworth, and Poole,

> differ from each other very widely in many very important opinions, yet unite[d] in the one great duty of unbounded *tolerance.*—If the day of darkness & tempest should come, it is most probable, that the influence of T. would be very great on the lower classes—it may therefore prove of no mean utility to the cause of Truth & Humanity, that he had spent some years in a society, where his natural impetuosity had been disciplined into patience, and salutary skepticism, and the slow energies of a *calculating* spirit.—(*CL* I 342)

Here is the complete Coleridge, dialectical, serpentine. Though a tactful approach was called for in writing to a friend who was also a person of importance in the area, and though Coleridge tended on occasion to tell correspondents what he thought they wanted to hear, this letter cannot be treated as a merely politic epistle. For one thing, Chubb was not only fond of Coleridge; he was also a man whose political views were extremely liberal. In the letter Coleridge is not, in short, sugarcoating his motives with a conservative argument meant to appeal to a stuffy merchant. On the contrary, he is being consistent, advocating, as he had in "Religious Musings" and the Bristol addresses, a program of political enlightenment intended neither to promote nor quite to prevent revolution, but to guide and control it if and when it should come—in this case, by befriending and disciplining the man accurately judged "superior to any other patriot," and therefore the likeliest potential leader in the event of a popular uprising against the Pitt government.[37]

"Here," as Richard Holmes remarks, "it is possible to feel that Coleridge was hedging his political bets."[38] It is also possible to feel, again, that in July–August 1797, a retributive revolution was more on Coleridge's mind than Thelwall's. What is certain is that only eighty-four days before he began *The Ancient Mariner,* the "retired" Coleridge was planning to take under his wing the most impressive of the English Jacobins, to influence him so as to make him the best possible leader if and when "the day of darkness & tempest" came to England—a day that inspired Coleridge with fewer hopes than fears, but which he was by no means ruling out.

Though, as we have seen, Thelwall was in almost full retreat from active politics, opinion in the neighborhood made the plan of moving so notorious a man to Stowey impossible. Tom Poole's introduction of Coleridge into the area

---

37. "Religious Musings" anticipates both this letter and Coleridge's later theory of the need for a "clerisy" (an elite of culture guardians and civilizing instructors of the rude populace). In lines 239–48 of "Religious Musings," we hear of "eloquent men," stung with pity by the sufferings of the oppressed, who "hush'd awhile with patient eye serene, / Shall watch the mad careering of the storm; / Then o'er the wild and wavy chaos rush / And tame the outrageous mass, with plastic might / Moulding Confusion" to the "perfect forms" they have seen in "bright visions" (*CPW* I 118).

38. *Coleridge: Early Visions,* 159.

had been bad enough; then came that suspicious "Frenchman," Wordsworth, also settled in under Poole's auspices. Thelwall would have been the last straw. The liberal Unitarian minister in Bridgwater, John Howell, to whom Coleridge first appealed on Thelwall's behalf, was powerless, and John Chubb, who had clout—he was not merely "liberal" but a close friend of Pitt's great parliamentary enemy, Charles James Fox—declined to help his friend Coleridge install the potential revolutionary leader in quarters near Stowey.

Writing to the Patriot at Swansea, Wales, on August 21, Coleridge spoke of Wordsworth's subletting of the house at Alfoxden, and of the worse calamities to be expected if Thelwall were to presently join their community:

> You cannot conceive the tumult, calumnies, & apparatus of threatened persecutions which this event has occasioned round about us. If *you* too should come, I am afraid, that even riots & dangerous riots might be the consequence . . .
> ["]what can it be less than plot & damned conspiracy—a school for the propagation of demagogy & atheism?["]. . . . When the *monstrosity* of the thing is gone off, & the people shall have begun to consider you, as a man whose mouth won't eat them—& whose pocket is better adapted for a bundle of sonnets than the transportation or ambush-place of a French army—then you may take a *house*—but indeed—I say it with a very sad, but a very clear conviction—at *present* I see that much evil & little good would result from your settling here. (*CL* I 343–44)

Coleridge was not being falsely alarmist, as one of the major historians of the period originally speculated.[39] In the event, the "monstrosity" of having England's most public Jacobin in the neighborhood did not evaporate, and Wordsworth's apparent offer to share the Alfoxden mansion with Thelwall and his wife merely increased *his* notoriety. In the end, no house could be found for Thelwall to rest his head. By September, the proscribed man had retreated all the way to a farmhouse in Llyswn, where Coleridge visited him on a "dart into Wales" (*CL* I 414) just prior to his departure to Germany with William and Dorothy Wordsworth. Coleridge had taken the Wordsworths with him to Wales, not without poetic result. "Liswyn farm" shows up in "Anecdote for Fathers," where the farmhouse, unlike that at "Kilve," has a "weathercock," still "glittering bright." It has also been suggested that some of the landscape surrounding Thelwall's farm appears in "Tintern Abbey." Some political thoughts supposedly evaded in "Tintern Abbey," and "withheld" in the "Anecdote"—thoughts about

39. The historian was E. P. Thompson. Five years later, he wrote, with wit and honesty: "I notice that the author of a recent book, *The Making of the English Working Class,* tends to sneer [page 164] at the sincerity of Coleridge's professions at this point. If he had speculated less, and carried his research a little further, he would have been of a different opinion. Coleridge was sincere. Those riots could have happened" ("Disenchantment or Default?" 162). Coleridge's letter to Thelwall was sent only one day after the plea to Chubb; but given the short distance to Bridgwater (only eight miles), he may have hand-delivered his letter or relied on the frequent mails. Chubb would have had time to respond—negatively—within twenty-four hours. On the mails, and on Chubb's having "the sense to decline helping Coleridge," see Berta Lawrence, *Wordsworth and Coleridge in Somerset* (32–33, 94), and her "John Chubb, a Friend of Coleridge."

the "five long years" between 1793 and 1798—may have been stirred by the visit to Thelwall, whose ideologically upright weather vane had survived the protest-silencing reactionary storms, to remain what Coleridge's Mariner calls a silent but "steady weathercock."[40]

But that visit took place in the late summer of 1798, an extraordinarily eventful year after Thelwall's visit to Alfoxden and Stowey: a year that saw virtually everyone who had opposed Pitt or the war with France in full retreat, their patriotism *British* now, in response to events both international and do-mestic. Back at Stowey a year earlier, in August of 1797, Coleridge had been awaiting, with mingled calculation and trepidation, the "darkness & tempest" that would accompany the "day" of domestic revolution. Shortly afterward, in the winter of 1797–1798, he had his ear even closer to the ground, monitoring the strange rumblings and confused noises that precede just such a day.

Whether or not, in those "five long years" between 1793 and 1798, revolution was feasible in England has been sharply, brilliantly, and inconclusively debated by historians. What is *not* hypothetical is that popular alienation and discontent ran deep and that—until the threat of a full-scale French invasion in the spring of 1798 created nationwide alarm and an upsurge of patriotism—the British government often feared its own people as much as the foreign enemy. In the winter of 1797–1798, that government was at its most vulnerable. His *Morning Post* contributions at this pivotal juncture suggest that Coleridge was once again ready for reformist action, perhaps prepared, if the Pitt government *did* fall, to work behind the scenes "To calm and guide / The swelling democratic tide." Firmly if temporarily remounted on what Thelwall reminds us was his friend's "darling hobby-horse, 'the republic of God's own making,'" Coleridge may have been anticipating not only the "storm or earthquake of national discord" (*F* I 218), but "that far deeper and more permanent revolution in the Moral World of which the recent changes in the Political World may be regarded as the pioneering whirlwind and storm."[41]

---

40. "The moonlight steeped in silentness / The steady weathercock" (lines 505–6). Cf. Marilyn Butler's historicization of "Anecdote for Fathers." She may risk losing Words-worth's *intended* point, and one doesn't have to agree that the poet is "withholding," or "falsifying." But her specific argument is ingenious, subtly caveated, and germane to my own general argument. As Butler notes, Wordsworth's original subtitle for the poem ("Showing how the Practice of Lying may be taught") was replaced in 1845 by an epigraph drawn from Apollo's warning against forcing the oracle: "Restrain your vio-lence, for I shall lie if you coerce me." While the editorial Wordsworth who substituted this epigraph goes on claiming that the child in the poem is lying (the boy seizes on the absence of a weather vane to explain his preference for the farm at Kilve), he does so, Butler argues, "more uneasily, for a child who speaks as an oracle is at some level telling the truth. In one code which Wordsworth either knew, or half-knew, or had once known, Llyswen indeed still in the ideological sense had its weathercock. By withholding the story's meaning, perhaps insisting falsely on its falseness, the editorializing poet finds a way . . . of averting the story's proper ending, its prophecy of a revolutionary future" ("Telling It Like a Story: The French Revolution as Narrative," 353–54).

41. *Samuel Taylor Coleridge's "Treatise on Method,"* ed. Alice D. Snyder, 68.

7

England a Dungeon

Every house a den, every man bound; the shadows are filld
With spectres, and the windows wove over with curses of iron. . . .
                                                    (Blake, *Europe*, 1794)

1

Given this frightening but exhilarating prologue to possible political upheaval, what actually happened? Of Coleridge's recurrent imagery in the letters of 1797 (hurricane, whirlwind, storm, the day of darkness and tempest), it might be said that, like earthquake and volcano, all are part of the Coleridgean natural and meteorological vocabulary of revolution, and that all yield, eventually, to the image of the dungeon-grate. But there is a transitional stage, marked less by fear than hope.

I have connected the drought and becalmment of the Mariner and his crew in a stagnant, silent sea with the silence and political inactivity of Coleridge, "retired" at Stowey, lamenting his own lot and that of his nation, its collective "tongue . . . wither'd at the root" through the "utter drought" (lines 131–32) imposed by Pitt's "gagging Acts." Then, in December 1797, just when Coleridge was working on the earlier sections of his ballad, came the crisis initiated by the Triple Assessment Bill and the possibility that the Pitt government might fall: developments intriguingly paralleled by the sudden shift (within two lines) between the utterly hopeless end of Part II of *The Ancient Mariner* ("Instead of the Cross the Albatross / About my neck was hung") and the hope-filled opening of Part III: "I saw a something in the Sky."

This something in the sky, "No bigger than my fist," echoes Elijah's "little cloud out of the sea, like a man's hand," the first sign of the drought-ending wind and rain. In the poem, of course, the hopeful sign in the sky turns out to be, not a biblical cloud heralding a drought-relieving storm (that longed-for rain comes only after the blessing of the water-snakes), but what the Mariner first takes to be a sail. As the mysterious ship approaches, the crew is incapable of speech, their tongues withered, their "throats unslak'd, with black lips bak'd":

> Then while thro' drouth all dumb they stood
> I bit my arm and suck'd the blood
> And cry'd, A sail! a sail!
>
> (lines 150–52)

The crew, dry mouths "Agape," hear the Mariner call out, and "they for joy did grin." But the ship moving steadily toward them without wind or tide is the spectre-bark bearing Death and his even more hideous companion, the harlot-hag later identified as Life-in-Death. As the gloss would later dramatically synopsize the terrifying reversal of expectations: "A flash of joy; And horror follows." The arrival of the spectre-bark, genetically the foundational element on which the poem was based,[1] provides the pivotal text:

> The western wave was all a flame,
> The day was well nigh done!
> Almost upon the western wave
> Rested the broad bright Sun;
> When that strange shape drove suddenly
> Betwixt us and the Sun.
>
> And strait the Sun was fleck'd with bars
> (Heaven's mother send us grace)
> As if thro' a dungeon grate he peer'd
> With broad and burning face.
>
> (lines 163–72)

So far as I am aware, the closest reading of these lines offered by a major critic occurs in George Herbert Clarke's well-known essay on the poem's Sun and Moon symbolism. Clarke's thesis is that the Mariner—"who is at once himself, Coleridge and all humanity—having sinned, both incurs punishment and seeks redemption." Anticipating Warren's thematic solar-lunar distinction, though without making the sun consistently malign, Clarke tells us that the Mariner "becomes anxiously aware of his relation to the God of Law (as symbolized by the Sun), and in his sub-consciousness earnestly entreats the forgiveness of the God of Love (represented by the Moon symbol)." The Mariner sins by killing the albatross, and, under the "bloody Sun," the "avenging process"

---

1. The source is Wordsworth. In the same account in which he records his suggestion that the Mariner kill an albatross and that regional "tutelary Spirits" take it upon themselves "to avenge the crime," Wordsworth tells us that "'The Ancient Mariner' was founded on a strange dream, which a friend of Coleridge had, who fancied he saw a skeleton ship with figures in it" (*Poetical Works* 1:361). For the strange dream of Coleridge's friend (an amiable bailiff named John Cruikshank), see Lowes, *The Road to Xanadu*, 155, 251–53. As Lowes notes, "on the evidence of the poem itself, . . . the skeleton-bark has evidently been dipped deep in the stuff of other dreams than Cruikshank's" (251). He means, essentially, Coleridge's dreams—dreams which, as I suggest and Lowes does not, include political nightmares.

begins: the ship is becalmed, the sailors hang the dead bird about the Mariner's neck, all are "suffering from drought and fear" when "at last the phantom vessel is descried." Of the crucial lines, Clarke writes: "Guilt and Fear have interposed themselves between God and the sinful Mariner and his mates, who find themselves now wholly in the power of Death and Life-in-Death," with the Mariner alone falling "to the lot of Life-in-Death."[2]

Some readers question the need for Guilt; none have ever questioned the presence of Fear at this moment, least of all the Mariner, whose "heart beat loud" (in the more forceful 1817 version, he exclaims: "Fear at my heart as at a cup, / My life-blood seemed to sip!"). Robert Barth, a Jesuit priest as well as an eminent Coleridgean, finds in the Mariner's vision of the fiery sun glaring through the masts of the spectre-bark "the terror of the infinite. . . . The Mariner is here experiencing an infinity of hell, imaged as imprisonment in a dungeon of fire."[3] But there are also finite dungeons, prisons for the living. The Mariner, the sole survivor of this terrifying voyage, is soon to be "wholly in the power," the specifically *arbitrary* power, of the living death to which he is sentenced by a mere throw of the dice. Though the leprous hag who wins the Mariner is not named "Life-in-Death" until 1817, even in 1798 she is "far liker Death" than her "fleshless" companion, the charnel-crusted skeleton, Death himself! Though no one has ever said it, the situation seems "political." Like slavery, prison is a prolonged life-in-death (as Byron, a great admirer of Coleridge's poetry, recognized in deliberately echoing *The Ancient Mariner* in Section VIII of *The Prisoner of Chillon*); and either or both, it seems to me, are among the fearful things that have "interposed themselves" between the peering sun and the Mariner and his mates—as the unexpected image of the dungeon-grate in an "apolitical" poem would tend to confirm.

There is an analogy, mentioned earlier, worth elaborating at this point. In "The Intimations Ode: A Timely Utterance," Marjorie Levinson performs a New Historicist contextualizing of Wordsworth's poem, exposing it as a "timely utterance" in a historical sense. Her most striking examples of images whose "historicity" Wordsworth had tried to repress are the Tree and Field of stanza IV and the "prison-house" of stanza V. Her argument is worth synopsizing in the present context since what she says about these images anticipates (though I discovered the resemblance belatedly) the precise point I make about the "dungeon grate" in *The Ancient Mariner.*

Commenting on the familiar and pivotal lines,

> But there's a Tree, of many, one,
> A single Field that I have looked upon,
> Both of them speak of something that is gone,

Levinson observes that of all the symbols generated by the French Revolution, "none was more prominent than the Tree of Liberty," a symbol with which Wordsworth, who had twice celebrated the Federation Feast in France, was

2. "Certain Symbols in *The Rime of the Ancient Mariner,*" 29–30, 38.
3. *Coleridge and the Power of Love,* 67–68.

thoroughly familiar. Having quoted the passage in *The Excursion* in which garlands are brought "to deck / The tree of liberty" (III.725–26), as well as Carlyle's description (in *The French Revolution*) of the feast with "tents pitched in the Champ-de-Mars" and many "Trees-of-Liberty," Levinson concludes:

> By associating Wordsworth's Tree and Field (Champ de Mars) with the emblems
> and events of a glorious and irrecoverable era, one is in a better position to ex-
> plain the abrupt intrusion of these images and the disproportionate emotion
> which the narrator brings to them, as well as their extreme specifity. The narrator
> thus indicates that his attempt to liberate the fond, pastoral memory from its
> original context ("There was a time [that is, *some, any* time]") has failed. The his-
> toricity of the imagery is as a return of the repressed.

By momentarily reassuming "their former and symbolic character," the natural tree and field reveal the poem's almost effaced political dimension. Two pages later, discussing the counter-Enlightenment faith that leads Wordsworth to turn against Nature in the fifth and sixth stanzas of the ode, Levinson synopsizes the poet's development of "a vision of mankind not just as Nature's 'foster' (rather than 'natural') children, but as Inmates of her indomitable 'prison-house,' a phrase which, eighteen lines preceding a reference to 'that imperial palace,' must bring to mind the Bastille. The prison, we learn, is life itself; Nature, which had meant Liberty in the context of the Enlightenment, is represented in the Ode as the supreme jailer."[4]

That Levinson is on to something significant I have little doubt. What *is* doubtful is that the "prison-house" (in its primary context a Platonic or Neo-platonic emblem of the soul's enclosure in the darkness of matter), *must* (a word that falls all-too-trippingly from postmodernist tongues) bring to mind the Bastille. Such an association was not inevitable for Levinson's mentor, McGann ("perhaps we glimpse a metaphoric after-image of the Bastille in 'Shades of the prison-house'—but perhaps not"), nor was it inevitable for Hazlitt, who quotes the ode to illustrate his generation's loss of "the bright dream of our youth; that glad dawn of the day-star of liberty; that spring-time of the world," as he put it in referring (in his great review of *The Excursion*) to the festive early days of the French Revolution (*Works* 4:116). Levinson and other New Historicists *must* see political implications in part because that is what they are looking for, and because they are too keen-eyed to lose sight of their quarry even when it is camouflaged by clouds of glory. She concedes that a historical reconstruction "is not always and necessarily the most important thing to do," but in the case of a poem that, like the ode, has been detached from its historical context and generalized, "it does seem to me," she writes, "most important right now and for the politics of Romantic scholarship to nudge the work toward a less literary register."[5]

4. *Wordsworth's Great Period Poems*, 93–94, 96.
5. Ibid., 100. Levinson's agreement is with Terry Eagleton, who, though observing that historical reconstruction is not "always and necessarily the best thing to do," is wary of any "literary" artifact that has been "detached by a certain hermeneutic practice

Fair enough; but, doubly politicized and made less "literary," the ode "must" indeed be historically referential. I believe it is, in ways both more persuasive than Levinson's, despite her "must," and more thematically germane to stanzas V–VIII of the ode. In Chapter 3, I referred to the most sensational moment in Coleridge's 1808 lecture against the Lancaster educational system, with its "punishments" so humiliating that no boy subject to them "will stand in fear of Newgate, or feel any horror at the thought of a slave ship!" Wordsworth seems to have remembered this juxtaposition. Four years later, Sara Hutchinson reports, "William" described the establishment of schools run on the opposing Bell system as, "with the exception of the abolition of the slave-trade, the most happy event of our times." For Wordsworth, as R. A. Foakes has recently demonstrated, education could be either liberating or imprisoning. But at the time he wrote both this stanza of the ode and the thirteen-book version of *The Prelude* (1804), school and narrow book-knowledge were, Foakes shows, "bound up with the idea of a prison" as opposed to what Wordsworth calls in *The Prelude* (II.251) the "discipline of love." In *The Prelude,* which begins with the poet's own escape "from a house of bondage," a "prison where he hath been long immured" (I.7–8), Wordsworth describes the "prodigy" in what Foakes calls "a curious image." The "discourse" of such a young bookworm "moves slow, / Massy and ponderous as a prison-door" (II.319–21). Foakes persuasively links this "confusing image" ("Is the door opening or closing? And on what? On the boy or the world outside?") with "the startling intrusion of the prison image" in stanza V of the ode—"Shades of the prison-house begin to close / Upon the growing Boy"—as well as with similar images associated, in both Coleridge and Wordsworth, with unnatural, imprisoning systems of education.[6]

This, surely, is more relevant to the thematic development of the middle stanzas of the ode than is Levinson's more specifically political prison. Nevertheless, while I do not wish to lose sight of the literariness of either the ode or *The Ancient Mariner,* I too "nudge" Coleridge's poem as Levinson does Wordsworth's in order to draw attention to the historicity of *its* imagery as a return of the repressed—in particular the image of the dungeon-grate, which, however overtly historical and "political" it may seem in detachment, has not yet served to draw down upon *The Ancient Mariner,* that "work of pure imagination," the full historicist treatment.

Given the danger of imaginative literature being historicized and, in some cases, tendentiously politicized, we may be grateful that *The Ancient Mariner* has

from its pragmatic context and subjected to a generalizing reinscription" (*Walter Benjamin; or Toward a Revolutionary Critique,* 122–23). For the circumspect comment of McGann, either anticipating Levinson or echoing her (with reservations) on the Wordsworthian "prison-house," see page 88 of *The Romantic Ideology* (a book whose polemical opening chapter is, however, riddled with its own "musts").

6. "'Thriving Prisoners': Coleridge, Wordsworth, and the Child at School," 194. Cf. my earlier connection (end of Chapter 2) of Crusoe's instruction of Friday with Coleridge's "child beneath its master's blow" and Wordsworth's image of "a master [brooding] o'er a slave."

escaped. Nevertheless, these two stanzas of the poem, with the sun setting and its face barred as by the grate of a dungeon, cluster together images the entangled roots of which are virtually *all* political—not only in the work of Coleridge, but of all the first-generation Romantics affected by what Shelley, a second-generation Romantic, could still call "the master theme of the epoch in which we live—the French Revolution."[7] Though Peter Kitson has located *The Ancient Mariner* within the general *conceptual* context of the revolutionary age, Coleridge's precise *imagery* here has to be placed, however briefly, in the context of the revolutionary cluster of sunrise and sunset, hope and despair, joy and horror.

Blake, whose "windows wove over with curses of iron" provide the epigraph for this chapter, was also responding imaginatively to revolutionary hopes twice blasted—by the Jacobin Terror in France and, specifically in these lines of *Europe,* by the Pitt government's first counterrevolutionary crackdown leading up to and including the treason trials of 1794. The initial promise and tragic failure of the French Revolution is also, of course, at the agitated heart of Wordsworth's *Prelude,* which traces the Revolution's promise and decline in imagery of sunrise and sunset, a cycle of despair compounded by the counter-reaction in his own country. The crisis he described, referring to 1798–1799, as "these times of fear," reflected both revolutionary "hopes o'erthrown" and the domestic selfishness and political repression of a time "Of dereliction and dismay" (*Prelude* II.449–57).

This is precisely the historical moment David Erdman felt Coleridge had "objectivized" in *The Ancient Mariner.* Though Wordsworth was writing about a period some eighteen months later, the analogue is certainly appropriate, since the sudden intrusion, at this climactic point of the 1799 version of *The Prelude,* of the destruction of the hopes aroused by the promise of the French Revolution derives directly from an "anxiously eager" letter Coleridge had sent Wordsworth in September of that year:

> My dear friend, I do entreat you go on with "The Recluse"; and I wish you would write a poem, in blank verse, addressed to those, who, in consequence of the complete failure of the French Revolution, have thrown up all hopes of the amelioration of mankind, and are sinking into an almost epicurean selfishness, disguising the same under the soft titles of domestic attachment and contempt for visionary *philosophes*. It would do great good, and might form a part of "The Recluse." (*CL* I 527)

In both the two-part *Prelude* of 1799 and the 1805 version of the poem, Wordsworth addressed Coleridge's important concerns point by point, recovering from dismay to reassert "a more than Roman confidence," a "faith" deriving from a mind and heart integrated with nature—despite the fact that

> good men
> On every side fall off we know not how
> To selfishness disguised in gentle names

7. *The Letters of Percy Bysshe Shelley* 1:504.

> Of peace and quiet and domestic love—
> Yet mingled, not unwillingly, with sneers
> On visionary minds.
>
>   (*Prelude* II.451–62)

Coleridge had particularly in mind, among other recent sneerers at "visionary minds," Sir James Mackintosh, an early and ardent supporter of the French Revolution. The author of *Vindiciae Gallicae* (1791), one of the more thoughtful pamphlets responding to Burke's *Reflections on the Revolution in France,* had just defecated on his old enthusiasms in a series of lectures at Lincoln's Inn in the spring of 1799. From his now Burkean perspective, Mackintosh dimissed the Revolution itself as "that conspiracy against God and man, the greatest scourge of the world, and the chief stain upon human annals." Though Coleridge, himself influenced by Burke, might have been able to accept these hyperboles (the last of which he had anticipated as early as the Bristol addresses), he had contempt for Mackintosh's gratuitous sneering at his former friends and "visionary" opinions. Suspicious of Mackintosh's motives in abandoning reform (*CN* I 947), Coleridge thought his lectures the work of a "great Dung-fly," a "ready warehouseman" of ideas.[8]

William Hazlitt had also attended these lectures, coming away considerably more impressed by Mackintosh's intellect if not by his less than humane and liberal politics. Readers of his *The Spirit of the Age* (1825) may be reminded of Coleridge's letter and of Wordsworth's lines in Hazlitt's (suprisingly gentle) strictures on Mackintosh's apostasy—though by 1825, Wordsworth and Coleridge were also firmly enlisted in Hazlitt's apostate ranks. More to the immediate point: in the same book, in the celebrated paragraph in which he characterized Wordsworth's "Muse" as "a levelling one," Hazlitt also perceptively identified the "revolutionary movement of our age," with its abrupt "political changes," as "the model on which" Wordsworth "formed and conducted" his poetry (*Works* 11:86–87).

Like Wordsworth, Coleridge, and innumerable others (including Wolfe Tone, for whom the French Revolution was to be "that morning star to liberty in Ireland"), Hazlitt depicted the ecstatic radical hopes of the 1790s in imagery of dawn and spring; unlike disillusioned Wordsworth and Coleridge, however, he remained faithful to "that bright dream of our youth," to that "glad dawn of the day-star of liberty," the springtime of the world "when France called her children to partake her equal blessings beneath her laughing skies" (*Works* 4:116). "For my part," he declared in 1827, "I set out in life with the French

---

8. *CL* I 588. Even though Mackintosh had recommended Coleridge to Daniel Stuart for the position on the *Morning Post* in December 1798, and had also promoted his interest with the Wedgwoods, he was unfairly lampooned in a poem Coleridge published in the *Morning Post* in 1800, "The Two Round Spaces on the Tombstone" (*CPW* I 353–55). The Latin epigraph prefacing the 1800 edition of *Lyrical Ballads* was apparently a private joke at Mackintosh's expense. And years later, in chapter 5 of the *Biographia,* Coleridge's attack on Hartleian associationism took the gratuitous form of a response to the despised Mackintosh.

Revolution, and that event had considerable influence on my early feelings, as on those of others. Youth then was doubly such. It was the dawn of a new era, a new impulse had been given to men's minds, and the sun of Liberty rose upon the sun of Life in the same day, and both were proud to run their race together" (*Works* 17:197).

Hazlitt is probably echoing Wordsworth's apogee of revolutionary "hope and joy," those celebrated lines extracted from *The Prelude* and printed by Coleridge in *The Friend* in 1809: "Bliss was it in that dawn to be alive, / But to be young was very heaven!" But having greeted the Revolution in rapture, and become a "patriot" and lover of the people with the guidance of Michel Beaupuy, Wordsworth was plunged into despair by the French leaders' betrayal of their own principles. To be sure, he long held, as did Coleridge and the Foxite Whigs, that France had been driven to revolutionary excesses by the warring monarchs allied against her; but the excesses were real. As is clear from his prudently withheld letter to the Bishop of Llandaff (written in early 1793), Wordsworth was untroubled by the executions of the French king and queen, necessary violence on the path to reform, a trifle in the larger millennial context. The terrible beauty of the Revolution was, however, beginning to lose its good looks. After shedding blood in their various domestic terrors (the repression of counterrevolution in Annette Vallon's district, the Vendée; the September massacres; the Jacobin Reign of Terror itself), the French—squandering what Wordsworth thought a second chance for redemption after the death of Robespierre to instead "become oppressors in their turn"—turned a war of self-defense into one of conquest, invading Spain, Italy, Holland, Germany, and—unforgivably—democratic Switzerland, converting it, at the point of Bonaparte's bayonets, into the "Helvetic Republic." And then sunset: the coronation of Napoleon as emperor, that

> last opprobrium, when we see the dog
> Returning to his vomit, when the sun
> That rose in splendour, . . .
> Sets like an opera phantom.
> (*Prelude* X.689–93, 791–94, 931–40)

For Coleridge, too—though there *is* that striking phrase in "The Destiny of Nations," "The Sun that rose on Freedom, rose in Blood"—the course of the Revolution cycles from hopeful sunrise to sanguinary sunset. Hazlitt, who spoke himself of the French dawn becoming "overcast" (*Works* 17:197), nicely telescopes the Coleridgean response to the revolutionary pattern of political hope and dejection in imagery drawn directly from poems like "Religious Musings," "The Destiny of Nations," the "Ode on the Departing Year," "France: An Ode," and "Fears in Solitude."[9] As Hazlitt concluded of Coleridge, "he hailed the

9. Responding to "Fears in Solitude," which Coleridge read to him while in Germany in 1798–1799, Clement Carlyon employed the same ubiquitous imagery. Writing in the early 1830s, he perceptively described the poet of "Fears in Solitude" as "struggling to

rising orb of liberty, since quenched in darkness and in blood" (*Works* 11:98–99). This imagery is not unrelated to the passage we are concerned with in *The Ancient Mariner.* Intriguingly enough, shortly after that poem was completed, Hazlitt, walking with the poet on the heaths overlooking the Bristol Channel, "pointed out to Coleridge's notice the bare masts of a vessel on the very edge of the horizon and within the red-orbed disc of the setting sun, like his own spectre-ship in the *Ancient Mariner*" (*Works* 17:120).

Had Wordsworth, who had been with them the day before, been along for the jaunt he might have been reminded not only of the spectre-bark obstructing the setting sun in his friend's poem, but also of lines inspired by a similar scene he had witnessed five years earlier. Wordsworth's unpublished lines, which begin "How sweet to walk along the woody steep," were written in the aftermath of the declarations of war between England and the nation that was still the home, not only of his republican ideals, but of Annette Vallon and their daughter Caroline— now endangered by British arms as well as domestic repression in the Vendée. In a jarring contrast between the natural beauty of sun and sea and the human history and ominous political reality that intrude upon the scene, Wordsworth describes himself gazing from the Isle of Wight at a summer (1793) sunset whose natural "Tranquillity" is violently interrupted, indeed canceled, by the sight and sound of the "proud" British fleet preparing for war with France. The "intrusion" could hardly be more striking, since Wordsworth had been hoping to return to Annette and Caroline. The descending "disc" is "lessened half," for "anchored vessels scattered" off Portsmouth "Darken with shadowy hulks" what should be a serene and beautiful sunset. In an anticipation of Thomas Hardy's "Channel Firing," there are also "sunset cannon," at the sound of which "The star of life appears to set in blood," while "Old ocean shudders in offended mood / Deepening with moral gloom his angry flood."[10]

Here the rising sun associated with France's blissful dawn is replaced by a descending disc ensanguined and perverted from its natural function as "the star of life." But Wordsworth's "moral" indignation on behalf of "offended" nature is not yet (in 1793, though the lines may have been written later)

---

devise an outlet from the storm, which had already gathered around the nations, and was overwhelming with still increasing darkness, the visions of Utopian felicity with which the drama of the French Revolution opened, and of which he had himself drunk so deeply" (*Early Years and Late Reflections* 1:141–42).

10. *Poetical Works* 1:308, lines 8–19. Wordsworth's "melancholy forebodings" on this occasion were still vivid a half-century later; see his preface to *Guilt and Sorrow* in *Poems, Chiefly of Early and Late Years* (1842). Kenneth Johnston discusses this and two related poems as interactions between "natural beauty and social structures" in "Wordsworth's Revolutions," 176–81. This scene reappears in both the 1805 and 1850 *Prelude,* but with much diminished dramatic intensity. The "shadowy hulks," the sun setting in "blood," and the morally "offended" ocean all disappear; and while both versions refer to the "unworthy service" of the fleet, we hear nothing in the final version (XI.315–30) of that service as something to which, in 1805, "The unhappy counsel of a few weak men / Had doomed it" (X.290–93).

directed at French excesses or (as, *still* later, it would be) at that "opera phantom" of a sunset crowning Napoleonic militarism and imperialism. Instead, the "moral gloom" from which violated nature takes its sober coloring is caused by *British* warships, the principal military arm of a government that had cast its counterrevolutionary shadow against the dawn of glad day from the outset. By the time Hazlitt pointed out to Coleridge another ship's masts circumscribed "within the red-orbed disc of the setting sun," most, though not all, of that had changed. The bloodying of the setting sun was now, in the poems of Coleridge and Wordsworth, attributed largely to France; but the spectre-bark of which Hazlitt was reminded—a "naked hulk" that intrudes its dungeon-grate-like masts between the Mariner and a sun previously described as "bloody"—still seems British, as in the darkening of that sun's face by the "shadowy hulks" of the British High Fleet five long years earlier.

The final turn of the Revolutionary wheel in this three-stage dialectical pattern is the phase of recovery, what Wordsworth calls in *The Excursion* "Despondency Corrected." This takes the form—as *The Prelude* argues, as Abrams demonstrates in *Natural Supernaturalism,* and as Kitson suggests in placing *The Ancient Mariner* in this context—of a reconstitution of hope, the reassertion of the greatness of the human mind and spirit, healed in large part as the result of a cognitive and imaginative transaction with a repossessed natural world, supposedly undarkened by the shadowy hulks of sociopolitical intrusion. This revolution and renovation—emotional, spiritual, imaginative—would take the form, in *The Ancient Mariner,* of the apparently unpremeditated blessing of the water-snakes.

Of course, for the "demystifying" New Historicists, such alleged triumphs of the inner life over the outer world are among the chief illusions, or distortions, of "the Romantic ideology." Despite my usual "Yes, but," I will soon be fleshing out my proposition that even the blessing of the snakes, that quintessentially "inner" and "spontaneous" act, may not be free of the outer world, "these times of fear." For the moment, aware of this recurrent pattern in the imagery of revolution and reaction, we return to the passage with which we began: the setting sun glaring through the rigging of the terrifying spectre-bark, "As if thro' a dungeon grate he peer'd."

The political lateness of the hour ("The day was well nigh done!") is suggested by the fact that the sun—so often the rising orb of Freedom's light, associated with the dawn of glad day in France—is "almost" setting. Though he failed to pursue the point, Robert Penn Warren seems to have intuited the historical context of this poem of allegedly "pure imagination." The sun, which had, he writes, "risen so promisingly and so gloriously 'like God's own head,' is suddenly 'the bloody Sun,' the sun of death—as though we had here a fable of the Enlightenment and the Age of Reason, whose fair promises had wound up in the blood-bath of the end of the century."[11] But what corresponds politically

11. "A Poem of Pure Imagination," 93.

to the interposing shape that suddenly looms up between the sunset and the sailors, flecking the sun and making it seem to peer through a dungeon-grate? The imagery, though it remains connected on the associational stream with the course of the Revolution in France, has more to do, I believe, with counter-revolutionary developments at home.

In terms of the political archetypes stored in Coleridge's *spiritus mundi,* the sun, however clouded or streaked, remains associated with Freedom and the *ideals* of the French Revolution. But a couplet from the original version of the "Ode on the Departing Year" symbolically links the British prime minister with an exaggerated response to that momentarily shadowed sun: "A cloud, O Freedom! cross'd thy orb of Light, / And sure he deem'd that orb was set in night."

As Coleridge's handwritten note to these lines confirms, "he" is William Pitt: enemy of freedom, betrayer of "the dove-eyed Maid," Peace. The "boastful bloody Son of Pride," Pitt here seizes on the passing of a single cloud to treacherously justify the conclusion that France's sun was set in night.[12] The French Revolution is also compared to a cloud-crossed sun in "The Destiny of Nations," a tale told to the French warrior-saint, Joan of Arc, by her tutelary power, a spirit who, leaving the Maid at poem's end, urges her to "Save thy Country!," assuring her that "Soon shall the Morning struggle into Day, / The stormy Morning into cloudless Noon" (*CPW* I 146).

In "To William Wordsworth" (1807), Coleridge depicted France in 1792 as a "becalméd bark," when, though a storm is impending, "no cloud / Is visible, or shadow on the main" (*CPW* I 405). But that French "Noon" was destined never to be "cloudless"; and it is the obscuring of the sun of Freedom that is our chief concern at the moment. Even when the French Revolution seemed to Coleridge a harbinger of mankind's "deliverance," the "dawning East" was, in fact, clouded: "The Sun was rising, though ye hid his light!" (*CPW* I 245). Though here, in the Recantation ode, the light-hider is Jacobin blasphemy, earlier it was, as we've just seen, Freedom-betraying, light-denying Pitt.

For radicals and reformers, Pitt's betrayal of freedom was both international and internal. *Internationally,* as the principal paymaster and champion of counterrevolution during the wars against France, Pitt, himself a "bloody Son"/sun, was responsible for driving the revolutionary nation into bloody reaction; it was the "shadowy hulks" of the British navy that darkened and bloodied the sun Wordsworth watched decline from the Isle of Wight in 1793. In Coleridge's other poem of 1798 entitled "Recantation," the stages of the French Revolution are jocoseriously "Illustrated in the Story of The Mad Ox," a fable in which the Pitt government is blamed for setting the British "bull-dog" on a creature that was originally "only glad" and frisking in the spring meadow, like any "beast of spirit." (Coleridge is perhaps recalling the most memorable analogy from Wordsworth's unsent "Letter" to the Bishop of Llandaff: that of the wild but natural

12. I quote from the ode as printed in the *Cambridge Intelligencer* (December 31, 1796) and from Coleridge's MS note, both printed in *CPW* I 163–64.

pent-up energy the newborn French Revolution shared with "the animal just released from its stall.")[13] Thus harried and pursued, the poor Ox *does* go "mad," committing excesses that must finally be dealt with. But, like Wordsworth, Fox, and many other early supporters of the Revolution, Coleridge still believed—in April 1798, when he called on Englishmen to repent "of the wrongs with which we stung / So fierce a foe to frenzy," and as late as July 1798, when this ballad was published in the *Morning Post*—that French excesses were largely attributable to counterrevolutionary goading, that "THEY DROVE THE POOR OX MAD."[14]

The handwritten note identifying Pitt as the enemy of freedom and peace impugns the treachery of "our Ministry" in its dealings with the French, and ends by calling on Englishmen to "declare their thoughts fearlessly by every method which the *remnant* of the Constitution allows" (*CPW* I 163–64n). The sarcasm points to the *internal* betrayal of freedom by Pitt and his Ministry, men convinced that they had reason to fear domestic discontents that, though they antedated the Revolution, had now escalated, energized by Freedom's dawn in France, to levels of dissension that tested, and quickly exceeded, limits established by an ordinarily tolerant government.

Ironically, but not surprisingly, this clarion call to Englishmen to "declare their thoughts fearlessly" never left Coleridge's desk. The allusion to Pitt's repeated violations of the Constitution (the emphasis on *remnant* is Coleridge's) embraces the treason trials of 1794, the initial suspension of habeas corpus (May 1794), and the passage of the Two Acts (December 1795). Repression escalated rapidly in March 1798 with the threat to renew that suspension (carried out within a month). Thus, the contemporary referent of the setting sun peering through the dungeon-grate would be neither Coleridge's horror of the slave trade nor of the past Terror in France, but rather the fear resulting from earlier constitutional violations as compounded and intensified by this demand for renewed suspension of habeas corpus—a demand made by Pitt during the invasion panic of March 1798, the very month in which Coleridge was finishing *The Ancient Mariner* (perhaps completed on March 23, though the poem remained in his hands until the second week of May).

13. *Letter to Llandaff*, in *The Prose Works of William Wordsworth*, ed. W. J. B. Owen and Jane Smyser, 1:38.

14. *CPW* I 299–303, 262. If Coleridge borrowed his animal imagery from Wordsworth's *Letter to Llandaff*, there was, as usual, reciprocity. In both the 1805 and 1850 versions of *The Prelude*, Wordsworth explained the Jacobin Reign of Terror in imagery that would seem to echo Coleridge's "Fears in Solitude" and his tale of the Mad Ox: "And thus beset with foes on every side, / The goaded land waxed mad" (X.311–12 [1805]; X.335–36 [1850]). In a characteristically succinct synopsis of the differing perspectives, Carl Woodring observes: "Burke believed the Revolution to contain seeds of inevitable despotism and imperial expansion. Charles James Fox and his steadily diminishing followers argued that the allied monarchs were driving peacefully inclined revolutionists to desperate extremes. It took both the excesses of the Jacobins and the fearful victories of Bonaparte to swing the popular press from Fox to Burke" (*Politics in English Romantic Poetry*, 14).

A crucial image for any political reading of *The Ancient Mariner*, this "strange surprizing" simile of the sun-flecking "bars" of a "dungeon grate" is, as noted earlier, the only image in the poem untracked by Lowes in *The Road to Xanadu*. It was, however, clearly anything but casual for Coleridge. In fact, in a handwritten correction in the 1798 edition of *Lyrical Ballads* he reinforced the image, replacing "Are those her naked ribs, which fleck'd / The sun that did behind them peer" (lines 177–78) with: "Are those her ribs which fleck'd the Sun / Like the bars of a dungeon grate?" (*CPW* I 194*n;* the lines in the 1817 version read: "Are those her ribs through which the Sun / Did peer, as through a grate?") Those naked ribs or (say) the grid of a fishnet are images we might expect from a nautical narrator. But *is* the dungeon-grate, however unexpected, "political"? Not, as we've seen, to Tillyard, or to House. Not even to Carl Woodring, who knows as well or better than anyone else that "prisons stank for Coleridge with a political stench," and that "as an anti-Pittite journalist he lived in sufficient danger to make his visions graphic." Yet Woodring feels that this particular dungeon-grate "probably had not acquired its methods of security directly from Pitt, Robespierre, or Admiral Lord Hood. . . . The poetic effect of the peering sun depends very much upon preference for the sun rather than for dungeons, a preference rather likely among readers of the poem. . . . If some of the poet's own dangerous voyaging was political, his Mariner's was not explicitly so."[15]

It is hard to take issue with what, despite the carefully chosen qualifying adverbs (*probably, directly,* and *explicitly*), constitutes an authoritative and witty dismissal of political significance in this passage and, indeed, in *The Ancient Mariner* as a whole. But on the basis of what, thanks to David Erdman, we now know about Coleridge's renewed political activism in the winter of 1797–1798, and the disappointing sequel, I would suggest that that dungeon-grate probably *had* acquired at least some of its methods of security from the first of Professor Woodring's trio. Indeed, the swift deterioration of the political situation in March and April 1798—a shift from hope to horror paralleled in the poem by the sudden appearance of the prison-like spectre-bark—may well have increased Coleridge's sense of danger to the point where his already rather obsessive images of dungeons became so graphic that a very real dungeon-grate intruded itself into his supernatural voyage—and may even have come to dominate the universe of the poem. Consider the following facts.

2

Daniel Stuart, the editor-owner of the *Morning Post,* had on January 12, 1798, dismissed "Ministers' sudden alarm" over the prospects of a French invasion as "designed to smother murmurs at the passing [on January 5] of the Triple Assessment" (*EOT* I lxxv). But he began to smother his own murmurs in February, and to definitely run scared after the arrest, on the final day of that month, of John Binns, Arthur O'Connor, the radical Irish priest James Coigley, and two

15. *Politics in the Poetry of Coleridge,* 54, 164–65.

associates at Margate as they were preparing to sail to France. The arrests, stemming from information supplied by Samuel Turner, a double agent in Hamburg, confirmed suspicions of an alliance among the leading radical groups—the London Corresponding Society, the United Englishmen, and, most troubling of all, those conspirators bent upon expediting another French invasion, the United Irishmen. It was the émigré Irish community in Hamburg, a gathering place for fleeing and conspiring English and Irish radicals, that had been infiltrated by Turner, a renegade United Irishman who, becoming a confidant of the wife of Lord Edward Fitzgerald (Fox's cousin), began reporting to Lord Downshire at the British Home Office in October 1797.[16]

Not suprisingly, then, the arrests also revealed treason: real treason, not the anti-Ministerial philosophizing Coleridge was inviting back in the sequestered dell in July 1797. A literally fatal paper was found in the pocket of the priest's greatcoat. Addressed from the "Secret Committee of England" to the French Directory, it expressed the hope that "the hero of Italy" (Bonaparte) and the *Armée de l'Angleterre* would shortly come to rescue them from the tyranny of the British government and establish "distinct republicks" in the British Isles. With (the French Government was assured) the "sacred flame of liberty . . . re-kindled," and making progress "even in the fleets and the armies" (a pointed allusion to the naval mutinies of the preceding year), "myriads will hail [the French] arrival with shouts of joy." Despite the government's own fear of popular unrest, this was wishful thinking. In the mass, Englishmen—urban and rural, rich and poor—were united in fearing, and determining to resist, a French invasion—both in 1798 and again during the panic of 1803.[17] Still, in the words of the Home Secretary, the Duke of Portland, in February 1798 the French were being invited by pro-Gallican traitors "to invade this kingdom—or at least that of Ireland." The document was to prove fatal not only to Coigley, who was hanged on June 8, 1798, but, legislatively, to the radical societies in England, now tarred as traitorous collaborators with both Irish rebels and French enemies.[18]

16. Turner's reports (under the alias "Richardson" since United Irishman leader Lord Edward Fitzgerald's wife was Pamela) are in the Public Record Office papers HO 100/75 (7–9). Citing the *Report of the Committee of Secrecy of the British House of Commons, printed the 15th of March 1799,* the *Annual Register* described Hamburg, a city under constant surveillance by the Pitt government, as "long . . . the receptacle of those disaffected persons who have fled from Great Britain or Ireland, either from apprehension of the consequences of the treasonable practices in which they have been engaged, or for the purpose of assisting the conspiracies carried on against their respective countries" *(Annual Register* 41 [1799], 224–25).

17. Readers of *The Making of the English Working Class* are given a vivid, and accurate, sense of mass alienation in the 1790s. But Yorkshire, the county that supplied most of Thompson's evidence, was an exception to the rule as far as loyalty was concerned. For an account of the "patriotism" of militia and volunteers, and its varied motivation, see the chapter entitled "Manpower" (283–319) in Linda Colley's *Britons.*

18. Portland to the King, March 3, 1798, in *The Later Correspondence of George III* 3:26. See the Public Record Office papers, HO 42/45, for "Proofs of the connection between

"Ministers' sudden alarm" now seemed to have considerable basis in fact. The electrifying arrests were covered in intimate detail in the *Morning Post* the following day, and within forty-eight hours Stuart found himself having to divulge his sources (supposedly Jacobin) to Pitt, Portland, and the Privy Council. At this session Stuart was either threatened or genuinely convinced of the likelihood of a French invasion. He was, of course, aware of the abortive invasion attempt of December 1796 and of the fiasco at Fishguard in the following year, and had, on January 20, 1798, mentioned to Coleridge the French lawyer Thilorier's "plan of invading England in Balloons" (*EOT* III 163*n*). Evidence of treachery, combined with accurate reports of French military activity in certain continental ports in early spring 1798, may have persuaded him that the present situation was considerably more ominous than anything the aerial Thilorier had in mind.

Whether convinced or capitulating, the slippery Stuart wisely began to ally his paper with the government's position. The *Morning Post* now expressed credence rather than skepticism about an imminent invasion, *and* accepted the Pitt Ministry's argument that domestic security demanded even more extreme measures. In the *Morning Post* of March 5, the anti-Ministerial Stuart performed a dramatic *volte face:*

> We understand that in a few days a motion will be made . . . for suspending the *Habeas Corpus Act,* founded, as it is said, on facts that have recently transpired.— Ministers having seen their error in suspending this Act once before without reason, will now, we presume, have good grounds for their conduct, before they take the step; and if they have good grounds, we hope they will proceed with alacrity. (*EOT* I lxxvii*n*)

Furthermore, Stuart may have confided whatever inside information he had been given to his star contributor, for in the previously mentioned letter to his brother written about March 10, Coleridge, though he attributes the "increased & increasing numbers" of "fiery & undisciplined spirits" chiefly to the "folly" of the present government, admits that "the Ministers may have had in their possession facts which may alter the whole state of the argument."[19]

Was an invasion imminent? It certainly made strategic sense. The French

---

the London Corresponding Society, the United Irish and the Irish rebels." The document found on Coigley, dated January 25, 1798, is cited by Goodwin (*The Friends of Liberty,* 436–37) from *State Trials,* vol. 26, columns 1250–52. Binns and O'Connor were eventually acquitted.

19. *CL* I 397. It is not easy to decipher the thinking of so mercurial a man as Coleridge, especially on the basis of letters occasionally reflecting what the writer imagined his correspondent wanted to hear. Only three years earlier, Coleridge's own fiery and undisciplined spirit had been engaged in detecting government plots; in the spring of 1798, all sarcasm spent, he seemed willing to acknowledge the possibility of pro-Gallican plots; a dozen years hence he would look back on the Ministry's abhorrence of the radicals of the nineties, when young enthusiasts "were *invested* [by the Pitt Government] with all the attributes of brooding conspiracy and hoary-headed treason" (*F* I 120–21; italics added).

imperium over a restive continent would always be under threat so long as Britain—counterrevolution's principal enemy and supplier of subsidies, arms, and sporadic injections of troops—remained independent. The English, unlike the "clumsy and grasping" Austrians, were, said Bonaparte, "courageous, meddling and energetic." "We must," he urged the Directory in 1797, "pull down the English monarchy. . . . Let us concentrate our efforts on building up our fleet and on destroying England. Once that is done Europe is at our feet."[20]

He was right; but the required naval equality let alone supremacy would elude the French throughout the Revolutionary and Napoleonic wars. That was precisely the case in the spring of 1798. We now know, as the British people and government could not, that the invasion panic of at least later March and April 1798 was over a phantom, both the French Directory and Bonaparte having decided—perhaps as early as February 23, certainly by March 25—that the fifty-thousand-man "Army of England" gathered near Brest under Bonaparte's command could neither be spared on the continent nor risked without adequate naval support in a cross-Channel invasion.[21]

There would of course be a smaller invasion of Ireland under General Humbert later in this Irish "Year of the French." But when Bonaparte did finally set sail, now in command of the thirty-one-thousand-man *Armée de l'Orient,* it was for neither England nor Ireland, but Egypt. Within a month he had conquered Egypt and begun an efficient colonization. But his supporting battleships, unable to enter the shallow harbor of Alexandria, were clustered in Abu Q'ir (Aboukir) Bay, a temporary and vulnerable anchorage that proved catastrophic. Following Lord Nelson's crushing defeat of the French fleet at Aboukir (the "Battle of the Nile," August 1), the former "hero of Italy" found himself and his army stranded in inhospitable country. Nelson's devastating victory (which quickly rallied Europe to form a Second Coalition against the French) virtually wiped out France's Mediterranean fleet and led Bonaparte, breaking out of his Egyptian "bondage," to abandon his own troops, just as the Directory, advised by Bonaparte and Tallyrand, would, in a momentous strategic blunder, unwisely abandon Humbert and the United Irishmen.[22]

20. Quoted in Michael Glover, *The Napoleonic Wars: An Illustrated History, 1792–1815,* 50.

21. Discussing the period during which preparations for the invasion of Great Britain came to an end, Georges Lefebvre concludes: "The military commanders had no faith in the invasion, and on 5 Ventose, Year VI [February 23, 1798], on his return from an inspection in the West, Bonaparte decided to abandon the project. . . . The navy declared itself impotent, and the Continental peace was too insecure for the Republic to deprive itself of an army and its best general" (*The French Revolution* 2:189, 216, 218).

22. The French naval disaster at Aboukir was epitomized in the fate of the commanding officer under Bonaparte, Admiral Brueys. A British sailor aboard the *Swiftsure,* one of the vessels engaging the French flagship, *L'Orient,* could see the admiral clearly in the vivid light provided by the "incessant flashes of the numerous guns." Glover quotes the report of Midshipman John Theophilus Lee: "The brave Brueys, having lost both his

But these events occurred in the summer and fall of 1798. Back in the spring, threat of a direct invasion of England seemed both real and prolonged. For much of the *Armée de l'Angleterre* stayed in its coastal positions even after the invasion plan had been abandoned. Lacking the necessary "naval supremacy" to invade England, "we can," said Bonaparte before assuming command of the *Armée de l'Orient*, "only abandon the expedition, while maintaining a pretence of it."[23] The bluff worked, so effectively that whatever the actual internal and external threats in March and April 1798, the practical results soon made themselves felt in Great Britain.

Even before the now acquiescent Opposition in Parliament succumbed to Pitt's demand for renewed suspension of habeas corpus (Tierney voted for it, Sheridan did not oppose, Fox voted against it), there was widespread alarm. In March, most of the Dublin-area leaders of the United Irishmen were rounded up and jailed, and arrests began in England, on grounds considerably more tenuous than planned insurrection. "Insolent and indecent liberties," the *Courier* of March 8 charged, began "to be taken throughout the kingdom with the characters of those persons who [had] forborne to support the Minister in his mad and merciless career" (*EOT* I lxxvii*n*). That kind of talk faded fast. On April 14, Stuart's *Morning Post* referred ominously to England being "menaced" not only from abroad but "at home." Nine days later, Stuart was acknowledging the need to "arrest those who would favour France." Between these two editorials, on April 20, George III sent a message to Parliament reporting "considerable and increasing activity in the ports of France, Flanders and Holland, with the avowed design of attempting the invasion of His Majesty's dominions" (*Parliamentary Register* [1798] LI, 4). Those dominions had to be protected not only from external but internal enemies, from Irish rebels and from those so-called "patriots," the English Jacobins. Now even Stuart seemed convinced of the presence of a potentially dangerous pro-Gallican minority among the English proponents of parliamentary reform.

These developments cannot have been comforting to Coleridge, a republican reformer if no "clubbist." As with the invasion, however, rumor counted for more than reality. Coleridge had been "deemed," as he frequently put it, not

---

legs, was seated with torniquets [sic] on the stumps in an armchair facing his enemies; and giving directions for extinguishing [a fire that had started near the mizzen chains], when a cannon ball from the SWIFTSURE put a period to his gallant life by nearly cutting him in two" (*The Napoleonic Wars*, 57).

The defeat at the Nile was compounded by the French failure to mount a force of sufficient size for the Irish expedition—a decision influenced by Bonaparte, who had been unimpressed by the United Irishmen he'd met in Paris. Two weeks after landing at Killala Bay, Co. Mayo, and enjoying some initial success, Humbert's skilled and courageous but vastly outnumbered force (about a thousand French soldiers reinforced by a small contingent of Irish peasants) was defeated by Cornwallis at Ballinamuck (September 8). A month later, a final tragic French expedition to Ireland was intercepted by Commodore Warren near Tory Island off the coast of Donegal (October 11). Among those taken prisoner was Wolfe Tone, who was to commit suicide in prison on November 19.

23. Quoted in Glover, *The Napoleonic Wars*, 53.

only a democrat but a seditionist, even a Jacobin. Whether or not he actually was, he *thought* he was on what he had called in 1795 the government's blacklist of "damn'd Jacobin pests." He had, after all, publicly labeled Pitt a betrayer of freedom who "kiss'd his country with Iscariot mouth," a "dark Nimrod," a detestable cold-blooded murdering monster "approaching lunacy," a Satanic apostate, and, best of all, a "cockatrice": a serpent who had lain the eggs of the Two Bills (now the Two Acts) in the "dunghill of despotism."[24] He therefore had plenty of reason to feel that insolent and indecent liberties might be taken with *him* at a time when men were being imprisoned for doubting pronouncements that female dancers sent from France might destroy Albion "in a more subtle and alarming warfare" than that of French gunboats.[25]

Recalling (expediently enough) that he was a "compleat Necessitarian" (*CL* I 137), Coleridge could point out, in "Fears in Solitude," that Pitt and his fellow Ministers were only "Poor drudges of chastising Providence." But he was hardly one of those who "dote with a mad idolatry," and in April 1798, when, with Opposition yielding to the general mood, suspension of habeas corpus was in fact renewed during the invasion alarm,

> all
> Who will not fall before their images,
> And yield them worship, they are enemies
> Even of their country!
> > Such have I been deemed.
> > > (*CPW* I 262)

And such a "Democrat & a Seditionist" (*CL* I 397)—though he did not share his friend and neighbor's reputation in the Bristol area as an anti-Pittite lecturer and journalist—was Wordsworth deemed, at least at Alfoxden House and its environs. Indeed, his very silence on political matters made Wordsworth, as Coleridge later said, all the more suspicious to the neighbors (*BL* I 189). Those

24. *L 1795* 331, 64, 9, 39, 301, 288; *CPW* I 83, 88. In a handwritten note of 1820, Coleridge said of the *Conciones ad Populum* that he saw little to regret or retract, with the exception of "some flame-coloured Epithets applied to Persons, as Mr Pitt & others, or rather to Personifications (for such they really were to *me*) . . ." (*L 1795* 25*n*). The same point is made in his 1817 "Apologetic Preface" to "Fire, Famine, and Slaughter" (*CPW* II 1100–1101). Though he did not name names, Coleridge did, in a 1794 letter to Southey, suggest that the stinging serpents of monarchy and aristocracy, symbolized as a "Cockatrice," ought to be killed (*CL* I 84).

25. In one of the (for us) more amusing arrests, James Perry, editor of the *Morning Chronicle,* was, on March 22, sentenced to three months in Newgate for failing to take with sufficient seriousness the Bishop of Durham's pronouncement in the House of Lords on the dangers presented by immoral French dancers. To Pitt, Perry's "impudent malignity" was one of "a chain of experiments made to try what their Lordships would bear," and Perry himself another of those editors who "praised the enemies of the country" and ridiculed the friends of the constitution. Erdman (*EOT* I lxxix) recapitulates the story from the *Parliamentary Register* V (1798), 327–28, 350–51, 354. Coleridge knew Perry, had dined with him, and had contributed his eleven *Sonnets on Eminent Characters* (December 1794–January 1795) to Perry's *Morning Chronicle.*

suspicions—which came to a head in March 1798, forcing the Wordsworths from Alfoxden—had been building for eight months: from the day after they moved in, and Thelwall arrived. The full context—the well-grounded fear of another French invasion attempt, and of pro-Gallican plotters in England— explains the famous Spy Nozy episode, which was at the time, however innately ludicrous, considerably less funny than Coleridge made it appear twenty years after in *Biographia Literaria*. Since that episode, in turn, provides the necessary context for the events of March 1798, we must briefly return to July–August 1797, beginning with Coleridge's famous reminiscence, and going on to supply the facts—many of which remained buried for years in the Home Office Papers, and thus unknown to Coleridge in his lifetime.

3

In Coleridge's account, one of the few amusing episodes in a decidedly un-funny book, the "dark guesses" of a "zealous" local inquisitor in Nether Stowey

> met with so congenial a soil in the grave alarm of a titled Dogberry of our neigh-borhood [the local magistrate, Sir Philip Hales, mistakenly thought by Coleridge to have instigated the investigation] that a SPY was actually sent down from the government *pour surveillance* of myself and my friend. There must have been not only abundance, but *variety* of these "honorable men" at the disposal of the Minis-ters: for this proved a very honest fellow. After three weeks' truly Indian perse-verance in tracking us . . . [and contriving, when we were outdoors] to be within hearing, . . . he not only rejected Sir Dogberry's request that he would try yet a little longer, but declared to him his belief, that both my friend and myself were as good subjects, for aught he could discover to the contrary, as any in His Maj-esty's dominions. He had repeatedly hid himself, he said, for hours together be-hind a bank at the sea-side (our favorite seat) and overheard our conversation. At first he fancied, that we were aware of our danger; for he often heard me talk of one *Spy Nozy*, which he was inclined to interpret of himself, and of a remarkable feature belonging to him; but he was speedily convinced that it was the name of a man who had made a book and lived long ago. (*BL* I 193–94)

Having almost certainly concocted this pun on Spinoza, our amused story-teller goes on at considerable length. Once, joining him on the road as he was returning from visiting Wordsworth, Spy Nozy tried to draw Coleridge out politically—only to be so thoroughly convinced that the man he was question-ing "was no friend of jacobinism" that the agent was allegedly made ashamed of his own play-acting. Others in the neighborhood were also questioned, but the upshot, in the words Coleridge creates for the landlord of the local inn, is conveyed in this bit of dialect: "'I have heard . . . Why, folks do say, your honor! as how he is a *Poet*, and that he is going to put Quantock and all about here in print; and as they be so much together, I suppose that the strange gentleman has some *consarn* in the business.[']—So ended this formidable inquisition. . . ." (*BL* I 195)

The collaborative "business," by the way, was not *Lyrical Ballads*, which, legend notwithstanding, didn't really get underway until Wordsworth's astonishing creative outburst in March 1798 on the heels of being given three months' notice to vacate Alfoxden. (Inspiration cooperated in a timely way with necessity. Wordsworth would soon be homeless, and if he and Dorothy wished to take up the proposal of Coleridge, who had the support of the Wedgwood annuity, that they all go to Germany, they would need the money from a joint volume.) In any case, since the "strange gentleman" *was* William Wordsworth and the "business" at hand the cross-fertilization of two great poets, most readers, grateful that English literature was permitted to advance, have been content to let Coleridge have his anecdote, inventions and jokes included. After all, the poets *were* innocent of treason, were they not? They were, in all senses but the expression of anti-Ministerial opinions that the Government chose to label "treason." But Coleridge immediately adds an important point, a detail that retains the jocularity while, finally, introducing the political atmosphere of the period.

"So ended this formidable inquisition, the latter part of which alone requires explanation." He goes on to explain that, as a poet, he had been seeking an epic subject, one that would permit "freedom for description, incident, and impassioned reflections on men, nature, and society, yet supply in itself a natural connection to the parts, and unity to the whole." He found such a subject in "a stream, traced from its source in the hills," dropping to a break or fall, to form a channel, thence flowing to a farm, a lonely cottage, down to "the hamlet, the villages, the market-town, the manufactories, and the seaport."

Readers may recognize in embryo the general plan of the cultural masterwork Coleridge was urging Wordsworth to undertake in 1797–1798, that philosophic epic that was to integrate "Nature, Man, and Society"—as Wordsworth described the plan in a letter written on the day after he was informed that his lease was to be terminated (*Letters: Early Years*, 212)—in a mutually beneficial and ultimately redemptive relationship. Coleridge's description also anticipates (retrospectively) the meandering and plunging "sacred river" of "Kubla Khan" as well as the sending forth of imagination, in "Frost at Midnight," to

> Sea, hill, and wood,
> This populous village! Sea, and hill, and wood,
> With all the numberless goings-on of life.
>
> (*CPW* I 240)

Though, like so many other projects, the epic poem with the "stream" as subject never materialized,[26] Coleridge made plein air studies in preparation

26. Having written the sonnet sequence *The River Duddon* (1820), Wordsworth subsequently realized that he was "trespassing upon ground" Coleridge had staked out in the passage just cited. He hoped Coleridge would read the Duddon sequence not as a "hindrance" but as a reminder "of his own more comprehensive design, and induce him to fulfil it," so that *The Brook* will, "ere long, murmur in concert with 'The Duddon'" (*Poetical Works* 3:503–4). What a world of psychodrama is concentrated in these words. Coleridge's project was magnificently, if unconsciously, carried out by Shelley, in "Mont Blanc," IV.

for it, an aesthetic process "revolutionary" in a sense undreamed of in the philosophy of the Home Office and of guessing neighbors. Coleridge walked in the Quantocks, "Through glooms, which never woodman trod"—excursions when, "like a man beloved of God" and (he seems anxious to persuade readers of the Recantation ode) "pursuing fancies holy," he wound his way by moonlight along the forested seacoast, "Inspired, *beyond the guess of folly,* / By each rude shape and wild unconquerable sound" (*CPW* I 244; italics added). In nocturnal expeditions that roused the suspicions of neighbors and government agents, Coleridge was observing the progress of the local stream flowing from Holford through Butterfly Combe and Holford Glen, the beautiful recess where he proposed "treason" as a topic to Thelwall, and eventually down to the sea at Kilve:

> With my pencil and memorandum book in my hand, I was *making studies,* as the artists call them, and often moulding my thoughts into verse, with the objects and imagery immediately before my senses. Many circumstances, evil and good, intervened to prevent the completion of the poem, which was to have been entitled "THE BROOK." Had I finished the work, it was my purpose in the heat of the moment to have dedicated it to our then committee of public safety as containing the charts and maps, with which I was to have supplied the French Government in aid of their plans of invasion. And these too for a tract of coast that from Clevedon to Minehead scarcely permits the approach of a fishing boat! (*BL* I 195–97)

The equation of the British Home Office with the notorious Committee of Public Safety in Jacobin France is a more than amusing touch, since both Coleridge and Wordsworth—at once ridiculing and fearing government spies and informers "engrossed," as Wordsworth put it rather too dismissively in 1795, by "sixpenny sedition shops" and "fire-side treason parties"—always held that the Pitt Ministry, in opposing Jacobinism, imitated it in undermining civil liberties, spying on its own citizens, and even seeking their blood.[27] The final remark, however, goes beyond legitimate protestations of innocence to a suggestion that any thought of such an invasion on that part of the coast was not merely unlikely, but simply laughable.

This arch dismissal of any possibility of an invasion on the Somerset coast is at least suspect. But Coleridge maintains this tone throughout the Spy Nozy story, which Wordsworth's biographer Mary Moorman finds "an extremely funny one." "And so, in retrospect, it is," says E. P. Thompson. "But when our sides have stopped shaking," we might want to look more closely at the incident in historical context.[28]

27. Wordsworth's dismissive phrases are from lines 64 and 66 of his abortive translation (undertaken with Francis Wrangham in 1795) of Juvenal's eighth satire (*William Wordsworth: The Poems,* ed. J. Hayden, 1:144).

28. Thompson, "Disenchantment or Default?" 156. The discussion that follows is less indebted to Thompson than to his follower in the study of the poets and politics of the 1790s, Nicholas Roe. The correspondence of Lysons, King, and Walsh is in the Public Record Office at Kew: Home Office Papers HO 42/41. A brief early account of the spy affair may be found in A. J. Eaglestone's 1908 article, "Wordsworth, Coleridge, and the

It was, after all, not a fishing boat but a huge French fleet that had tried to land in Ireland in December 1796. And, on a much smaller scale, there was the actual landing of February 1797, when a French ship violated the Welsh coast of His Majesty's dominions, landing a force of 1,200–1,400 men near Fishguard on the Pembrokeshire coast. Within two days the unimpressive attempt collapsed, and the French invaders—the "Black Legion" and its veteran American commander, the South Carolinian "democrat" and adventurer, Colonel William Tate—were taken prisoner. Understandably, however, there was widespread alarm, including a bank panic in London (February 25). Disturbing revelations emerged from the questioning: not only that the original French plan, designed by General Hoche himself, had called for a landing on the very coast Coleridge pronounced unapproachable, but that Tate's assignment of highest priority had been to attack and set afire the major city of Bristol, and to attempt to "raise an insurrection" among disaffected Englishmen.[29] Though these instructions were not published until 1798, word may have leaked. Within ten days of the local militia leader's account of the questioning, concluding with his assurance to the Duke of Portland of his volunteers' "spirit of loyalty," a Bristol newspaper was sounding the tocsin: "Rouse, British Spirits, rouse! now is the time for Exertion! The Enemy is insulting your Coasts; and is, perhaps, encouraged in that daring Insolence, by the presumptuous hopes that there are Englishmen so debased as to be ready to lend an assisting Hand towards enslaving their Country."[30]

Though, according to an official government estimate of coastal defenses made as late as January 1797, "the Coasts of the Bristol Channel . . . probably do not enter into the Contemplation of an Enemy," the Fishguard incident, reminding west-coasters of the earlier French invasion attempt in Ireland, helps, as Clive Emsley remarks, "to explain why," in mid-1797, the people around Stowey and Alfoxden "assumed from the antics of Wordsworth and Coleridge that they were French spies," and why the Duke of Portland was "sufficiently impressed to direct an agent to investigate." The west coast had once seemed safe from invasion; "now men flocked to the colours of the local volunteers and the government was inundated with requests for additional protection by land and sea."[31]

The *Monthly Magazine* of March 1797 dismissed the landing in Wales as a misconceived effort "to create an alarm on the British coast" (231). Among

---

Spy." See also F. M. Todd, *Politics and the Poet: A Study of Wordsworth*, 96 and appendix B, 299–31. The fullest and most up-to-date account is that of Roe, both in *Wordsworth and Coleridge* (258–62) and in his two *Wordsworth Circle* articles: "Who Was Spy Nozy?" and "Coleridge, Wordsworth, and the French Invasion Scare."

29. *Authentic Copies of the Instructions Given by General Hoche to Colonel Tate Previous to His Landing on the Coast of South Wales, in the Beginning of 1797* (London, 1798). On the Fishguard fiasco, see Commander E. H. Stuart Jones, R. N., *The Last Invasion of Britain;* for the London panic, see Lefebvre, *The French Revolution* 2:193–94.

30. *Felix Farley's Bristol Journal,* March 4, 1797.

31. *British Society and the French Wars, 1793–1815,* 56–57.

those genuinely alarmed by events and with a sharpened eye for pro-Gallican Englishmen was Dr. Daniel Lysons of Bath. In the second week of August, he thought he had damaging information about the occupants of a certain mansion house, speculative but certainly worth passing on to the Duke of Portland at the Home Office. The source of his information was less than direct. Lysons had heard from his cook, who had learned from James Mogg, a former employee at Alfoxden, that Thomas Jones, a present employee, had been startled by some vehement but unspecified political talk at a dinner party the Wordsworths hosted in late July for a dozen guests including Coleridge and a demonstrative but unidentified man who stood up after dessert to hold forth in the manner of a public orator. Considering that neither he nor his sources knew that the after-dinner speaker was none other than Citizen John Thelwall, Lysons managed to make his report quite ominous.

In his August 11 letter to Portland (one written three days earlier has not survived), Lysons referred to "an emigrant family, who have contrived to get possession of a Mansion House at Alfoxden." The "master of the House," who has "no wife with him, but only a woman who passes for his Sister," entertains visitors who "go about the country upon their nocturnal or diurnal expeditions." They "have also a Portfolio in which they enter their observations, which they have been heard to say were almost finished," and for which they were to be "rewarded." Most significantly, they and their guests were "very attentive to the River near them." Lysons' conjecture, which convinced him it was "necessary to acquaint your Grace" with these doings, was that "These people may *possibly* be under Agents to some principal at Bristol."

There is no indication of who Lysons thought the spymaster in Bristol might have been. It is, however, an indication of the mixture of legitimate alarm and paranoia in the air that the Home Office promptly responded by sending from London an experienced government agent to check out this hearsay. It would have been a juicier story had Lysons's sources identified one of the guests as the former anti-Pittite lecturer in Bristol, Samuel Taylor Coleridge, a man they knew. Unlike others in the neighborhood, they apparently did *not* know that the short man with "dark cropt hair" and white hat was the far more notorious John Thelwall, who had been in Bristol just before coming to visit the poets and stopped there again on the return trip, where he met supporters and friends. Given the ignorance of these potentially explosive facts, it is ironic that the agent dispatched from the Home Office was none other than James Walsh, the spy who had been hounding Thelwall since 1794: the man assigned to provoke disturbances at Thelwall's lectures, the very man who had identified Thelwall to the officers sent to arrest him on the notorious charge of high treason in 1794.[32]

Why he hadn't followed Thelwall west in the first place we don't know. Perhaps the famous man—who had traveled from London to Stowey on foot, part of his "Pedestrian Excursion" to collect accurate information on wages

32. See Mrs. Thelwall's *The Life of John Thelwall*, 96, 157.

paid to workers in the "manufacturing system"—was being watched by other agents.[33] In any case, Walsh quickly went to work. Having questioned Mogg, "by no means the most intelligent Man in the World," Walsh focused on the particular attention these "French people" and one of their guests had paid to the brook and to the Parrett River, especially the inquiry as to whether either "was Navigable to the Sea." Later, they had been sighted "examining the Brook quite down to the Sea." Coleridge's note-taking for his projected poem *The Brook* had suddenly become of pressing if nonliterary interest to a British Ministry expecting a second French invasion attempt on the Somerset coast. Walsh was sent a £20 bank note for purposes of tongue-loosening and instructed by his superior at the Home Office, John King, to "immediately proceed" to the Alfoxden-Stowey neighborhood, there to make discreet inquiries, being careful "above all . . . not to give [the suspects] any cause of alarm, that if necessary they may be found on the spot."

Walsh arrived at the Globe Inn, Stowey, on August 15. Within minutes, he overheard a Mr. Woodhouse asking the landlord if he had "seen any of those Rascalls from Alfoxton." He had. The next question pricked up Walsh's already alert ears. Woodhouse asked "if *Thelwall* was gone." Before waiting for the landlord's answer, Walsh quickly asked "if they meant the famous Thelwall." They did. He had been "down some time," with the "Nest of them" at Alfoxden, where they suspected he was still to be found. Walsh probed: he had heard somebody say at Bridgwater that they were French people. But both Woodhouse and the landlord were sure on that point, and another: "No. No. They are not French, but they are people that will do as much harm, as All the French can do." This isn't exactly what Coleridge would later have the landlord say in the *Biographia* version. But it also exploded the most sinister version of the French theory. "I think," the perspicacious Walsh concluded his report, "that this will turn out no French Affair but a mischiefuous gang of disaffected Englishmen."

Walsh added that he had just procured the name of "the person who took" the house at Alfoxden. "His name is *Wordsworth* a Name I think known to Mr. Ford," Richard Ford being a Bow Street magistrate who may have come to know of Wordsworth because of the letters he sent across the channel to Annette. Thelwall had departed the neighborhood, but Walsh stayed on for an additional day (Coleridge's three weeks of "Indian perseverance" probably reflects the activities of prying neighbors) to spy on the "Sett of violent Democrats" at Alfoxden. Though he may well have thought them *potential* fifth columnists, disaffected and debased enough to assist enemies disembarking in the area, he observed no charting of inlets to accommodate a French landing party. Apparently satisfied that no treason was afoot, Walsh departed the area on August 16.

Though they had not been directly questioned, let alone charged with espio-

33. The excursion, announced in the February 1797 *Monthly Magazine* (145–46), was later reported on in Thelwall's series of articles for that magazine between August 1799 and April 1800. See Pollin, "John Thelwall's Marginalia," 76, *n*16.

nage, the gossip about the Wordsworths and their suspicious friends reached their landlady, the widowed mother of the infant owner of Alfoxden. Though she did nothing overt at the time, she may have decided as early as the fall of 1797 that the Wordsworths' days were numbered. In any case, rumors continued. The inevitable denouement came in March 1798. Having been, as Coleridge said, "caballed against *so long and so loudly*" (*CL* I 403), Wordsworth could not survive the renewed and much more intense invasion panic of that month. On the same day (March 5) that even Stuart called for alacrity in jailing suspects without indictment or trial, "Allfoxden's musing tenant" (in the phrase of Thelwall, whose visit the previous summer had proven a catalyst for neighborhood suspicion) received notice that after midsummer, when his lease ran out, he would have to muse elsewhere.[34]

Wordsworth had come into the neighborhood under a cloud of suspicion and he left it the same way. A taciturn man who kept to himself, he lacked the disarming conviviality of Coleridge, suspicion of whom was tempered by his having a "normal" family and an outgoing personality. "As to *Coleridge,* there is not so much harm in *him,* for he is a whirl-brain that talks whatever comes uppermost; but that——————! he is the *dark* traitor. *You never hear HIM say a syllable on the subject.*"[35] An early instance of a politically pregnant "not said,"

34. Poole appealed to the landlady, Mrs. Lancelot St. Albyn, in a September 16, 1797, letter in which he explained the presence of Thelwall and defended the thorough "respectability" of Wordsworth, a man "who only wishes to live in tranquillity." Unpersuaded, she *may* have decided, as early as that autumn, to eventually terminate the Wordsworths' tenancy. What is certain is that on March 5, 1798, she refused to allow the Wordsworths to stay beyond July (*BL* I 193n; Berta Lawrence, *Wordsworth and Coleridge in Somerset,* 151, 155).

Alongside a citation (in an unpublished memoir compiled by Barron Field) of him being, as Coleridge said, "caballed against so long and so loudly," Wordsworth is alleged to have written: "A mistake. *Not the occasion* of my removal. Annoyances I had none. The facts mentioned by Coleridge of a spy, etc., came not to my knowledge till I had left the neighbourhood. I was not refused a continuance. I never applied for one" (cited in George McLean Harper, *William Wordsworth: His Life, Works, and Influence* 1:250n). If he actually wrote this, Wordsworth was being forgetful or dishonest. He was even more annoyed by the publication, in 1847, of Joseph Cottle's *Reminiscences of Samuel Taylor Coleridge and Robert Southey,* in which Cottle reprints (177) the letter to him containing Coleridge's remark about Wordsworth being "caballed against *so long and so loud*" that he was forced to leave Alfoxden.

Given all this, it *is* odd to find Coleridge, finally back from Germany, writing to Poole in March 1800: "I would to God I could get Wordsworth to re-take Alfoxden—the Society of so great a Being is of priceless Value—but he will never quit the North of England" (*CL* I 582). In the event, Coleridge moved to Keswick to be near Wordsworth, by then ensconced at Dove Cottage in Grasmere.

35. *BL* I 189. Despite his firsthand experience in France, Wordsworth was only briefly activist in England. Still, his political reticence surely reflects prudence (familial concern mixed with fear of a repressive government) rather than lack of interest. On the very day habeas corpus was first suspended (May 23, 1794), Richard Wordsworth wrote to his brother about the dangers of expressing his politics freely. Five days later, Dorothy

this mimicking of a local busybody is both the funniest and the most credible moment in Coleridge's retelling of the Spy Nozy episode. The mimickry is in fact repeated by De Quincey, reporting local gossip in one of his *Tait's* articles. In his version, too, Coleridge is a "rattle-brain" and Wordsworth close-lipped on the subject of politics "from year's end to year's end." But the context is ominous: neighborhood discussion of "the probabilities that Wordsworth and Coleridge might be traitors and in correspondence with the French Directory."[36]

Coleridge too, all joking aside, must have been aware in the spring of 1798 of the reverberations of the incidents of July–August 1797 as they affected his own current situation. As Nicholas Roe remarks, concluding his discussion of the period: "The 'Spy Nozy' incident, which with hindsight appears so humorously mistaken, was dependent on a complex sequence of contemporary events and—at the time—was a serious concern for the Home Office. In this perspective, it helps to establish the position of Wordsworth and Coleridge at Alfoxden and Stowey up to their departure for Germany a year later in August 1798."[37]

Government investigation of the Alfoxden "nest" or "Sett" cannot have failed to have had some impact on Coleridge. In Walsh's final report of August 16, 1797, Coleridge had been described as a writer lately from Bristol, "reckoned a Man of superior Ability," but nevertheless one of this mischievous gang of disaffected Englishmen gathered in the Alfoxden-Stowey neighborhood. Walsh's ignorance even of Coleridge's name (which he misspelled "Coldridge" in his report) "perhaps indicates," as Roe suggests, "that the Home Office was ignorant of his political activities at Bristol too." Perhaps; though Tom Poole himself had similarly misspelled Coleridge's name in the opening line of the awed and awful poem of September 1795 he addressed to his new friend, the eloquent Bristol lecturer, after his first visit to Stowey: "Hail to thee Coldridge, youth of various powers!"[38] In any case, by the spring of 1798, the vari-powered

---

responded, reassuring Richard of "William's caution about expressing his political opinions" (*Letters: Early Years,* 121). He would have learned caution regarding the mails because of his need to communicate to Annette across the English Channel during wartime. "On one subject we are habitually silent," Coleridge said in May 1798; "—we found our data dissimilar, & never renewed the subject" (*CL* I 410). The context suggests that the "subject" was religion, though some have identified it as politics. It is, however, hard to imagine that Wordsworth, living in daily intercourse with the poet who had just written the Recantation ode and "Fears in Solitude," would be altogether silent on *that* subject. He may not have been an activist, and overt political engagement even in his poetry receded after the move from Racedown to Alfoxden. Still, as Harper remarks, "We have every reason to distrust the testimony of strangers, and even his own deprecatory remarks in old age, to the effect that he was not at that time [1797–1798] occupied with politics" (*William Wordsworth: His Life* 1:257).

36. *Recollections of the Lakes and the Lake Poets,* 176–77.

37. *Wordsworth and Coleridge,* 258.

38. Ibid., 261. However bad as verse, the poem (quoted by Lawrence, *Wordsworth and Coleridge in Somerset,* 55) reveals that the eloquence that moved Poole was in large part political: Hail to thee Coldridge, youth of various powers! / I love to hear thy soul pour forth the line, / To hear it sing of love and liberty / As if fresh-breathing from the hand divine."

Coldridge had resurfaced as an anti-Pittite journalist publishing in the *Morning Post,* the prominent and very popular London newspaper whose owner-editor was, in March, being questioned by Pitt and the Privy Council.

4

In short, however humorous the confusion of poetic note-taking with espionage in August 1797, or Coleridge's subsequent anecdotalizing of the Spy Nozy affair, surveillance and the possibility of government repression were nothing to laugh at in early 1798. On January 30 Coleridge, discussing with Thelwall correspondence between them that had failed to arrive, alluded ominously to surveillance, adding, "I have lately had a letter from me to Mr Wedgewood [either Tom or Josiah Wedgwood] intercepted, and I suspect the *country* post masters grievously" (*CL* I 382; note the simultaneously ironic yet cautious blaming of local functionaries rather than the Home Office). By March, Wordsworth, experiencing a burst of creative power, was thinking little of politics, even on the heels of his politically motivated eviction. Coleridge was more concerned in that portentous month. By then, chains and dungeon-grates were threatening to become more than the metaphors that clanked in his and Wordsworth's political—and supposedly apolitical—poems.

And Coleridge was a man by no means as undeterred by the "clank of Chains" as he later claimed in the well-known 1803 letter to Sir George and Lady Beaumont. His half-Christian, half-Godwinian emphasis on patience notwithstanding, this self-confessed "Slave of Impulse" (*CL* I 106) had enough of Alhadra's "warm-blooded imprudence" to be, as Thelwall said, reckless on the pulpit. But while he would recall for his aristocratic friends the contemplated moment during the Bristol days when he "might leap on the wall & stand in the breach, the first and the only one" (*CL* II 1001), it was in fact neither he, as he admits in a sonnet, nor Godwinian "closet" revolutionaries "sketching mimic war," but Thelwall who "mid thickest fire / Leap[ed] on the wall" (*CPW* II 1090), thereby gaining a familiarity with dungeons that was more than literary. While he was far too hard on himself in acknowledging a "coward heart" (*CPW* I 107), it seems fair to say that to "any real possibility of personal danger," Coleridge "invariably reacted with caution."[39] Certainly, he did not view prison with the equanimity and afflatus of Thelwall, who could console himself in Newgate with such thoughts as these:

> Within the dungeon's noxious gloom
>   The Patriot still, with dauntless breast,
> The cheerful aspect can assume—
>   And smile—in conscious Virtue blest![40]

39. Lucyle Werkmeister and P. M. Zall, "Possible Additions to Coleridge's 'Sonnets on Eminent Characters,'" 123. See also *L 1795* xlvii*n.*

40. Thelwall's lines, from one of his *Poems Written in Close Confinement in the Tower and Newgate, under a Charge of High Treason,* are quoted by Thompson, *The Making of the English Working Class,* 136.

Neither in his life nor in his poetry (not even in "This Lime-tree Bower my Prison") do we find in Coleridge a hint of the Romantics' agoraphobic enthusiasm for the Happy Prison. As a merely vicarious sufferer of the imprisonment of Thelwall, Horne Tooke, and Thomas Hardy, Coleridge painted, in his lecture *On the Present War,* a graphic picture of life under a Liberty Tree stripped of its boughs. "We can be torn from the bleeding breast of domestic affections," he cried; "we can be thrown into foul and damp dungeons" (*L 1795* 62). A year later, on the eve of the Stowey retirement, it was to Thelwall that Coleridge announced: "I am not *fit* for *public* Life . . . meantime do *you* uplift the torch dreadlessly" (*CL* I 277). Was Coleridge recalling these words—and acknowledging both his difference from Thelwall at that time and his own self-division between engagement and withdrawal—in Alhadra's description of her gentler half? After listening to the Moorish woman's tale of her sufferings in an Inquisition dungeon, Maria asks: "But your husband?" Alhadra replies: "A month's imprisonment would kill him, lady!"

> He hath a lion's courage,
> But is not stern enough for fortitude,
> *Unfit* for boisterous times, with gentle heart
> He worships Nature in the hill and valley,
> Not knowing what he loves, but loves it all![41]

Later in the play, Coleridge will have to momentarily split Alhadra's personality in order, as he admits in a letter to Thelwall, to put in her mouth his own "wish" to escape from the responsibility of action, a wish embodied as the dream of being fed, like Elijah, by ravens, and floating off in a skiff.[42] Elsewhere in the play it is clearly Albert (an advocate of repentance rather than physical punishment) with whom Coleridge identifies. But in Alhadra's response about imprisonment we surely see in her husband, Ferdinand, the publicly "unfit" S.T.C., nature doctrine, universal benevolence, and all. In fact, years later, in the conclusion to *Aids to Reflection,* Coleridge quotes these pantheistic lines about Ferdinand's nature-worship as referring to what "for a brief period was my own state" (404). Earlier in this work, quoting the same passage, Coleridge had been even more orthodox: "The Reader will, of course, understand, that I am here speaking in the assumed character of a mere Naturalist, to whom no light of revelation had been vouchsafed" (353).

The defensiveness is largely justified. My suggestion about Coleridge's identification with Ferdinand has less to do with mere "naturalist" doctrine, about which Coleridge always had reservations, than with their shared fear of prisons. That shared fear seems stressed by the eerie circumstances of Ferdinand's death at the hands of the treacherous Osorio. He is thrust down a deep chasm ("A hellish pit! O God—'tis like my night-mair!") in the furthest recess of an "inhuman cavern" described as "too bad a *prison house* for goblins." Both

41. *CPW* II 528–29; italics added.
42. *CL* I 350; *Osorio* V.i.49–56 (*CPW* II 584); cf. *W* 52, for another reference to Elijah's miraculous feeding in the wilderness.

nightmare and fulfillment are footnoted by an obviously involved author. We are told first that "Prophetical dreams" involve "dim ideas connected with vivid feelings"; then that the actual murder is "an important instance how dreams and Prophecies cooperate to their own completion."[43] In this personal connection, it seems significant that the only lines subsequently incorporated into *Osorio* which appeared first in the Gutch Memorandum Book are lines involving death and imprisonment. The starkest entry—especially in the case of a man who had retired from politics to tend his garden—is inserted, ominously enough, between a "Tartarean forest" of poison trees and a "gallows." It reads:

> a Dungeon
> In darkness I remained—the neighb'ring Clock
> Told me that now the rising Sun shone lovely on my garden.
>
> (*CN* I 152)

Once again, as when warships obstructed Wordsworth's view of the sun from the Isle of Wight, a political obstruction darkens the sun and violates the organic rhythms of nature. But here the imagery is closer to the case of the Mariner, who, along with his shipmates, is cut off from the sun by a symbolic dungeon-grate. A version of the notebook lines recurs in Alhadra's description of the Velez "prison house," and the "dungeon" into which she was cast, with

> no bed, no fire, no ray of light,
> No touch, no sound of comfort! The black air,
> It was a toil to breathe it! . . .
> . . . .
> In darkness I remain'd, counting the clocks
> Which haply told me that the blessed Sun
> Was rising on my garden.
>
> (*CPW* II 527–28)

Coleridge's imaginative shrinking from the Nightmare Life-in-Death in the form of a dungeon may well have been put to a practical test by the ominous developments of March 1798. His reaction supports my suggestion that some of his own "vivid feelings," dreams, and prophecies centered on the prison house of a very real "hellish" Pitt (Ferdinand's "pit" being, I should think, yet another pun on the prime minister's name), and that he wished to avoid the fulfillment of the "night-mair" that entered an 1802 notebook as a cryptic six-word fragment: "My being in the Bristol Newgate—" (*CN* I 1110). For within a week of Stuart's leader supporting the renewed suspension of habeas corpus, and the news that Wordsworth's lease was, for patently political reasons, not being renewed, William, Dorothy, and Coleridge had, apparently at Coleridge's urg-

---

43. *CPW* II 565, 570*n*1. There is a self-fulfilling dream in *The Ancient Mariner* (lines 291–92), and its importance as a Wordsworthian motif is confirmed by the deleted final stanza of "Strange Fits of Passion," the first of the "Lucy" poems. Ferdinand's nightmare in *Osorio* seems to be a horrifying echo of Clarence's veridical dream in *Richard III* (I.iv) or of Eve's dream in *Paradise Lost*.

ing, made their ambitious and perhaps fearful plans to leave England and spend the next two years in Germany.[44]

I am not denying the validity of the given motives—to master German philosophy, "to acquire the German language and to furnish ourselves with a tolerable stock of information in natural science," as Wordsworth put it—nor the fact that such a plan had been "germinating in Coleridge's mind for over two years." But when one of the best biographers of Coleridge's early years notes this, and then goes on to discuss the actual trip as a purely intellectual enterprise, he forgets that the letter in which Coleridge first mentioned such a plan was the same letter in which he announced, "After No. 12, I shall cease to cry the state of the political Atmosphere."[45] In other words, the Watchman had watched in vain; his private journal had failed, and he, soon to be followed by the national Tribune, Thelwall, was driven into political "retirement." Now, in March 1798, with the internal and external crisis at its height and Stuart himself forced to capitulate, a major public bastion of opposition, the *Morning Post*, had, in its own way, failed, and the "political Atmosphere" was at its most stifling.

Nor would this be the first time that the former Pantisocrat had, in an iron time, planned to sail to other climes "o'er the ocean swell" (*CPW* I 68). Sixty years ago J. R. MacGillivray argued that, as a Pantisocrat, Coleridge was one of those with radical sympathies "who by 1794 had full cause to fear that the choice lay between freedom in America and compulsory emigration to Mr Pitt's ideal colony at Botany Bay," and John Colmer has remarked of the earlier nineties that "preoccupation with Pantisocracy certainly saved Coleridge from the 'pitfalls of sedition.'" More recently, it has been observed by an anonymous *TLS* reviewer (judging from the style, E. P. Thompson) that Coleridge's radical trajectory in the mid-nineties, "if it had not been arrested by the retirement of Stowey, would almost certainly have led him to prison," and that this was an important factor in Coleridge's decision to give up politics in order to tend his own garden: "The undulating Quantocks were more inviting than Botany Bay."[46]

44. The plan to go to Germany was worked out between March 9 and 11, 1798. As late as March 6, Wordsworth was "utterly unable to say where we will be" after mid-summer. Coleridge arrived at Alfoxden on the 9th and, two days later, the plans were firm. See Wordsworth, *Letters: Early Years*, 188, 189. According to R. L. Brett and A. R. Jones, after the Wordsworths "had discussed various moves, Coleridge put forward the ambitious proposal that both their families should embark on a two-year visit to Germany" (Introduction to *Lyrical Ballads*, xix–xx). Wordsworth's eviction, John E. Jordan deduces, provided the stimulus both to publish *Lyrical Ballads* and to depart for Germany (*Why the "Lyrical Ballads"? The Background, Writing, and Character of Wordsworth's 1798 "Lyrical Ballads,"* 21, 29–32). If, as seems increasingly likely, Griggs was accurate in tentatively dating Coleridge's letter to his brother George March 10, 1798, that would place this crucial document of political withdrawal squarely within these two critical days.

45. Wordsworth, *Letters: Early Years*, 213. *CL* I 208. Hanson, *The Life of S. T. Coleridge*, 262–63.

46. MacGillivray, "The Pantisocratic Scheme and Its Immediate Background," 144; Colmer, *Coleridge: Critic of Society*, 8; Thompson [?], "Bliss Was It in That Dawn: The Matter of Coleridge's Revolutionary Youth," 932.

But the Quantocks had been rumbling as well as undulating in December–January 1797–1798, only to grow suddenly and ominously still in March. That, at this juncture, prison was much on Coleridge's mind is suggested even by the material he selected to accompany *The Ancient Mariner* in *Lyrical Ballads*.

He extracted two passages from *Osorio*. Together they formed a single unit, which Coleridge described to the publisher of *Lyrical Ballads* as having "no sort of reference to my Tragedy," but constituting "a Tale in itself, as the ancient Mariner" (*CL* I 412). The first extract is Albert's lamentation about what man has done to his fellow-man. Himself cast into the Velez castle dungeon, he meditates on the cruelty of imprisonment, inflicted upon a "poor brother . . . / Most innocent, perhaps—and what if guilty?/ Is this the only cure?":

> uncomforted
> And friendless solitude, groaning and tears,
> And savage faces, at the clanking hour,
> Seen through the steams and vapour of his dungeon,
> By the lamp's dismal twilight! So he lies
> Circled with evil, till his very soul
> Unmoulds its essence. . . .

He invokes the antithesis of this deforming brutality: the healing ministrations of "thou, O Nature!," praying that her "soft influences" be poured on him

> Till he relent, and can no more endure
> To be a jarring and a dissonant thing,
> Amid this general dance and minstrelsy;
> But bursting into tears, wins back his way,
> His angry spirit heal'd and harmoniz'd
> By the benignant touch of Love and Beauty.

And what *if* "innocent," one wants to ask; but this piece, entitled "The Dungeon" in *Lyrical Ballads*, calls upon the prisoner to "relent," to win back his way to acceptance, to reconcile his "jarring" dissonance into something resembling the harmony of the Mariner's post–snake-blessing world, including the merry "minstrelsy" of the wedding feast.

"The Dungeon" is accompanied by "The Foster-mother's Tale." The latter, which immediately follows *The Ancient Mariner* in the 1798 edition of *Lyrical Ballads*, echoes the ballad's "rumbling" imagery, associated in the last chapter with Coleridge's and Alhadra's political earthquakes. The "tale" is of a previous tenant of the Velez dungeon, a "youth" who "was seized / And cast into that hole" because he knew too much. While this nameless young man and Lord Velez were "chained in discourse," an ominous event occurred:

> The earth heaved under them with such a groan,
> That the wall tottered, and had well nigh fallen
> Right on their heads.

So "sore frightened" was the tyrant that he "made confession" of the evils that "brought this judgment." The recipient of this indiscretion was instantly imprisoned. However, with the help of the narrator's father-in-law, the young man escaped to the new world, where, "'tis supposed, / He liv'd and died among the savage men"—roughing it, but at least free, one might surmise, not only from the Velez dungeon but also from the prisons awaiting supposedly conspiring traitors during the most repressive five years in British history.[47] These poems not only accompany *The Ancient Mariner* in *Lyrical Ballads;* they also immediately follow "This Lime-tree Bower my Prison" and immediately precede *The Ancient Mariner* in all editions of Coleridge's poetry. Thus they offer a significant political context in which to place that ballad's "dungeon grate."

That context is reinforced by a similar contribution to *Lyrical Ballads* from Wordsworth, a companion piece to Coleridge's "The Dungeon" entitled "The Convict." This poem, written in 1794–1796, made an unimpressive debut in the *Morning Post* of December 14, 1797, over the name *Mortimer* (Marmaduke's name in contemporaneous manuscripts of *The Borderers*), and now appeared, never to be reprinted, in the 1798 edition of *Lyrical Ballads*. It recaptures the dungeon imagery and—in its earliest, antimonarchical, version, in which the convict's nightmares are contrasted to the serene slumber of a guilty king, fresh "from the dark synod, or blood-reeking field"—even the revolutionary ardor of a passage in Wordsworth's "Guilt and Sorrow" where the "heroes of Truth" are exhorted to "uptear / The oppressor's dungeon from its deepest base" and, "undaunted," rear the "Herculean mace" of Reason "High o'er the towers of Pride" (*Poetical Works* I 340–41). This call to action anticipates Alhadra's curtain lines in *Osorio*. More intriguingly, "The Convict" itself throws baleful light on *The Ancient Mariner,* particularly on the setting sun peering through that dungeon-grate.

Wordsworth's poem (*Poetical Works* I 312–14) opens with another setting sun, this one, as in the Isle of Wight lines, initially positive: "The glory of evening was spread through the west." But, with even more startling abruptness than the cancellation of a beautiful sunset by the "shadowy" hulks of British warships in 1793, the scene of natural beauty is eclipsed and we find the narrator gazing at a dungeon cell:

> The thick ribb'd walls that o'ershadow the gate
> Resound; and the dungeons unfold;
> I pause; and at length, through the glimmering grate,
> The outcast of pity behold.
>
> (lines 9–12)

This pitiable creature, his eyes intent "On the fetters that link him to death," is also frightful. The narrator pierces to the man's heart and finds "More terrible images there," but his external appearance is nightmarish enough: "His bones

47. *CPW* I 282–85; cf. *CPW* II 527–28 and 586–87 for the passages in their contexts in *Osorio,* Acts IV and V. "The Foster-mother's Tale," though excluded from the acting version of *Remorse,* was printed as a "dramatic fragment" in an appendix to the second edition of the play in 1813.

are consumed, and his life-blood is dried," while "his crime . . . / Still blackens and grows" (lines 16–24).

The stark and sudden contrast between the "glory of evening . . . spread through the west" and the convict seen "through the glimmering grate" curiously resembles the sudden shift from hope to horror at the moment in *The Ancient Mariner* when the sign in the sky is revealed as the spectre-bark through whose skeletal rigging the setting sun peers as if through a dungeon-grate. The mysterious guilt and ever-blackening "crime" may remind readers of the never-fully-redeemed Mariner; while Wordsworth's horrific images of blackness and the convict's consumed bones recall Coleridge's skeleton Death, his "bones . . . black with many a crack," and covered with "charnel crust" (*The Ancient Mariner*, lines 169–85). Like the Coleridge of the 1798 *Ancient Mariner*, Wordsworth lays on the Gothic horrors with a trowel. Weighed down by "his fetters at night" and suffering in this "comfortless vault of disease," the half-sleeping wretch, "the terror" leaping at his heart, is awakened as the "jail-mastiff howls at the dull clanking chains" (lines 32–41).

The situation seems a bit hopeless. Then, no less suddenly, the narrator reveals himself as "no idle intruder," but a benevolent friend "whose first wish is the wish to be good," and who "Is come as a brother thy sorrows to share." He is not a detached spectator, he is *involved*. The rough Coleridgean analogue—the simple goodness and fraternal love exhibited by the Mariner in blessing the water-snakes, a benevolence endorsed and didacticized by the moral—is enhanced by the final lines of Wordsworth's poem. "My care," the narrator tells the silent convict, "if the arm of the mighty were mine, / Would plant thee where yet thou might'st blossom again." The lines may convey either a Godwinian penal-reformist wish that the convict might be transported to Australia, or (if only the speaker had "the arm of the mighty," itself presumably armed with Truth's "Herculean mace") a more radical dream of freedom. Either way, the final line's verbs, *plant* and *blossom*—reminiscent of Thelwall's account of how "the blossoms of sensibility began to unfold themselves" as the result of a sympathy-inducing response to nature—are "the first words of positive, natural, organic process to enter the poem since the first quatrain and constitute a shorthand symbolism, as we might now recognize, for Wordsworth's faith in a moral interdependence between the world of nature and the world of mankind."[48]

There is no need to belabor the obvious connection between this "interdependence" and the Mariner's snake-blessing and subsequent moral about loving "Both man and bird and beast." Wordsworth's faith in a moral interdependence between the world of nature and the world of mankind, though merely Godwinian when he first wrote the poem, is close enough to Coleridge's on this point. In any case, whether one sees an analogue between Wordsworth's poem, unsuccessful and never reprinted, and Coleridge's, successful and endlessly

48. Kenneth Johnston, "Wordsworth's *Lyrical Ballads*," 155–56. Johnston's comparison, however, is between "The Convict" and "Tintern Abbey," not *The Ancient Mariner*. Thelwall's remark, from *The Peripatetic*, has earlier been cited in Chapter 5 above.

reprinted, enough has been said to suggest that dungeons were on the minds of both men who put together *Lyrical Ballads* in the spring of 1798.

In fact, however, the man really obsessed by dungeons was Coleridge. If one is, like Mary Moorman, "curious" about the appearance in the *Morning Post* of this early and mediocre poem in December 1797, at a time when Wordsworth "was already the author of other and superior poetry," the explanation is that "Coleridge sent it in as part of his own contract with Daniel Stuart, the editor."[49] Since Wordsworth always feared that poems "connected with political subjects" would be "injurious to sale of the Work" (*Letters: Early Years,* 309), it was probably Coleridge who wanted "The Convict" in *Lyrical Ballads.* Did he connect it not only with the *Osorio* excerpts but with *The Ancient Mariner?* Whether he did so consciously or not, it seems fair to speculate that the "dungeon grate" in that ballad—a "poem of six hundred lines without the glimmering of a reference to any body politic," according to Tillyard—is not only *not* a casual simile, but may be at least as "political" as the dungeoned convict beheld "through the glimmering grate" in the Wordsworth poem Coleridge sent to the *Morning Post* at the outset of his political reengagement in December 1797.

Such poetic imagery, however incidental it may at first seem in *The Ancient Mariner,* clearly coincides with the political and personal history of the time. Whatever speculation may be involved, this much we can definitely say about Coleridge in the spring of 1798: amused wordplay on Spy Nozy (if there actually *had* been any in 1797) and grimmer puns on Pitt's name, as well as high-spirited public praise of that worthy by his cohorts Fire, Famine, and Slaughter, had yielded to an unmistakable mood of disengagement (solemnized into "recantation" by the timely cooperation of the French, whose invasion of Switzerland alienated most British admirers of the Revolution), and to a variety of "fears in solitude" that included such unalluring possibilities as peering through a more-than-metaphorical dungeon-grate or (in Coleridge's own parallel) playing Bathsheba's inconvenient and expendable husband to Pitt's David in the event of a French invasion.

The latter was a possibility Coleridge took seriously as early as January 1798. In a characteristically serpentine letter written to Josiah Wedgwood on the fifth of that month, the day the Triple Assessment was passed, he lamented his increasing "Temptations," as a "hired paragraph-scribbler," to supply sensationalistic and "vindictive" anti-Ministerial material to the *Morning Post,* since nothing else seems to please and interest "my Employers." Though of all things,

---

49. Moorman, *William Wordsworth: A Biography* 1:352. Two other poems signed "Mortimer" appeared in the *Morning Post* in April and May 1798. Though included in Coleridge's *Literary Remains,* both poems are by Wordsworth, and are to be found among his early manuscripts. Moorman concludes: Wordsworth seems to have given Coleridge "a free hand with his old note-books" (352). For evidence that Coleridge eventually drew on seven Wordsworth poems for the *Morning Post* in the spring of 1798, see Robert S. Woof, "Wordsworth's Poetry and Stuart's Newspapers, 1797–1803." One of these poems, entitled "Sonnet," contains the lines: "Haply my bolder tongue may then reveal / The prison annals of a life of tears" (*Poetical Works* 1:308).

"I most dislike party politics—yet this sort of gypsie jargon I am compelled to fire away." Coleridge may have a point, but hardly enough of one to persuade us that all the vindictive glee of the "War Eclogue," to be published three days later, or the urgency of his calls for "the removal of the present Ministers" on January 2 and 20, is to be attributed to the partisan demands of Daniel Stuart!

Doubtless trying to put the touch on Josiah for a larger annuity from the Wedgwood brothers, Coleridge claims in the letter that he is still considering the Unitarian post since, despite its tendency to sectarianize and narrow the intellect, the ministry is at least "comparatively" better than "the Press, considered as a *Trade*." In addition, were he to become a preacher,

> by Law I shall be exempted from military service—to which, Heaven only knows how soon we may be dragged. For I think it not improbable, that in the case of an invasion our government would serve all, whom they chose to suspect of disaffection, in the same way that good King David served Uriah—'Set ye Uriah in the forefront of the hottest battle, & retire ye from him, that he may be smitten & die.'" (*CL* I 367, citing 2 Samuel 11:15)

Indeed, after discussing the invasion panic of the spring of 1798, E. P. Thompson flatly declares: "The poets, when they went to Germany, were hopping the draft."[50] Or fleeing the alternative possibility: imprisonment as potential "traitors." In a letter Thompson quotes on the same page, the local militia commander assures the Lord Lieutenant of Somerset that, though he is sure of his men's "Loyalty," he also holds it "of the highest Importance to use every Means in my Power for investigating (as far as it is possible) the real State of every Man's Feelings, previous to his being entrusted with [Government] Arms." Though neither harbored traitorous impulses, it is difficult to imagine Wordsworth, who was being drummed out of the neighborhood, or Coleridge, a recently resurgent anti-Pittite journalist firing away his vindictive gypsie jargon, passing such a security check with flying colors. Whatever the other varied motivations for departing the country, it was also time—especially after the passage, in April 1798, of the Defense of the Realm Act—to bail out of a worrisome if not intolerable political situation. Germany must have seemed an ideal solution. Emulating the "moving" moon and its attendant "star or two" in the most tension-relieving moment in *The Ancient Mariner* (line 256), Coleridge and the Wordsworths seemed eager to be able to say they "no where did abide."

Considering Coleridge's "career of Sedition" (*CL* II 1001) since his college days, and the display of what might be taken as vestigial or resurgent Jacobinism in his *Morning Post* contributions of the months just past, fear would have been justified. For the hunt *was* on. Arrests of both disaffected Englishmen and

50. "Disenchantment or Default?" 168. Coleridge's most recent biographer concurs. The French invasion of Switzerland had unsettled everything, and given added "urgency" to the contemplated trip to Germany, "threatened like England herself with invasion." The "whole Continent might soon be closed to English visitors. Coleridge even expected that he and Wordsworth might soon be drafted into the army" (Holmes, *Coleridge: Early Visions*, 196).

of insurrection-planning Irishmen began in March. In the following month, Thomas Evans, secretary of the London Corresponding Society, and the surviving committee members of that spy-infiltrated organization were arrested. On April 18 Evans was jailed on a charge of high treason. The following day, the sixteen remaining delegates were "rounded up in the course of a heated discussion as to what action they should take"—join the Volunteers, assist the French, or go to ground—in the event of a French invasion. Whatever its nuances, the debate was ended by the Bow Street Runners, who burst into the room and arrested the entire committee on a general warrant. Evans, by his own account (reminiscent of Alhadra's), "was conveyed to the Bastile, and there confined many months in a cell, with the accommodation of a bog of straw, a blanket, and rug; denied books, pen, ink, paper, candle, and much of the time access to fire."[51]

Within little more than a year of the Margate arrests, and in the aftermath of the failed Irish rebellion revealed and compromised by information extracted from O'Connor and supplied by the Hamburg double agent, the LCS and other clubs proscribed by name were defunct, the abolition of the societies becoming law on July 12, 1799. Thanks to the fear of a French invasion, intensified by the document found in Coigley's greatcoat providing belated proof of the treason the government had always hyperbolically attributed to the radical societies, the Pitt Ministry had at last succeeded in crushing the popular radical movement that had been worrying it for a decade. As Goodwin remarks in his magisterial study of the rise and suppression of the protest movement: "The United Englishmen, the United Scotsmen, the United Britons, the United Irish and the London Corresponding Society . . . found a common legislative grave as a result of their collaboration in the Irish rebellion."[52] By 1799 many of the old leaders were either in prison or, like the dreadless but much-hounded Thelwall, in semivoluntary exile.

5

Fear, dread, and pursuit obviously figure enormously in *The Ancient Mariner.* At the conclusion of Part I of the ballad, the Wedding Guest, noting the ghastly look on the face of the haunted storyteller, invokes divine help: "God help thee, ancyent Marinere! / From the fiends that plague thee thus" (lines 77–78). This terror of being pursued by avenging forces is no less dramatic in Part VI, in the form of another simile located at a pivotal point in the poem: this time as immediate preludium to the Mariner's return to his "own countrée" (line 472).

"Soon" his cheek will be fanned by a gentle, miraculous wind, "Like a

51. Iain McCalman focuses on Evans as the representative "artisan revolutionary" in *Radical Underworld.* But my present source for Evans's account of his confinement is Thompson, *The Making of the English Working Class,* 171, 174; additional details are supplied by Goodwin, *The Friends of Liberty,* 446–47. For a close study of the government controllers and their agents, the spies who infiltrated the clubs, see Mary Thale, ed., *Selections from the Papers of the London Corresponding Society, 1792–1799.*

52. *The Friends of Liberty,* 454.

meadow-gale of spring" that "mingled strangely with my fears, / Yet . . . felt like a welcoming" (lines 461–64). At this moment, however, the Mariner, just awakening from the trance in which the two Voices conversed about his fate, looks about. The weather is gentle, the night calm, the moon high; but the lifeless crew is standing in place:

> All stood together on the deck,
>   For a charnel-dungeon fitter:
> All fix'd on me their stony eyes
>   That in the moon did glitter.
>   (lines 439–42)

So much for theories about the *consistently* (not merely predominantly) benign aegis of the moon. His shipmates' dying curse had not passed away, and the Mariner is unable to lift his eyes from theirs in order to pray. Yet "in its time"—"And now," in the 1817 version, accompanied by the unpersuasive gloss that "The curse is finally expiated" (*CPW* I 203)—"the spell was snapt," and he was able to move his eyes. He "look'd far-forth, but little saw / Of what might else be seen," afraid to look because he feels

> Like one, that on a lonely road
>   Doth walk in fear and dread,
> And having once turn'd round, walks on
>   And turns no more his head:
> Because he knows a frightful fiend
>   Doth close behind him tread.
>   (lines 451–56)

His visual perspective is limited because of the terror he has experienced and which still grips him. Anyone who has walked a lonely road in fear will respond to Coleridge's compelling simile. But whatever else it evokes, this anything-but-dreadless fear of fiends in pursuit is not utterly apolitical—a point perhaps reinforced by a related simile added to the poem in 1817 and identifying the ship-pursuing storm-blast as "tyrannous."[53] The "hot pursuing fiends" of "Religious Musings" who hound "Fear" before he is "transfigured with a dreadless awe" are the agents of political repression (*CPW* I 111–12). Coleridge and Wordsworth actually *were* pursued by spying neighbors and a government agent in July–August 1797, and Coleridge's boss, Daniel Stuart, had been summoned before the Privy Council in March 1798. In Italy in 1804 (if we are to believe the account he gave to Joseph Cottle), Coleridge, whose "reputation" had been brought to the attention of Jerome Bonaparte, was himself ushered

---

53. In lines added to the *Sibylline Leaves* edition, a related "pursuit"-simile was used to ~~d~~escribe the ship as it "drove fast" toward the South Pole: "With sloping masts and dipping ~~prow,~~ As who pursued with yell and blow / Still treads the shadow of his foe" (lines 45– ~~49). Pursued~~ is ambiguous here, the ship is at least as much pursued as pursuing. In ~~the "Tem~~pest strong" played the mariners like freaks and drove them along ~~(lines 41–44~~). In 1817, the "STORM-BLAST" that drove them was personified ~~as a "tyrannical~~": "he / Was tyrannous and strong" (lines 41–42).

into the presence and warned that if he had "written anything against my brother Napoleon, . . . my advice is that you leave Italy as soon as you possibly can." Coleridge took the advice, now certain that he had not been paranoid in earlier suspecting that he was being trailed through Italy by the agents of Napoleon, a telescope-eyed "vulture" who "could descend from the most dazzling heights to pounce on the leveret in the brake, or even on the field-mouse amid the grass." The "tyrant's vindictive appetite" had been whetted, this particular field mouse was convinced, by the series of anti-Napoleonic essays he had published two years earlier in the *Morning Post,* and which Bonaparte, expecting to be praised, probably *had* read.[54]

In early 1798, when he wrote the "fear-and-dread" stanza, Coleridge, along with many other friends of liberty, had even more reason to feel exposed to hostile power. Political as well as supernatural fear haunts the lines in which the Mariner is compared to a man walking in dread, afraid, having looked back once, to look again, knowing "a frightful fiend / Doth close behind him tread." Both Shelleys, in *Frankenstein* and *The Triumph of Life,* allude to this stanza, which Jeffrey Robinson has recently called "the period's touchstone passage," an epitome of "the entire world of pursuit and of power." Twenty pages later, Robinson himself "pursues" the Romantic theme of wandering, persecution, and separation by comparing poems by Thelwall and Coleridge, who, having "experienced persecution to a lesser degree," sympathized with the Patriot's "experience and burden." Of Coleridge, Robinson says:

> He weaves in Thelwallian themes only to deny reference to their original political and personal significance. . . . It is not enough to say that [the dispossessed fig-

54. See *BL* I 216–17. Jerome Bonaparte's warning is reported by Coleridge's publisher, Cottle, in *Reminiscences of Samuel Taylor Coleridge and Robert Southey,* 310–11; see also *BL* I 216n and *CN* II 2785 and *n.* Coleridge claimed, in an 1803 letter to his brother George, that in 1800 the representative of the French consulate in London had asked Stuart when Coleridge's announced "Character" of Bonaparte would appear. Stuart was told, says Coleridge, that "the question was asked at the instance of Bonaparte himself, who had been extremely impressed" with the first part of Coleridge's March 1800 "Pitt and Bonaparte" (*EOT* I 219–27) and was "very anxious to see his own [Character]— which, no doubt he expected, would be a pure eulogy" (*CL* II 1007). The "Bonaparte" half never materialized, but the First Consul would not have been pleased by the three-part "Comparison" of contemporary France with Augustan Rome that appeared in the *Morning Post* in September–October 1802.

These essays, in which Coleridge compared ancient Rome and Bonaparte's France as republics rigidified into iron-handed tyrannies, are reprinted by Erdman (*EOT* I 311–38), who also discusses Coleridge's statements about possible revenge by Bonaparte. According to Stuart (*EOT* I 402–3), Coleridge's essays were translated into French, and probably *were* read by the First Consul. In a letter of May 1802 to Addington, Pitt himself, knowing that Bonaparte was in the habit of having British newspaper reports on France and himself translated and brought to him daily, referred to "*the pacificator of Europe*" taking it into his head "to send an army . . . to avenge himself for some newspaper paragraph" (quoted in Derek Jarrett, *Pitt the Younger,* 204). Though Bonaparte was indeed angered by attacks on him in the British press, there were of course weightier reasons to believe that the 1802 Treaty of Amiens was fragile, that renewed war was virtually inevitable.

ures we find in the poems of Wordsworth, Coleridge, and Thelwall] are wanderers or simply alienated beings. They are often persecuted as well. This means not only that they are lonely or misunderstood, but that their loneliness has the claustral burdens of the political prisoner. From this point of view Coleridge's use of imagination . . . becomes a solution to the plight of the persecuted radical.[55]

In the Coleridgean "solution," loneliness is not only "annulled by imagination," says Robinson, it is "turned into a virtue." When, for example, Coleridge, "imprisoned" in the lime-tree bower and separated from his friends, moralizes about the heart kept "Awake to Love and Beauty!" he is "transforming separation from a condition of political persecution"—evident in the poem ("Maria") in which Thelwall gazed "thro' my grated dungeon" longing to glimpse his wife and child—"to a newly preferred condition of being—the solitary 'liberty' of contemplation and the feeling of love." The same transformation occurs in the final stanza of the Recantation ode and in the turning-point scene of the poem from which "the period's touchstone passage" comes. At that point, however, though love's redemptive process has begun, Coleridge's Mariner is still a pursued and terrified outcast. Like Dante, pursued in hell by a vulture-winged "black devil," or Wordsworth's war-terrified sailor in "Salisbury Plain" (both echoed in this passage), the Mariner is in dread of the vindictive forces that have marked him out for punishment: a fear which, for Coleridge at the time, would have had less to do with Dante's black devil than with that arbitrary entity worse than an "omnipotent Devil," the despotic Pitt Ministry.[56]

Given the plausibility of Thompson's suggestion that Coleridge and Wordsworth were evading a possible military draft in going to Germany, there is a chance that even Wordsworth's tour of the Wye on the eve of departure may have been an evasion of "pursuing" authorities. Citing the speaker's description of himself in "Tintern Abbey" as

> more like a man
> Flying from something that he dreads than one
> Who sought the thing he loved

55. *The Current of Romantic Passion*, 48, 66–67.

56. *L 1795* 295. The lines from *The Ancient Mariner* are both Dantesque and Wordsworthian. Someone penciled in the margin alongside this passage in Coleridge's own copy of *Sibylline Leaves*, "From Dante." The indefatigable Lowes took the hint and tracked the allusion, quoting *Inferno* XXI.25–30 from the J. A. Carlyle prose translation: "Then I turned round, like one who longs to see what he must shun, and who is dashed with sudden fear, so that he puts not off his flight to look; and behind us I saw a black Demon come running up the cliff" (Lowes, *The Road to Xanadu*, 200*n*, 480–83). The next two stanzas describe the black *diavol* skimming along the rock with outstretched wings—a bit like the Napoleonic vulture pursuing the Coleridgean field mouse. Two lines in Wordsworth's "Salisbury Plain"—"Till then as if his terror dogged his road / He fled, and often backward cast his face" (lines 127–28)—also anticipate Coleridge's lines, especially since Wordsworth's fleeing man is a sailor. Perhaps both poets are echoing the *Inferno* passage. For Dantesque symbolism in *The Ancient Mariner*, see A. A. Mendilow, "Symbolism in Coleridge and the Dantesque Element in *The Ancient Mariner*."

(a simile she might well have connected with the flight-from-a-"dreadful-fiend" simile in *The Ancient Mariner*), Marjorie Levinson speculates that if Wordsworth "was, or felt himself to be, a fugitive," the sojourn in Germany might turn out to be "an extended expatriation," and the tour of the Wye Valley

> a valediction to Nature and to England. A pilgrimage to the Lakes would, of course, have made a more satisfying narrative; Wales seems to have been chosen for practical reasons. Wordsworth, already at Bristol [to which he would return to give Cottle "Tintern Abbey," to add to *Lyrical Ballads*], probably lacked the time for a Northern holiday. Besides, if Wordsworth *were* on the lam, it would have been dangerous to return to his native region where he could be easily identified.[57]

Though, like my own extended argument, this is speculative, the political atmosphere at the time justifies such speculation. Wordsworth had reason to worry—James Chandler and Marilyn Butler notwithstanding, the Wordsworth of 1798 had not quite achieved a consistently conservative line on key social and political issues. (Indeed, David Erdman, basing his argument on the republican "Sonnets to Liberty," insists that, as late as 1802, Wordsworth, like Blake at the time, "saw the threat of Napoleonic invasion as a prophetic moment when national community could restore a true Commonwealth.")[58] But if Levinson's wild surmise about Wordsworth being "on the lam" is in part justified, such a surmise would be even more justified in the case of Coleridge, who, unlike Wordsworth, had pursued (whatever his rhythmic shifts between retirement and engagement) a politically activist career, and who had recently been attacking Pitt and calling for a change of government in the pages of the *Morning Post*.

It is at "a dear ransom," according to the gloss, that the Mariner, seeing the approaching ship, "freeth his speech from the bonds of thirst." He frees it, we recall, by biting his arm and sucking the blood in order to cry out. This is, as Humphry House has noted, "his one tremendous effort: it is a moment of terrible hope for him and for the whole crew. But the hope is blasted, not just negatively, but positively, appallingly blasted."[59] The brief hope of the anti-Pittites in the winter of 1797–1798 was no less appallingly blasted. We can only wonder how dearly Coleridge imagined he might have to pay for having freed his own speech in his recent hopeful and violently anti-Ministerial contributions to the *Morning Post*.

Whether we attribute to realism or paranoia Coleridge's sense of vulnerability and of being pursued—his explicitly expressed fear of having letters intercepted, or of being placed in the front lines in the case of a French invasion, or his nightmare of being clapped into a dungeon—he does seem to have believed that his Bristol career and his contributions to Stuart's anti-Ministerial

57. *Wordsworth's Great Period Poems*, 22.
58. "Milton! Thou Shouldst Be Living." On Wordsworthian Toryism by 1798, see James K. Chandler's examination of Burke's impact on the poet, *Wordsworth's Second Nature: A Study of the Poetry and Politics*, and Butler, *Romantics, Rebels, and Reactionaries*.
59. *Coleridge*, 95.

newspaper had fixed him on a wide sea, exposed to the government's arbitrary hostility. Discussing the killing of the albatross, the act that provokes "the fiends that plague" him and that focuses the crew's hostile attention on the Mariner, Michael Cooke speaks of an "assertion of individual primacy, perhaps even of human dignity," and of the Mariner having "undertaken the adventure of individuality."[60] Coleridge's anti-Pittite journalism in December and January 1798 was also an adventure, inadequate as an expression of his political feelings but one that ran the risk of a dungeon-grate at its end.

And so we end by returning to the image of the dungeon. In response to James Thomson's poetic certainty that "Fortune," whatever else she might deny, "cannot" rob one of "free Nature's Grace" or shut the windows of the sky, Coleridge, fighting at the time against the Two Bills in Bristol rather than languishing apathetically in the dungeon of the Castle of Indolence, noted that, "alas!" Fortune "*can* deny us all this" by confining us in "Great Cities." But his preference for rural to urban living is certainly expressed in an extreme and, for a political lecturer recently accused of treason, revealing trope, one reminiscent of Blake's "windows wove over with curses of iron." Those who live in the city because they need work are described as being forced, "fettered and handcuffed," into a "felon-crowded Dungeon"— precisely the imagery he used in *The Plot Discovered* to describe England as a whole after the passage of the Two Acts (*CL* I 154–55, *L 1795* 314–15). It begins to seem less and less "strange and surprizing" that, in the winter of 1797–1798, Coleridge, again temporarily out of political "retirement" and writing against the Pitt Ministry for the *Morning Post,* should again contradict the certainty that Fortune cannot "bar" us from enjoying nature—this time by replacing Thomson's Fortune, who "cannot shut the Windows of the Sky / Through which the Morning shews her dewy face," with a Nightmare Hag who rolls dice to determine the Mariner's fortune, and whose ship "drove suddenly / Betwixt us and the Sun," flecking his "burning face" with "bars / (Heaven's mother send us grace) / As if thro' a dungeon grate he peer'd." Against that imprisoning Hag, pagan Fortune and the Madonna alike have neither a window of opportunity nor, despite the Mariner's parenthetical interjection, a "prayer."

Though I do not believe I *am,* it is possible that I *may* be overestimating Coleridge's fears in 1798. He was, after all, simply writing a few articles, submitting a few poems. Indeed, as his lectures and *The Watchman,* and, more recently, *Osorio* and his *Morning Post* journalism, all suggest, Coleridge felt a frustrating discrepancy between his political hopes and the power of his pen, retired or active, to expedite those hopes. Revealingly enough, even *that* discrepancy betwixt Coleridge and the sun of liberty was depicted in the same obsessive imagery. In a dramatic anticipation of poststructuralism's loss of faith in language's power to refer to actual things or to express ideas and feelings (what Wittgenstein has called "the cage" and others, including Fredric Jameson, "the prison-house of language"), Coleridge, in a notebook entry lamenting "the

60. *The Romantic Will,* 31, 32.

inadequacy of Words to Feeling, of the symbol to the Being," fuses the powerlessness of language with the powerlessness of the political prisoner: "O what then are Words, but articulated Sighs of a Prisoner heard from his Dungeon! powerful only as they express their utter impotence!" (*CN* II 2998).

Though Coleridge's *Morning Post* essays were unsigned and the poetic effusions attributed to one "Laberius," what Cooke calls the Mariner's "exposure of identity" seems relevant.[61] After all, discovering the author's identity would have posed no problem whatever to the Privy Council, which had already hauled Stuart in once for questioning. Whatever Bonaparte's reading habits in 1802, including reading Coleridge's *Morning Post* articles in translation, the *Morning Post* was, we know, closely scrutinized by William Pitt in 1798. It was time to get some wind in the sails. Not, like the Mariner, in order to return to "mine own countrée"— though, on the level of symbolically displaced politics, the snake-blessing is precisely an act of loyalist "repatriation"—but to get out of it and to pursue one's old course in a country new. The stanza in *The Ancient Mariner* immediately following the springing up of the welcoming wind opens, "Swiftly, swiftly flew the ship" (line 465); Coleridge and the Wordsworths planned to be aboard one soon.

61. Ibid., 33.

8

Benedictions in the Cosmic Dungeon: *Enforced* Love in the Mariner's Nightmare Universe

1

Coleridge was working on *The Ancient Mariner* through the winter of Pitt's discontent, the news of the French invasion of Switzerland, and the Margate arrests and subsequent panic. Though apparently completed on March 23, the manuscript was in his hands through the mass arrests of April, until it was finally given to Cottle in the second week of May.[1] This period saw the poet move from indifference to active politics, to ardent opposition to the government (even, in the "War Eclogue," to reaffirmed partisan ferocity), only, hopes blasted, to swing quite rapidly (in the letter to George of mid-March and "The Recantation: An Ode," published in the *Morning Post* of April 16) to a solemn political lavabo. This took the form of a disengagement based on a rejection of all forms of human government in favor of the pursuit of true liberty, to be found, according to the prose "Argument" added to the ode in 1802, by "the individual man, so far as he is pure, and inflamed with the love and adoration of God in Nature."[2]

I have been arguing for Coleridge's partly conscious, partly unconscious, incorporation into the poem of contemporary political events. He would have us believe that we should look less to political than to psychological and religious developments for an explanation of his oscillation between the patriotic indignation he defended, and vented, in the winter and the nature-induced benevolent quietism we hear of in February and, especially, in March and April.

1. Though Coleridge kept calling the ballad "finished" (*CL* I 357, 368, 387), it was still only "340 lines" as late as February 18. The truly finished poem, which, as Wordsworth said, "grew and grew," turned out, of course, to be over 600 lines. The poem was probably begun on the "dark and cloudy evening" of November 13, 1797, and finished, according to both Hanson (*The Life of S. T. Coleridge,* 253) and Chambers ("Some Dates in Coleridge's *Annus Mirabilis*") on March 23, 1798. For Wordsworth's "grew and grew" remark, see Christopher Wordsworth, *Memoirs of William Wordsworth* 1:108.

2. *CPW* I 244. Written in late March 1798, "Recantation" was published in April, when the Bow Street Runners were at their busiest. The *Morning Post,* as Erdman and Woodring were the first to document, was then in retreat on issues of domestic freedom.

I submit that at least the acceleration of this benevolent quietism is a direct result of political developments, and further suggest that we may find a sublimated parallel in the benediction his Mariner pronounces on the water-snakes.

"I love fields & woods & mountains with almost a visionary fondness—and as that fondness [has] increased, therefore I should wish to be the means of implanting it in others—and to destroy the bad passions not by combating them, but by keeping them in inaction" (*CL* I 397). This—the thesis of the March letter to George—is, in essence, the "moral" of *The Ancient Mariner*, later glossed by Coleridge as the imperative "to teach by his own example, love and reverence to all things that God made and loveth" (*CPW* I 209).

The problem, as Lowes said long ago, is that "the 'moral' of the poem, *outside the poem*, will not hold water." Consequence and cause, "*in terms of the world of reality*, are ridiculously incommensurable."[3] This "problem," whether of logical inconsequence or of incommensurable suffering, was powerfully and influentially emphasized by Edward E. Bostetter. His pioneering essay (1962) substituted for Warren's sacramental cosmos a nightmarish universe said to reflect Coleridge's own repressed fears of a world that was irrational and anything but benevolent. Bostetter thus takes the objection to the moral a considerable step further than Lowes; for him, the real "problem" is that in the terrifying world of the poem, the moral becomes (in a neat pun) "inescapably ironic." In the context of an arbitrary universe ruled by the "throw of the dice" and an "avenging Jehovah,"

> the moral tag carries the concealed threat that even the most trivial violations of his love will bring ruthless and prolonged punishment. The way to avoid conscious or unconscious sin is to withdraw from active life to humble ourselves in prayer. At best, the "love" of God is the love of the benevolent despot, the paternal tyrant, the "great Father" to whom each bends. We love not through joy and spontaneous participation in the "One Life" but through fear and enforced obedience.

When the poem is read less for its verisimilitude and morality than for its symbolic evocativeness and psychological depth, Bostetter's approach itself may seem too narrowly "logical." Nevertheless, in its rigorous examination of the "astonishing implications of the dice game," an arbitrary game that "surely . . . knocks out any attempts to impose a systematic philosophic system, be it necessitarian, Christian, or Platonic on the poem," and in its conclusion that the "total impression . . . we get of the universe in the *Rime* is of unpredictable despotic forces," Bostetter's argument seems to me not only unchallengeable but fruitful in one way he fails to consider.[4]

That "way" involves, predictably, the political analogue I have been tracing. What better way have we to reconcile Bostetter's statements about "fear and enforced obedience" as well as "unpredictable despotic forces" with what we know to have been the poet's very different conception of God—God, not as the Miltonic deity, still less as a Blakean Nobodaddy, but as a just, loving,

---

3. *The Road to Xanadu*, 274, 275; italics in original.
4. "The Nightmare World of *The Ancient Mariner*," 114, 115, 118.

infinitely benevolent Parent? True, under the familiar system of optimism descended from the *felix culpa* doctrine Coleridge inherited from Milton, Hartley, and Priestley, partial evil educes perfect good. But *The Ancient Mariner*—in which, because of the shooting of an albatross, two hundred men die, an innocent boy "doth crazy go," and the protagonist is doomed to a proto-Yeatsian purgatory of eternal reenactment of his crime—seems a classic case of overkill.

Leave it to the principal modern denigrator of "Milton's God" to see the injustice in all this. Having killed the bird, William Empson declared in 1964, the Mariner is "struck down by guilt as by the Furies." While he has no wish to "weaken the obvious violence of the effect," Empson thinks it a "sad lack of sturdiness in the modern world to obscure [an] equally obvious reflection: 'how free from guilt he is, according to our own beliefs.'" Those of us not in the "why-all-this-pother-about-a-bird?" camp and less skeptical of the sacramental bond uniting us all to the one life within us and abroad may not share Empson's "beliefs." But then there are *Coleridge's* beliefs to consider. As is clear from the poem to which the famous phrase, "O! the one Life within us and abroad," was later added, Coleridge had far too hair-triggered a moral censor to permit him, no matter how liberated his imagination, to project the gigantic blasphemy Bostetter describes. In that poem, "The Eolian Harp," an ominously over-scrupulous Coleridge records himself as being reproved by his religiously orthodox bride for his unchristian philosophizing, "These shapings of the unregenerate mind" (*CPW* I 101, 102).

Those shapings were benign; consider, with Bostetter, the motiveless malignity of the skeleton Death and his hideous companion aboard the spectre-bark. They cast dice to determine the fate of the Mariner and his crew; the consequence is the penitential life-in-death suffered by the Mariner for the sin or "crime"—as both the gloss and Wordsworth's account of the poem's genesis will later put it—of killing the albatross. One does not have to agree with Empson's insistence that the Mariner is free of guilt, or accept his prosaic argument that the creature was "obviously" slain to provide food for a crew reduced to eating worm-infested biscuits, in order to agree in part at least with Lowes and Bostetter on the incommensurable relation, in the world of reality, between cause and consequence and to be disturbed by the Nobodaddy-tyranny implicit in that arbitrary "throw of the dice." Coleridge, we can be sure, would have been in accord with Einsteinian theodicy. "I shall never believe that God plays dice with the world," said Einstein, whose related axiom (*Raffiniert ist der Herr Gott, aber Boshaft ist er nicht*) is inscribed in Fine Hall, Princeton University: "The Lord God is subtle, but malicious he is not."

The implications of the dice game go to the problematic heart not only of *The Ancient Mariner* but of Coleridge's belief in both a divine order and the freedom of the human will. Given the "ridiculously" disproportionate nature of the punishment, one can only wonder about the systematic moral structure of the universe presented. The forces at work seem remorseless but arbitrary, even haphazard: rather than a harmonious universe presided over by a loving God, we *do* seem to be in a "nightmare world" in which supernatural retribution is weird and unpredictable—at best capricious, at worst malicious. The rolling of the (loaded) dice is ruthlessly arbitrary and the gloating of the victorious hag—"'The game is done! I've won, I've won!' / Quoth she, and whistled thrice" (lines 193–94)—stunning in its sadistic glee.

That hag is a personification of "Nightmare," a realm with which this poet was all too familiar. No matter how profound Coleridge's need to "discover" and bear Christian witness to a benign, intelligible cosmos, it was disturbed and undermined by an equally profound awareness of his own guilt-ridden and often terror-filled inner world—a world of which this poem seems a macro-cosmic, and in part politicized, projection. The poem has its "moral," but providential belief in Christian redemption is troubled if not shattered by suffering of a sort not unknown to Coleridge: the agony of an isolated and outcast soul,

> Alone on a wide wide sea:
> So lonely 'twas that God himself
> Scarce seemed there to be
>   (lines 631–33),

and subjected to primordial forces so beyond his control as to cast doubt not only on moral tags about love and prayer, but on the freedom of the human will itself.

It is possible to resign oneself to the workings of Greek Fate or of Judeo-Christian Providence; but Coleridge, however acutely conscious of limits on volition and of dark abysses in the human psyche, clung always to a vestigial belief in individual free will. If it is a testimony to his honesty and imaginative integrity that his greatest poem should virtually eclipse that article of faith, it is, in turn, a testimony to his faith that he should supply a "moral" and a pious gloss in an attempt to retrieve what was lost. Together they would "explain" the meaning of an uncanny poem which—less providential than capricious, and lacking in much evidence of human freedom—had been curbed and ruddered by the shaping imagination rather than submitted to rational or religious control.

In "The Prospects of the Anglican Church," Cardinal Newman, alert as always to the dangers of corrosive skepticism in individual religious inquiry, chastised Coleridge for having "indulged a liberty of speculation which no Christian can tolerate, and advanced conclusions which were often heathen rather than Christian," by allowing himself to be lured away from religious "Truth" by the dangerous enchantments of "*Imagination* of the Truth."[5] Cole-ridge's orthodox "explanation" of *The Ancient Mariner* in moral and gloss seems almost an anticipatory response to this orthodox but accurate charge—a charge remarkably similar to that implicit in the admonishing glance cast in "The Eolian Harp" by Sara, that "meek daughter in the family of Christ," who evidently (as Byron later said of a character based on his own wife) "*looked* a

5. *Essays Critical and Historical*, 268.

lecture, / Each eye a sermon, and her brow a homily" (*Don Juan* I.xv). And it is precisely this need to render the chaotic orderly and the heathen orthodox that must be kept in mind as we—to quote Byron's famous chuckle at Coleridge's "metaphysics" in the "Dedication" to *Don Juan*—"explain his Explanation."[6]

The dilemma is simple: where on earth did Coleridge, an optimistic believer in a benevolent deity, find the model for a supernatural force that, despite his best explanatory efforts, still seems capricious, tyrannical, even malevolent? One key to my proposed solution to the dilemma lies in the homily that occasioned Coleridge's remark that "my *sermons* spread a sort of sanctity over my *Sedition*" (*CL* I 179). At that time (January 31, 1796) he contrasted the early "uncorrupted" belief in a benevolent God to the later growth of a conception of "a capricious or malignant" deity. Such corrupted religion had a sociopolitical origin, "in Terror, and the Hopes of averting supposed Malignity. Thus Wretchedness and Tyranny assisted to corrupt Religion, and corrupted Religion aids and confirms Tyranny and Wretchedness" (*L 1795* 350).

This interconnection of religious terror and political tyranny underlies the fifth of Coleridge's *Lectures on Revealed Religion* of 1795. There, attacking the doctrine that "Sin is of so heinous a nature that God cannot pardon it without an adequate Satisfaction being made to his justice, and the honour of his Laws and Governments"—a doctrine which appears to him "not to be Blasphemy only because it is nonsense"—Coleridge said:

> He who foresees and permits what he might have prevented predestines. And is this the all-loving Parent of the Universe, who mocks the Victims of his Government with a semblance of Justice and predestines to Guilt whom he had doomed to Damnation—and what is Justice? Is it not "the best means of producing the greatest Happiness["]? And is this effected by infinite Punishment and eternal Reprobation? . . . Should I not honor [such a] Deity by being an Atheist? He who denies my existence would be my friend compared with the man who publickly calumniated me as capricious and a Tyrant! The Calvinist, who from his Childhood has associated with the notion of Deity everything gloomy, everything terrible, is not an Atheist only because he cannot make himself certain that there is not a God! As a man who for many years had been confined in a dark and noisome Dungeon, of which he never saw the Guard, may perhaps be prevented from endeavoring to burst the prison door by the whisper of Terror. There may be a Jailer, and if he intercept me, ah! that deeper Cell and those fearful Torments! (*L 1795* 204–5)

Laws, Government, Tyrant, Victims, Punishment, a semblance of Justice, Dungeon, Guard, whisper of Terror, Jailer, Cell. . . . Even if we didn't know that Coleridge, whose early sermons were typically "*peppered with Politics*" (*CL* I 176),

---

6. Responding to the publication of *Biographia Literaria,* Byron referred to "Coleridge," who "has lately taken wing, / But like a hawk encumbered with his hood,— / Explaining metaphysics to the nation— / I wish he would explain his Explanation" (*Don Juan,* Dedication, II). In Shelley's "Letter to Maria Gisborne" (1820), a Coleridge blinded by his own mental light is similarly depicted as "A cloud-encircled meteor of the air, / A hooded [originally, "blinded"] eagle among blinking owls" (lines 207–8).

could never really separate the themes of his "Lay-sermons" or "Moral and Political Lectures," the terminology here would reveal the *political* parallel of the capricious theological tyranny that so repelled the then-Dissenting theologian. One recalls—and Coleridge had just been discussing the "absurdity" of Gnosticism, and its doctrine that the soul is "imprisoned in the Body" (*L 1795* 197)—the Gnostic vision of "the Soul trapped and lost in the labyrinth of the world, seeking to escape, and frightened back by the gatekeepers of the cosmic prison, the terrible Archons."[7] And it is just this kind of cosmic Dungeon that we enter, it seems to me, in the rather Gnostic vision of penitential terror entitled *The Rime of the Ancient Mariner.* It is a vision—as Wordsworth aptly put it—of "spectral persecution" (*Poetical Works* I 361), persecution only partially alleviated because the Mariner himself, the sole survivor of the voyage, is only partially redeemed.

Now, given Coleridge's incapacity for blasphemy; given, too, the England of the 1790s, and, especially, the political events of the months during which Coleridge was working on the poem, where could a confirmed anti-Pittite have found a better, or a more uncomfortably immediate, model for his capricious Tyrant, "unpredictable despotic forces," and imprisoning universe than in William Pitt and his increasingly arbitrary police state?

In *Osorio,* the Inquisition of "Holy Church" stood, just this side of sedition, for Pitt's inquisition. In phrases contorted by caution, Coleridge had, in *The Plot Discovered,* referred to a Hanoverian law of 1793 "which assumes the infallibility of the Pope, and the power of the inquisition." He hopes and struggles to believe that George III has not been its author, "lest an unbidden and unwelcome suspicion force its way into our bosoms, that they, who ordered such a measure in Hanover, must wish it in England" (*L 1795* 289–90). The "suspicion" had considerable basis. For one thing, Coleridge probably knew that the king, as Elector of Hanover, was behind the Hanoverian censorship law of December 1793; for another, he was far from blind to what was going on around him. The "suspicion" proved to be all too justified; and, secure behind what was, in *Osorio,* a simple substitution of locale and century, and, in *The Ancient Mariner,* a late medieval and supernatural setting and an almost indecipherable symbolic universe, Coleridge may have felt free to drop his guarding qualifications and take for granted, as did Blake and the brilliant political cartoonist James Gillray, the equation of the two inquisitions.[8]

More probably, the terrifying world of *The Ancient Mariner* is both a projection of inner terrors and a largely unconscious displacement and resituation of the contemporary public world, marked by Coleridge's fearful response to political developments. His "night-mair" about "being in the Bristol Newgate"

7. Hans Jonas, *The Gnostic Religion*, xiii.

8. Blake called the Bishop of Llandaff, Richard Watson, "an Inquisitor" of the official "State Religion" (see his Watson Marginalia in *The Poetry and Prose of William Blake*). As early as 1793, Gillray accurately predicted a "British Inquisition" with a "Black List of English Jacobins." See Erdman, *Prophet against Empire,* 263.

(*CN* I 1110) is just one of the nightmares regarding the arbitrary counterrevolutionary inquisition which both Coleridge and Wordsworth connected with the September Massacres and the full-scale drama following that dress rehearsal: the French Reign of Terror of 1793–1794. "Most melancholy at that time, O friend" (writes Wordsworth, addressing Coleridge),

> Were my day-thoughts, my dreams were miserable;
> Through months, through years, long after the last beat
> Of those atrocities (I speak bare truth,
> As if to thee alone in private talk)
> I scarcely had one night of quiet sleep,
> Such ghastly visions had I of despair,
> And tyranny, and implements of death,
> And long orations which in dreams I pleaded
> Before unjust tribunals.
>
> (*Prelude* X.392–412)

From 1793 to 1798, and perhaps most intensely in the spring of the latter year, the tyranny and unjust tribunals most immediately troubling the dreams of Coleridge were English rather than French. Thus, while my "political" reading has some relation to that of Robert Maniquis, I suggest that it is not the French but the *domestic* political Terror that would be most likely to consciously or unconsciously enter into the arbitrary and punitive nightmare-world of *The Ancient Mariner.* Back in 1795, in the opening lecture in his theological series, Coleridge had noted that "a malignant Deity the experience of all our senses shows to be an absurdity" (*L 1795* 105). And the doctrine of God's inability to forgive sin without "adequate Satisfaction" appeared to him "not to be Blasphemy only because it is nonsense" (*L 1795* 204). But it is this very absurdity and nonsense which governs the "ridiculously incommensurable"—almost Kafkaesque—world of Coleridge's greatest poem, a poem of political as well as supernatural "terror."

In that world, even the ambiguous "Second Voice" ("a softer voice, / As soft as honey-dew") insists that "the man hath penance done / And penance more will do." In the poem's most beautiful stanza, the moving moon went up the sky "softly," and this Voice seems to convey the same gentle, benign, redemptive power. Indeed, Christian readers almost automatically connect the vengeful "First Voice" with Law, God's judgment, and the Old Testament; the Second, "softer voice," with Love, God's forgiveness, and the New Testament. The contrast works to a considerable degree; but we ought to remember not only that this is simplistic theology, but that in the poem neither Voice is particularly forgiving. The very content and cadence of "the man hath penance done,/ And penance more will do," recalls the marked countenance of Cain, which "told in a strange and burning language of agonies that had been, and were, and were still to continue to be"—in Coleridge's "The Wanderings of Cain," a work manifestly related to *The Ancient Mariner* and written at the same time (*CPW* I 289). In addition, the "still small Voice" of the Lord, the Old Testament inner voice that haunts Coleridge (*CL* I 78, 395; III 156, 216), can often be more demanding than the louder, ostensibly more severe voice of outer condemnation. Finally, as Coleridge reminds us, "prospects of pain and evil to others, and in general all deep feelings of revenge, are commonly expressed in a few words, ironically tame and mild" (*CPW* II 1098). Thus, even though Coleridge (like Albert in *Osorio*) distinguishes between punishment and penance, the softer Second Voice of *The Ancient Mariner* may resemble that "whisper of Terror" that frightens prisoners back into the "deeper Cell" of the cosmic dungeon (*L 1795* 205). For Coleridge, this would be just another manifestation of that "malignant Deity" he considered a blasphemous absurdity.

Speaking of blasphemous absurdity: when Coleridge said that under the provisions of Pitt's Treasonable Practices Bill "even the son of God could be condemned," he was perhaps recalling the sardonic Lord Justice Braxfield's defense of "the most perfect constitution ever created." Told by one of his victims that Jesus was a reformer, the sarcastic and brutal destroyer of the Scottish Enlightenment replied, notoriously, "Muckle he made o' that. He waur hangit tae!" Of this Treason Bill, Coleridge declared: "I paid it too much reverence when I honored its nonsense with the ceremony of refutation" (*L 1795* 292). But again, this was the "nonsense" under which His Majesty's dominions were in fact to be governed within three weeks (the Two Acts were passed on December 18, 1795) of Coleridge's lecture, a lecture that clarifies the link between a despotic Ministry and a corrupt notion of God:

> If these Ministers believe . . . that this Constitution as it at present exists is the best possible, they must likewise believe either that there is no God, or if there be a God, that he is not all-powerful or not benevolent. For this said summum bonum as it at present exists, doth evidently prevent little evil and produce much. An omnipotent Devil in a good humour would grant a much better extreme of possible good. (*L 1795* 295)

And this government's disregard of the *remnant* of constitutional protection of individual liberty was reaching its peak, one must remember, in the month Coleridge was finishing *The Ancient Mariner.*

Coleridge's reaction to Pitt's escalation of political terror in March 1798 has already been discussed. In the critically important letter written on or about the day the Wordsworths accepted his plan to go to Germany, Coleridge categorically rejects all things French, especially the Revolution, figured of course as the wind, fire, and earthquake of Elijah. And, he continues the biblical allusion, "now (believing that no calamities are permitted but as the means of Good) I wrap my face in my mantle & wait with a subdued & patient thought, expecting to hear 'the still small Voice,' which is of God" (*CL* I 395). I've earlier noted the ambiguity inherent in that still small voice; but even if one were to take this characteristic recoil almost completely at face value, it still seems *somewhat* suspect. It is indeed a convenient logical consequence of this mixture of spiritual serenity and Optimistic Necessitarianism (a quietist doctrine scorned on occasion by the meliorist half of Coleridge) that those in Opposition who—like Coleridge himself in December and January—expected real change from change of government, became, in April, "Dupes of a deep delusion" who "fondly . . . attach"

> A radical causation to a few
> Poor drudges of chastising Providence,
> Who borrow all their hues and qualities
> From our own folly and rank wickedness,
> Which gave them birth and nursed them.
> (*CPW* I 262)

Admission of personal membership in the brotherhood of folly and wickedness is an authentic insight for any political thinker. But surely the "all" is excessive, an indication perhaps that the wondrous ways of Providence can become indistinguishable from an understandable excuse for retreating from active Opposition. It is not an isolated phenomenon. The same reaction that allows Coleridge to accept Pitt and his Ministers as creatures of "chastising Providence," requiring, not "indignation" against them as "instruments of Evil," but rather "contemplation" of their uses "in the great process of divine Benevolence" (*CPW* I 101, 262, 116*n*), has its secular version in the pseudoreligious confidence of some contemporary academic Marxists who, in what Edward Said calls "cloistral seclusion from the inhospitable world of real politics," talk and write endlessly about politics while trusting in a Utopian vision of Marxism, a teleological allegory subsuming all antagonisms in a painlessly achieved classless society.[9]

In short, Coleridge's "providential politics" in "Fears in Solitude" is neither the first nor the last instance of a transcendental teleology that, embracing oppressed and oppressors alike and treating the latter as passing phenomena, serves to depoliticize even a revolutionary ideology. And where does theoretical justification, genuine insight, or rationalization in the face of disappointed hopes, end, and an expediency based on fear of reprisal begin? We may, I think, detect some political as well as philosophic wishful thinking in the adverb when Coleridge describes himself in "Fears in Solitude" as a man who, having engaged in some "youthful . . . folly," is now "*securely* wise." For by April, Pitt, having survived the domestic crisis of the winter, was once again firmly in control. "The general zeal and spirit of the country," he informed Lord Camden on the twenty-first of that month, "is everything that we can wish."[10]

In the wake of the French advance into the Swiss Cantons, the massing of the *Armée de l'Angleterre* under Bonaparte, and the Margate arrests, the nationwide fear of invasion rallied the country behind the prime minister. Writing to Lord Mornington in April, William Eden, Lord Auckland, echoed Pitt's judgment in the letter to Camden. While he acknowledged that his Irish-born friend

9. "Opponents, Audiences, Constituencies, and Community," 20–22. Said is critiquing Fredric Jameson's teleological argument in *The Political Unconscious*. See also Jean-Pierre Mileur, *The Critical Romance: The Critic as Reader, Writer, Hero,* especially the notes on 208–9 and 219–20.

10. *The Later Correspondence of George III* 3:49*n*. "Fears in Solitude," lines 14–16; italics added. This claim to secure wisdom was a deposit subsequently drawn upon—in *The Friend, The Statesman's Manual,* and the second *Lay Sermon.* Later Coleridge frequently cited "Fears in Solitude" as evidence of his loyalism, of his veneration of "my country and its laws" (*LS* 122*n*).

had reason to worry about his large estates in an Ireland still threatened by Jacobinism, all, proclaimed Auckland, was again well in England: "With respect to this good old island, I can say with extreme pleasure and confidence that I have never seen it so rightly disposed. There certainly exist in London, Manchester, and other places, clubs and secret societies of men connected and affiliated as 'United English[men]' on grounds of the wildest and blood-iest democracy. But they are few in number, and composed of the refuse of mankind."[11]

By the end of April, a good deal of the most noisome "refuse" had already been collected. With her potential "traitors" transported, jailed, silenced, or convinced of the need for national solidarity in the "good cause," Britannia stood ready to repel the revolutionary invader. Within a few short months, the war was nationalized; the living legend of "helmsman" Pitt, the lean inflexible "pilot that weathered the storm," was born.[12] As the nation's leader in a time of peril, the prime minister was impregnable, and, with the Habeas Corpus Act suspended, the arbitrary power of the police was virtually unlimited.

A close reading of the letter of early March, taking into account some hyper-bolic breast-beating for the benefit of conservative brother George, reveals that Coleridge is making a kind of culminating statement rather than saying much that is new. Indeed, the withdrawal into an internal spirituality, the recoil from things public and political, is at the very heart of the Coleridgean rhythm (or apostate illusion, if we accept some versions of the old radical and/or New Historicist critique of the Romantic ideology). In "Religious Musings," he had pivoted from evocations of the French Revolution, "the Giant Frenzy / Uproot-ing empires with his whirlwind arm," and the unconquerable Hag, "black Ruin . . . / Nursing the impatient earthquake," directly (the very next line) into religious quietude: "O return! / Pure Faith! meek Piety!" (*CPW* I 121). The same recoil and purgation occurs in the Epode that concludes the violently prophetic "Ode on the Departing Year":

> Away, my soul, away!
> I unpartaking of the evil thing,
>   With daily prayer and daily toil
>   Soliciting for food my scanty soil,
> Have wail'd my country with a loud Lament.
> Now I recentre my immortal mind
>   In the deep Sabbath of meek self-content;
> Cleans'd from the vaporous passions that bedim
> God's Image, sister of the Seraphim.
>
> (*CPW* I 168)

11. Auckland to Mornington, in *The Wellesley Papers: The Life and Correspondence of Richard Colley Wellesley, Marquess Wellesley, etc.* . . . 1:52–53.

12. Depicted since 1793 as the "helmsman" of the British Ship of State, Pitt was honored on May 28, 1802 (his forty-third birthday) as "The Pilot that weathered the Storm," the title of the hymn of praise composed for the occasion by George Canning and sung, in Pitt's absence, by more than eight hundred guests.

In the March letter to his brother, once again "unpartaking of the evil thing," Coleridge is prayerfully recentering his mind, cleansed of the political passions that bedim God's image, in the "deep Sabbath" of humble retirement. This religiously inspired, Elijah-echoing, withdrawal from political activism is nothing new under the Coleridgean political sun. What *is* new, I have been suggesting all along, is that after the Margate arrests some ten days prior to this letter and the impending suspension of habeas corpus, now supported even by Stuart, there was a serious possibility of a dungeon-grate coming, not only "betwixt" the Mariner and "the Sun," but also between S.T.C. and the sun. I turn now to the "submerged" parallel to Coleridge's reaction in the crucial—and moonlit—act of his Mariner.

2

The situation leading up to the benediction recalls the stagnant calm preceding the arrival of the spectre-bark. Utterly passive, the Mariner "look'd" at the sea and the corpse-strewn deck, both "rotting": "a million million slimy things / Liv'd on—and so did I." He "look'd" to heaven and tried to pray—like *Hamlet*'s Claudius, in vain:

> or ever a prayer had gusht,
> A wicked whisper came and made
> My heart as dry as dust.

But the static monotony of the ocean desert ("the sky and the sea, and the sea and the sky / Lay like a load on my weary eye") and the longing for extinction ("And yet I could not die") is broken by that extraordinarily lovely ascending movement:

> The moving Moon went up the sky,
> And no where did abide:
> Softly she was going up
> And a star or two beside.
> (lines 255–58)

The feverous Mariner is tormented yet static, the cooling moon serene yet mobile. Her cool beams bemock the "sultry" ocean as if spreading it with "morning frosts" (later, "April hoar-frost"),

> But where the ship's huge shadow lay,
> The charméd water burnt alway
> A still and awful red.

Once the Mariner's perspective ranges out "Beyond" that aquatic Inferno recalling his initial "hellish" act, he can see the once slimy things as creatures sharing the luminous mobility of the moon—a change from hot loathsomeness to cool beauty John Keats seems to have remembered, and reversed, in *Lamia* (I.47–51, 146–72). Antiphonally, the Mariner is *then* able, in one of the truly splendid moments in Romantic poetry, to perceive them as even more vividly beautiful "*Within*" the red shadow of the ship:

> Beyond the shadow of the ship
>   I watch'd the water-snakes:
> They mov'd in tracks of shining white:
>   And when they rear'd, the elfish light
>   Fell off in hoary flakes.
>
> Within the shadow of the ship
>   I watch'd their rich attire:
> Blue, glossy green, and velvet black
>   They coil'd and swam; and every track
>   Was a flash of golden fire.
>   (lines 264–73)

Despite Irving Babbitt's amusing but reductive reference to the Mariner "admiring the color of water snakes," this is surely the imaginative high-water mark of the poem, perhaps the imaginative apex in all of Coleridge. But the passage goes on, to the conclusion of Part IV of the ballad:

> O happy living things! no tongue
>   Their beauty might declare:
> A spring of love gusht from my heart,
>   And I bless'd them unaware!
> Sure my kind saint took pity on me,
>   And I bless'd them unaware.
>
> The self-same moment I could pray;
>   And from my neck so free
> The Albatross fell off, and sank
>   Like lead into the sea.
>   (lines 274–83)

Ian Wylie's recent tracing of the radical political, even millennial, implications of Coleridge's interest in contemporary natural science concludes with a discussion of these "miraculous" stanzas. "Seen as creatures of decay until this moment," writes Wylie,

the spontaneously generated "slimy shapes" now appear as immature sea-snakes, held for the symbolic duration of the curse in the first stage of their life cycle. As the moon rises, it invigorates the ocean and evokes a glittering response in this young life. . . . Wherever the light of the moon falls the spell of the decaying burning sea is broken and life returns. The sea-snakes mature in the enlivened water, and as they disturb the myriads of luminescent larvae the water shines brightly. . . . The light of the moon transforms the uncreated parasites of a decaying ocean into protoplastic larval forms, imbued with vitality to grow and develop. For a few moments the phosphoreal oils burn in the ship's shadow where the moonlight cannot penetrate, but as the ocean begins to teem with life, the snakes fill the darkness with their own luminescence and dispel the redness of the corrupted water. . . . As the creative, living light at last overcomes the decaying fires around the spellbound ship, it elicits in the mariner an overflowing affirmation of life. At this moment of oneness between God and man, the burden of his old world is transformed by the plastic power of his imagination, and in place of death there is now life.[13]

Wylie's brilliantly documented treatment of the movement from generation to restoration, from death to life, traces, in naturalistic terms of the ambiguous decay and vitality of marine luminescence, the religious pattern most readers acknowledge in these stanzas: a new perception in which ugliness is transformed to beauty by means of a self-transcending, spirit-renewing act of grace, gratuitous and, ultimately, divine in origin.[14]

Not all readers have followed Coleridge's Christian paradigm, a redemptive process culminating in the prayer that causes the albatross to fall from the Mariner's neck. The act relieving him of the burden of his transgression, an admiration of water-snakes through which the Mariner "obtains subrationally and unconsciously . . . the equivalent of Christian charity," was condemned many years ago by Babbitt as a confused and bogus claim to a "religious seriousness that at bottom [the poem] does not possess."[15] But while it has come under that and subsequent attack, the "conversion" experience enacted here—as John Beer, Anthony Harding, Robert Barth, and others have shown— is lacking in neither psychological verisimilitude nor parallels. "When the albatross falls from the Mariner's neck," writes Beer, "the moment of relief is cognate with that in *The Pilgrim's Progress* when Christian, after many initial trials, comes to the cross and feels his burden, loosed from his shoulders, tumble away into the mouth of the nearby sepulchre. Even the imagery is not dissimilar. 'He looked therefore, and looked again, even till the springs that were in his head sent the waters down his cheeks.'"

"And in real life," as Beer continues, there was the example of John Woolman, the American Quaker whom Coleridge pronounced a man who not only "believes in 'the Voice within' but lives by it" (*CL* III 156), and whose spiritual autobiography Coleridge referred to approvingly in a letter of February 1797 (*CL* I 302). In his spiritual *Journal*, synopsized by Beer, Woolman describes "how his first religious stirrings came through remorse at killing a mother-robin on her nest; later he speaks of 'feeling the spring of Divine love opened'; and still later, of the 'well of living-waters; or the springing up of the living-waters' as the sign of a good Quaker meeting. By such usages, the biblical imagery of springs and waters had been drawn effortlessly into the language of personal religious experience."[16]

13. *Young Coleridge and the Philosophers of Nature*, 160–61.
14. Anthony John Harding stresses the blessing's origin in God, "acting perhaps through some 'kind saint'" (*Coleridge and the Idea of Love: Aspects of Relationship in Coleridge's Thought and Writing*, 63). Father Barth has emphasized in particular the "conversion" or "renewal" of the Mariner's heart as "a gratuitous act of God"—the source of power, the *natura naturans*, "revealing itself through the *natura naturata*," the aggregate of phenomena (*Coleridge and the Power of Love*, 65, 69, 70).
15. "The Problem of the Imagination," 120–21.
16. *Coleridge's Poetic Intelligence*, 160–61. Beer quotes from pages 35–36 of the 1678 edition of Bunyan's *Pilgrim's Progress* and from John Woolman's *Journal* (Dublin, 1776), 3, 4, 12, 22, 28.

But having persuaded us of the parallel with the Mariner, Beer goes on, two paragraphs later, to observe that, while the Mariner can thus far be regarded as a representative convert, when we "look more closely" at some of his detailed experiences—

> and more particularly at the language and imagery with which they are described—we begin to see that the implications of his "conversion" range much further. Within that fairly simple awakening there is being indicated the work of a more subtle and intricate transformation of the psyche, particularly relevant to the circumstances of the time when the poem was written. We recognize certain points of contact, in other words, between the Mariner's experiences and those of the young men who had come to a sense of hopeless isolation as a result of the political events of the time, including the aftermath of the French Revolution and the declaration of war on France by England.

A framing context for this intriguing generalization was established with a rhetorical question a dozen pages earlier—"Was this a world in which it was possible for human beings to be changed and where the French hopes would be realized in a new order?"—followed up by the interesting suggestion that *The Ancient Mariner* "was originally placed as the opening poem to *Lyrical Ballads*" to signal the correspondence between the Mariner's experiences, chief of which is the rescue from apathy and despondency, and "those of Wordsworth and Coleridge during the years after the French Revolution." Thus, the Mariner's "final state could be said to give a tone to the collection as a whole."[17]

But despite these valuable insights, Beer says absolutely nothing specific about the possible political implications of the very experiences, language, and imagery to which he draws our attention as indicative of "a more subtle and intricate transformation of the psyche" relevant to "political events" of the period. Thematically if not linguistically, this is what Kitson's 1989 essay *does* supply. But I wish to simultaneously extend and narrow his argument, focusing on the precise events emphasized earlier.

In the closed world of the poem, the Mariner's blessing of the water-snakes seems as unpremeditated and unforced as his earlier gratuitous cruelty in killing the companionable albatross. Now a symmetrical act of sympathy, a change of heart and a cleansing of what Blake called "the doors of perception," enables him to see the universe as sacred and beautiful, thus initiating the movement from isolation to communion, or (in Blakean terms) from Innocence through Experience to Organized Innocence. This Romantic paradigm has immense appeal. Yet it is not necessary to crudely historicize this scene in order to draw out its possible political implications.

Though it was to have many thematic progeny, the sudden vision in all their vivid beauty of the water-snakes earlier despised as loathsome reptilian life generated from the rotting ocean is like nothing else in literature. Yet the situation, as Ian Wylie has shown, is not without precedent in the eighteenth-century naturalists and not quite without its Coleridgean precursor. In "The

17. Ibid., 161, 150, 175. Incidentally, it was France that first declared war on England.

Destiny of Nations," a fragment with deep political implications, the formerly "slimy" Protoplast, transfigured by "Love," is suddenly beheld standing "beauteous" on the "charméd wave" (*CPW* I 141). When the Mariner envisions as beautiful, and then blesses, the previously slimy water-snakes, is Coleridge (consciously or unconsciously) going beyond this passage in "The Destiny of Nations" to its political implications to present us with a symbolic equivalent of the repudiation of his own indignant hatred of "cockatrice" Pitt and the other "slimy" miscreated things flourishing in the pestful calms of despotism? It was, as Tillyard says, "only through the destruction of his old state of mind that the Mariner was able to achieve the new, enlarged state of mind that could include the water-snakes in its sympathies." Though Tillyard's conviction that the poem is without a glimmering of politics prevented him from making any such connection, this internal renovation and transformation parallels not only Wordsworth's recovery from despair in the French Revolutionary Books of *The Prelude* but also the renunciation by Shelley's shackled Titan of his hatred of tyrannical Jupiter: "I wish no living thing to suffer pain."[18]

On the level of sublimated politics, this sympathetically enlarged, renovated, and reintegrating state of mind would parallel Coleridge's Christian or Necessitarian renunciation of all hatred of Pitt and his fellow "drudges of chastising Providence." The Mariner hates those "million million [later 'thousand thousand'] slimy things" that "crawl with legs" on the rotting and "slimy Sea" (lines 121, 230). Later in this turning-point section of the poem, Part IV, these slimy crawlers become simply "water-snakes," then "happy living things" (lines 265, 274), and, finally (in the gloss), "God's creatures of the great calm." Not only does this recall (echo and revoke) the gloss on the crawling things ("He despiseth the creatures of the calm"), it specifically incorporates the previously loathsome things within the economy of God's creation—just as, in "Fears in Solitude," the previously loathsome Ministers of the Pitt government become creatures operating within an Optimistic design of "chastising Providence": *God's* ministers, as it were.

This acceptance of evil can seem quietist to the point of blandness, or profoundly Christian. In both the blessing of the water-snakes and in "Fears in Solitude," Coleridge echoes the benevolent Necessitarianism of Joseph Priestley, a rational determinist and materialist who nevertheless accepted divine revelation. What he called his "belief in the doctrine of an overruling Providence" led Priestley to the conviction that what appears repellent or noxious is actually subservient to the benign Creator's grand scheme. Priestley's *Essay on First Principles of Government* (1768) and his influential "Introductory Essay" (1775) to *Hartley's Theory of the Human Mind* (his condensed version of Hartley's 1749 *Observations on Man*), reveal a Unitarian fusion of Hartleian associationism and Optimistic Necessitarianism in which human action, determined rather than free, is guided in conformity with God's design. Thus, even apparent evil educes ultimate good, and bad men can serve benign ends. Not that, say, the

18. Tillyard, *Five Poems*, 72–73. Shelley, *Prometheus Unbound* I 305. See Appendix.

members of the malign Pitt government are conscious of their part in the divine plan. But all—water-snakes and Ministers—are part of God's universe, instruments of his will and, as participants in creation, themselves sympathy-inducing tenants, as Thelwall put it, "of this many-peopled sphere."

In fact, this suggested equation between the Pitt Ministry and the water-snakes might illuminate Coleridge's ambiguous remark that in *The Ancient Mariner* he "ought not to have inculcate[d] humanity to beasts."[19] By "inculcate" he may have meant simply instill or attribute, but as a classicist Coleridge would also be likely to have in mind the Latin root, *inculcatus,* the past participle of *inculcare:* to tread in, or down, or under-heel (*-calx*). That is, either he "ought not to have" anthropomorphized beasts or that he "ought not to have" reduced human beings to beasts, as he had earlier reduced Pitt (*L 1795* 288) to that fabulous and fatal serpent whose mere glance can kill, the "cockatrice," whose root (*calcatrix,* from the Latin *calcare,* to tread) also leads etymologically to *calx,* "heel." The most famous heel in Western tradition is the "heel" bruised by the Satanic serpent, its head in turn to be bruised by the mother of us all, our instinctive hostility to snakes biblically explained by this curse in which God "put enmity between" humankind and "the serpent" (Genesis 3:15).

Given his remark about "inculcating," and the traditional enmity between human beings and snakes, it may not be all that strange that those "slimy things" that crawl "Upon the slimy sea" (lines 121–22) should resemble cockatrice Pitt, that "Satanic apostate" who had turned against liberty, and a Ministry that had flourished in the "pestful calms" of despotism: all of them creatures whom, in the spring of 1798, Coleridge might have been less anxious to inculcate than to cultivate in order to mitigate the "enmity between" himself and men with the power to "bruise" *him.*

Little of this can have been completely conscious, though the pattern of power and the repellent need to bow before it if one is not to be crushed has a long, and bestial, lineage in Coleridge. Back in "Religious Musings," the "wretched Many," bent beneath their loads, "gape at pageant Power,"

> before whose purple pomp
> Who falls not prostrate dies! And where by night,
> Fast by each precious fountain on green herbs
> The lion couches: or hyaena dips
> Deep in the lucid stream his bloody jaws;
> Or serpent plants his vast moon-glittering bulk,
> Caught in whose monstrous twine Behemoth yells,
> His bones loud-crashing!
>
> (*CPW* I 118–19)

The bestiary of "pageant Power" is a transparent allegorizing of the Pitt Ministry, as Charles Lamb confirms in his letter protesting the excesses of the assault: "Snakes, Lions, hyenas and behemoths, is carrying your resentment

---

19. This comment on the poem was recorded by Hartley Coleridge in his review of his father's *Poetical Works* (1834), 28.

beyond bounds" (*Letters* I 8). But Coleridge stuck to his stridency, including that constricting serpent glittering in the moonlight in an altogether less appealing way than the water-snakes coiling and swimming in the moonlit turning-point scene of *The Ancient Mariner.*

Again, I am not claiming that the Mariner's loving embrace of the water-snakes consciously allegorizes Coleridge's enforced prostration—in lieu of being crushed—before the Pitt Ministry in the spring of 1798. After all, in this same spring, Coleridge once again overtly reduced Pitt and his Ministers to "Hyaenas, that in the murky den / Whine o'er their prey and mangle while they whine" (*CPW* I 247*n*): an inculcation of humanity to beasts that occurs in the sixth stanza of the Recantation ode, dropped when the poem was reprinted as "France: An Ode" in 1802. But at the very least, Coleridge's remark about inculcating humanity to beasts in *The Ancient Mariner* reaffirms the obvious: that both revulsion and Christian love have as their central objects, not sea-birds and water-snakes, but human beings—with the blessing of the snakes suggesting at once a loving and/or fearful embrace of the previously despised, including, in the present reading, one's political enemies.

The benediction emerges in such a both/and reading as an extremely curious and problematic participant in the whole Romantic program: "Love of Nature leading to Love of Mankind," to quote the subtitle to Book VIII of *The Prelude.* That was the never-proven but never-abandoned credo of Wordsworth— who, incidentally, retained his detestation while deleting his "inculcation" of the Pitt Ministry of 1793–1798 as "vermin working out of reach" to "undermine / Justice, and make an end of Liberty." Those undermining vermin had put Hardy, Tooke, and Thelwall on trial; jailed, transported, or hounded various activists into political retirement; and, most "base," set Home Office agents and informers on disaffected Englishmen like himself and Coleridge, innocents driven abroad in reaction to a Gallophobic hysteria they themselves (ironically enough) had begun to share. Wordsworth's charges—identical to those leveled against the Pitt Ministry in Coleridge's *Morning Post* "Essay on Party Spirit"—are repeated, though the "vermin" disappear, in the 1850 version of *The Prelude.*[20]

For Coleridge, the movement, itself serpentine, between revulsion and providential acceptance, even love, is not only a religious and a philosophic but a *political* movement. Christians who have promulgated truth, preached the "rights of Man," and "defied 'wickedness in high places,'" must calmly endure ignominy, wretchedness, pain, even death. But they are, Coleridge continued in this December 1796 epistolary sermon to the activist Thelwall, "to feel nothing but sorrow, and pity, and love for those who inflicted [these torments]; wishing

20. *Prelude* X.654–57. In this, the 1805 version, the Ministers "Thirsted to make the guardian crook of law / A tool of murder" (X.646–47); in the 1850 version, they "Acted, or seemed at least to act, like men / Thirsting . . .", and the "vermin"-image is dropped (XI.61–73). Wordsworth, in the words of Coleridge's "Essay on Party Spirit," held that Pitt and his Ministers, "in order to oppose Jacobinism . . . imitated it in its worst features: in personal slander, in illegal violence, and even in the thirst for blood."

their Oppressors to be altogether such as they, 'excepting these bonds'" (*CL* I 282–83).

If so, is it simply that "the Author recalls himself," as he would in a 1797 footnote added to "Religious Musings," "from his indignation against the instruments of Evil, to contemplate the *uses* of these Evils in the great process of divine Benevolence" (*CPW* I 116*n*)? Or—as the implicit protest, in "Fears in Solitude," against being "deemed" an "enemy" of his country may suggest—is this snake-blessing a symbolic ritual beneath which we may discern Coleridge's own strategic retreat (in "the Hopes of averting . . . Malignity") from the offensive anti-Ministerial position he had recently taken in the *Morning Post*? For the exception mentioned in the letter to Thelwall ("excepting these bonds") draws our attention to a hard reality of which Thelwall—released two years earlier from the Tower, where he had been a Job comforted by a patience-urging Godwin—hardly needed to be reminded: namely, that the "bonds" (the dungeon-grate and clanking fetters) were unabstract instruments of evil firmly in the hands of an oppressive government.

Without for a moment denying the genuineness of the "benevolence & quietness growing within" Coleridge, I merely suggest that the specter of the dungeon was at least a participating partner in the chastening, subduing, and aversion-softening effect of a Nature moralized by Akenside, Wordsworth, Thelwall, and Coleridge himself. Indeed, while Bostetter's earlier-cited remarks carry no intentional political implication (by "active life" he means no more than what is represented by the wedding feast), we may well wonder to what degree "fear and enforced obedience" motivated Coleridge's political oscillations. I refer particularly to his decision in March 1798 to "withdraw himself from active life" in the world of politics—a world he had only recently reentered—in order to "humble himself in prayer," even to plan to withdraw physically by leaving a country to which he believed the Pitt Ministry deemed him hostile.

I have no wish to reductively distort what virtually all readers from 1798 on have agreed are the finest stanzas in *The Ancient Mariner,* a passage enshrining an epiphanic moment registered in subsequent poems from "Tintern Abbey" to Yeats's "A Dialogue of Self and Soul" and "Vacillation" (though Yeatsian beatitude, significantly, is secular and autonomous) as well as in Auden's elegy for Yeats. The blessing of the water-snakes *may* be the supreme imaginative and intuitive act of *The Ancient Mariner:* the recovery of creative joy through an affirmation of "the one Life within us and abroad." But in its full context, that blessing, its impulse retrospectively attributed to a pitying "kind saint," and followed immediately by conscious prayer, seems in its own way as ominous as "unregenerate" Coleridge's meek submission to his upbraiding and orthodox bride in "The Eolian Harp." My resistance here is supported by the arguments of Bostetter and, more recently, of Camille Paglia—arguments to which I shall be adding a few political twists.

Bostetter's point about the poem's moral (that it suggests that we "love not through joy and spontaneous participation in the 'One Life' but through fear and enforced obedience," a succumbing to the despotic Father-God) leads to the more challenging but related argument of Camille Paglia. From her psychoanalytic, iconoclastically half-feminist perspective, the "blessing" of the water-snakes is less a moving religious conversion-experience than an anxiety-induced collapse, Christian and Wordsworthian, that undercuts Coleridge's penetration into the daemonic, chthonian life embodied by the primordial water-snakes. The Mariner's response to them is, she writes,

> embarrassingly simplistic. "A spring of love" gushes from his heart, and he blesses them. The moment he can pray, the albatross falls from his neck and into the sea. How dreadful to see our shaman-poet unmasked, cranking the bellows of afflatus like a stagehand. Coleridge is overcome by anxiety and surrenders to Wordsworth and to Christianity. Love and prayer are a ludicrously inadequate response to the chthonian horror that Coleridge has summoned from the dark heart of existence. . . . Having introduced a benevolent emotion into his daemonic poem, Coleridge is at a loss how to proceed. A new cast of characters is hustled in—seraphs, a Pilot, a Hermit. There is confused dialogue, a fuzzy twisting and turning. Here is the point: the moment the Mariner prays, the moment good rather than evil triumphs, the poem falls apart. At the end of part IV Coleridge is overwhelmed with fear at what he has written and vainly attempts to turn his poem in a redemptive direction.

In Paglia's fusion of Freudian and Jungian terms, the "superego acts to obscure" what has come from the poet's "amoral id." What has surfaced from the teeming id is the terrifying revelation of being alone on a wide, wide sea, beneath which a Jehovah-obliterating "vampire mother . . . rises from the slime of nature," whirling the Mariner about "in the maelstrom of chthonian nature" (images that intriguingly recall those I've earlier identified as specifically revolutionary in Coleridge). Given these powerful up-thunderings and whirlpools, the Mariner's desperate clinging to the "frail twig" of prayer and "communal churchgoing" is, says Paglia, a futile "Christian finale," a "smokescreen" which cannot, despite Coleridge's "vigorous efforts to steer the poem in a morally acceptable direction," conceal from the stunned Wedding Guest "the terrible revelation of Coleridge's daemonic dream-vision."

Of the religious thoughts, or afterthoughts, in *Robinson Crusoe*, James Joyce declared: "They decorate the figure of the rude sailor neither more nor less than the votive talismans which hang about the neck and from the outstretched hands of a miracle-working Madonna."[21] Employing similar imagery to similar purpose, Paglia notes that, nineteen years after he wrote *The Ancient Mariner,* Coleridge

> added the marginal glosses still adorning the poem. These dithery festoons are afterthoughts, revisions that often depart crucially in tone from the text they "explain." We hear in them the Christian Coleridge trying to soften the daemonic Coleridge, exactly as the older, Urizenic Wordsworth "corrected" his early nature

21. "Daniel Defoe," 11–12.

poetry. By rationalization and moralization, Coleridge strove to put out the daemonic fires of his own imagination.[22]

The first of my "political twists" is the suggestion that the snake-blessing may be the supreme act of Coleridge's cleansing of his vaporous *political* passions: his transformation of radical politics into what he called in 1805 "spiritual Revolution" (*CN* II 2547). If so, it would certainly be the most imaginatively appealing dramatization of his transformation of politics into poetry. But there is a problem: a collapse paralleling (on the political level) the regresssion, rationalization, and moralizing described with such élan by Paglia in her presentation of a Coleridge "overwhelmed with fear"—a variation on and extension of that "fear and enforced obedience" to which Bostetter refers.

Such a fearful reaction implies some degree of calculation. Yet this blessing and the ability, in "that self-same moment," to "pray," have been, until quite recently, almost universally accepted as acts both spontaneous and essentially moral. Are they? The repeated verbs suggest otherwise. The Mariner "look'd" and "look'd and "look'd," then "watch'd" and "watch'd," until, finally, he "bless'd" the snakes, "unaware." We may recall, as John Beer does, Bunyan's Christian, who "looked . . . , and looked again," or Wordsworth's response to the jocund "host, of golden daffodils." His "I gazed—and gazed—but little thought / What wealth the show to me had brought," genuinely expresses the immediacy of experience rather than any "thought" (that will come later, when on his "pensive" couch he lies), let alone calculation. The same would *seem* to be true of the Mariner's repeated watching and looking at the "happy living things" swimming in their tracks of "golden fire." Yet the Mariner's is a more prolonged and less intense gazing, and it may issue in a benediction and a prayer less redemptive than fearful, less active than acquiescent.

The effect of the verb sequence is reinforced by the diurnal, almost seasonal, modulation of the water-snakes' opalescent colors, with the morning hoar-frost and white flakes of elfish light kindling—not in direct moonlight but in the moon-illumined shadow of the ship—into the more vivid flashes of "golden fire." Taken together, the evolution of colors and the Mariner's verbal repetitions suggest less suddenness than we tend to remember. The full spectrum of his acts of will—from the first two blood-acts, "I shot" and "I bit," through "I . . . cry'd" out, "I look'd," "I watch'd," "I bless'd"—form a continuum. A new level of perception is attained, a change certainly occurs; but the change is not instantaneous and not quite "moral," despite the dragging in of the "kind saint."

Though "that self-same moment I could pray," atonement is not fully achieved with the benediction, or ever. Discussing the punishment of a crime as the theme at the "core of the poem," Tillyard speaks of the Mariner's "fulfillment of a frightful penance: he issues out of his prison like a prisoner who has served his time."[23] But the Mariner is a lifer. The crime is never fully expiated—not after the blessing of the snakes, nor, a moment later, when the albatross "fell

22. For the passages quoted from Paglia, see *Sexual Personae*, 326–28.
23. *Five Poems*, 67, 68.

off, and sank / Like lead into the sea"; not after the encounter with the Hermit, who does *not* "shrieve" the Mariner's soul effectively enough to fully "wash away / The Albatross's blood," but only temporarily relieves him by becoming the first in a long line of auditors to a tale "wrench'd" from the sufferer "With a woeful agony";[24] not even after the latest compelled listeners, the Wedding Guest and the poem's audience, have heard the compulsive retelling and are left as "stunn'd" as both the Mariner and the Wedding Guest and "sadder" as well as "wiser." If the blessing of the water-snakes had been efficacious in the sense of being truly redemptive, it would obviously not have been necessary (as a number of commentators have noted) for the poem to go on and on—in what most readers find a rather confusing way.

In short, the Mariner's is a case, in Freud's grim phrase, of "Analysis Interminable": a case, in Michael Cooke's distinction, less moral than ontological. "Morally, we expiate our actions," says Cooke; "ontologically, we contain them and recognize in them the idea of ourselves as expressed in those actions, and, with reservations that are no more than analytical, as satisfied by them." Applied to the Mariner, this seems, at first, unpersuasive. But it is crucial to remember, as Cooke does, that the tale "originates in response to the question 'What manner of man art thou?' The Ancient Mariner is more than remembering, he is identifying himself, the person who includes the water snake blessing without excluding the shooting of the albatross."[25]

Indeed, though Cooke does not raise the issue, his point about inclusion is reinforced by the often overlooked fact that the snake-blessing impulse "does *not* take place because of the light cast on the snakes by the moon—comments by Warren, Clarke, and a host of other critics to the contrary notwithstanding." Rather, the snakes are transformed, if not *by*, at least *within*, "the red fiery light" of the shadowed water, water symbolically reddened by, precisely, the shed blood of the albatross.[26] And it might be added that the Mariner, who identifies himself as the man who blessed the snakes without excluding his shooting of the bird, is also the man who freed his speech from the "bonds" of thirst by drinking his own blood.

24. In all versions of the poem, the Hermit "crossed his brow" (line 575; *cross'd* in 1798 ed., line 608) in response to the Mariner's plea to "shrieve me." Though the gesture may have been meant to grant the request for absolution, it might just as easily signify a blessing conveying something like "Heaven defend us!" The crossing is brief, in any case, and is instantly followed by "'Say quick,' quoth he, 'I bid thee say / What manner of man art thou?'" (lines 609–10). The later gloss implies, in what follows the semicolon, that he *has* been shriven, but emphasizes the penitential suffering still to be borne: "The ancient Mariner earnestly entreateth the Hermit to shrieve him; and the penance of life falls on him" (*CPW* I 208).

25. *The Romantic Will*, 36, 38.

26. Oddly, the critic I'm quoting, Elliott B. Gose, Jr., having made the important point about the Mariner's "conversion" occurring as the snakes are transformed by the "red fiery light," goes on to cite several passages involving blood—all interesting, but none referring to the blood of the albatross that symbolically stains sea and sun ("Coleridge and the Luminous Gloom").

The political application of these points touched on by Cooke and Gose would stress a similar ontological or existential continuity in Coleridge, a subtle undercurrent of consistency (however oscillating or ambivalent) in which political obsessions persist unreconciled beneath the humble, often too-much-protesting, retirements into benign quietism. The snake-blesser is the same man who sheds blood: the bird's, and—later, in order to cry out—his own. The activist who vents indignant and prophetic wrath is the same man who recoils into benevolent quietude, only to break out of retirement, retreat again, return, and so on, in a back-and-forth rhythm that he himself compared to the movements of a long-legged water-insect and a serpent.

Accordingly, one might ask if the "slimy things" that had crawled upon the slimy sea and evoked revulsion are now, simply (or simplistically, grotesque legs shed) beautiful "happy things" to be blessed? Or do they too reflect and contain the sustained dialectic between expressions of hatred and necessary vengeance, on the one hand, and tolerance, even love, on the other? Through an act of enlarged sympathy, the Mariner blesses snakes which, on the level of my political argument, have been generated out of slime associated with the pestful despotism presided over by snake-Pitt as "cockatrice." That fabulous creature is associated by Coleridge with the "Diminution of civil Freedom" against which the prophet Samuel warned the ancient Israelites. Disregarding him, they later "severely repented of it so that there was among them this figurative Remark. A cockatrice is a Dragon with a Crown on his head, and hatched by a Viper on a Cock's Egg. The Viper was a symbol of Ingratitude among them and a Cock's Egg of Credulity" (*L 1795* 134). A year earlier, in the privacy of a letter to Southey, his fellow "sturdy Republican," Coleridge had regicidally telescoped the king and his ministers, monarchy and "Loath'd Aristocracy," in the same image, urging a very different sort of "sympathy" than that expressed in the snake-blessing—sympathy as homeopathic medicine and a talisman against tyranny: "The Cockatrice is emblematic of Monarchy—a *monster* generated by *Ingratitude* on *Absurdity*. When Serpents *sting*, the only remedy is—to *kill* the *Serpent*, and *besmear* the *Wound* with the *Fat*. Would you desire better *Sympathy*?" (*CL* I 84).

The gap or aporia in *The Ancient Mariner*—its apparent failure to sustain the dialectic between vengeance and sympathy, hatred and love—is emphasized in Robert Maniquis's remarks relating revolutionary Terror to this "poem about violence and its symbolic transformations." The killing of the albatross and "the sacrificial sacrament imitated" by hanging the slain bird about the Mariner's neck "must," he writes, "be got beyond"—

> in an act of love imagined without any primitive memory of *necessary* violence at its center. When that act of love is complete, the albatross falls from the Mariner's neck and the sacrificial memorial of violence falls away.
>
> The framed narrative of *The Ancient Mariner* provides the perfect distancing from this most self-conscious of all romantic poems about the mythic imagination of violence. . . . The Wedding Guest is unforgettably silenced by the story. But the Wedding Guest is not both a wiser and a sadder man because the violence wit-

nessed and all its subsequent—and disastrous—transformations have left him with any new symbology. He has only the injunction to love in the poem[;] it is only by a thaumaturgic act of love that both violence and its sacrificial sublimations are got beyond. Yet Coleridge himself thought that injunction an inadequate issue out of the poem's symbolic complexity.[27]

What is ostensibly missing in *The Ancient Mariner*—the oscillating continuity or sustained dialectic between "love" and the "necessary violence" at its center— can be demonstrated by glancing at the subsequent history of the two most gleefully vengeful poems Coleridge ever wrote, the "War Eclogue: Fire, Famine, and Slaughter" and "The Raven." After examining Coleridge's subsequent revisions, and revisionings, of those two poems, as well as the revisioning implicit in the gloss added in the same year (1817) to *The Ancient Mariner* itself, we will be in a better position to return to the ambiguous blessing of the snakes.

3

Both poems appeared, as earlier noted, in the *Morning Post* during the period of Coleridge's political reengagement and his ongoing composition of *The Ancient Mariner.* The first imagines the enraged multitude seizing and dismembering Pitt "and his brood" on earth, with hellfire clinging to the damned prime minister "everlastingly." The second vents sardonic glee at the destruction of those who made a ship of the oak that housed the raven and his family. Both fables, the first rather more explicitly, are political and anti-Pittite; and both were later the occasions of apologia. In 1817, in *Sibylline Leaves,* an "antidote" was "annexed" to "The Raven" in the form of a couplet responding to the anticipated question: was the bird's revenge *truly* "sweet"?

> We must not think so; but forget and forgive,
> And what Heaven gives life to, we'll still let it live.

One might applaud Coleridge's Christian endorsement of his doctrine of the one Life if one weren't embarrassed by the mealy-mouthed auto-suppression that amounts to imposing mind-forged manacles on his own satiric Muse. Serpentine Coleridge himself was, characteristically, divided about this live-and-let-live "antidote." In now, nineteen years later, leaving the unjust oppressors to Heaven, was he purging himself of that vengeance which is the Lord's, *or* timidly recanting that "salutary wrath" advocated in "Religious Musings" (*CPW* I 112) and put into secular action by Alhadra, the avenging heroine of *Osorio,* and by Coleridge himself when he published his political fable on March 10, 1798, in the *Morning Post?* More the latter it would seem, for the couplet appended as an antidote to "The Raven" was itself not allowed to stand without commentary. The endlessly dialectical reviser was compelled to scribble in the margin a manuscript note beginning: "Added thro' cowardly fear of the Goody." Both internal (Coleridge's own moral censor) and external, the Goody betrays a "Hollow" where the "Heart of Faith ought to be." Coleridge defines it in the manuscript note as "this alarm concerning Christian morality,

27. "Holy Savagery and Wild Justice," 390, 391.

that will not permit even a Raven to be a Raven, nor a Fox a Fox"—with the addition of the extra-poetic animal suggesting a pun on the name of Pitt's great enemy in Parliament (*CPW* I 171*n*). Perhaps the timid Goody, refusing to accept what even the "Heart of Faith" reveals (that there is genuine evil in the world), will also not permit a slimy, crawling, and grotesquely "legged" sea-reptile, or a "cockatrice" Pitt, to remain just that, unredeemed and unblessed.

Aside from the well-known and endlessly discussed preamble to "Kubla Khan," the most notorious of all Coleridgean apologias specifically involves Pitt. It is, of course, the "Apologetic Preface" added in this same year, 1817, to "Fire, Famine, and Slaughter." In defending the "anonymous" author from the atrocious "malignity" of heart said to have motivated the poem, Coleridge distinguished between "serious" and "imagined" or fanciful desire for revenge. Ironically, he himself associates the "round and round" whirling motion that characterizes the sinking of the ships in both *The Ancient Mariner* and "The Raven" with the obsessiveness of a "rooted hatred, an inveterate thirst of revenge," which "eddies round its favourite object," moving restlessly "round and round" (*CPW* II 1099).

This is just one indication among many that, whatever the subtle, sophisticated, and serpentine truths of this belated preface, Coleridge protests far too much when he claims that at the time he wrote or published "Fire, Famine, and Slaughter," he was so far from wishing *real* harm to the prime minister that he would have been ready, "had Mr Pitt's person been in hazard, to interpose my own body, and defend his life at the risk of my own" (*CPW* II 1101). The point is that Coleridge *still* reprinted the poem. And a handwritten note he added at the end of the "Apologetic Preface" in a copy of the 1829 edition of *Sibylline Leaves* reaffirms the continuity we have been tracing. He found the preface (which he'd described a dozen years earlier as his "happiest effort" in prose composition) "a work creditable to the head and heart of the Author, tho' he happens to be the same person, only a few stone lighter and with chestnut instead of silver hair, with his Critic and Eulogist" (*CPW* II 1097, 1108).

Since, again in 1829, the poem was reprinted, Coleridge might have added that the silver-haired and chestnut-haired man was the "same person" as the raven-haired youth who had written "Fire, Famine, and Slaughter" in the first place. Not, of course, that what Max Schulz calls the "many" or "multivisaged" Coleridges—poet, journalist, lecturer, preacher, apostate, addicted "failure," damaged archangel, religious oracle, philosopher, Highgate sage—are to be reduced to an essential, individual personality, in accord with what James Clifford criticizes as the biographical drive to deliver, at the "expense of plenitude," a "shaped life" consistent with the "myth of personal coherence." But there *is* continuity as well as discontinuity, protean shiftings balanced by a simultaneous Coleridgean respect for a "self," evident in his "pertinacious hold on it through all his quick changes of fictive personalities."[28] Thus, the triadic Coleridge—

28. Schulz, "The Many Coleridges," 22, 23, quoting James Clifford's "'Hanging Up Looking Glasses at Odd Corners': Ethnobiographical Prospects," 46–47.

young, middle-aged, old; political activist, poet, conservative moralist—can no more be dismembered than Yeats's great-rooted blossomer can be reduced to merely leaf, or blossom, or bole; or Yeats himself to the raven-plumed boy, or lover, or sixty-year-old smiling public man of that very Coleridgean poem, "Among School Children."[29] To refocus these considerations on the years that concern us: The Coleridge of 1795–1798 who sees evil as part of Providence's plan and who preaches love of one's tyrannical oppressors is the "same person" who promulgates truth, defies wickedness in high places, longs to make a Pitt-fall, and even works to that end—at least until no choice but affrighted disen-gagement (or "loyalism," or "repatriation," or capitulation) seems viable.

The secondary elaborations on, and revisionings of, "The Raven" and "Fire, Famine, and Slaughter" are characteristic of Coleridge. For even more psycho-logically complex reasons, he held back his second-best-known poem, "Kubla Khan," for almost twenty years, finally publishing it in 1816, and then only "at the request of a poet of great and deserved celebrity [Byron, through his publisher, John Murray], and, as far as the Author's own opinions are con-cerned, rather as a psychological curiosity, than on the grounds of any sup-posed *poetic* merits." This defensive apologetic preface was itself preceded by the equally disarming designation of the poem as "A VISION IN A DREAM. A FRAGMENT" (*CPW* I 295). Of course, *without* the preface few readers would take "Kubla Khan," a magnificent assertion of creative inspiration, to be either fragmentary or lacking in poetic merit. *With* the preface, we *do* notice the fragmentary nature of a work divided between vivid, visionary experience and, with the introduction of the retrospective "I" (". . . in a vision once I saw . . ."), after-the-fact commentary. In addition, if we linger elegiacally on "once" and on the opening word of "Could I revive within me . . . ," the poem, this self-designated "psychological curiosity," seems to go beyond sublime ambiguity to suggest creative failure.[30]

"Kubla Khan" was by 1816, when it was finally published together with *Chris-tabel* and "The Pains of Sleep," famous by word of mouth. But *The Rime of the Ancient Mariner* had long been out there in public, famous but maligned as fragmentary and incoherent by a number of reviewers. They included the author's estranged friend Robert Southey (who thought many of the stanzas in this "Dutch attempt at German sublimity" in themselves "laboriously beautiful; but in connection . . . absurd or unintelligible") and, most painfully for Cole-ridge, Wordsworth himself. His perceptive but less-than-gracious comments (in his preface to the second edition of *Lyrical Ballads*) on the "great defects" in the "Poem of my Friend," especially the charge that "the events[,] having no

29. Like "Tintern Abbey," Yeats's "Among School Children" and "A Prayer for My Daughter" take off from Coleridge's "Frost at Midnight."

30. The most recent discussions of the relation of the introductory material to the poem are David Perkins's "The Imaginative Vision of 'Kubla Khan': On Coleridge's Introductory Note" and commentaries by James Holt McGraven, Jr., Norman Fruman, and Patricia Skarda, all in Richard E. Matlack, ed., *Approaches to Teaching Coleridge's Poetry and Prose*, 62–68, 89–101, 134–46.

necessary connection[,] do not produce each other," seem, in retrospect, to have made something like the later gloss inevitable. Whatever the ambiguous genesis and final shape of "Kubla Khan," *The Ancient Mariner,* defensive Coleridge would show, was *not* disconnected, *not* "A FRAGMENT."

The endlessly dialectical, or serpentine, nature of Coleridgean unity-within-diversity, which every reader of Coleridge recognizes, is notoriously reflected in the relationship between *The Ancient Mariner* and its prose gloss, rather different texts by the same yet different author in different guises. This learned prose commentary, though often eloquent and sometimes beautiful, has irritated as many readers as it has pleased. His editorial commentary concerned above all with the supernatural figures and events in the poem, this notably pious glossist has more than a little to do with the Mariner who, in response to the protean terror and beauty of the world he has experienced, simply blesses the water-snakes and prays, prompted by his guardian angel, his "Goody."

For at least some antithetical readers, the Mariner's benediction of the snakes has seemed less redemptive than regressive, a retreat into Christian moralism. If so, it might be said to anticipate both the didactic moral that even Coleridge felt had obtruded too openly on the reader as well as the prose gloss, which an increasing number of contemporary critics, many following the early lead of B. R. McElderry, Jr., and later of Bostetter and Empson, find less a clarification of the poem than a revisionary moralistic simplification. The point is sufficiently germane to my own reading of the blessing of the water-snakes to justify a brief sampling of recent critical response to this complex interplay between the poem and what Lawrence Lipking accurately calls "the most famous marginal gloss in English."

Discussing "Versioning," which he defines as the editorial decision to print, not an eclectic critical edition of a literary text, but "two or more radically differing versions that exhibit quite distinct ideologies, aesthetic perspectives, or rhetorical strategies," Donald Reiman notes that "students of the English Romantics are especially interested in discovering what elements bind youth to age and what happens to a poem when a writer revises it after he leaves the chamber of maiden thought." What Reiman calls "versioning" was finally, in 1993, applied to the various texts of *The Ancient Mariner* in the edition of Martin Wallen. Surprisingly, though he mentions the early and late texts of *The Ancient Mariner* on the next page, Reiman does not discuss the gloss.[31] Wallen and others have, beginning with Wordsworth, who, anticipating much subsequent criticism, regarded it as superfluous and an afterthought.

In his important 1932 article, "Coleridge's Revisions of *The Ancient Mariner,*" McElderry drew attention to deletions and insertions *and* to the fact that the gloss often supplies information not available, indeed "not paralleled," in either the 1798 or the 1817 version of the poem. Only from the gloss, for example, could we know that by justifying his killing of the albatross, his shipmates "make themselves accomplices in the crime" (gloss to lines 99–102, 1817

31. "'Versioning': The Presentation of Multiple Texts," 169, 171, 172.

version). On a *supernatural* moralistic level—and it is on this level that the gloss most "adds to the text"—there is the role of the angels. For example, the polar daemon now "obeys" the angels, and a stanza has been inserted in which a "troop of spirits blest" descends—a "blessed troop of angelic spirits," according to the gloss, "sent down by the invocation of the guardian saint" (lines 347–49 and gloss). This, says McElderry, "has all the appearance of an afterthought," as do many other of the glossist's moral "clarifications": thoughts not present in the poet's mind in 1798 when he wrote the poem.[32]

Emphasizing the terrors of the Mariner's nightmare universe, Bostetter draws attention to Coleridge's covert fear of the "terrifying activity of the unconscious," a distrust which caused him to increasingly rely on the "conscious will" to impose an order he could not find. Bostetter's has been the position followed by those critical of the once-dominant reading of the poem offered by Robert Penn Warren. In Max Schulz's synopsis of the critical history of *The Ancient Mariner:*

> The overarching critical division has been between the Warrenists, who would read the poem as a confirmation of a supernatural benevolent universe, and the Bostetterites, who are skeptical of the intelligibility of that universe. The aim in much recent criticism has been to chip away at the inconsistencies and contradictions inherent in these standard positions, in the hope of clarifying, if not resolving, the basic conflicts. The other tactic is to place the contrary worlds of the poem in irresolvable tension to one another.[33]

It is also possible to move beyond the crux, as Jerome McGann does, or as James Boulger does in his introduction to the *Twentieth Century Interpretations* volume on the poem. He too criticizes the "archly pious" moral and the "vague" and misleading gloss, Coleridge's excuse for both being "that he was afraid of his own vision, or at least a part of it." Yet the world of the poem "is neither a clear presentation of a sacramental universe, nor a merely meaningless nightmare vision, but is rather an original parable in epic structure of the uneasy religious skepticism and faith that has been with us since Newton and Kant."[34]

Yet, precisely because that "uneasy" tension between skepticism and faith continues to be "with us," it is less the "trimming" balance than the self-division in both Coleridge and his poem that has attracted most of the recent critical attention. What Bostetter refers to as Coleridge's increasing reliance on the order-imposing will suggests the relationship, seldom the perfectly integrated one divided Coleridge sought, between the imaginatively liberated poet and the prose writer, philosopher, and theologian. In discussing Coleridge's poetic decline, L. D. Berkoben has examined at length this tension between the

32. "Coleridge's Revisions of *The Ancient Mariner*," 88–89. McElderry concludes that the nature of the revisions in 1800 and, above all, in 1817, "gives rise to the conviction that the poem lived in Coleridge's mind as an alterable thing, a thing becoming, not absolutely achieved" (92): an insight that anticipates, among others, the New Historicists.

33. "Samuel Taylor Coleridge," 386–87. This rich bibliographical essay suggests leads and provides useful synopses of current criticism.

34. Introduction to *Twentieth-Century Interpretations of "The Ancient Mariner,"* 20.

moral and rational thinker who wanted to believe in a benevolent cosmic harmony and the imaginative explorer who, departing like his Mariner from a morally and rationally ordered world, encounters a natural world less benign than terrifying, a universe presided over by supernatural forces more punitive than redemptive.[35] Indeed, for an increasing number of readers, the endlessly discussed "moral" seems added *to,* rather than an integral part *of,* the poem. Like the gloss, it is perceived as in less-than-harmonious accord with what actually happens to the Mariner: terrifying events that compel few contemporary readers to discern a moral pattern or providential design, or to imagine praying to the supposedly loving but apparently capricious "great Father" who presides over the world the poem presents.

The implication, that no "moral" or pedantic/causal gloss could "gloss" over the mysterious terrors of the world of *The Ancient Mariner,* is made explicit by critics focusing on the glossist and the gloss. I've already quoted Paglia on the marginal commentaries as so many festooned afterthoughts. Women seem to have been particularly, and skeptically, receptive to the intricacies of the dialectic between poem and editorial "explanation." In 1973, Sarah Dyck examined the dramatic perspectives of the Mariner (who vitally experiences something he cannot fully comprehend), of the Wedding Guest (whose response to the Mariner's tale is a stunned silence that leaves him sadder but wiser), and of the later prose glossist (who, she says, introduces, articulates, and emphasizes the moral theme). The result, however, is a mystery that "will not be systematized."[36]

Four years later, Raimonda Modiano, stressing the "limits of expression," noted the contrast between the Mariner's "pain and inexplicable suffering" and the "perfectly orthodox moral" with which he caps his public attempt to conceptualize, Christianize, and convey that untranslatable private experience to his auditor, "a dry moral that falls flat even on the Wedding Guest's ears":

> The narrative moves from a world commanded by Death and Life-in-Death to one where a "saint" is supposed to "take pity" on the Mariner, and finally does, as the Mariner interprets it, when he blesses the water snakes. The Mariner turns to traditional concepts, such as heaven, hell, and religious rituals of blessing and praying. . . . [Thus] the moral represents the culmination of a tendency that is apparent throughout the Mariner's tale and is only given a more emphatic form toward the end.

The Mariner, Modiano writes, is "in many ways a Wedding Guest himself, and his exchange with his auditor reflects an inner conflict":

> Like the Wedding Guest, the Mariner desires to make sense of chance and irrationality in terms of accepted myths in order to maintain control over an experience that borders on madness. . . . When the Mariner delivers his closing moral, the Wedding Guest is "stunned" and "of sense forlorn," a state hardly suitable for the wise lesson of love and prayer the Mariner tries to teach him. . . . On the other hand, the tale which ends with the moral is a tale gone wrong for the Mari-

35. *Coleridge's Decline as a Poet.*
36. "Perspective in *The Rime of The Ancient Mariner.*"

ner too, and he is the first to feel it. The memory of green ice, slimy water snakes, and the revengeful specter-bark continues to haunt the mind and demands a new story.

The gap between the Mariner's lived experience and a constructed narrative intended to "provide a Christian abstract of a far more mysterious and in part untranslatable episode of his past" is a discrepancy extendable to the verbal strategy resorted to by Coleridge himself in the explanatory gloss, a gloss Modiano returned to in a 1985 essay on Coleridge's marginalia.[37]

In "Guilt and Samuel Taylor Coleridge," a chapter in her book on Romantic irony, Anne K. Mellor establishes the ironic and irreconcilable tension between two opposing Romantic visions of the world. On the one hand, we have an ontological reality that is dynamic, unstable, unconscious, amoral and charged with destructive and creative force; on the other, a moral order sanctioned by Christian theology: a world that is intelligible, coherent, orderly. What most engages her, as it has other recent commentators on the philosophic and artistic legacy of the French Revolution, is the Romantics' alienated and irresolute stance toward "a universe founded in chaos and incomprehension rather than in a divinely ordained teleology." She finds Coleridge ambivalent and guilt-ridden, torn between conflicting allegiances to the abundant but chaotic imagination (which she labels "Free Life") and the understanding, with its limiting systems ("Confining Form"). Applying this familiar dialectic of freedom and constraint, Dionysian poet and Apollonian moralist, to *The Ancient Mariner*, Mellor sees Coleridge's instinctive retreat from the unpredictable, active universe into a comforting Christian orthodoxy embodied in the "painful tension" between the 1798 tale of the "Mariner's inexplicable, agonizing, joyful experience of a chaotic universe" and the 1817 glossist's Christian vision of "an ordered and just universe," which is "sensible, rational, moral."[38] Though, in general, Mellor has less to say of the "agonizing" than of the "enthusiastic" responses of the Romantics to change and chaos, it is clear that *The Ancient Mariner*'s gloss is inadequate to its universe.

Suavely steering between the limiting-moral and no-moral critical positions, Frances Ferguson notes that the gloss, "in assuming that things must be significant and interpretable, finds significance and interpretability, but only by reading ahead of—or beyond—the main text." Writing in the early 1980s, reader-response critic Kathleen M. Wheeler declared the gloss a parody of the passive reader imposing a moralistic interpretation on a poetic narrative demanding an altogether more profound imaginative response. Most recently, Martin Wallen concludes the "Commentary" to his "Experimental Edition" by focusing on the marginal gloss, a gloss that "can make its moral interpretation only because

37. "Words and 'Languageless' Meanings: Limits of Expression in *The Rime of The Ancient Mariner*," 40–41; "Coleridge's Marginalia." Like Dyck, Modiano offers not only her own interpretation but also a useful recapitulation of previous critical positions on the gloss, study of which began in earnest with McElderry in 1932, followed by Huntington Brown in 1945, with "The Gloss to *The Rime of the Ancient Mariner*."

38. *English Romantic Irony*, vii, 143–48.

it maintains a faith in a moral universe." The gloss causes the poem to take on "an entirely new shape," splitting itself into "two contrasting voices." The commentary it provides "is compelling and seductive in its claim to explain the essential meaning of the poem, and yet it imposes an interpretation at odds with much of the Mariner's narration." The effect of the gloss's account "is indeed a clearer explanation of why things happen as they do. But the Mariner's experience is in continual violation of the explainable." The effect of Wallen's edition is to make this compulsively revised poem (perhaps more than the evidence warrants) inexplicable, unstable, and indeterminate, though its "endless textual recasting" is, as Wallen notes, analogous to "the Mariner's endless wandering."[39]

One could go on with examples of the tendency, especially marked in the work of poststructural ironists and deconstructionists, to see the relationship between poem and gloss as that between irreducible experience, on the one hand, and book learning or Christian superimposition or secondary interpretation, on the other, the latter (unsurprisingly) doomed to failure in the attempt to achieve closure, to resolve the poem's indeterminacy, to make it— and the cosmos—cohere. Many of these recent critics advance arguments that are challenging, even brilliant. A few alter, without utterly obliterating, traditional ways of looking at *The Ancient Mariner,* and, like those who approve of the gloss, all agree that Coleridge's addition of this logical and *theo*logical running prose commentary significantly affects our reading of the poem.

Though Anthony Harding and Robert Barth have emphasized Christian love in Coleridge's poetry, few if any *theoretically* oriented critics (with the exception of Jonathan Arac) seem willing to entertain the idea that poetry, however important to Coleridge, was in fact less important than theology, a preoccupation to which even the Muse was subordinate. That point had been stressed in the past by such critics as Basil Willey and W. J. Bate, who argued that poetry was "incidental" to other Coleridgean interests, especially the theological concerns that so preoccupied him. Robert Penn Warren, while he renewed our understanding of "the theological bases" of Coleridge's criticism, failed, Arac points out, to acknowledge that "for Coleridge's writing religion was not just the base, but was even more the center and ultimate goal." Indeed, the displacement of the aesthetic sphere by the religious accounts in large part for the "notorious fact that Coleridge's most productive years as a prose writer were extremely lean poetically."[40]

39. Ferguson, "Coleridge and the Deluded Reader." Wallen, *Coleridge's Ancient Mariner,* 141, 134, 135, 110. Wallen's approach was adumbrated in his earlier article, "Return and Representation: The Revisions of *The Ancient Mariner.*" Wheeler devotes her entire discussion of the poem in *The Creative Mind in Coleridge's Poetry* (42–64) to the addition of the gloss. See also Wendy Wall's "Interpreting Poetic Shadows: The Gloss of *The Rime of the Ancient Mariner.*"

40. Willey, *Samuel Taylor Coleridge,* ix, 257. Bate, *Coleridge,* 40–41. Arac, "Coleridge and New Criticism Reconsidered: Repetition and Exclusion," 84–85. In *Coleridge and the Inspired Word,* Harding emphasizes the centrality of Christianity for Coleridge, for whom

Naturally enough, Arac connects these thoughts with the addition of the prose gloss to *The Ancient Mariner*. He quotes Walter Pater, who, in 1889, had observed that the revisions and addition of the gloss in the *Sibylline Leaves* edition had succeeded in "connecting . . . the chief poem of Coleridge with his philosophy," making it his "one great complete work, the one really finished thing, in a life of many beginnings." Acknowledging the point, Arac suggests that the revisions and the gloss "may also, however, have afforded a haven from which Coleridge was unwilling or unable to set out again, . . . a completion [marking] the terminal domestication of Coleridge's poetic wanderings, the ultimate correction of error through revision."[41] Politically, such corrective "domestication" amounts to repatriation. As an act of "completion," this termination of wandering seems to me related to what Arac describes two paragraphs later as the poem's "move toward unity and away from history." The New Historicists would presumably agree. What seems admirable about Arac's remarks is his unfashionable acknowledgment of Coleridge's conception of religion as "the center and ultimate goal." Predictably, most of the deconstructionists and other indeterminists who discuss the gloss refuse even to take into account the remote possibility that the glossist's exercise of what is clearly a theological imagination may in fact complete the poem, making it genuinely less chaotic.

That was the line taken in general by McElderry, an argument advanced in greater detail by Lawrence Lipking. Though fully sensitive to the "civilized scholastic voice" and "pious certainty" of a glossist out to superimpose reflective interpretive order on shocking and unpredictable experience, Lipking nevertheless concludes, alluding to Coleridge's own attraction to the pausing and advancing "motion of a serpent":

> The tension between the two ways of construing the mariner's tale—between experiencing it and interpreting it—is recreated by the eye of every reader, as it snakes back and forth between the text and the margin, interrupting and interpenetrating one script with another, and striving to make a simultaneous order out of two different phases of seeing. . . . [F]inally the ballad and gloss conclude together; for the mariner's own last understanding of his story, the need to love and reverence all things for the sake of that God who "made and loveth all," is identical with the last statement in the margin. As a divided consciousness might be healed by a moment of prayer, so a divided text is healed by a moral intelligible to the wise and simple heart alike. And the reader joins in that union. No longer stunned by wonders, he should rise from the ordeal of this serpentine text exhausted, perhaps, but sadder and wiser.[42]

---

the "human character of Imagination" was grounded on the Bible's assertion of the finite will's responsibility to what Coleridge called "an Absolute Will" (73). Barth's *Coleridge and the Power of Love* grows organically out of his earlier studies of Coleridge's religious thought (*Coleridge and Christian Doctrine* [1969]) and of his extension of that thought (*The Symbolic Imagination* [1977]).

41. Pater, *Appreciations*, 100, 101. Arac, "Coleridge and New Criticism," 85.

42. "The Marginal Gloss: Notes and Asides on Poe, Valery, *The Ancient Mariner*, etc. . . . ," 615, 621.

Not every reader will join in that union or agree that divided consciousness and divided text have been healed by the moral. Nevertheless, like the other discussions just mentioned, Lipking's perceptive article (to whose serpentine imagery I will recur in my own uroboric rondure) draws attention to Coleridge's problematic attempt to reconcile precisely those ambiguities and tensions, those benign and malevolent forces, that give the poem its terrible beauty and power. One can argue, as Lipking and Humphry House do, that, though banal when detached from its context, the moral has meaning "*because it has been lived.*"[43] Ultimately, however, *The Ancient Mariner* incarnates a serpentine mystery that, for many readers, cannot be stabilized by any symbolic categorization, made to fit any moral system—not even Coleridge's own theistic and often desperately optimistic world view.

4

My original interest in these text-gloss discussions was less focused on *The Ancient Mariner* than on the peripheral light they cast on the relationship among the 1799, 1805 and 1850 texts of Wordsworth's *Prelude,* and on such Coleridgean "revisions" as the "Apologies" later appended, in the same year the gloss was added to *The Ancient Mariner,* to the "War Eclogue" and "The Raven." At this point, however, the dialectic informing the Mariner's vital experience, the poet's structuring narrative, the moral tag, and the even-more-moralistic glossist's later editorial commentary, also seems to illuminate Coleridge's rejection—in March–April 1798—of political hatred and salutary wrath, replaced by an instrumental or "Priestleyan" acceptance of Pitt, his Ministers, and "constituted power" as chastening elements in God's grand providential design. Viewed in the light of the moralizing and stabilizing optimism so many contemporary critics have attributed to the reflective parts of the Mariner's tale and, of course, to the learned gloss, the movement, in the snake-blessing passage, from revulsion to love, takes on another aspect. The moralistic imprimatur added to the sudden burst of love that impels the Mariner to bless the water-snakes, an impulse attributed to a guardian angel, "my kind saint," seems not only a kind of premature—and notably orthodox—"gloss" on the experience but also a sign that the blessing is a more complicated—more suspect, and perhaps more "political"—act than originally meets the eye.

At the risk of diminishing the imaginative validity of that ostensibly glorious moment, I have therefore come to suspect that part of its "ontological inclusiveness," and part of its conscious or unconscious genesis, was indeed political. The blessing and prayer may be another instance of something "added through cowardly fear"—fear either of the internal censor, the "Goody," or of "unpredictable despotic forces" closer to home than the regions presided over by the Polar Spirit. Either way, the result is an act perhaps more prudent than spontaneous. For on the political level, the "spring of love" that "gusht" from the Mariner's heart and took the form of that blessing seems not quite so

43. House, *Coleridge,* 92.

unpremeditated, unanalyzed, and "moral" when we consider the *Watchman*-like watchfulness leading up to it and the unbroken agony following it, reflections of the contemporary tensions, oscillations, and fearful submission of its author. With the blessing of the snakes, at least on this submerged political level, the venerable distinction between morality and prudential calculation may well blur. Perhaps Coleridge, following his own earlier reeducation plan for Thelwall, has here entered into a state of mind in which "his natural impetuosity ha[s] been disciplined into patience . . . and the slow energies of a *calculating* spirit" (*CL* I 344).

It has been accurately observed that "in creating the Inquisitor, Francesco," in *Osorio*, Coleridge "must certainly have thought of Pitt."[44] The benevolent quietism of Coleridge and the snake-blessing of his Mariner, converging in March of 1798 and issuing in "a spring of love," appear more complicatedly "spontaneous" (a word that etymologically brackets "independence" [*spontaneus*] and "binding" [*spons, spondere*]) when we recall the boast of snake-Pitt's counterpart in *Osorio* to his spy: "Yes! Yes! I have the key of all their lives. / If a man·fears me, he is forced to love me" (*CPW* II 560).

No abstract metaphor, this "key" fits into a very literal dungeon lock. And the language of the second line suggests a parallel Coleridge may or may not have intended. For with this juxtaposition of fear and love, Francesco resembles the Miltonic God about whom Adam (buffeted by Michael's catalog of woe before being promised that "paradise within" which Peter Kitson finds at the heart of *The Ancient Mariner*) comes to certain prudential conclusions at the end of *Paradise Lost:* "Henceforth I learn, that to obey is best, / And love with fear the only God." Though this God is, Adam adds, "Merciful over all his works, with good / Still overcoming evil," that evil includes, in the passage from Revelation (2:10) Milton is echoing, the trials and tribulations deriving from the power of "the devil" to "cast some of you into prison" (an image more than metaphoric for a man who had, in 1660 and in very real danger of death or imprisonment, been hidden by his friends and protected by Marvell from a Restoration government seeking out regicides and their great defender).[45] The faithful, promised an eventual "crown of life," are to "fear none of those things," yet we *are* to "love with fear" this God upon whose Providence we "sole depend" (*Paradise Lost* XII.561–66).

Like the supernatural forces at work in *The Ancient Mariner,* this seems a God who is perhaps more punitive than redemptive, and who is certainly more an object of "fear" than his providential minion, the devil, who actually casts us

44. Arnold B. Fox, "Political and Biographical Background of Coleridge's *Osorio*," 261.

45. Milton actually spent at least the autumn of 1660 in a Restoration prison; the record of his release (December 17) refers to his "having now laid long in custody." But whatever his fear of confinement and, for some time afterward, assassination, Milton, as Byron notes in *Don Juan* (Dedication, X), never prostrated himself before power. Indeed, he rejected royal overtures in 1663, preferring, as he told his wife, "to live and die an honest man."

"into prison." Once again, we are faced with "power" before which we must prostrate ourselves if we are to survive—or if we are to avoid prison, one of "those things" Coleridge could never bring himself not to "fear." The Coleridgean equivalent to Michael, Milton's cautionary archangel, may therefore be less the seraph-men who help guide the Mariner's ship home than the "kind saint" to whom the Mariner attributes the snake-blessing impulse and who seems, on a political level, to be the cautiously Christian or affrighted side— the glossist or "Goody"—in Coleridge. The "Argument" that preceded the poem in 1798 referred to the "strange things that befell" the protagonist, "and in what manner the Ancyent Marinere came back to his own Country."[46] The homecoming of the poem's protagonist may seem far removed from the contemporary drama of political "repatriation." But whatever the Mariner's "strange" experiences and the "manner" in which he came back to his own country, the repatriation of Samuel Taylor Coleridge in the spring of 1798 was anything *but* apolitical.

46. This is the conclusion of the 1798 "Argument," prefatory material revised in 1800 and dropped altogether after 1802. The wording is almost identical in the more "moral" argument ("how the Ancient Mariner *cruelly* and in contempt of the laws of hospitality, killed a Sea-bird; and how he was followed by many and strange *Judgments*...") introducing the poem in the 1800 edition of *Lyrical Ballads*. Though, pace Empson and others, the killing of the albatross was never value free, the moral and visionary emphasis in the 1800 version may reflect Coleridge's reading of Wordsworth's "Hart-Leap Well." Written in January or February 1800 and chosen by Wordsworth to begin volume 2 of the 1800 edition of *Lyrical Ballads*, "Hart-Leap Well" presents a slain creature closely resembling the albatross: "This beast not unobserv'd by Nature fell, / His death was mourn'd by sympathy divine." And more than mourned, for the hart was avenged by a "Being" who "Maintains a deep and reverential care / For them the quiet creatures whom he loves." In a final "lesson" recalling the "moral" of *The Ancient Mariner* and anticipating the conclusion of the Intimations ode, we are "Never to blend our pleasure or our pride / With sorrow of the meanest thing that feels." I quote the poem (lines 163–68, 177–80) from the Brett-Jones edition of *Lyrical Ballads*, 127–33.

Conclusion

When British Freedom for an happier land
Spread her broad wings, that flutter'd with affright,
ERSKINE! thy voice she heard, and paus'd her flight
Sublime of hope, for dreadless thou didst stand. . . .

(CPW I 79)

1

The event the epigraph speaks of took place in 1794. With the passage through Parliament of the Two Bills in December 1795, the eloquence of Thomas Erskine—the successful defender of Thomas Hardy, Horne Tooke, and the even more dreadless Thelwall—was of little avail.[1] Sporadically but inexorably, repression intensified. By March 1798, as Coleridge had prophesied in *The Plot Discovered*, the time had come when "British Liberty leaves her cell by permission, and walks abroad to take the air between two jailors; fettered, and handcuffed, and with a gagg in her mouth!!!" Whether or not it was indisputable that, with the Treason and Sedition Acts on the books, the country had become "a vast aviary, and all the honest are incaged within it" (*L 1795* 314–15), it would be considerably less hyperbolic a characterization during the invasion panic of the spring of 1798, when the immediate targets of Gallophobic hysteria were not only English Jacobins, but anyone suspected of harboring anti-Ministerial impulses.

Ever a bird, British Liberty had flapped her creaking quill feathers briefly in the winter of 1797–1798 only to find, particularly after the Margate arrests and the intensified invasion alarm, that (Richard Lovelace notwithstanding) "iron bars" and suspended habeas corpus *do* make a "cage." By the time he had finished his greatest poem, British freedom seemed, to the Friends of Liberty, as dead as Coleridge's albatross. Or, if still alive in the breasts of individuals, the affrighted bird certainly no longer had any reason to "pause her flight"—not, this time, to the banks of the Susquehanna, but to the universities of Germany.

---

1. Not that Erskine was rendered dumb; his 1797 pamphlet against the war enjoyed "infinite popularity," according to William Hayley (*Memoirs of Life and Writing* 1:497). Still, his protest against the Gagging Acts had cost him the deanship of the Scottish Faculty of Advocates. As Erdman notes (*Prophet against Empire*, 303n), Erskine was ousted by Pitt's man Dundas.

Though to readers safely distanced from the Pittite inquisition it may seem not so, to Coleridge, who thought himself akin to Shakespeare's prince, England between 1793 and 1798 occasionally seemed as much a prison as Denmark did to Hamlet. If, as Coleridge admitted, the "moral" of *The Ancient Mariner* had too obtrusively insinuated itself into what "ought to" have been a work of "pure imagination," why should we resist the idea that his political hopes and dungeon-haunted fears similarly intruded themselves into a poem composed during the height of the domestic and international crisis? How, really, could it be otherwise in the case of a man for whom poetic, moral, and political concerns were often indistinguishable, a man whose philosophy and critical theory stressed again and again the special power of "the poet, described in *ideal* perfection, to bring the whole soul of man into activity" (*BL* II 15–16)? The "poetic genius . . . sustains and modifies the images, thoughts, and emotions of the poet's own mind" (*BL* II 15), but the whole soul comes into play.

Even if exclusion, or "privatizing" evasion, of all moral and political thought were intended in a work of "pure imagination," it would be virtually impossible. As young Coleridge had learned from Hartley, thought and imagination can "curb and rudder," but cannot arbitrarily eliminate, the "streamy nature of association."[2] Nor was the world of politics ever really remote from Coleridge's dialectical Muse. A man haunted by that material world—specifically by the French Revolution and its seismic and atmospheric repercussions in England in the 1790s—could not simply turn off the current of political ideas and images. That would be true even when he took up a poem as ostensibly removed from that world as seems humanly possible—a poem taken up, perhaps, *precisely* because it *was* distanced from the body politic, but which, nevertheless, atmospherically and symbolically registers that body's convulsions during the period the poem was being written and revised.

The Ancient Mariner would not be unique in this regard. New Historicists have described Wordsworth's "Tintern Abbey" as (in Kenneth Johnston's words) "one of the most powerfully *de*politicized poems in the language—and, by that token, a uniquely political one." Norman Rudich and Marilyn Butler, also cited in the "Critical Introduction," present Coleridge's shift from what Butler calls "a public to a private focus in response to political events" as itself having "an acknowledged political significance"—specifically, the move from anti-Ministerial radicalism to "loyalism." In such poems, politics are effaced, internalized—or intrusive. We *expect* the intrusion of war and war's alarms into the "green and silent spot," the still dell, of "Fears in Solitude," a poem of "repatriation" written in wartime and "During the Alarm of an Invasion." But the "sound of the World without" (*CL* III 216) also intrudes into that most intimate of poems,

2. This notebook phrase of Coleridge's is quoted by Lowes. Its implications lie, he claims, not only at the roots of his study of the ways of Coleridge's imagination, but "at the very roots of art"—provided we remember that the associative faculty *is* "curbed and ruddered by the disposing imagination" (*The Road to Xanadu,* 68). The debate between Abrams and Culler, discussed in my "Critical Introduction," turns on precisely this point.

the Dejection ode, in the form of the groans of wounded and freezing soldiers: a description lifted from such earlier, overtly political poems as "The Destiny of Nations" and "Fears in Solitude" (*CPW* I 368; cf. 138, 260).

As Keith Thomas has shown in recontextualizing "Dejection: An Ode," this "unexpected" vision of war at once connects the poem to politics and recoils back to "a second vision purely lyrical and privative." From the "groans" of wounded soldiers, to "But hush," followed by "a pause of deepest silence" in which the wind "tells another tale, with sounds less deep and loud" (the moaning and crying of Wordsworth's lost Lucy Gray), there is a complex dialectical sequence that

> starkly dramatizes the lyric's tropological reduction of politics to an image of private solitary consciousness. In effect, the little girl . . . defeats this army, but she is essentially continuous with it in character even as she transcendentalizes it. The wounded retreating army may re-sound Coleridge's own Horatian retreat from the strife of the public world, but in having this army cede to the image of Lucy Gray Coleridge lyricizes public fears, threats, and anxious hopes by transforming them into the private predicament of a solitary isolated self. This lyrical transformation is all the more powerful for the polarity of the two images: from collective, male, reactive behavior, Coleridge moves to individual, female, active behavior. Lucy Gray has braved the storm at her own peril, but she moans and screams in order to be rescued, . . . to "make her mother *hear*. . . . [I]t is at this site of lyric's putative victory that the subordinated forces regroup and re-exert their power."[3]

Even the pleasure-domed garden of Kubla, with "walls and towers girdled round," is not immune to threats from within and without. Quite aside from the verbal associations Woodring remarks between Kubla's edifice and that erected by Pitt's oratorical wizardry, as well as the insights of Norman Rudich and the intriguing interplay Marilyn Butler notes between Kubla's garden and Aloadin's in Southey's *Thalaba*, there is intrinsic evidence. The "sunny spots of greenery" are cut "athwart" by a "deep romantic chasm" in whose dark abysm pulses a volcanic fountain, and the entire sanctuary, though fortified by walls and towers, is threatened by "Ancestral voices prophesying war!" As Jerome McGann notes, "the entire project of Imagination in this poem is continually threatened and haunted by fearful images of evil and destruction. The Khan's civilization has been fashioned with the sword and is destined to a similarly violent end."[4] In short, while this precariously balanced poem accepts the Wordsworthian ministry of fear as the price for its imaginative resolutions, the excited reverie in and of Coleridge's most paradisal garden is as "interrupted" as the poet himself claimed to be by the famous visitor from Porlock.

The characteristic rhythm of Coleridge Agonistes takes the form of an oscillation between engagement and retreat, with both movements haunted by a still small voice urging subdued retirement . . . or whispering of terror . . . or reminding the remorseful man of his duty. Against the letter to George of March

---

3. "The Politics of Coleridge's 'Dejection: An Ode,'" 9.
4. *The Romantic Ideology,* 102–3.

1798 should be set this lament of 1809: "I found in my Books and my own meditations a sort of high-walled Garden, which excluded the very sound of the World without. But the Voice within could not be thrust out—the sense of Duty unperformed" (*CL* III 216). He is ostensibly speaking of his unfulfilled promise as a poet, but the sense of "Duty unperformed" may reflect not only the inner voice but also guilt at having selfishly tried to exclude the "very sound" of the "World without" by retreating to an inner, imaginative, literally *quiet*ist "garden" undisturbed by the commotions of contemporary history. Even here the Coleridgean rhythm—a central motif in the poems, as Max Schulz, D. G. James, Kelvin Everest, and others have shown—seems not only psychological and poetic but political.[5]

In the case of *The Ancient Mariner*, we have a work begun (in November 1797) in the epicycle of "retirement" and then troubled by the political rumbles affecting its author, and the nation, in the extended course of its composition. But to choose to "escape" in a *ship*—emblematic, as W. H. Auden says in his study of Romantic iconography, of an internally and externally threatened society[6]—is in itself significant, especially since Coleridgean retreat is usually to a "Valley of Seclusion" *away* from the sea (*CPW* I 106). When, in "The Eolian Harp," the sea *is* mentioned, it is "distant" and its "stilly murmur" tells us of "silence" (*CPW* I 100).

The Ancient Mariner, though it has its own "silences," presents a dramatic contrast. Having retired to Stowey to cultivate his garden, Coleridge set his Mariner aboard a ship emblematic in both a societal and personal sense. *Societally*, the ship would be internally threatened—by its own burden of guilt, the crimes of Albion under the Pitt Ministry—and externally threatened, by that chief source of revolutionary convulsion, the French Revolution, and its English repercussions. On a *personal* level, from his garden retreat at Stowey, Coleridge sends his Mariner off—in a poem presumably embodying his escapist impulses at the time—on a dangerous voyage in which the protagonist, experiencing a series of radical shifts, is utterly exposed, "alone on a wide, wide sea"; subjected to fierce cold and tongue-withering drought; appalled by the spectre-bark whose masts against the sun resemble a dungeon-grate; then placed at the mercy of the terrifying penitential universe into which that dungeon-grate opens—or, to be more accurate, closes. If this is escapism, something has intruded itself into the fantasy.

The two "intrusions" I have focused on—the dungeon-grate and the submarine rumbling and explosion that sink the Mariner's warped and fiendish ship in a whirl—are, as I hope I have shown, connected on the associational stream

5. See James's *The Romantic Comedy*, 155–61, and Schulz's "Coleridge Agonistes," 268–77. Despite its title, the article never mentions Milton's dramatic poem; but it is a penetrating psychological examination of the Coleridgean rhythm of engagement and remorseful disengagement from "reality." As noted earlier, in *Coleridge's Secret Ministry* Everest traces this dialectic in the "Conversation Poems" of 1795–1798.

6. Of the archetype of the ship, Auden observes that it is "only used as a metaphor for society in danger from within or without. When society is normal the image is the City or the Garden" (*The Enchaféd Flood; or, The Romantic Iconography of the Sea*, 18).

with Coleridgean politics, itself part of a larger pattern of imagery Coleridge shares with Wordsworth and other English Romantics responding to the international and domestic impact of the French Revolution. The killing of the albatross is no less an "intrusion," a moral violation. Here we are faced with the penetration of perverse cruelty into a world—at *that* moment at least, for its protean randomness before and after is notable—of apparent natural and supernatural harmony. The killing of the bird was, according to Wordsworth, his idea. It would not be an alien theme for a poet whose principal motifs include the tranquillity-shattering intrusion of human history and politics into the world of natural beauty. In addition to recording that sunset-darkening intrusion of British warships in the Isle of Wight lines, Wordsworth also gives us, in the mutilation of the hazel bower in "Nutting," a sudden and perverse violation of nature leading to new discovery: the penitent recognition, resembling that of the repentant slayer of the albatross, that "there is a spirit in the woods." The same theme, as just noted, informs "Hart-Leap Well."

The very fact that I have associated the albatross at different times with freedom and the victims of slavery indicates that, while its implications are related, this great symbolic bird cannot be crudely politicized. Nor am I saying that *The Ancient Mariner* is a calculated political allegory. And if allegory says one thing, "while in disguise" it means another, and symbolism means what it says and has another hidden meaning besides, I am not even arguing that the poem is a kind of Blakean prophecy with politics as one of its intentional layers of meaning.[7] But *The Ancient Mariner* may well be an attempted escape from the dungeon England had become for a man of Coleridge's political views. I say "attempted" since the escape, though a near-miraculous triumph of the transfiguring imagination, was far from complete. The poem remains, simultaneously, a reflection, even incorporation, of the breezeless, tongue-withering calms of despotism that had silenced Pitt's opponents (of whom it might be said, as it is of the stricken mariners, "thro' drouth all dumb they stood"), and had finally, after a brief resurgence of hope in the winter of 1797–1798, rendered Coleridge himself, like the poem's windless ocean, "Still as a Slave before his Lord." This, the most overtly "political" image in the poem, may provide a final distillation of my thesis.

The words are those of the "Second Voice," immediately following the soft but ominous announcement that "the man hath penance done, / And penance more will do":

> Still as a Slave before his Lord,
>   The Ocean hath no blast:
> His great bright eye most silently
>   Up to the moon is cast—
>   (lines 419–22)

7. For Coleridge's negative remarks on "allegoric writing," see *Coleridge's Miscellaneous Criticism*, ed. Raysor, 30–31. John Gatta, Jr., has argued that the real target was crudely mechanical interpretation of allegory; see his "Coleridge and Allegory."

Though the ocean's "Lord" is the moon, that heavenly body is female, both here and in the famous "Softly she was going up. . . ." Though its designation as a female "Lord" appropriately makes the personified Moon loving as well as sovereign, it remains an odd and unexpected description. The problem is the result of what I have been calling "intrusion." Coleridge's lovely simile of the ocean under the gracious aegis of the female moon (twice identified as "she" in the next stanza) has been invaded and subverted by thoughts of enslaving despotism. The primary subliminal image evoked is that of a human slave—for the author of "On the Slave Trade," probably a black slave—still, silent, and submissive before his master: a Friday-Crusoe relationship, a reader of the first part of this project might say. On the level of "submerged" politics being explored at the moment, the simile evokes *two* images.

The first is that of an ocean resembling Coleridgean politics during the nineties—an ocean depicted in the poem as either stagnant and motionless or tempest-driven. Now, though the "Ocean hath no blast," the ship stirs with an "uneasy motion," moving "Backwards and forwards," only to make a "sudden bound" that flings the blood into the Mariner's head and makes him swoon (lines 390–97). However agitated or becalmed, the ocean is, at this pivotal moment, pictured as being brought under the control both of a serene lunar imagination and of Christianity. An ocean made "still" before its "Lord" surely echoes Jesus' calming of the sea with that haunting imperative, "Peace, be still." But this Christian serenity is subverted by the image of the submissive slave, with the gentle Jesus replaced by those "unpredictable despotic forces" Bostetter associates with an "avenging Jehovah," the "paternal tyrant . . . to whom each bends."

Such language is as political as it is theological. In a related image in "Fears in Solitude," Coleridge had fretted over being "deemed"—by the members of the Pitt Ministry, those drudges of "chastising Providence"—an enemy of his country because he was not among those who "fall before their images, / And yield them worship." In short, in the still-as-a-slave-before-his-lord analogy, the ocean's immobility, combined with the ship's uneasy oscillations and sudden dizzying bound, together suggest the characteristic rhythm of Coleridge's shifting politics in this troubled decade. Thus, the second, and ontologically complementary, image is of the political Coleridge himself in the spring of 1798, subjected to *enforced* quiescence and obedience, his own Mariner-like bright eye "cast" up subserviently to the moon as the alternative to peering, like the sun, "thro' a dungeon grate"—if in fact it *is* an alternative once one has been made "Still as a Slave before his Lord."[8] However intentionally "beautiful" or even "religious" the analogy of the ocean "Still as a Slave before his Lord," the

8. The ocean's "great bright eye" recalls the "glittering eye" of the "bright-eyed Marinere" (lines 17, 24), which in turn recalls the many descriptions of Coleridge's own mesmeric glittering eye. Coleridge's figure of speech in the quatrain given the Second Voice echoes a couplet in Sir John Davies's poem *Orchestra:* "For his great chrystal eye is always cast / Up to the moon, and on her fixéd fast." But Davies has no "Slave-Lord" simile.

simile, though curbed and ruddered by a lunar imagination, deconstructs itself, emerging simultaneously as a negative image of submission and capitulation.

2

Carl Woodring declared that when David Erdman "reasons that Coleridge was 'objectifying the dereliction and dismay of the times in an imaginatively controlled nightmare *The Ancient Mariner*,' he goes beyond what we can demonstrate to the skeptical."[9] Just as he argues only against *The Ancient Mariner* being "explicitly" political, here Woodring does not deny Erdman's statement, only its capacity of being demonstrated to the skeptical. But I have, in effect, taken my thesis from Erdman's remark and from Lowell's detection in the poem of "fetters clanking," and have here attempted one approach to such a demonstration. In doing so, I have ventured far beyond, but also *beneath*, the text of the poem, a poem whose political elements remain, for the most part, under the surface. Several crucial images, however, break through that surface in a return of the politically repressed. Like "Destruction," the undersea dragon in the "Ode on the Departing Year," or Yeats's rough beast in "The Second Coming," or Camille Paglia's "vampire mother who rises up from the slime of nature," submerged images—deriving in part from the "streamy nature of association," yet reflecting the material history of the period—ascend from the depths of the unconscious.

Like that suppressed "stream" that issues from the not-quite-breathless mouth of the drowned Friday in Coetzee's *Foe*, the political images in Coleridge's poem erupt from "nether seas up-thundering," surprising us when they surface at several critical moments. They take the form of what Raimonda Modiano calls "strikingly unusual analogies," though she, like virtually every other scholarly reader, rules out any social or political resonance in such analogies, however striking or unusual—however "strange" and "surprizing"—they may be. And yet, given the political situation in England, and the events that made the SW1"clank of Chains" (Coleridge's phrase, anticipating Lowell's "fetters clanking") and the "whisper of Terror" so much more audible during the last three weeks the poet was working on *The Ancient Mariner*, it would have been even more strange and surprising if images of oppression and submission, threat and capitulation, had *not* found their way into the poem. Though Modiano rejects any "social" referentiality in its imagery, the poem's most haunting phenomena (she singles out, along with the green ice, the "slimy water snakes" and the "revengeful specter-bark") *do*, as she says, break the piously moralistic frame of the tale and "demand a new story."[10]

---

9. *Politics in the Poetry of Coleridge*, 33.

10. "Words and 'Languageless' Meanings," 54, 41. Modiano emphasizes the physicality of these similes, but not their possible historical references. Of even the dungeon-grate stanza, she writes as if this, like the poem's other "essentially concrete" analogies, has nothing to do with the "social" connotations of the word *dungeon*: "The reference to a dungeon grate emphasizes the physical appearance of the sun" (55). Those familiar

The "new story" I have told is largely political. But despite the extrinsic— and intrinsic—evidence presented here, I am not proposing that *The Ancient Mariner* should suddenly be recategorized as one of Coleridge's "political" texts. For most readers, including *this* reader as a classroom teacher, the poem will continue to thrill, terrify, and delight as an essentially "apolitical" work of the imagination. That will probably remain the case—at least in most intrinsic readings, though, on New Historicist grounds, its very lack of overt political content probably *makes* the poem "political" given the politically charged circumstances in which it was written.

Yet even an intrinsic reading, having to account for *all* the elements in the poem, cannot simply ignore or normatively tame the more "unusual," or "intrusive," items. This is especially so when the elements in question are significant features of the poem, two of them dramatic transformations and turning-points. Indeed, the three phenomena I have focused on here—the underwater convulsion that sinks the Mariner's ship, the likening of the spectre-bark's masts silhouetted against the sun to a political "dungeon grate," and the blessing of the water-snakes—are among the most resonant symbols in the nightmare universe of *The Ancient Mariner*, with the last—the snake-blessing—the crux of *any* interpretation, traditional or subversive. By way of confirming the unfixable nature of this poem's elusive scenes and symbols, I will end by adding (with the help of Camille Paglia, Carl Woodring, and Frances Ferguson) a final twist to this, the most serpentine and endlessly elusive moment of them all.

I have been stressing the perhaps unconscious compulsion behind the "unaware" blessing of the water-snakes, a variation on that "enforced obedience" emphasized by Bostetter. He juxtaposes "love" and "enforced obedience" with "fear." "Fear" is referred to by Paglia as well. Even while celebrating the fiery energy of the "daemonic" realm, she associates the brilliantly veined water-snakes with the green snake, the "blue-veined" lamia Geraldine, in Coleridge's *Christabel*,[11] and—describing the primordial power and terrible beauty the Mariner's water-snakes manifest—actually refers to the daemonic world's "chthonian horror," even to its "evil."

From Paglia's psychoanalytical and Nietzschean perspective, presumably be-

---

with jails may see the image more feelingly. Anya Taylor's students at the John Jay School of Criminal Justice in New York City, many of whom "have siblings or children in jail," find *The Ancient Mariner* particularly "accessible," responding especially to "the provocative and descriptive metaphors (as of the sun looking through the grate)" ("Teaching *Ancient Mariner* and *Christabel* to Students of Criminal Justice," 128, 129).

11. Coleridge does not use "veined" to describe the snakes; yet Paglia asks: "Why are the sea snakes veins? Because . . . all great lines in *The Ancient Mariner* look forward to 'Christabel,' where the vampire has exquisite 'blue-veined feet'" (*Sexual Personae*, 326). Though I do not deny Paglia's insight, her importation of "veins" into *The Ancient Mariner* reveals a rather too palpable design. I am reminded, though, of the most vivid lines in Coleridge's sonnet "To the River Otter," in which the color of the tinted waters is intensified by the sand of the river bed, which, "veined with various dyes / Gleamed through thy bright transparence" (*CPW* I 48).

yond conventional good and evil, to "bless" those snakes is to shrink from the abyss of sexual and ontological reality in a gesture of weak piety. On our political level, the blessing of serpentine evil—and Coleridge had depicted "cockatrice" Pitt and his Ministers as miscreated "slimy shapes" flourishing in the ocean-poisoning and pestful calms of despotism—is a no-less-serious shrinking from "evil." In this case, paradoxically, that shrinking takes the apparent form of a providential and loving embrace, though the love involved *may* be— as Coleridge's comment on his own "antidote" to "The Raven" suggests—the "cowardly" work of "the Goody," afraid to call evil evil, a snake a snake. Camille Paglia is right to associate the water-snakes with the serpentine Geraldine, a connection I would reinforce. In *Christabel,* as Carl Woodring notes, "Sir Leoline complacently embraces the foul Geraldine, and assures all listeners—in the face of Bard Bracy's prophetic dream and poetic instinct—that 'arms more strong than harp or song' will crush the serpentine evil that threatens them. The Bard is a dreamier but surer guide than the Baron: he knows when the garden has a snake in it."[12]

Woodring immediately adds, in these the closing pages of his book, "we would follow politics too slavishly if we attempted to explain or illustrate the situation of Bard, Baron, and snake by reference to a trying experiment deeply felt by Coleridge, the situation of Bard, England, and Pitt." That is true; at the same time, however, it is no accident that such a parallel between this snake in the garden (recently and specifically linked with Satan by Stuart Peterfreund, who argues that Geraldine's name is an anagram of "dire angel") and that "Satanic apostate," William Pitt, would be even peripherally suggested by the closest reader of overt politics in Coleridge's poetry. Indeed, Geraldine's power to "control Christabel's speech," figured, as Anne K. Mellor has recently observed, "as the poison of a snake," may not be unrelated to the similar power of "cockatrice" Pitt, a serpent whose glance could kill, and whose Gagging Acts effectively controlled the speech of even his most Abdiel-like opponents.[13]

12. *Politics in the Poetry of Coleridge,* 222–23.

13. Peterfreund, "The Way of Immanence: Coleridge and the Problem of Evil." As a cockatrice, a serpent whose looks kill, Satanic Pitt is also a kind of male Medusa, a figure connected with Geraldine in the famous terror-stricken response of Shelley. In the manuscript version of "Christabel" that Coleridge sent to Byron in October 1815, when Geraldine unbinds her cincture, we find that "her bosom and half her side" ("a sight to dream of, not to tell," in the published version) "Are lean and old and foul of hue." When these lines were read to Shelley by Byron, the effect was sensational. In Thomas Medwin's version, it "conjured up some frightful woman of an acquaintance of his at home, a kind of Medusa, who was suspected of having eyes in her breasts" (*Conversations of Lord Byron,* 149). In John Polidori's account, Shelley, "suddenly shrieking, and putting his hands to his head, ran out of the room with a candle." Looking at Mary Shelley, he had "suddenly thought of a woman he had heard of who had eyes instead of nipples, which, taking hold of his mind, horrified him" (*The Diary of John William Polidori,* 128).

In *Romanticism and Gender,* Mellor cites—as examples of the definition of female "characters" or "principles" as "an evil to be eradicated or overcome"—Blake's "Female Will" and two Coleridgean representations: "the female power that wins the Ancient

Indeed, Woodring continues by remarking that one can resist reading "practical politics . . . allegorically" into *Christabel* and *The Ancient Mariner* "without believing that a poem suspected of reference to life outside the poem should be cut dead." He had observed on the preceding page that "politics were an expansive, amorphous part of Coleridge's 'one Life within us and abroad'" and that, "as poet, he did not wish to divorce the ethics of politics from the ethics of love." Now he concludes that his own study has sought "to establish the political life as one corresponding actuality for the imagined worlds of Sir Leoline and of the Mariner who learned to love 'All things both great and small.'"[14]

My twist on the theme has been to suggest that the Mariner's blessing of the water-snakes may be as suspect as Sir Leoline's misguided embrace of the snake Geraldine; that, on the "submerged" level I have been discussing, the embrace of the "one Life" and the extension of "love" to "all things both great and small" may be, in the case of the snake-blessing, a reflex of the Goody taking the form of a move less philosophic, moralistic, or genuinely Christian than strategic and political: in short, a capitulation.

If so, certain apparently unlikely parallels emerge between the snake-blessing and earlier, specifically political images. Once again, though in a far more imaginatively acceptable form, Coleridge might be hanging up in the "chamber of Penitences" the fragments of his "squeaking baby-trumpet of sedition." In "Religious Musings," he who, faced with "pageant Power" and "purple pomp," "falls not prostrate dies!" (*CPW* I 118–19). In "Fears in Solitude," all who will not "fall before" the "images" of Pitt and his Ministry and "yield them worship" are pronounced "enemies" of their country.

Though publicly professing his loyalism in "Fears in Solitude," Coleridge did not enlist himself among the abject and blasphemous worshipers falling before political "images." Perhaps echoing these very lines in *Biographia Literaria,* he later condemned the littleness of spirit, the "arrogance of pusillanimity," which "lifts up the idol of a mortal's fancy and commands us to fall down and worship it as a work of divine wisdom, an ancile or palladium fallen from heaven" (*BL* I 138). The Latin terms—the security of ancient Rome was connected with that of the shield (*ancile*) and the image of Pallas Athene (*Palladium*) brought by Aeneus from Troy—confirm the political nature of such blasphemous worship. That perceptive atheist and unreconstructed radical, John Thelwall, sarcastically fusing Coleridge's religious conservatism with his later support of other "established systems of *legitimate* despotism," scribbled in the margin beside this passage: "Baptise the idol by the name of orthodoxy, and the worship becomes legitimate devotion."[15]

In the benediction of the water-snakes, a ritual at once religious and (if I am

---

Mariner is a leprous 'Nightmare,' Life-in-Death, while Geraldine's ability to control Christabel's speech is figured in the patriarchal discourse of the Narrator as the poison of a snake" (28).

14. *Politics in the Poetry of Coleridge*, 223–24.

15. Pollin, "John Thelwall's Marginalia," 80, 93.

right) "political," we may have an act of "legitimate devotion" less spiritually orthodox than—as Thelwall would put it—politically apostate, and even blasphemous. For in that snake-blessing, Coleridge, another slave stilled before his lord, may unconsciously be purging his salutary wrath, making his peace with the satanic idol who presided over the Pitt Ministry's dismantling of the constitution: a daemon he described as worse than "an omnipotent Devil" (*L 1795* 295), and who was never worthier of that adjective than in the spring of 1798. "We are told," writes Frances Ferguson, who concludes her richly perspectival article with a reference to the "devil," that the Mariner's

> redemption or conversion occurs when he blesses the sea snakes. But if it seem like a conversion for a man who killed a rather appealing bird to see beauty in snakes, there is also room for a different interpretation. The bird is spoken of in part 5 of the poem as something of a Christ figure, and we all know about the spiritual connotations of snakes. The Mariner's conversion, then, may be a redemption, or, merely a deluded capitulation to the devil. For Coleridge, as for the Ancient Mariner, the problem is that one cannot know better even about whether or not one is knowing better.[16]

True enough. On this occasion, however, coming from the perspective of the political developments of November 1797–April 1798, I have chosen to argue—serpentinely, to be sure—the capitulation theme.

3

I confess, in conclusion, that in doing so I have in large part gone against my own grain, though also driven by that "Yes, but" of the true trimmer. I don't *want* to resist John Thelwall, "contemplating, with enamoured eye, the varied beauties of creation," his heart "soothed and meliorated," the "blossoms of sensibility" unfolding themselves as he awakens to a "sympathetic feeling for every sentient tennant of this many-peopled sphere." I don't *want* to resist the letter to his brother George in which Coleridge describes a "visionary fondness" for nature and a "benevolence growing within" him that de-activates "the bad passions"; nor resist the lines he quotes there from Wordsworth about the man who, taught to love "things that hold / An inarticulate Language," and which excite "no disquietude, / No vengeance & no hatred," finds a "kindred Joy" in which "he looks round— / He seeks for Good & finds the Good he seeks." I don't *want* to resist, and, happily, *cannot* fully resist, the great peroration in which Coleridge, having long and vainly pursued collective "liberty"

16. "Coleridge and the Deluded Reader," 635. The same point is made by Donald Ault in his foreword to the "Experimental Edition" of Martin Wallen (who, incidentally, finds "no clear indication," outside the gloss, that the "slimy things" and the water-snakes are even "the same animals"). Ault writes: "The scene in which the Mariner supposedly undergoes redemptive transformation when he blesses the water-snakes (which appear in this form only at this point in the poem) becomes excessively problematic. The powerfully ambivalent associations snakes have in Christian and non-Christian myths raise the issue of what it is the Mariner is committing himself to" (*Coleridge's Ancient Mariner*, 118–19, xiii).

through "forms of human government," finds at last that "guide of homeless winds, and playmate of the waves!"

> And there I felt thee!—on that sea-cliff's verge,
>   Whose pines, scarce travelled by the breeze above,
> Had made one murmur with the distant surge!
> Yes, while I stood and gazed, my temples bare,
> And shot my being through earth, sea, and air,
>   Possessing all things with intensest love,
>   O Liberty! my spirit felt thee there.
>   (*CPW* I 247)

The poem, Coleridge's Recantation ode, ends as it had begun, with the poet's despair of government as the vehicle of achieving liberty—a despair engendered not only by the French violation of democratic Switzerland and the personally menacing repression at home, but by the conviction that political freedom is inseparable from the moral or spiritual freedom lost when liberty is confused with license and when "the individuals making up a nation have broken their life-giving bond with Nature."[17] But "What," we may wonder with a perceptive contemporary commentator (possibly Robert Southey), "does Mr. Coleridge mean by liberty in this passage? or what connexion has it with the subject of civil freedom?"[18] The implication, given the ode's political context, is that the word has been transformed utterly by being displaced from the public to a private realm. As Morton Paley has noted, the question "cut close enough for Coleridge to reply."[19] He did so privately, in Sir George Beaumont's copy of the quarto edition including this poem, along with "Frost at Midnight" and "Fears in Solitude." There (p. 18), he referred to "*unfounded* Objections" that made it seem "as if I had confounded moral with political Freedom—but surely the object of this stanza is to show, that true political Freedom can only arise out of moral Freedom."

"Interesting as it may be in its own right," says Paley, "this proposition is not the argument of the last stanza." According to the ode, Liberty never breathed its soul "in forms of human pow'r," but rather "speedest on subtle pinions, / To live amid the winds, and move upon the waves" (lines 91–92, 97–98). The poem, Paley continues, "does involve a rejection of the political realm and a semantic juggling of 'Liberty.'" He quotes Abrams, according to whom the "resolution of this poem is intelligible only if we recognize that it turns on the conversion of the political concepts, slavery and liberty, into the metaphors of the mind in relation to nature." Positioning himself between Abrams and the New Historicists, if somewhat closer to the latter, Paley concludes that "in the poem's end" ("an exemplary Romantic situation," as Abrams remarks of poetic "rondure"),

17. Woodring, *Politics in the Poetry of Coleridge*, 186.
18. *The Critical Review* 26 (1799), 474. Cited in Reiman, ed., *Romantics Reviewed* Part A, *The Lake Poets* 1:312.
19. "Apocalypse and Millenium," 32.

is its beginning, with the poet alone on the seacliff experiencing the unity of his own being with the forces of Nature. Significantly, the poet does not link these, as he does in the "Monody on the Death of Chatterton," with a human community; nor does any Cot or heart-honour'd Maid [as in "The Eolian Harp"] await him now. His situation is much like that in the end of the *Ode on the Departing Year,* with the forces of Nature being substituted for the purely spiritual ones of the earlier ode. The ideal of domesticity has disappeared, the apocalyptic become historicized in the past, the millennial shown to be an illusion.[20]

As we have seen, the inward turn of the first-generation Romantics, the disenchanted "flight" or defaulting "retreat" from politics and history, first critiqued by Byron and Shelley, has come under increasingly cold-eyed historicist scrutiny. One may read this final stanza—which, as Kelvin Everest also says, displaces Coleridge's political vision into "a personal, elemental unity with nature" and, as Angela Esterhammer says, "locates Liberty in an unpopulated landscape, representing it not as a word that is heard, but a spirit that is felt"— as a repudiation not only of republicanism but also of "human liberty" altogether.[21] In this climax, writes Alan Liu, Coleridge "*seems*" to affirm "Liberty," but

> like blind Lear on the sea-cliff's verge, or like some ancient mariner on the verge of feeling love for sea snakes, the poet says Yes to natural Liberty only in the spirit of alienation from human liberty. *The* sea-verge at the time, after all, looked eastward not with intensest love but with hate toward the expected French invasion. Natural liberty was freedom *from* the liberty-become-repression of France as well as of the land behind the poet's back: Pitt's England. The Ode on France, we may thus say, is a poem of pure marginality—the opposition mentality forced into a borderline stand neither here nor there in the social world.[22]

Yes, but. . . . One *may* "thus say," and be astutely and even absolutely correct—but at the cost of at least *seeming* to remain unmoved, not only by any politics-transcending conviction, but by the linguistic power of this, the sublime rondural conclusion of the finest poem Coleridge ever published in the *Morning Post,* and one of the great "moments" in Romantic poetry. As Geoffrey Hartman, Hillis Miller, and even Stephen Greenblatt might warn (in passages such as those cited in my "Critical Introduction"), a reader both brilliant and accurate, as Liu is here, can be so much in touch with material reality and historical "resonance" that the linguistic reality, the "wonder," loses its palpability.[23] In any case, since the final stanza of this ode has always seemed to me as

20. Ibid. For Abrams's comment on poetic "rondure," see *Natural Supernaturalism,* 363, 364.

21. Everest, *Coleridge's Secret Ministry,* 38. Esterhammer, "Speech Acts and Living Words," 81.

22. *Wordsworth,* 418.

23. In his self-questioning epilogue, Liu has his interlocutor ask him: "Is it not true that the 'facts' you have perused in your researches have often moved you more than any literature—least of all that of your chosen poet—could ever do?" The accusation is that he is "alive to the materiality of the past in a way that you are not alive to literature even

compelling as the response to the beauty of the water-snakes and considerably more persuasive than their blessing (which evokes as much "but" as "Yes"), I have advanced with a reasonably clear conscience this negative response to the Mariner's benediction.

That negative response, I discover at the end, fuses Bostetter's *ironic* argument about "fear and enforced obedience" as a bowing down to "the paternal tyrant, the 'great Father'" and Camille Paglia's *psychoanalytic* argument that the snake blessing is a fearful retreat from the chthonian Female to a Christian moralism, with E. P. Thompson's leftist *political* argument, that "capitulation by the Jacobin poets to the traditional, paternalistic culture was *in fact* inimical to the sources of their art."[24]

This bowing down to a patriarchal deity is not peripheral. It is the Mariner's central and final "stance," one as submissive as Friday's before *his* providential savior and "master"—himself an image of "Defoe's God," visualized by Harold Bloom "coping with the universe as Crusoe makes do on his island, but with teeming millions of adoring Fridays where Crusoe enjoys the devotion of just one."[25] In the stanza immediately preceding the poem's explicit "moral," Coleridge's aged Mariner tells the Wedding Guest that, for him, it is "sweeter than the Marriage-feast"

> To walk together to the Kirk,
> And all together pray,
> While each to his great Father bends.
> (lines 634–40)

Echoing and partially reversing this passage, Wordsworth describes the "conflict of sensations" aroused in him when he would find himself in an English church, exulting in French triumphs:

> When in the congregation, bending all
> To their great Father, prayers were offered up,
> Or praises for our country's victories,

he, "only, like an uninvited guest," "Fed on the day of vengeance yet to come!" (*Prelude* X.260–74).

It seems safe to say that the distinguished annotators of the Norton "Critical Edition" of the 1799, 1805, and 1850 texts of *The Prelude* have missed at least part of the point in simply remarking of the "bending all / To their great Father" phrase: "for Wordsworth, as for the Mariner, shared worship is symbolic of harmony." One of those editors and annotators, Jonathan Wordsworth, subsequently and rightly observed of this passage that it is "memorable for its study

in your most imaginative moment. . . . You are a *believer* in history, and literature is only your testament. Can you say this is untruth?" Liu's answer to his own question—"It is not the whole of the truth. But it is part of it" (501)—is at once honest and evasive, and it does tend to confirm the fact that he is more "alive" to history than to literature.

24. "Disenchantment or Default?" 173.

25. Introduction to *Eighteenth-Century British Fiction*, 3.

of alienation."[26] For in 1793–1794, tormented Wordsworth, far from joining his countrymen in bending to their great Father, religious or nationalistic, stood apart from any symbolic harmony, feeding himself on the promise of salutary wrath—an epitome of the revolutionary break with eighteenth-century patriarchal tradition.[27] If my political argument has any merit, it is precisely this righteous and wrathful indignation that Coleridge, through the Mariner, eschews in order to fall back on inherited tradition—less, perhaps, in the passage preceding the moral, or even in the moral itself, than in the blessing of the water-snakes.

It hardly needs to be added that any conversion or repatriation or "bending" capitulation subliminally represented by that blessing (the work, as Beer says, of "a more subtle and intricate transformation of the psyche") is imaginatively preferable to the snapping of the squeaking baby-trumpet of sedition, and the hanging up of its fragments in the chamber of penitences. It is also preferable to falling "prostrate" before "Power" and "foul Oppression" as the alternative to being "Caught" in the "monstrous twine" of that bone-crushing "serpent" whose "vast moon-glittering bulk" slithers bombastically and politically through "Religious Musings" (*CPW* I 118–19).

Yet the difference may well be one of degree and tone, not necessarily of political kind. It may even be that, just as the miscreated "slimy shapes" fouling the Pacific in "The Destiny of Nations" anticipated the "slimy things" that "crawl with legs / Upon the slimy Sea," so the strident anti-Ministerial passage from "Religious Musings" anticipates the exquisite imagery of moonlight and snakes at the turning-point of *The Ancient Mariner.* There is more than one transformation here. It is worth mentioning that the "beauty" of the snakes is the result not only of altered light and perception but of actual appearance. That the creatures originally "crawl *with legs*" upon the slimy sea may be felt, to quote William Empson, "as an outrage against Nature herself." By the time the Mariner "attains such a pure sympathy with Nature that he loves them for the beauty of their movement," they have "turned into water-snakes; it was very lucky for the Mariner that all their legs dropped off, because he could not have loved them if they had still been crawly—though the hypocrisy of the doctrine insists that he could or should have loved them however crawly they were."[28] Empson does not make the political point, so I will. By the time he completed

26. *The Prelude: 1799, 1805, 1850,* ed. Jonathan Wordsworth et al., 372*n;* Jonathan Wordsworth, "Wordsworth's 'Dim and Perilous Way,'" 217.

27. For late eighteenth-century Europeans, the patriarchal familial model embraced father, king, and God. One of the leading new cultural historians, Lynn Hunt, offers an astute analysis of the revolutionary connection between "private sphere" and "public arena" in *The Family Romance of the French Revolution.* In keeping with her Freudian title, she cites Freud's point, from *Totem and Taboo,* that the psychoanalysis of individuals teaches us that "the god of each of them is formed in the likeness of his father," and that "at bottom God is nothing other than an exalted father." The same, she adds, "might be said of the law and of social organization generally" (7).

28. Introduction to *Coleridge's Verse,* 40–41.

The Ancient Mariner, Coleridge, responding to both the benevolence growing "within [him]" and the menacing political situation rapidly developing all around him, managed to find William Pitt and his Ministers less crawly and more lovable.

Even without the addition of Empson (a critic at once acute and facetious), Bostetter, Paglia, and Thompson make strange bedfellows. As the merging of such disparate but perceptive arguments should suggest, my submerged political thesis here has led me on as "strange and surprizing" an adventure as my earlier exploration of the slavery "theme" in Defoe and Coleridge. As mentioned at the outset, the exploration as a whole, reading and writing alike, has emulated the "motion of a serpent," as advocated by Coleridge in the chapter of *Biographia Literaria* devoted to *Lyrical Ballads:*

> The reader should be carried forward, not merely or chiefly by the mechanical impulse of curiosity, or by a restless desire to arrive at the final solution; but by the pleasurable activity of mind excited by the attractions of the journey itself. Like the motion of a serpent, which the Egyptians made the emblem of intellectual power, . . . at every step he pauses and half recedes, and from the retrogressive movement collects the force which again carries him onward. (*BL* II 14)

At the end of my journey, I am by no means sure that I am not what Frances Ferguson calls a "deluded reader." If so, I will certainly not be, like Crusoe and the Mariner, "Alone, alone, all, all alone." And I will have been carried forward by the pleasurable activity of mind excited by the journey itself, an enjoyment I hope at least some of my readers will have shared. If not, there is the consolation that *The Rime of the Ancient Mariner* has survived with its interpretation-defeating mystery intact, a poem to be read, re-created, and wondered about anew when the critics who would reduce it to their own theoretical perspectives and cultural biases are themselves reduced to footnotes.

We began with Yeats and, rounding this book's elaborate whorl, may fittingly end with him as well. Evoking, as Coleridge did in March 1798, the political implications of the whirlwind and earthquake experienced by Elijah before he heard the far subtler yet more powerful "still small voice of God," Yeats compares the delicate aesthetic labor that goes into the making of a poem with divine creativity itself: "Politics, for a vision-seeking man, can be but half-achievement, a choice of an almost easy kind of skill instead of that which is, of all those not impossible, the most difficult. Is it not certain that the Creator yawns in earthquake and thunder and other popular displays, but toils in rounding the elaborate spiral of a shell[?]"[29]

Yes, but. . . . In his haughty, "quietist" dismissal of the facile and the vulgar, Yeats gives fair warning to those who would too easily repoliticize art at the expense of what has been achieved by painstaking aesthetic transformation. Yet, as I have argued in "Revolutions French and Russian: Burke, Wordsworth, and the Genesis of Yeats's 'The Second Coming,'" it is critically self-limiting to

29. *Autobiographies,* 240.

dismiss the political genesis of even Yeats's *most* "vision-seeking" poem. The same is true of *The Ancient Mariner,* a "work of pure imagination" almost miraculously generated out of closely related revolutionary materials: that often slimy sea of politics that reappears in the ballad in displaced form.

To politically recontextualize poems, even the most visionary poems, need not necessarily be to vulgarize or limit them. Envisioning *The Ancient Mariner* multiperspectivally and from another level on the spiral of appreciation, we are in a better position to reaffirm, even enhance, its status as a great—though not quite the *same*—work of art. Though I would like to think that my own "toil" has not been in vain, I would concede, even insist, that my argument, once it has been absorbed, can largely be left behind as, once again, we respond to *The Ancient Mariner* itself, that wonderful if not quite "supernatural" creation that emerged from the political convulsions of the 1790s.

APPENDIX

The Mariner, Prometheus, and the Yeatsian Self

Of all readers of Coleridge's major poems it may be Shelley who best enacts what Eliot calls the first and highest form of criticism by masterfully re-creating—in *Alastor,* "Mont Blanc," *Prometheus Unbound,* and "Adonais"—such poems as "Kubla Khan" and *The Ancient Mariner.* The Visionary Poet's supernatural boat journey in *Alastor* is obviously indebted to Coleridge's ballad, along with the allegorical boat journey in Southey's *Thalaba.* But Shelley's subtlest imitation—focused on *The Ancient Mariner*'s crucial event, the blessing of the water-snakes—occurs, I would suggest, in his own masterwork, *Prometheus Unbound.* Appropriately, Shelley's disciple, W. B. Yeats, perhaps building on *Prometheus Unbound,* has his own antithetical variation on that blessing in what is arguably his central poem, "A Dialogue of Self and Soul." These interconnections seem worth sketching in an appendix since both later works cast light on *The Ancient Mariner* and its pivotal if problematic shift to an all-embracing love.

The Shelleyan version of reintegrating reversal comes early, indeed in the hero's opening soliloquy. In an instinctive change of heart, Prometheus "recalls" (remembers and is soon to revoke) his curse against the tyrant and paradoxically "prostrate slave" who has chained him in the Caucasus. "Disdain. Ah no! I pity thee." He prophesies Jupiter's inevitable "Ruin," but

> in grief,
> Not exultation, for I hate no more,
> . . . .
> . . . changed so that aught evil wish
> Is dead within. . . .
>
> (I.52–53, 70–71)

"O happy *living things!,*" the Mariner had cried out, suddenly perceiving as beautiful the slimy things he had earlier despised. "I wish no *living thing* to suffer pain" (I.305), says Prometheus at the equivalent moment, withdrawing his curse upon Jupiter, and substituting love for hatred. Hearing this renunciation, "Earth," the Mother of the Titans, mistakenly imagines that the most stalwart of her sons has at last capitulated to the tyrant "to whom all things of Earth and Heaven do bow / In fear and worship" (I.284–85). Her heart is "rent" with "misery" that "Jove at length should vanquish thee" (306–9). Ione (who, with her sister Panthea, has long been seated at the chained Titan's feet) reassures the attendant Echoes: "Fear not—'tis but a passing spasm, / The

Titan is unvanquished still" (314–15). While the revocation of hatred is no passing spasm, Ione is right about the main point; Prometheus remains indomitable. Though Ione's perspective is limited, it is, in this sense, less limited than that of Earth.

Earth's limitation is made abundantly clear in act 3, when the tyrant falls, vanquished by—precisely—Prometheus's moral choice to renounce hatred: an unpremeditated choice by which (though of *this* effect he is as "unaware" as the Mariner in his act of benediction) he releases the full power of love in the beautiful form of his female *epipsyche,* Asia, the long-exiled sister of Ione and Panthea. By choosing to take no vengeance, Prometheus "keeps himself," as Donald Reiman has noted, "from becoming another Jupiter."[1]

This refusal of the oppressed to become an oppressor in his turn has—as my echo of Wordsworth's judgment of the French would indicate—an overt historical context. Employing the imagery of the preceding generation, Shelley in *Prometheus Unbound* depicts France's cycle from dawn to bloody denouement in domestic terror and foreign conquest. According to two semichoruses of the Furies sent by Jupiter to torment the hero, the "disenchanted nation" (France), throwing off the spell of monarchy, "springs like day from desolation," dedicated to "Truth" and "Freedom" in fraternal love. But all too soon, those ideals are perverted: "See how kindred murder kin" when, in the "vintage-time for Death and Sin,"

> Blood, like new wine, bubbles within
> Till Despair smothers
> The struggling World, which slaves and tyrants win.
> (I.567–77)

The historical context, then, is one Shelley shares with his immediate precursors, Wordsworth and Coleridge. To again quote Donald Reiman:

> As Shelley had seen in the course of the French Revolution, when the oppressed lack the capacity to love and forgive, they soon turn into new oppressors who are basically indistinguishable from the old. Prometheus' decision to turn from self-centered hatred to outgoing love marks the moment in human history that breaks the old meaningless cycle of oppression and retribution—"the despot's rage, the slave's revenge"—and introduces a new order based on forgiveness and equality. Prometheus becomes an ideal far different from a vengeful rebel, a Jupiter-out-of-office; he becomes a purified symbol of human creativity, offering men something to emulate that will change their conceptions of what they are and what they can and ought to become.[2]

As he acknowledges in his preface, Shelley was aware of the degree to which *Prometheus Unbound* had been "tinged" and "modified" as a result of his study of "contemporary writings," particularly the works of those "who stand in the foremost ranks" of his own age. Certain "forms," he continued, were due "less to the peculiarities" of individual minds than to "the peculiarity of the moral

1. *Percy Bysshe Shelley,* 82.
2. Ibid.

and intellectual condition of the minds among which they were produced."[3]
The historical age dominated by what Shelley called "the master-theme of the
epoch in which we live—the French Revolution" is the proper context in which
to read both *Prometheus Unbound* and *The Ancient Mariner,* as well as Southey's
Thalaba. And no "moral and intellectual" motif was more a part of the Roman-
tic zeitgeist than the transformation of divisive hatred into a self-integrating
and encompassing love. Shelley may well be remembering that Thalaba eventu-
ally pardons rather than kills the tyrant who had murdered his father. But by
having Prometheus, in revoking his curse against the tyrant, echo the Mariner's
conversion, specifically the refusal to exclude from sympathy any "living thing,"
Shelley in effect recognized the "political" dimension of the blessing of the
water-snakes in *The Ancient Mariner.*

In stressing the capitulation theme rather than the reintegration theme, I
may seem as limited in perspective as Shelley's mistaken Earth. And yet, there
are crucial differences between the Mariner's "conversion" and that of
Prometheus—several of them differences emphasized in Yeats's reworking of
the Coleridgean "blessing" in "A Dialogue of Self and Soul."

To begin with, both Prometheus and Asia (the latter in act 2, in De-
mogorgon's cave) recognize that Jupiter, for all his seeming omnipotence, is a
"slave" doomed by an inexorable cycle to eventually fall. It is this clairvoyant
perspective that justifies and perhaps motivates the Farseer's pivotal act of
forgiveness and renunciation of the curse, the latter a moral flaw that had for a
time made him resemble his vindictive foe. The second point is that Jupiter is in
fact overthrown. The creator of the Mariner, the repatriated "loyalist" of "Fears
in Solitude," had no such assurances of the eventual defeat of the forces either
of foreign oppression or of domestic *re*pression. In Shelley's drama, "Heaven's
Despotism," a now defeated "Conquest," is "dragged Captive through the
Deep." So announces Demogorgon in his great concluding speech, in which he
describes triumphant Love, a kind of secularized Holy Spirit, in terms that
almost evoke a regenerated Coleridgean albatross: "Love from its awful throne
of patient power / In the wise heart," having endured agony, "springs / And
folds over the world its healing wings" (V.556–61).

"Gentleness, Virtue, Wisdom and Endurance" are the "seals" of the assur-
ance that "bars the pit over Destruction's strength"; nevertheless, Eternity her-
self, with "infirm hand," might in the future "free / The serpent that would
clasp her with his length." Should that happen, Demogorgon promises—in
that litany of resonant infinitives that concludes *Prometheus Unbound*—"spells
by which to reassume / An Empire o'er the disentangled Doom":

> To suffer woes which Hope thinks infinite;
> To forgive wrongs darker than Death or Night;
> To defy Power which seems Omnipotent;

3. Preface to *Prometheus Unbound,* in *Shelley's Poetry and Prose,* ed. Donald H. Reiman
and Sharon B. Powers, 133–34.

> To love, and bear; to hope, till Hope creates
> From its own wreck the thing it contemplates;
>   Neither to change nor falter nor repent:
> This, like thy glory, Titan, is to be
> Good, great and joyous, beautiful and free;
> This is alone Life, Joy, Empire and Victory.
>   (V.556–78)

Injustices are to be endured, wrongs forgiven; but Shelley still insists that destructive power is to be defied rather than yielded to, and that the defier (in an intriguing echo of Milton's rebellious Satan) is not to change, falter, or repent.[4] And he remains aware that imprisoning tyranny, itself imprisoned in act 4, always threatens to break free in the form of a constricting "serpent" resembling the bone-crushing "serpent" of tyrannical (Pittite) "power" in Coleridge's "Religious Musings," a poem Shelley knew well.

Though we remain threatened by dark forces, the world—at the end of act 3 and the great coda of act 4 of *Prometheus Unbound*—is utterly redeemed by the transfiguring and regenerative power of love. In *The Ancient Mariner* that transfiguration is less than complete. The previously despised reptiles are now recognized as fellow-creatures and the Mariner, as alienated as Prometheus was before *his* "conversion," seems reintegrated—internally, and with the world around him. He loves, he prays; and yet the Mariner, never fully redeemed, continues "to suffer woes" that seem "infinite"—"woeful agonies" that, apparently, no amount of repentance and willingness to "bend" to the "great Father" can terminate. For he experiences an agonizing reenactment of guilt he is condemned to repeat "again and yet again."

I am deliberately echoing Self's peroration in Yeats's "A Dialogue of Self and Soul," a quite different version of Eternal Recurrence that, in turn, echoes with a difference the blessing of the water-snakes. A "spring of love" gushes from the Mariner's heart as he looks upon the previously repellent, "slimy" water-snakes, and "blessed them unaware." With vitalistic relish, the Yeatsian Self embraces the primordial slime itself, "If it be life to pitch / Into the frogspawn. . . ." And Self is content, in an "ontological" recapitulation,

> to follow to its source
> Every event in action or in thought;
> Measure the lot; forgive myself the lot!
> When such as I cast out remorse
> So great a sweetness flows into the breast
> We must laugh and we must sing,
> We are blest by everything,
> Everything we look upon is blest.

4. Though Prometheus had said of his curse just before revoking it, "It doth repent me," he also refers to his sufferings as "unrepentent pains" (I.303, 427). Here, in Demogorgon's speech, Shelley echoes the Satan who defiantly cries out that no matter what "the Potent Victor" has inflicted or "Can else inflict," he does not "repent or change" (*Paradise Lost* I.94–96).

"Repentance keeps my heart impure," Yeats says in "Sun and Stream at Glendalough"; here, his dialectical triumph is over his own self-division, a reaffirmation of autonomy in which remorse is "cast out," reversing the defiling image earlier "cast upon" him by the "mirror of malicious eyes." Along with the "malicious eye" of the deformed figure who would mislead the quester at the outset of Browning's heroic but cyclical rather than millennial "Childe Roland to the Dark Tower Came," Yeats's phrase may recall the fixed, accusing eyes of the Mariner's dead shipmates—stony eyes that in the moon did glitter. In Yeats's poem, that passive mirror has turned lamp, and Christian redemption has been—magnificently or blasphemously—secularized, with the autonomous Romantic imagination as redeemer. The sweetness that "flows into" the self-forgiving breast displaces the infusion (*infundere:* "to pour in") of Christian grace through divine forgiveness.

In Yeats's secular, Nietzschean variation on the beatitude theme, there are no mirroring or guilt-projecting eyes, no pitying "kind saint" in attendance, no conventional prayer. Soul had earlier announced that "only the dead can be forgiven," but Yeats's audacious Nietzschean Self, measuring the lot, forgives *himself* the lot, casting out the heart-muddying "remorse" the Mariner is condemned to relive in an endless series of rending reenactments of his "crime." Despite Yeats's indebtedness to the blessing of the water-snakes (as well as to Blake's related Romantic-spiritual axiom, "Every thing that lives is holy"), the differences between Coleridge's Mariner and the Yeatsian Self are obvious. But what, to return to Shelley, is the difference between the changes of heart experienced by Prometheus and those experienced by the Mariner?

Mother Earth was wrong: the indomitable Prometheus was not vanquished, he did not capitulate. Trying to persuade the Titan to reveal the secret of Jupiter's overthrow, "fear of which perplexes the Supreme," Mercury enjoins him—echoing the same lines in the *Mariner* echoed earlier by Earth and still earlier in Wordsworth's very different tableau of communal prayer—to "bend thy soul in prayer" to "the great Father" (I.371–76, 354). He does not. The fate of the Mariner, on the other hand, suggests that, for all his outpouring of "love," he is something less than Reiman's Prometheus—"a purified symbol of human creativity" for us all to emulate as a model of perspectival change. The Mariner's final vision is, however moving, both simplistic and submissive; despite the agony he continues to suffer, he is reduced to "bending" in fearful reverence to a "great Father" who seems—even worse than Jupiter—*un*willing to terminate the sufferings of what is in this case a *repentant* sinner. Such a compensation-exacting God Coleridge himself had pronounced a "blasphemous absurdity," a veritable symbol of the punitive Tyrant.

In the world of 1798, exacting tyranny took the form of William Pitt and his cabinet, those "slimy shapes" flourishing in the stagnant sea of despotism. To "bless" such creatures and then provide an orthodox imprimatur may be an expression of love, but it may also be an expression of the cowardice of what Coleridge called "the Goody." For those snakes have a lineage in "cockatrice" Pitt. The constricting tyrannical "serpent" consigned to the "pit" in *Prometheus*

Unbound may be the very bone-crushing "serpent" shrunk from in "Religious Musings"; and both may be related, on the "political" level of interpretation, with the snakes blessed—perhaps with less unpremeditation than political fear, less compassion than capitulation—at the turning point of *The Ancient Mariner.* Though Shelley's Prometheus does not lie, as Earth mistakenly thought, "fallen and vanquished," Coleridge's Mariner *may*—a submission initiated by the very act most readers see as his moment of triumph. And while Prometheus never bends to the great Father, the Mariner goes on to make such bending the primary occupation of his life.

Works Cited

Excluding the works of Coleridge and Defoe, all primary and secondary texts cited are given below.

Abrams, M. H. "The Deconstructive Angel" (1977). In *Doing Things with Texts*, 237–52.

———. *Doing Things with Texts: Essays in Criticism and Critical Theory*. New York and London: Norton, 1989.

———. "English Romanticism: The Spirit of the Age" (1963). In *The Correspondent Breeze: Essays on English Romanticism*, 44–75. New York: Norton, 1984.

———. *The Mirror and the Lamp: Romantic Theory and the Critical Tradition*. New York: Norton, 1953.

———. *Natural Supernaturalism: Tradition and Revolution in Romantic Literature*. New York: Norton, 1971.

———. "On Political Readings of *Lyrical Ballads*." In *Doing Things with Texts*, 364–91.

———. "Rationality and Imagination in Cultural History: A Reply to Wayne Booth." *Critical Inquiry* 2 (1976): 447–64.

———. "A Reply." In *High Romantic Argument: Essays for M. H. Abrams,* edited by Lawrence Lipking, 164–75. Ithaca and London: Cornell University Press, 1981.

———. "What Is a Humanistic Criticism?" *The Bookpress* 3.5 (1993): 1–2, 7–8, 12–14. (Shortened version of the first Heinrich and Alice Schneider Memorial Lecture, delivered at Cornell University on March 31, 1993.)

Alam, Fakrul. "Religious and Linguistic Colonialism in Defoe's Fiction." *North Dakota Quarterly* 55 (1987): 116–23.

Althusser, Louis, and Etienne Balibar. *Reading Capital,* translated by Ben Brewster. New York: Pantheon Books, 1970.

Anderson, Hans. "The Paradox of Trade and Morality in Defoe." *Philological Quarterly* 39 (1941): 23–46.

Arac, Jonathan. "Coleridge and New Criticism Reconsidered: Repetition and Exclusion." In *Critical Genealogies: Historical Situations for Postmodern Literary Studies*, 81–95. New York and London: Columbia University Press, 1989.

Armitage, W. H. G. "Joseph Mather: Poet of the Filesmiths." *Notes and Queries* 195 (1950): 320–22.

Asante, Molefi Kete. "Multiculturalism: An Exchange" (1991). In *Debating PC: The Controversy over Political Correctness on College Campuses,* edited by Paul Berman, 299–311. New York: Laurel, 1992.

Asimov, Isaac. *Asimov's Guide to Shakespeare.* 2 vols. in one. New York: Avenel Books, 1978 [1970].

Aspinall, Arthur, ed. *The Later Correspondence of George III.* 5 vols. Cambridge and New York: Cambridge University Press, 1970.

Auden, W. H. *The Enchaféd Flood; or, The Romantic Iconography of the Sea.* New York: Vintage, 1951.

Aufderheide, Patricia, ed. *Beyond PC: Toward a Politics of Understanding.* St. Paul, Minn.: Graywolf Press, 1992.

Ault, Donald. Foreword to Martin Wallen, *Coleridge's Ancient Mariner: An Experimental Edition of Texts and Revisions, 1798–1828.* Barrytown, N.Y.: Station Hill Literary Editions, 1993.

Authentic Copies of the Instructions Given by General Hoche to Colonel Tate Previous to His Landing on the Coast of South Wales, in the Beginning of 1797. London, 1798.

Ayers, Robert W. "*Robinson Crusoe:* 'Allusive Allegorick History.'" *PMLA* 82 (1967): 399–407.

Ayling, Stanley. *Life of Charles James Fox.* London: John Murray, 1991.

Babbitt, Irving. "The Problem of the Imagination: Coleridge." In *On Being Creative and Other Essays,* 97–133. Boston: Houghton Mifflin, 1932.

Backscheider, Paula. *Daniel Defoe: His Life.* Baltimore and London: Johns Hopkins University Press, 1989.

Baine, Rodney M. "Daniel Defoe and Robert Drury's *Journal.*" *Texas Studies in Literature and Language* 16 (1974): 479–91.

———. *Daniel Defoe and the Supernatural.* Athens: University of Georgia Press, 1968.

Baker, Herschel. *William Hazlitt.* Cambridge, Mass., and London: Harvard University Press, 1962.

Barber, Benjamin R. *An Aristocracy of Everyone: The Politics of Education and the Future of America.* New York: Ballantine Books, 1992.

Barry, Kevin. *Language, Music, and the Sign: A Study of Aesthetics, Poetics, and Poetic Practice from Collins to Coleridge.* Cambridge and New York: Cambridge University Press, 1987.

Barth, Robert, S.J. *Coleridge and the Power of Love.* Columbia and London: University of Missouri Press, 1988.

Barth, Robert, S.J., and John L. Mahoney, eds. *Coleridge, Keats, and the Imagination: Romanticism and Adam's Dream.* Columbia and London: University of Missouri Press, 1990.

Bate, Walter Jackson. *Coleridge.* New York and London: Macmillan, 1968.

Beer, John B. *Coleridge's Poetic Intelligence.* London and Basingstoke: Macmillan, 1974.

———. *Coleridge the Visionary.* New York: Macmillan, Collier, 1962 [1959].

———, ed. *Coleridge's Writings.* Princeton: Princeton University Press, 1991–.

Behn, Aphra. *Oroonoko; or, The History of the Royal Slave* (1688). Edited by Lore Metzger. New York: Norton, 1973.

Bell, Derrick. *Faces at the Bottom of the Well: The Permanence of Racism.* New York: Basic Books, 1992.

Bell, Ian A. *Defoe's Fiction.* London and Totowa, N.J.: Barnes and Noble, 1985.

Benjamin, Edwin B. "Symbolic Elements in *Robinson Crusoe.*" *Philological Quarterly* 30 (1951): 205–11.

Berkoben, L. D. *Coleridge's Decline as a Poet.* The Hague: Mouton, 1975.

Berman, Paul, ed. *Debating PC: The Controversy over Political Correctness on College Campuses.* New York: Laurel, 1992.

Bernal, Martin. *Black Athena: The Afroasiatic Roots of Classical Civilization.* 2 vols. New Brunswick and London: Rutgers University Press, 1987, 1991.

Berubé, Michael. "Public Image Limited: Political Correctness and the Media's Big Lie" (1991). In *Debating PC: The Controversy over Political Correctness on College Campuses,* edited by Paul Berman, 124–49. New York: Laurel, 1992.

Bewell, Alan. *Wordsworth and the Enlightenment: Nature and Society in the Experimental Poetry.* New Haven and London: Yale University Press, 1988.

Bishop, Elizabeth. "Crusoe in England." In *Geography III.* New York: Farrar, Straus and Giroux, 1976.

Blake, William. *The Letters of William Blake.* Edited by Geoffrey Keynes. Cambridge, Mass., and London: Harvard University Press, 1970.

———. *The Poetry and Prose of William Blake.* Edited by David V. Erdman, Commentary by Harold Bloom. Garden City, N.Y.: Doubleday, 1965.

Blewitt, David. *Defoe's Art of Fiction: Robinson Crusoe, Moll Flanders, Col. Jack, and Roxanne.* Toronto: University of Toronto Press, 1979.

Bloom, Allan. *The Closing of the American Mind: How Higher Education Has Failed Democracy and Impoverished the Souls of Today's Students.* New York: Simon and Schuster, 1987.

Bloom, Harold. "The Internalization of Quest Romance" (1968). In *The Ringers in the Tower: Studies in Romantic Tradition,* 13–35. Chicago and London: University of Chicago Press, 1971.

———. Introduction to *Eighteenth-Century British Fiction.* The Critical Cosmos Series. New York: Chelsea House, 1988.

Blumenbach, Johann Friedrich. *De Generis Humani Varietate Nativa.* 3d ed. Göttingen, 1795 [1775]. Translated by T. Bendyshe. London, 1865.

———. *The Institutions of Physiology.* Translated by John Elliotson. Philadelphia, 1817.

———. *A Manual of the Elements of Natural History.* London, 1825.

Boase, T. R. S. "Shipwrecks in English Romantic Poetry." *Journal of the Warburg and Courtauld Institute* 22 (1959): 332–46.

Bodkin, Maud. *Archetypal Patterns in Poetry: Psychological Studies of Imagination.* Oxford and New York: Oxford University Press, 1934.

Boime, Albert. *The Art of Exclusion: Representing Blacks in the Nineteenth Century.* Washington, D.C.: The Smithsonian Institution, 1990.

Booth, Wayne. "M. H. Abrams: Historian as Critic, Critic as Pluralist." *Critical Inquiry* 2 (1976): 411–45.

Borrow, George. *Lavengro: The Scholar, the Gypsy, the Priest.* 2 vols. London, 1851.

Bostetter, Edward E. "The Nightmare World of *The Ancient Mariner*" (1962). In *The Romantic Ventriloquists.* Seattle: University of Washington Press, 1963.

Boulger, James D. Introduction to *Twentieth-Century Interpretations of "The Rime of the Ancient Mariner,"* edited by Boulger. Englewood Cliffs, N.J.: Prentice-Hall, 1969.

Bové, Paul A. *In the Wake of Theory.* Hanover and London: Wesleyan University Press, 1992.

Bowra, C. M. "*The Ancient Mariner.*" In *The Romantic Imagination,* 51–75. Oxford and New York: Oxford University Press, 1961 [1949].

Brackman, Harold. *Farrakhan's Reign of Historical Error: The Truth Behind "The Secret Relationship between Blacks and Jews."* Simon Wiesenthal Center Reports, 1992.

Braverman, Richard. "Crusoe's Legacy." *Studies in the Novel* 18 (1986): 1–26.

Brett, R. L., and A. R. Jones, eds. *Lyrical Ballads: Wordsworth and Coleridge.* 2d. ed. London and New York: Routledge, 1991.

Brinkley, Robert A. "Vagrant and Hermit: Milton and the Politics of 'Tintern Abbey.'" *The Wordsworth Circle* 16 (1985): 126–33.

Bromwich, David. "Burke, Wordsworth, and the Defense of History." In *A Choice of Inheritance.* Cambridge, Mass., and London: Harvard University Press, 1989.

———. *Politics by Other Means: Higher Education and Group Thinking.* New Haven and London: Yale University Press, 1992.

Brown, Huntington. "The Gloss to *The Rime of the Ancient Mariner.*" *Modern Language Quarterly* 6 (1945): 319–24.

Brown, Laura. "The Romance of Empire: *Oroonoko* and the Trade in Slaves." In *The New Eighteenth Century: Theory, Politics, English Literature,* edited by Felicity Nussbaum and Laura Brown, 40–61. New York and London: Methuen, 1987.

Brown, Philip Anthony. *The French Revolution in English History.* New York: C. Lockwood and Son, 1918.

Burke, Edmund. *The Correspondence of Edmund Burke.* 10 vols. Thomas Copeland, general editor. Cambridge and New York: Cambridge University Press; Chicago and London: University of Chicago Press, 1958–1978.

———. *The Writings and Speeches of Edmund Burke.* 12 vols. Paul Langford, general editor. Oxford: Clarendon Press, 1981.

Burnet, Thomas. *Telluris theoria sacra: Orbis nostri originem et mutationes generales, quas aut iam subuit, aut olim subiturus est, complectens.* 2 vols. London, 1681, 1689. Translated as *Theory of the Earth . . .* London, 1684, 1690.

Butler, Marilyn. "Godwin, Burke, and *Caleb Williams.*" *Essays in Criticism* 32 (1982): 237–57.

———. "Plotting the Revolution: The Political Narratives of Romantic Poetry and Criticism." In *Romantic Revolutions: Criticism and Theory,* edited by Kenneth Johnston et al., 133–57. Bloomington and Indianapolis: University of Indiana Press, 1990.

———. "Repossessing the Past: The Case for an Open Literary History" (1989). In *Rethinking Historicism: Critical Readings in Romantic History,* Marjorie Levinson et al., 64–84. Oxford: Basil Blackwell, 1989.

———. *Romantics, Rebels, and Reactionaries: English Literature and Its Background, 1760–1830.* Oxford and New York: Oxford University Press, 1981.

———. "Telling It Like a Story: The French Revolution as Narrative." *Studies in Romanticism* 28 (1989): 344–64.

Byron, Lord. *Don Juan and Other Satirical Poems*. Edited by Louis I. Bredvold. New York: Odyssey Press, 1935.

Calleo, David P. *Coleridge and the Idea of the Modern State*. New Haven and London: Yale University Press, 1966.

———. "Coleridge on Napoleon." *Yale French Studies* 26 (1960–1961): 83–93.

Carlyon, Clement. *Early Years and Late Reflections*. 2 vols. London, 1836.

Cavell, Stanley. *Must We Mean What We Say?* New York: Scribner's, 1969.

Césaire, Aimé. *Cahier d'un retour au pays natal* (1939). Translated as *Return to My Native Land*. Preface by André Breton. Paris: Livre-Poche-Bilingue, 1971 [1947, 1956].

Cestre, Charles. *John Thelwall: A Pioneer of Democracy and Social Reform in England during the French Revolution*. New York: Charles Scribner's Sons, 1906.

Chambers, E. K. "Some Dates in Coleridge's *Annus Mirabilis*." In *A Sheaf of Studies*, 42–51. Oxford and New York: Oxford University Press, 1942.

Chandler, James K. *Wordsworth's Second Nature: A Study of the Poetry and Politics*. Chicago and London: University of Chicago Press, 1984.

Christensen, Jerome. "Once an Apostate Always an Apostate." *Studies in Romanticism* 21 (1982): 461–64.

Christophe, Robert. *Napoleon on Elba*. Translated by Len Ortzen. London: Macdonald, 1964 [1959].

Clarke, George Herbert. "Certain Symbols in *The Rime of the Ancient Mariner*." *Queen's Quarterly* 40 (1933): 27–45.

Clarkson, Thomas. *The History of the Rise, Progress, and Accomplishment of the Abolition of the African Slave-Trade by the British Parliament*. 2 vols. London, 1807.

Clifford, James. "'Hanging Up Looking Glasses at Odd Corners': Ethnobiographical Prospects." In *Studies in Bibliography*, edited by Daniel Aaron, 41–56. Cambridge and New York: Cambridge University Press, 1978.

Coburn, Kathleen, ed. *The Letters of Sara Hutchinson from 1800 to 1835*. Toronto: University of Toronto Press, 1954.

Coetzee, J. M. *Foe*. New York: Viking Penguin, 1987 [1986].

———. *In the Heart of the Country*. New York: Viking Penguin, 1982.

Coleridge, Hartley. Review of *Coleridge's Poetical Works* (1834). *Quarterly Review* 52 (1834): 28.

Colley, Linda. *Britons: Forging the Nation, 1707–1837*. New Haven and London: Yale University Press, 1992.

Colmer, John. *Coleridge: Critic of Society*. Oxford: Clarendon Press, 1959.

Colvin, Anne Hutta. "The Celluloid Crusoe: A Study of Cinematic Robinsonades." *Dissertation Abstracts Index* 50(6): December 1989, 1464A–1464B.

Cone, Carl B. *Burke and the Nature of Politics*. 2 vols. Lexington: University of Kentucky Press, 1957–1964.

———. *The English Jacobins*. New York: Scribners, 1968.

Cooke, Michael. *The Romantic Will*. New Haven and London: Yale University Press, 1976.

Cooper, Anna Julia. *A Voice from the South*. Oxford and New York: Oxford University Press, 1988.

Copley, Stephen, and John Whale, eds. *Beyond Romanticism: Approaches to Texts and Contexts, 1780–1832.* London and New York: Routledge, 1992.

Cottle, Joseph. *Reminiscences of Samuel Taylor Coleridge and Robert Southey.* Highgate: Lime Tree Bower Press, 1970 [1847].

Courtney, Winifred F. "Nevis, West Indies, and the English Romantic Writers." *Charles Lamb Bulletin* 71 (1990): 248–53.

Cowper, William. "Verses Supposed to Be Written by Alexander Selkirk." In *The Poems of William Cowper,* edited by John D. Baird and Charles Ryskam. Oxford and New York: Oxford University Press, 1980.

Crews, Frederick. *The Critics Bear It Away: American Fiction and the Academy.* New York: Random House, 1992.

———. *Skeptical Engagements.* Oxford and New York: Oxford University Press, 1988.

Culler, Jonathan. "Human Limits: A Response to M. H. Abrams." *The Bookpress* 3.6 (1993): 1, 3, 13.

Damrosch, Leopold. "Myth and Fiction in *Robinson Crusoe.*" In *God's Plot and Man's Stories,* 187–212. Chicago and London: University of Chicago Press, 1985.

Darlington, Beth. "Two Early Texts: *A Night-Piece* and *The Discharged Soldier.*" In *Bicentenary Wordsworth Studies,* edited by Jonathan Wordsworth, 425–48. Ithaca and London: Cornell University Press, 1970.

Davies, Lindsay. "The Poem, the Gloss, and the Critic: Discourse and Subjectivity in *The Rime of the Ancient Mariner.*" *Forum for Modern Language Studies* 26 (1990): 259–71.

Davis, David Brion. *The Problem of Slavery in the Age of Revolution, 1770–1823.* Ithaca and London: Cornell University Press, 1975.

De Man, Paul. *The Resistance to Theory.* Minneapolis: University of Minnesota Press, 1986.

———. "Wordsworth and Hölderlin." In *The Rhetoric of Romanticism.* New York and London: Columbia University Press, 1984.

De Quincey, Thomas. *Recollections of the Lakes and the Lake Poets.* Edited by David Wright. Harmondsworth, Middlesex: Penguin Books, 1970 [1834].

Derrida, Jacques. *Of Grammatology.* Translated by Gayatri Spivak. Baltimore and London: Johns Hopkins University Press, 1976.

Dickstein, Morris. *Double Agent: The Critic and Society.* Oxford and New York: Oxford University Press, 1992.

Diop, Cheikh Anta. *Civilization or Barbarism: An Authentic Anthropology.* New York: L. Hill Books, 1991 [1981].

Dobrée, Bonamy. *English Literature in the Early Eighteenth Century, 1700–1740.* Oxford and New York: Oxford University Press, 1959.

Donoghue, Denis. *The Pure Good of Theory: The Bucknell Lectures in Literary Theory.* Cambridge, Mass., and Oxford: Basil Blackwell, 1992.

———. "The Values of *Moll Flanders.*" *Sewanee Review* 71 (1963): 287–303; reprinted in *England, Their England.* New York: Random House, 1988.

"Dorrington, Edward." See below, under Quarll, Philip.

Douglass, Frederick. *The Narrative of the Life of Frederick Douglass, An American Slave*. Boston, 1845.

Doyle, William. *The Oxford History of the French Revolution*. Oxford and New York: Oxford University Press, 1989.

Drinkwater, John. *Charles James Fox*. London: Ernest Benn, 1928.

Dworkin, Ronald. *Law's Empire*. Cambridge: Belknap Press of Harvard University Press, 1986.

Dyck, Sarah. "Perspective in *The Rime of the Ancient Mariner*." *Studies in English Literature* 13 (1973): 591–604.

Dykes, Eva Beatrice. *The Negro in English Romantic Thought; or, A Study of Sympathy for the Oppressed*. Washington, D.C.: The Associated Publisher, 1942.

Eaglestone, A. J. "Wordsworth, Coleridge, and the Spy" (1908). Reprinted in *Coleridge: Studies by Several Hands on the Hundredth Anniversary of His Death*, edited by Edmund Blunden and E. L. Griggs. London: Constable, 1934.

Eagleton, Terry. *Walter Benjamin; or, Toward a Revolutionary Critique*. London: Routledge, 1980.

Ebbatson, J. B. "Coleridge's Mariner and the Rights of Man." *Studies in Romanticism* 11 (1972): 171–206.

Egerton, Douglas. Letter to author, December 13, 1991.

Ehrman, John. *The Younger Pitt*. 2 vols. Stanford: Stanford University Press, 1983.

Elliott, Marianne. *Partners in Revolution: United Irishmen and France*. New Haven and London: Yale University Press, 1982.

Ellis, Frank H. Introduction to *Twentieth-Century Interpretations of "Robinson Crusoe."* Englewood Cliffs, N.J.: Prentice-Hall, 1969.

Ellison, Ralph. *Invisible Man*. New York: Random House, 1952.

Empson, William. "*The Ancient Mariner*." *Critical Quarterly* 6 (1964): 298–319.

Empson, William, and David Pirie, eds. *Coleridge's Verse: A Selection*. New York: Schocken, 1973 [1972].

Emsley, Clive. *British Society and the French Wars, 1793–1815*. London and Totowa, N.J.: Rowman and Littlefield, 1979.

———. "The Impact of the French Revolution on British Politics." In *The French Revolution and British Culture*, edited by Ceri Crossley and Ian Small, 31–62. Oxford and New York: Oxford University Press, 1989.

Erdman, David V. *Blake: Prophet against Empire*. 3d ed. Princeton: Princeton University Press, 1977 [1954].

———. "Coleridge on George Washington: Newly Discovered Essays of 1800." *Bulletin of the New York Public Library* 61 (1957): 81–97.

———. *Commerce des Lumières: John Oswald and the British in Paris*. Columbia and London: University of Missouri Press, 1987.

———. "The Dawn of Universal Patriotism: William Wordsworth among the British in Revolutionary France." In *The Age of William Wordsworth: Critical Essays on Romantic Tradition*, edited by Kenneth R. Johnston and Gene W. Ruoff, 3–20. New Brunswick and London: Rutgers University Press, 1987.

———. "Milton! Thou Shouldst Be Living." *The Wordsworth Circle* 19 (1988): 2–8.

————. *The Political Coleridge.* In press.

————. "Treason Trials in the Early Romantic Period." *The Wordsworth Circle* 19 (1988): 76–82.

Esterhammer, Angela. "Speech Acts and Living Words: On Performative Language in Coleridge's Poems of 1798." *The Wordsworth Circle* 24 (1993): 79–83.

Everest, Kelvin. *Coleridge's Secret Ministry: The Context of the Conversation Poems, 1795–1798.* New York: Barnes and Noble, 1979.

Ferguson, Frances. "Coleridge and the Deluded Reader." *Georgia Review* 31 (1977): 617–35.

Fischer, Michael. "Morality and History in Coleridge's Political Theory." *Studies in Romanticism* 21 (1982): 457–60.

Fish, Stanley. "The Common Touch; or, One Size Fits All" (1990). In *The Politics of Liberal Education,* edited by Darryl J. Gless and Barbara Herrnstein Smith, 241–66. Durham and London: Duke University Press, 1992.

Fletcher, Pauline, and John Murphy, eds. *Wordsworth in Context.* London and Toronto: Associated University Presses, 1992. [Selected papers originally presented in April 1990 at a Bucknell University conference entitled "Revolutionary Romanticism, 1790–1990."]

Foakes, R. A. "'Thriving Prisoners': Coleridge, Wordsworth, and the Child at School." *Studies in Romanticism* 28 (1989): 187–206.

Forster, John. *The Life of Charles Dickens.* 3 vols. Philadelphia: Lippincott, 1874.

Foucault, Michel. *Discipline and Punish: The Birth of the Prison.* Translated by Alan Sheridan. New York: Vintage Books, 1977.

————. *Language, Counter-Memory, Practice: Selected Essays and Interviews.* Edited by Donald F. Bouchard. Translated by Bouchard and Sherry Simon. Ithaca and London: Cornell University Press, 1977.

Fox, Arnold B. "Political and Biographical Background of Coleridge's *Osorio.*" *Journal of English and German Philology* 61 (1962): 258–67.

Franklin, John Hope. *Race and History: Selected Essays, 1938–1988.* Baton Rouge: Louisiana State University Press, 1989.

Freeman, Douglas Southall. *R. E. Lee.* 4 vols. New York: Charles Scribner's Sons, 1934–1935.

Fry, E. F. "Correspondence." *The New Republic,* December 10, 1990, 4–5.

Frye, Northrop. *Myth and Metaphor: Selected Essays, 1974–1988.* Charlottesville and London: The University Press of Virginia, 1990.

Gadamer, Hans George. *Truth and Method.* New York: Seabury Press, 1975.

Gardner, Martin. *The Annotated Ancient Mariner, Illustrated by Gustave Doré.* Cleveland and New York: Meridian Books, 1968.

Gates, Henry Louis, Jr. "Beware of the New Pharaohs." *Newsweek,* September 23, 1991, 47.

————. *Loose Canons: Notes on the Culture Wars.* Oxford and New York: Oxford University Press, 1992.

Gatta, John, Jr. "Coleridge and Allegory." *Modern Language Quarterly* 38 (1977): 62–77.

Gay, Peter. *Freud: A Life for Our Time.* New York and London: Norton, 1988.

————, ed. *The Freud Reader.* New York and London: Norton, 1989.

Gettman, Royal A. Introduction to *"The Rime of the Ancient Mariner": A Handbook.* San Francisco: Wadsworth, 1961.

Gildon, Charles. *The Life and Strange Surprizing Adventures of Mr. D——De F— of London, Hosier.* Published as *Robinson Crusoe Examin'd and Criticis'd* (London, 1719). Edited by Paul Dottin. London and Paris: Dent, 1923.

Gill, Stephen. *William Wordsworth: A Life.* Oxford and New York: Oxford University Press, 1989.

Gillman, James. *The Life of Samuel Taylor Coleridge.* 2 vols. London, 1838.

Girard, René. *Violence and the Sacred.* Translated by Patrick Gregory. Baltimore and London: Johns Hopkins University Press, 1977.

Giraudoux, Jean. *Suzanne et le Pacifique.* Paris: Emile-Paul Frères, 1921.

Giroux, Henry. "Liberal Arts Education and the Struggle for Public Life: Dreaming about Democracy" (1989). In *The Politics of Liberal Education,* edited by Darryl J. Gless and Barbara Herrnstein Smith, 120–44. Durham and London: Duke University Press, 1992.

Gless, Darryl J., and Barbara Herrnstein Smith, eds. *The Politics of Liberal Education.* Durham and London: Duke University Press, 1992.

Glover, Michael. *The Napoleonic Wars: An Illustrated History, 1792–1815.* New York: Hippocrene Books, 1978.

Godwin, William. *Caleb Williams.* 3d ed. 1797. Edited by David McCracken. Oxford and New York: Oxford University Press, 1970.

Goodheart, Eugene. *The Skeptic Disposition: Deconstruction, Ideology, and Other Matters.* Princeton: Princeton University Press, 1991.

Goodson, A. C. "Burke's Orpheus and Coleridge's Contrary Understanding." *The Wordsworth Circle* 22 (1991): 52–58.

Goodwin, Albert. *The Friends of Liberty: The English Democratic Movement and the War of Ideas.* Cambridge, Mass., and London: Harvard University Press, 1979.

Gordimer, Nadine. "The Power of a Well-Told Tale." Interview with Nadine Gordimer by Paul Gray and Bruce W. Nelan. *Time,* October 14, 1991, 91–92.

Gose, Elliot B., Jr. "Coleridge and the Luminous Gloom." *PMLA* 75 (1960): 238–44.

Gould, Stephen Jay. *The Mismeasure of Man.* New York and London: Norton, 1981.

Graff, Gerald. *Beyond the Culture Wars: How Teaching the Conflicts Can Revitalize American Education.* New York: Norton, 1992.

Gramsci, Antonio. *Prison Notebooks.* Vol. 1. New York and London: Columbia University Press, 1992.

Green, Martin. *The Robinson Crusoe Story.* University Park and London: University of Pennsylvania Press, 1990.

Green, Peter. *Alexander to Actium: The Historical Evolution of the Hellenistic Age.* Berkeley and Los Angeles: University of California Press, 1990.

Green, Walon, and Christopher Logue, screenwriters. *Crusoe* (1988) [film].

Greenblatt, Stephen. "Culture." In *Critical Terms for Literary Study.* Edited by Frank Lentricchia and Thomas McLaughlin, 225–32. Chicago and London: University of Chicago Press, 1990.

————. *Marvellous Possessions: The Wonder of the New World.* Chicago and London: University of Chicago Press, 1991.

————. *Representing the English Rennaissance.* Berkeley and Los Angeles: University of California Press, 1988.

————. "Resonance and Wonder." In *Learning to Curse: Essays in Early Modern Culture.* London: Routledge, 1990.

Greene, John C. *The Death of Adam.* New York: New American Library, 1961 [1959].

Gross, Lawrence, Cary Nelson, and Paula Treichler, eds. *Cultural Studies.* New York and London: Routledge, 1992.

Haeger, J. H. "Coleridge's Speculations on Race." *Studies in Romanticism* 13 (1974): 333–57.

Halewood, William. "Religion and Invention in *Robinson Crusoe.*" *Essays in Criticism* 14 (1964): 339–51.

Hanftängel, Ernst. *Hitler: The Missing Years.* London: Eyre and Spottiswoode, 1957.

Hanley, Keith, and Raman Selden, eds. *Revolution and English Romanticism: Vision and Rhetoric.* New York: St. Martin's Press, 1990.

Hanson, Lawrence. *The Life of S. T. Coleridge: The Early Years.* New York: Russell and Russell, 1962 [1938].

Harding, Anthony John. *Coleridge and the Idea of Love: Aspects of Relationship in Coleridge's Thought and Writing.* London and New York: Cambridge University Press, 1974.

————. *Coleridge and the Inspired Word.* Kingston: McGill-Queen's University Press, 1985.

Harper, George McLean, *William Wordsworth: His Life, Works, and Influence.* 2 vols. New York: Russell and Russell, 1960 [1929].

Harris, Daniel. "What Is the Politically Correct?" *Salmagundi* 90–91 (1991): 45–55.

Hartman, Geoffrey H. "Criticism and Restitution." *Tikkun* 4 (1989): 29–31.

————. *Minor Prophecies: The Literary Essay in the Culture Wars.* Cambridge, Mass., and London: Harvard University Press, 1990.

————. "The State of the Art of Criticism." In *The Future of Literary Theory,* edited by Ralph Cohen, 86–101. New York and London: Routledge, 1989.

Hausermann, Hans W. "Life and Thought in *Robinson Crusoe.*" *Review of English Studies* 11 (1935): 299–312.

Hayley, William. *Memoirs of Life and Writing.* 2 vols. Edited by J. Johnson. London, 1823.

Hazlitt, William. *The Complete Works of William Hazlitt.* 21 vols. Edited by P. P. Howe. London and Toronto: Dent, 1930–1934.

Heffernan, James A. W. "The English Romantic Perception of Color." In *Images of Romanticism: Verbal and Visual Affinities,* edited by Karl Kroeber and William Walling, 133–48. New Haven and London: Yale University Press, 1978.

Hegel, G. W. F. *The Logic of Hegel.* Translated by W. Wallace. Oxford and Fairlawn, N.J., 1892.

Hill, Christopher. *A Nation of Change and Novelty: Radical Politics, Religion, and Literature in Seventeenth-Century England.* London and New York: Routledge, 1990.

Hilton, Boyd. *The Age of Atonement: The Influence of Evangelicalism on Social and Economic Thought, 1795–1865.* Oxford and New York: Oxford University Press, 1988.

Hirsch, E. D., Jr. *Cultural Literacy: What Every American Needs to Know.* Boston: Houghton Mifflin, 1987.

Hodgson, John. "Coleridge's 'Coeli Enarrant' and a Source in *Robinson Crusoe.*" *English Language Notes* 25 (1987): 40–44.

Holmes, Richard. *Coleridge: Early Visions.* New York: Viking, 1990.

Honan, Park. *Jane Austen: Her Life.* New York: St. Martin's Press, 1987.

Hope, A. D. "Man Friday." In *The Age of Reason.* Melbourne: Melbourne University Press, 1985.

Horse Capture, George P. "An American Indian Perspective." In *Seeds of Change: A Quincentennial Commemoration, Five Hundred Years Since Columbus,* edited by Herman J. Viola and Carolyn Margolis, 186–207. Washington and London: Smithsonian Institution Press, 1991.

House, Humphry. *Coleridge: The Clark Lectures, 1951–1952.* London: Rupert Hart-Davis, 1953.

Howe, Irving. "History and the Novel." *The New Republic,* September 3, 1990, 29–34.

Hubback, Edith C. *Jane Austen's Sailor Brothers.* London: J. Lane, 1906.

Hughes, Robert. *Culture of Complaint: The Fraying of America.* New York: New York Public Library/Oxford University Press, 1993.

Hulme, Peter. *Colonial Encounters: Europe and the Native Caribbean, 1492–1797.* London and New York: Methuen, 1986.

Hume, David. "Of National Characters." In volume 1 of *Essays and Treatises on Several Subjects.* 2 vols. Edinburgh, 1825.

Hunt, Lynn. *The Family Romance of the French Revolution.* Berkeley and Los Angeles: University of California Press, 1992.

Hunter, J. Paul. *The Reluctant Pilgrim: Defoe's Emblematic Method and Quest for Form in "Robinson Crusoe."* Baltimore and London: Johns Hopkins University Press, 1966.

James, C. L. R. *The Black Jacobins: Toussaint L'Ouverture and the San Domingo Revolution.* 2d ed., rev. New York: Vintage, 1963 [1938].

James, D. G. *The Romantic Comedy.* Oxford and New York: Oxford University Press, 1963 [1948].

Jameson, Fredric. *The Political Unconscious: Narrative as a Socially Symbolic Act.* Ithaca and London: Cornell University Press, 1981.

Jarrett, Derek. *Pitt the Younger.* New York: Charles Scribner's Sons, 1974.

Jefferson, Thomas. *Thomas Jefferson: Writings.* New York: The Library of America, 1984.

Johnson, Barbara. Editor's Preface to "The Pedagogical Imperative: Teaching as a Literary Genre," a special issue of *Yale French Studies* 63 (1982): iii–vii.

Johnston, Kenneth R. "Philanthropy or Treason? Wordsworth as 'Active Partisan.'" *Studies in Romanticism* 25 (1986): 371–409.

———. "The Politics of 'Tintern Abbey.'" *The Wordsworth Circle* 14 (1983): 6–14.

———. *Wordsworth and "The Recluse."* New Haven and London: Yale University Press, 1984.

———. "Wordsworth's *Lyrical Ballads*." In *The Age of William Wordsworth*, edited by Johnston and Gene W. Ruoff, 133–59.

———. "Wordsworth's Revolutions, 1793–1798." In *Revolution and English Romanticism: Vision and Rhetoric*, edited by Keith Hanley and Raman Selden, 169–204. New York: St. Martin's Press, 1990.

Johnston, Kenneth R., and Gene W. Ruoff, eds. *The Age of William Wordsworth: Critical Essays on Romantic Tradition*. New Brunswick and London: Rutgers University Press, 1987.

Johnston, Kenneth R. et al., eds. *Romantic Revolutions: Criticism and Theory*. Bloomington and Indianapolis: University of Indiana Press, 1990.

Jonas, Hans. *The Gnostic Religion*. Boston: Houghton Mifflin, 1963.

Jones, Alun R. See Wordsworth, William, below.

Jones, E. H. Stuart, R. N. *The Invasion that Failed: The French Expedition to Ireland, 1796*. Oxford and New York: Oxford University Press, 1950.

———. *The Last Invasion of Britain*. Cardiff: University of Wales Press, 1950.

Jordan, John E. *Why the "Lyrical Ballads"? The Background, Writing, and Character of Wordsworth's 1798 "Lyrical Ballads."* Berkeley and Los Angeles: University of California Press, 1976.

Jordan, Winthrop. *White over Black: American Attitudes toward the Negro, 1550–1812*. Chapel Hill and London: University of North Carolina Press, 1968.

Joyce, James. "Daniel Defoe." Trieste Lecture, translated and edited by Joseph Prescott. *Buffalo Studies* 1 (1964): 7–25.

Jump, Harriet Devine. "High Sentiments of Liberty: Coleridge's Unacknowledged Debt to Akenside." *Studies in Romanticism* 28 (1989): 207–24.

Kant, Immanuel. *Observations on the Feelings of the Beautiful and the Sublime*. Translated by John T. Goldthwait. Los Angeles and New York: University of California Press, 1991 [1960].

Kaplan, Richard. "Defoe's Views on Slavery and Racial Prejudice." Ph.D. diss., New York University, 1970.

Kazin, Alfred. *On Native Grounds: An Interpretation of Modern Literature*. New York: Reynal and Hitchcock, 1942.

———. "The Way We Live Now." *New York Review of Books*, April 22, 1993, 3–4.

Keane, Patrick. "On Truth and Lie in Nietzsche." *Salmagundi* 29 (1975): 67–94.

———. "Revolutions French and Russian: Burke, Wordsworth, and the Genesis of Yeats's 'The Second Coming.'" *Bulletin of Research in the Humanities* 82 (1979): 18–52.

———. "Time's Ruins and the Mansions of Eternity." *Bulletin of Research in the Humanities* 86 (1983): 33–66.

———. *Yeats's Interactions with Tradition*. Columbia and London: University of Missouri Press, 1987.

Keats, John. *The Poems of John Keats*. Edited by Jack Stillinger. Cambridge: The Belknap Press of Harvard University Press, 1978.

Kecht, Maria-Regina, ed. *Pedagogy Is Politics: Literary Theory and Critical Teaching*. Urbana and Chicago: University of Illinois Press, 1992.

Kelly, Patrick. "Day and Night: Mystery and Error in Coleridge's *The Rime of the Ancient Mariner*." *English Studies in Canada* 11 (1985): 295–310.

Kemp, Wolfgang. *The Desire of My Eyes: A Life of John Ruskin*. Translated by Jan van Heurck. London: HarperCollins, 1991 [1983].

Kennedy, Roger G. *Orders from France: The Americans and the French in a Revolutionary World, 1780–1820*. New York: Knopf, 1989.

Kimball, Roger. "The Periphery v. The Center: The MLA in Chicago" (1991). In *Debating PC: The Controversy over Political Correctness on College Campuses*, edited by Paul Berman, 61–84. New York: Laurel, 1992.

Kitson, Peter. "Coleridge, Milton, and the Millennium." *The Wordsworth Circle* 18 (1987): 61–66.

———. "Coleridge, the French Revolution, and *The Ancient Mariner*: Collective Guilt and Individual Salvation." *Yearbook of English Studies* 19 (1989): 197–207.

Klingender, F. D. "Coleridge on *Robinson Crusoe*." *Times Literary Supplement*, February 1, 1936, 96.

Kroeber, Karl. *Romantic Fantasy and Science Fiction*. New Haven and London: Yale University Press, 1988.

Kroeber, Karl, and William Walling, eds. *Images of Romanticism: Verbal and Visual Affinities*. New Haven and London: Yale University Press, 1978.

Kucich, Greg. "Ironic Apocalypse in Romanticism and the French Revolution." In *Revolution and English Romanticism: Vision and Rhetoric*, edited by Keith Hanley and Raman Selden, 67–88. New York: St. Martin's Press, 1990.

Lacan, Jacques. *Ecrits: A Selection*. Translated by Alan Sheridan. London: Tavistock, 1977.

Lamb, Charles. *The Letters of Charles and Mary Anne Lamb*. 3 vols. Edited by Edwin W. Marrs, Jr. Ithaca and London: Cornell University Press, 1975–1978.

Landor, Walter Savage. *The Complete Works of Walter Savage Landor*. 3 vols. Edited by Stephen Wheeler. London: Chapman and Hall, 1935.

Lawrence, Berta. "John Chubb, a Friend of Coleridge." *Charles Lamb Bulletin* 27 (1979): 51–55.

———. *Wordsworth and Coleridge in Somerset*. Bristol: Newton Abbot, David and Charles, 1970.

Leask, Nigel. *The Politics of Imagination in Coleridge's Critical Thought*. London: Macmillan, 1988.

Lefebvre, George. *The French Revolution*. 2 vols. Translated by J. H. Stewart and James Friguglietti. New York and London: Columbia University Press, 1964.

Lentricchia, Frank. *Criticism and Social Change*. Chicago and London: University of Chicago Press, 1985.

Levere, Trevor H. *Poetry Realized in Nature: Samuel Taylor Coleridge and Early Nineteenth-Century Science*. Cambridge and New York: Cambridge University Press, 1981.

Levin, Richard. "The Poetics and Politics of Bardicide." *PMLA* 105 (1990): 491–502.

Levinson, Marjorie. *Wordsworth's Great Period Poems: Four Essays.* Cambridge and New York: Cambridge University Press, 1986.

Levinson, Marjorie et al. *Rethinking Historicism: Critical Readings in Romantic History.* Oxford: Basil Blackwell, 1989.

Lichtveld, L. A. M. *Crusoe's Only Isle.* Tobago, n.d.

Lipking, Lawrence. "The Marginal Gloss: Notes and Asides on Poe, Valery, *The Ancient Mariner,* etc. . . ." *Critical Inquiry* 3 (1977): 609–55.

Liu, Alan. *Wordsworth: The Sense of History.* Stanford: Stanford University Press, 1989.

Losh, James, trans. Benjamin Constant's *Observations on the Strength of the Present Government of France, and of the Necessity of Rallying Round It.* Bath, 1797.

Lowes, John Livingston. *The Road to Xanadu: A Study in the Ways of the Imagination.* Boston: Houghton Mifflin, 1964 [1927].

Lyotard, Jean-François. "The Unconscious, History, and Phrases: Notes on *The Political Unconscious.*" *New Orleans Review* 11 (1984): 73–79.

McCalman, Iain. *Radical Underworld: Prophets, Revolutionaries, and Pornographers in London, 1795–1840.* Cambridge and New York: Cambridge University Press, 1989.

Maccoby, Simon. *English Radicalism, 1786–1832.* London: Allen and Unwin, 1955.

McElderry, B. R. "Coleridge's Revisions of *The Ancient Mariner.*" *Studies in Philology* 29 (1932): 68–94.

McGann, Jerome J. "Introduction: A Point of Reference." In *Historical Studies and Literary Criticism.* Madison: University of Wisconsin Press, 1985.

———. "The Meaning of *The Ancient Mariner.*" *Critical Inquiry* 8 (1981): 35–66.

———. *The Romantic Ideology: A Critical Investigation.* Chicago and London: University of Chicago Press, 1983.

———. *Social Values and Poetic Acts: The Historical Judgment of Literary Work.* Cambridge, Mass., and London: Harvard University Press, 1988.

———. "The Third World of Criticism." In *Rethinking Historicism: Critical Readings in Romantic History,* edited by Marjorie Levinson et al., 85–107. Oxford: Basil Blackwell, 1989.

MacGillivray, J. R. "The Pantisocratic Scheme and Its Immediate Background." In *Studies in English,* edited by M. W. Wallace, 131–69. Toronto: University of Toronto Press, 1931.

Macherey, Pierre. *A Theory of Literary Production.* Translated by Geoffrey Wall. London and Boston: Routledge and Kegan Paul, 1978 [1966].

Mackiewicz, Wolfgang. *Providenz und Adaption in Defoe's "Robinson Crusoe": Ein Beitrag zum Problem des Pragmatischen Puritanismus.* Frankfurt am Main, 1981.

McKillop, Alan Dugald. *The Background of Thomson's Seasons.* Minneapolis and London: University of Minnesota Press, 1942.

Magnus, Bernd, Stanley Stewart, and Jean-Pierre Mileur. *Nietzsche's Case: Philosophy as/and Literature.* New York and London: Routledge, 1993.

Magnuson, Paul. *Coleridge and Wordsworth: The Lyrical Dialogue.* Princeton: Princeton University Press, 1988.

————. *Coleridge's Nightmare Poetry.* Charlottesville and London: University Press of Virginia, 1974.

————. "The Politics of 'Frost at Midnight.'" *The Wordsworth Circle* 22 (1991): 3–11.

————. "Teaching the Coleridge-Wordsworth Dialogue." In *Approaches to Teaching Coleridge's Poetry and Prose,* edited by Richard E. Matlack, 76–82. New York: Modern Language Association of America, 1991.

Mahan, Alfred Thayer. *The Influence of Sea Power on the French Revolution and Empire.* 2 vols. London, 1892.

Manceron, Claude. *Age of the French Revolution.* Vol. 2, *The Wind from America, 1778–1781.* New York: Knopf, 1978 [1974].

Maniquis, Robert M. "Holy Savagery and Wild Justice: English Romanticism and the Terror." *Studies in Romanticism* 28 (1989): 365–95.

Mannix, Daniel P., and Malcolm Cowley. *Black Cargoes: A History of the Atlantic Slave Trade, 1518–1865.* New York: Viking Press, 1962.

Marsh, Florence G. "The Ocean-Desert: *The Ancient Mariner* and *The Waste Land.*" *Essays in Criticism* 9 (1959): 126–33.

Martin, Bernard. *"The Ancient Mariner" and the "Authentic Narrative."* London: Heinemann, 1949.

Martin, C. G. "The Dating of S. T. Coleridge's 'Fire, Famine and Slaughter.'" *Notes and Queries,* n.s., 19 (1992): 289–90.

Martin, Charles. *Passages from Friday.* Omaha: Abattoir Press, 1983.

Marx, Karl. *Capital: A Critique of Political Economy.* 2 vols. Translated by Samuel Moore and Edward Aveling. New York: Random House, 1906.

Marx, Karl, and Friedrich Engels. *The German Ideology.* London: Lawrence and Wishart, 1970.

Marzorati, Gerald. [Report on the rebirth of European liberalism in 1989.] *International Herald Tribune,* July 11, 1990.

Maser, Werner. *Adolf Hitler: Legende, Mythos, Wirklichkeit.* Munich: Bechtle, 1989.

Matlack, Richard E., ed. *Approaches to Teaching Coleridge's Poetry and Prose.* New York: Modern Language Association of America, 1991.

Matthews, G. M. "A Volcano's Voice in Shelley." *Journal of English Literary History* 24 (1957): 191–228.

Maxwell, Kenneth. "¡Adiós Columbus!" *New York Review of Books,* January 28, 1993, 38–45.

Mays, J. C. C. "Reflections on Having Edited Coleridge's Poems." In *Romantic Revisions,* edited by Robert Brinkley and Keith Hanley, 136–53. Cambridge and New York: Cambridge University Press, 1993.

Medwin, Thomas. *Conversations of Lord Byron.* 2d ed. London, 1824.

Meier, Thomas Keith. *Defoe and the Defense of Commercials.* English Studies Monograph Series, no. 38. Victoria, B.C.: University of Victoria, 1987.

Mellor, Anne K. *English Romantic Irony.* Cambridge, Mass., and London: Harvard University Press, 1980.

————. *Romanticism and Gender.* New York and London: Routledge, 1993.

Mendilow, A. A. "Symbolism in Coleridge and the Dantesque Element in *The Ancient Mariner.*" *Scripta Hierosolymitana: Publications of the Hebrew University, Jerusalem* 2 (1955): 25–81.

Mileur, Jean-Pierre. *The Critical Romance. The Critic as Reader, Writer, Hero.* Madison: University of Wisconsin Press, 1991.

Miller, J. Hillis. "The Critic as Host." In *Deconstruction and Criticism,* edited by Harold Bloom et al., 217–53. New York: Continuum, 1979.

———. "The Function of Literary Theory at the Present Time." In *The Future of Literary Theory,* edited by Ralph Cohen, 102–11. New York and London: Routledge, 1989.

———. "Just Reading: Kleist's 'Der Findling.'" In *Versions of Pygmalion.* Cambridge: Harvard University Press, 1990.

———. "Stevens' Rock and Criticism as Cure." *Georgia Review* 30 (1976): 330–48.

Miller, John T. *Ideology and Enlightenment: The Social and Political Thought of Samuel Taylor Coleridge.* New York: Garland, 1987.

Milton, John. *Poetical Works.* Edited by Douglas Bush. Oxford and New York: Oxford University Press, 1966.

———. *The Works of John Milton.* 18 vols. New York and London: Columbia University Press, 1931–1938.

Modiano, Raimonda. *Coleridge and the Concept of Nature.* Tallahassee: Florida State University Press, 1985.

———. "Coleridge's Marginalia." *TEXT: Transactions of the Society for Textual Scholarship* 2 (1985): 257–68.

———. "Metaphysical Debate in Coleridge's Political Theory." *Studies in Romanticism* 21 (1982): 465–74.

———. "Words and 'Languageless' Meanings: Limits of Expression in *The Rime of the Ancient Mariner.*" *Modern Language Quarterly* 38 (1977): 40–61.

Monk, Samuel Holt. Introduction to *Colonel Jack.* Edited by Monk. Oxford and New York: Oxford University Press, 1965.

Moore, C. A. "Whig Panegyric Verse." *PMLA* 41 (1926): 389–96.

Moore, George. *Avowals.* London: Heinemann, 1924.

Moore, John Robert. *Checklist of the Writings of Daniel Defoe.* Hamden, Conn.: Greenwood, 1971 [1960].

———. *Daniel Defoe: Citizen of the Modern World.* Chicago and London: University of Chicago Press, 1958.

———. "*The Tempest* and *Robinson Crusoe.*" *Review of English Studies* 21 (1945): 52–56.

Moorman, Mary. *William Wordsworth: A Biography.* 2 vols. Vol. 1, *The Early Years, 1770–1803.* Oxford: Clarendon Press, 1957.

Morrison, Anthea. "Samuel Taylor Coleridge's Greek Prize Poem on the Slave Trade." In *An Infinite Complexity: Essays in Romanticism,* edited by J. R. Watson, 145–60. Edinburgh and New York: Edinburgh University Press and Columbia University Press, 1983.

Morrow, John. "Coleridge and the English Revolution." *Political Science* 40 (1988): 128–41.

————. Introduction to *On Politics and Society*. Edited by Morrow. Vol. 1 of *Coleridge's Writings*. John Beer, general editor. Princeton: Princeton University Press, 1991.

Muldoon, Paul. *Madoc: A Mystery*. New York: Farrar, Straus and Giroux, 1991 [1990].

Neill, Diana. *A Short History of the English Novel*. New York: Collier Books, 1964.

Newman, Cardinal John Henry. "The Prospects of the Anglican Church." In *Essays Critical and Historical*. London, 1897.

Newman, Gerald. *The Rise of English Nationalism: A Cultural History, 1740–1830*. New York: St. Martin's Press, 1987.

Nietzsche, Friedrich. *The Antichrist*. In *The Portable Nietzsche*, edited by Walter Kaufmann. New York: Viking, 1968 [1954].

————. *The Gay Science*. Translated by Walter Kaufmann. New York: Vintage, 1974.

————. *On the Genealogy of Morals/Ecce Homo*. Translated by Walter Kaufmann. New York: Vintage, 1967.

————. *The Will to Power*. Translated by Walter Kaufmann and R. J. Hollingdale. New York: Random House, 1967.

Nodier, Charles. Introduction to *The Swiss Family Robinson*. Translated by W.H.D.A. London, 1870.

Nolan, Alan T. *Lee Considered: General Robert E. Lee and Civil War History*. Chapel Hill and London: University of North Carolina Press, 1991.

Norris, Christopher. *What's Wrong with Postmodernism: Critical Theory and the Ends of Philosophy*. Baltimore and London: Johns Hopkins University Press, 1990.

Novak, Maximillian E. "Crusoe the King and the Political Evolution of His Island." *Studies in English Literature* 2 (1962): 337–50.

————. *Defoe and the Nature of Man*. Oxford and New York: Oxford University Press, 1963.

————. *Economics and the Fiction of Daniel Defoe*. Berkeley and Los Angeles: University of California Press, 1962.

————. "Imaginary Islands and Real Beasts: The Imaginative Genesis of *Robinson Crusoe*." In *Realism, Myth, and History in Defoe's Fiction*, 23–46. Lincoln: University of Nebraska Press, 1983.

————. "*Robinson Crusoe* and Economic Utopia." *Kenyon Review* 25 (1963): 474–90.

————. "Robinson Crusoe's 'Original Sin.'" *Studies in English Literature* 1 (1961): 19–29.

————, ed. *English Literature in the Age of Disguise*. Berkeley and Los Angeles: University of California Press, 1977.

O'Brien, Conor Cruise. *The Great Melody: A Thematic Biography and Commented Anthology of Edmund Burke*. Chicago and London: University of Chicago Press, 1992.

Onuf, Peter S., ed. *Jeffersonian Legacies*. Charlottesville and London: University Press of Virginia, 1993.

Orwell, George. "Politics and the English Language." In *A Collection of Essays*. Garden City, N.Y.: Doubleday Anchor, 1954 [1953].

Ower, John. "The 'Death-Fires,' the 'Fire-Flags,' and the Corposant in *The Rime of the Ancient Mariner.*" *Philological Quarterly* 70 (1991): 199–218.

Paglia, Camille. *Sexual Personae: Art and Decadence from Nefertiti to Emily Dickinson.* New Haven and London: Yale University Press, 1990.

Paley, Morton D. "Apocalypse and Millennium in the Poetry of Coleridge." *The Wordsworth Circle* 23 (1992): 24–34.

Palmer, R. R. *The Age of the Democratic Revolution: A Political History of Europe and America, 1760–1800.* 2 vols. Princeton: Princeton University Press, 1959, 1964.

Parker, A. Reeve. "Wordsworth's Whelming Tide: Coleridge and the Art of Analogy." In *Forms of Lyric: Selected Papers from the English Institute,* edited by Reubon A. Brower, 75–102. New York and London: Columbia University Press, 1970.

Parliamentary Committee Reports. (Specific reports cited in text.)

The Parliamentary History of England. 36 vols. (1806–1820). Edited by William Cobbett. 1st series, vols. 27–35. London: Longman and Co., 1813–1819.

Pater, Walter. *Appreciations.* London, 1889.

Patterson, Annabel. *Censorship and Interpretation.* Rev. ed. Madison: University of Wisconsin Press, 1990 [1984].

———. *Reading between the Lines.* Madison: University of Wisconsin Press, 1993.

Patterson, Orlando. *Freedom: Freedom in the Making of Western Culture.* New York: Basic Books, 1991. [The first of two projected volumes.]

Paul-Emile, Barbara. "Samuel Taylor Coleridge as Abolitionist." *Ariel: A Review of International English Studies* 5 (1974): 59–75.

Paulson, Ronald. *Representations of Revolution.* New Haven and London: Yale University Press, 1983.

———. "Turner's Graffiti: The Sun and Its Glosses." In *Images of Romanticism: Verbal and Visual Affinities,* edited by Karl Kroeber and William Walling, 167–88. New Haven and London: Yale University Press, 1978.

Pease, Donald A. "New Americanists: Revisionist Interventions into the Canon." *boundary 2* 17 (1990): 1–37.

Perkins, David. "The Imaginative Vision of 'Kubla Khan': On Coleridge's Introductory Note." In *Coleridge, Keats, and the Imagination: Romanticism and Adam's Dream,* edited by Robert Barth, S.J., and John L. Mahoney, 97–108. Columbia and London: University of Missouri Press, 1990.

Peterfreund, Stuart. "The Way of Immanence: Coleridge and the Problem of Evil." *English Language History* 55 (1988): 125–58.

Piper, H. W. "*The Ancient Mariner:* Biblical Allegory, Poetic Symbolism, and Religious Crisis." *Southern Review* 10 (1977): 232–42.

Pirie, David. "Textual Commentary" and "Notes." In *Coleridge's Verse: A Selection,* edited by William Empson and David Pirie, 207–16, 222–43. New York: Schocken, 1973 [1972].

Poe, Edgar Allan. "The Black Cat." In *Prose Tales (First Series) by Edgar Allan Poe.* Boston: Dana Estes, 1856.

Polidori, John. *The Diary of John William Polidori.* Edited by W. M. Rossetti. London: Elkin Mathews, 1911.

Pollack, Frederick. "To the Unknown Reader." *Salmagundi* 88–89 (1990–1991): 496–509.

Pollin, Burton R., assisted by Redmond Burke. "John Thelwall's Marginalia in a Copy of Coleridge's *Biographia Literaria.*" *Bulletin of the New York Public Library* 74 (1970): 73–94.

Pollock, John. *Wilberforce.* London: Constable, 1977.

Pope, Alexander. *The Poems of Alexander Pope: A One Volume Edition of the Twickenham Pope.* Edited by John Butt. London: Methuen, 1963.

Pope-Hennessy, James. *Sins of the Fathers: A Study of the Atlantic Slave Traders, 1441–1807.* London: Weidenfeld and Nicholson, 1967.

Pound, Ezra. *The Cantos of Ezra Pound.* New York: New Directions, 1970.

Priestley, Joseph. *An Essay on First Principles of Government; and on the nature of political, civil, and religious liberty.* London, 1768.

———. Introductory Essay to *Hartley's Theory of the Human Mind, on the principle of the Association of Ideas.* . . . London, 1775.

———. *The Present State of Europe compared with Ancient Prophecies; a Sermon preached at the Gravel Pit Meeting in Hackney, February 28, 1794, Being the Day appointed for a General Fast.* London, 1794.

Public Record Office. Home Office Papers. (Specific documents cited in text.)

Purinton, Marjean D. "Wordsworth's *The Borderers* and the Ideology of Revolution." *The Wordsworth Circle* 23 (1992): 97–108.

Quarll, Philip. *The England Hermit; or, Unparalleled Sufferings, and Surprizing Adventures, of Mr. Philip Quarll, who was lately discovered on an uninhabited Island in the South-sea; where he had lived above fifty years, without any human assistance.* London, 1786 [1727]. (The narrative is signed "Ed. Dorrington.")

Rajan, Tillotama. *Dark Interpreter: The Discourse of Romanticism.* Ithaca and London: Cornell University Press, 1980.

Ramazani, Jahan. *Yeats and the Poetry of Death: Elegy, Self-Elegy, and the Sublime.* New Haven and London: Yale University Press, 1990.

Rauch, Jonathan. *Kindly Inquisitors: The New Attacks on Free Thought.* Chicago and London: University of Chicago Press, 1993.

Rediker, Marcus. *Between the Devil and the Deep Blue Sea: Merchant Seamen, Pirates, and the Anglo-American Maritime World, 1700–1750.* Cambridge and New York: Cambridge University Press, 1987.

Reiman, Donald H. "The Bollingen Coleridge" and "'Versioning': The Presentation of Multiple Texts." In *Romantic Texts and Contexts.* Columbia and London: University of Missouri Press, 1987, 69–84, 167–80.

———. "Coleridge and the Art of Equivocation." *Studies in Romanticism* 25 (1986): 325–50.

———. *Percy Bysshe Shelley.* New York: Twayne, 1969.

———, ed. *The Romantics Reviewed.* Part A, *The Lake Poets.* 2 vols. New York and London: Garland, 1972.

Retamar, Roberto Fernández. *Caliban and Other Essays.* Translated by Edward Baker. Minneapolis: University of Minnesota Press, 1989.

Richetti, John. *Daniel Defoe*. Boston: Twayne, 1987.

———. *Defoe's Narratives: Situations and Structures*. Oxford and New York: Oxford University Press, 1975.

Roberts, Warren. *Jane Austen and the French Revolution*. New York: St. Martin's Press, 1988.

Robinson, Jeffrey. *The Current of Romantic Passion*. Madison: University of Wisconsin Press, 1991.

———. *Radical Literary Education: A Classroom Experiment with Wordsworth's "Ode."* Madison: University of Wisconsin Press, 1987.

Roe, Nicholas. "Coleridge, Wordsworth, and the French Invasion Scare." *The Wordsworth Circle* 17 (1986): 142–48.

———. "Who Was Spy Nozy?" *The Wordsworth Circle* 15 (1984): 46–50.

———. *Wordsworth and Coleridge: The Radical Years*. Oxford and New York: Oxford University Press, 1988.

Rogers, Pat. *"Robinson Crusoe."* Unwin Critical Library Series. London and Boston: Allen and Unwin, 1979.

Rorty, Richard. *Philosophy and the Mirror of Nature*. Princeton: Princeton University Press, 1979.

———. "Two Cheers for the Cultural Left." In *The Politics of Liberal Education*, edited by Darryl J. Gless and Barbara Herrnstein Smith, 213–40. Durham, N.C., and London: Duke University Press, 1992.

Rousseau, Jean-Jacques. *Emilius and Sophia; or, A New System of Education*. London, 1762. [First English translation of *Émile*.]

Rubenstein, Chris. "A New Identity for the Mariner." Paper delivered at the Coleridge Summer Conference, 1990.

Rudich, Norman. "'Kubla Khan,' a Political Poem." *Romantisme* 8 (1974): 50–56.

Rushdie, Salman. *Haroun and the Sea of Stories*. New York: Granta Books/ Viking, 1990.

Ruskin, John. *Modern Painters*. 5 vols. Vol. 21 in the St. Mark's edition of *John Ruskin's Works*. Boston: Dana Estes, n.d.

Said, Edward. *Culture and Imperialism*. New York: Knopf, 1993.

———. "Opponents, Audiences, Constituencies, and Community." In *The Politics of Interpretation*, edited by W. J. T. Mitchell, 7–32. Chicago and London: University of Chicago Press, 1983.

———. "The Politics of Knowledge" (1987). In *Debating PC: The Controversy over Political Correctness on College Campuses*, edited by Paul Berman, 172–89. New York: Laurel, 1992.

Sale, Kirkpatrick. *The Conquest of Paradise: Christopher Columbus and the Columbian Legacy*. New York: Knopf, 1990.

Sandford, Mrs. Henry. *Thomas Poole and His Friends*. 2 vols. London, 1888.

Sayre, Robert. "The Young Coleridge: Romantic Utopianism and the French Revolution." *Studies in Romanticism* 28 (1989): 397–415.

Schlesinger, Arthur, Jr. *The Disuniting of America: Reflections on a Multicultural Society*. New York and London: Norton, 1992.

Schonhorn, Manuel. "Defoe: The Literature of Politics and the Politics of Some Fictions." In *English Literature in the Age of Disguise,* edited by Maximillian Novak. Berkeley and Los Angeles: University of California Press, 1977.

———. *Defoe's Politics: Parliament, Power, Kingship, and "Robinson Crusoe."* Oxford and New York: Oxford University Press, 1991.

Schulz, Max F. "Coleridge Agonistes." *Journal of English and German Philology* 61 (1962): 268–77.

———. "The Many Coleridges." In *Approaches to Teaching Coleridge's Poetry and Prose,* edited by Richard E. Matlack, 18–30. New York: Modern Language Association of America, 1991.

———. *The Poetic Voices of Coleridge: A Study of His Desire for Spontaneity and Passion for Order.* Detroit: Wayne State University Press, 1964.

———. "Samuel Taylor Coleridge." In *English Romantic Poets: A Review of Research and Criticism,* 4th ed., edited by Frank Jordan, 341–463. New York: Modern Language Association of America, 1985.

Searle, John. "The Storm over the University" (1990). In *Debating PC: The Controversy over Political Correctness on College Campuses,* edited by Paul Berman, 85–123. New York: Laurel, 1992.

Seidel, Michael. *"Robinson Crusoe": Island Myths and the Novel.* Boston: Twayne, 1991.

Sewell, Elizabeth. "Coleridge on Revolution." *Studies in Romanticism* 11 (1972): 342–59.

Shakespeare, William. *Othello* and *The Tempest.* In *William Shakespeare: The Complete Works.* Alfred Harbage, general editor. Baltimore: Penguin, 1969.

Shelley, Percy Bysshe. *The Letters of Percy Bysshe Shelley.* 2 vols. Edited by Frederick Jones. Oxford and New York: Oxford University Press, 1964.

———. *Shelley's Poetry and Prose.* Edited by Donald H. Reiman and Sharon B. Powers. New York: Norton, 1977.

Shelvocke, Captain George. *A Voyage round the World by the Way of the Great South Sea. . . .* London, 1726.

Sheridan, Richard B. *Sugar and Slavery: An Economic History of the British West Indies, 1623–1775.* Baltimore and London: Johns Hopkins University Press, 1974.

Sill, Geoffrey. *Defoe and the Idea of Fiction, 1713–1719.* Newark: University of Delaware Press, 1983.

Simpson, David. *Irony and Authority in Romantic Poetry.* London: Rowman and Littlefield, 1979.

———. *Wordsworth's Historical Imagination: The Poetry of Displacement.* New York and London: Methuen, 1987.

Smith, Barbara Herrnstein. "Value/Evaluation." *South Atlantic Quarterly* 86 (1987): 445–55.

Southey, Robert. "Lyrical Ballads." *The Critical Review* 24 (1798): 197–204.

———. *The Poetical Works of Robert Southey.* 10 vols. Boston, 1863.

———. *Thalaba the Destroyer.* 2 vols. London, 1801.

Spanos, William V. *The End of Education: Toward Posthumanism*. Minneapolis: University of Minnesota Press, 1993.

———. "The Genealogy of Humanism." *The Bookpress* 3.7 (1993): 1, 16–17, 20.

———. *Repetitions: The Postmodern Occasion in Literature and Culture*. Baton Rouge: Louisiana State University Press, 1987.

Stamm, Rudolph G. "Daniel Defoe: An Artist in the Puritan Tradition," *Philological Quarterly* 15 (1936): 225–45.

Stanhope, Earl. *Life of Pitt*. 2 vols. London, 1861.

Starr, G. A. *Defoe and Spiritual Autobiography*. Princeton: Princeton University Press, 1965.

Sterne, Laurence. *Tristram Shandy*. Edited by James A. Work. New York: Odyssey Press, 1940.

Stevens, Wallace. *The Collected Poems of Wallace Stevens*. New York: Knopf, 1954.

Stillinger, Jack. "The Multiple Versions of Coleridge's Poems: How Many *Mariners* Did Coleridge Write?" *Studies in Romanticism* 31 (1992): 127–46.

Stimpson, Catherine R. "Multiculturalism: A Big Word at the Presses." *New York Times Book Review*, September 22, 1991, 1.

Strauss, Leo. Epilogue to *Essays in the Scientific Study of Politics*. Chicago and London: University of Chicago Press, 1962.

Sultana, Donald. "Coleridge's Political Papers in Malta." In *New Approaches to Coleridge: Biographical and Critical Essays*, edited by Sultana, 212–40. London and Totowa, N.J.: Barnes and Noble, 1981.

———. *Samuel Taylor Coleridge in Malta and Italy*. New York: Barnes and Noble, 1969.

Sutherland, James. *Daniel Defoe: A Critical Study*. Cambridge and New York: Cambridge University Press, 1971.

———. *Defoe*. Philadelphia and New York: Lippincott, 1938.

Swift, Jonathan. *Gulliver's Travels*. Edited by Robert A. Greenberg. New York: Norton, 1970.

Tarnas, Richard. *The Passion of the Western Mind: Understanding the Ideas that Have Shaped Our World View*. New York: Harmony Books, 1991.

Tawney, R. H. "The Study of Economic History" (1933). In *History and Society: Essays by R. H. Tawney*, edited by J. Winter, 47–65. London: Routledge, 1978.

Taylor, Anya. "Teaching *Ancient Mariner* and *Christabel* to Students of Criminal Justice." In *Approaches to Teaching Coleridge's Poetry and Prose*, edited by Richard E. Matlack, 134–46. New York: Modern Language Association of America, 1991.

Tennyson, Lord Alfred. *The Poems of Tennyson*. Edited by Christopher Ricks. London: Longmans, 1969.

Thale, Mary, ed. *Selections from the Papers of the London Corresponding Society, 1792–1799*. Cambridge and New York: Cambridge University Press, 1983.

Thelwall, Cecil Boyle. *The Life of John Thelwall by his Widow*. 2 vols. London, 1837.

Thelwall, John. Marginalia on Coleridge's *Biographia Literaria*. See Pollin, Burton R., above.

———. *Peaceful Discussion, and Not Tumultuary Violence the Means of Redressing National Grievances*. London, 1795.

————. *The Peripatetic: or Sketches of the Heart of Nature and Society; in a Series of Politico-Sentimental Journals in Verse and Prose. . . .* 3 vols. London, 1793.

————. *Poems, Chiefly Written in Retirement.* 2d ed. Hereford, 1801.

————. *Poems Written in Close Confinement in the Tower and Newgate, under a Charge of High Treason.* London, 1795.

————. *The Tribune.* 3 vols. London, 1795–1796.

Thomas, Keith G. "The Politics of Coleridge's 'Dejection: An Ode.'" Unpublished essay, c. 1987.

[Thompson, E. P.?]. "Bliss Was It in That Dawn: The Matter of Coleridge's Revolutionary Youth." *Times Literary Supplement,* June 8, 1971, 929–32.

Thompson, E. P. "Disenchantement or Default? A Lay Sermon." In *Power and Consciousness,* edited by Conor Cruise O'Brien and William Dean Vanech, 149–81. New York: New York University Press, 1969.

————. *The Making of the English Working Class.* New York: Random House, Vintage, 1966 [1963].

Thompson, J. M., ed. and trans. *Napoleon Self-Revealed: Three Hundred Selected Letters.* Boston and New York: Houghton Mifflin, 1934.

Thompson, Thomas Perronet. Comments on Coleridge's *Table Talk. Westminster Review* 22 (1835): 531–37.

Thomson, James. *"The Seasons" and "The Castle of Indolence."* Edited by James Sambrook. Oxford and New York: Oxford University Press, 1972.

Thoreau, Henry David. *Walden; or, Life in the Woods.* New York: Signet, 1960.

Ticknor, George. *Life, Letters, and Journals of George Ticknor.* 2 vols. Boston and New York: Houghton and Mifflin, 1909.

Tillyard. E. M. W. *The Elizabethan World Picture.* New York: Vintage Books, n.d. [1943].

————. *Five Poems, 1470–1870.* London: Chatto and Windus, 1948.

Todd, F. M. *Politics and the Poet: A Study of Wordsworth.* London: Methuen, 1957.

Tone, W. T. W. *Life of Theobold Wolfe Tone.* 2 vols. Washington, 1826.

Tournier, Michel. *Vendredi: ou Les limbes du Pacifique.* Paris: Gallimard, 1967.

Trevelyan, G. M. *History of England.* Vol. 3, *From Utrecht to Modern Times.* 3d ed. Garden City, N.Y.: Doubleday, 1953.

Twitchell, James B. *Romantic Horizons: Aspects of the Sublime in English Poetry and Painting, 1770–1850.* Columbia and London: University of Missouri Press, 1983.

Veeser, H. Aram, ed. *The New Historicism.* New York and London: Routledge, 1989.

Vendler, Helen. "Lowell in the Classroom." *The Harvard Advocate* 93 (1979): 26–28.

————. "'Tintern Abbey': Two Assaults" (1990). In *Wordsworth in Context,* edited by Pauline Fletcher and John Murphy, 173–90. London and Toronto: Associated University Presses, 1992.

Vlastos, Gregory. *Socrates, Ironist and Moral Philosopher.* Ithaca and London: Cornell University Press, 1991.

Walcott, Derek. "Crusoe's Journal." In *The Gulf: Poems by Derek Walcott.* New York: Farrar, Straus and Giroux, 1970.

Wall, Wendy. "Interpreting Poetic Shadows: The Gloss of *The Rime of the Ancient Mariner.*" *Criticism* 29 (1987): 179–95.

Wallen, Martin. *Coleridge's Ancient Mariner: An Experimental Edition of Texts and Revisions, 1798–1828.* Barrytown, N.Y.: Station Hill Literary Editions, 1993.

———. "Return and Representation: The Revisions of *The Ancient Mariner.*" *The Wordsworth Circle* 17 (1986): 148–56.

Walvin, James. *England, Slaves, and Freedom, 1776–1838.* Jackson: University Press of Mississippi, 1986.

Ware, Malcolm. "Coleridge's 'Spectre-Bark': A Slave Ship?" *Philological Quarterly* 40 (1961): 589–93.

Warren, Robert Penn. "A Conversation with Cleanth Brooks." In *The Possibilities of Order: Cleanth Brooks and His Work,* edited by Lewis Simpson. Baton Rouge: Louisiana State University Press, 1976.

———. "A Poem of Pure Imagination: An Experiment in Reading." In *The Rime of the Ancient Mariner,* by Samuel Taylor Coleridge, 61–148. New York: Reynal and Hitchcock, 1946.

Watkins, Daniel. "History as Demon in Coleridge's *The Rime of the Ancient Mariner.*" *Papers on Language and Literature* 24 (1988): 23–33.

Watt, Ian. *The Rise of the Novel: Studies in Defoe, Richardson, and Fielding.* Berkeley and Los Angeles: University of California Press, 1967.

The Wellesley Papers: The Life and Correspondence of Richard Colley Wellesley, Marquess Wellesley, etc. . . . 2 vols. London: H. Jenkins, 1914.

Wells, Roger. *Insurrection: The British Experience, 1795–1803.* Gloucester: A. Sutton, 1983.

Werkmeister, Lucyle, and P. M. Zall. "Possible Additions to Coleridge's 'Sonnets on Eminent Characters.'" *Studies in Romanticism* 8 (1969): 121–27.

West, Cornel. "Diverse New World" (1991). In *Debating PC: The Controversy over Political Correctness on College Campuses,* edited by Paul Berman, 326–32. New York: Laurel, 1992.

———. *Race Matters.* Boston: Beacon Press, 1993.

Whalley, George. "On Editing Coleridge's Marginalia." In *Editing Texts of the Romantic Period,* edited by John D. Baird, 89–116. Toronto: University of Toronto Press, 1972.

Wheeler, Kathleen. *The Creative Mind in Coleridge's Poetry.* London: Heinemann, 1981.

———. *Sources, Processes, and Methods in Coleridge's "Biographia Literaria."* Cambridge and New York: Cambridge University Press, 1980.

Willey, Basil. *Samuel Taylor Coleridge.* New York: Norton, 1971.

Williams, Bernard. *Shame and Necessity.* Berkeley and Los Angeles: University of California Press, 1993.

Williams, Eric. *Capitalism and Slavery.* New York: Capricorn Books, 1966 [1964].

Williams, John. *Wordsworth: Romantic Poetry and Revolutionary Politics.* Manchester and New York: Manchester University Press and St. Martin's Press, 1989.

Williams, Raymond. *Marxism and Literature.* Oxford and New York: Oxford University Press, 1977.

Winders, James A. *Gender, Theory, and the Canon*. Madison: University of Wisconsin Press, 1991.

Woodring, Carl. *Politics in English Romantic Poetry*. Cambridge, Mass., and London: Harvard University Press, 1970.

———. *Politics in the Poetry of Coleridge*. Madison: University of Wisconsin Press, 1961.

———, ed. "Coleridge: The Politics of the Imagination." *Studies in Romanticism* 21 (1982): 447–74.

Woodward, C. Vann. Reply in "'Illiberal Education': An Exchange." *The New York Review of Books*, July 18, 1991, 74–76.

Woof, Robert S. "Wordsworth's Poetry and Stuart's Newspapers, 1797–1803." *Studies in Bibliography* 15 (1962): 149–89.

Woolf, Virginia. *The Second Common Reader*. New York: Harcourt, Brace, 1932.

Wordsworth, Christopher. *Memoirs of William Wordsworth*. 2 vols. London, 1851.

Wordsworth, Dorothy. *Journals of Dorothy Wordsworth*. Edited by Mary Moorman. Oxford and New York: Oxford University Press, 1971.

Wordsworth, Jonathan. *Ancestral Voices: Fifty Books from the Romantic Period*. London and New York: Woodstock Books, 1991.

———. "Wordsworth's 'Dim and Perilous Way.'" In *Revolution and English Romanticism: Vision and Rhetoric*, edited by Keith Hanley and Raman Selden, 205–23. New York: St. Martin's Press, 1990.

Wordsworth, William. *The Letters of William and Dorothy Wordsworth: The Early Years, 1787–1805*. Edited by Ernest de Selincourt. Revised by Chester Shaver. Oxford: Clarendon Press, 1967. *The Later Years, 1821–1853*. 4 vols. Revised by Alan G. Hill. Oxford: Clarendon Press, 1978–1988.

———. *The Poetical Works of William Wordsworth*. 5 vols. Edited by Ernest de Selincourt and Helen Darbishire. Oxford and New York: Oxford University Press, 1940–1949.

———. *The Prelude: 1799, 1805, 1850*. Edited by Jonathan Wordsworth, M. H. Abrams, and Stephen Gill. New York: Norton, 1979.

———. *The Prose Works of William Wordsworth*. 3 vols. Edited by Alexander B. Grosart. London, 1876.

———. *The Prose Works of William Wordsworth*. Vol. 1. Edited by W. J. B. Owen and Jane Smyser. Oxford, 1974.

———. *William Wordsworth: The Poems*. 2 vols. Edited by J. Hayden. New Haven and London: Yale University Press, 1977.

———. *Wordsworth's Poems of 1807*. Edited by Alun R. Jones. Atlantic Highlands, N.J.: Humanities Press International, 1987.

———. See also Brett, R. L., and A. R. Jones above.

Worrall, David. *Radical Culture: Discourse, Resistance, and Surveillance, 1790–1820*. Detroit: Wayne State University Press, 1992.

Wright, Ronald. *Stolen Continents: The Americas through Indian Eyes, since 1492*. Boston: Houghton Mifflin, 1992.

Wylie, Ian. *Young Coleridge and the Philosophers of Nature*. Oxford and New York: Oxford University Press, 1989.

Yeats, W. B. *Autobiographies.* London: Macmillan, 1955.

———. *Uncollected Prose by W. B. Yeats.* Vol. 1. Edited by John B. Frayne. New York and London: Columbia University Press, 1970.

———. *The Variorum Edition of the Poems of W. B. Yeats.* Edited by Peter Allt and Russell K. Alspach. New York, 1957.

Young, Edward. *Night Thoughts.* Edited by Stephen Cornford. Cambridge and New York: Cambridge University Press, 1989.

Zeitz, Lisa M. "'A Checker-Work of Providence': The Shaping of *Robinson Crusoe.*" *English Studies in Canada* 9 (1983): 255–71.

Index

PERMISSIONS

Excerpts from the following copyrighted works have been reprinted by permission:

"Crusoe in England," from *The Complete Poems, 1927–1979,* by Elizabeth Bishop. Copyright © 1979, 1983, by Alice Helen Methfessel. Reprinted by permission of Farrar, Straus & Giroux, Inc.

Foe, by J. M. Coetzee. Copyright © 1986 by J. M. Coetzee. Reprinted by permission of Viking Penguin, a division of Penguin Books USA, Inc.

"Man Friday," from *The Age of Reason,* by A. D. Hope. Reprinted by permission of the Melbourne University Press.

"Passages from Friday," from *Steal the Bacon,* by Charles Martin. Reprinted by permission of Charles Martin and the Johns Hopkins University Press.